AN EXPLORER'S GUIDE

The Blue Ridge and Smoky Mountains

AN EXPLORER'S GUIDE

The Blue Ridge and Smoky Mountains

Jim Hargan

With photographs by the author

The Countryman Press ✳ Woodstock Vermont

FIRST EDITION

DEDICATION
To my wife, Kasey—and to everyone else who faces life as an explorer.

We welcome your comments and suggestions. Please contact Explorer's Guide Editor, The Countryman Press, P.O. Box 748, Woodstock, Vermont 05091, or e-mail countrymanpress@wwnorton.com.

ISBN: 0-88150-484-X
ISSN: 1538-8395

Maps by Moore Creative Design © 2002 The Countryman Press
Cover and interior design by Bodenweber Design
Text composition by Melinda Belter
Cover photographs by Jim Hargan

Published by The Countryman Press, P.O. Box 748, Woodstock, Vermont 05091

Distributed by W. W. Norton & Company, Inc., 500 Fifth Avenue, New York, NY 10110

Printed in the United States of America

10 9 8 7 6 5 4 3 2 1

EXPLORE WITH US!

Welcome to the first edition of *The Blue Ridge and Smoky Mountains: An Explorer's Guide,* the definitive guide to the tallest mountains in the East. It's the perfect companion for exploring the Great Smoky Mountains National Park, the Blue Ridge Parkway, and all the ridges in between. Here, you'll find thorough coverage for both sides of the Tennessee–North Carolina state line, with detailed listings on the best sight-seeing, outdoor activities, restaurants, shopping, and B&Bs. Like all Explorer's Guides, this book is an old-fashioned, classic traveler's guide, where an experienced and knowledgeable expert helps you find your way around in a new area or explore some fascinating corners of a familiar one.

WHAT'S WHERE

In the beginning of the book you'll find an alphabetical listing of special highlights and important information that you may want to reference quickly. You'll find advice on everything from Area Codes to Wildlife.

LODGING

We've selected lodging places for inclusion in this book based on their merit alone; we do not charge innkeepers for inclusion. **Prices:** Please don't hold us or the respective innkeepers responsible for the rates listed as of press time in early 2002. Changes are inevitable. At the time of this writing, the state and local room tax ranged from 6 to 11 percent.

RESTAURANTS

In most chapters please note the distinction between *Eating Out* and *Dining Out.* By their nature, restaurants included in the *Eating Out* group are generally inexpensive. A range of prices is included for each entry.

KEY TO SYMBOLS

✎ **Child-friendly.** The crayon denotes a family-friendly place or event that welcomes young children. Most B&Bs prohibit children under 12.

&. **Handicapped access.** The wheelchair icon denotes a place with full Americans with Disabilities Act (ADA) standard access, still distressingly rare in these remote areas.

☂ **Rainy day.** The umbrella icon points out places where you can entertain yourself but still stay dry in bad weather.

☙ **Pets.** The dog's paw icon identifies lodgings that allow pets—still the exception to the rule. Accommodations that accept pets may still charge an extra fee or restrict pets to certain areas, as well as require advance notice.

Author's Choice: Sidebars mark the author's personal favorites in each chapter—a subjective selection, but good guidance when you only have a day or so to spend in an area.

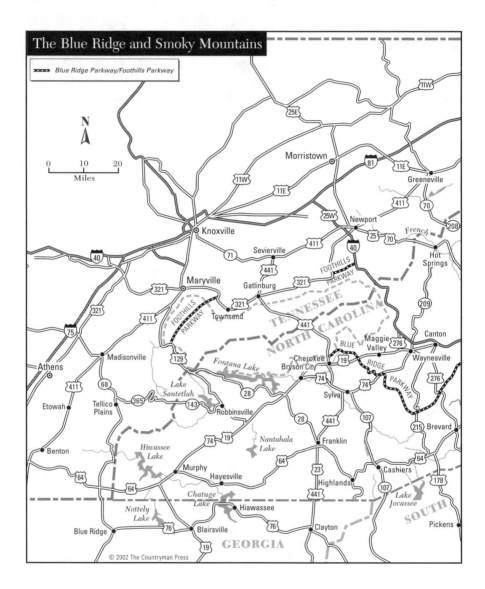

The Blue Ridge and Smoky Mountains

▆▆▆ *Blue Ridge Parkway/Foothills Parkway*

N

0   10   20
Miles

© 2002 The Countryman Press

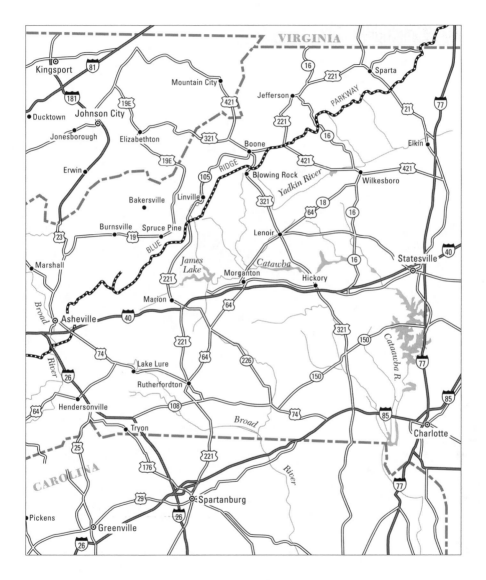

The Blue Ridge and Smoky Mountains Regions

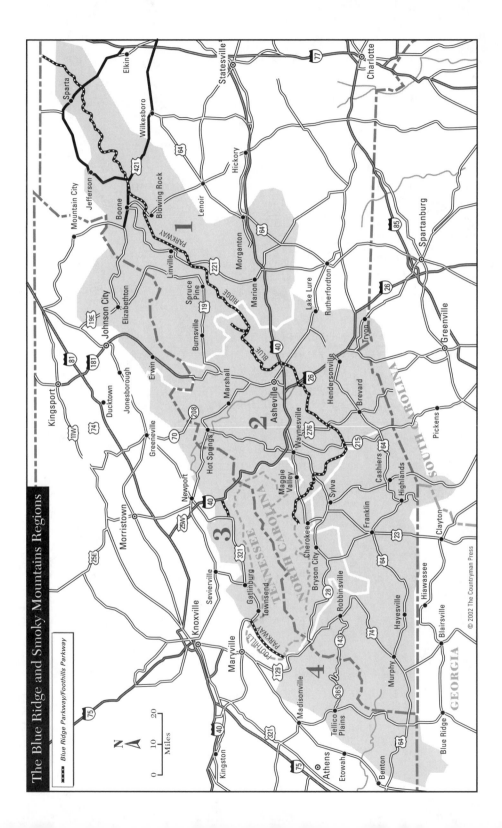

Blue Ridge Parkway/Foothills Parkway

N

0 10 20
Miles

© 2002 The Countryman Press

CONTENTS

10   INTRODUCTION

15   WHAT'S WHERE IN THE BLUE RIDGE & SMOKY MOUNTAINS

1 The Northern Mountains

39   THE BLUE RIDGE PARKWAY ENTERS NORTH CAROLINA

51   THE BLUE RIDGE PARKWAY: BLOWING ROCK & GRANDFATHER
MOUNTAIN

73   BEHIND THE BLUE RIDGE: BOONE & BANNER ELK

95   BEHIND THE BLUE RIDGE: SPRUCE PINE & BURNSVILLE

113   THE MOUNTAINS OF NORTHERN TENNESSEE

129   BENEATH THE BLUE RIDGE: THE CATAWBA RIVER VALLEY

2 Asheville's Mountains

153   ASHEVILLE & THE BLUE RIDGE PARKWAY

187   WAYNESVILLE & THE BLUE RIDGE PARKWAY

203   ASHEVILLE'S RUGGED HINTERLANDS

221   THE BLUE RIDGE: CHIMNEY ROCK & SALUDA

241   THE BLUE RIDGE: HENDERSONVILLE & BREVARD

3 Great Smoky Mountains National Park

273   GATLINBURG & THE NORTHEAST QUADRANT

295   TOWNSEND, CADES COVE & THE NORTHWEST QUADRANT

317   BRYSON CITY & THE SOUTHWEST QUADRANT

337   CHEROKEE & THE SOUTHEAST QUADRANT

4 South of the Smokies

359   NEAR THE PARK: SYLVA & DILLSBORO

377   THE BLUE RIDGE: CASHIERS & HIGHLANDS

395   FRANKLIN & THE NANTAHALA MOUNTAINS

409   THE NORTHERN UNICOIS: ROBBINSVILLE & TELLICO PLAINS

426   THE SOUTHERN UNICOIS: MURPHY & THE COPPER BASIN

444   INDEX

INTRODUCTION

Some travel experiences are for passive enjoyment, for being gently led from meal to pastime to meal. Not so the Smokies. The Blue Ridge and Smoky Mountains are for involvement—for finding the perfect little inn with broad views from an antiques-furnished room, for discovering the wonderful meal superbly prepared at a little roadhouse, for digging up the odd little corner, the unforgettable museum, the remarkable site. The Blue Ridge and Smoky Mountains are for exploring.

And this is a guide for explorers. It is a guide for finding your way down a winding mountain road to a beautiful river, a quiet log cabin, or a wide view. It seeks out the memorable, the unique, and the worthwhile—whether it be a place to visit, a place to shop, a place to eat, or a place to stay. It excludes the ordinary or routine places—after all, there are plenty of those back home. And, unlike many guides, it doesn't charge fees or accept advertising. This is a collection of personal recommendations.

This guide centers on two of the most popular national park lands in the nation: Great Smoky Mountains National Park and the Blue Ridge Parkway. In doing so it covers the 40 highest peaks of the East, the most biodiverse forests in temperate North America, scores of waterfalls, and hundreds of panoramic views. However, this guide goes well beyond the boundaries of the national parks to cover all of the surrounding mountains and forests, the small towns and the settled valleys. In it you'll find tidy county seats, brick-front downtowns little changed in half a century, artists' colonies hidden away in remote valleys, and well-tended farms and old log cabins that welcome overnight visitors. You'll find the homes of Carl Sandburg and Daniel Boone, the summer estate of an aristocratic South Carolina governor, and the log cabin of a frontiersman North Carolina governor. And you'll find lots of outdoor activities as well—whitewater and stillwater adventures, horseback riding, fishing, rock climbing, snow skiing, and golf.

Specifically, this guide covers the most rugged areas of the South's two great mountain ranges, the Blue Ridge and the Smokies/Unakas. The Blue Ridge, with its long series of gray cliffs facing toward the distant Atlantic, defines the eastern edge of the region. A set of mile-high ridges define the western edge, variously named (from south to north) the Unicoi Mountains, the Great Smoky Mountains, the Bald Mountains, the Unaka Mountains, the Yellow Mountains, and the Stone Mountains. Together, these are commonly called the Unakas (you-NAY-kuhs) by geologists, and the Smokies by ordinary folk; this book splits the difference and calls them the Smokies/Unakas.

This guide divides this 10,000-square-mile area (larger than New Jersey) into 20 chapters. Each chapter takes in a coherent area with a good range of sites, activities, and places to stay. The chapters are grouped into four broad areas ("The Northern Mountains," "Asheville's Mountains," "Great Smoky Mountain National Park," and "South of the Smokies"), each a major region worthy of a long trip. Great Smoky Mountains National Park gets four chapters to itself, making up one of the four regions. The Blue Ridge Parkway, more than 250 miles long and very skinny, also gets four chapters, spread throughout the first half of the book; these chapters always have "Blue Ridge Parkway" in their titles. The remaining chapters cover the areas between the two great national parks—frequently as rugged, as wildly beautiful, and as entertaining as the parks themselves.

This guide gains strength from being part of an established series known for its high standards—The Countryman Press's Explorer's Guide series. *The Blue Ridge and Smoky Mountains* shares a format polished from long experience and honed to the needs of adventurous travelers. Each chapter covers an area that can be conveniently explored from any of its listed inns. The chapter starts with an overview, then follows with general descriptions of exploring the scenery *(Wandering Around)*, the major areas of natural scenic beauty *(Wild Places)*, and the major settled places *(Villages)*; these topic headings let you go straight to the parts that interest you. After that, the chapter gets down to specifics: sites and attractions worth a visit *(To See)*; outdoor activities *(To Do)*; the most interesting and unique of the area's best lodging *(Lodging)*; places to get good, fresh food prepared from scratch *(Where to Eat)*; places with regular evening entertainment *(Entertainment)*; unique shops and worthwhile shopping districts *(Selective Shopping)*; and some of the best of the annual festivals *(Special Events)*.

Readers experienced with our New England guides will immediately notice that this guide spends a lot more time in the woods and a lot less time in the towns. Travelers experienced with the American South will see nothing odd in this; in much of the South, the woods are the good part. Yet this guide finds much to recommend in the towns and villages of the Blue Ridge and Smoky Mountains. Most remarkable are the busy, well-tended brick-front downtowns that appear in one country town after another, from Sparta, NC, in the far north to Copperhill, TN, 290 miles south. Equally amazing are the artists' colonies spread throughout these hills, from Penland, NC, with its hundred or more studios to Tellico Plains, TN, with a dozen impressive local crafters. Not surprisingly, good shopping can be found in some unexpected places.

Author Jim Hargan lives deep in the Blue Ridge and Smoky Mountains, near the small county seat of Burnsville, NC (see "Behind the Blue Ridge: Spruce Pine and Burnsville"). A travel photographer and writer with a background in geography, he's been involved with the Smokies since vacationing there as a small boy and attending one of the mountain universities (see Western Carolina University under *To See—Cultural Sites* in "Near the Park: Sylva and Dillsboro). The Blue Ridge and Smoky Mountains region remains one of his core specialties (Great Britain being the other), and he brings his own local insights to his recommendations.

The Deep Mountains. In the middle of the American South, two great mountain ranges run parallel with each other. Their heads point northeast, toward the great cities of the Atlantic seaboard; their tails point southwest, toward the empty pine flatlands of Georgia and Alabama. The easternmost of the two, the Blue Ridge, lies 300 miles from the Atlantic coast, stretching from southern Pennsylvania deep into the

South without a break. It faces the settled coast with a steep eastern face from Virginia to northern Georgia, a wall that intimidated early settlers and protected the Cherokees—for a few early decades, at least.

The western ridge is higher but more broken, appearing in fits and starts. Beginning in southern Virginia, it borders a wide inland valley with a mile-high range that stretches to the Georgia border. During the pioneer era its various chunks acquired different names: the Bald Mountains, the Unaka Mountains, the Stone Mountains, the Unicoi Mountains, and the Smoky Mountains. During the colonial era the British, unaware of the breaks in this great barrier, knew the entire range as the Smoky Mountains, a common parlance to this day; however, 20th-century geologists decided to rename them the Unaka Mountains. This book calls them the Smokies/Unakas.

Between these two great barrier ridges lies a knotted tangle of mountains, a great mass of ridgelines and valleys that run in all directions at once, paying little heed to the needs of little humans scurrying from one town to another. Some of these in-betweeners are as modest as an Ozark mountain, while others rival, and even surpass, all other eastern ridges in elevation and ruggedness. Only in the great central bowl around Asheville, NC, do these in-betweener ranges fail altogether, leaving a Piedmont-like countryside.

These are the great mountains of the American South: the Blue Ridge Mountains and the Smokies/Unakas and the ridges that jumble between them. Higher and steeper than any other eastern range, they penetrate far enough south to gain a rich mantle of vegetation of astonishing richness and variety; yet their highest peaks reach so far into the cool upper atmosphere as to be clothed in subarctic forests. Ridge after receding ridge charms the visitor, as do the wisps of smoke rising from the cabins in the valleys far below. It is little wonder that the great national parks within these mountains attract 25 million visitors a year. Yet there remains plenty of friendly little valleys where old-fashioned hospitality awaits visitors. This book is a guide to those valleys and the great peaks that look down on them.

Appalachians or Alleghenies? Are these really the Appalachian Mountains? Or are they the Alleghenies? Or perhaps the Alleghenies are farther west, and the "Appalachians" include them, the Great Valley (Knoxville and Chattanooga, TN), the Smokies/Unakas, and the Blue Ridge. All such usages can be found in contemporary writing. So what's the real name of these mountains?

In 1565 French cartographer Jacques Le Moyne published a map of Florida in which he identified a mountain range, far to Florida's north, which he labeled the "Montes Apalatchi." Evidently the Apalachee Indians of the Florida Panhandle had boasted to Le Moyne that they owned these mountains, an obvious tall tale. At any rate, both Le Moyne and his Florida informants had been referring to the Georgia Blue Ridge, not the entire mountain chain that stretches from Alabama to Nova Scotia. However, five years later Gerard Mercator repeated the name "Montes Apalatchi" on his landmark map, the term stuck, and the mountains became known as the Appalachians.

If only the story was that simple. The fact was, the name "Appalachian" was a silly one and nobody liked it. By the late 1700s it had died out in favor of the "Allegheny Mountains," and "Appalachian" disappeared from use. By the late 19th century, only antiquarians knew the meaning of the term *Appalachian*.

And that is exactly where it came from. In 1861, Swiss geographer Arnold Guyot revived the term and applied it to "the Appalachian Mountain System," which he identified as consisting of the eastern mountains (the Blue Ridge and Smokies/Unakas), the Great Valley of Tennessee (Knoxville and Chattanooga, TN), and a plateau escarpment farther west whose heavily dissected edge has a mountainous look. The mountain people disliked Guyot's new terms (if they ever heard of them) and continued to use "Allegheny" well into the 20th century (one of North Carolina's mountain counties is named "Allegheny"). But it was no use, as academics of the era had their own ideas. Twentieth-century geographers followed Guyot's lead and ignored common usage, even taking the liberty of moving the term *Allegheny* westward from the Blue Ridge to the plateau escarpment. Sociologists followed, professing to discover a unified social and cultural region in Guyot's "Appalachian Mountain System." They dubbed this purported region "Appalachia," a place they described as characterized by social atavism and extreme poverty, "a strange land inhabited by a peculiar people," as one writer put it. No wonder terms remain confusing.

With all this, readers will be pleased to learn that both the names "Blue Ridge" and "Smoky Mountains" are authentic early terms, in common usage by the mid–18th century. Cherokee names still abound, and some, such as Nantahala (nanta-HAY-la) and Unaka (you-NAY-ka) retain their original pronunciation.

About This Book. Unlike many other guidebooks, Explorer's Guides are not collections of paid advertising. No entry has been charged a fee or allowed to supply copy. Rather, these entries are the personal recommendations of the author, a geographer, travel specialist, and longtime resident of the Blue Ridge and Smoky Mountains.

This guide does all it can to include phone numbers, addresses, and prices that are accurate as of press time. However, you can be safely assured that by the time you read this book, some of this information will inevitably be out of date—especially the prices. Use them for comparison, with each other and your budget. Make a little inflation adjustment in your head; these prices were quoted to the author in early 2001.

Also included are some—but by no means all—relevant web sites. In general, we list web sites for chambers of commerce and other tourism agencies, along with sites that have their own domain name and unique, informational content. (See also *Web Sites* in "What's Where in the Blue Ridge and Smoky Mountains.")

Here are a few notes about the organization of this book.

Wandering Around—The one thing you can always rely on in the Blue Ridge and Smoky Mountains is first-rate sight-seeing. This section orients you to an area's scenic qualities while steering you toward the best of the roads and trails.

Villages—Of course, the American South doesn't really have villages in the northern sense. More typical is a small county seat with a courthouse and a brick-front downtown, surrounded by many miles of dispersed farms and houses in which settlements are names on the map without specific centers. The mountains are no different. This section describes all places with well-defined centers that a visitor might want to visit or stumble into by accident, plus a few dispersed settlements that have notable sites mentioned elsewhere in the text. In congested areas, this section gives tips on parking.

Wild Places—In the Blue Ridge and Smoky Mountains, settled areas can be widely separated islands in a sea of trees—"Ploughed Spaces" or "Paved Spaces" in an area where wild lands are the norm. This section describes, in broad terms, the qualities of the giant wild tracts of publicly accessible lands and follows this with the best of the parks and picnic areas. (New visitors should note that picnicking is an excellent alternative in a region where restaurants are far apart and may not be very good.)

To See—Worthwhile destinations are listed here. To be included, a place must be unique and interesting in some mountainy way—the sort of thing you traveled here to see. After all, there are plenty of water slides and miniature golf places back home. Listed places must be reasonably authentic and not exploitative to either the mountain folk or their own customers. You won't find any salted gem mines or "hillbilly hoe-downs" in these pages (but there are several authentic local gem mines and mountain music venues).

To Do—These entries list outdoor activities for those who get antsy with too much relaxing. This book tries to include all outdoor sports that are quiet and noninvasive, as well as some golf courses and ski slopes.

Lodging—Only independent, local establishments with high standards of comfort, cleanliness, and hospitality are listed. Not all worthy establishments can be mentioned; this book tries to give a good selection of different types of places, emphasizing character and uniqueness. Unless otherwise noted, listed lodgings have private baths for all rooms. All rates listed are for two people in one room for one night, unless noted otherwise. By definition, all "Bed & Breakfast" listings include breakfast in the room rate unless listed otherwise. We made a special effort to find places that are disabled accessible, family friendly, and/or pet friendly, but we were not always able to find such places for each chapter.

Where to Eat—This section emphasizes food made fresh from scratch, using fresh ingredients. It lists places in two categories: casual, inexpensive places in *Eating Out,* and formal, expensive places in *Dining Out.* In *Eating Out,* the occasional catered (premade) side is allowed if the price is right and the atmosphere nice; in *Dining Out,* catered or precooked food is unforgivable.

Entertainment—The Blue Ridge and Smoky Mountains are not noted for their lively night club scene. This section lists places that have authentic mountain music and bluegrass ("mountain music" being the old-time folk music on which bluegrass is based), as well as summer theater, regular classical music schedules, and miscellaneous neat stuff.

Selective Shopping—As with other sections, this one emphasizes the unique and unusual. Rather than a complete listing, it's typically a few suggestions to help get you started in the right direction. Sometimes it lists individual shops; in other places it gives a general description of a shopping district as an aid in exploration. You'll find a lot of crafts galleries listed, as this region is a major center of the Fine Crafts movement.

Special Events—Again, this is not a complete listing but a selection of especially worthwhile annual events and festivals.

WHAT'S WHERE IN THE BLUE RIDGE AND SMOKY MOUNTAINS

AREA CODES No fewer than six area codes extend into the Blue Ridge and Smoky Mountains from nearby urban areas. In North Carolina, most areas are in the **828** code, while the northernmost mountain counties are in **336.** In Tennessee, the southern and the northern Smokies/Unakas use **423,** while the central Smokies/Unakas are included with Knoxville, TN's, **865.** South Carolina's mountains are in area code **864,** while the northern Georgia mountains are in **706.**

AIRPORTS There are six airports with scheduled passenger service in or near this region, five of which have jet service. Most visitors will want to fly into either Asheville, NC (see **Asheville Regional Airport** under *Getting There* in "Asheville and the Blue Ridge Parkway"), or Knoxville, TN (see **McGhee Tyson Airport** under *Getting There* in "Townsend, Cades Cove, and the Northwest Quadrant"). However, there are some exceptions: Greenville/Spartanburg, SC (**Greenville-Spartanburg International Airport),** is the closest to Brevard and Cashiers/Highlands, NC; Chattanooga, TN (**Chattanooga Metropolitan Airport**), is closer to Copperhill, TN, and Murphy, NC; and Tri-Cities (Johnson City, Bristol, and Kingsport, all in Tennessee; **Tri-Cities Airport**) is closest to the northernmost counties. Hickory, NC (**Hickory Regional Airport),** has regular commuter flights from Charlotte, NC (**Charlotte-Douglas International Airport),** and leaves you just underneath the Blue Ridge near Boone and Morganton, NC. Bargain hunters should consider flying into the nearest major hubs (either Charlotte, NC, or Atlanta, GA); and driving from there into the mountains (typically 2 to 4 hours). In any case, expect to rent a car; these mountains have virtually no regional or local bus service.

AMTRAK There is no passenger train service to these mountains; not even Chattanooga, TN, gets a choo-choo these days. The closest approach is at Greenville and Spartanburg, SC, about 45 minutes south of **Asheville,** NC, where **The Crescent** stops twice a day.

AMUSEMENT PARKS This book does not cover amusement or theme parks, as a modern intrusion from the outside having nothing to do with mountain wilderness or culture. However, there are several such parks of varying quality within this region. For those who like such things, look for amusement parks **outside the main gates of Great Smoky Mountains National Park,** at Gatlinburg and Pigeon Forge, TN, and at Cherokee and Maggie Valley, NC—Pigeon Forge's **Dollywood** being the largest and best of this bunch. Aficionados of **Wild West attractions** will find three to choose from, at Boone, Maggie Valley, and Franklin (all in NC). The Boone Wild West attraction features a **historic steam locomotive** that was in local commercial use through most of the first half of the 20th century [see The ET & WNC (Tweetsie) Railroad under *To See—Historic Sites* in "The Mountains of Northern Tennessee"].

ANTIQUES Antiques lovers used to the rich selections in the Virginia Blue Ridge and the mountains of New England may find this region disappointing. Truth is, most of these valleys were unspeakably poor until the 1950s and 1960s, and folks did not buy a lot of fancy furniture. However, this is a good area to look for **old farm implements;** animal-drawn plowing did not die out in most of these valleys until the 1960s and 1970s.

APPALACHIAN TRAIL (AT) Blazed in the 1930s as the world's first long-distance recreational footpath, the Appalachian Trail stretches for well over 2,000 miles along the East's wildest and toughest mountains, from Georgia to Maine. Although officially part of the national park system (as a National Scenic Trail), the AT is mainly a private volunteer effort, blazed and maintained by 31 hiking clubs that make up the **Appalachian Trail Conference.** This book covers 365 miles of the trail, including the ultra-popular stretch through Great Smoky Mountains National Park. Various chapters include rewarding day hikes along bits of the trail. For more information contact the Appalachian Trail Conference (304-535-6331), 799 Washington Street, Harpers Ferry, WV 25425.

APPLES Cherokees introduced apple growing to the Blue Ridge and Smoky Mountains in the early 18th century, having picked it up from the Creeks (who had learned it from Spanish missions in "La Florida"). While English settlers dismissed apple horticulture as impractical in the cold mountain climate, the Cherokees learned to grow trees in special valleys turned warm by persistent air inversions. Nineteenth-century mountain folk took up the Cherokee techniques in a big way, creating the beginnings of a mountain apple industry. Today, the **Brevard,** NC, area has the largest commercial orchards in the region (see **Apple Country** under *Wandering Around— Exploring by Car* in "The Blue Ridge: Chimney Rock and Saluda"), while a fine heritage orchard is open to the public at **Altapass,** along the Blue Ridge Parkway (see **The Orchard at Altapass** under *To See—Along the Blue Ridge Parkway* in "The Blue Ridge Parkway: Blowing Rock and Grandfather Mountain"). U-pick-ems are a common sight around Brevard and are found in most parts of this region; look to pick apples in late August through early October.

ARTISTS AND ART GALLERIES In the 1920s and 1930s, folk crafts were widely seen as a way of bringing hard cash into the remote mountain coves. Folk art schools and guilds founded in that era to support the economic development of poor mountain families, today survive as centers of the Fine Crafts movement, dominated by university-educated artists building on mountain traditions. Major schools survive at Penland (see **Penland School of Crafts** under *To See—Cultural Sites* in "Behind the Blue Ridge: Spruce Pine and Burnsville") and Brasstown (see **John C. Campbell Folk School** under *To See—Cultural Sites* in "The Southern Unicois: Murphy and the Copper Basin") in North Carolina,

while the **Highland's Crafts Guild** promotes craft artists from its headquarters in Asheville, NC (see **The Folk Art Center and Allenstand Craft Shop** under *To See—Along the Blue Ridge Parkway* in "Asheville and the Blue Ridge Parkway").

BALDS, GRASSY While most of these mountains are covered in dense forest, an occasional grassy meadow will cling to a high ridgeline. Known as "grassy balds," these high meadows furnish wide panoramas across swaths of wildflowers, framed in the spring by bushes purple with Catawba rhododendrons and orange with flame azaleas. These balds may be as small as a few dozen acres but may also sweep for miles along a high ridge. Their origin is unclear. Grassy balds were far more common in the 19th century, when a hundred thousand cattle grazed along the crest of the Great Smoky Mountains every summer. Left ungrazed, these great fields have been returning to forest since the start of the 20th century. The grassy balds may have been created by the Cherokees, burned out to create wildlife habitat for hunting. Or they may have been formed by grazing elk and buffalo in the 16th through 18th centuries, then maintained by cattle after the elk and buffalo had been hunted to extinction in this region. The largest surviving grassy balds are in **The Roan Highlands** (see The Roan Highlands on the Appalachian Trail under *Wandering Around—Exploring on Foot* in "Behind the Blue Ridge: Spruce Pine and Burnsville").

BALDS, ROCKY Unlike grassy balds, rocky balds are a completely natural phenomenon. Common to the Blue Ridge, a rocky bald consists of a broad expanse of smoothly curving, exposed bedrock elevated at any possible angle from dead flat to totally vertical. A typical rocky bald will extend from 1 to 5 acres, with the bare rock covered by patches of moss and an occasional dwarfed pine. The rock looks like granite but isn't; it's *gneiss* (pronounced nice), a metamorphosed granite whose peculiar geology causes this unusual formation. Along the Blue Ridge, this ancient gneiss has been compressed under immense pressure for most of the last quarter billion years, only to be raised up and exposed by erosion during the past 50 million or so years. This great relief of pressure has allowed the gneiss to expand like a spring, in the stateliest of slow motion, exfoliating in thinly compressed layers. This exfoliation is just fast enough to slough off soil as quickly as it forms, leaving the

bedrock smooth and bare. Needless to say, rocky balds furnish some of the most dramatic views anywhere. One of the most impressive sights along the Blue Ridge is an entire dome of rock exposed in this way, such as **Looking Glass Rock** visible for miles from the **Blue Ridge Parkway** (see *Wandering Around—Exploring by Car* in "Waynesville and the Blue Ridge Parkway").

BARBEQUE People who've heard of the wondrous qualities of North Carolina barbeque will be disappointed to learn that this rich and varied tradition seldom extends into the mountains. The famously piquant, slow-cooked Piedmont barbeque with its vinegar-cayenne baste and its coleslaw made fresh with the barbeque sauce is hard to find in these parts. But good barbeque, slow-cooked over wood, does exist in the mountains, and we highlight it when we find it.

BED & BREAKFASTS A rare sight 15 years ago, B&Bs are now found in every part of the Blue Ridge and Smoky Mountains except Cherokee, NC. They are generally price-competitive with local motels and a whole lot nicer. Small and friendly, these small lodgings offer a good way to relax and meet the locals. A typical mountain B&B will have a wide porch with rocking chairs and a view over a garden, a great room with comfortable sofas and chairs grouped around a wood fire, a friendly group of guests who swap experiences over a luxurious breakfast or an evening glass of wine, and a gregarious host who never seems to tire of meeting new people and giving a helping hand to visitors.

By the way, you might want to check the Internet for a B&B web site before calling for a reservation. Although this book seldom lists web sites for inns and B&Bs (addresses tend to change too often), nearly all of them have one, and most show photos of the individual rooms.

BERRY PICKING Wild berries are available for the picking throughout the public lands of the Blue Ridge and Smoky Mountains. Old fields and grassy balds offer **wild strawberries** in June, then **blackberries** in mid-August, with **blueberries** in the high grassy balds in late August and early September. Wild strawberries, tiny and intensely flavored, hide low among the grasses in old fields. Blackberries grow on thorny canes in old fields and are full of chiggers (see *Bugs*). Blueberries grow on low, woody bushes on grassy and rocky balds and like the cool, wet weather above 4,000 feet. There are lots of other edible berries; look for a **ranger-led talk** in a national park or forest. You can collect up to a gallon of each type of berry per day without a permit in the national park and forest lands—free fun that kids love.

BICYCLING The region offers wonderful opportunities for bicyclists. Back roads, increasingly paved, offer lovely scenery and light traffic, with a down side of narrow, shoulderless lanes and the occasional mean farm dog. The premiere road-biking experience is the **Blue Ridge Parkway,** where the scenery is nonstop and wide shoulders, gentle curves, and frequent pullovers reduce traffic problems. The huge tracts of **national forest land** found throughout this region offer many miles of trail biking, mainly down old logging roads. Finally, a few places offer dedicated bicycle trails, most notably Nantahala National Forest's **Tsali Recreation Area** (see *Wild Places—Recreation Areas* in "Bryson City and the Southwest Quadrant"). For those who don't travel with their bicycles, this book lists bicycle rentals in most areas.

THE BLUE RIDGE PARKWAY The 469-mile Blue Ridge Parkway stretches from the southern edge of the Shenandoah National Park (in Virginia, near Washington, DC), to the North Carolina gateway of Great Smoky Mountains National Park. More than 250 miles of the parkway cross this book's region, following the crest of the Blue Ridge from the North Carolina–Virginia state line to Asheville, NC, then climbing a series of remote mile-high peaks over to the Smokies. Constructed between 1936 and 1989, the parkway was originally intended as a Depression make-work project, with a long-range goal of bringing tourist dollars to the depressed mountain coves of Virginia

and North Carolina. By this standard, it's a roaring success; the parkway attracts 15 million recreation visitors a year, the greatest number of any National Park Service property.

Built and operated by the National Park Service, the parkway's typical thousand-foot width has been carefully and unobtrusively landscaped over its entire length, for a continuously beautiful drive. The effect is subtle but remarkable. Grassy verges curve into forests, giving views deep into the trees; split-rail fences line pastures and farmlands; forests drop away suddenly to reveal wide and dramatic mountain views over low stone walls. Bridges, tunnels, and abutments are clad in hand-laid stonework, done by artisans brought in from Europe. Commercial intrusion is virtually nonexistent, and modern buildings are a rare sight. The National Park Service furnishes a small number of concession areas, widely spaced, where food, gasoline, and lodging are available.

BUGS First the good news. The Blue Ridge and Smoky Mountains are largely free of swarming blackflies, midges, and mosquitoes—the kind of insects that form clouds around your face and fill your nose when you try to breathe. What's more, flies and roaches are less of a nuisance here than in warmer parts of the South. This is not to say that these mountains are free of all pests. You are likely to get **chiggers**—microscopic larvae that burrow into your skin—anytime you sit on the ground in even slightly warm weather. **Ticks** are very common and likely to jump on you anytime you brush against a plant in warm weather. Chigger bites itch like crazy and can last for weeks if you have an allergic reaction (most people do). Ticks spread diseases, some of them crippling or fatal. Your best defense against both chiggers and ticks is to wear long sleeves and long pants and spray insect repellant around your neck, belt, and cuffs.

BUS SERVICE There is only one scheduled passenger bus route in this region, a **Greyhound Bus Lines** line from Greenville, SC, to Asheville, NC, then northward out of the mountains into Tennessee. Along the way, the bus stops at the mountain towns of Hendersonville, NC, and Waynesville, NC.

CABIN RENTALS Cabin rentals have long been a tradition in these mountains and have become increasingly popular in recent years. In some places, small compounds of log cabins, recently built in traditional styles and luxuriously furnished, have been springing up faster than chain motels. A rental cabin can be a pleasant retreat for a couple, with its ample space, separate living room, and porch; for a family with kids, it can also be a major money saver, allowing breakfasts and dinners at home, and picnic lunches on the road. This book includes a selection of good cabin compounds throughout the region. Many of these cabins can be rented for only a night or two; others require rental periods of up to a week.

CAMPING Campgrounds are found in abundance throughout this region. The national parks and forests contain scores of public campgrounds, generally cheap and scenic but without hookups. (The popular campgrounds within Great Smoky Mountains National Park don't even have showers.) While many of the public campgrounds stay booked all summer, you can always find a good site in a remote, beautiful little national forest campground down a gravel road somewhere; ask a ranger at the nearest district station (listed under *Guidance* in appropriate chapters). Private campgrounds are the best bet for RVers who insist on electricity and running water.

CANOEING AND KAYAKING This region has abundant whitewater and stillwater, with suitable streams in nearly every chapter. Famous whitewater streams include the **Ocoee River,** site of the 1996 Summer Olympics; the **Nantahala River,** well known as a training ground for Olympic medalists; and the **Chatooga River,** made famous in the novel *Deliverance.* Two other rivers, the **New River** and the **French Broad River,** offer excellent areas for long, scenic canoe trips and are perfect for overnight camping. Places to hire canoes and kayaks, join a whitewater rafting party, or have your boat shuttled to a drop-off point are noted throughout this book.

CHEROKEES This entire region was the core home of the Cherokees, centering on the fertile valleys of the Little Tennessee River south of the Great Smoky Mountains. The Cherokees lived in villages ranging from a half-dozen to several score houses made of logs and surrounded by cultivated fields. These were organized along clan lines, similar to the Scottish Highlands but without the constant warfare; Cherokee villages shared a traditional legal code, enforced through consensus and the leadership of chiefs. Until the wars of the late 18th century, the Cherokees had three major settlement areas: an area of villages in the South Carolina upstate, a second area in the deep mountains to the immediate south of the Smokies, and a third area ("Overhill") at the foot of the mountains in Tennessee. The more northern mountains, around present-day Burnsville, NC, and Boone, NC, were kept as a hunting ground.

In the late 18th century, the Cherokees tried to defeat the European invaders in battle, with disastrous consequences. After that, tribal consensus swung toward working within the invaders' legal system. Led by wealthy Europeanized chiefs, the tribe formed itself into a quasi-autonomous legal entity known as the **Cherokee Nation,** located in northern Georgia, southeastern Tennessee, and the westernmost corner of the North Carolina mountains. In 1838, President Andrew Jackson's administration expelled the Cherokee Nation to Oklahoma, forcing the Cherokees into a deadly winter march known as The Trail of Tears.

About 600 Cherokees remained in the deep coves of the Smokies, and their descendants still live, work, and thrive in these mountains. The **Eastern Band** of the Cherokee Nation, some 10,000 strong, inhabits a sizable reservation, properly called the **Qualla Boundary,** located on the North Carolina side of Great Smoky Mountains National Park.

CHILDREN, ESPECIALLY FOR The author spent many a summer as a child in these mountains and vividly remembers the things he found the most fun: splashing in mountain streams, exploring the forests, picking berries, visiting log cabins, sifting for rubies, and climbing around on rocky crags with dramatic views. Whitewater rafting hadn't been invented yet, else that would have made the list as well. Rustic cabins were a lot neater than motel rooms, especially on cool, rainy days when we played board games by the wood fire. Home-cooked suppers at our cabins were more fun for us than

eating out, and picnics in a national park were more fun than burgers in a tourist town. Museums could be patience testers, but log cabins and pioneer log farms were endlessly fascinating—particularly those with farm animals, or gristmills that worked. We liked to walk down short, easy trails, particularly to cliffs or waterfalls; or just get out of the car and run around. We gained these tastes as small children and retained them as teenagers; perhaps if we had first seen the mountains at age 14 we would have been too cool for any of this.

This region is jammed with child-appropriate, family-friendly stuff. The text makes a serious effort to mention anything that will challenge a child's patience, endurance, or safety, making it easy to judge what's right for your kids. Restaurants, lodgings, and attractions that are of particular interest to families are marked with the ✐ symbol. Please note that most B&Bs do not accept children under 12; the text notes those that do with a crayon icon.

COUNTRY STORES As towns thrive and prosper, country stores decline and disappear. However, country stores continue to survive in some of our most remote rural areas, serving the needs of residents who live too far from town. Others, such as the famous **Mast General Store** (see *To See—Historic Sites* in "Behind the Blue Ridge: Boone and Banner Elk") near Boone, NC, have survived and thrived by combining the tourist trade into their local business. This book mentions a number of general stores.

DRY COUNTIES These mountain regions are a patchwork of local liquor laws. Both North Carolina and Tennessee allow local options on beer, wine, and liquor sales, and North Carolina still has a socialized liquor control system. Depending on where you are,

you may be able to buy wine and beer but not liquor, liquor but not wine or beer, wine or beer in a store but not a restaurant, or in a restaurant but not a store—or all sales may be banned outright. That is, except for golf clubs, tennis clubs, and hotels and restaurants within 3 miles of the Blue Ridge Parkway. This book tries to include whether wine is available at a fine dining spot, but it's best to check in advance.

EMERGENCIES, MEDICAL There is nothing more frightening than having a serious medical emergency and not knowing where the nearest emergency room is. For this reason, each chapter introduction includes the location of the nearest emergency room, as well as the walk-in clinic if one exists.

FALL FOLIAGE The Blue Ridge and Smoky Mountains have one of America's outstanding autumn color displays—the result of a large variety of species spread over a large range of elevations and habitats. Look for color to begin in early October and to reach its peak in the middle of the month. From then, colors will last until the first strong wind, generally in the third or fourth week of October. In most years, color is nearly gone by early November.

FISHING This region is a wonderful place for fly-fishing, and this book tries to include contact information for guides. You'll need a state fishing license everywhere but within the **Cherokee Reservation,** where you'll need a tribal license instead.

HIKING Sooner or later, nearly everyone gets out of the car and walks through the woods. The Blue Ridge and Smoky Mountains are laced with footpaths, up creeks and along ridges. There are thousands of miles of walking trails to choose from, with good choices in every chapter of this book. *Wandering Around* contains a suggestion or two, very rewarding and not particularly difficult. Other sections will mention still more trails, each with a brief indication of the type of scenery as well as their difficulty and length.

HIGHWAYS AND ROADS This region is crossed by **I-40** from east to west, and by **I-26** from north to south; they intersect at Asheville, NC. At this writing, I-26 north of Asheville is under construction, but largely completed; the completed segments are marked as **US 23** for the time being.

Apart from interstates and U.S. highways, this book follows a welter of road types. State highways are designated as NC 80 or TN 70. Although these are supposed to be main highways, some are no better than local roads with fancy signs, and three of them in North Carolina are **gravel surfaced** (NC 281, NC 197, and NC 90). Local roads have names in Ten-

nessee, Georgia, and South Carolina but four-digit numbers in North Carolina (see *Highways and Roads in North Carolina*). National Park Service roads are always designated with names. National Forest Service roads are designated with numbers, such as FS 712; please note that many Forest Service roads are not passable for passenger cars.

The mountains being what they are, this book frequently recommends touring on gravel-surfaced roads. These roads have been improved by pounding in a mixture of gravel and rock dust, the rock dust acting as a temporary cement. Gravel roads form potholes and washboardlike ridges if not graded once or twice a year, a condition most apt to occur on Forest Service roads. The text will highlight known problems. In general, if a road starts looking too rough for you, don't hesitate to turn around and go back.

HIGHWAYS AND ROADS IN NORTH CAROLINA Unlike other states, North Carolina has no local roads. All of its rural roads are state roads, from the largest freeway down to the roughest dirt rut. The state's Department of Transportation (known as NCDOT, or NickDot) distinguishes "state highways" from "state roads." **State highways** are considered major thoroughfares, with regular state highway signs and two- or three-digit numbers, such as NC 90 or NC 197. **State roads** have four-digit numbers, typically marked on stop signs with those little home address stick-on numbers. In this book, state roads are denoted as, for example, SSR 1300 or SSR 1407, the SSR standing for "state secondary road." This guide tries very hard to get the state road numbers right, because—unlike road names—they are almost always present at intersections. However, don't expect locals to direct you to an SSR number; no one in North Carolina pays attention to them.

HORSEBACK RIDING Most parts of this region have at least one horseback riding stable. Some offer trail rides on their own property, while others outfit longer expeditions on national forest lands. Nearly every chapter lists at least one stable. In addition, there are several listed accommodations that offer stabling to people who travel with their horses.

HUNTING The main hunting season runs from **September through January.** Remember that hunting is allowed in all national forest lands, including the 16 wilderness areas (see *Public Lands: Wilderness*) in this region; always wear hunter orange anytime you enter these areas during the season. If you wish to avoid hunting areas altogether, stay in the 3 national parks and the 11 state parks (which, fortunately, offer plenty of outdoor opportunity). Hunting is also prohibited on Sunday in the state of North Carolina, making that a good day to enjoy God's creation (but wear hunter orange anyway, just in case).

INFORMATION As much as we like to be encyclopedic in our coverage, we admit that there is nothing like fresh, local information. Each chapter of this book lists the relevant chambers of commerce, along with their toll-free number and web site. We also describe local tourist information centers, so you can drop by and talk to someone friendly and in the know.

LAKES There are no natural lakes in this region: all of the lakes are man-made, mostly for hydropower. Typically, these lakes drown a steep-sided mountain valley, twisting upstream for miles through roadless areas into steep-sided woodlands, poking little inlets up side valleys. In many cases the shores are national forest lands with no restrictions on boat-side camping. However, other lakes are privately owned—and this may include the lake's surface as well as the surrounding shore. This book will point out interesting opportunities as they arise, as well as give contact information for lake-oriented fishing guides.

LOG CABINS While most of us associate log cabins with the first generations of settlers, log construction continued in the mountains into the early 20th century. This was not a matter of isolation or tradition, so much as saving money; logs were free, while milled studs required scarce dollars. Great Smoky Mountains National Park displays a superbly crafted log cabin built by its owner in 1902 (see **Mountain Farm Museum** under *To See—Historic Sites* in "Cherokee and the Southeast Quadrant").

In these parts, all vernacular log cabins were built with *planked* logs—that is, logs that had their vertical sides hewn flat. Planking reduced rot by allowing rainwater to run straight down rather than bead up on the underside of a round log. While barns frequently used round logs, a round log cabin is invariably modern.

This book sometimes describes a log cabin in terms of its *cribs*. A crib is the rectangle made when the logs are fit together; doors and windows are then cut out of the cribs. The simplest cabins had one crib, covered with a roof. Larger cabins had two cribs, and the cribs could be placed together to form a two-room cabin, separated by a chimney (a rare form in the South), or (most commonly) separated by a roofed central breezeway, or *dogtrot*.

Log cabins were an important part of mountain life—but today, most log cabins you will see are either carefully restored museum pieces or abandoned hulks. Not so with **log barns;** keep an eye peeled for log barns still in use along any back road and particularly in the areas covered by "The Northern Mountains."

LOST Even with the best maps (see *Maps: USGS Topos*) you are likely to get lost once you stray from a main highway. On these twisting roads, even the sharpest explorers lose their sense of direction. Your best defense is a **compass**—one of those round ones you stick on your dashboard. Pay attention to it along several twists, and take an average. This will at least tell

you if you are going generally toward your destination or away from it. And relax. How bad can it be? Getting lost is an adventure, not a disaster.

MAPS: ROAD MAPS Even really good road maps can be insufficient help in the mountains. Main highways are easy enough to follow, but back roads are a twisty maze, frequently with no regular names. Once you start exploring a back road, your folding highway map won't help you much. **DeLorme's** atlases and gazetteers (1-800-575-2244; www.delorme.com) show all the back roads as well as the shapes of the mountains, giving extra clues for your party's navigator to analyze. Unfortunately, you'll have to buy four individual state volumes to cover the entire Blue Ridge and Smoky Mountains region; this will give you a bonus (possibly unneeded and unwanted) of incredibly detailed coverage from the Atlantic seaboard to the Mississippi River. A computer street atlas of the United States is much cheaper, if you can get used to using your laptop in a moving car. But whatever map you use, be prepared to get lost (see *Lost*) every once in a while.

MAPS: USGS TOPOGRAPHIC MAPS Of course, no serious outdoors enthusiast will step away from the parking lot without a U.S. Geological Survey (USGS) topographic map showing every detail of mountain slope at 2⅔ inches to the mile. Unfortunately, the USGS hasn't gotten around to updating some of these mountain topos since the Great Depression; the mountain slopes haven't changed much, but don't expect anything else to be very accurate. The good news: the **U.S. Forest Service** has marked up black-and-white copies of the USGS maps with their own information, providing accurate local road data as well as showing Forest Service roads, trails, recreation sites, and land ownership. To get these first-rate maps, inquire with the ranger at the local Forest Service district station, listed under *Guidance* in appropriate chapters; each office has the maps for their area, and no other.

MOUNTAINTOPS Nearly all of the region is covered in dense forest. You can walk for miles along a high ridgeline without ever having a view. Of course, the forests are a prime attraction of these mountains, endlessly varied and with more tree species than are found in Europe. However, the occasional overwhelmingly dramatic panorama is certainly welcome, the more so if you don't have to hike all day to find it. The best views are from balds (see *Balds, Grassy*), great sweeps of open grass or rocky ground. Other views are intentionally created and maintained by the National Park Service, within Great Smoky Mountains National Park or along the Blue Ridge Parkway. This book highlights the best of the views, both roadside and from the easier paths.

MUSIC This guide tries to find and describe worthwhile music venues throughout the region. These range from rural dance halls, to weekend bluegrass jams, to large-scale classical

music festivals. Mountain music is featured most often (see *Music, Mountain*), along with bluegrass—the local favorite, more popular than Nashville-style country. Classical music, along with jazz, is found near the universities, and Brevard, NC, hosts a major classical music festival every summer (see **Brevard Music Center** under *To See—Cultural Sites* in "The Blue Ridge: Hendersonville and Brevard").

MUSIC, MOUNTAIN Mountain music isn't bluegrass, and it definitely isn't country. Mountain music is the music people knew before radios came along, the music they used to play deep in the coves and hollows. Mountain music was already a fast-disappearing anachronism when Mars Hill, NC, native Bascom Lamar Lunsford started his vast collection of mountain folk music, mixing heavily with nationally circulating sheet music and radio broadcasts. Today it represents a carefully preserved folk tradition, still popular and readily available throughout this region. This book cites mountain music venues wherever it can.

PETS Only a few B&Bs will allow pets, and these are highlighted in the text with the pet-friendly symbol 🐾. You'll have better luck with a cabin rental, which fortunately are very common in this area, but verify in advance that your pet will be welcome. Of the places that allow pets, many charge an extra fee or restrict pets to special units. Great Smoky Mountains National Park prohibits pets on all hiking trails, with no exceptions, and requires dogs to be kept on a leash at all times anywhere else.

PUBLIC LANDS: THE NATIONAL PARK SERVICE The National Park Service (NPS), a bureau of the U.S. Department of the Interior, maintains three properties in this region: Great Smoky Mountains National Park, the Blue Ridge Parkway, and the **Carl Sandburg Home** National Historic Site (see *To See—Historic Sites* in "The Blue Ridge: Hendersonville and Brevard"). Each has its own management style. Great Smoky Mountains National Park—the only designated "national park" of the three and the most visited national park in America—has always been maintained as a wilderness park with the emphasis on hiking, camping, picnicking, and fishing. The Blue Ridge Parkway (the most visited property managed by the National Park Service) is more purely recreational, with hotels, restaurants, and even gas stations along its length. The Carl Sandburg Home, small and little visited, faithfully preserves the great poet's historic antebellum estate the way he knew it—including an active goat farm. However, all three share one major characteristic with each other and every other NPS property. They are all preserves, each safeguarding a precious resource for the future. All prohibit hunting, gathering plants, rockhounding, and picking wildflowers.

PUBLIC LANDS: THE NATIONAL FOREST SERVICE People frequently confuse the National Forest Service (NFS) with the National Park Service (NPS)—yet the two agencies couldn't be more different. While the NPS preserves our finest natural and historic lands, the NFS—part of the U.S. Department of Agriculture—manages forest lands for sustainable exploitation. The NFS logs many of its tracts, getting much of its operating revenues from timber sales. It allows hunting on virtually all of its lands, including congressionally declared wildernesses. The actual type of use given to any tract of national forest land—logging, recreation, preservation—is set by a plan that is revised every eight years.

This region has five national forests, any one of which dwarfs the local national parks in size: **Cherokee National Forest** in Tennessee, **Chattahoochee National Forest** in Georgia, **Sumter National Forest** in South Carolina, **Nantahala National Forest** in the southern half of the North Carolina mountains, and **Pisgah National Forest** in the northern half of the North Carolina mountains. Nearly every chapter in this book includes huge tracts of national forest land, some with many wonderful things to do and see.

PUBLIC LANDS: WILDERNESS Maybe only God can make a tree (see **Joyce Kilmer Memorial Forest** under *Wild Places—The Great Forests* in "The Northern Unicois: Robbinsville and Tellico Plains"), but only the U.S. Congress can create a wilderness. Under the Wilderness Act of 1964, Congress sets aside large, contiguous tracts of federal land as perpetual wilderness preserves. Each of the tracts remains under the management of their original agency but is managed under rules that prohibit all logging, all mechanization, and all roads. There are 16 congressionally declared wildernesses in this book, totaling 185,000 acres (289 square miles), all of which are managed by the National Forest Service and allow hunting (see *Hunting*). Typically, these are the most rugged, remote, and beautiful areas of the mountains—very special places.

RAILROADS Railroading buffs find the Blue Ridge railroads to be particularly fascinating—and with good reason. Rugged topography, thousands of feet of climbing, and an irregular, unpredictable geology posed special challenges. Some railroads, such as the narrow-gauge **Tweetsie** (see The ET & WNC Railroad under *To See—Historic Sites* in "The Mountains of Northern Tennessee"), mastered the terrain by conforming to it; others, such as the ultramodern **Clinchfield** (see The Clinchfield Railroad Loops under *To See—Historic Sites* in "The Blue Ridge Parkway: Blowing Rock and Grandfather Mountain"), blasted through in uncompromising straight lines. The big timber companies built elaborate but extremely temporary railroads throughout these mountains, and some of the old grades survive as modern auto roads (see **Driving the Little River Railroad** under *Wandering Around—Exploring by Car* in "Townsend, Cades Cove, and the Northwest Quadrant"). You can get a good long taste of an old-fashioned mountain railroad on the 53-mile-long **Great Smoky Mountain Railroad**

in Bryson City (see *To See—Other* in "Bryson City and the Southwest Quadrant"), which runs passenger excursions by day and freight by night.

ROCKHOUNDING Eons ago, columns of molten magma broke into veins throughout the mountain bedrock, crystallizing out quartz, garnets, rubies, sapphires, beryl, and gold along with the granite. None of these valuable minerals have been found in large quantities, although optimists formed small commercial mines in the 19th century. Instead, the mountains have always been mined for the cruder minerals associated with such magmatic intrusion: **granite, feldspar, mica,** and **kaolin** are all still mined. In past decades, rockhounds have loved the old abandoned feldspar and mica mines for the occasional precious stone or valuable specimen found in the tailings. Today, few sites allow such casual and dangerous trespassing. Instead, entrepreneurs offer sites where tourists can sift for rubies, selling buckets of "pay dirt" salted with cheap foreign stones (which they will cut for you, for a fee). There are a few authentic **ruby mines,** as well as an excellent **placer gold mine,** that offer unsalted dirt from on-site. See **Thermal City Gold Mine** under *To Do—Gold Mining* in "Beneath the Blue Ridge: The Catawba River Valley"; **Old Pressley Sapphire Mine** under *To Do—Gem Mining* in "Waynesville and the Blue Ridge Parkway"; and **Mason's Ruby and Sapphire Mine** and **Sheffield Mine** under *To Do—Gem Mining* in "Franklin and the Nantahala Mountains."

Old-fashioned rockhounding remains legal on national forest lands, with many restrictions. If this is your interest, inquire at the local **ranger**

district station (these are listed under *Guidance* in appropriate chapters).

SIX-THOUSAND-FOOT PEAKS Most of the East's mountains are less than 4,000 feet high. Of those that rise higher, a handful reach the mile-high mark, and only 41 top 6,000 feet. Of these 41 "6-ers," 40 are within this region, including the 1st through 16th tallest peaks. (The 17th tallest peak in the East, Mount Washington, is located in

New Hampshire.) Bagging 6-ers is catching on as a hobby, akin to bagging Scottish Munros or Coloradan 14-ers, only easier. If you're looking for a reason to choose one mountain walk over another, bagging 6-ers will lead you to many great places, and the **Tennessee Eastman Hiking and Canoeing Club** will give (well, sell) you a neat patch ($5 for a patch, plus a lot of walking; tehcc.org/beyo6000.htm). This guide points out the locations of all 40 of the six thousand-footers.

SKIING, DOWNHILL Many people think that the southern Smokies and Blue Ridge are too far south for skiing. They're right; snow seldom sticks around more than a week or so at even the highest elevations, and cold rain is much more common than fleecy blizzards. However, a number of ski slopes stay in business using manufactured snow. Mostly the result of a speculative boom in the 1960s, some of these slopes are old and unpleasant, while others keep themselves up. None are particularly fancy. Winter skiing is not an environmentally friendly sport, as it carves great scars on hillsides and breaks the winter silence with the sideshow roar of diesel generators and massive snowblowers. However, this book lists several of the better slopes, for those so inclined. See **Ski Beech** and **Sugar Mountain** under *To Do— Skiing* in "Behind the Blue Ridge: Boone and Banner Elk"; **Wolf Laurel** under *To Do—Skiing* in "Asheville's Rugged Hinterlands"; and **Ober Gatlinburg** under *To Do—Skiing* in "Gatlinburg and the Northeast Quadrant."

WALKING Frequently the best way to enjoy the mountains is to get out and walk around. Each chapter of this Explorer's Guide offers a few good walks, mainly short and easy, that highlight major features of the locale. This listing is by no means encyclopedic; rather, it's more by the way of a sampler, oriented toward the rushed traveler who doesn't have time to spend on a long, hard hike. There are numerous specialized hiking guides for the enthusiast, starting with Backcountry Guides' *Fifty Hikes in the Mountains of North Carolina Mountains* and *Fifty Hikes in the Tennessee Mountains.*

WATERFALLS Erosion—50 million years' worth—has not yet smoothed away all the rock ledges in these mountain valleys. Waterfalls abound throughout this region, ranging from a half-dozen feet high to more than 400. Many require difficult hikes down gorges, but some can be reached down an easy path, and a few can be viewed from the roadside. The text highlights dozens of these waterfalls, with a listing in nearly every chapter.

WEATHER These mountains have long been a summer retreat because of their famously cool weather—but your results may vary. In general, temperatures are cooler farther north and at higher elevations. Lower elevations are hotter, as are places farther south. The lowest elevations and hottest temperatures are along the base of the Smokies in Tennessee, where 90°F temperatures can linger late into August. Temperatures are lower on the North Carolina side, with 90° a regular event along the low elevations of the Little Tennessee River and the Tuckaseegee Valley, and a rarity on the 4,000-foot crest of the Blue Ridge near Cashiers, NC, and Highlands, NC. Asheville, NC, suffers from air inversions and is quite hot. North of Asheville, temperatures seldom reach 90°, and the mile-high peaks—Roan Mountain, Mount Mitchell, Elk Mountain—are always cool. At this writing (2001), we've had 10 years of hot, dry summers; before then, such hot weather was rare and summer rain frequent. To sum up: Escape the heat by going uphill and north. Expect hot weather below 2,000 feet.

There is life after summer. The hot weather can start in mid-June but normally waits politely for the Fourth of July weekend; it can linger into September but normally departs by late August. Spring and fall are cool, with highs between 40° and 65°F, and lows occasionally dipping below freezing. Consistent freezing weather starts sometime in November, with most days having highs between 25° and 35°F. Snow can happen any time between late October and late April, with January through March getting the worst of it. January snows are fluffy and clean, while April snows are a soggy mess.

WEB SITES These web sites cover most or all of the Blue Ridge and Smoky Mountains. Sites specific to a limited area are included in the chapter listings.

Great Smoky Mountains National Park Official Web Site (www.nps.gov/grsm/). This official National Park Service (NPS) site gives general information about the park, such as travel basics, campgrounds, and facilities. Click on "In Depth" to visit a much larger NPS site dedicated to the Smokies, with a very wide range of information.

John William Uhler's Great Smoky Mountains National Park (www.great.smoky.mountains. national-park.com/). This excellent site contains all the basic information on the park, in a well-organized format that loads fast. Uhler runs a series of similar web sites on other national parks, supported by discrete advertising.

The Blue Ridge Parkway Official Site (www.nps.gov/blri/). As with the Great Smoky Mountains' site, this official National Park Service site offers basic information on facilities, campgrounds, lodgings, and fees and an "In Depth" link to a larger and more elaborately detailed site.

Kathy Bilton's Appalachian Trail Site (www.fred.net/kathy/at.html). Kathy Bilton has run this enthusiasts' site since 1994, making it the oldest web site on the subject. It's mainly a links site nowadays, with hundreds of trail-related links in a fast-loading and well-organized format.

www.mtbikewnc.com This personal web site—run by Jordan Mitchell, an Asheville, NC, area resident and enthusiastic mountain biker —gives a lot of information about biking the western mountains of North Carolina, including detailed trail descriptions.

www.nctrout.com This thorough and well-designed site, run by a Marion, NC, fly-fisherman, covers all of the western North Carolina mountains with information on locations, flies, techniques, regulations, links to other sites, and fishing in Great Smoky Mountains National Park.

www.swimmingholes.org Tom Hillegass' wonderfully detailed exploration of the East's best wilderness swimming includes 37 locations within this book's coverage areas. Anyone who wants a cool dip in a mountain stream would do well to consult these web pages.

www.ncroads.com (www.ncroads.com/index.html). This hobby site describes most of the state and U.S. highways in North Carolina in detail, including history and scenery. Huge and easy to navigate, it's a great place to start planning a scenic drive or bicycle ride. And it will answer any question you might have about how those crazy highway numbers got assigned.

WHITEWATER RAFTING This region includes the **Ocoee Whitewater Center,** the1996 Summer Olympics whitewater competition site in Tennessee, as well as the **Nantahala Outdoor Center** in Bryson City, NC, the training site of several of our American whitewater medalists. No wonder whitewater rafting listings appear in nearly every chapter of this book. Rivers range from Class II (a few easy ripples), through Class III and IV (fun, and more fun), to Class V (expect to get very, very wet). Outfitters will put your group into a raft with other customers, put you in the river, and pick you up (typically 6 miles downstream). Some outfitters put a guide in each raft, some in each group of rafts, and some just put you in and let you float—it depends on the difficulty of the river and how much you pay. With few exceptions these are family-friendly excursions, although infants and toddlers are not allowed, and the more violent rivers may have higher age restrictions. Most of the outfitters also rent and shuttle **kayaks,** and offer kayaking lessons.

Two long Class II rivers, the **French Broad** and **New Rivers,** offer miles and miles of easy **canoeing.** This allows a family group to hire a canoe, paddle gently downstream, and camp for the night along the way. A good weekend trip might cover 30 miles of stunning river scenery, quite a contrast to a whitewater 6-mile thrill ride. The New River, the more popular of the two, flows gently through rugged wilderness gorges and narrow pastoral valleys, while the French Broad (upstream from Asheville, NC) meanders through a wide farming valley framed by tall peaks. (Downstream from Asheville, the French Broad is a Class IV whitewater stream.)

WILDFLOWERS Wildflower season starts late in the mountains, with daffodils finally beginning to decorate the drab winter roadsides in mid-April. By mid-May all the trees are in leaf and the spring wildflowers are underway in earnest. The high grassy balds become colorful by the end of May, with the rhododendrons and azaleas bursting out in mid-June. At that time, natural rhododendron "gardens" in the mile-

high grassy balds become dotted with clouds of purple, framing the wonderful views. Color fades slowly into August, then bursts out again in mid-September as the goldenrods and asters make one last fine show under the turning leaves. These will remain until late October, before the last of the blooms fade and winter returns.

WILDLIFE Bears, of course. People are sometimes surprised to learn that bears are common enough to be hunted in parts of our national forests (and a bear hunt is a massive enterprise, resembling a military search-and-destroy mission). Bears are also common enough that you might walk up to one by accident in the backcountry; treat it as very, very dangerous and get away without showing panic or fear. The infamous begging bears of Great Smoky Mountains National Park are less of a pest now than in the past but are still to be avoided as dangerous.

Wildlife is common but timid. The author has seen, on his small rural property, foxes, groundhogs, rabbits, skunks, turkeys, and a bobcat—a pretty typical cross-section. Deer are also common, particularly in the national parks. Rangers offer regular wildlife walks in all the national parks and forests, with schedules available at park offices and web sites.

The Northern Mountains

THE BLUE RIDGE PARKWAY ENTERS
NORTH CAROLINA

THE BLUE RIDGE PARKWAY:
BLOWING ROCK & GRANDFATHER
MOUNTAIN

BEHIND THE BLUE RIDGE:
BOONE & BANNER ELK

BEHIND THE BLUE RIDGE:
SPRUCE PINE & BURNSVILLE

THE MOUNTAINS OF NORTHERN
TENNESSEE

BENEATH THE BLUE RIDGE:
THE CATAWBA RIVER VALLEY

THE NORTHERN MOUNTAINS

At their northern end, the Blue Ridge and Smokies/Unakas draw together and grow taller, and the high valleys between them become narrow and rugged. The New River drains the northernmost part of this area—a wide, rolling valley that becomes increasingly higher and more rugged toward its south. The first of many mile-high peaks appear at the end of the New River's drainage and the start of the Tennessee River's drainage. From this high watershed all the way south to Georgia, the Tennessee River and its tributaries drain the land west of the Blue Ridge.

Here the Blue Ridge Parkway follows the Blue Ridge on its 469-mile journey from Virginia's Shenandoah National Park to Great Smoky Mountains National Park in North Carolina (see The Blue Ridge Parkway and the Heintooga Spur Road under *Wandering Around—Exploring by Car* in "Cherokee and the Southeast Quadrant"). Conceived in the mid-1930s as a work relief project for desperately poor mountain counties, its location along the Blue Ridge was far from assured. Tennessee's aggressive and powerful congressional delegation lobbied hard to place it along the Smokies/Unakas instead, but their heavy-handed power plays alienated the National Park Service, while North Carolina's State Road Department (now NCDOT) officials quietly finessed the federal park bureaucracy. The result: a beautifully landscaped route, with roadworks clad in hand-cut stone, stretching through remote and stunning scenery. Typically miles from any settlement (the exceptions being Blowing Rock, NC, and Asheville, NC), the parkway winds slowly through mountain farms and high meadows, across torrential rivers and quiet creeks, through ancient forests, and along high cliffs with wide views. Sometimes the parkway hugs the Blue Ridge; in other places it strays for miles.

In this area the Blue Ridge Parkway follows the actual Blue Ridge very closely. Typical of this old and unusual mountain, the Blue Ridge's eastern slope is a rugged and clifflike wilderness covered in trees and nearly empty of people, while its western slope is a series of grass-covered hills, with more farms than forests. When the parkway follows the eastern side of the Blue Ridge it slabs across rugged wilderness with wide views, as at Grandfather Mountain. When it follows the western side, it rolls through pastoral countryside with wide meadows, as it does near Linville, NC, and Sparta, NC. And when it follows the crest of the Blue Ridge, as it does in Doughton Park, NC, it yields the best of both worlds—rolling ridgeline meadows with wide views over rugged mountains and peaceful little farms.

The main town of this region is Boone, NC, a college town shaded by the 5,000-
foot peaks of the Tennessee River–New River divide. Boone has 13,500 residents in
its own right, while the downtown campus of Appalachian State University adds another 11,000 students during the school year. Only a half-dozen miles away, the historic and
exclusive resort town of Blowing Rock adds additional sophistication to the region, and
ski resorts top the mile-high peaks to their immediate south. This whole area makes
up a small complex of intensely developed vacation lands with a wide choice of first-
class services; northward and southward stretch traditional mountain lands, little
affected by tourism or its sprawling development. In these surrounding lands, attractive
little county seats such as Burnsville, NC, Jefferson, NC, and Elizabethton, TN, offer
a quieter and more authentic mountain experience.

This area received European settlement much earlier than other southern mountain
districts. For one thing, it had no permanent Cherokee settlement, as the Cherokees
held it as a sacred hunting reserve. For another, Daniel Boone lived there. Born in 1734
in Pennsylvania, at age 14 he accompanied his father, mother, and siblings to their
new home in North Carolina's upper Piedmont. Daniel grew up as a hunter and frontier explorer; when he married, he moved to a log cabin even farther west, at the edge
of Cherokee lands at the base of the Blue Ridge. Not much of a farmer, Daniel spent
his time hunting and exploring the wild mountain lands, eventually learning every
track between the Yadkin and the Tennessee Valley. Boone used this knowledge to blaze
the tracks, eventually known as the Wilderness Road, that would run through modern-day Boone and into Tennessee and Kentucky. An organized group of settlers used
these tracks to enter the Cherokee hunting lands, lease a large area from tribal leaders, and establish the Watauga Colony, forming their own courts and laws at present-day
Elizabethton.

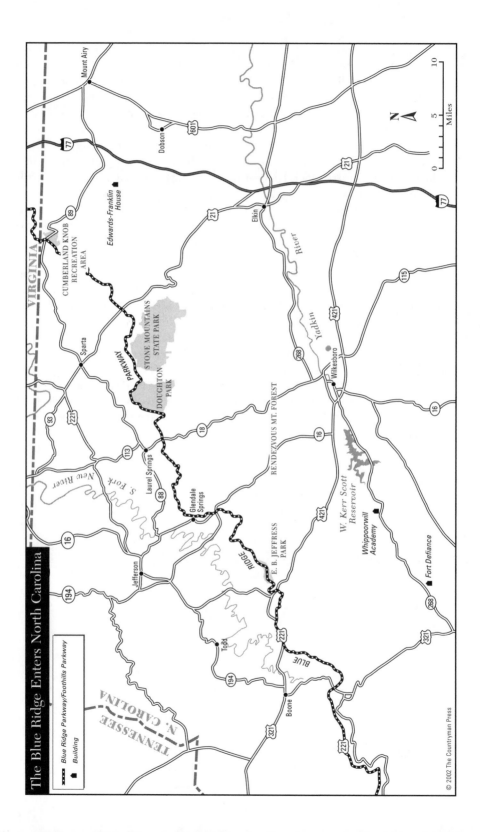

The Blue Ridge Enters North Carolina

Blue Ridge Parkway/Foothills Parkway
Building

© 2002 The Countryman Press

THE BLUE RIDGE PARKWAY ENTERS NORTH CAROLINA

The first 75 miles of North Carolina's Blue Ridge Parkway passes through one of the mountains' least-visited corners. On the eastern, Atlantic side of the parkway the land drops straight down to a series of rugged, broken mountains covered in thick forest and lightly settled. On its western side, the land rolls away in gentle hills covered in farms and pastures, broken only occasionally by an isolated massif large enough to be called a mountain. Despite its pastoral appearance, this western plateau is merely a high, wide bowl blocked by mountains in all directions, difficult to reach and little visited. In the areas traversed by this section of parkway, only one town has a definite center with a downtown, the handsome county seat of Sparta, NC. The scenery, on and off the parkway, is almost without exception beautiful and little touched by the tourist industry. Nevertheless, there are ample facilities for the most discerning traveler, with a good selection of B&Bs and restaurants.

GUIDANCE Allegheny County Chamber of Commerce (336-372-5473; 1-800-372-5473), 348 South Main Street, P.O. Box 1237, Sparta, NC 28675. This is the only tourist information center that treats the Blue Ridge Crest region as its central concern. Ashe County's chamber covers the Glendale Springs, NC, area (see **Ashe County Chamber of Commerce and Visitors Center** under *Guidance* in "Behind the Blue Ridge: Boone and Banner Elk").

GETTING THERE *By car:* This area is best approached from I-77. Take NC 89 (exit 100) if you're trying to reach the north end of the Blue Ridge Parkway or Sparta, NC, from the north. Take US 21 (exit 83) to reach Stone Mountain State Park or Sparta from the south.

By air: **Charlotte/Douglas International Airport** (704-359-4000), in Charlotte, NC, is probably your best bet. A major regional hub, it's only a hundred miles from Sparta, NC, straight up I-77. Piedmont Triad Airport in Greensboro, NC (336-665-5600), also has good service and is about the same distance away.

MEDICAL EMERGENCIES Allegheny Memorial Hospital (336-372-5511), 233 Doctors Street, Sparta, NC. This small regional hospital is located just north of Sparta off NC 18. If you are in the Glendale Springs area, **Ashe Memorial**

Hospital (336-246-7101), in Jefferson, NC, is probably closest (see *Medical Emergencies* in "Behind the Blue Ridge: Boone and Banner Elk"). At the south end of this section of the parkway, use **Watauga Medical Center** (828-262-4100; 1-800-443-7385) in Boone, NC (see *Medical Emergencies* in "Behind the Blue Ridge: Boone and Banner Elk").

✳ Wandering Around

EXPLORING BY CAR The Blue Ridge Parkway. At 14.8 miles east of Sparta on NC 18, turn south onto the Blue Ridge Parkway. Follow the parkway southward for 75 miles to the US 321 exit at Blowing Rock.

Along this route the Blue Ridge is a sharp barrier of hard old rock, a 2,000-foot escarpment facing the Atlantic and gentle hills rolling westward. When the parkway follows the crest, its scenery is wild and its views are long, with deep forests and sharp crags. When the road swerves west, it suddenly enters a land of gentle hills, lush meadows, and rich farmlands. The first site, only a mile from **NC 18,** is **Cumberland Knob Recreation Area** (see *To See—The Blue Ridge Parkway*), with a good view from its visitors center. For the next 12 miles you'll be on the first segment of the Blue Ridge Parkway ever built, in 1935; the last segment, **Grandfather Mountain** (see **Linn Cove Viaduct** under *To See—Along the Blue Ridge Parkway* in "The Blue Ridge Parkway: Blowing Rock and Grandfather Mountain"), opened in 1987. On this original stretch, **Fox Hunter's Paradise Overlook** gives wide views, and a lovely path circles a millpond. The parkway regains the crest just in time for a spectacular view over the edge to **Stone Mountain** (see Stone Mountain State Park under *Wild Places—The Great Forests*); use **US 21** to visit this remarkable site. **Brinegar Cabin** (milepost 238.5) on the left, one of the parkway's most attractive and worthwhile log cabins, marks the beginning of **Doughton Park** (see *To See—The Blue Ridge Parkway*), with its beautiful mountain meadow walks (see Doughton Park Walks). After Doughton Park there's more farmland, then the **Sheets Cabin** (milepost 252.3), a log cabin built in 1815 and

THE PARKWAY IS LINED WITH MILES OF SPLIT-RAIL FENCE LIKE THIS ONE

occupied until 1940. The parkway passes the **Northwest Trading Post** (see *Selective Shopping—Glendale Springs*), a local crafts shop, then wonderful views from **Jumpinoff Rocks and The Lump** (see *To See—The Blue Ridge Parkway*). Beyond The Lump, the parkway swerves behind the crest for wide views westward over the New River Valley to **Mount Jefferson** (see Mount Jefferson State Natural Area under *Wild Places—Recreation Areas* in "Behind the Blue Ridge: Boone and Banner Elk"), at **Mount Jefferson Overlook** (milepost 266.8). The parkway enters **E. B. Jeffress Park** (see *To See—The Blue Ridge Parkway*) at **Cascades Overlook,** with its fine waterfall walk and log cabin. The final 20 miles of this section passes a series of crest overlooks in both directions; look especially for eastward views from **Grandview Overlook** (milepost 281.4) and westward views from **Raven Rocks Overlook** (milepost 289.5).

EXPLORING ON FOOT Stone Mountain Paths. Loop trails poke around the interesting back corners of Stone Mountain State Park's unusual collection of granitic domes. Formed as one large *pluton*, or underground dome-shaped magma intrusion, today this exposed granite mound rises up to a thousand feet above its valley floor, appearing as a series of bare rock monadnocks broken by rugged little stream valleys. Even though these peaks aren't very high by North Carolina standards, their steep sides and rocky terrain can make the paths difficult and tiring. The most popular and difficult trail is the **4½-mile loop** that climbs Stone Mountain itself—the easternmost and largest of the three monadnocks. Starting at the **Hutchinson Homestead** (see Stone Mountain: Hutchinson

DOUGHTON PARK WALKS

The mile or more of mountaintop meadows at Doughton Park provide wonderful places to walk—pleasant scenery, lots of wildflowers, magnificent views—and the going is much easier than one deserves on any Blue Ridge mountaintop. The walk past Wildcat Cliffs to Fodderstack Knob, with a trailhead at the lodge, is the most popular, and deservedly so. The cliff-top views **at Wildcat Cliffs** (only a short distance from the parking lot) give a wide sweep down the 2,000-foot escarpment of the Blue Ridge and over the wide plains of the Piedmont; at the base of the cliffs, a single log cabin breaks the forest. A level 1-mile round-trip leads from there to **Fodderstack Knob,** a rocky bald with the characteristic Japanese garden look, framing another wide view. South from the lodge, a path is hardly needed through the wide meadows that crown the mountain for a mile—though one exists, just in case. On this long summit you'll come across wide and ever-changing views, many wildflowers, rocky outcrops, and dwarfed and twisted trees. The picnic area's access road parallels the summit meadows on their western downhill side, allowing picnickers to stroll up from their tables into the meadows at any point. For those who want a longer walk, the 8-mile **Bluff Mountain Trail** starts at the Brinegar Cabin and follows the **Blue Ridge Crest** (including the summit meadows) to **Basin Cove Overlook**—a good walk for those who can arrange a car shuttle.

Homestead and Garden Creek Church under *To See—Historic Sites*), the path strolls easily up the grassy valley with great views toward the cliff face of Stone Mountain, then follows a forested stream uphill for a mile or so to the park's most impressive waterfall, **Stone Mountain Falls.** From here the path becomes quite steep, although it climbs the mountain's least difficult side. Surprisingly, the top is forested, but with wide and changing views from the cliff edges that surround the mile-long summit. At the far end of the summit the trail descends exposed rock at an improbably steep grade to reach the parking lot. Another, much easier loop visits the other two monadnocks, **Cedar Rock** and **Wolf Rock**—actually two sides of the same summit. Much lower and shorter (although still difficult in places), this loop furnishes good scenery and great views. Start the loop from the **Stone Mountain Loop Trail,** a short distance east of the Hutchinson Homestead; it returns to the parking lot.

✳ Villages

Sparta, NC. The small county seat of Sparta (population 1,817), 7 miles west of the Blue Ridge Parkway's US 21 exit, serves as the main market town for the area. It occupies a high mountain bowl at an elevation of 2,900 feet, surrounded by small mountains (or large hills) with peaks scarcely 500 feet above the valley floor. It is very much a throwback to an earlier era. Its central grid of four blocks by three blocks centers on a three-block brick-front downtown that still functions as the main shopping district. A handsome old courthouse, with a historic jail, sits at the main intersection at the center of town. Few towns in the region are as uninfluenced (some would say unspoiled) by the tourism industry.

Glendale Springs, NC. Just off the Blue Ridge Parkway's NC 16 exit, Glendale Springs is a rural settlement best known for the spectacular fresco of the Last Supper in its tiny Episcopalian church (see **The Parish of the Holy Communion** under *To See—Cultural Sites*). Visited by 60,000 people a year, Ben Long's moving 1980 Renaissance-style fresco has generated a small local tourism industry, and something resembling a town has grown up near the church during the past 20 years. You'll find a number of places to eat, sleep, shop, and gas up within a mile of the church.

✳ Wild Places

THE GREAT FORESTS & **Stone Mountain State Park** (336-957-8185), 3042 Frank Parkway, Roaring Gap, NC. A remarkable granite dome sits at the foot of the Blue Ridge Crest, just downhill from the parkway's US 21 exit. Here the mountains drop steeply to a valley 1,500 feet below; from there, an oval dome 20 miles long and a mile wide rises a thousand feet nearly straight up. Erosion has cut the dome into several subpeaks, carved stream valleys into its flanks, and covered much of it with thin soil and thick forest. However, the dome's tallest point remains an isolated monadnock, a thousand-foot mass of nearly bare rock—Stone Mountain.

Since 1969, when Hanes underwear king R. Phillip Hanes donated the core holdings to the state, North Carolina has worked to preserve this unique formation and enough of the surrounding mountains to form a viable wilderness ecosys-

STONE MOUNTAIN AS VIEWED FROM THE WEST

tem. They now protect 21 square miles of unique Blue Ridge backcountry. Park access is down a back road that follows the valley separating the dome area from the mountain wall to its north, forming a semicircle around the strange granitic formations at the park's center. At its center are ample picnic areas, primitive campsites, historic sites (see **Stone Mountain: Hutchinson Homestead and Garden Creek Church** under *To See—Historic Sites*), and a network of loop trails exploring the granite dome area (see **Stone Mountain Paths** under *Wandering Around—Exploring on Foot)*—including paths to waterfalls and views both of and from Stone Mountain. The Blue Ridge slopes that tower above the granite dome to its north have only one public footpath, a rugged, rocky path to backpacking camps; the rest of the backcountry remains little-visited wilderness. Free admission.

✳ Wild Places

Picnicking on the Blue Ridge Parkway. Picnickers will find many good sites along this 75-mile stretch of the parkway. From north to south, these include:

Cumberland Knob Recreation Area (milepost 217.5). See *To See—Along the Blue Ridge Parkway.*

Little Glade Mill Pond (milepost 230.1) has five picnic tables and a short path by a pond.

Doughton Park (milepost 241.1). See *To See—Along the Blue Ridge Parkway.*

The Cascade Picnic Area (milepost 271.9). See E. B. Jeffress Park under *To See—Along the Blue Ridge Parkway.*

ALONG THE BLUE RIDGE PARKWAY Cumberland Knob Recreation Area.
This thousand-acre tract was the first segment of the Blue Ridge Parkway opened
to the public and was also the site of the dedication ceremony in 1935. It's a forested knob located a mile south of the Virginia border, adjacent to the parkway's NC
18 exit. It has a visitors center with exhibits and a nice picnic area. It offers two
pleasant trails, a 1-mile stroll to the top of Cumberland Knob (only 2,840 feet, but
the highest point in the area), and a more strenuous 2-mile loop down to **Gully
Creek**—the latter an 800-foot return climb, offering mountain views, deep
forests, attractive small waterfalls, and a log barn.

Doughton Park. Originally named Bluff Mountain, this 6,000-acre Blue Ridge
Parkway tract includes 6 miles of the Blue Ridge Crest and the watershed beneath
it. Typical of all the Blue Ridge, the Atlantic side is a rugged, broken drop of 2,000
feet, while the western side is little more than rolling hills. Along this stretch, the
crest is especially notable for its large meadows and heaths and its rocky outcrops
with wide views. Paths link the meadows and the outcrops, forming multiple loops
that plummet into the stream basin beneath and climb back out again. At the center is a classic parkway recreation area—picnic area, camping area, gas station,
store, two coffee shops, and a motel-style lodge.

At the north end is the **Brinegar Cabin** (milepost 238.5), built in 1885 and one
of the loveliest log cabins in the region; it's the site of weaving demonstrations during the summer. In 2 miles the parkway enters meadows, with a parking area and
path on the left (milepost 240.6). You'll reach the main area of meadows, heaths,
rocky outcrops, and grand views in another half mile; take the road to the lodge on
the left. The stunning **Fodderstack Knob** trail (see Doughton Park Walks under
Wandering Around—Exploring on Foot), with its panoramic view centering on a
log cabin far below, starts at the lodge. The meadows follow the ridgeline from the
lodge south toward the picnic area, extending for nearly a mile along the crest of
the Blue Ridge. Along this stretch the parkway descends the gentle western side
of the mountain, staying discreetly out of the wild and windy views. The meadows
end at a cliff, and the parkway drops below it to a narrow spine passing more overlooks with impressive views back toward the mountain.

Jumpinoff Rocks and The Lump. The Jumpinoff Rocks are a set of outcrops
that form a rocky bald on the crest of the Blue Ridge with wide views over the valley far below. The level half-mile walk leads through galax and wildflowers; you'll
find it at the **Jumpinoff Rocks Overlook** (milepost 260.3), just north of the parkway's NC 16 exit. Four miles farther south, The Lump (milepost 264.4) is a knob-
by peninsula that projects a thousand feet out from the crest of the Blue Ridge.
Covered in meadows and surrounded by 2,000-foot drops, The Lump affords
views both wide and spectacular. It's a short walk up a small hill from the overlook
parking lot; in the summer, it's a good chance you'll see people flying powered
model airplanes from it.

E. B. Jeffress Park. This 500-acre park, actually part of the Blue Ridge Parkway,
is named after the 1935 North Carolina Department of Roads chief who champi-
oned the parkway and insisted that it be a free road instead of a toll road. Located along the parkway just north of its intersection with US 421, it preserves a 2.3-

mile stretch of the Blue Ridge Crest with a typically steep plummet on its Atlantic side and gentle swale toward the back. A late-19th-century log cabin and a rough log structure used as a church and revival site sit in a flower-studded meadow by the roadside (park at the **Thomkins Knob Overlook** and follow the path). A half mile north, the **Cascade Picnic Area** has well-kept tables with excellent views over the edge of the Blue Ridge toward the Piedmont. However, the park's most popular site is the **1-mile loop path** that leads from the picnic area through jun-glelike old-growth forests and heavy rhododendrons to **Cascade Falls,** a lacy waterfall over a 50-foot gray outcrop.

HISTORIC SITES ✔ **Stone Mountain: Hutchinson Homestead** and **Garden Creek Baptist Church** (336-957-8185), Stone Mountain State Park. Located within **Stone Mountain State Park** (see *Wild Places—The Great Forests*), these two historic sites present a picture of late-19th-century community life in the Blue Ridge area. **Hutchinson Homestead** is a mid-19th-century farm in scenic mead-ows underneath the cliffs of Stone Mountain. Preserved for decades as a park maintenance area, it was restored in 1998 to its original form as a pioneer farm-stead. It has a log cabin, barn, corn crib, meat house, and blacksmith shop, all fur-nished in-period. Stunning views over the meadows to the massive monadnock, Stone Mountain, add to its charm. A mile down the park road, the 1897 **Garden Creek Baptist Church** gives a rare opportunity to visit an authentic 19th-centu-ry country church. Nearly unchanged in over a century, the small crackerbox building is of unpainted clapboards and has a lovely display of day lilies in early summer. It's still used for Sunday services in warm weather.

The Edwards-Franklin House (336-786-8359), Blevin's Store, NC. Open the second weekend each month, April through September. Built in 1799, this hand-some white wood farmhouse with a full porch and shake roof has its original dec-orative painting on the doors, mantels, and wainscoting. Owned by the Surry County Historical Society, it's 12 miles off the parkway's NC 18 exit at the edge of the Blue Ridge Mountains, in the back road community of Blevins Store, NC. Its location way down a back road gives you a chance to see the Blue Ridge back-country and the scenic **Fisher River Valley;** go 0.65 mile east on NC 18; then right 5.2 miles on NC 89; then right 5.2 miles on Hidden Valley Road (SSR 1338), following Fisher River; then left onto Haystack Road (SSR 1331).

Whippoorwill Academy and Village (Tom Dooley Museum) (336-973-3237), 11929 NC 268 West, Ferguson, NC. Located at the edge of the twisted Blue Ridge Mountains, it's 12 miles from the parkway's US 421 exit as the crow flies, and 32 miles as the crow drives a car down good-quality highways. Take US 421 about 20 miles to the Piedmont town of Wilkesboro, NC, then go west on NC 281 another 12 miles or so. Open Saturday and Sunday 3 PM–5 PM; closed January through March. Free admission (donations appreciated). This open-air museum, a collection of late-19th-century buildings with fascinating exhibits, marks the hometown of "Tom Dooley"—Tom Dula, the subject of the mountain folk song made popular by the Kingston Trio. Tom, a Civil War veteran and lady's man, was unfortunate enough to have planned to elope with Laura Foster the night she was stabbed through the heart. Even a defense by North Carolina's popular Civil War governor Zeb Vance (see **Vance Birthplace State Historic Site** under *To See—*

Historic Sites in "Asheville and the Blue Ridge Parkway") didn't save the poor boy from the hangman's noose. The old one-room schoolhouse of unpainted clapboard (called the Whippoorwill Academy for its remoteness), authentically furnished downstairs, has a museum to local-boy-made-bad Dula in its loft. Also on site is a general store with period products and locally canned goods, a replica of an 18th-century smokehouse with local art exhibits, a forge and weaving shed, a chapel, and an authentic reconstruction of the home of another famous local boy—**Daniel Boone,** who lived here with his wife in the 1760s.

Fort Defiance (828-754-0782), NC 268, Lenoir, NC. Open April through October, on the first and third Sunday, 2 PM–5 PM. Not a fort at all but the 18th-century home of Revolutionary War hero General William Lenoir, this simple, handsome Colonial homestead is located on NC 268, the scenic state highway that runs along the foot of the Blue Ridge between US 321 and US 421. Twice a month, costumed docents give tours of this authentically furnished house, including 250 items of General Lenoir's. The site is beautiful and the drive well worthwhile for scenic interest; time it right and you can combine it with a visit to Tom Dooley's hometown (see **Whippoorwill Academy and Village**, above), just 9 miles east on NC 268.

CULTURAL SITES The Parish of the Holy Communion (The Churches of the Frescoes) (336-982-3076). Open any reasonable time. Free admission. These two rural parish churches close to the parkway's NC 16 exit at Glendale Springs are noted for their exquisite frescoes in the classic Italian Renaissance manner. These two modest Episcopalian churches are simple wood buildings constructed between 1901 and 1905 and still serve congregations in Ashe County. Artist Ben Long created the frescoes between 1971 and 1980, choosing themes that mirrored the annual cycle of the Episcopalian liturgy. The larger of the two churches, **St. Mary's Church** (in West Jefferson, NC), has three large frescoes, each depicting a stage in the life of Christ: *Mary Great with Child, John the Baptist,* and *The Mystery of Faith.* The tiny **Holy Trinity Church** (on NC 16 in Glendale Springs, NC) is decorated with one giant fresco behind the altar, a moving and original interpretation of the Last Supper. These remarkable works of art have become an attraction—or perhaps a pilgrimage site—of great popularity, receiving 60,000 visitors a year.

FRESCOES OF THE LAST SUPPER ARE ON VIEW AT HOLY TRINITY EPISCOPAL CHURCH IN GLENDALE SPRINGS.

GARDENS AND PARKS ✥ **Rendezvous Mountain Educational State Forest** (336-667-5072), 1956 Rendezvous Mountain Road, Purlear, NC. Open March through November, Tuesday through Sunday; closed December through February. Free admission. This 3,000-acre mountaintop forest sits in the Blue Ridge Mountains, 12 miles east of the parkway's NC 16 exit. The "educational" part is a 150-acre open-air museum developed and run by the North Carolina Forest Service (a state agency that promotes silviculture and good forestry practices). Oriented toward children and families, the museum's four loop paths lead through exhibits on forest ecology and logging practices. Loops include "talking trees" who explain who they are and how they fit in the forest, a fire tower and Civilian Conservation Corps (CCC) cabin with fine views, and a logging demonstration with an operating sawmill. Much of the museum area is located on the summit of Rendezvous Mountain, with excellent views from the picnic area. The remainder of the tract preserves a beautiful old-growth oak-and-hickory forest, with 20 miles of hiking, horseback riding, and mountain biking trails.

✳ To Do

BICYCLING Buffalo Bob's Mountain Store (336-372-2433). This gift shop by the Blue Ridge Parkway at milepost 232 rents bicycles.

GOLF Old Beau Golf Club (336-363-3333), US 21, Roaring Gap, NC. Open all year. $45 weekdays, $60 weekends. A short distance off the parkway on US 21, this resort's 18-hole course is remarkably scenic, with wide mountain views.

HORSEBACK RIDING Mountain View Riding Stables (866-686-8724), 6345 Elk Creek–Darby Road, Darby, NC. Open daily all year. Reservations required. $45 for 2 hours, $75 for 4 hours. These stables are in a rural and mountainous area about 15 miles south of the Blue Ridge Parkway's US 421 exit. Located in the remote tangle of mountains beneath the Blue Ridge, this stable offers trail rides graded by degree of difficulty, from easy, scenic meadow ridges to strenuous mountain climbs.

✳ Lodging

COUNTRY INNS Glendale Springs Inn (336-982-2103; 1-800-287-1206), 7414 NC 16, Glendale Springs, NC 28629. This historic 1892 country inn sits a quarter of a mile off the Blue Ridge Parkway on NC 16. It's a large, gabled Victorian structure with a wide front porch, furnished throughout in a turn-of-the-century style. Downstairs is a full-service gourmet restaurant (see **Glendale Springs Inn and Restaurant** under *Dining Out*) and one guest room; upstairs are four more guest rooms and private commons for inn guests, off limits to restaurant patrons. Next door, a recently built guest lodge looks like a country cottage, with its own full porch; it has four more rooms, furnished in a country style. Some rooms have whirlpool tubs and fireplaces. $95–115.

BED & BREAKFASTS Burgiss Farm Bed & Breakfast (1-800-233-1505), Elk Knob Road, Laurel Springs. This 1899 farmhouse sits on 200 acres, 3 miles off the Blue Ridge Parkway's NC 18 exit. Handsome and well kept, it's surrounded by lawns and framed by wood fences and green hills. The 1,200 square feet of living space is available to only one party at a time and includes two bedrooms and an ample common area in an informal country decor. Amenities include a large stone fireplace, hot tub, bumper pool, and satellite TV. Guests have their choice of seven different hearty, full breakfasts.

The Burgiss Farm also includes the **Burgiss Barn Mountain Music Jamboree** (see *Entertainment*), a unique and lively Saturday-night mountain music venue with homestyle barbeque. $90 per room for the first night; $80 for each additional night.

✐ **Briar Patch B&B** (336-352-4177), 150 Wild Rose Trail, Dobson, NC 28717 (13 miles south of the Blue Ridge Parkway's NC 18 exit). This quiet three-room B&B occupies a new two-story log home at the foot of the Blue Ridge Mountains in the remote hill country south of NC 89. You'll find it not far from the historic **Edwards-Franklin House** (see *To See—Historic Sites*). The planked farm-style house has two wide front porches overlooking 48 wooded acres. Comfortably furnished in a country style, the rooms range from cozy to roomy; two have private half-baths, sharing a shower. $70–75.

Doughton-Hall Bed & Breakfast (336-359-2341), 12668 NC 18 South, Laurel Springs, NC 28644. Located less than 2 miles from the parkway's NC 18 exit, Doughton-Hall occupies the 1898 National Register–listed home of Robert L. Doughton, the powerful congressman who helped write the Social Security Act and who brought the Blue Ridge Parkway to North Carolina. Tucked into a quiet rural location and surrounded by lawns, this red-trimmed Queen Anne house has wide wraparound porches. Its common areas, and four guest rooms with whirlpool tubs, are furnished with antiques. Guests are greeted with wine and hors d'oeuvres when they arrive, and are given a full breakfast at the time they choose. $80.

Inn of the Red Thread (336-372-8743), 110 Mountain Hearth Drive, Sparta, NC 28675. Open all year. This modern log lodge sits by the Blue Ridge Parkway near its exit with US 21. Made of local hemlock logs and featuring hardwood floors, the lodge has a common living room and restaurant-style dining room. Its seven guest rooms consist of three normal-sized inn rooms, a suite, and three log cabins (no kitchens). All rooms are en suite and furnished in antiques; the suite and the cabins have fireplaces and whirlpool tubs, and the cabins have porches. Rooms $90–95; suite $110–140; cabins $120–140; includes full breakfast.

CABIN RENTALS ✐ **Fall Creek Cabins** (336-877-3131), P.O. Box 190, Fleetwood, NC 28626. Seven cedar log cabins sit on 54 acres deep in the Blue Ridge Mountains, not 5 miles from the parkway's intersection with US 421. These modern two-story cabins, all individually decorated, have full porches and wood floors, as well as fireplaces and hot tubs; some have mountain views, while others look out on forests or streams. $160–185.

Adele's Cabins at Turkey Hill (828-265-1213). These three modern log cabins sit near the top of the Blue Ridge, 2 miles from the parkway's exit onto US 421. All are carefully decorated, and have full front porches, hardwood floors, and fireplaces. The views are of the wooded property or over the mountains toward the parkway. $140–160.

✳ **Where to Eat**

EATING OUT **The Blue Ridge Café** (336-372-8670), 38 South Main Street, Sparta, NC. This small café in downtown Sparta is next door to the town's emporium-style antiques store, in the

Smithey's Building (see **Blue Ridge Plaza** under *Selective Shopping*).

The Pines Restaurant (336-372-4148), 501 South Main Street, Sparta, NC. This Southern-style eatery on the south edge of Sparta, 7 miles off the parkway on US 21, offers fresh country cooking and hand-chopped barbeque.

DINING OUT Glendale Springs Inn and Restaurant (336-982-2103; 1-800-287-1206), 7414 NC 16, Glendale Springs, NC. Open for lunch and dinner; closed Wednesday. This historic 1892 inn, a quarter mile off the Blue Ridge Parkway, offers casual fine dining. Guests are seated in three turn-of-the-century-style dining rooms, including one overlooking the garden that grows fresh herbs for the kitchen; on a pleasant summer's day, tables are available on the wide porch as well. The menu emphasizes a wide choice fresh seafood, as well as chicken, pork, and beef, typically prepared with an appropriate sauce or married with complementary tastes. All desserts made fresh by the restaurant's pastry chef. Extensive wine list, with most bottles less than $25. Entrées, served with soup or salad: $11–12.

✷ Entertainment

𝄢 ♪ **Burgiss Barn Mountain Music Jamboree** (336-384-4079; 1-800-233-1505), 429 Woodland Trails, Lansing, NC. Located just off the Blue Ridge Parkway, 3 miles north on NC 18 to NC 113. Open Saturday 7 PM–11 PM. Adults $6, children under 14 free. Barbeque dinner $5–7 extra. This large, plain modern barn hosts a dinner and a bluegrass and mountain music dance every Saturday night. Bands from all over the mountains furnish the music, and the food is cooked fresh in a large

pit barbeque. The 200-acre **Burgiss Farm Bed & Breakfast** (see *Lodging*) is next door.

✷ Selective Shopping

This deeply rural section of the Blue Ridge defines the periphery of this region's market areas. Its residents are used to driving some distance for even basic goods, while tourists tend to pass through on the parkway without straying from it. First-rate shopping is available in abundance at Blowing Rock, NC (see *Selective Shopping* in "The Blue Ridge Parkway: Blowing Rock and Grandfather Mountain"), at the southern end of this section of the parkway.

Blue Ridge Plaza (336-372-8670), 38 South Main Street, Sparta, NC. This emporium-style antiques and collectibles store occupies the old Smithey's Building in the center of downtown Sparta.

Northwest Trading Post (336-982-2543). This gift shop, looking like an old country store, fronts the Blue Ridge Parkway at milepost 259 near Glendale Springs, NC. Open April through October. Run by the Northwest Development Association as a nonprofit shop to promote local mountain crafts, it features handmade arts and craft items, as well as baked goods, from the northwestern counties of North Carolina's Blue Ridge.

✷ Special Events

June: **Allegheny Quilters' Show and Blue Ridge Mountain Craft Fair** (336-363-2312), Sparta, NC. *Third weekend in June.* Free admission. This Friday and Saturday event combines a crafts show and a quilters' meet with live bluegrass and mountain music, at the county fairgrounds in Sparta, NC.

June–July: **Sparta Lions Club Horse Shows** (336-359-8160), Sparta, NC. Held at the county fairgrounds during the *last weekend in June* and the *first two weekends in July.* $5 for each weekend event. Three different horse shows run on three consecutive weekends: The first is a draft horse show held Friday night only, featuring a horse-pull competition. The second is an English and western show on the following Saturday. On the third weekend, a Game Show with barrel racing and pole bending is held on Friday night and Saturday.

July: **Allegheny Fiddler's Convention,** 334 Reynolds Road, Sparta, NC. *Third weekend in July.* Friday night $6, Saturday $7, both days $10. Old-time mountain and bluegrass bands come from all over to compete for cash prizes at the county fairgrounds. There's also a dance competition.

September: **Mountain Heritage Festival** (1-800-372-5473), Sparta, NC. This annual street fair in downtown Sparta features live bluegrass and mountain music, crafts demonstrations, a hundred or more arts and crafts booths, and food vendors.

First Saturday in October: **Sonker Festival at the Edwards-Franklin House**, Blevins Store, NC. A "sonker" is a deep-dish fruit pie. This festival celebrates the sonker with old-time mountain music (and lots of home-cooked sonkers) at this Surry County 18th-century house at the foot of the Blue Ridge.

THE BLUE RIDGE PARKWAY: BLOWING ROCK & GRANDFATHER MOUNTAIN

This 50-mile stretch of the crest of the Blue Ridge has been attracting summer visitors since the late 19th century. First the resort village of Blowing Rock, NC, emerged on the Blue Ridge Crest just south of Boone, NC; then, 12 miles down the crest, a mountain family settled the summer-cottage village of Linville, NC, and surrounded it with thousands of acres of wilderness preserve. Many of the hard-scrabble ridgetop farms were absorbed into large estates surrounding summer homes—later to become parts of the Blue Ridge Parkway, further preserving the crest scenery. Another 12 miles down, the spectacular Linville Falls attracted more summer cottages; and 12 miles below that, Little Switzerland, NC, became a magnet for early-20th-century car-driving tourists.

This section of the Blue Ridge Parkway is varied and exciting, with rugged, wild scenery alternating rapidly with more settled and pastoral views. Off the parkway, Blowing Rock remains the focus of interest. Still a popular resort appealing to the wealthy, it features a good selection of gourmet restaurants, luxurious small B&Bs, and fascinating shops.

GUIDANCE Blowing Rock Chamber of Commerce (828-295-7851; 1-800-295-7851), P.O. Box 406, Blowing Rock, NC 28605. This chamber runs a visitors center a half block from downtown, in an old house.

GETTING THERE *By car:* The Blowing Rock, NC, area is best approached via US 321, a reasonably good highway that extends south from I-81 and north from I-40 and Charlotte, NC.

By air: You have a choice of three airports, two regional and one international. **Hickory Regional Airport** (828-323-7408; see also *Guidance* in "Beneath the Blue Ridge: The Catawba River Valley") is 35 miles south of Boone and gets several commuter hops a day from Charlotte, NC. **Charlotte/Douglas International Airport** (704-359-4000) itself is another 40 miles south of Hickory, and the flights are usually much cheaper. Don't neglect to check out **Tri-Cities Airport**

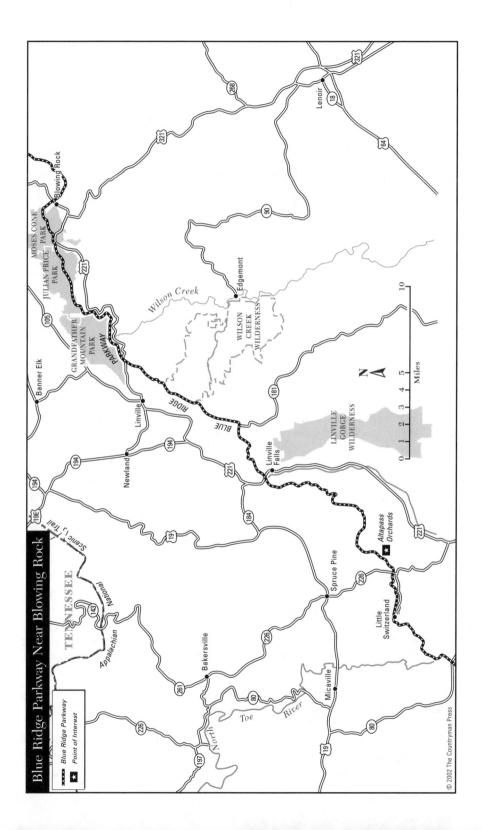

Blue Ridge Parkway Near Blowing Rock

••••• Blue Ridge Parkway
★ Point of Interest

© 2002 The Countryman Press

(423-325-6000), only 45 miles west of Boone in Johnson City, TN; much bigger than Hickory's airport, its fares may be cheaper than Charlotte's.

By bus or train: There is no scheduled bus or train service in this area.

MEDICAL EMERGENCIES In Blowing Rock, NC, or along the northern half of this section of the parkway, **Watauga Medical Center** (828-262-4100; 1-800-443-7385) is in nearby Boone, NC (see *Medical Emergencies* in "Behind the Blue Ridge: Boone and Banner Elk"). At the south end of this section of the parkway, **Spruce Pine Hospital** (828-765-4201) is your best bet (see *Medical Emergencies* in "Behind the Blue Ridge: Spruce Pine and Burnsville".

✳ Wandering Around

EXPLORING BY CAR **The Blue Ridge Parkway.** *Leg 1:* Enter the Blue Ridge Parkway at US 321 in Blowing Rock, NC, and go south 20 miles to NC 181.

Leg 2: Continue south 32 miles to NC 18. Burnsville, NC (see *Villages* in "Behind the Blue Ridge: Spruce Pine and Burnsville"), is 20 miles north via US 19E.

The parkway immediately enters the civilized meadows of **Moses Cone Park** (see *To See—The Blue Ridge Parkway*), with its 1890s neoclassical mansion (now a crafts center) and miles of carriage trails. From there the parkway passes into **Julian Price Park** (see *To See—The Blue Ridge Parkway*), with its lovely lake views, then enters more rugged scenery as it approaches **Grandfather Mountain** (see **Grandfather Mountain Park—The Backcountry** under *Wild Places— The Great Forests*), the tallest peak on the Blue Ridge at 5,960 feet. The parkway slabs the high eastern slopes of Grandfather, a wild and impressive drive of wide views and great crags, with viaducts over the most rugged cliffs (see **Linn Cove Viaduct** under *To See—The Blue Ridge Parkway*), and a downhill view over the **Wilson Creek National Wild and Scenic River** (see *Wild Places—The Great Forests*). Beyond, US 221 leads right to the entrance of **Grandfather Mountain Park** (see *To See—The Blue Ridge Parkway*); at this intersection, **Beacon Heights Overlook** gives one of the best views of Grandfather Mountain, plus a little side trail leading a half mile to another viewpoint. In 3 more miles, the **Flat Rock Overlook** (see *To See—The Blue Ridge Parkway*) parking lot on the right marks a short, worthwhile walk to a gardenlike rocky bald.

Past NC 181, the scenery become more pastoral, passing meadows and farms with pleasant views over split-rail fences. A spur road to the left leads to the giant **Linville Falls waterfall** (see

COWS GRAZE IN THE PASTURES BELOW THE MANOR HOUSE AT MOSES CONE PARK.

Linville Falls Recreation Area under *To See—The Blue Ridge Parkway*) at the mouth of the **Linville Gorge Wilderness** (see *Wild Places—The Great Forests* in "Beneath the Blue Ridge: The Catawba River Valley"). Beyond Linville Falls the scenery becomes rugged again. Look for impressive gorge views over the Catawba River to your left, climaxing with the dizzying view from **Chestoa Overlook** in 3 miles, and a 270-degree panorama from **Bear Den Overlook** 2 miles later. After Bear Den, look for your first of many views over the 2-mile-long **Orchard at Altapass** (see *To See—The Blue Ridge Parkway*), a stunningly beautiful heritage orchard with hayrides, a café and gift shop, and free live music on summer weekends. The historic **Clinchfield Railroad Loops** (see *To See—Historic Sites*) are visible below, as is the gravel roadbed of the 1913 predecessor to the parkway, the **Crest of the Blue Ridge Highway** (see *To See—Historic Sites*). At the NC 226 intersection the **Museum of North Carolina Minerals** (see *To See—The Blue Ridge Parkway*) and services at **Spruce Pine,** NC (see *Villages* in "Behind the Blue Ridge: Spruce Pine and Burnsville"), are to the right. From there the parkway parallels the settlement of **Little Switzerland,** NC, then enters another wild and rugged area with fine views in all directions. The parkway passes **Crabtree Falls Recreation Area** (see *To See—The Blue Ridge Parkway*), then reaches **Black Mountain Overlook** for the parkway's best view of **Mount Mitchell** (see Mount Mitchell State Park under *To See—Along the Blue Ridge Parkway* in "Asheville and the Blue Ridge Parkway"), the tallest peak in the East. NC 80, the end of this section of the parkway, is 2 miles away. The easiest way to get back to Blowing Rock is to return the way you came.

EXPLORING ON FOOT **Daniel Boone Scout Trail** (828-733-4337; 1-800-468-7325). This National Recreation Trail runs from the peak of Grandfather Mountain through the Grandfather Park backcountry to the Blue Ridge Parkway. It is owned and maintained by the private **Grandfather Mountain Park** (see *To See—The Blue Ridge Parkway*), and admission fees pay for its upkeep and patrol; hikers are required to pay the fee. Hikers who start on the parkway and walk uphill can get permits in Blowing Rock, NC, at half price (see High Mountain Expeditions under *To Do—Rafting and Kayaking*)—but face an uphill climb on the Boone trail of 2,000 feet in 2.6 miles. Many hikers find that it's worth it; the trail features high meadows and cliffs with stunning views, through scenery so rugged that the trail uses cables and ladders to cross it. Uphill hikers can get a good taste of the **Grandfather Mountain Park backcountry** (see *Wild Places—The Great Forests*) by taking the **Nuwati Trail** instead, a short distance before the Boone trail. Nuwati climbs gently and evenly for 1.2 miles to **Storyteller's Rock** for first-rate views over this virgin backcountry. On the return hike, **Cragway Trail** branches off to the right, to climb 500 feet in a mile. Here you reach the Boone trail, passing through crags and boulder fields with wide views.

Tanawha Trail. The Blue Ridge Parkway engineers built this 12-mile hiking trail as part of the viaduct project in 1987, and to the same high standards. Staying on the parkway properties throughout, this moderately easy path wanders through every type of Blue Ridge scenery, from rough crags to soft meadows. It starts at the **Linn Cove Viaduct** Visitors Center (see *To See—The Blue Ridge Parkway*), then passes under the viaduct, giving a close view of the bridge and the ecology it protects. It ascends a boulder wall using stone steps, then passes by a small waterfall on a flagstoned path—the headwaters of **Wilson Creek National Wild and Scenic River** (see *Wild Places—The Great Forests*). It climbs up to **Rough Ridge** and crosses its rare and fragile mountain heather ecology on a 200-foot boardwalk, with continuous panoramic views off the Blue Ridge, over the viaduct and the Wilson Creek watershed and into the **Piedmont.** Beyond, the path goes through New England–style forests and Blue Ridge–style rhododendron tunnels as it approaches **Julian Price Park** (see *To See—The Blue Ridge Parkway*), then passes through a long series of old meadows, fields, and apple orchards before ending at the **Boone Fork Overlook** (milepost 297.1). This makes a fine 1-day hike if you can arrange to be picked up.

✳ Villages

Blowing Rock, NC. This village sits in a shallow bowl just behind the crest of the Blue Ridge, a short distance off the parkway. It's been around since the 1890s, a resort town from the first, and many of its buildings are historic. The model for novelist Jan Karon's "Mitford," Blowing Rock's old village center remains attractive and busy, with a four-block downtown and a city park at its center. It has always been a gathering place for the wealthy, so that both quality and price tend to be high. Parking can be difficult, even in the off-season, and you may find yourself forced into a hilly two- or three-block walk to reach the downtown shops.

Linville, NC. Linville was founded as a resort town in the 1890s, about the same time as Blowing Rock; it was the Linville resort company that constructed US 221 between the two towns, the earliest auto road in the mountains. Linville was conceived as a summer village around the **Eseeola Lodge** (see *Lodging—Resorts*), and a collection of early summer homes still exists at the far end of the lodge. In those days, the resort company controlled the entire valley surrounding Linville, including Grandfather Mountain, and managed it as a wilderness park of great beauty. Today, that resort company survives as **Grandfather Mountain Park** (see *To See—The Blue Ridge Parkway*), still a privately owned wilderness park, while Linville has declined into a sleepy village with little beyond the typical roadside services.

Linville Falls, NC. Twelve miles south of Linville on US 221, and just off the Blue Ridge Parkway, Linville Falls is the third in this series of 19th-century Blue Ridge resorts, and the least-successful survivor in the series. Formed on the **Crest of the Blue Ridge Highway** (see *To See—Historic Sites*), it was expected to be a major tourist stop, as visitors took time to visit the **Linville Falls waterfall** (see Linville Falls Recreation Area under *To See—The Blue Ridge Parkway*). Today it is little more than a name on a crossroads, with a couple of restaurants and handful of motels; a group of stone buildings and a wide scattering of 19th-century summer houses attest to its historic origins. Linville Falls is the most convenient village for both the Linville Falls waterfall and the **Linville Gorge Wilderness** (see *Wild Places—The Great Forests* in "Beneath the Blue Ridge: The Catawba River Valley"), justly popular for its wild, craggy beauty.

Little Switzerland, NC. The western end of the abandoned **Crest of the Blue Ridge Highway** (see *To See—Historic Sites*) continued as a toll road to nowhere as late as the mid-1920s. Passing above the cliffs of the Blue Ridge, this early auto road gave flatlanders easy access to cool summer air and wide views. It still does, and the settlement of Little Switzerland has formed from the people attracted to this high perch. Unlike the other villages in this chapter, Little Switzerland is a linear settlement of a type familiar in the automobile era, stretched along NC 226A (as this section of the Crest of the Blue Ridge Highway is now designated) mainly as a series of motels and restaurants. The town center consists of four or five interesting shops gathered around the post office.

✳ Wild Places

THE GREAT FORESTS 🐾 **Grandfather Mountain Park—The Backcountry** (828-733-4337; 1-800-468-7325). Privately owned Grandfather Mountain Park (see *To See—The Blue Ridge Parkway*) supports more than 4,000 acres of primitive backcountry as an environmental preserve, centered on the 5,900-foot central ridge of Grandfather Mountain. This unique area has been managed as a preserve since it became part of the **Eseeola Lodge** (see *Lodging—Resorts*) property in 1892 and is still owned by the heirs of the founding family. Today the preserve is run in partnership with The Nature Conservancy and the United Nations—it's the world's only privately owned International Biosphere Reserve.

Viewed from any direction, Grandfather Mountain's most distinctive characteristic is the line of rugged cliffs and bare rock along its main crest and extending down its side ridges. Up close, these become the center of a fantasy landscape of broken rock and sheer drops, with nonstop views that change constantly. These outcrops and boulder fields nurture 16 distinct habitats, creating one of North America's most biologically diverse environments. The preserve shelters 42 rare and endangered species, with 11 listed as globally imperiled—including the beautiful wildflowers Heller's blazing star, Gray's lily, and pink-shelled azalea.

The Grandfather backcountry is open to hikers and campers only. The park maintains a 13-mile system of trails, some in territory so rugged that cables and ladders have been permanently installed. As this is an admission-supported park, you have to pay to hike in it. You can buy a hiking permit (adults $6, children $3) at several local stores, including **High Mountain Expeditions** (see *To Do—Rafting and Kayaking*); these permits allow hikers to ascend the trails from the valley up. There are two routes for this, both of them spectacular and strenuous. The east-side route, starting on the Blue Ridge Parkway, is shorter, less difficult, and more popular (see **Daniel Boone Scout Trail** under *Wandering Around—Exploring on Foot*). The west-side route, starting on NC 105, is a mile longer and 400 feet higher; it passes the view of an old man's profile that gave Grandfather Mountain its name. If you pay the full park admission fee ($12 adults, $6 children), you get to start at the **Mile High Swinging Bridge** (see Grandfather Mountain Park under *To See—The Blue Ridge Parkway*) and take a thousand feet off your climb; from there, the ladder-and-cable ascent of the 5,940-foot peak is only a mile away and 600 feet uphill.

Wilson Creek National Wild and Scenic River. Wilson Creek Wild and Scenic River drains the southeast slope of Grandfather Mountain, dropping 4,000 feet in a 23-mile run through **Pisgah National Forest** to its end at the **Johns River,** the upper edge of the **Piedmont.** It drains a rugged and little-visited watershed, remarkable for its waterfalls, cliffs, and gorges. From the Piedmont, **NC 90** winds slowly northward to the heart of this region to end at its center, in the rural community of **Edgemont.** From there, good gravel roads and rough national forest tracks twist uphill in various directions; Blowing Rock, Linville, and Linville Falls, NC, are all possible destinations.

Wilson Creek has two halves. The uphill, from Grandfather Mountain to Edgemont, is remote and rugged, with much of the western watershed protected in **Wilson Creek Wilderness Study Area.** The downhill half, starting at the **Mortimer Recreation Area (Wilson Creak Area)** (see *Wild Places—Picnic Areas*), is a deep gorge famous for its Class II to V whitewater. Pleasantly enough, a good road **(SSR 1328)** runs along the bottom of the gorge, making it easy to park, sunbathe on a rock, and watch the more vigorous among us kayak through the rapids.

Many of the best sight-seeing opportunities are in the 21-square-mile Wilderness Study Area. Containing much of the western half of Wilson Creek's watershed, it's a tangled series of rugged ridges and V-shaped valleys. It has over 30 miles of Forest Service–maintained trails (including 10 miles of the **Mountain-to-Sea Trail**), leading to six waterfalls and three clifftop views. **Forest Service Road 464,** a good gravel road, follows a ridgeline uphill through the center of the study area, starting at **NC 90** in **Edgemont** and ending 11.4 miles later, where **NC 181** intersects with the Blue Ridge Parkway. It's a lovely forest drive with several good views and access to a number of good trails, including **Darkside Cliffs Trail,** a nearly level mile-long round-trip to a cliff view of Grandfather Mountain and the Wilson Creek basin.

RECREATION AREAS Bass Lake. This lovely little lake, in **Moses Cone Park** (see *To See—The Blue Ridge Highway*) and adjacent to the village of Blowing Rock, NC, is ringed by carriage paths that are wide, flat, and immaculately kept. Popular with joggers, it's a wonderful place to stroll and unwind for those staying in Blowing Rock. It has its own parking lot, 0.5 mile west of downtown on US 221. A first-rate picnic area, run by the North Carolina Department of Motor Vehicles, is just across US 221 from the lake.

PICNIC AREAS Blowing Rock, NC. The village offers two convenient and attractive picnic areas. The town park at the center of downtown is convenient for shoppers and gives nice views of Main Street. **Broyhill Park and Annie Cannon Gardens** (see *To See—Gardens and Parks*) has large and lovely gardens as well as a challenging waterfall hike; you'll find the picnic tables at its north end, two blocks west of downtown off US 221, on the left.

The Blue Ridge Parkway. On this section of the parkway, picnic areas are located at **Julian Price Park, Linville Falls Recreation Area,** and **Crabtree Falls Recreation Area** (see *To See—The Blue Ridge Parkway*), all three of which are large and well kept.

Mortimer Recreation Area (Wilson Creek Area). This pretty Pisgah National Forest recreation site is in the Wilson Creek area (see **Wilson Creek National Wild and Scenic River** under *Wild Places—The Great Forests*), on NC 90 at the rural settlement of Edgemont. It has a nice riverside picnic area as well as tent camping. It's at the site of a large Civilian Conservation Corps (CCC) camp and marks the head of the scenic **Wilson Creek Gorge.** Two other national forest recreation sites in this remote area also offer picnicking; named **Mulberry** and **Boone's Fork,** both are off NC 90 east of Edgemont, along SSR 1368.

✳ To See

ALONG THE BLUE RIDGE PARKWAY *From Blowing Rock to NC 80* ☙ **Moses Cone Park** (828-295-7938; milepost 294). In the 1890s, Greensboro, NC, denim manufacturer Moses Cone and his wife, Bertha, started to accumulate a large estate along the crest of the Blue Ridge above the new resort village of Blowing Rock, NC. The Cones built a summer home for themselves second only to the Biltmore House (see *To See—Along the Blue Ridge Parkway* in "Asheville and the Blue Ridge Parkway") in resplendence, with Grecian columns framing a view that not even the Vanderbilts could command. The Cones converted the tired old farmlands they had purchased into wildflower meadows and laced these mead-ows with miles of carriage paths. Without any close heirs, they willed their estate to their favorite charity, a Greensboro hospital, under the condition that it remain intact, a recreation ground for the American people. In 1949 the hospital did the best thing for meeting the Cones' wishes; they donated it to the National Park Ser-vice, making it part of the Blue Ridge Parkway—the present Moses Cone Park.

This is not a wild place. It is a cultured place, a cultivated place, a place where a man-made landscape of great beauty and richness spreads over thousands of acres. At its base, lovely **Bass Lake** (see *Wild Places—Recreation Areas*) sits on the edge of Blowing Rock, ringed by carefully planned carriage paths. From it, mead-owlands stretch uphill, broken and framed by forests and rhododendrons, woven by carriage paths, to reach the simple and elegant mansion, now a crafts center run by the **Southern Highlands Craft Guild.** Crossing the parkway behind the manor, the meadows continue uphill, as the carriage path forks toward two high-peak views—a 3-mile switchback to **Flat Top** and a 5-mile spiral to **Rich Mountain.**

THE MANOR HOUSE AT MOSES CONE PARK NEAR BLOWING ROCK

The manor and its crafts center get much of the visitor attention—deservedly so, with its shop of fine crafts from throughout the Appalachians, its summer crafts demonstrations, and its wide views from a porch well outfitted with rockers. However, the **carriage paths** are the real marvel of the park. Evenly and gently sloped, they wander through the carefully planned landscape in a series of amazing turns and twists, switchbacks, loops, and spirals. They allow a modern walker to meander up the face of the Blue Ridge while hardly breaking a sweat. The paths are also open to horses, which can be hired in Blowing Rock (see **Blowing Rock Stables** under *To Do—Horseback Riding*).

Julian Price Park (milepost 297). Part of the Blue Ridge Parkway, 6.5-square-mile Julian Price Park fills the gap between **Moses Cone Park** (see above) and the privately owned **Grandfather Mountain Park** (see *Wild Places—The Great Forests*). It does this in the most literal sense, filling in the mountainous spaces between these two better-known areas; and it does it in a more literal sense as well, being less tame and civilized than Moses Cone Park, yet not so wild as the windswept cliffs of Grandfather Mountain. It is more of a typical Blue Ridge landscape, with fields left from grazing and woods left from logging, crossed by trails that are rough and rolling. The middle of the park is taken up by a plateau surrounded by slightly taller peaks, containing a pleasant lake, a large picnic area framed by split-rail fences, and a campground. The parkway runs close by the edge of the lake and over its stone dam—a popular and scenic stop. From the picnic area a path runs 2.5 miles (round-trip) along Boones Fork to a pretty 25-foot waterfall, from there connecting to a number of rougher backcountry trails.

&. **Linn Cove Viaduct** (milepost 304). As you approach from Blowing Rock, NC, you'll see the viaduct as you travel beyond the **Rough Ridge Overlook** (milepost 303); then, a mile later, you'll be on it with no opportunity to stop and admire it. To get a good look, stop at the **Yonalossee Overlook** (milepost 303.5), where a roadside path leads to its beginning and the view you see in postcards. Once you've crossed

THE LINN COVE VIADUCT AS VIEWED FROM YONALOSSEE OVERLOOK ON THE EAST SLOPE OF GRANDFATHER MOUNTAIN.

GRANDFATHER MOUNTAIN PARK

✎ (828-733-2013; 1-800-468-7325), US 221 (1 mile north of the Parkway),
Linville, NC.Open daily. Summer: 8 AM–7 PM; winter: 8 AM–5 PM. Adults $12,
children $6. Hiking permit half price. Owned by noted conservationist Hugh
Morton and his family, Grandfather Mountain Park is described as "a scenic
travel attraction"—a theme park where the themes are nature, the environment, and incredible natural beauty. There's a spectacular drive up, a nature
center, a first-rate habitat zoo, and a mile-high suspension bridge. Four thousand acres of the park is a permanently protected wilderness preserve (see
Grandfather Mountain Park—The Backcountry under *Wild Places—The
Great Forests),* recognized by the United Nations as an International Biosphere Reserve (the only such privately owned tract in the world).

The attraction and centers on a 2.2-mile road that climbs a thousand feet up
the mountain in eight tight switchbacks. This section of the Blue Ridge Crest
has spectacular, sheer cliffs facing west, getting larger as the mountain gets
higher. The road gains views of these cliffs on its westward curves (including
a **cliff-top picnic area**), while eastward curves wander through lovely forests
broken by large rock formations. The road's last 0.5 mile swags steeply up the
mountain with wide views over high meadows.

Halfway up is the outstanding **habitat zoo,** open to visitors at no extra charge.
Grandfather's large animal enclosures feature native mountain animals in
their actual habitats, with the human visitors separated by moats or elevated
walks. Animals include black bear, bear cubs, deer, panther, and river otter
(with an underwater viewing area), as well as golden eagles and bald eagles.
The adjacent **nature center** presents the history of Grandfather Mountain
(both natural and human) in a museum designed by the Smithsonian's former
chief of natural history exhibits. It includes a section on Daniel Boone, a display of North Carolina minerals and gems, and an operating real-time weather station. Works of art, rather than dead things, illustrate the flora and fauna
of Grandfather: Paul Marchand's artificial wildflowers, songbird woodcarv-
ings by Bill Chrisman, Hugh Morton's photographs of endangered species.
There's also a **restaurant.**

The road ends at almost exactly 1 mile in elevation, in an area of great open
views, meadows, spruce-fir forests, cliffs, and strange rock formations. In the
middle of it all is the **Mile High Swinging Bridge,** almost a hundred yards
long, crossing a rocky chasm 80 feet deep. An easy 2.5-mile walk goes
through the chasm under the bridge, then through boreal forests and across
rocky outcrops to a viewpoint overlooking the Blue Ridge Parkway.

it, you'll reach the Linn Cove Viaduct **Visitors Center** on the left on the opposite side, with an information desk and exhibits. A disabled-accessible trail leads a short distance to an overlook.

One of the most remarkable and important bridges of its era, the Linn Cove Viaduct came about through an environmental dispute between the National Park Service and a local man. In the late 1960s the Park Service tried to replace its 1930s-era right-of-way (never used) with a much higher route, slashing across the virgin preserve of Grandfather Mountain Park (see *Wild Places—The Great Forests*) in giant cuts and fills. The local man—Hugh Morton, owner of Grandfather Mountain—was determined to protect his mountain. Although the Park Service believed it had the right to simply condemn Morton's land, they quickly found out that this power did not extend to relocating the right-of-way; yet they refused to budge from their concept of a high-mountain slash. Finally the governor of North Carolina forced a compromise, a middle route that avoided environmental problems by bridging them. The longest of these bridges is the Linn Cove Viaduct.

The viaduct took a radical new approach to protecting the environment. It's set on towering pillars, installed without a construction road, each one disturbing only a tiny 50-foot circle of land. Every roadway section was precast in concrete and lifted into position; when one section was attached to a pillar the work crews would move onto it to move the next section into position, cantilevering out from the pillars. The roadway sections curve slightly to conform to the environmental needs of the land below. The resulting bridge is beautiful, a soft line curving gently against the wild mountain.

THE UPPER FALLS SEEN FROM THE CHIMNEY VIEW OVERLOOK

Flat Rock Overlook (milepost 308). You have to work for this view, but it's worth it. A half-mile circular walk takes you to a large rocky bald with the beauty of a Japanese garden, its dwarfed pines and azaleas (May through June blooms) framing 270-degree panoramic views that include Grandfather Mountain.

Linville Falls Recreation Area (milepost 317). The Blue Ridge Parkway has a large recreation area along the **Linville River,** centering on the tall plunge of Linville Falls. As the parkway approaches the river, it enters lovely meadows with split-rail fences. A spur road to the left leads 1.5 miles to the waterfall; just beyond, a side road leads directly to the riverside picnic area, where you can get a good view of the parkway crossing the Linville River high above on a stone-clad arched bridge. The picnic area is nice, and the **Linville River Bridge** is impressive, but the waterfall is the real attraction.

The **trails to Linville Falls** start at a small visitors center at the end of the spur. The falls occur as the Linville River reaches the upper edge of

THE ORCHARD
AT ALTAPASS

THE ORCHARDS AT ALTAPASS WITH LINVILLE MOUNTAIN
IN THE DISTANCE

✐ (1-888-765-9531), milepost 329, Little Switzerland, NC. Free admission. Weekend music free. Hayrides $3. At the turn of the 20th century, the Clinchfield Railroad built an amazing grade up the face of the Blue Ridge, with 17 tunnels in 23 miles of hairpin loops (see The Clinchfield Railroad Loops under *Historic Sites).* Above the last loop, the railroad planted an apple orchard that followed the crest of the Blue Ridge for 2 miles. Then, in the 1930s, the Blue Ridge Parkway passed through the middle of the orchard—2 miles of sweeping views over large apple trees heavy with fruit, one of the great sights of the parkway.

Sixty years later the orchard had suffered from years of neglect, the trees ignored and allowed to grow wild. In 1994 Kit Carson Trubey bought the orchard to restore and preserve it, under the management of her brother and sister-in-law Bill and Judy Carson. Their plan: Restore the orchard and welcome in the public.

Today, it's a wonderful place. The heritage apple trees, nearly a century old, are again healthy and beautiful, framing unimaginable views with bright, red fruit in huge clusters. **Hay-ride tours** wind through the orchard, with orchard storytellers relating the lively history of this important pass. In-season, warm weekend afternoons ring to the sounds of local country musicians in **free concerts** near the apple packing house. Behind the packing house is a **monarch butterfly garden** (the staff hand raises monarchs in a special area of the packing house), an **herb garden,** and a **spring wetland.** The packing house holds a remarkable **gift shop,** with apple products made in the orchard, local honeys and preserves, crafts from local crafters (four of whom have been declared North Carolina Living Treasures), and neat stuff from all over. It also has a small **café** if you are feeling peckish.

Linville Gorge (see Linville Gorge Wilderness under *Wild Places—The Great Forests* in "Beneath the Blue Ridge: The Catawba River Valley") and plunges straight down into it. The trails spread out in fingers from the visitors center to various viewpoints, starting as paths along both banks of the river. The left-bank paths lead first to a ledge and pool at the top of the waterfall, with a view out over the gorge and a lovely little cascade upstream. Then the path continues to a view toward the falls from the gorge rim and two views over the gorge. The right-bank paths lead to a rim-top view toward the waterfall, then a drop to the bottom of the gorge for a view from beneath. The shortest walk is a mile round-trip, while visiting all six overlooks will require about 5 miles of walking.

✎ ⅃ **Museum of North Carolina Minerals** (828-765-2761), Little Switzerland, NC. Located by the parkway's exit onto NC 226, at milepost 331. Open daily, May through October. Free admission. This small museum, built of local stone in the shape of a cottage, marks the center of North Carolina's mountain mining industry. Erected in 1953 as a joint project between the parkway and the state of North Carolina, Park Service experts designed the exhibits with extensive input from local gem collectors and mining industry officials. Displays included careful descriptions of the mountain mining industry, the minerals extracted, and the rare and fascinating gemstones that resulted as a by-product. The most interesting displays are those of the local gem collectors, a fascinating exhibit of rare stones and strange crystals.

By the time you visit the museum, this may have changed, updated to reflect the passage of a half century of time. Then again, it may not. At this writing, the 1953 exhibits are all still there, an immaculately kept window into the mid–20th century.

Crabtree Falls Recreation Area (milepost 340). This recreation area contains a picnic area, a snack bar and store, a gas pump, and a campground. Its main feature of interest is a 2.5-mile loop trail to **Upper Crabtree Falls,** a beautiful cascade popular with photographers and valued by waterfall aficionados. The return requires a 500-foot climb.

HISTORIC SITES The Clinchfield Railroad Loops (milepost 329). The Clinchfield Railroad, built in the first decade of the 20th century, climbs the Blue Ridge in an bewildering series of loops and tunnels just beneath the **Orchard at Altapass** (see *To See—The Blue Ridge Parkway*). The Clinchfield's plan was to link the Atlantic South with the Midwest by attacking the Appalachian barrier head on, using all the techniques of modern engineering. Building north from Marion (see *Villages* in "Beneath the Blue Ridge: The Catawba River Valley"), they pushed their road straight up the sheer face of the Blue Ridge; in the 6 linear miles between the bottom and the crest, they built 23 miles of road with five hairpin curves and 17 tunnels. Although enormously expensive to build, this superbly engineered road gave the Clinchfield a short, direct route between two major markets, while their competitors meandered around the mountains. The road, now part of the CSX System, remains a heavily used freight line. The Blue Ridge Parkway parallels it closely for 4 miles, from milepost 327 to milepost 331; look for it from the **North Cove Valley Overlook** (milepost 327.4), **Altapass Orchards Overlook** (milepost 328.4), and **Table Rock Overlook** (milepost

329.8) (also see *Wandering Around* in "Beneath the Blue Ridge: The Catawba River Valley."

The Crest of the Blue Ridge Highway. In 1910, North Carolina State Geologist Dr. Joseph Hyde Pratt came up with a wonderful idea—a scenic road following the crest of the Blue Ridge, specifically designed to attract wealthy adventurers driving their newfangled automobiles. This was at a time when farmers struggled down muddy ruts to get their crops to railheads, and through highways were a starry-eyed dream. Spend state money on a tourist road? However, the toll road would pay for itself and would bring in out-of-state money to some of the state's poorest areas. The state approved Pratt's plan, dubbed it the "Crest of the Blue Ridge Highway," and built a chunk of it before World War I ended construction.

In a very real sense, the modern Blue Ridge Parkway is the realization of Dr. Pratt's vision. A section of the original Crest of the Blue Ridge Highway still survives, paralleling the Blue Ridge Parkway from Altapass to Little Switzerland, NC. To follow it, exit the parkway at McKinney Gap, NC (milepost 327.7), go under the parkway, and turn right onto SR 1567 to the Orchard at Altapass (see *To See—The Blue Ridge Parkway*). This gravel section must look very much like it did in 1913, passing through the heart of the orchards, then continuing (across the parkway) through farmlands. At its end, turn left onto NC 226 to return to the parkway; or continue under the parkway and take a right onto NC 226A through Little Switzerland, another section of the Crest highway, still charging tolls in the mid-1920s.

GARDENS AND PARKS **Broyhill Park and Annie Cannon Gardens,** Blowing Rock, NC. Located one block west of downtown. A large and attractive park that any town would be proud of, it has informal gardens and a gazebo around a lovely lake. Below the dam lies Annie Cannon Gardens, a native flower garden. Downstream from the garden, a hiking path leads steeply downhill to two high and beautiful waterfalls, a worthwhile if strenuous hike (3 miles round-trip, 800-foot climb).

The Blowing Rock (828-295-7111), US 321, Blowing Rock, NC. Open daily, March through December; weekends, January and February. Adults $5. This privately owned attraction features a 1-acre garden and short trails around the rock formation that gave the village of Blowing Rock its name. The views are excellent. A large gift shop is on the premises.

OTHER ✍ **Linville Caverns** (828-756-4171; 1-800-419-0540). Located south of Linville Falls on US 221 in Marion, NC. Open daily 9–5, March through November; weekends only, December through February. Adults $5, children $3, seniors $4. This show cave features elaborate dripstone formations along nearly level paths. It's lighted in the most natural way possible, to better show off the subtle colors and shapes of the strange rock formations. Endangered eastern pipistrelle bats, harmless and tiny, are found in this cave. The attractive park-style reception building, made of stone and gray wood, has a nice gift shop.

✷ To Do

GOLF Golfers may think it odd that no courses are listed for the Blowing Rock or Grandfather Mountain area—considering that several are clearly visible from the main road. In fact there are six golf courses, all of them either largely or completely closed to casual visitors. The two listed courses are some distance south of the ritzily exclusive Blowing Rock area.

Blue Ridge Country Club (828-756-7001; 1-800-845-8430) is near Linville Falls, NC, on US 221. Open all year. $35–45. This 18-hole course, built in 1995, features wide mountain views and a mountain river in play on 8 of the holes.

Mount Mitchell Golf Club (828-675-5454), 7590 NC 80 South, Burnsville (just off the NC 80 exit from the Blue Ridge Parkway). Open April through November. $48–59. This 18-hole course sits at the foot of Mount Mitchell and offers wide views toward the East's highest peak.

HORSEBACK RIDING Blowing Rock Stables (828-295-7847). Located on the western edge of the village of Blowing Rock, NC, off US 221, this stable offers trail rides through stunning **Moses Cone Park** (see *To See—The Blue Ridge Parkway*).

RAFTING AND KAYAKING High Mountain Expeditions (828-295-4200; 1-800-262-9036), Main Street, Blowing Rock, NC. Located downtown, this outfitter furnishes rafting trips ($49–67)—calm, family-oriented floats on the **Watauga River,** or wild, whitewater trips on the **Nolichucky River.** They also offer a whole lot of other stuff: cave tours ($45), hiking tours ($35–75), mountain biking tours

($35–75), mountain bike rentals ($19 for 1 hour, $29 for 8 hours), stillwater (mountain lake) kayaking tours, and—note this, hikers—shuttle services.

ROCK CLIMBING High South Mountain Guides (828-963-7579), Linville, NC. This guide service centers in the **Linville Gorge Wilderness** area (see *Wild Places—The Great Forests* in "Beneath the Blue Ridge: The Catawba River Valley") and will provide equipment. An instructional session takes students to **Table Rock** (see *Wandering Around* in "Beneath the Blue Ridge: The Catawba River Valley").

✷ Lodging

RESORTS Westglow Spa (828-295-4463; 1-800-562-0807), 2845 US 221 South, Blowing Rock, NC 28605. Located 3 miles west of Blowing Rock, Westglow is a European-style spa in a beautifully restored 1916 mansion surrounded by 20 landscaped acres. This National Register classical-style house, with Greek columns framing the front porch, served as the summer home of American impressionist artist Elliott Daingerfield, who named it Westglow. Seven bedroom suites are furnished almost entirely in antiques; more modest cottages near the mansion have lower prices. The three meals a day are healthy, balanced—and gourmet. Spa services are both wide ranging and less structured than at many American-style spas; a new Life Enhancement Center contains an indoor pool, a full choice of weight and exercise equipment, whirlpools, saunas, a hair and nail salon, an aerobics studio, and a poolside café, with a tennis court nearby. Unlike other prices quoted in this book, these include taxes and gratuities, as well as access to the fully staffed spa facilities. Mansion: $816–906 per night for two adults in one room. Cottages and lodge: $712–790 per night for two adults in one room. Significant discounts for stays longer than one night.

✦ **Clear Creek Guest Ranch** (828-675-4510; 1-800-651-4510), 100 Clear Creek Road, Burnsville, NC 28714. This stunningly beautiful classic dude ranch sits in the shadows of Mount Mitchell, the tallest peak in the East, on a back road at the far southern end of this section of the parkway. The large property has meadows, streams, mountains, and wide, wide views. It also has horses. The tariff includes a full slate of trail rides and ranch activities, both on the ranch and in adjacent Pisgah National Forest. Accommodations are in log-sided cabins, new and immaculately kept, with full front porches and one to three bedrooms. Hearty ranch meals are served three times a day, family style in the central lodge, or on the trail, or at an outdoors barbeque (including a weekly steak barbeque). The ranch has wide decks spreading downhill from the lodge to surround a pool, as well as a stocked pond. This family friendly resort offers a full program from children age 5 and up. $370 per night for two adults in one room. Rates include three meals and a full program of trail rides.

✦ **Eseeola Lodge** (828-733-4311; 1-800-742-6717), 175 Linville Avenue, Linville, NC 28646. Open May through October. In existence since 1892, the Eseeola remains a summer playground for the wealthy. It's surrounded by the historic summer homes of its early-20th-century patrons, whose heirs still own the Eseeola. The present lodge, dating from 1926 and on the National Register, has 24 elegant rooms with all amenities. All rooms have private porches, and many have separate living rooms. The rates include breakfast and dinner (coat and tie required) at the lodge's gourmet restaurant; menus change daily and always include a choice from seven entrées. Guests have access to tennis courts, exercise rooms, and a fishing lake (all at a separate charge), and there's a day camp for children. Guests also have access to the 18-hole private course ($80 per round), little changed since Donald Ross designed it in 1924. Rooms $300–335; suites $400–450. Price includes two meals a day.

BED & BREAKFASTS Crippen's Country Inn (828-295-3487; 1-877-295-3487), 239 Sunset Drive, Blowing Rock, NC 28605. Located in a restored turn-of-the-century home, Crippen's offers a European-style experience in the center of Blowing Rock. Located between downtown and US 321 on quiet Sunset Drive, it's a large bungalow-style structure with a full front porch, green clapboarding and shingle gables, and a lovely little garden in the postage-stamp area between the porch and the stone wall bordering the sidewalk. Inside, two front parlors are comfortably furnished with sofas, fireplaces, art on the walls, and coffee table books. The right-hand parlor opens up into a comfortable and intimate bar with a good selection of cognacs and single malts, part of the superb restaurant that comes alive in the evening (see *Dining Out*). Upstairs are the rooms, each carefully and comfortably furnished with modern and antique furniture and quilts on the beds. Standard rooms are normal in size; deluxe rooms are large enough to have roomy sitting areas with sofas. The continental breakfast, served in the restaurant, consists of baked goodies made on the premises. Rooms $99–149; cottage $159–179.

Gideon Ridge Inn (828-295-3644), 202 Gideon Ridge Road, Blowing Rock, NC 28605. Located just south of Blowing Rock off US 321, near the entrance to the Blowing Rock attraction (see *To See—Gardens and Parks*), the inn straddles the Blue Ridge, with sweeping views off the edge of the world. This low stone building sits amid 5 acres of native gardens, accessible from wide stone terraces. While the terraces, with their expansive views framed by gardens, serve as the focal point for the common areas, there is also a large library with a stone fireplace and a breakfast room with original art. Rooms are comfortably furnished with country-style antiques and reproductions; the least-expensive rooms are modest upstairs rooms with views from dormer windows, but most rooms are larger, with a choice of amenities such as terrace doors, whirlpool baths, and fireplaces. $125–285, including full breakfast and afternoon tea.

The Inn at Ragged Gardens (828-295-9703), 203 Sunset Drive, Blowing Rock, NC 28605. This elegant B&B, a short stroll from downtown Blowing

THE GARDENS AT THE INN AT RAGGED GARDENS

Rock, is surrounded by gardens and walled off from the world. It's a large, square manor, clad in shingles, with an oversized porte cochere topped by a balcony/deck. The large common rooms are elegantly furnished with Edwardian antiques—a spirit carried into the 12 individually decorated rooms, each with a turn-of-the-century theme. Rooms range from standard size to large; each has a fireplace, a goosedown comforter, bathrobes, and seasonal fresh flowers, and the majority have private balconies, whirlpool baths, and sitting areas. Breakfast includes homemade granola and bread, plus a choice of two hot entrées. There's also an evening wine serving with hors d'oeuvres, and two stocked butler's pantries for guests who need munchies. $170–310.

Springhaven Inn (828-295-6967), P.O. Box 2726, Main Street, Blowing Rock, NC 28605. Located at the south edge of downtown Blowing Rock, this little B&B occupies a stagecoach inn built in the earliest days of the village; Martha Mitchell was one of its guests. It's a handsome shingle-sided two-story structure with wide porches overlooking Main Street, on a lot surrounded by giant pines. Decorated throughout with antiques, the five rooms all have private baths. Breakfast is typically fruit, muffins or breads, and a breakfast casserole. $69–99.

Maple Lodge Bed & Breakfast (828-295-3331), 152 Sunset Drive, Blowing Rock, NC 28605. This 11-room early-20th-century inn is just behind downtown Blowing Rock. Separated from the street by a white picket fence and surrounded by wildflower gardens, this simple and attractive two-story Colonial structure is furnished with antiques, including a library with a fireplace and two parlors. The rooms are also furnished with antiques and oriental rugs; some are quite large, with sitting areas, while others are cozier. A full breakfast is served in the dining room overlooking the wildflower garden. $90–180, depending on size and season; weekday discounts.

&. **Stone Pillar Bed & Breakfast** (828-295-4141; 1-800-962-9955), 144 Pine Street, Blowing Rock, NC 28605. Located just off downtown Blowing Rock, this 1920s-era home is furnished with antiques, including its six guest rooms. Although the cheapest room is very small, other rooms are comfortable and beautifully decorated. May through October: $65–110; November through April: $60–95.

Rocksberry Bed & Breakfast (828-295-3311), 445 Rocking Horse Lane, P.O. Box 1417, Blowing Rock, NC 28605. This seven-room B&B occupies a large old mountain farmhouse, white clapboard with a two-story porch, down a back lane close to Blowing Rock. It's on its own private road, surrounded by 3 acres of tree-shaded landscaping and gardens, including fruit trees and berry patches. It's furnished throughout with antiques, including the seven guest rooms. $120–130, including full breakfast.

The Alpine Inn (828-765-5380), Highway 226A, P.O. Box 477, Little Switzerland, NC 28749. Located just off the Blue Ridge Parkway, this modest inn was built in 1929 and once furnished lodgings to the Blue Ridge Parkway workers. Today it is a homey and well-kept low-cost B&B with 14 rooms, nearly all with breathtaking panoramic views from their balconies. $50.

CABIN RENTALS ✐ **Bear Den Creekside Cabins** (828-765-2888), Route 3, Box 284, Spruce Pine, NC 28777. Open all year. Located on a remote stretch of the Blue Ridge Parkway between Linville Falls and Little Switzerland, NC, this set of modern pine log cabins with oak floors is part of a 400-acre camping resort with a lake, a sand beach, canoes, and lots of on-site walking paths. The comfortable and fully furnished cabins—each with full kitchen, fireplace, whirlpool bath, and front porch—are isolated from the camping area, along a creek. There are also some "campin' cabins," described by the owners as "tents with a tin roof." $110–200 per night; 2-night minimum; price depends on cabin size and season.

✳ Where to Eat

EATING OUT Storie Street Grille (828-295-7075), Main Street, Blowing Rock, NC. This downtown storefront restaurant prides itself on its fresh food prepared from scratch. Soups, sandwiches, and special entrées are prepared to order with imagination and flair—definitely a good Main Street choice.

The Original Emporium Restaurant (828-295-7661). Located south of Blowing Rock, NC, on US 321. If you're looking for a beer, a burger, and a view, this popular restaurant is definitely your spot. The menu may be fairly standard, but the burgers, salads, and sandwiches are fresh and good. And the view . . . well, it's the kind of view you came here for, with a large deck hanging over the edge of the Blue Ridge just a wee bit, giving an unobstructed 180-degree panorama down into the Catawba Valley.

The Gamekeepers Restaurant

(828-963-7400). Located in a remote mountainous area north of Blowing Rock, across from the Yonalossee Resort; from Blowing Rock, just follow the signs to the Yonalossee. The Gamekeepers occupies a large wooded site, well up from its country road. Its menu puts a modern twist on mountain favorites, featuring game, fish, vegetarian entrées, and fresh seasonal vegetables cooked on a wood-fired grill. The winding drive out is beautiful, passing through and then along the boundaries of **Moses Cone Park** (see *To See—The Blue Ridge Parkway*).

Famous Louise's Rockhouse Restaurant (828-765-2702). This landmark stone building, by the Blue Ridge Parkway on US 221 in Linville Falls, NC, once furnished a hearty good time to the parkway's Works Progress Administration (WPA) construction crews—an endeavor helped by its position straddling three county

CRIPPEN'S COUNTRY INN AND RESTAURANT

(828-295-3487; 1-877-295-3487), 239 Sunset Drive, Blowing Rock, NC. Open for dinner only. Open daily July through October; June: Tuesday through Sunday; November through May: Thursday through Sunday. Owners Jimmy and Carolyn Crippen and chef James Welch have created one of the finest and most exciting restaurants in the mountains, in this beautifully restored boardinghouse off downtown Blowing Rock. Occupying much of the first floor of this fine European-style inn, the restaurant features an elegant, yet casual atmosphere. A wide front porch welcomes diners, as does a comfortable small bar facing a parlor sitting area. The roomy dining area has old-fashioned full-length windows and wood floors, simple wood furniture, and fine art on the walls. Each evening's menu is unique, selected from Chef Welch's large repertoire of adventurous, boldly flavored creations. Entrées center around beef and seafood (with chicken, duck, pork, lamb, and pasta also appearing on the menu). You might dine on grilled pork tenderloin marinated with rosemary and garlic, served with a rosemary-zinfandel sauce, a mash of goat cheese and chives, and baby vegetables; or (Jimmy's favorite) a grilled beef tenderloin, crusted with espresso and infused with bittersweet chocolate, served with an Irish Cream sauce, French beans, and walnut–goat cheese au gratin potatoes. In addition to several decadent desserts, they also offer handmade ice creams and sorbets, fine brandies, single malt scotches, ports and dessert wines, and fine cigars (smoking on the porch only). The menu is á la carte. Appetizers $7–14; soups and salads $5–8; entrées $16–26.

lines, which discouraged unwanted snooping by county sheriffs. Now it's a popular Southern-style restaurant serving good home-style food three meals a day.

Chalet Restaurant at Switzerland Inn (828-765-2153). Just off the Blue Ridge Parkway at milepost 334 in Little Switzerland, NC. Open for lunch and dinner, this restaurant is part of the Switzerland Inn. Nicely decorated, it's mainly noted for its panoramic views off the Blue Ridge, which at this point is directly underfoot. The straightforward menu has many old favorites and some pleasant surprises as well—local trout smoked on the premises, a knockwurst and bratwurst plate on fresh sauerkraut, a bowtie pasta dish with andouille sausage, chicken, and shrimp in a tomato creole sauce. They have a Friday prime rib and seafood buffet for the all-you-can-eat crowd, and a Saturday outdoor barbeque during the summer (weather permitting).

DINING OUT The Riverwood (828-295-4162), 7179 Valley Boulevard (US 321), Blowing Rock, NC. Open for dinner, Wednesday through Saturday. The Riverwood wanders through a 70-year-old house with three intimate dining rooms and a full bar. Appetizers include grilled venison sausage served with caramelized shallots and a sun-dried blueberry-Madeira sauce, and seared tempeh and mushrooms with a caraway–sun-dried tomato sauce on bowtie pasta. Entrées (which include house salad, vegetables, and bread) include baked mountain trout with an apple-almond-basil stuffing, beef tenderloin tournedos marinated in herbs and red wines, served with shallot mashed potatoes; and vegetarian entrées. Entrées $15–23.

✷ Entertainment
The Blowing Rock Stage Company (828-295-9627), Blowing Rock, NC. This nonprofit professional theater company performs four plays (two of them musicals) each summer season.

Geneva Hall (828-668-7223), Little Switzerland's town hall hosts weekly clogging all summer long, just across from the Switzerland Inn (see **Chalet Restaurant at Switzerland Inn** under *Eating Out*).

✷ Selective Shopping
Blowing Rock, NC
Blowing Rock's elegant little downtown stretches along four blocks of Business US 321, opposite the town park. It's built up from numerous small buildings—old brick fronts, houses, renovated gas stations, even a vacant lot or two—now given over to catering to the needs of the village's well-heeled visitors. Galleries, gift shops, antiques shops, and restaurants dominate the street.

⊤ Main Street Gallery/Expressions Craft Guild (828-295-7839). Located downtown in an old stone building across from the post office, this fine-crafts cooperative features a wide selection of local artists' pottery, jewelry, glass, wood, fiber, and photography. It's owned and managed by its members, and a member should be on the floor willing to talk with you when you drop in.

Man in the Moon (828-295-3699). This downtown shop is a rarity—a gift shop where men want to stay longer than their wives. No sports memorabilia or NASCAR souvenirs here, just a wide range of doodads and whatchamacallits tailored to men's tastes. Be sure to come in to enjoy the large

ARTIST'S POTTERY AT EXPRESSIONS GALLERY

kinetic sculptures with marbles dropping down copper rails. Now if they would just add a selection of power tools . . .

↑ **Sunset Tees and Hattery** (828-295-9326),. Another masculine favorite in downtown Blowing Rock, Sunset Tees features a huge selection of first-rate men's hats in a large room in the back. There's plenty of cowboy hats and baseball caps—but also bowlers, top hats, berets, jazzy hats, Sunday-go-to-meeting hats, leather hats, cloth hats, straw hats, and lots of felt hats. A fun shop.

Lenoir, NC
Bolick Family Pottery (828-295-3862), 4884 Bolick Road. You'll find this studio by heading 3 miles south of Blowing Rock on US 321, then driving left on Blackberry Road (SSR 1500) for 0.5 mile. Open Monday through Saturday 8–5, Sunday 1–5. Fifth-generation potter Lula Owens Bolick and her husband, Glenn, moved from Seagrove, NC, to this spot down a back road near Blowing Rock in 1973. They

specialize in traditional shapes—mugs, bowls, pitchers, candle holders, tea sets—in colors of gray, oatmeal, and cobalt blue.

Linville, NC
One World Bookstore and Soup Bar (828-733-8897). Open Wednesday through Saturday 11–4. This unique shop down a residential street in Linville combines a bookshop specializing in regional, Native American, cooking, health, childrens', and metaphysical titles, with a soup bar offering fresh homemade soup, baked goods, and fresh coffee. It also has local art, pottery, antiques, and gifts.

Little Switzerland, NC
Trillium Gallery (828-765-0024). Located in the set of shops associated with the Switzerland Inn (see Chalet Restaurant at Switzerland Inn under *Eating Out*), off the Blue Ridge Parkway at milepost 334. Open May through October every day, 9–5. Trillium Gallery represents a dozen or more local fine crafters, including some associated with the **Penland School of Crafts** (see *To See—Cultural Sites* in "Behind the Blue Ridge: Spruce Pine and Burnsville"). You'll find original works of art in pottery, basketry, glass, and jewelry. The Trillium sits in an interesting collection of shops, including a crafts shop and a gem shop.

Grassy Mountain Bookshop (828-765-9070). This bookshop at the center of Little Switzerland (on NC 226A) specializes in used, rare, and out-of-print books. Open May through October every day, 10–5.

✳ **Special Events**
♪ *January:* **Blowing Rock Winterfest** (828-295-9168; 1-888-465-0366), Blowing Rock, NC. Mid-January. For a

3-day weekend during the coldest part of the year, the village of Blowing Rock, NC, celebrates the fun part of winter, with hayrides and hot chocolate, bonfires, a parade, dog sledding, ice sculpting, street musicians, dances, live jazz, live theater, a chili cook-off—and (hopefully) lots of snow.

May–October: **Blowing Rock Art in the Park,** Blowing Rock, NC. One Saturday a month, this juried art show features a hundred contributors in downtown Blowing Rock's beautiful park.

June: **Singing on the Mountain** (828-733-2013; 1-800-468-7325), Linville, NC. *Fourth Sunday in June.* Free admission. Held annually since 1924, this all-day gospel sing and church bazaar at the foot of **Grandfather Mountain** (see *To See—The Blue Ridge Parkway*) features a dozen gospel groups.

July: **Grandfather Mountain Highland Games and Gathering of the Clans** (828-733-1333), Linville, NC. *Second weekend in July.* For nearly half a century, the Grandfather Mountain Highland Games have been held on **MacRae Meadows** at **Grandfather Mountain Park** (see *Wild Places—The Great Forests*). A highly popular 5-day celebration with attendance in the tens of thousands. Events include classic Scottish athletics, bagpipe demonstrations and competitions, Highland dancing, a 5-mile foot race and a marathon up Grandfather Mountain, ceilidhs (Celtic jam sessions), Scottish harp, Scottish fiddling, Gaelic song, and sheep herding demonstrations. There are a large number of vendors and clan tents. The games are sponsored by the nonprofit Grandfather Mountain Highland Games, Inc., which uses proceeds to run the games and a scholarship fund. Each day requires a separate ticket, as do many special events; tickets typically range from $10–20 apiece, and event-wide passes are not available.

July–August: **Blowing Rock Charity Horse Show** (828-295-9861) Blowing Rock, NC. *Late July through mid-August.* An annual event since 1923, this horse show consists of two AA-rated Hunter/Jumper shows (at 5 days each) and one A-rated 4-day Saddlebred Show. Although the emphasis is on fun, the first Hunter/Jumper show is a World Champion Hunter Rider event, and the Saddlebred show is part of the American Saddlebred Grand National Series. Charities supported include the local volunteer fire department and rescue squad, Moses Cone trail maintenance (see **Moses Cone Park** under *To See—The Blue Ridge Parkway*), and a riding program for the disabled.

August: **Grandfather Mountain Amateur and Professional Camera Clinic** (828-733-2013; 1-800-468-7325), Linville, NC. *Third weekend in August.* Free admission. (Participants must register for free admission to the park.) For over half a century, **Grandfather Mountain Park** (see *To See—The Blue Ridge Parkway*) has hosted this annual photojournalism convention, open to all serious photographers.

BEHIND THE BLUE RIDGE:
BOONE & BANNER ELK

On the back of the Blue Ridge, westward from Blowing Rock, NC (see Villages in "The Blue Ridge Parkway: Blowing Rock and Grandfather Mountain"), the Watauga and New Rivers drain a wide, perched bowl of a valley. Each river runs in a separate direction—the New River northward toward the Ohio River, the Watauga River westward toward the Tennessee River. Nevertheless, their headwaters come within a few hundred yards of each other in a wide, level gap at the center of this region. This location, long a wilderness crossroads, now holds the college town of Boone, NC.

North Carolinian Daniel Boone explored this high, mountainous bowl in the years before the American Revolution. He wasn't the first European to do so; he was just the most important. His pa, Squire Boone, had created a prosperous farmstead at the foot of the Blue Ridge, and young Daniel spent his youth poking up every little game trail he could find within a 2-week walking distance. Daniel established reasonably good trails up the Blue Ridge into the Watauga lands and helped European settlers find their way into these Cherokee hunting grounds (in violation of English laws). The settlers negotiated a private peace with the Cherokee chiefs (money played a large part in the transaction) and settled down the Watauga into Tennessee. Boone went on to blaze more trails, moving on into western Virginia and the empty Kentucky hunting lands.

Today, the town of Boone sits at the center of this rugged valley, a small town with a busy brick-front downtown and a largish state university, Appalachian State. Nearby, the settlement of Valle Crucis (Valley Crew-sis), NC, preserves a lively and beautiful historic landscape that mixes farmhouses from Boone's era with general stores from the 1930s. Still farther back, a couple of those 5,000-foot peaks harbor ski slopes—about as snowy and nicely kept as you'll find in the warm latitudes of the American South. To the north of Boone stretches beautiful rural countryside, little visited by tourists, dominated by the ancient New River and the little county seat of Jefferson, NC.

GUIDANCE **Boone Convention and Visitor's Bureau** (828-262-3516; 1-800-852-9506), 208 Howard Street, Boone, NC 28607. Located in downtown Boone, on a back street, this friendly staff at this information desk will answer questions about the town of Boone and its surrounding area.

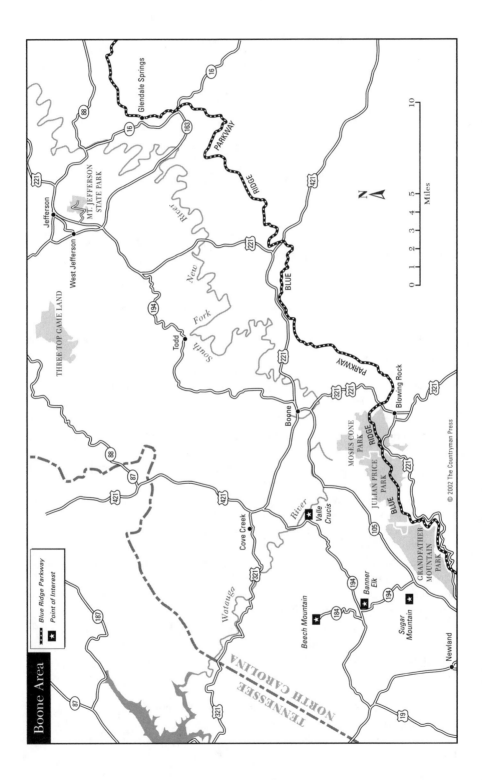

Boone Area

Blue Ridge Parkway
Point of Interest

THREE TOP GAME LAND

Jefferson

West Jefferson

MT. JEFFERSON
STATE PARK

Glendale Springs

New

Fork

South

River

221
88
16
163
16

RIDGE

PARKWAY

Todd

194

221

BLUE

421

Boone

221
321
221

PARKWAY

Blowing Rock

221

MOSES CONE
PARK

RIDGE

221

JULIAN PRICE
PARK

BLUE

221

Cove Creek

321

321

River

Valle
Crucis

105

Watauga

GRANDFATHER
MOUNTAIN
PARK

© 2002 The Countryman Press

87

88

421

187

87

TENNESSEE
NORTH CAROLINA

321

Beech Mountain

184

194

Banner
Elk

194

Sugar
Mountain

Newland

19

N

Miles

0 1 2 3 4 5   10

© 2002 The Countryman Press

Beech Mountain Chamber of Commerce (828-387-9383; 1-800-468-5506), 403A Beech Mountain Parkway, Beech Mountain, NC 28604. This small-town chamber welcomes visitors from an office within City Hall. You'll find it at the top of the mountain on the left on NC 184. Open Monday through Friday 9–4.

Avery/Banner Elk Chamber of Commerce (828-898-5605; 1-800-972-2183), P.O. Box 335, Banner Elk, NC 28604. Covering all of Avery County (the rural areas west of Valle Crucis), this visitors center is hidden away in the shopping center at the corner of NC 105 and NC 184.

Ashe County Chamber of Commerce and Visitors Center (336-246-9550), 6 North Jefferson Avenue, West Jefferson, NC 28694. Located off the main highway in West Jefferson's redbrick downtown, this visitors center offers help and advice for the Jefferson area.

GETTING THERE *By car:* The main highways into this region are US 321 and US 421, which converge at Boone, NC. Within the region, NC 105 (a surprisingly unattractive roadway) is the easiest way to drive south from Boone to Banner Elk, NC, while US 221 is the easiest route north from Boone to Jefferson, NC.

By air: You have a choice of three airports, two regional and one international. **Hickory Regional Airport** (828-323-7408; see also *Guidance* in "Beneath the Blue Ridge: The Catawba River Valley") is only 35 miles south of Boone and gets several commuter hops a day from Charlotte, NC. **Charlotte/Douglas International Airport** (704-359-4000) itself is another 40 miles south of Hickory, and the flights are usually much cheaper. Don't neglect to check out **Tri-Cities Airport** (423-325-6000), only 45 miles west of Boone in Johnson City, TN; much bigger than Hickory's airport, its fares may be cheaper than Charlotte's.

By bus or train: There is no scheduled bus service and no passenger train service in this region.

MEDICAL EMERGENCIES **Watauga Medical Center** (828-262-4100; 1-800-443-7385), 336 Deerfield Road, Boone, NC. This full-service regional hospital, with a wide range of surgical and medical specialties, offers 24/7 emergency-room services at its main building. It's located 2 miles south of Boone on US 221/321, then a block north on Deerfield Road.

Ashe Memorial Hospital (336-246-7101), 200 Hospital Avenue, Jefferson, NC. This full-service 76-bed hospital with a 24/7 emergency room serves the rural northwest corner of the North Carolina mountains from its campus at the center of Jefferson.

✳ Wandering Around

EXPLORING BY CAR **NC 194.** *Leg 1:* Starting at Jefferson, NC, take Business US 221 through West Jefferson, NC, to US 221; take a right onto NC 194; follow 194 to Boone, NC.

    Leg 2: Continue on NC 194, coterminous with US 421 through Boone; continue on NC 194 when it turns left off US 321/421; continue to Banner Elk, NC.

    Leg 3: Turn right off NC 194 onto NC 184, climbing to Beech Mountain, NC.

NC 194 passes through the center of this region for 48 miles, from Jefferson to Boone, then on to Valle Crucis and Banner Elk. It's a slow and twisty road but exceptionally pretty, with pastoral vistas over streamside meadows framed by low mountains and dotted with old barns and farmhouses. Start at the northern end of this region, at **Jefferson,** lightly built with scattered businesses and homes, and dominated by its great domed redbrick courthouse. In 2 miles **Business US 221** reaches **West Jefferson,** a busy little former rail depot, with a three block red-brick downtown that is coming back to life. As the road narrows and enters the mountains, it climbs a little valley then switchbacks down to the National Register village of **Todd,** NC (see **Todd National Historic District** under *To See—Historic Sites*), a tiny collection of historic buildings off the road on the left. On a side lane through Todd, the **South Fork of the New River** (see *Wild Places—The Great Rivers*) makes one of its characteristic 180-degree curves, doubling back on itself around steep mountain slopes. Eleven miles later, **NC 194** twists out of the mountains to reach **US 221/421** at Boone.

NC 194 follows **US 421** through **Boone,** a busy college town, passing right up the middle of its crowded downtown (see *Villages* and *Selective Shopping*) and out the other side. Five miles beyond Boone, NC 194 turns off the main highway to the left and once more becomes a mountain road, curving down to the wide mead-ows of the **Watauga River** at **Valle Crucis,** passing the **Mast General Store** (see *To See—Historic Sites*). The pastoral beauty and historic structures continue for 7 miles past the Mast Store as the road twists sharply around meadows and up mountain slopes to **Banner Elk** (see *Villages*).

On the far side of Banner Elk, this route climbs **NC 184** to **Beech Mountain,** NC (see *Villages*), using five switchbacks in 3 miles to rise 1,400 feet above the val-ley. The road tops out at 5,000 feet above sea level, at the center of the highest vil-lage in the East; to the right, **Blackberry Ridge Road** leads a short distance to superior views. The main road continues through the village to switchback down the back of the mountain, with more good views. You'll find **Ski Beech** (see *To Do—Skiing*) down this way, where a summer ride up a ski lift leads to a mile-high panorama.

EXPLORING ON FOOT Mount Jefferson Summit. This mile-long walk along the summit of 4,600-foot Mount Jefferson climbs 350 feet in elevation on its way to two spectacular viewpoints. It starts at the picnic area on the top of the moun-tain in **Mount Jefferson State Park** (see Mount Jefferson State Natural Area under *Wild Places—Recreation Areas*), a mile outside Jefferson, NC. The trail proceeds along an old roadbed at the far end of the picnic area, climbing uphill at a fairly steep 15 percent grade—mercifully, for only a thousand feet or so—to a viewpoint at the highest point of Mount Jefferson. The trail continues along a high rocky ridge, forested with tough old hardwoods, for another half mile to **Luther Rock,** a rocky outcrop and cliff with wide views over Jefferson and northward over the New River Valley. A loop returns through rhododendron tunnels.

☙ **Lee and Vivian Reynolds Greenway Trail (The Boone Greenway).** This 2.2-mile (one way) urban greenway follows the headwaters of the New River just east of Boone, NC. The paved and gravel trails of this attractive and well-kept riverside walk cross the river three times via handsome pedestrian bridges to find wildflower fields, river glades, and vistas. Popular with locals and college students, it has plenty of benches for enjoying the view. The upstream end is the easier to find; take US 321 south 2 miles from downtown Boone to a left turn onto Deerfield Road, then four blocks to a left onto State Farm Road, then one block to the start of the greenway.

✳ Villages

Boone, NC. This college town and county seat sits in a high valley straddling the headwaters of the Watauga and the New Rivers. Not that many years ago it was a sleepy mountain town, but the explosive growth of **Appalachian State University** has left Boone bursting at the seams with 13,400 residents, its overflow sprawling down US 321 toward Blowing Rock and NC 105 toward Banner Elk. This is a lot of people for a mountain town that can only be reached via two-lane highways, and traffic can be bad. On the bright side, it has a neat downtown shopping district and plenty of interesting shops and restaurants. The compact campus of 13,000 students, Appalachian State sits only three blocks from downtown, paralleling it along a stream and up the opposite mountain slope. The university-sponsored **Appalachian Summer Festival** (see *Special Events*) brings a wide variety of performing artists and lecturers into Boone each July.

Valle Crucis, NC. This rural settlement is nearly unique in the Appalachians—a popular tourist destination that remains unspoiled by success. Pronounced Valley Crew-sis, it's a dispersed rural settlement along the Watauga River, its center 9 miles west of Boone, NC, on back roads. It has become popular for its lush pastoral scenery, historic buildings, unique small shops and B&B inns, and its general store and post office, the famous **Mast General Store** (see *To See—Historic Sites*). It has a prosperous look more common to New England than Appalachia, but there's nothing fake about it; this area has been settled since the late 1700s, and surviving buildings date from that earliest period. To find it from Boone, take NC 105 west from Boone 4.75 miles to Broadstone Road (SSR 1112), just over the Watauga River, and turn right. Valle Crucis stretches along Broadstone Road 2.8 miles to NC 194 and the Mast General Store, generally taken as the center of the village.

Banner Elk, NC. For many years a quiet little village centered on a small liberal arts college, today Banner Elk is Main Street for the **Sugar Mountain and Beech Mountain ski slopes** (see *To Do—Skiing*). Banner Elk's original village center sits at the intersection of NC 194 and NC 184, by tiny **Lees-McRae College,** and this remains the best place to look for shops, cafés, or quaint old B&Bs. It's also the location of **Mill Pond** (see *Wild Places—Picnic Areas*), a scenic picnic spot run by the college and open to the public. Modern-day Banner Elk scatters south from its old center along NC 184 for 2.6 miles to the entrance to Sugar Mountain, then beyond another 1.5 miles to the urban sprawl along NC 105.

Beech Mountain, NC. In all likelihood the highest town in the East, Beech Mountain's town hall sits just barely above 5,000 feet in elevation—and a third of a mile higher into the sky than nearby Boone, NC. This ski village is reached by taking NC 184 north from Banner Elk, NC, and straight up five switchbacks and 1,500 feet. The village, a small scattering of modest shops and motels surrounded by condos and second homes, sits on a high, flat shelf about 200 feet shy of the summit. The ski slope starts some distance downhill (toward the back of the

THE ASHE COUNTY COURTHOUSE IN JEFFERSON

mountain) and rises directly behind the town hall, making it easy to watch the skiers from the little town square. In fact, the town government provides a children's sledding slope behind the town hall, complete with artificial snow. The temperature difference between Beech Mountain and lower-lying towns is marked; Beech Mountain is long-sleeve cool and breezy in the warmest of summer weather. The mountain is an isolated mile-high peak surrounded by much lower terrain, so good views are a given from just about anywhere near the village center.

Jefferson and **West Jefferson, NC.** Twenty-five miles north of Boone, NC, and far off the beaten tourist paths, these little-developed redbrick sister towns retain their old mountain look and feel. They complement each other; Jefferson, with 1,400 residents, has the government functions and the historic domed courthouse; while West Jefferson, with 1,000 residents, has the downtown main street (called Jefferson Street). Once a railroad depot, West Jefferson's old-fashioned downtown is surprisingly interesting, with a scattering of galleries representing local artists. Mount Jefferson looms above both towns, a state park with magnificent views from four overlooks (see **Mount Jefferson State Natural Area** under *Wild Places— Recreation Areas*).

✷ Wild Places

THE GREAT FORESTS Wild places abound along the Blue Ridge, a scant half-dozen miles to the south of Boone, NC, including some of the most remarkable in the Southern Appalachians: All are described in the previous chapter, "The Blue Ridge Parkway: Blowing Rock and Grandfather Mountain," devoted to the Blue Ridge Parkway as it runs through this area (see that chapter's introduction). They include the privately owned scenic park at Grandfather Mountain (see Grandfather Mountain Park—The Backcountry under *Wild Places—The Great Forests*), the Blue Ridge Parkway with its stunning views (see The Blue Ridge Parkway under *Wandering Around—Exploring by Car*), and the deep woods and waterfalls of Pisgah National Forest (see Wilson Creek National Wild and Scenic River under *Wild Places—The Great Forests*).

Once you've backed away from the Blue Ridge, large public wild places become scarce. Much of the Watauga and New River Valleys has been heavily settled and farmed since the time of Daniel Boone in the late 18th century; the lovely pastoral landscapes are dotted with historic buildings, but wilderness has long since given way to woodlots. To the south, the high, wild peaks of Sugar and Beech Mountains have been converted to ski-oriented tourist attractions and thickly built up, their former wilderness dissected by closely spaced roads and small building lots.

To the north of Boone, tall mountains still retain their wild character. Forests tend to be old and lovely, with rich and diverse ecosystems; the scenery is dotted with beautiful waterfalls, odd little perched valleys, and impressive cliffs. Unfortunately for travelers, virtually all of these wild places are privately owned and closed to the public. Only one large tract welcomes visitors to explore at their leisure—**Three Top Mountains Game Lands,** near Todd, NC. A second tract, The Nature Conservancy's **Bluff Mountain Preserve,** is open only to guided walks (which, fortunately, occur all summer long).

Three Top Mountain Game Lands (919-733-7291), 1701 Mail Service Center, Raleigh, NC. Take NC 194 north of Boone to Todd, then head north on Three Top Road for 8.7 miles. The public access parking lot is on the right, just before a bridge over Three Top Creek. This 2,300-acre tract (about 3.6 square miles) between Todd and Jefferson, NC, preserves the impressive 4,800-foot craggy peak known as **Three Tops** and its surrounding slopes. The tract's public hiking trails lead through rich forests to wildflower meadows, crags, and views. The Nature Conservancy started assembling this impressive tract in 1989 from a mosaic of donations, cooperative local owners, and a couple of busted subdivisions; expect some of the lower walking to be on old subdivision tracks. It's currently owned by the North Carolina Wildlife Resources Commission, whose main mission is maintaining public land for hunting and fishing.

Bluff Mountain Preserve (The Nature Conservancy) (919-403-8558), One University Place, 4705 University Drive, Suite 290, Durham, NC. This 2,000-acre privately owned preserve, located in the same mountain range as the **Three Top Mountain Game Lands** (see above), protects an unusual flat-bottomed valley perched just below the 4,800-foot peak of Bluff Mountain. The site offers wonderful views from rocky outcrops, and a variety of beautiful and unusual ecosystems—a mature hemlock forest, a dwarf oak forest, rocky bald plant communities, and a rare example of the Southern Appalachian fen, protected in the high valley. Owned and managed by The Nature Conservancy, Bluff Mountain is not open for casual visits from the public. However, both The Nature Conservancy and the **Ashe County Chamber of Commerce** (see *Guidance*) host regular guided walks.

THE GREAT RIVERS The South Fork of the New River. The most remarkable thing about this river is the way it meanders, acting as if it is lazily wandering through a level plain before finally reaching an ocean. This is not the case. The New River rises more than 3,100 feet above sea level, just behind the Blue Ridge, and follows the Blue Ridge for nearly 90 miles. Of course, those are meandering river miles; the actual linear distance covered is 29.43 miles. Those distance-tripling meanders reduce the slope of the river to the point where canoes commonly replace kayaks; much of the river is stillwater, and most of its rapids are a mild Class I. Despite their flatlands shapes and slopes, these meanders have managed to cut straight down into the hard rock of the Blue Ridge, leaving the river surrounded by clifflike slopes. Occasionally the river will make a sharp 180-degree curve, cutting a gorge that doubles back on itself. The easy paddling couples with the prime mountain scenery to offer 90 miles of day explorations and overnight adventures.

This stretch of river has long enjoyed the reputation as the second oldest river in the world, and the oldest in North America—claims repeated by President Clinton when he declared it a National Heritage River from its banks near Jefferson, NC, in 1998. Some have objected to this, claiming that there is no agreed-upon measure of a river's age, and even if there was, it has never been used in a world survey. Well, picky, picky, picky. Those 90 miles of meanders formed when the New River flowed through a flat plain. The meanders cut into the rock as the mountains rose underneath them—in this case the Blue Ridge Mountains, 220 million years old. You do the math.

RECREATION AREAS Mount Jefferson State Natural Area (336-246-9653), SSR 1152, Mount Jefferson State Park Road (off US 221), Jefferson, NC. This isolated mountain rises just south of Jefferson, its peak 1,400 feet above the wide valleys that surround it. A paved lane climbs the west slope of Mount Jefferson in seven switchbacks, with two overlooks giving broad views over West Jefferson and Bluff Mountain. At the top is a tree-shaded picnic area, a nature trail, and walking paths along the narrow half-mile-long summit to two more overlooks (see also **Mount Jefferson Summit** under *Wandering Around—Exploring on Foot*).

PICNIC AREAS Mill Pond Picnic Area, Banner Elk, NC. This lovely little picnic area sits in the village center. It's a landmark along NC 184, with a barn-red cottage sitting under great trees by the reflecting surface of the small lake. Its scattered lakeside tables are a great place to picnic, or just sit and relax.

Howard Knob Park, Boone, NC. From downtown Boone, head uphill on Waters Street (away from the university) to its end, then continue steeply uphill on Junaluska Road; when it tops out, go right to Howard Knob Park. This 6-acre county park sits high above Boone. Its main feature is a large outcrop and cliff with stunning views over Boone and Valle Crucis, NC. It can be difficult to find but is worth the effort.

✳ To See

HISTORIC SITES Todd National Historic District. Located halfway between Boone and Jefferson, NC, on NC 194 (see *Wandering Around—Exploring by Car*), Todd is a former depot town on a long-defunct mountain railroad that followed the New River to Jefferson and over the mountains to Virginia. A bit of a ghost town, Todd today is a collection of late-19th- and early-20th-century vernacular buildings that somehow manage to preserve the look and feel of an old rural railroad siding village. While most of the buildings are private, the general

MAST GENERAL STORE

✏ ☎ (828-963-6511), NC 194, Valle Crucis, NC. Open Monday through Saturday 7–6, Sunday 1–5. You may have seen various Mast General Stores selling outdoor and gift items in downtown Boone, Hendersonville, Asheville, and Waynesville, NC. Make no mistake; the 19th-century frame store at the center of Valle Crucis is the real Mast General Store and always has been—the primary general store for the community of Valle Crucis since 1882 (when it replaced a smaller structure across the street). This National Register structure is really a collection of white clapboard buildings sort of stuck together, with doorways passing through common walls on the inside. The outside has a false front, plate-glass windows, a wood boardwalk, and a hand-crank gas pump that no longer works. Inside, it combines the items needed by the Valle Crucis community—groceries, mail, fishing licenses, burning permits, and a checkers set by a potbellied stove—with local canned jellies and honeys, barrels of marbles, bulk candy, local arts, outdoor products, and all sorts of other stuff. The Mast family owned it until 1973 and is still involved in its management. Its current owners, John and Faye Cooper, have taken the Masts' longtime formula of "Everything from Cradles to Caskets" and used it to create a general-store marketing powerhouse with branches in five mountain towns. However, they've kept the original Mast General Store true to its heritage, one of the few general stores to make it successfully into the 21st century.

THE MAST STORE IS LISTED ON THE NATIONAL REGISTER OF HISTORIC PLACES.

store is still going strong, and the depot houses a local crafts gallery and New River outfitter (see **Appalachian Adventures** under *To Do—Whitewater Adventures*). The New River comes right up to the town's lower edge and makes one of its unique hairpin turns around a cliff. It was at this point that the railroad started following the New River, and its old grade is now a narrow country lane with sweeping river views; you can rent bicycles at the depot for a lovely riverside jaunt.

✈ **Hickory Ridge Homestead** (828-264-2120), 591 Horn In The West Drive, Boone, NC. Located by the **Horn In The West** amphitheater (see *Cultural Sites*) and **Daniel Boone Gardens** (see *Gardens and Parks*); go east of downtown on US 421 and turn right (south) onto Horn In The West Drive. Open summer: Tuesday through Sunday 1–8:30; spring and fall: Saturday 9–4, Sunday 1–4; closed in winter. $2 per person. This living history museum in Boone re-creates a late-18th-century pioneer farmstead. Owned by the Southern Appalachian Historical Association, it preserves two historic log cabins and several outbuildings on an attractive wooded slope near the center of town. The buildings are beautifully and authentically furnished, and have period vegetable and herb gardens. Guides in period clothing explain the pioneer way of life, demonstrate crafts, and perform authentic music. Visitors are invited to participate in activities such as carding and spinning wool, weaving on a 185-year-old loom, candle making, and cooking over an open hearth. Summer visitors should look into an evening visit followed by a performance of Horn In The West—for the same cost as a ticket to Horn In The West alone.

CULTURAL SITES Appalachian State University (828-262-2000), Boone, NC. The parklike main campus of Appalachian State University (ASU) stretches the length of central Boone, along a stream two blocks downhill from downtown. Compact and modern, the 50 or more university buildings squeeze onto a 75-acre site, landscaped with a plentiful number of hardwood trees and rhododendrons. The attractive campus is studded with sculptures and contains several galleries of student and faculty art. On-campus accommodations are available at the tree-shaded, hill-top **Broyhill Inn,** with a first-rate restaurant (see *Lodging—Hotels* and *Dining Out*). A member campus of the University of North Carolina, ASU has nearly 13,000 students and 175 degree programs.

&. ↑ **The Appalachian Cultural Museum** (828-262-3117), University Hall, Appalachian State University, is located off US 321 south of Boone; take US 321 south from downtown, turning left onto University Hall Road. Open Tuesday through Saturday 10–5, Sunday 1–5; closed Monday. Adults $4; free on Tuesday. Sponsored by Appalachian State University, this museum has exhibits on every aspect of Appalachian history and culture: Blue Ridge geology; Native American settlement and culture; early settlers; Daniel Boone; Daniel Boone's mythologizer, James Daugherty; the Civil War; African Americans in Appalachia; moonshine (including an authentic hundred-year-old still); mountain crafts and music; storytelling; a reconstructed general store from 1911; NASCAR racing; the local ski industry; and modern logging and tourism (including an exhibit on a failed theme park, Land of Oz, on Beech Mountain). Of particular note is a gallery of self-portraits of local people, ranging from professional artists to ordinary folk.

Horn In The West (828-262-2120; 1-888-825-6747), 591 Horn In The West Drive, Boone. For over half a century, the Southern Appalachian Historical Association has presented Kermit Hunter's large-scale outdoor musical drama of the early settlement of the Watauga Valley, centering on Daniel Boone and the American Revolution. Held six evenings a week throughout the summer, the performance is preceded by an evening tour of the historically authentic reconstructed pioneer farmstead, **Hickory Ridge Homestead** (see *Historic Sites*)—actually an extension of the performance, with period-costumed guides demonstrating the pioneer way of life.

⊤ **The Jones House Community and Cultural Center** (828-262-4576), 604 West King Street, Boone, NC. Open Wednesday through Saturday noon–5. Free admission. This 1908 local doctor's home sits incongruously in the center of Boone's brick storefront downtown, a genteel white clapboard mansion with a wide porch overlooking its high lawn toward busy King Street. Today, this National Register structure is owned by the town of Boone and run by the Watauga County Arts Council. While much of this large house is given over to community center uses, several rooms serve as a gallery for local artists, while other rooms are furnished in-period. It's definitely worthwhile to take a time out from King Street shopping and pop up for a visit.

⊤ **The Turchin Center for the Visual Arts** (828-262-3017), Boone, NC. Under construction at the time of writing, the Turchin Center in downtown Boone should be open by the time you visit. Affiliated with **Appalachian State University** (see *Cultural Sites*), this arts center occupies the hundred-year-old octagonal brick Methodist church that has long been a prominent downtown landmark. Meant as a center for campus-community interaction, it should have a main gallery and six smaller galleries, plus two terraces for displaying sculpture, a lecture hall, and a wing for classrooms and studios.

GARDENS AND PARKS Daniel Boone Gardens (828-264-6390). Open May through October 9–6; 9–8 on days when there are **Horn In The West** (see *Cultural Sites*) performances. Closed November through April. $4. Owned and run by the nonprofit Garden Club of North Carolina on land contributed by Horn In The West (Southern Appalachian Historical Association), Daniel Boone Gardens presents native Appalachian plants in a free-flowing, informal landscape. First open in 1966, the gardens have had more than three decades of growth and improvement, offering season-long displays of every native flower imaginable. The gardens now include a bog garden, a fern garden, a sunken rock garden with a tiny pond, a mountain spring, a reflecting pool, and a meditation garden. The large wrought iron entrance gate with the initials "DB" were handmade by artist and Daniel Boone descendant Daniel Boone VI.

✳ To Do

BICYCLING Magic Cycles (828-265-2211), 208 Faculty Street #1, Boone, NC. This full-service bicycle shop, located south of downtown Boone on Faculty Street just off US 321, offers both mountain bike rentals and guided bicycle trips. The Boone area has a wide variety of bicycle paths and trails, and this is a good place to find out about them all. Rentals: $15 for 4 hours; $25 for 8 hours; $30 for 24 hours; $60 for 3 days. Guided trips: $50 per person; minimum of 2 people.

Beech Mountain Biking Trails (828-387-2795), 325 Beech Mountain Parkway, Beech Mountain, NC. The **Beech Mountain Biking Club** maintains more than 30 miles of mountain biking trails on the high slopes of Beech Mountain—many (or most) on a busted subdivision abandoned since the 1970s. These trails offer a wide range of technical challenges and mountain scenery. The **Beech Mountain Chamber of Commerce** (see *Guidance*) offers a good brochure with very clear and detailed maps.

FISHING Whitetop Laurel Fly Shop (366-246-3475), 210 South Jefferson Avenue, West Jefferson, NC. This full-service fly-fishing shop at the center of West Jefferson offers guide trips throughout the **New River** region.

GOLF Village of Sugar Mountain Golf Course (828-898-6464), Sugar Mountain Drive, Banner Elk, NC. Open April through October. $22. This 1974 18-hole course, designed by Duane Francis and Arnold Palmer, sits just beneath the ski slope at Sugar Mountain.

Willow Creek Public Golf Course (828-963-6865), Bairds Creek Road, NC 105, Boone, NC. Open May through October. $14. Part of a resort development, this nine-hole course west of Boone off NC 105 features country scenery and well-kept fairways.

Boone Golf Club (828-264-8760), 433 Fairway Drive (US 321), Boone, NC. Open April through October. $43 weekdays, $48 weekends. This 18-hole course, situated just south of Boone, was designed in 1959 by Ellis Maples.

Hawksnest Golf Resort (828-963-6565), 2058 Skyland Drive, Seven

Devils, NC. Open April through October. $35 weekdays, $39 weekends. This 4,200-foot-high 18-hole course offers stunning scenery and lots of dramatic elevation change.

Jefferson Landing on the New River (336-982-7767), NC16/88, Jefferson, NC. Open mid-March through mid-November. $42 weekdays, $62 weekends. This 18-hole course, built in 1991 on the site of a former dairy farm, offers wide views toward Mount Jefferson, as well as water hazards on 15 holes.

Mountain Aire (336-877-4716), 1104 Golf Course Road, West Jefferson, NC. Open mid-March through mid-December. $32 weekdays, $39 weekends. This 18-hole course, built in 1950 in the remote mountains near Jefferson, offers first-rate scenery.

HORSEBACK RIDING Banner Elk Stables (828-898-5424) offers trail riding along the slopes of Beech Mountain, from their stables at the end of Shomaker Road in Banner Elk. $15 per hour.

Smith Quarter Horse Farm (828-898-4932). A mile outside Banner Elk off NC 194, this stable offers trail rides on the slopes of Beech Mountain.

ROCK CLIMBING Footsloggers (828-262-5111), 139 South Depot Street, Boone, NC. Tower open spring through fall, noon–5. Tower: $9 plus rentals. This downtown Boone outdoor store, in addition to offering a full line of climbing gear and encyclopedic knowledge of local routes, has a 35-foot climbing tower and an enclosed bouldering cave.

Appalachian Challenge (828-898-6484; 1-888-844-7238), Banner Elk, NC. This whitewater outfitter also offers guide services and instruction for rock climbing and cave exploring (the latter in Virginia and Tennessee caves).

Edge of the World (828-898-9550; 1-800-789-3343), Banner Elk, NC. Another whitewater outfitter offering day-long rock climbing and rappelling instructional trips (adults $75).

SKIING ✔ Ski Beech (828-387-2011; 1-800-438-2093), 1007 Beech Mountain Parkway, Beech Mountain, NC. Open daily 8:30 AM–10 PM. Lift tickets $28–45 adults; $21–32 children and seniors. Located downhill behind the village center, Ski Beech starts a group of two-story 1960s alpine vernacular buildings grouped around an outdoor skating rink, with a snack bar and a number of shops. The main lodge is up a set of outdoor wooden stairs—a rambling, 1960s-style three-story structure with broad and impressive views from many decks and windows. The whole complex is clean and well kept, full of adults and families with children. Its run is 3,600 feet with a drop of 750 feet from a summit of 5,505 feet to a base of 4,700 feet, the highest ski elevations in the Smoky Mountains region (and probably in the East).

✔ Sugar Mountain (828-898-4521; 1-800-784-2768), Banner Elk, NC. Open daily 9 AM–10 PM. Lift tickets $33–49 adult; $27–37 children. The Sugar Mountain ski lodge is easily accessible from NC 184 in Banner Elk, not that far a distance uphill or off the main road. It's a three-story wood building with gray pressboard paneling in an early 1970s style, perhaps a bit down at the heals but very clean. It is busy with adults and families but handles crowds well. It has the longest run and the farthest drop in the area—1½ miles and

1,200 feet from a summit at 5,300 feet to a base at 4,100 feet.

WHITEWATER ADVENTURES The Watauga River and the New River—both rising from the town of Boone, NC—offer radically different whitewater opportunities. The **South Fork of the New River** (see *Wild Places— The Great Rivers*) meanders through a cliff-sided gorge, but with so many twists that its 30 miles of travel is lengthened to 90 miles of riverbed of an exceedingly gentle gradient and with hardly any rapids. Indeed, it almost qualifies as stillwater, and most people prefer to travel along it in canoes. It is so stunningly beautiful that it has been declared both a National Wild and Scenic River and a National Heritage River, and at 90 miles it allows some great overnight canoe trips. The **Watauga River** offers shorter and more action-packed runs, with some Class II and III rapids to get your adrenaline running.

✔ Appalachian Adventures (336-877-8800), NC 194, Todd, NC. Located in the 1888 train depot at the historic center of Todd, midway between Boone and Jefferson, NC, Appalachian Adventures furnishes tubing, kayaking, and canoeing on the **South Fork of the New River,** as well as bicycling on the scenic lanes in the area.

✔ Appalachian Challenge (828-898-6484; 1-888-844-7238), Banner Elk, NC. This Banner Elk guide service offers whitewater rafting on the mild and beautiful **Watauga River** (adults $39, children $29)**,** and special trips on the technically challenging **Wilson Creek.** They also offer guide services for rock climbing and cave exploring (the latter in Virginia and Tennessee caves).

⚶ **Edge of the World** (828-898-9550; 1-800-789-3343), Banner Elk, NC. This Banner Elk guide service sponsors guided raft floats on Class II to III rapids on the **Watauga River;** the 4-hour trip includes a fried chicken lunch made fresh that morning (adults $52, children $42; includes lunch). Also see *Rock Climbing*.

⚶ **Wahoo's Adventures** (828-262-5774; 1-800-444-7238), Boone, NC. Wahoo's offers a wide range of rafting experiences throughout the Smokies, with branches in Gatlinburg and Ducktown as well as their flagship location in Boone. In the Boone area, they offer gentle family trips on the **New River** and the **Watauga River,** and fierce rapid-runners on **Wilson Creek, Russell Creek,** and the **Watauga River Gorge.**

⚶ **Zaloos Canoes** (336-246-3066; 1-800-535-4027), 3874 NC 16 South, Jefferson, NC. Located on the South Fork of the New River, at the corner of NC 16 and NC 88 (5 miles east of Jefferson), Zaloos offers tubing and canoe trips (including camping trips) along the **New River.**

✳ Lodging

HOTELS The Broyhill Inn and Conference Center (828-262-2204; 1-800-951-8048), 775 Bodenheimer Drive, Boone, NC 28607. A full-service 83-room inn and conference center on the attractive campus of Appalachian State University. This modern building sits on a parklike hilltop landscaped to appear like a mountaintop meadow. Its charming dining room (see *Dining Out*) with a large wood-burning fireplace, has sweeping mountain views over a small sculpture garden. Roomy and comfortable common areas are decorated with local art. A recent renovation

has turned the formerly spartan rooms into the comfortable quarters you'd expect from a high-end business hotel, including computer data ports in every room. Winter and spring: $90–95 for standard rooms, $130–175 for suites. Summer and fall: $135 for standard rooms, $165–220 for suites. The tariff does not include meals; however, this can be changed by adding a fixed surcharge of $40–50.

The Mast Farm Inn (828-963-5857; 1-888-963-5857), P.O. Box 704, Valle Crucis, NC 28691. This popular and respected small country inn at the heart of Valle Crucis has so many historic buildings that it's listed on the National Register as a Historic District. The 1880s farmhouse holds nine comfortable rooms furnished in country antiques. Adjacent historic log cabins and farm outbuildings, original to the site and as old as 1812, have roomy cottage accommodations furnished with mountain country antiques; one- and two-bedroom floor plans have separate living rooms and wet bars, but no kitchens. The grounds are beautifully landscaped, and the farmhouse's wide wraparound porch is a perfect place to sit and rock. Their restaurant

ENJOYING A CUP OF COFFEE ON THE PORCH OF THE MAST FARM INN

is noted for its organic gourmet regional cuisine. Rooms $125–195; cottages $195–380.

✏ **Archers Mountain Inn** (828-898-9004; 1-888-827-6155), 2489 Beech Mountain Parkway, Banner Elk, NC 28604. Halfway up Beech Mountain, this group of 1970s vintage lodge buildings offers a wide variety of room types (and prices). All rooms are individually decorated with antiques and reproductions, typically in a country or farmhouse style, and all rooms have fireplaces and either a deck or porch. Features available in some rooms include separate sitting areas, kitchens, structural cedar beams, whirlpool baths, feather beds, and private mountain-view porches. The lodge's restaurant, **The Jackalope View** (see *Dining Out*), is first rate and has a weekend jazz bar. $70–195, includes full breakfast.

BED & BREAKFASTS Lovill House Inn (828-264-4204; 1-800-849-9466), 404 Old Bristol Road, Boone, NC 28607. Open all year, this four-diamond AAA-rated inn retains the look and feel of the mountain countryside while sitting on the edge of downtown Boone. Its 11 acres of property has a perennial flower garden, barn, strtheam, and waterfall, with woodland views on all sides. The 1875 Victorian farmhouse with wraparound porches and rockers, built by one of Boone's most prominent citizens, has hardwood pine and maple floors, and wormy chestnut moldings and doors. Public areas are elegant and roomy, with lovely period antiques. The six en suite rooms are large, with fireplaces (half wood, half gas) and elegant antiques and reproductions. An outbuilding, once a feed store on the

19th-century farm, has been renovated as a self-catering cottage, carrying the same theme of 19th-century country elegance. A full gourmet breakfast is served in the sunny dining room, and a social hour—by the fire in bad weather, on the porch in good—greets guests in the evening. $125–185.

Window Views B&B (828-963-8081; 1-800-963-4484), 204 Stoneleigh Lane, Boone, NC 28607. This two-room private home B&B perches on a high mountainside with stunning panoramas from the decks and full-length windows of this 1992 house. A large common room lets out onto a deck with an unobstructed 180-degree panorama over Valle Crucis and the valley of the Watauga River. The bright, cozy rooms, decorated with modern furniture and antiques, have similarly wide views through glass French doors that lead to decks. Afternoon cookies are served on the deck, and a full breakfast in the morning. $75–100, including full breakfast.

The Baird House (828-297-4055; 1-800-297-1342), 1451 Watauga River Road, Valle Crucis, NC 28679. Open all year. This 1790 farmhouse sits on 16 acres, including 500 feet of **Watauga River** frontage. A pristine, early example of planked lumber construction, the Baird house boasts a stunning two-story-high porch with round columns, a center dogtrot-style hall, and the original 18th-century planking on the walls of one of the elegantly furnished common rooms. The guest rooms are elegantly furnished with antiques and reproductions typical of prosperous 19th-century farms. Two rooms are in the main house, while three more rooms (one a kitchenette) occupy a renovated 20th-century outbuilding; by the time you read this, two additional rooms may have been added to the main house. $95–145, including a full country breakfast.

Mast Gap Inn (828-297-5287), 1914 Mast Gap Road, Sugar Grove, NC 28679. This classic three-room B&B occupies a 1937 farmhouse in a pastoral location on NC 194 just north of Valle Crucis (see NC 194 under *Wandering Around—Exploring by Car*). Beautifully restored, common areas are comfortably furnished with a mixture of antiques and modern furniture. The bright and cozy bedrooms also emphasize comfort, with goose down comforters. There is a hosted social hour every evening with hors d'oeuvres and beverages, coffee and pastries before breakfast, and a full gourmet breakfast by Cordon Bleu–trained innkeeper and chef Jody Leonard. $99–125, including breakfast.

Alta Vista (828-963-5247), 2839 Broadstone Road, Valle Crucis, NC 28691. Located upstairs from Valle Crucis's **Gallery Alta Vista** (see *Selective Shopping*), this comfy B&B has large rooms with country antique furniture, bead-board walls and ceilings—and lots of original art on the walls. In fact, having this fine gallery on site is part of the charm of this 1923 brick bungalow in the center of the settlement. Another aspect of its charm—the large front porch overlooking the Watauga River and the old general store now occupied by the Mast General Store Annex. An upstairs common sitting room serves as the venue for the full hot breakfast, as well as a great place to sit and read. $110.

Bluestone Lodge (828-963-5177), Bluestone Wild Road, P.O. Box 736, Valle Crucis, NC 28691. Located down a side lane in Valle Crucis, this four-room B&B is in a three-story modern home with decks and mountain views on all three floors. The well-landscaped property has an outdoor pool with mountain views, a sunroom, and an indoor hot tub and sauna. Rooms are large and well decorated, each with its own theme. $96–167.

♿ **Azalea Inn** (828-898-8195), P.O. Box 1151, Banner Elk, NC 28604. Open all year. This large 1937 bungalow, rated three diamonds by AAA, sits at the very center of the village of Banner Elk, by a stone Works Progress Administration (WPA) school built the same year and still in use. This roomy and cheerful house, with country antiques and quilts, has wormy chestnut trim in the front parlor, while three other common rooms offer sunny places to relax. Within the main house are two downstairs rooms, plus one upstairs room with a strange and wonderful attic-tunnel sitting area. An addition has more rooms, including one with a whirlpool bath and a full-sized private porch. A detached cottage, over a garage, offers a high level of self-catering. $99 and up.

🐾 **Banner Elk Inn Bed & Breakfast** (828-898-6223), 407 Main Street East (NC 194 West), Banner Elk, NC 28604. Open all year. Built in 1912 as a country church, this large wooden house was moved to Banner Elk from a site farther up the mountain to take advantage of the new auto road—now the Old Toll Road east of town. Beautifully restored, this pink house with green shutters recalls the elegant, comfortable living of a country lawyer or doctor. A breakfast area is flooded with light from large windows; plush chairs face a fire; stained bead-board covers the walls and ceilings. Two standard rooms are ample sized, while a two-bedroom suite offers comfortable quarters for families or couples traveling together. A honeymoon suite, taking up most of the low-ceilinged attic, offers special privacy (and a whirlpool bath) for those willing to take on the extra-steep and narrow steps. Pets must be arranged for in advance. Rooms $95–145; two-bedroom suite $140–180.

The River Farm Inn (336-877-1728), 179 River Run Bridge Road, Box 2, Fleetwood, NC 28626. This renovated 19th-century dairy barn sits on a beautifully landscaped property on the South Fork of the New River, off a lovely country lane in the community of Fleetwood, 17 miles northeast of Boone, NC. The beautifully renovated barn holds two large suites, each elegantly decorated with antiques, and each with a full kitchen. A nearby building holds a third suite, while a modern log cabin is also available. Suites $175–195; cabin $250; includes continental breakfast.

Buffalo Tavern Bed & Breakfast (336-877-2873; 1-877-615-9678), 958 West Buffalo Road, West Jefferson, NC 28694. Built in the 1870s, this large wooden house in the rural Bluff Mountain area (6 miles west of Jefferson) was a popular 19th-century coaching inn and Prohibition-era tavern. Today it's an elegant three-room B&B surrounded by azaleas, its first- and second-story porches shaded by large old trees. It's decorated in the country Victorian style, and all rooms have down comforters and log fireplaces. A gourmet breakfast is served by candlelight in the dining room. $115–135.

French Knob Inn (336-246-5177), 133 Ferguson Road (NC 163), West Jefferson, NC 28694. This three-room B&B sits in a scenic location amid the low mountains of the New River Valley, 5 miles south of Jefferson. In this modern farm-style home with dormers, the rooms and common areas are elegantly decorated with Victorian antiques and reproductions. Two of the three rooms are large, with whirlpool tubs. $95–150.

CABIN RENTALS The Cottages of Glowing Hearth (828-963-8800; 1-888-232-5080), 171 Glowing Hearth Lane, Vilas, NC 28692. Open all year, this remote Baird Creek site, up winding paved roads, is an easy, scenic 10-minute drive from Valle Crucis to the west and Boone to the east; ask for directions. Bill and Pam Moffit host five luxurious cottages on 40 acres of mountaintop land offering sweeping views in all directions. The 1500-square-foot modern cabins are reminiscent of farmhouses with picket rails and covered porches, but with 18-foot peaked ceilings and broad windows facing the view. Comfortable main living areas include plush sofas and chairs, a wood-burning fireplace, and a fully equipped kitchen. The master bedroom features a four-poster king bed and whirlpool bath. From $200.

✳ Where to Eat

EATING OUT Red Onion Café (828-264-5470), 227 Hardin Street, Boone, NC. Open 11–9 weekdays, 11–10 weekends. This downtown casual restaurant reuses a 1960s-era barbeque as an upmarket sandwich, salad, and pasta café. A tuna salad features grilled and marinated yellowfin tuna on mixed greens with hearts of palms, mushrooms, olives, scallions, and tomatoes; a less extraordinary mayonnaise-y tuna salad is available too. Personal-sized pizzas on whole wheat crusts come with a variety of toppings, from traditional and pesto to South-western and creole. Desserts are made on the premises. Sandwiches and salads $6.95–7.95; pastas, 10-inch pizzas, and specialties $9.95–15.95.

Our Daily Bread (828-264-0173), 627 West King Street, Boone, NC. Open Monday through Friday 8–6, Saturday 9–5; closed Sunday. When Sam and Jennifer Parker bought this small downtown storefront café in the center of Boone, they knew what they wanted—fresh produce from local farms, lots of choice, and great food prepared from scratch. Their menu centers on breakfasts, soups, salads, and 25 different sandwiches, including 12 vegetarian choices and grilled cheese made with local farm cheese (and under $3). Their carefully decorated interior is bright and welcoming, with plenty of blond hardwood. Breakfast $1.45–3.95; lunch $2.25–5.50.

✔ **Dan'l Boone Inn** (828-264-8657), 130 Hardin Street, Boone, NC. Open June through October: 11:30 AM–9 PM weekdays, 8 AM–9 PM weekends. November through May: 5 PM–8 PM weekdays, 8 AM–8 PM weekends. A popular family eatery since 1959, occupying a large former boardinghouse at the south edge of downtown Boone. Inside, it's plain and straightforward, with several large rooms paneled in tongue-in-groove pine. Fried chicken, corn, whipped potatoes (with lumps), green beans (soft, with fatback, Southern style), country fried steak and gravy, coleslaw, a superb country ham on biscuit, baked apples, gravy—all are served family-style. Beverage, soup or salad, and dessert are also included. You take what you want, and if the bowl goes empty they bring you some more. Dinner: adults $12; children under 12, $0–6, depending on age. Breakfast:

adults $8; children under 12, $0–5, depending on age.

The Caribbean Café (828-265-2233), 489-B West King Street, Boone, NC. Open daily 11:30 AM–1 AM. This downtown storefront tavern has been popular with students and locals for years. Its jazzy, bright decor combines Caribbean themes with pub memorabilia. Specializing in a wide range of microbrews and imported beers, particularly British pub favorites such as Theakston Old Peculier and Marston Old Speckled Hen. Entrées have a West Indian flair, including jerk chicken (with coconut rice, Cuban black beans, and plantains), shrimp riders (sautéed with onions and peppers served with a rum sauce over saffron rice), and warm smoked salmon with a tomatillo sauce. The menu also includes a build-your-own-pasta section and a full range of salads, sandwiches, and vegetarian dishes. $5–12.

The Corner Palate (828-898-8668). Located at the corner of NC 184 and NC 194 (between Sugar Mountain and Beech Mountain). Open for lunch and dinner; may keep shortened hours in the winter. A casual atmosphere with an intelligent, imaginative menu. The more casual pub area is in the back; the quiet and atmospheric dining room in front. Both feature a gourmet approach to all meals, combining fresh local ingredients and a creative interpretation to popular American dishes. Specials change daily. Lunch $5–10; dinner $8–20.

DINING OUT The Broyhill Inn (828-262-2204; 1-800-951-6048), 775 Bodenheimer Drive, Boone, NC. Open all year. The newly renovated Broyhill Inn (see *Lodging—Hotels*), on a hilltop inside Appalachian State

University, now sports an elegant dining area off the main lobby anchored by a giant hearth at one end and a glass wall at the other, with a view over the inn's sculpture garden and parklike grounds to Howard's Knob and the mountains beyond. Breakfasts can be either a buffet or à la carte, while lunches center on an ample buffet, and a Sunday brunch buffet includes an omelet chef. However, dinners are the main event, elegant entrées served with live piano and a crackling wood fire. Appetizers might include a wild mushroom ragout in puff pastry or sautéed Maryland-style crabcakes. Entrées—served with potato, mixed green salad or freshly made soup, and vegetables—include farm-raised quail stuffed with wild rice; grilled rainbow trout with baby shrimp, leeks, and amaretto butter; and braised veal shank with a white wine tomato demiglaze. Dinner $10–22; lunch and breakfast also available.

The Jackalope View (828-898-9004; 1-888-827-6155), 2489 Beech Mountain Parkway (NC 184), Beech Mountain, NC. The first thing you notice at the Jackalope View is—the view. Located halfway up Beech Mountain, this casual fine dining restaurant at **Archers Mountain Inn** (see *Lodging—Hotels*) has glass walls and a deck hanging over a 180-degree open south-facing panorama toward Sugar Mountain and the Blue Ridge. Three wine cellars offer 300 different wines (with a large selection under $25 a bottle), and 28 wines by the glass. The menu presents exotic and original preparation of beef, trout, fresh seafood, and game. A venison an black bean chili comes with house-made tortilla chips on the side; a risotto includes lump crab, Shiitake mushrooms, and asparagus. A mountain trout is crusted with walnuts and almonds and drizzled with citrus butter; a veal chop may be grilled, stuffed with prosciutto and Gorgonzola cheese, and served with a Marsala mushroom sauce. Upstairs is a large and comfortable bar with even more great views, a wide selection of microbrews, and live jazz on weekends.

✳ Selective Shopping
Boone, NC
Stretching for four long blocks along US 321/421, downtown Boone marks the former location of Daniel Boone's Wilderness Trail. Today it's a classic turn-of-the-century brick-front town, lively and active with interesting shops. The main street is a simple two-laner with parallel parking, named King Street; behind it on the downhill side is alleylike Howard Street, where most of the off-street parking is to be found; Appalachian State University starts on the next block down. With a 13,000-student university two blocks downhill, parking spaces are scarce and regulations are aggressively enforced. However, there's a trick to it; stop by the **Chamber of Commerce** on the western end of Howard Avenue and get a permit that lets you park to shop downtown.

Farmers Hardware (828-264-8801), 661 West King Street. Farmer's Hardware, part of Boone since 1924, is special. And not just for its classic Main Street storefront, with well-worn hardwood floors, old wooden cabinetry, and wide stairs descending downward in the middle of the store. In addition to hardware, a housewares department offers the sort of kitchen ware you normally find only in specialty catalogs and a section of wild-bird houses and feeders. Inside the old safe are a range of fine decorative items. Then down the stairs, behind the paints section, is another strange and funky selection of pottery and garden decorations.

Row by Row Bookshop (828-265-2154), 641 West King Street. This modest used bookshop, the last in a series of small alternative shops occupying the same downtown Boone storefront, deserves a visit from any book lover. Its books are well kept and well organized, with a wide range of unusual topics—from a wall full of obscure history titles to a good selection of hardbound mysteries and science fiction. It's a good place to look for first editions, or just for a nice reading copy of that long-out-of-print title.

The Watauga County Farmer's Market. Open May through October on Saturday morning. Held at the **Horn In The West** (see *To See—Cultural Sites*) for more than 25 years, the Farmer's Market features fresh locally grown produce and local crafts. Go there for organically grown produce, fresh herbs, fruits, flowers, honey, eggs, preserves, fresh-baked goods, bedding plants, and farm crafts. You can talk with the actual growers, buy some baked goodies and have a picnic at the adjacent Horn In The West picnic area.

Valle Crucis, NC
Gallery Alta Vista (828-963-5247), 2839 Broadstone Road. This lovely gallery occupies the parlors and dining room of a large 1923 farmhouse. It features a large selection of realistic and impressionistic watercolors and oils, mainly by local and regional artists, but also by artists from around the nation and the world. It's a good place to browse for fine art original paintings of mountain scenes, as the technical quality and originality are consistently high.

West Jefferson, NC
De Pree Studio and Gallery (336-246-7399; 1-877-639-5808), 109 North Jefferson Avenue. Open weekdays 9–5, Saturday 9–4. This large and beautiful gallery occupies a 1930s brick storefront in the town center. Its roomy display areas highlight the paintings of co-owner Lenore De Pree, brilliantly colored scenes of Blue Ridge life and landscapes, stylistically influenced by medieval Persian art. The gallery also features large and small wood sculptures by local artist Tom Sternal, and handwoven Persian rugs.

Ashe County Cheese Company (336-246-2501), 106 East Main Street. The mountain region's only cheese manufacturer has been in business in West Jefferson since 1930. They offer factory tours, fresh cheese for sale, and a gift shop.

✳ Special Events

June–August: **Horn in the West** (828-262-2120; 1-888-825-6747), 591 Horn in the West Drive, Boone, NC. This venerable outdoor drama presents the story of the area's settlements (see *To See—Cultural Sites*). **Lees-McRae Summer Theater** (828-898-8721), Lees-McRae College, Banner Elk, NC. Adults $18, children $10. Lees-McRae College (see *Villages—Banner Elk*), a small liberal arts college, sponsors this summer theater festival. They typically perform three musicals, each for a 5-day run toward the end of a month.

July: **An Appalachian Summer Festival** (828-262-4046; 1-800-841-2787). Affiliated with Appalachian State University at Boone, this festival fills the July calendar with music, dance, and the visual arts. Music is the main focus, with classical symphonic performances, pop orchestras, jazz, and mountain music, and a mix of regional and national performers. Modern dance and serious theater stud the program, along with lecture series, workshops, and visual-art displays. The festival ends with an outdoor fireworks concert featuring a major headliner.

Third Saturday in July: **Doc Watson Music Fest,** Historic Cove Creek High School, Sugar Grove, NC. This annual celebration of Doc Watson is held on the lawn of the old Cove Creek High School, not too far from Doc Watson's home, as a fundraiser to establish the **Doc and Marie Watson Museum** inside the old school. The 2-day event features music by Doc Watson and his friends—about 20 bluegrass and mountain bands in all. Crafts vendors are present (with the emphasis on music), and food is available.

First Saturday in August: **Firefly Festival,** Boone, NC. Held at the **Hickory Ridge Homestead** (see *To See—Historic Sites),* Boone's annual Firefly Festival, a fundraiser for this outdoor museum of 18th-century life, includes storytellers, musicians, mountain crafters, and folk artists, with guides dressed as 18th-century pioneers.

Mid-August: **Barbershop Bonanza (Barbershop Quartet Competition and Show),** Boone, NC. This annual Boone event features a day of barbershop quartet competitions, followed by an evening performance by the winners.

Mid-September weekend: **Cove Creek Farm Heritage Days,** Historic Cove Creek High School, Sugar Grove, NC. This fundraiser for Cove Creek Preservation and Development, patterned after the local agricultural fairs of a hundred years ago, features mountain music and clogging, farm exhibits, farm crafts demonstrations, old-time games and activities, a petting zoo, local crafts, and a canning competition. The day after the fair, local farms open their doors to strangers for afternoon farm tours.

☙ *Third weekend in September:* **Banner Elk Woolly Worm Festival,** Banner Elk, NC. For the last quarter of a century, this celebration of the furry caterpillar has drawn more than 15,000 people every year. Although there are vendors and food, the main interest centers on the worm races—50 heats of the worms racing up strings, bringing cash prizes to their owners. When a champion is finally declared, the festival's official forecaster uses its stripes to predict the coming winter weather. It's a fundraiser for local schools, held on the elementary school grounds at the center of the village.

Last weekend in September: **Old Boone Streetfest** (828-262-4532), Boone, NC. This street fair celebrating downtown Boone features free concerts on the Jones House lawn (see *To See—Cultural Sites)* and near the Turchin Center (see *To See—Cultural Sites),* and crafts vendors and food on Howard Street.

November–December: **Cut and Choose Christmas Tree Celebration** (828-264-3061). Sixteen Watauga County Christmas-tree growers organize this old-fashioned family Christmas tree-cutting celebration, holding a special welcome for families coming from the warm flatlands to choose a tree and maybe see some pre-Christmas snow. A brochure describes each farm in detail and gives directions.

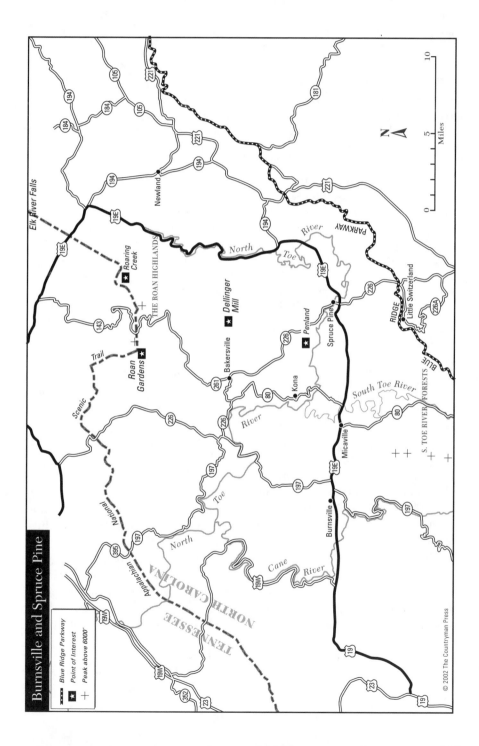

Burnsville and Spruce Pine

Blue Ridge Parkway
Point of Interest
Peak above 6000'

N

Miles
0   5   10

© 2002 The Countryman Press

BEHIND THE BLUE RIDGE:
SPRUCE PINE & BURNSVILLE

The Toe and the Cane Rivers drain some of the East's tallest mountains. The Black Mountains, with 10 peaks above 6,000 feet, sit on the south edge of the Toe-Cane drainage. The Highlands of Roan, with three peaks above 6,000 feet, loom over the north edge of the drainage, with miles of mountaintop meadows and hundreds of acres of natural rhododendron gardens. Between these two great ranges is a broken land of 4,000-foot peaks and 2,000-foot valleys, a land little visited by tourists. On the west, the Cane River and its tributaries drain rich, narrow valleys with bottomland farms beneath tall peaks; here the lovely little county seat of Burnsville gathers around an old town square still dominated by its 170-year-old inn. Farther east, the South Toe River drains northward off the forested slopes of Mount Mitchell, the tallest peak in the East, and enters a difficult and broken country linked to the notorious events of Frankie and Charlie Silver. Still farther east, the North Toe River drains a rough and forested land, dominated by feldspar, rock, and gravel mining, and centered around the terraced town of Spruce Pine. Here the famous Clinchfield Railroad cuts through the mountains by following the North Toe River as it merges with the South Toe and the Cane, to become the roaring Nolichucky River, powerful enough to carve a deep gorge through the mountains and out into the plains of Tennessee.

GUIDANCE **Yancey County Chamber of Commerce.** (828-682-7413; 1-800-948-1632), 106 West Main Street, Burnsville, NC 28714. The chamber runs an attractive visitors center in a restored early gas station on the western edge of downtown Burnsville.

Mitchell County Chamber of Commerce. (828-765-9483; 1-800-227-3912), 79 Parkway Road, Spruce Pine, NC 28777. This chamber, which covers the Spruce Pine and Bakersville, NC, areas, maintains an information desk for visitors just off the Blue Ridge Parkway in the **Museum of North Carolina Minerals** (see *To See—The Blue Ridge Parkway* in "The Blue Ridge Parkway: Blowing Rock and Grandfather Mountain").

Toecane Ranger District, Pisgah National Forest. (828-682-6146), US 19E Bypass, P.O. Box 128, Burnsville, NC 28714. This small ranger station, the administrative headquarters for Pisgah National Forest in the Toe and Cane River Valleys, maintains an information desk and welcomes travelers with questions.

GETTING THERE *By car:* The Toe and Cane River Valleys are linked by US 19, marked as US 19E over much of this segment. It runs from Mars Hill, north of Asheville, through Burnsville, Micaville, and Spruce Pine, NC, then into Tennessee near Elizabethton, TN.

By air: The closest airports are **Asheville Regional Airport** (see *Getting There* in "Asheville and the Blue Ridge Parkway") and **Tri-Cities Airport** in Johnson City, TN (see *Getting There* in "The Mountains of Northern Tennessee").

By bus or train: The Clinchfield Railroad eliminated passenger service on what had been one of the most scenic rides in the East over half a century ago. Bus service is long gone as well. You'll need a private car to see this region.

MEDICAL EMERGENCIES **Spruce Pine Hospital** (828-765-4201), 125 Hospital Drive, Spruce Pine, NC. Located off US 19E on the south edge of Spruce Pine, this small regional hospital furnishes the only 24/7 emergency-room services in the region.

✳ Wandering Around

EXPLORING BY CAR **NC 80.** *Leg 1:* From the NC 80 exit from the Blue Ridge Parkway (see *Wandering Around—Exploring by Car* in "The Blue Ridge Parkway: Blowing Rock and Grandfather Mountain"), take NC 80 north 28.3 miles to its end at Loafers Glory, NC. Sections are very twisty and narrow.

Leg 2: Turn right onto NC 226; go 2.6 miles east to Bakersville, NC, then turn left onto NC 261; go 12.8 miles to the top of Roan Mountain at Carvers Gap, at the Tennessee state line. The total drive is 43.6 miles.

From the parkway, **NC 80** quickly drops into the lovely South Toe River Valley, with fine views over the river to **Mount Mitchell** (see Mount Mitchell State Park under *To See—Along the Blue Ridge Parkway* in "Asheville and the Blue Ridge Parkway"), the highest peak in the East. From here the highway descends through the scattered rural community of **Celo,** NC, noted for its fine-crafts community, and reaching the old railroad siding town of **Micaville,** NC (see *Villages*), in 14 miles. After that, NC 80 becomes a narrow country lane of astonishing twistiness, coiling past cemeteries and churches, through forests, and into fields with wide mountainy views. A new bridge crosses high above the **South Toe River,** with views of the historic **Clinchfield Railroad** running through its gorge (see The Clinchfield Railroad Loops under *To See—Historic Sites* in "The Blue Ridge Parkway: Blowing Rock and Grandfather Mountain"). Just beyond, country lanes lead 5 miles to the famous craft school and artists' colony at **Penland,** NC (see **Penland School of Crafts** under *To See—Cultural Sites*). Then NC 80 reaches the attractive village of **Kona,** NC, with excellent views, a neat artist's gallery, and a **museum to Frankie and Charlie Silver** in an old church (see Kona, NC, under *To See—Historic Sites*).

Seven twisty, view-studded miles later, NC 80 ends at the settlement of **Loafers Glory,** NC, named for the gang of old-timers who once gathered in front of its (now defunct) general store. The charming, down-at-the-heels county seat of **Bakersville,** NC (see *Villages*), is just beyond; **Dellinger's Mill** (see *To See—Historic Sites*), a 1901 overshot waterwheel still in operation, is 4 miles west.

North of Bakersville, the route sweeps through lovely rural valleys, then climbs up to the mile-high **Carvers Gap** deep in the **Roan Highlands** (see *Wild Places—The Great Forests*). At the top, wide mountain meadows sweep uphill to the right, with incredible panoramic views (see The Roan Highlands on the Appalachian Trail under *Exploring on Foot*). To the left, a paved side road leads to **Roan Mountain Gardens** (see *To See— Gardens and Parks*), a 600-acre natural rhododendron garden with wide views from two 6,000-foot peaks. Crossing into Tennessee, the highway becomes **TN 143,** a ledge carved into the cliflike side of **Roan Mountain,** descending steeply with incredible views.

NC 197. Pick up NC 197 north of Asheville, NC, at Barnardsville, NC, and follow it 52 miles to its end at Indian Grave Gap, at the Tennessee state line. Very twisty and part gravel.

THE BLACK MOUNTAINS AS SEEN FROM THE LICKSKILLET COMMUNITY IN CANE RIVER

This spectacular and remote state road follows the major rivers of the region: the Cone, the Toe, and the Nolichucky. Like nearby NC 80, NC 197 is remarkably primitive for a road marked as a major highway. In fact, a section of it is gravel—one of the few dirt-surfaced state highways left anywhere in the South. It gives the drive a certain charm. From **Barnardsville** the highway is straight and easy at first, but quickly becomes a switchbacked gravel track as it climbs 2,000 feet up to **Cane River Gap,** then descends more switchbacks with views toward the **Black Mountains.** NC 197 finally regains its paved surface and crosses the **Cane River** (already quite large), then hugs the river for 11 miles, with many lovely views. The road enters the outskirts of **Burnsville,** NC (see *Villages*), whose town square is worth visiting, then passes a small textile mill (they make sailcloth) as it climbs **Green Mountain,** giving good views both north and south.

Past Burnsville, the highway continues through attractive rural countryside for a half-dozen miles, then reaches the wide and beautiful **Toe River** for another long riverside drive. At the community of **Red Hill,** NC (whose general store makes good sandwiches), it turns away from the river to twist through remote and beautiful farmland. It regains the **Toe River** at **Relief,** NC, following it for another mile or so downstream, then turns sharply right to once again twist into the mountains. The road finds the river again (now merged with the Cane and dubbed the **Nolichucky River**) at **Poplar,** NC, where the Forest Service maintains a kayak launch site at the start of the **Nolichucky Gorge** (see *Wild Places—The Great Forests*). From Poplar, the highway swerves and switchbacks uphill to cross the **Unaka Mountains** into Tennessee at 3,370-foot **Indian Grave Gap. Erwin, TN,** is 7 miles ahead on TN 395.

EXPLORING ON FOOT **The Roan Highlands on the Appalachian Trail (AT).** Starting at **Carvers Gap** on NC 216 (see NC 80 under *Exploring by Car*), this walk goes eastward through the wide meadows of the Roan Highlands to the northernmost 6,000-foot summit in the South, **Grassy Ridge Bald** (see The Roan Highlands under *Wild Places—The Great Forests*). This undulating trail is a 5-mile round-trip, with a thousand feet of climbing (a third of it on the way back). Park in the Forest Service picnic area on the left side of the road and take the AT across the road, through a split-rail fence, and into the mountaintop meadows. Both the views and the wind will increase steadily as you climb 300 feet up **Round Bald,** reaching the first of several 360-degree views from its summit in 0.4 mile. The trail continues down to a small gap, then uphill to **Jane Bald** (1.1 miles), staying in grassy meadows with wildflowers and wide views the entire way. After a shallow gap, the trail starts on a long climb (600 feet in 0.75 mile) up Grassy Ridge Bald; when the AT slabs off the ridge crest to the left, continue on the side trail along the ridge. After passing through thick rhododendrons, the trail tops out on the 6,200-foot summit, with a full-circle view from the top of the world. Return the way you came.

The Overmountain Victory Trail. In the colonial era, a footpath known as Brights Trace crossed the Roan Highlands at Yellow Gap, now a remote national forest tract. In September 1780 the frontier militia followed Bright's Trace to unite with Piedmont militias in an attack on British forces at Kings Mountain, SC—one of the most important American victories in the Revolution. The surviving segment of Bright's Trace is commemorated as part of the **Overmountain Victory National Historic Trail.**

This walk, a 5-mile round-trip with a 1,200-foot climb, takes the Overmountain Victory Trail from the end of the motorable Roaring Creek Road (SSR 1132), where a turnaround area offers wide views over the head of Roaring Creek Valley. Roaring Creek Road is a left turn off US 19E fourteen miles eastward from Spruce Pine, NC; there's an Overmountain Victory plaque at the proper intersection. The trailhead is at the end of the road in 4.6 miles, the last part of which is a steep gravel road.

Now part of Pisgah National Forest, this area was a private farm until the mid-1990s. It's still covered in meadows, with an apple orchard and a bright red barn. The formal trail follows a gated Forest Service road gently uphill through forests. A much more interesting alternative takes an informal trail downhill into the fields, then follow it up through wildflower meadows and apple orchards to the barn. Now an Appalachian Trail (AT) shelter, the barn gives a panoramic view over Roaring Creek Valley and toward the Blue Ridge beyond. To continue, take the blue-blazed trail east, recovering the Overmountain Trail in couple of hundred yards. The path continues uphill through open woods to **Yellow Mountain Gap** on the crest of the Roan. Here you'll intersect with the AT, in the broad ridgetop meadows so characteristic of the Roan Highlands (see *Wild Places—The Great Forests*). Head east along the AT, going steeply uphill through wide-open meadows, to reach the peak of **Little Hump Mountain,** with panoramas in all directions. Return the way you came.

✳ Villages

Burnsville, NC. This beautiful little village has a classic town square, a large, well-kept strolling space with lawns, trees, and flowers centering around its statue of an early-19th-century sea captain (Otway Burns, the town's namesake). Grouped around the square are the county courthouse, city hall, public library, and the town's 170-year-old coaching inn, the **Nu Wray Inn** (see *Lodging—Country Inns and Hotels*). There are several nice restaurants, gift shops, and crafts galleries. Parking is free, with overflow parking two blocks west of the square.

Micaville, NC. This tiny town sits along the South Toe River, bypassed by US 19E, halfway between Burnsville and Spruce Pine, NC. It was for many years an important siding on the Yancey Railroad, a spur from the Clinchfield (see The

Clinchfield Railroad Loops under *To See—Historic Sites* in "The Blue Ridge Parkway: Blowing Rock and Grandfather Mountain"), and it is from those early years that much of Micaville's small center dates. During the 1970s the Yancey Railroad was abandoned so quickly that the tracks were left behind with a pony engine still sitting on them (which is there to this day). The old **Micaville General Store,** attractively restored, is now a combination realty office and crafts cooperative, while the **Micaville Grille** across the street is popular with locals.

Spruce Pine, NC. This railroad town along the North Toe River has long been supported by mineral mining, particularly feldspar. The mining continues today, with a large strip mine scarring the mountainside immediately above downtown, and another strip mine greeting tourists who approach the town from the west on US 19E. Modern Spruce Pine, still dominated by mining, is struggling—with some

THE BURNSVILLE TOWN SQUARE, DECORATED FOR AUTUMN

success—to create an interesting and vibrant downtown. Downtown Spruce Pine consists of two long blocks paralleling the riverside depot (still active with freight trains), with a lower level facing the depot and an upper level one story above that. A number of interesting shops occupy both levels, and there's plenty of free parking by the depot.

Bakersville, NC. The seat of Mitchell County, Bakersville is a tiny town with a scant one-block downtown next to its old courthouse. Located on NC 216 ten miles north of its much larger sibling, Spruce Pine, Bakersville is best known for the large number of fine-crafts artists who live in the surrounding valleys.

LOOKING TOWARD MOUNT MITCHELL FROM THE SUMMIT OF ROAN MOUNTAIN

THE ROAN HIGHLANDS

The 15,000 protected acres of the Highlands of Roan contain the largest concentration of grassy mountaintop balds in the East, 600 acres of natural rhododendron gardens, large tracts of Canadian-style spruce-fir forests, and more rare species than Great Smoky Mountains National Park. John Fraser discovered the Catawba rhododendron here in 1787, and great early scientists such as Asa Gray and Elisha Mitchell studied its unique environments in the early 1800s, Gray calling it "without doubt the most beautiful mountain east of the Rockies."

The Roan Highlands consist of a single wall of remote, high mountains along the North Carolina–Tennessee state line, stretching from **Hughes Gap** (SSR 1330, Buladean Road) eastward to the deep gap that carries US 19E. Most of the highlands are within Pisgah National Forest, with significant tracts protected by the Southern Appalachians Highlands Conservancy, The Nature Conservancy, and the State of Tennessee. Made up of hard old rocks more characteristic of the Blue Ridge than the Smokies, the crest of the Roan Highlands stays above 4,000 feet for nearly its entire length, with 5 miles of it more than a mile high. Its three peaks that top 6,000 feet are the last in the

※ Wild Places

THE GREAT FORESTS **South Toe River Forests.** South of Burnsville and Micaville, NC, looms the tallest summit in the East, **Mount Mitchell** (see Mount Mitchell and the Black Mountains under "Asheville and the Blue Ridge Parkway"), one of the ten 6,000-foot peaks in the **Black Mountains.** The Blacks typically rise 3,000 feet above the Toe River in a linear distance of 3 miles, creating an unbroken barrier 7 miles long. While much of the area was logged, the very steepness spared large tracts along these slopes, and some trails climb through old-

Appalachian Mountains that exceed this height until Mount Washington in New Hampshire, 800 miles to the north.

Despite heavy exploitation between 1890 and 1940, the Roan Highlands look much the same today as they did 160 years ago. In 1836, Mitchell wrote, "The top of the Roan may be described as a vast meadow without a tree to obstruct this prospect, where a person may gallop his horse for a mile or two with Carolina at his feet on one side and Tennessee on the other, and a green ocean of mountains rising in tremendous billows immediately around him." Gray rocky crags stick out of the knee-high grasses; wildflowers form carpets whipped by winds that average 25 miles per hour. Most astonishing are the panoramas, frequently extending in a complete circle around the viewer, continuing unbroken for mile after mile. Even the bureaucracy of the U.S. Department of Agriculture is impressed, writing in a 1974 planning document, "There is no other area that offers such extensive panoramic views of the high country of the Southern Appalachians. Unique is not, in this sense, misleading."

Only one road crosses the Roan Highlands: NC 216/TN 143 makes the climb at mile-high **Carvers Gap** (see NC 80 under *Wandering Around—Exploring by Car).* Carvers Gap is the Roan's main access point for recreationalists, with a side road leading west to **Roan Mountain Gardens** (see *To See—Gardens and Parks),* and the **Appalachian Trail** (AT) leading east through miles of open meadows (see The Roan Highlands on the Appalachian Trail under *Wandering Around—Exploring on Foot).* The crest of the Roan is followed closely by the AT for its entire length, a very difficult through-walk that traverses 2,000-foot climbs up over steep and rocky paths. Side trails tend to be even more challenging, and the rugged slopes are seldom visited. One notable exception is the head of **Roaring Creek Valley;** extremely scenic and easily reached, it is the location of a colonial-era trace that the Overmountain militia followed on their secret march to attack the British at King's Mountain (see The Overmountain Victory Trail under *Wandering Around—Exploring on Foot).*

growth forests. Five paths make the 3,000-foot climb up the face of the Blacks, all of them scenic, and all of them difficult day-long slogs. The whole wall of the Blacks can be admired from the South Toe River at **Carolina Hemlocks Recreation Area** (see *Recreation Areas*), a great swimming hole.

Nolichucky Gorge. At the end of their long run, the Toe and the Cane Rivers merge to become the **Nolichucky River,** large enough to carve a gorge straight through the high Unaka Mountains. Pisgah National Forest owns nearly all of the land on both sides of the gorge, as well as the gorge itself. No roads or paths penetrate the bottom of the gorge—just the **Clinchfield Railroad** (see The Clinchfield Railroad Loops under *To See— Historic Sites* in "The Blue Ridge Parkway: Blowing Rock and Grandfather Mountain"), hugging tight to the riverbank and still under heavy use as a through-goods line (ludicrously dangerous for walking). A small village, known as **Lost Cove,** thrived for many years at the bottom of the gorge with no car access of any sort—until the railroad ceased passenger service, and its inhabitants had to walk in and out.

THE BLACK MOUNTAINS AS SEEN FROM THE SOUTH TOE RIVER

Good gorge-top views can be found from the easily accessible top of **Flat-top Mountain,** a large Pisgah National Forest tract on the west side of the gorge. Here a good gravel road leads to an old farm site near the top of the mountain. The shortest of climbs uphill leads to broad meadows (maintained by the Forest Service for wildlife), stretching for a mile along the rolling top of this tablelike mountain. Views include wide panoramas west over the Nolichucky Gorge to the Highlands of Roan, then east toward the Bald Mountains. The marked footpath leads downhill to the remains of Lost Cove village—a very difficult walk by all accounts.

The access road to Flattop Mountain, Howell Branch Road (SSR 1415), starts 5.3 miles along US 19W on the North Carolina side of the state line; when you pass through a gate after 1.2 miles, you'll be on the gravel Forest Service Road 278 for 3 more miles to its end at a closed gate. This is the old farmstead; the path is uphill to your right.

RECREATION AREAS Carolina Hemlocks Recreation Area. Open April through November. $3 per car. This picnic and camping area on NC 80 (see *Wandering Around—Exploring by Car*) is maintained by Pisgah National Forest adjacent to its large **South Toe River** holdings (see South Toe River Forests under *The Great Forests*). Its main attraction is a long and lovely stretch of the South Toe River, with wonderful views toward Mount Mitchell (the tallest peak in the East) and several good swimming holes. There's also a riverside path and a nature trail.

Elk River Falls Recreation Area. Open all year. Free admission. Located off US 19E near the North Carolina–Tennessee border, this lovely little recreation area offers several picnic tables, a long stretch of the Elk River with grassy banks for fishing, and a large waterfall, where this wide and powerful river pours over a 50-foot rock ledge. A short path clambers down to the base of the falls, and a long rocky spur leads out to a fine view.

PICNIC AREAS Ray-Cort Recreation Park, Burnsville, NC. To find this county park, take the side street north from the town square about five blocks. The park centers on a handsome small mountain stream flowing gently through a tree-shaded draw, with picnic tables scattered along its length. It has a fine large play-

ground, as well as volleyball and basketball courts. Picnic tables are under the
trees surrounded by closely cropped grass, or under shelters (including one made
of stone and logs, with a shake roof).

Riverside Park, Spruce Pine, NC. Located across the **North Toe River** from
downtown Spruce Pine, and linked to it by a 410-foot footbridge, Riverside Park
offers a shelter and a row of shaded picnic shelters, as well as a paved walking/
jogging loop that runs by the river.

✳ To See

HISTORIC SITES **Kona, NC (Frankie and Charlie Silver).** Kona resident
Frankie Silver (Mrs. Francis Stewart Silver) may not have been the first woman
hanged in North Carolina, but she was certainly the most notorious. Three days
before Christmas 1832, in her Kona log cabin and with her infant daughter looking on, the petite 18-year-old chopped husband Charlie into pieces and burned
him in the fireplace. The mountain folk song "Ballad of Frankie Silver" attributed
the murder to jealousy—but the real motive was Charlie's brutal abuse of his wife.
Best-selling author Sharyn McCrumb, whose grandparents lived nearby, has writ-
ten a fine novel, *The Ballad of Frankie Silver.*

Modern-day Kona is a lovely little mountain settlement straddling scenic NC
80 (see *Wandering Around—Exploring by Car*) 6 miles north of US 19E. Kona
occupies a set of meadowy hilltops that drop from the old Baptist church, past the
new Baptist church, then straight down to the gorge of the **Toe River** and the
Clinchfield Railroad below (see The Clinchfield Railroad Loops under *To See—
Historic Sites* in "The Blue Ridge Parkway: Blowing Rock and Grandfather Mountain"). The old Baptist church sits by NC 80, surrounded by the **Silver Cemetery.**
The Silver family gives pride of place to their common ancestor, Revolutionary
War veteran George Silver, who received the surrounding square mile of land as
reward for his service in the Patriot army. However, most tourists are interested in
his grandson Charlie's graves—three of them, as they kept finding bits of Charlie
hidden in the snow. The Silver Cemetery is extremely well kept, with banks covered in wildflowers, and offers broad views westward from its grassy top. The old
wooden church serves as a museum for the Silver clan, with many interesting
exhibits on the notorious murder. South of the cemetery is the colorful **Mountain
Hill Country Gallery,** the working studio of painters Pat and Dan Dowd.

By the way, that infant daughter survived, was raised by Frankie's mother, and
prospered as much as anyone could in the mountains after the Civil War; she has
left more than a hundred known descendants.

The McElroy House (Rush Wray Museum of Yancey County History) (828-
682-3671), Burnsville, NC. Located two blocks off Burnsville's town square above
the Yancey County Visitors Center (see Yancey County Chamber of Commerce
under *Guidance*), this large 1840s-era farmhouse is home to the Rush Wray
Museum of Yancey County History. It's now a simple and attractive home, but in
the antebellum era it was the fanciest mansion in this poor, remote corner of the
world. During the Civil War it served as the headquarters for the Home Guard,
the state forces charged with securing the (largely Unionist) mountain coves and
hollows for the Confederacy (see **Shelton Laurel Backcountry Area** under

MUSEUM DIRECTOR JIM PRIESMEYER IN HISTORIC GARB, IN ONE OF THE PERIOD ROOMS AT THE McELROY HOUSE

Wild Places—The Bald Mountain Highlands in "Asheville's Rugged Hinterlands"). Today, its kitchen and living area have been restored to exhibit early mountain farm life, while other exhibits are being prepared on Cane River archeological sites, the Civil War in the Toe and Cane Valleys, and the history and people of the McElroy House. Traditional food and craft demonstrations are made throughout summer and fall; call for details.

Dellinger Mill (828-688-1009), Bakersville, NC. The mill is 4 miles east of Bakersville on Cane Creek Road (SSR 1211). Open June through September: every third Saturday 10–5; October through November: Monday through Saturday 10–5. This operating overshot water mill has been grinding corn for the Bakersville area since 1867. Still owned by its original family, the current National Register structure was built of chestnut in 1901, when the original mill was washed out in a flood. All but the flume and milldam are original to the 1901 structure, including the giant metal overshot wheel and the huge granite millstones. This is a working mill, producing stone-ground corn throughout the corn harvest season.

CULTURAL SITES Penland School of Crafts (828-765-2359), 816 Penland School Road, Penland, NC. Campus tours are available, by appointment, on Tuesday and Thursday. Gallery and visitors center open Tuesday through Saturday 10–noon and 1–5, Sunday noon–5; closed Monday. Campus tours Tuesday and Thursday by appointment. One of the most distinguished crafts schools in America, Penland was founded as a weaver's cooperative in 1923 by local schoolteacher Lucy Morgan. Miss Morgan brought in instructors to improve the weavers' skills—and was surprised by the outpouring of interest in professional-level crafts instruction.

A DISPLAY OF GLASS AND CERAMICS AT THE PENLAND GALLERY, PENLAND SCHOOL OF CRAFTS

In 1929, she formally opened the Penland School to offer regular schedules of instruction. Over the years, nine other crafts areas have been added: books and paper, clay, drawing, glass, iron, metals, photography, printmaking, and wood.

Then as now, Penland is a serious school for crafts professionals and dedicated
amateurs. Completely residential, its classes, studios, and student buildings wander over a pastoral 400-acre campus 5 miles northwest of Spruce Pine, NC. Straddling both sides of a twisting country lane, the campus has an informal, slightly shabby look, with buildings of every conceivable 20th-century style. Intense summer programs are 1 to 2 weeks in length, while autumn and spring see 8-week in-depth sessions in selected subjects. An old school houses the gallery and visitors center, with excellent rotating displays of affiliated artists.

GARDENS AND PARKS ✿ ♿ **Roan Mountain Gardens.** Located just off NC 216 on the North Carolina–Tennessee state line (see *Wandering Around—Exploring by Car*). Closed in winter. $3 per car. Six hundred acres of natural rhododendron gardens cover two 6,000-foot peaks deep within Pisgah National Forest and offer a mile of high ridgetop meadows and rhododendron balds with stunning views. Managed as a park by the U.S. Forest Service (who levies an admissions charge), this site has three major activity areas. First after the entrance station is a ridgetop parking lot with picnic tables; a trail leads over meadows to the site of a long-gone 1880s hotel, and left uphill to more meadow views. It is here that the **Appalachian Trial** climbs to its last two Southern peaks above 6,000 feet—**Roan High Knob** (6,285 feet, 18th highest in the East), a short hill walk to the east, and **Grassy Ridge Bald** (6,180 feet, 27th highest), a handful of miles farther on (see The Roan Highlands on the Appalachian Trail under *Wandering Around—Exploring on Foot*). A half mile up the road, a small information booth, toilets, and picnic area on the left mark the center of the gardens. Here a disabled-accessible trail loops 0.3 mile through spectacular rhododendrons (blooming mid- to late June), with a platform giving wide views across the Toe River Valley to the Black Mountains. Continuing to the end of the road and the park's third and final picnic area, an easy walking path leads 1.2 miles round-trip to **Roan High Bluff,** at 6,367 feet the 12th highest summit in the East. Here a platform built over rocky crags gives a cliff-top view over the broken mountains of the Toe River Valley.

✴ To Do

FISHING Main Street Outpost (828-682-1206), 120 West Main Street, Burnsville, NC. Located just off the town square, this attractive outdoor shop offers fly-fishing guide service as well as guided hiking trips and shuttle service.

GOLF Grassy Creek Golf and Country Club (828-765-7436), 101 Golf Course Road (NC 226), Spruce Pine, NC. Open April through October. $34–39. This 18-hole course, built in 1957 by Ross Taylor, sits a mile south of Spruce Pine, near the Blue

Ridge Parkway. You'll find it a hilly course with good views of the surrounding mountains.

Mountain Glen Golf Course (828-733-5804), NC 194, Newland, NC. $45. This well-kept 18-hole course, located a few miles north of Newland off NC 194, offers surprisingly level fairways and water hazards on 16 holes.

HORSEBACK RIDING Springmaid Mountain (828-765-2353), 2171 Henredon Road, Spruce Pine, NC. $12–17. These stables offer 1- and 1½-hour trail rides on their own 400-acre property, south of Spruce Pine near Altapass.

THE OUTDOOR LIFE Toe River Lodge (828-682-9335), Rt. 1, Box 299, Green Mountain, NC. This outfitter has 117 acres and caters to those who long for a true outdoor experience. Located on the banks of the Toe River near NC 197 (see *Wandering Around—Exploring by Car*) in the remote mountains north of Burnsville, NC, the lodge offers single-day and overnight clinics and guide services in kayaking (costs vary), fly-fishing ($175–250 for 1 day; $550 for 2 days with accommodation), and upland bird hunting ($200–300). Accommodation is in canvas tents set on wood platforms near a mountain stream, with a pavilion nearby where meals are served. Guests can mix and match the lodge's specialties, with fly-fishing float trips or kayaking instruction on the Class III and IV waters of **Nolichucky Gorge** (see *Wild Places—The Great Forests*), only 4 miles away.

✳ Lodging

COUNTRY INNS AND HOTELS The Nu Wray Inn (828-682-2329; 1-800-368-9729), Town Square, Burnsville, NC 28714. Open all year. No one knows exactly how old Burnsville's Nu Wray Inn may be. It appeared in the history books in 1833, when its first innkeeper sold it to Milton Penland. Then, 35 years later, Penland sold it to Garrett Ray, who changed its name to the Ray Hotel. When Garrett's children inherited it in 1912, they refurbished it and renamed it the Nu Wray Inn. And so it remains today: one of the oldest and most gracious historic hotels in the Smokies.

The Nu Wray Inn occupies a fine old three-story white frame structure, its full height brick-columned entry porch facing the town square. Behind the inn is a large, well-maintained garden. Its 32 en suite rooms are comfortably furnished with country antiques, and there's a large guest lounge on each floor. Guests are welcomed with an authentic English tea in the afternoon, and greet the new day with a choice of English, Southern, or continental breakfast. $70–95.

Pinebridge Inn (828-765-5543; 1-800-365-5059), 207 Pinebridge Avenue, Spruce Pine, NC 28777. This three-diamond AAA-rated hotel occupies a 1920s two-story brick high school in the center of Spruce Pine, in a quiet residential neighborhood. Well landscaped and kept, the 44-room hotel is linked with Spruce Pine's terraced downtown by a lighted 400-foot footbridge across the North Toe River. The hotel's two buildings, separated by a courtyard, are lovely 1920s-vintage school-district Gothic, and the rooms retain their high ceilings and large windows. Next door, the former gymnasium, a plain modern structure, houses a recreation center under separate management. Wooded riverside parks, also adjacent to the inn, offer walking and jogging paths. Rooms $59–70; suites $84; housekeeping units $139; includes continental breakfast.

RESORTS The Panes: A Residential Spa Retreat (828-682-4157), Route 3, Box 312A, Burnsville 28714. This three-room facility sits in the remote, little-visited mountains west of Burnsville. Owned by a lifetime massage therapist and her craftsman husband, the Panes combines luxurious accommodations featuring fine woodwork and stained glass with a wide range of spa services. The main house, a rambling modern structure with wide

THE NU WRAY INN ON TOWN SQUARE IN BURNSVILLE

decks, has only one room—a huge suite with skylights, stained glass, a whirlpool tub, a steam room, a separate sitting room, and two porches. Two meals a day, plus a massage or facial are included. Also on the property are a 150-year-old log cabin and a beautifully crafted modern cabin, both with full kitchens. An outdoor hot tub, set in the main house's beautiful gardens, is available to all guests. Main house: $325 per couple, including two meals and some spa services. Cabins: $125–225 per couple, no meals or spa services included. Spa services: $45–90 each.

BED & BREAKFASTS The Terrell House (828-682-4505), 109 Robertson Street, Burnsville, NC 28714. Built in the early 1900s as a dormitory for a private girls' school, this large Colonial-style home sits on a quiet residential street. Reminiscent of an old plantation house, it's clad in white clapboard and surrounded by well-kept gardens; white columns hold a two-story roof over its front porch. Common areas include a back garden with a gazebo, a cozy parlor with late-

Victorian antiques and facing sofas, and a formal dining room where a full breakfast is served on fine china. The six guest rooms are furnished individually in country-style antiques and reproductions. $75–85.

The Wray House (828-682-0445; 1-877-258-8222), 2 South Main Street, Burnsville, NC 28714. Open all year. This beautiful gingerbread Victorian house sits just off Burnsville's town square. Looking like a quaint cottage from the street, in fact it's deceptively large and comfortable, with five guest rooms and four common areas. The sitting room, furnished in comfortable Edwardian antiques, is the venue for before-breakfast coffee and afternoon tea, while a breakfast room overlooks the rear garden; there's even a formal dining room, excellent for business meetings. The guest rooms are individually furnished with antiques in a variety of styles. $75–115, including full country-style breakfast.

✔ **The Celo Inn** (828-675-5132), 1 Seven Mile Ridge Road, Burnsville, NC 28714. This five-room B&B occupies a long two-story log frame building, sitting by the **South Toe River,** in a grove of old trees. Located in the remote Celo community, about 8 miles south of Burnsville on NC 80 and not far from the Blue Ridge Parkway, the inn is well known and well respected in the small but national caliber artists' community that spreads itself throughout Celo. The inn is particularly welcoming to cyclists. $30–75.

✐ **Estes Mountain Retreat** (828-682-7264), Route 10, Box 500, Bakers Creek Road, Burnsville, NC 28714. This modern log cabin sits off a quiet back road in the high mountains west of Burnsville. This planked white cedar structure sits on 4 acres at 3,800 feet—high enough for good views off its wide front porch, and high enough to be noticeably cooler than Asheville. Both of its two en suite rooms are roomy and comfortable, with simple country furnishings and handmade quilts on the beds. $59–72, including full breakfast and homemade dessert in the evening.

✐ **Richmond Inn Bed & Breakfast** (828-765-6993; 1-877-765-6993), 51 Pine Avenue, Spruce Pine, NC 28777. Rated three diamonds by AAA, this eight-room B&B sits on a residential back lane, three blocks uphill from downtown Spruce Pine. It's a large, white clapboard Dutch Colonial house from the mid–20th century, sitting on a high stone terrace with dormers, bay windows, and a wide porch looking out over Spruce Pine to the mountains beyond. Guests share a comfortable parlor, furnished with antiques in a restrained country style. Rooms range from comfortable sized to large and are individually decorated with antiques. A full breakfast is served in a formal dining room overlooking the garden.

CABIN RENTALS Laurel Oaks Farm (828-688-2650; 1-800-528-7356), 7334 NC 80, Bakersville, NC 28705. These two cabins sit on a sheep farm in the wooded hills south of Bakersville, on scenic NC 80 (see *Wandering Around—Exploring by Car*). One is modern and one an old-style log cabin. Both are comfortable and fully equipped and have views from their porches. The farm has two trout ponds, on-property walking paths, and a border on the **Toe River,** as well as a sheep herd and a llama. $85–130.

✳ Where to Eat

EATING OUT *✐* ♿ **The Nu Wray Inn** (828-682-2329; 1-800-368-9729), Town Square, Burnsville, NC. Breakfast: 8–9:30 daily; lunch: Sunday 11:30–2. Dinner: 5:30–8. The dining area of this 150-year-old inn (see *Lodging—Country Inns and Hotels*) has been recently remodeled to an elegant restaurant-style room, with individual tables grouped around the large fireplace. Breakfasts include a choice among a traditional English breakfast, hearty Southern-style, or continental. Dinners are hearty country food with an ample selection of vegetables and other sides served family style; entrées include fried chicken, country ham, English-style roast beef, or trout. Breakfast $6.95; evening meals and Sunday lunch $12.95.

The Garden Deli (828-682-3946), 107 Town Square, Burnsville, NC. Open Monday through Saturday 11–2. A Burnsville lunchtime fixture since 1987, the Garden Deli features patio seating shaded by willows and wisterias, overlooking the lovely town square. Inside seating for this year-round café is in a wood-paneled room with bay windows and a large fireplace.

Offering soups, salads, deli-style sandwiches, and a selection of freshly made sides and desserts. Specialty items include pork barbeque pit-smoked on the premises. $3–5.

Afternoon Delight (828-765-7164), 14701 NC 226 South, Spruce Pine, NC. Located along NC 226 a few miles south of Spruce Pine, between the Blue Ridge Parkway and the Wal-Mart. Open Monday and Wednesday through Saturday 7 AM–9 PM; Sunday 9 AM–3 PM. Despite its name, this is an all-day, full-menu restaurant with a tilt toward Southern-style food. Breakfast gives a choice of menu service or a full buffet, all reasonably priced, while the lunch menu offers a selection of sandwiches and salads. Dinners also include sandwiches, plus entrées such as slow-cooked roast beef, grilled pork chops, country fried steak, and (of course) fried chicken. Breakfast $2–4; lunch $3–5; salads and sandwiches as a dinner $6–7; full dinners $9–13.

✳ Entertainment

Parkway Playhouse (828-682-4285), Burnsville, NC. Founded in 1947 as a summer outlet for Greensboro university students, the Parkway Playhouse is the state's oldest continuously operating theater. Now a semiprofessional company, it features a combination of old Broadway standards, childrens' plays, and Appalachian-themed plays from its giant barnlike theater down a (well-signposted) back street in Burnsville. Plays start at 8 PM, most summer weekends. Reservations are required; call on weekday afternoons.

Young's Mountain Music), Micaville, NC. The large nondescript building is located just off US 19E, halfway between Burnsville and Spruce Pine

on the Yancey-Mitchell county line. Open Saturday, from 7 PM. $2 donation. A revered mountain tradition, Young's is noted as a venue for authentic, old-time (pre-bluegrass) Appalachian music from serious local musicians. It features live mountain music and dancing (clogging, two-step, line, and square) every Saturday night, with nonalcoholic beverages, a snack bar, and homemade desserts.

✳ Selective Shopping

Burnsville, NC

Hayden Gallery (828-682-7998; 866-442-9336), 7 South Main Street. Located just off Burnsville's town square in a plain old brick commercial building, this well-known and respected crafts gallery assembles the work of a number of local fine-arts and crafts artists—potters, glass artists, jewelry artisans, visual artists, and creators of garden art. In addition, they maintain a gallery of fine antiques.

Zebulon Gallery (828-682-0598), 4 West Main Street. Located on Burnsville's town square, this fine-crafts gallery specializes in handmade American crafts art and folk art, much of it from local artists.

The Country Peddler (828-682-7819), 3 Town Square. This small shop on Burnsville's town square sells custom-made quilts, as well as quilting supplies and patterns—a good source for those who want a real Appalachian quilt instead of something from an Asian sweatshop.

Micaville, NC

CraftPride Gallery (828-675-5470), 3961 NC 80 South, Burnsville. Open May through November, Monday and Thursday through Saturday 10–5. Located 5 miles south of Micaville on

NC 80, this roadside arts and crafts gallery has a variety of work by local and regional artists.

Toe River Crafts (828-675-4555), NC 80 South, Burnsville. Open Friday and Saturday 10–5, Sunday noon–5. Limited off-season hours. This modest old board-and-batten building, 7 miles south of Micaville on NC 80, is home to a cooperative of local artisans who specialize in a variety of contemporary crafts. Staffed by cooperative members, this gallery features pottery, woodworking, textiles, fibers, glass, paper, metals, toys, photography, prints, watercolors, and needlework.

Spruce Pine, NC

Twisted Laurel Gallery (828-765-1562), 221 Locust Street. Open April through December: Tuesday through Saturday 10–5; January through March: Friday and Saturday 10–5. Established in 1989 by third-generation clockmaker Luther Stroup, this downtown gallery, just across from the railroad depot, features the work of more than 130 crafts artists, all from the Spruce Pine and Penland area. Beautifully displayed in this large, airy storefront, the art covers just about every medium and style imaginable, with a particularly rich selection of glass art.

Blue Moon Book Store (828-766-5000), 271 Oak Avenue. Open Monday through Saturday 10–6. Located on the upper level of Spruce Pine's terraced downtown, this large storefront bookstore offers a wide selection of regional titles and children's books, used books, art (particularly note cards) by local crafters, and a good café. Blue Moon sponsors a program of music, storytelling, and readings in the store all year long.

Bakersville, NC

Potters of the Roan. P.O. Box 554. This cooperative unites 11 potters—all with ties to the **Penland School** (see *To See—Cultural Sites*)—with studios scattered throughout the mountain valleys surrounding Bakersville. All 11 members open their studios (many of them in extraordinarily scenic locations) to the public. For a brochure giving contact information, a map and directions, and pictures of the work of all 11 potters, contact the cooperative at pottersoftheroan@hotmail.com, or ask the Mitchell County Chamber of Commerce (see *Guidance*).

✳ Special Events

First weekend in May: **Spring Studio Tour**. The nonprofit Toe River Arts Council sponsors this annual event featuring more than 50 studios and galleries open to the public, spread throughout the Burnsville and Spruce Pine, NC, areas.

Last Saturday in May: **Spring Arts Festival**, Burnsville, NC. This annual arts festival, held in front of the Yancey County Courthouse, combines local artists, live art demonstrations, and food sponsored by local nonprofits.

First Saturday in June: **Avery Heritage Fest**, Newland, NC. Held in Newland's beautiful town square, in front of the old Avery County Courthouse, this festival emphasizes genealogy and mountain history, with local history writers, genealogy tents, Civil and Revolutionary War reenactors, and an authentic 19th-century circuit-riding preacher. The local church serves up a barbeque lunch.

✐ Fourth of July: **Burnsville Fourth of July Celebration,** Burnsville, NC.

This lively town square celebration includes an all-day band competition, crafts booths, local nonprofits selling home-made items and food, fire trucks, a wagon train, and special activities for children. **Spruce Pine Independence Day Celebration,** Spruce Pine, NC. This downtown street celebration includes square dancing, food, and fireworks. It's preceded by a 3-day town-wide sidewalk sale.

Last weekend in July: **Rhododendron Festival**, Bakersville, NC. For more than a half century, the little mountain town of Bakersville has celebrated the magnificent rhododendron display with a large street fair, including street dancing, a car show, a beauty pageant, and a number of bicycling events.

↑ ✐ ⚬ *First weekend in August:* **Mount Mitchell Crafts Fair**, Mount Burnsville, NC. Free admission. This town-square crafts fair, founded in 1956, features moe than 200 local and regional crafts artists, selected by the Crafts Fair Selection Committee for quality, originality, and variety. There is ongoing bandstand entertainment that emphasizes mountain music and dance, as well as a number of food vendors.

Mid- to late September: **Overmountain Victory Trail March,** Little Switzerland, NC. Every year the Overmountain Victory Trail Association commemorates America's amazing Revolutionary War victory at King's Mountain, SC, by reenacting the frontier militia's cross-mountain march. The festivities start with a mid-September reenactors' camp at the **Museum of North Carolina Minerals,** in Little Switzerland (see *To See—The Blue Ridge Parkway* in "The Blue Ridge Parkway: Blowing Rock and Grandfather Mountain"), in which both British and Patriot sides plot strategies, drill, and practice shooting their black powder muskets. Then a week later (roughly around the anniversary of the events on September 25), the frontier militia marches across the mountains to dinner and encampment at Spruce Pine, NC, followed by a march at the **Orchard at Altapass,** in Little Switzerland (see *To See—The Blue Ridge Parkway*).

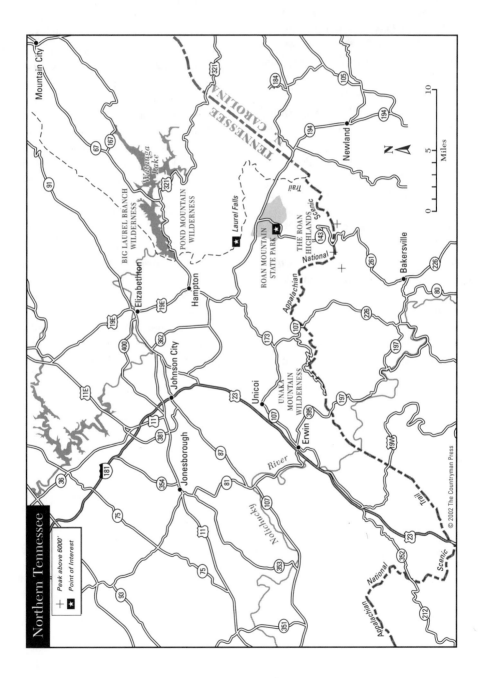

Northern Tennessee

+ Peak above 6000'
★ Point of Interest

Mountain City

67
167
91

Waranga Lake

BIG LAUREL BRANCH
WILDERNESS

321

POND MOUNTAIN
WILDERNESS

Laurel Falls ★

Elizabethton

19E

Hampton

19E

19E

400

362

Johnson City

11E

11W

11

381

Jonesborough

354

87

81

107

Nolichucky

River

75

111

93

75

353

351

TENNESSEE

N. CAROLINA

184

321

105

Newland

194

194

★ ROAN MOUNTAIN
STATE PARK

THE ROAN
HIGHLANDS

143

261

Bakersville

226

80

Appalachian

National

Scenic

Trail

+

+

173

107

226

197

Unicoi

UNAKA
MOUNTAIN
WILDERNESS

107

395

197

Erwin

19W

23

23

352

212

Appalachian

National

Scenic

Trail

N

0   5   10

Miles

© 2002 The Countryman Press

THE MOUNTAINS OF NORTHERN TENNESSEE

The Tennessee–North Carolina state line follows a series of 5- and 6,000-foot peaks, with a 4,000-foot drop down to the valleys of East Tennessee. It's an impressive sight, but it doesn't end there. Yet more mountains rise to 3- and 4,000 feet—some a rough jumble, others running straight as a stick for many miles. The four wild places give a good sampling: Big Laurel Branch Wilderness for a linear mountain with craggy views, Pond Mountain Wilderness for a rough jumble of wild lands, Unaka Mountain Wilderness for a 5,000-foot state line ridge, and the famous Highlands of Roan for 6,000-foot peaks, rhododendron gardens, and crestline grassy balds.

This is also a land of deep history. Settled in the 18th century, Elizabethton has a 1770s "mansion" with its original interior, a reconstructed fort, an 1887 covered bridge, and a historic district of antebellum and Victorian houses. Nearby Erwin has strong links to one the Appalachian's great railroads, the Clinchfield, still one of the East's great freight lines. Just outside town, the Nolichucky River Gorge is increasingly prized for its challenging whitewater and stunning scenery.

GUIDANCE Elizabethton-Carter County Chamber of Commerce (423-547-3850; 1-888-547-3852), 500 East Bypass, P.O. Box 190, Elizabethton, TN 37644. The chamber maintains a welcome center that includes picnic facilities, on the eastern edge of Elizabethton, on US19E/321.

Unicoi County Chamber of Commerce (423-743-3000), 100 South Main Avenue, Erwin, TN 37650. This chamber maintains a visitors center and information desk in one of downtown Erwin's restored historic buildings.

Watauga Ranger District, Cherokee National Forest (423-735-1500), P.O. Box 400 (TN 173 north of town center), Unicoi, TN. 8 AM–4:30 PM, Mon–Fri. This large modern office, just east of US 23 (future I-26) off exit 23, has a friendly information desk and bookshop, with complete information on the forests in this chapter.

GETTING THERE *By car:* I-181/US 23 provides freeway access to Erwin, TN, and the western parts of this area. US 19E and US 321, mostly four-lane, link Elizabethton, Roan Mountain, and Lake Watauga, TN, to the rest of the world.

By air: **Tri-Cities Airport** (423-325-6000), 2525 Highway 75, Blountville, TN. The "Tri-Cities" are Johnson City, Kingsport, and Bristol, TN. The airport is located in Tennessee's Great Valley, in the middle of the triangle formed by the three cities, off I-81's exit 63. This is about 25 miles west of this region, and much farther from any other area covered in this book. Tri-Cities has four commuter airlines furnishing nonstops to six different hubs, so it's not uncommon to find good and/or cheap connections.

By bus or train: **Greyhound Bus Lines** (1-800-229-9424) service runs to Johnson City, TN, immediately outside this area. There are no passenger trains in East Tennessee (not even Chattanooga!).

MEDICAL EMERGENCIES **Sycamore Shoals Hospital** (423-542-1300), 1501 West Elk Avenue (US 321), Elizabethton, TN. Elizabethton's 121-bed hospital offers full emergency-room services from its facility on the west end of town.

Unicoi County Memorial Hospital (423-743-3141), Greenway Circle, Erwin, TN. Erwin's 48-bed hospital has full emergency-room services. It's located in town, 1 mile south of downtown via NC 81 (former US 23) and two blocks to the left.

✳ Wandering Around

EXPLORING BY CAR **The Unaka Mountains.** The Unaka Mountains loom 3,000 feet above Erwin, TN. This drive circles around the Unakas, explores the historic railroad town of Erwin and its surrounding valleys, then climbs up to the very top of the mountain for some wonderful views from the Appalachian Trail (AT).

THE VIEW SOUTH FROM UNAKA MOUNTAIN TOWARD THE BLACK MOUNTAINS OF NORTH CAROLINA

Start on **US 23** at the North Carolina–Tennessee state line, a place known as **Sams Gap.** The **AT** crosses here, and a short walk up to the west leads to some nice views from an old cemetery. From here you can see the US 23 freeway slabbing down a side ridge, blowing through everything in its path (it's destined to become part of I-26); to its left, the old U.S. highway drops straight down into the valley, steeply and with many curves. Take the new freeway down toward Erwin for many fine, wide views. The official overlook is definitely worth a stop, with a short ridgeline path to a variety of views up to the Unakas and down into the settled valleys.

When you reach the bottom, take the first **Erwin** (see *Villages*) exit and follow **TN 81** through this well-kept railroad town; as you pass along its classic small-town Main Street, the railroad yards are a block to your left. Continue out of town on **TN 107,** quickly passing through suburbs to regain mountain valley scenery. The county's worthwhile **Heritage Museum** (see *To See—Cultural Sites*) is 3 miles from Erwin at the old Federal Fish Hatchery, with exhibits on the **Clinchfield Railroad,** local history, and a log one-room schoolhouse. The small town of **Unicoi,** TN, is 5 miles from Erwin, off NC 107 to the left, with an antiques shop and a couple of restaurants.

Continue on NC 107 through lovely mountain valleys. When you begin to climb out of the valley (12 miles from Erwin) look for a gravel road on your right, possibly marked with a brown recreation sign. This is the **Unaka Mountain Scenic Road**—a rough gravel road, badly maintained by the U.S. Forest Service. It's unsafe in bad weather, but in good, dry weather you should be able to get the family station wagon up it with a lot of dust and jolts. It's worth it. After the first switchback look for a parking area on the right and a short trail to the hundred-foot-tall **Red Fork Falls,** noted for its sunset rainbows. From there the road runs through dense valley forests, then climbs to a ridgeline in two hairpin switchbacks. Two more hairpin switchbacks ladder you up to **Stamping Ground,** a high rocky-heath bald with unusual gardenlike vegetation and breathtaking views over the **Unaka Mountain Wilderness** (see *Wild Places—The Great Forests*). This is the high point, and a good place to turn a passenger car around. High clearance four-wheel-drive vehicles can continue for more views at Beauty Spot, with the road ending at TN 395.

EXPLORING ON FOOT Laurel Falls on the Appalachian Trail (AT). This short section of the Appalachian Trail follows an old logging railroad grade along the rim of the **Laurel Fork Gorge,** to end at lovely Laurel Falls. The trail is approximately 2 miles long with no meaningful elevation change until the steep and difficult plunge down to the foot of the falls; the walk out on the railroad bed is worthwhile in itself. The trailhead parking is in Dennis Cove, a twisting 3-mile drive up paved Dennis Cove Road (FS 50), which intersects US 321 five miles south of Elizabethton in the small town of **Hampton,** TN, marked by a brown recreation sign. Take the AT to the left (north), along a level railroad grade. The trail quickly enters Pond Mountain Wilderness (see *Wild Places—The Great Forests)* and follows **Laurel Fork,** an impressively large and violent stream, noted for its trout fishing. After 0.75 mile the trail drops steeply into a gorge, crosses the stream at an impressive footbridge on two rock piers, then climbs to a ledge in a sheer quartzite cliff in a flight of 60 stone steps. The AT regains the old railroad grade, only to drop off it again and plunge down into the gorge, reaching Laurel Falls after 265 very difficult stone steps. Laurel Fork stair-steps down a 30-foot thickness of plunging quartzite, forming a waterfall about as wide as it is high and framed by gray-white cliffs. Return the way you came.

Historic Elizabethton Walking Tour (423-547-3850; 1-888-547-3852). Elizabethton's Chamber of Commerce has established one of the nicest and best-marked historic town walks of these mountains. An excellent brochure is available from the chamber, just east of town on US 19E/321 (see *Guidance*). The short path, starting at City Hall downtown, wanders past 30 historic buildings and sites along this small town's three-block downtown and along the Doe River. Highlights include elegant southern mansions, lovely riverside parks, an authentic covered bridge, and a red 1921 fire engine (not to mention the tallest fir tree in Tennessee, in front of one of those mansions).

✳ Villages

Erwin, TN. You'll find Erwin just off the new US 23 freeway (which will be redesignated I-26 at some time in the future), at the foot of the Unaka Mountains and not far from the Tennessee–North Carolina line. Erwin is, and always has been, an industrial town. It is in no way polluted, defaced, or ugly; but neither does it make much of an attempt to put on a pretty face for visitors. Founded as Unicoi County's seat in 1879, Erwin became a small city when, in 1908, the Clinchfield Railroad chose it as its major repair yard (a big deal in the days of temperamental steam engines), and later its corporate headquarters. The Clinchfield's bold attempt to slice straight through the heart of the Appalachians was a financial success (see **The Clinchfield Railroad Loops** under *To See—Historic Sites* in "The Blue Ridge Parkway: Blowing Rock and Grandfather Mountain"), and Erwin thrived along with its railroad. During this period, Southern Potteries operated a successful hand-painted china factory in Erwin, turning out the Blue Ridge China now prized by collectors. However, the pottery closed in 1957 (a victim of postwar foreign competition), and the Clinchfield offices closed in 1983 when the CSX System bought out the railroad. Not that Erwin suffered much from these closures; it had already acquired a new major industry—uranium processing (mainly for navel ships). CSX still maintains a yard in Erwin, servicing the very busy line that the Clinchfield built. Erwin has an attractive, old-fashioned downtown with several shops that are worth a visit.

✳ Wild Places

THE GREAT FORESTS Big Laurel Branch Wilderness. Cliffs rise straight up out of still lake water; a stream plummets over the edge and falls 50 feet straight down. Such is the dramatic edge of the Big Laurel Branch Wilderness, taking up the southernmost 10 square miles of heavily wooded **Iron Mountain** (with an additional 8 square miles of the mountain classed as a "roadless area"). Iron Mountain climbs 1,400 feet above the waters of Lakes Watauga and Wilbur, then extends northeast, straight and true, with a narrow crest that never swerves. Big Laurel Branch itself is a bowl-shaped drainage cut into the southern edge of the mountain, trail-less and inaccessible to all but the most experienced cross-

Viewed from the main highway, Elizabethton appears to be a modest factory town, a bit on the skids. However, Elizabethton holds a secret: Turn off the highway and wander into its center and a charming historic village opens up—a brick-front downtown with a riverfront park, a beautiful white clapboard covered bridge reflected in a weir, a line of **Victorian and antebellum homes,** and a large veterans monument in a circle by the **old brick courthouse.** Elizabethton's center looks as if it would be more at home in New England than in the rural South.

Located at the confluence of the **Watauga and Doe Rivers,** Elizabethton was one of the earliest transmountain settlements south of Virginia. These settlers were well west of any law or government, in Cherokee lands where settlement was prohibited by British law; so they formed the Watauga Association, to establish and enforce laws and lease land from the Cherokees. The association held its first court under a sycamore tree near the current downtown, a site marked by a section of the original tree (which died in 1987). Guarded by the British army at nearby Fort Watauga and with good fords over two difficult rivers, Elizabethton became an important frontier settlement. The old fort, at Sycamore Shoals on the western edge of town, has been reconstructed and now houses a local museum (see **Sycamore Shoals State Historic Site** under *To See—Historic Sites).*

Elizabethton remained small throughout most of the 19th century, acquiring several antebellum mansions that still stand today, as well as a fine covered bridge that still crosses the Doe River in a single 134-foot span (see **Doe River Covered Bridge** under *To See—Historic Sites).* However, the town quickly became a lumbering and factory center when the railroad arrived in the late 1880s. The first railroad was the famous **"Tweetsie" Railroad** [see The ET & WNC (Tweetsie) Railroad under *To See—Historic Sites),* a narrow gauge that crossed the mountains from Boone, NC. Two large rayon factories furnished prosperity during the 1920s and still dominate the town's industrial suburbs.

country hikers. However, the **Appalachian Trail** follows Iron Mountain through the wilderness, furnishing good access and a first-rate day hike. You can pick up the trail at **Watauga Dam,** and follow it uphill along the crest for approximately 4 miles to a trail shelter, a fairly steady climb of 1,200 feet. The trail passes through a varied and interesting dry hardwood forest broken by large outcrops and cliffs with dramatic views down to the lake below. The trail shelter, located at the edge of the wilderness area, has a particularly wide and impressive cliff-top view.

Pond Mountain Wilderness. Pond Mountain is not a linear mountain like that found in the Big Laurel Branch Wilderness (see above); instead, it's a wild jumble of peaks and valleys, ridges that run every which way, valleys perched on high crests, outcrops projecting from deep forests, and gorges cut straight through ridges. From the valley below it doesn't look taller than linear Iron Mountain, but it is—a 2,200-foot climb from nearby Watauga Lake to its vaguely crescent-shaped crest. The U.S. Congress has protected nearly 11 square miles of this difficult area.

Of the many interesting features of this wilderness area, the strangest may be the deep gorge carved through its western edge by Laurel Creek, a gorge that includes a couple of deep horseshoe curves at the center of the crest line. **Laurel Creek Gorge** features an impressive waterfall, sheer cliffs, and some strange rock formations, as well as a historic railroad bed. The Appalachian Trail follows that old railbed for a fine hike (see Laurel Falls on the Appalachian Trail under *Wandering Around—Exploring on Foot*), then curves around to the top of Pond Mountain for some wide views.

Highlands of Roan. Nearly 10 miles of the Roan Mountain crest is covered with wide grassy balds and rhododendron heaths; one heath forms a 600-acre natural garden that turns brilliant pink every June. With three peaks above 6,000 feet and 6 miles of mile-high crest, the Highlands of Roan, straddling the Tennessee–North Carolina state line, make up one of the great sights of the Southern Appalachians. With 23 square miles of protected land, there's plenty to see:

On the Tennessee side, Hampton Creek Cove State Natural Area (see *To See— Gardens and Parks*) includes an operating mountain farm that merges with the forests above, its access track leading still higher to the grassy balds along its crest.

Nearby, Tennessee's **Roan Mountain State Park** (see *Recreation Areas*) protects 2,000 acres along the lower slopes, including a reconstructed 19th-century farmstead, the **Dave Miller Homestead** (see *To See—Historic Sites*).

From Roan Mountain State Park, TN 143 climbs mile-high Carvers Gap to enter North Carolina, an impressive scenic drive (see **NC 80** under *Wandering Around—Exploring by Car* in "Behind the Blue Ridge: Spruce Pine and Burnsville").

From Carvers Gap, the **Appalachian Trail** heads east through wide-open meadows, on one of the most breathtaking walks in the East (see The Roan Highlands on the Appalachian Trail under *Wandering Around—Exploring on Foot* in "Behind the Blue Ridge: Spruce Pine and Burnsville").

Also from Carvers Gap, a paved road leads west along the crest to a 600-acre rhododendron garden with wide views, in North Carolina's **Pisgah National Forest** (see The Roan Highlands under *Wild Places—The Great Forests* in "Behind the Blue Ridge: Spruce Pine and Burnsville").

A long drive around on the North Carolina side leads to the head of Roaring Creek Valley, with stunning views and a walk along the Revolutionary War–era **Overmountain Victory Trail** (see *Wandering Around—Exploring on Foot* in "Behind the Blue Ridge: Spruce Pine and Burnsville").

Unaka Mountain Wilderness. The 5,160-foot peak of Unaka Mountain looms

above Erwin, TN, its summit clothed in black-green firs and spruces. The **Unaka**
Mountain Scenic Road (see The Unaka Mountains under *Wandering Around—
Exploring by Car*) follows its crest, linking a series of heaths and grassy balds with
wide views, and paralleled by the Appalachian Trail on its uphill side. Downhill
from this stretches the Unaka Mountain Wilderness, known for its rugged terrain,
steep cliffs, dramatic waterfalls, and wide views from heath balds. It's a surprisingly popular place for hikers, with its beauty outweighing its remoteness and difficulty. One popular trail starts at the wilderness's low point, **Rock Creek Recreation Area** (see *Picnic Areas*), and climbs a thousand feet in a 5-mile round-trip
to **Rock Creek Falls,** a beautiful cliff cascade. Another trail from the same recreation area climbs the exposed backbone of **Rattlesnake Ridge** to reach the scenic drive after a 2,500-foot climb and many spectacular views (6 miles round-trip).

RECREATION AREAS **Roan Mountain State Park.** This Tennessee state park
preserves 3 square miles of the middle slopes of the Roan Highlands. It has an
attractive visitors center graced by an old-fashioned overshot wheel, a number of
hiking trails, and several good picnic areas. Considered a "resort park," it has a set
of 30 cabins (see **Roan Mountain State Park Cabins** under *Lodging—Cabin
Rentals*), as well as tennis courts and a swimming pool. Roan Mountain is particularly noted for its wide-ranging program of activities, including workshops in traditional mountain crafts, a spring **Naturalists Rally** and a summer **Rhododendron Festival** (see both under *Special Events*). The state park is 10 miles from
the crest of Roan Mountain and its famous gardens (see **Roan Mountain Gardens** in *To See—Gardens and Parks* in "Behind the Blue Ridge: Spruce Pine and
Burnsville") via TN 143—among the most spectacular 10 miles in the mountains.

Wilbur Lake and Watauga Dam Recreation Areas. Six miles east of Elizabethton via Siam Road, then right on Iron Bridge Road; follow the signs for
Watauga Dam. The Tennessee Valley Authority (TVA) maintains a large and
attractive recreation area stretching from Wilbur Dam, along the 3-mile length of
Wilbur Lake, then over a gap to a hill above Watauga Lake. It starts with views of
Wilbur Dam, a 1912 concrete structure 77 feet high, with a canoe launch at its
foot. From there the road closely follows the banks of narrow Wilbur Lake, with
several picnic areas, boat launches, and places to park and fish. The scenery here
is particularly attractive, with cliffs rising out of the opposite shore of the lake, and
the impressive, 50-foot Little Laurel Branch Waterfall opposite one of the picnic
areas. Beyond, the road climbs Iron Mountain Gap to meet the Appalachian Trail
(AT), with a few roadside parking spaces. You can follow the AT right 1 mile to
cross the top of Watauga Dam (see To See, Big Dammed Lakes), while to the left
it enters Big Laurel Branch Wilderness (see The Great Forests) On the other side
of the gap, the park road drops to the Watauga Lake at Overlook Recreation Area,
a well-kept TVA picnic site with wide views from a glassed overlook and a short
trail to a view over the 330-foot earthen Watauga Dam.

PICNIC AREAS **Rock Creek Recreation Area,** Erwin, TN. This attractive picnic and camping area, heavily shaded, sits on TN 395 at the lowermost edge of the
Unaka Mountain Wilderness (see *The Great Forests*) and serves as one of the
wilderness's trailheads.

Shook Branch Recreation Area. This Cherokee National Forest picnic area marks the place where the **Appalachian Trail** crosses US 321, eight miles southeast of Elizabethton, TN. It's located on **Lake Watauga** and offers pleasant lake views, as well as access to the **Pond Mountain Wilderness** (see *The Great Forests*).

✳ To See

BIG DAMMED LAKES Lake Watauga. This Tennessee Valley Authority (TVA) lake covers just 10 square miles but has a hundred miles of shoreline—half of it public land. With miles of fiddly little indents and coves and lots of forested shoreline, it's a fun lake to explore. It has numerous recreation sites for picnicking, boat launching, and camping, the three largest being along US 321 twenty-one miles east of Elizabethton, TN. The TVA built Watauga Dam in 1948 for flood control and hydropower. This earthen dam stands 100 yards high and 1,000 feet wide at the top; you can visit the dam by hiking out the Appalachian Trail from Iron Mountain Gap or view it from above at Overlook Recreation Area (see *Wild Places—Recreation Areas*).On the road to the dam, **Lake Wilbur Picnic Area** gives views of Little Laurel Branch throwing itself out of the wilderness area and over a 50-foot cliff, into the lake below.

HISTORIC SITES Doe River Covered Bridge, Elizabethton, TN. In continuous use since its construction in 1882, this 134-foot wood-truss bridge spans the Doe River a block south of downtown Elizabethton. Clad in white clapboard, the bridge looks absurdly elongated and flimsy—but it has survived intact the deadly floods of 1901 and 1998, when more modern structures were swept away. The secret of its success: its massive trusses, constructed of coupled 8x8 oak beams that tower 10 feet over the deck. The trusses suspend the deck across the entire width of the river, far above the highest floodwaters. The white clapboard cover exists for one reason only—to protect the wood truss from rot forming at the slanted joints. Because of its wood cover, this bridge remains strong enough to carry cars after 120 years and two major floods.

The bridge is flanked by lovely riverside parks on both banks, and framed on its downstream side by a weir that fed a 19th-century millrace. On the Elizabethton bank, rows of beautifully kept Victorian houses stretch along the river, facing across the road to the park. A block north is Elizabethton's reviving brick-front downtown, with several antiques shops. A walk through the park along the river is a delight; the views are simply beautiful, particularly in the fall when brilliant colors frame the bridge.

Sycamore Shoals State Historic Site (615-543-5808), 1651 West Elk Avenue, Elizabethton, TN. Park is open 8 AM–dusk; visitors center is open Monday through Saturday 8–4:30, Sunday 1–4:30. Free admission. On the western outskirts of Elizabethton, Sycamore Shoals was the center of the colonial transmountain settlement of Watauga. The British built **Fort Watauga** here in the early 1770s to control a frontier that was supposedly closed to white settlement; however, white settlement had already begun, and the settlers relied on the fort for safety. Sycamore Shoals became one of the most important frontier sites of the Revolutionary War period. It was here that the private Transylvania Corporation, made up of North Carolina land speculators, bought Kentucky and western Tennessee from a group of Cherokee chiefs; years later, it was here that settlers sheltered from Cherokee attacks during the American Revolution; and it was here that the Overmountain Boys mustered for their successful march to King's Mountain, SC, to defeat a loyalist army poised to harry the mountain settlements. Today Sycamore Shoals is a small, well-kept state park centered around a reconstruction of Fort Watauga and a small museum with a number of rotating local displays. In mid-July, an outdoor drama featuring local actors tells the story of the Watauga settlement (see **The Wataugans Outdoor Drama** under *Entertainment*). Sycamore Shoals offers a full calendar of activities, including some very imaginative ones (September's Flint Knapping Day comes to mind; see **Special Events at Sycamore Shoals** under *Entertainment*). The park is on a rolling, tree-shaded site by the Watauga River and has good day-use facilities, including a picnic area and a riverside jogging path.

The Carter Mansion (615-543-6140), 1651 West Elk Street, Elizabethton, TN. Located at the end of Broad Street (US 321); go straight through the traffic light at US 19E and continue for one block. (The contact information is for Sycamore Shoals, which administers the site.) Tours daily May through August; arrange at Sycamore Shoals State Historic Site (see above). Free admission. The oldest frame house in Tennessee, the Carter Mansion was built by John Carter, a leader of the Watauga Association, in 1780. Astonishingly, over 90 percent of the interior of this modest frontier "mansion" date from the original 1780 construction. This includes the hand-carved paneling, the crown molding, and the chair rails—and it definitely includes the two landscape paintings over the fireplaces, executed directly on the wall paneling. It also includes the plumbing; there isn't any, and never has been! Last occupied in 1966, the State of Tennessee acquired it in 1973 with 4.6 acres of land and restored it to its original appearance in 1978.

The Dave Miller Farmstead. You'll find this farmstead adjacent to Roan Mountain State Park (see *Wild Places—Recreation Areas*), on TN 143, 3 miles south of the village of Roan Mountain. Try to stop by on a summer's Saturday between noon and 2 PM, when artists and musicians are present. Open Memorial Day through Labor Day, Wednesday through Sunday 9–5. Free admission. This lovely early 20th-century farmstead, immaculate white with stylish little gable dormers over its front porch, is the successor to two pioneer log cabins, the homes of the Millers since 1870. The first cabin was on land leased from Roan Mountain's land baron, General John Wilder (see **General Wilder's Bed & Breakfast** under *Lodging*); the Millers bought their farm from the general in 1904 and built the second cabin. The present house succeeded it, the home of later generations of Millers. Now it's an open-air museum, demonstrating a turn-of-the-century mountain farmstead.

The ET & WNC (Tweetsie) Railroad, Elizabethton, TN. Although the initials stood for "East Tennessee and Western North Carolina," to mountain folk they stood for "eat 'taters and wear no clothes." It was also known as the "Tweetsie" for the peculiar sound made by the whistle of its main steam engine (see **Tweetsie Railroad** in *To Do—Family Adventure*). One of the great legendary lines of the Southern Appalachians, the Tweetsie was a narrow-gauge railroad originally built to haul iron ore from a mine north of Spruce Pine, NC (see *Villages* in "Behind the Blue Ridge: Spruce Pine and Burnsville") to Johnson City, TN; eventually it was extended as far as Boone, NC. A friendly, local line that wandered slowly through the mountains, it linked communities in a way that the more serious-minded Clinchfield did not (see The Clinchfield Railroad Loops under *To See—Historic Sites* in "The Blue Ridge Parkway: Blowing Rock and Grandfather Mountain"). The Tweetsie's crew (the same men for many years) would take orders from locals along the line and deliver the goods to their door. The Tweetsie survived surprisingly late into the 20th century, losing its line to Boone in a 1944 flood and closing its last section in 1950. However, in a sense it survives to this day—as the roadbeds of US 19E, NC 194, and NC 105, all major highways.

With most of its bed superseded by highways, little remains to be seen—with one spectacular exception: the **Doe River Gorge.** To visit this exception, call the Doe River Christian Camp and Conference Center (423-928-8936) to get permission to park your car on their land and walk through their property (and to get directions to the trailhead, near the village of Roan Mountain). Oh, and don't forget your flashlight—the railbed trail immediately dives into a long tunnel (the first of three) to enter the rugged Doe River Gorge. From it traverses 2.4 miles of stunning cliff-sided gorge scenery, with spectacular views and lots of railroad artifacts along the way. Turn around when you reach a rickety trestle; no wood structure can be trusted after half a century's abandonment in the heavy damp of the Southern Appalachians.

CULTURAL SITES Heritage Museum (423-743-9449). Unicoi County's Heritage Museum is located in the 1903 Superintendent's Residence of the U.S. Fish Hatchery, off US 23's exit 19 between Erwin and Unicoi, TN. Open May through October, Tuesday through Sunday 1 PM–5 PM. Free admission. Nine of the museum's 10 rooms are open to the public. Railroad buffs will head immediately to the Railroad Room on the second floor, with exhibits on the old **Clinchfield Railroad** (see The Clinchfield Railroad Loops under *To See—Historic Sites* in "The Blue Ridge Parkway: Blowing Rock and Grandfather Mountain"). The Clinchfield was (and remains) one of the greatest lines in the East, running straight through the Appalachians like a hot wire through butter; formerly an independent company headquartered in Erwin, it's now a heavily used main line for the CSX System. In the next room is a reconstruction of Erwin's Main Street, from about the period when the fish hatchery (and the Clinchfield) were built. Other rooms display home-canned and -preserved food; another type of preserve—artifacts of nature, including a stuffed bear (killed by accident); period furniture; local arts and crafts; turn-of-the-century costumes; and just a lot of neat stuff. Individual rooms are sponsored by local civic organizations. A one-room log schoolhouse sits outside (moved in from Greasy Cove), and a nature trail is on the property.

GARDENS AND PARKS Hampton Creek Cove State Natural Area (615-532-0436) is located at the end of Hampton Creek Road, which starts at the village of Roan Mountain. Unique among the State of Tennessee's 60 natural areas, Hampton Creek Cove contains a working farm, still run by the family that has farmed this land for the last century. A state-owned part of the 15,000-acre Highlands of Roan, Hampton Creek demonstrates mountain farming practices that conserve natural ecosystems and improve biodiversity. A track runs uphill through the farmlands and into the woods above, eventually reaching the famous ridgetop meadows of the Roan at the **Overmountain Victory Trail** (see *Wandering Around—Exploring on Foot* in "Behind the Blue Ridge: Spruce Pine and Burnsville").

✳ To Do

FAMILY ADVENTURE ✓ **The Tweetsie Railroad**. (828-264-9061; 1-800-526-5740), Blowing Rock, NC. Adults, $23; children under 13, $16. Open daily 9–6, June through August; Friday through Sunday 9–6 during May, September, and October; closed Nov through May. This circa-1960 cowboy theme park, named after the region's historic narrow gauge railroad [see **The ET & WNC (Tweetsie) Railroad** in *To See—Historic Sites*], includes rides on a 3-mile closed-loop railroad, with the train pulled by the real Tweetsie Railroad's #12 engine, built in 1917. (She's aided by a second steam engine, the White Pass & Yukon Railroad's #190 "Yukon Queen," dating from 1943.) Some of the rolling stock comes from the ET & WNC, too. The train takes you to a tourist attraction featuring Hollywood-style Old West buildings, shoot-em-ups, and can-can dancers.

FISHING Journey's Edge (423-772-3177), Roan Mountain, TN. This outfitter offers local guide services for fly-fishing ($150 per day), backpacking ($75 per day), and hunting ($250 per day).

GOLF Elizabethton Municipal Golf Course (423-542-8051), Golf Club Road, Elizabethton, TN. $15–23. This fairly hilly 18-hole par-72 course overlooks the Watauga River on the west side of the City of Elizabethton, off US 321.

Buffalo Valley Golf Course (423-743-5021), 90 Country Club Drive, Unicoi, TN. $17–19. Eight miles north of Erwin, TN, this 18-hole public course sits on the level floor of the oddly riverless valley that stretches north from Erwin to Johnson City, TN. It in an attractive rural location, convenient to the US 23 freeway that's destined to become I-26 someday.

HORSEBACK RIDING Wilderness Ranch, Inc. (423-768-3030; 1-800-381-6751), 168 Wilderness Trail, Butler, TN. Located in the mountains northeast of Elizabethton, TN, Wilderness Ranch offers trail rides ($20 per hour), covered-wagon rides, and hayrides on its property. Also on the property is **Mountain Lake Wilderness Resort** (see *Lodging—Cabin Rentals*), which rents cabins.

STILLWATER ADVENTURES Watauga Kayaking (423-542-6777), 1409 Broad Street, Elizabethton, TN. Watauga Kayaking offers calm-water lake and river tours on area waters, including **Lake Watauga,** for a quiet and peaceful enjoyment of nature. They also rent kayaks for calm-water use.

WHITEWATER ADVENTURES Cherokee Adventures, Inc. (423-743-7733; 1-800-445-7238), 2000 Jonesborough Road, Erwin, TN. $16–36 half day, $31–63 whole day. This outfitter specializes in fully guided trips on the **Nolichucky River**— wild rides on the **Nolichucky Gorge,** or gentle, scenic floats farther downstream. Most floats include lunch. With 50 riverside acres, they have packages that combine primitive camping or simple cabin accommodations with meals and float trips. They also offer mountain bike tours and a roping school.

B-Cliff Whitewater Rafting (423-542-2262; 1-800-592-2262), 390 Wilbur Dam Road, Elizabethton, TN. Open Memorial Day through Labor Day. $30. B-Cliff offers whitewater rafting and kayaking on the **Watauga River** 5 miles east of Elizabethton.

Nantahala Outdoor Center at Erwin, TN (423-743-7400; 1-800-232-7238), 4 Jones Branch Road, Erwin, TN. This major regional company, headquartered in Bryson City, NC (see *To Do—Rafting and Kayaking* in "Bryson City and the Southwest Quadrant"), maintains an outpost at the head of the **Nolichucky Gorge,** 4 miles south of Erwin—a base for trips through the Nolichucky Gorge.

USA Raft (423-743-7111; 1-800-872-7238), 2 Jones Branch Road, Erwin, TN. This West Virginia whitewater rafting chain operates an outpost at the mouth of the **Nolichucky Gorge,** 4 miles south of Erwin.

✳ Lodging

BED & BREAKFASTS 🖉 🐾 **Iron Mountain Inn** (423-768-2446; 1-888-781-2399), 138 Moreland Drive, P.O. Box 30, Butler, TN 37640. Open all year. This modern log structure sits on 140 acres in the Iron Mountains, 12 miles south of Mountain City, TN. It has a porch and a deck with views, a great room with a fireplace, and a library. Its four rooms, individually decorated and themed, have handmade quilts and whirlpool baths; two rooms have steam showers, and three

have private balconies. Guests are treated to afternoon refreshments as well as a three-course breakfast, and the cookie jar is always full. Dinner and picnic lunches are available with 24 hours notice (for a fee). Pets and small children require prior arrangement. $125–250, including full breakfast. Rates are lower on weekdays and off-season, higher on weekends, in October, and on holidays. AAA discounts.

Doe River Inn (423-416-0777), 217 Academy Street, Elizabethton, TN 37643. This 1894 Victorian house faces the Doe River in Elizabethton's historic district, within site of the town's famous covered bridge (see *To See— Historic Sites*). Built on the site of the original ford over the Doe River, it was once known as "The Crossover." Today's inn has two rooms, each elegantly furnished with antiques and with its own bath. Common rooms, also furnished in high Victorian style, include a living room, a sunroom, and a formal dining room, where a full breakfast is served.

General Wilder's Bed & Breakfast (423-772-3102), 200 Main Street, Roan Mountain, TN 37687. Built in 1880, this National Register–listed Victorian country house was probably the most elegant structure in the rural Doe River area. It's original owner, Civil War general John Thomas Wilder, built it as he formed his plans to exploit his 7,000-acre property on the crest of the Roan Highlands—the core of today's national forest holdings. It's a simple two-story white frame house with a hipped-roof front porch and simple gingerbread details, located at the center of this mountain-gorge village, several blocks removed from US 19E. Its four rooms with private baths are elegantly furnished with Victorian antiques to a level of comfort that General Wilder would appreciate. $79–99, including breakfast.

🐾 ✍ **Mountain Harbour B&B** (423-772-9494; 866-772-9494), 9151 Highway 19E, Roan Mountain, TN 37687. This four-room B&B inn is in a farmhouse-style home with stained clapboarding, dormers, and a wraparound porch. The four rooms, ranging in size from cozy to large, are individually furnished in a country-antiques style. The largest room has a whirlpool tub and a fireplace. Two rooms are en suite, while two other rooms share a bath. $70–120.

CABIN RENTALS 🐾✍ **Roan Mountain State Park Cabins** (423-772-0190; 1-800-250-8620), 1015 Highway 143, Roan Mountain, TN 37687. This 2,000-acre state park has 30 rustic cabins available by the day. Each cabin is a modern-built structure in a classic park style with full front porch, living room, full kitchen, and two bedrooms. They are attractively set in a wooded glade, with a stream nearby and a large, well-kept lawn area. Ten cabins are available with phones. Only one cabin is approved for pets. $65–95.

🐾 ✍ **Mountain Lake Wilderness Resort** (423-768-3030; 1-800-381-6751), 166 Wilderness Trail, P.O. Box 300, Butler, TN 37640. These modern log cabins are on the site of Wilderness Ranch, an outdoors family resort with horseback rides, hayrides, exotic animals, covered-wagon rides, and a wagon-train ride. Each cabin has a full front porch, living room with fireplace, full kitchen, and two bedrooms, with a picnic area outside. Pets require prior approval and an extra $10 per night fee. $85; discounts for longer stays.

Cherokee Forest Mountain Cabins

(423-768-4484), 1423 TN 167, Butler, TN 37640. Open all year. These two modern log cabins are located at the far northern end of Watauga Lake, near Butler. Both have wide views from their front porches, with wood-finished interiors furnished in a simple, elegant country style. Living areas have cathedral ceilings and fireplaces, and kitchens are full sized. $130–170; discounts for longer stays.

Bee Cliff Cabins (423-542-6033), 106 Bee Cliff Lane, Elizabethton, TN 37643. These three cabins are located on a rural stretch of the Watauga River, convenient to **Wilbur Lake** (see *Wild Places—Recreation Areas*), 5 miles east of Elizabethton. Like an old-time fish camp, the modest log-sided cabins group around the central drive, sharing a common dock on the river. Inside, they are simply and comfortably furnished, wood-walled, with full kitchens. $75; discounts for longer stays.

✳ Where to Eat

EATING OUT Ridgewood Barbeque (423-538-7543), 900 Elizabethton Highway, Bluff City, TN. Open for lunch and dinner Tuesday through Sunday; closed Monday. The Proffit family of Bluff City founded this popular pit barbeque in 1948 and still own it today. They run a friendly, family-oriented place, sitting underneath the last of the mountain ridges on the old US 19E (now called Elizabethton Highway), 7 miles north of Elizabethton, TN. They barbeque pork and beef in the two original pits, using their own sauce recipe and slicing it to order. The sides are made fresh as well.

The Coffee Company (423-542-3438; 1-800-358-3709), 444 East Elk Street, Elizabethton, TN. Open for breakfast and lunch. This coffee shop in downtown Elizabethton serves breakfast and lunch along with a full line of coffees roasted on the premises. Breakfasts are limited to muffins and other goodies baked fresh each morning. Lunches are more elaborate, with homemade soups, sandwiches, desserts, and a daily special.

✳ Entertainment

Special Events at Sycamore Shoals (423-543-5808), Elizabethton, TN. This fascinating historic site (see *To See—Historic Sites*) runs a full slate of events, with something happening every month. Its reconstructed fort hosts several reenactments, including the famous **Overmountain March** each September 23 (see *Special Events* in "Behind the Blue Ridge: Spruce Pine and Burnsville"). There is a **Native American Festival** in June, a fine arts show in July, a **Celtic Festival** in September, and a **quilt show** in October.

The Wataugans Outdoor Drama (423-543-5808) is held in July at **Sycamore Shoals State Historic Site** (see *To See—Historic Sites*). Adults $5, children $3. Tennessee's official outdoor drama and the oldest outdoor drama in the state, "The Wataugans" tells the story of the 18th-century Watauga Settlements that brought Europeans into the lands now known as Tennessee.

The Elizabethton Twins (423-547-6440), 208 North Holly Lane, Elizabethton, TN. Elizabethton is one of only two cities in this guide to have its own minor league team (Asheville is the other; see The Asheville Tourists under *Entertainment—Asheville* in "Asheville and the Blue Ridge Parkway"). A farm team of the Minnesota Twins since 1937, the Elizabethton Twins are part of the rookie-level Appalachian League, one of America's last remaining old-time small-town leagues.

✳ Selective Shopping

Duck Crossing Antique Mall (423-542-3055), 515 East Elk Avenue, Elizabethton, TN. Open Monday through Saturday 10–5. Antiques dealers and gift items inhabit this three-story building in downtown Elizabethton.

Farmhouse Gallery and Garden (423-743-8799; 1-800-952-6043), 21 Covered Bridge Lane, Unicoi, TN. Located north of Unicoi on Erwin Highway, the Farmhouse Gallery features the wildlife art of Johnny Lynch. The gallery is in a restored log cabin surrounded by 3 acres of perennial and water gardens, and set in a 75-acre preserve. The complex includes an events venue for weddings, meetings, and such.

The Hanging Elephant (423-743-9661), 219 South Main Street, Erwin. TN. This downtown Erwin shop offers antiques and collectibles, including Blue Ridge Pottery—hand-painted china made in an Erwin factory from the 1920s through the 1950s.

✳ Special Events

Easter: **Peters Hollow Egg Fight** (423-547-3852), Elizabethton, TN. This annual event, held at **Sycamore Shoals** (see *To See—Historic Sites*), started in 1823 when an Easter egg hunt got out of hand. Or maybe it was a competition to see who's hen laid the strongest egg; traditions vary. Some people like to watch, while others join in.

April: **Fiddlers and Fiddleheads**

Festival (423-743-8799), 21 Covered Bridge Lane, Unicoi, TN. *Late April.* Held 10–9. Free admission. This annual event at Johnny Lynch's **Farmhouse Gallery and Garden** (see *Selective Shopping*) features music, a vintage car show, antiques sales, flower sales, storytelling, and food.

First weekend in May: **Roan Mountain (State Park) Spring Naturalists Rally** (423-772-0190), Roan Mountain, TN. Roan Mountain State Park sponsors a weekend of nighttime nature lectures and daytime naturalist-led hikes through the early-spring wildflowers.

Second weekend in May: **Unicoi Strawberry Festival,** Unicoi, TN. This street fair in the small town of Unicoi (5 miles north of Erwin, TN), celebrates the strawberry with live entertainment, a Sunday gospel sing, crafts and fair booths, a city-wide yard sale, and strawberries.

Early June: **Covered Bridge Celebration,** Elizabethton, TN. Elizabethton celebrates its beautiful old covered bridge (see Doe River Covered Bridge under *To See—Historic*

Sites) with a 4-day annual festival.

June and July: **Annual Rhododendron Festival at Roan Mountain State Park** (423-772-0190), Roan Mountain, TN. *Last weekend in June.* This annual festival celebrates the peak of the rhododendron display, particularly spectacular in nearby **Roan Mountain Gardens** (see *To See—Gardens and Parks* in "Behind the Blue Ridge: Spruce Pine and Burnsville"), part of Pisgah National Forest across the line in North Carolina. This 2-day event includes old-time mountain music, clogging, crafts, and food. There's another **Rhododendron Festival** held during the *last weekend in July* on the other side of the mountain, at **Bakersville** (see *Special Events* in "Behind the Blue Ridge: Spruce Pine and Burnsville"). A true festival enthusiast will want to take in both.

First weekend in October: **Unicoi County Apple Festival,** Erwin, TN. This 2-day street fair takes over downtown Erwin, with 300 crafts and food exhibits, live music, and (of course) plenty of apples.

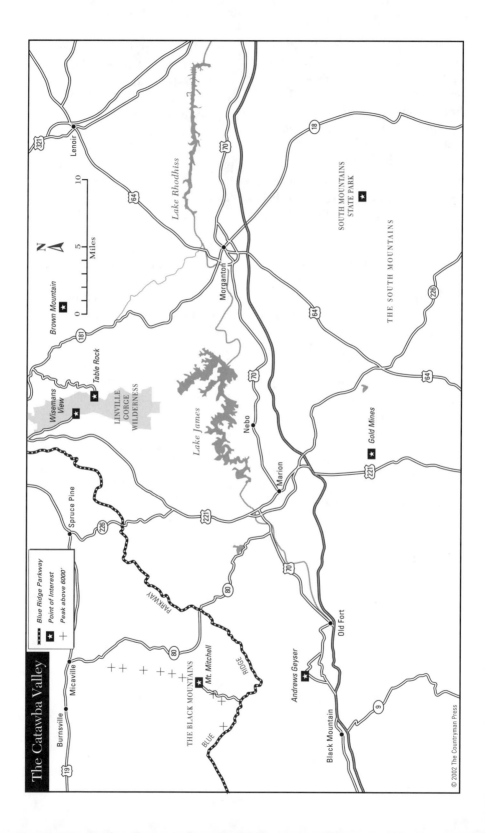

The Catawba Valley

Blue Ridge Parkway
Point of Interest
Peak above 6000'

© 2002 The Countryman Press

BENEATH THE BLUE RIDGE: THE CATAWBA RIVER VALLEY

The mountains begin, and the Piedmont ends, in the valley of the Catawba River. One of the great rivers of the South, the Catawba rises from the upper slopes of the Blue Ridge 15 miles east of Asheville, NC, near the town of Black Mountain (see *Villages* in "Ashville and the Blue Ridge Parkway"). It then drops steeply to Old Fort, NC, and flows eastward into a wide, rolling valley, past the redbrick centers of Marion and Morganton, NC, then out into the Piedmont. The cliffs of the Blue Ridge loom 6 or 8 miles north of the valley bottom; the rugged peaks and clefts of the South Mountains lie the same distance south.

The Catawba Valley has always been the main approach to the Smokies from the thickly settled areas of North Carolina. First wagons, then trains, went up it to reach the rich mountain forests; today, a flood of cars and trucks follow I-40 in their path. Before the Civil War, some of those wagons carried the North Carolina Supreme Court to Morganton every summer, escaping the downstate heat; the state supreme court's graceful little courthouse still sits in the middle of Morganton's old-fashioned downtown. After the war, furniture manufacturers built factories along the rail yards beneath the cliffs of the Blue Ridge, the perfect distance between mountain hardwoods and downstate markets. More than a hundred years later, furniture manufacturing still leads a laundry list of clean mill industries that continue to dominate the Catawba Valley economy. Today, you'll find an axis of urban and industrial development stretching lengthways along the I-40 corridor; however, leave the interstate corridor to the north or south, and the modern development drops away as you climb out of the valley floor and into the mountains.

GUIDANCE Burke County Travel and Tourism Commission (828-433-6793; 1-888-462-2921), 102 East Union Street, Morganton, NC 28655. Open Monday through Friday 10–4, Saturday 10–1. Headquartered in Morganton's fine Old Courthouse, this small agency is delighted to help walk-in visitors with their trips to the eastern half of the Catawba Valley.

McDowell County Tourism Development Authority (828-652-1103; 1-888-233-6111), P.O. Box 1028, Marion, NC 28752. McDowell County Tourism Development occupies a large, modern hilltop visitors center by a minor exit on US 221 as it bypasses Marion on its west. Covering the western half of the Catawba Valley, it offers friendly help and advice, a small but interesting display of local art and minerals, and a sweeping view north toward the Blue Ridge.

Old Fort Chamber of Commerce (828-668-7223), Old Fort, NC. Open Tuesday through Saturday 10–4. The town of Old Fort's local chamber offers visitors help and guidance from the railroad depot at the west end of town. It also includes a small **railroad museum.**

✍ **Pisgah National Forest, Grandfather Ranger District** (828-652-2144), 109 East Lawing Drive, Nebo, NC 28761. Open normal business hours. Pisgah National Forest includes an arc of large mountainous tracts along the slopes and side ridges of the Blue Ridge, all along the northern edge of the Catawba Valley. The ranger station for these lands is a large, new building by exit 90 on I-40, at Nebo. It contains a staffed visitors center with a full range of maps and pamphlets, as well as a small bookstore and exhibits on forestry.

GETTING THERE *By car:* I-40 runs up the center of the Catawba Valley for its entire length. With rugged mountains lining the valley's north and south edges, I-40 is the easiest approach no matter what direction you're coming from.

By bus: **Greyhound Bus Lines** (1-800-229-9424) schedules daily service through the Catawba Valley, with stops in both Marion and Morganton, NC. Both of these towns have taxi services and car rentals; check with their visitors centers (see *Guidance*) for details.

By air: **Hickory Regional Airport** (828-323-7408), 25 miles east of Morganton, NC, at the small Piedmont city of Hickory, NC, has five scheduled commuter flights a day (fewer on weekends) from Charlotte, NC, via **U.S. Airways Express.** Car rentals are inside the terminal. Charlotte's major international airport, **Charlotte/Douglas International Airport** (704-359-4000) is 75 miles from Morganton via four-lane highway.

MEDICAL EMERGENCIES Grace Hospital (828-438-2000), 2201 South Sterling Street, Morganton, NC. This major regional hospital, serving the eastern half of the Catawba Valley, is located by I-40, at the NC 18 exit.

The McDowell Hospital (828-659-5000), 100 Rankin Drive, Marion, NC. This fair-sized local hospital with 24/7 emergency-room service sits by I-40 at exit 81 (Sugar Hill Road), 3 miles south of Marion, and is convenient to the western half of the Catawba Valley.

✳ Wandering Around

EXPLORING BY CAR OR BICYCLE *Note:* You can rent bicycles in Black Mountain, NC (see Epic Cycles under *To Do—Bicycling* in "Asheville and the Blue Ridge Parkway").

✍ **The Swannanoa Grade.** *Leg 1:* From Old Fort, NC, take US 70 west 0.25 mile; turn right onto Old US 70 (SSR 1400) and drive 2.5 miles; turn right onto Mill Creek Road (SSR 1407) and drive 5.25 miles to Old US 70 (SSR 1400). *Cars* continue straight to Black Mountain, NC, and I-40.

Leg 2 (for bicycles only): Turn left as you regain Old US 70, at the white gate. Follow the concrete road, former US 70, now abandoned, downhill for 3.4 miles.

Built in the 1870s with convict labor, the steep railroad known as the **Swannanoa Grade** takes 10 miles to cover a distance that a crow could fly in just over

4. In doing so it climbs a thousand feet in elevation, loops back on itself five times, and goes through seven tunnels with a total underground distance of 0.75 mile. More to the point, most of these engineering wonders (and the rugged scenery that brought them into existence) can be easily viewed by car-bound visitors—just as well, as there's been no passenger service on this line for a half century.

Start at downtown **Old Fort** (see *Villages*), where two small museums give historic perspective—on pioneer life at the **Mountain Gateway Museum** (see *To See—Cultural Sites*), and on 19th-century railroading at the **Old Fort Railroad Museum** (see *To See—Cultural Sites*). After that, follow the signs westward to Andrews Geyser. You'll be on the former main highway as far as the classic Civilian Conservation Corps (CCC)–built **Old Fort Picnic Area** (see *Wild Places—Picnic Areas*), then up the pastoral Mill Creek Valley as far as **Andrews Geyser** (see *To See—Historic Sites*). The railroad built the "geyser" (a 30-foot fountain) to impress passengers disembarking at a resort hotel; passengers and hotel are long gone, but the "geyser" remains, kept in operation by dedicated local residents. The geyser is placed in the center of three pigtail loops, and railroad enthusiasts will enjoy tracing the railroad on its mountain-slope gyrations. From Andrews Geyser the road climbs the Blue Ridge as a good gravel lane through **Pisgah National Forest** lands. Attractive hardwood forests surround the road all the way up, except for a small orchard (privately owned) at the luxurious **Inn on Mill Creek** (see *Lodging—Bed and Breakfasts*); the small pond behind the inn is the source of Andrews Geyser.

A bit farther you suddenly regain the old paved main highway, open to the right but gated to the left. The gated leftward road is **Old US 70;** a half-mile walk down its concrete surface will lead to a series of four railroad tunnels, as well as a good view. From here, cars should complete the drive by following the old concrete road to the right to **Black Mountain**, NC, and **I-40.** However, bicyclists can follow the abandoned highway downhill for wonderful views and a close look at those railroad tunnels. The old highway circles back to the **Old Fort Picnic Area.**

A WATERFALL ON JACOB'S FORK ON THE HIGH SHOALS FALLS TRAIL

EXPLORING ON FOOT **Waterfalls and Views in the South Mountains.** The South Mountains offer a wide variety of first-rate walks and hikes; these two, each steep but short, lead to an 80-foot waterfall and a wide panorama. Both are reached from the **Jacob Fork Picnic Area** (see South Mountains Picnic Areas under *Wild Places— Picnic Areas*), within **South Mountains State Park,** and are well sign-posted.

Start by following the signs to the **High Shoals Falls Trail,** a well-built waterfall walk that will take you on a 2-mile round-trip with many, many steps.

WISEMAN'S VIEW, LOOKING SOUTH DOWN LINVILLE GORGE IN SPRING

EXPLORING BY CAR: THE RIM OF LINVILLE GORGE

Leg 1: From Linville Falls, NC, on US 221, go east on NC 183 for 0.8 mile; then turn right onto Kistler Memorial Highway (SSR 1239) and drive 4 miles to Wiseman's View. Return to NC 183. *Leg 2:* Continue heading east (turn right) on NC 183 for 4 miles; turn right onto NC 181 and drive 3 miles; turn right at Table Rock Road (SSR 1265) and drive 6.3 miles; then turn right at the fork and drive 1.4 miles to Table Rock Picnic Area. Return to NC 181. *Leg 3:* Turn right onto NC 181 and drive 23 miles to Morganton, NC.

This drive explores both rims of rugged **Linville Gorge,** the first eastern forest to be declared a wilderness area. It starts at the rural community of **Linville Falls,** NC, noted for its handsome stone buildings constructed by the stonemasons who built the Blue Ridge Parkway, and for its simple, turn-of-the-century farm-style houses built as summer homes by an early generation of tourists. Outside the village, this route follows the gravel, poorly maintained

Go straight to the falls by taking the left fork of this loop trail—the one marked WARNING: STEEP AND RUGGED PATH. The path follows the violent little **High Shoals Creek** for a short distance, then turns suddenly and crosses an astonishing field of truck-sized boulders on a long, stepped boardwalk. Here the stream breaks up around the boulders, forming many small waterfalls. From this point up it's all steps, flight after flight, until you reach a large viewing platform at the base of 80-foot **High Shoals Falls**—where the powerful stream plunges straight down

Kistler Memorial Highway along the western edge of the **Linville Gorge Wilderness.** This verbosely named back road follows the ridgeline that defines the edge of the wilderness, running through a dry oak forest for the most part. The first path on the left (parking) leads to **Linville Falls waterfall** (see Linville Falls Recreation Area under *To See—The Blue Ridge Parkway* in "The Blue Ridge Parkway: Blowing Rock and Grandfather Mountain"), and all the later paths on the left descend steeply to the gorge bottom. Stop at **Wiseman's View** on the left, and take the short, easy path to impressive cliff-top views over the gorge. Beyond Wiseman's View, the Kistler Highway may be impassable to passenger cars; return the way you came.

The route continues through rural countryside to the unremarkable mountaintop settlement of Jonas Ridge, where a brown recreation sign points down the road to **Table Rock Picnic Area** (see *Wild Places—Picnic Areas).* This good-quality Forest Service gravel road slowly winds its way through a large, handsome hardwood forest. The final mile climbs up seven switchbacks to reach the other side of the Linville Gorge, almost opposite Wiseman's View, at the lovely, tree-shaded picnic area. Here, footpaths stretch north and south along the gorge rim to spectacular cliff-top views and strange geological formations at **Table Rock** and the **Chimneys** (see Table Rock Walks on the Linville Gorge Rim under *Wandering Around—Exploring on Foot).* Return the way you came.

The final leg follows **NC 181** downhill to **Morganton**. In 2 miles, the trailhead for **Upper Creek Falls** is on the left, with **Bark House Picnic Area** (see *Wild Places—Picnic Areas)* just beyond. For the next 5 miles the highway follows the top of **Ripshin Ridge,** with excellent views back toward Table Rock and the Chimneys—here more impressive than ever. At the bottom of the mountain, commercial nurseries keep large fields of blooming trees, an amazing sight in the spring. NC 181 leads to the center of **Morganton,** with its early-19th-century courthouse once used by the North Carolina Supreme Court for its summer sessions.

over a vertical gray cliff to a large, deep pool. The steps continue upward, hugging the cliffs near the falls, to reach the top, where you'll find a narrow view over the falls into the gorge. The loop trail continues on through second-growth forest; it's more fun to return the way you came, appreciating the fine cliff scenery from a leisured descent.

If you still have the energy, take the **Chestnut Knob Overlook Trail** on the way back for great views across a deep gorge to High Shoals Falls and beyond;

you'll pass the trailhead on your return to the picnic area. This trail ascends the dry hemlock and pine forests of the steep south-facing slopes, climbing a thousand feet in 2 miles, to reach the wide cliff-top views at Chestnut Knob. Here, more than anywhere else in North Carolina, you can see the end of the mountains, the sudden plunge to the Piedmont and the endless plains of the Deep South. Return the way you came.

Table Rock Walks on the Linville Gorge Rim. Table Rock Picnic Area (see *Wild Places—Picnic Areas*) gives access to one of the most interesting and spectacular day hikes in the area, following the rocky, cliff-lined rim of Linville Gorge. To the north, the **Table Rock Trail** climbs steeply (500 feet in a half mile) to the cliff-lined, flat-topped Table Rock, a remarkable mesalike formation protruding 600 feet above the trees of the surrounding ridge. The **Chimneys Trail** heads south along the rim to the rocky hoodoos known as The Chimneys. Much easier and only slightly longer, this path is a gentle ridgetop ramgle along an exposed rocky cliff with wide views.

✳ Villages

Morganton, NC. Founded in the late 1700s as the pioneer settlement of Morganborough, Morganton gained its prosperity as a furniture mill town in the 19th century. The mountain hardwood forests furnished the raw material, and the railroad shipped out the final product. This is still the arrangement—Morganton and its suburbs retain the corporate headquarters of major furniture manufacturers Henredon and Drexel Heritage. (Alas, neither has a public showroom.) Late-19th-century Morganton also gained major medical centers, and for similar reasons—good rail access and closeness to the healthy air of the mountains. Today the late-19th-century campuses of the Broughton Hospital (a state psychiatric hospital) and the North Carolina School for the Deaf make up a large National Register Historic District (see **Morganton's National Historic Districts** under *To See—Historic Sites*), occupying the same hill on the south end of town. It's a gentle place of stately old buildings, wooded glades, and wide mountain views over grassy meadows.

Settled since the middle of the 18th century, Morganton has several worthwhile historic sites (see *To See—Historic Sites*). However, its main attraction is its downtown—a classic small-town Main Street, anchored by lovely Courthouse Square, which is dominated by its old courthouse, now a historic museum (see **Old Burke County Courthouse** under *To See—Historic Sites*). A good-quality shopping district, full of active, interesting stores and cafés, runs along the north side of Courthouse Square, while two sets of historic buildings are being renovated into more shops nearby. Parking is plentiful and free, with lots of street parking as well as large municipal lots behind the storefronts.

Marion, NC. This thriving county seat sits on an important railroad junction, where two major freight lines fight their separate ways up the face of the Blue Ridge. It centers on a four-blocks-long downtown of two-story brick storefronts from the late 19th century and a golden brick 1920s courthouse faced with 12-foot windows. Downtown shops still center mainly on the old small-town standbys, well kept but lacking restoration. However, the little downtown has character and

improves a bit every year, as projects such as the **Shamrock Inn** (see *Lodging—*
Bed and Breakfasts) and **Eagle Hotel** (see **The Crooked Door** under *Eating Out*) restore the buildings one by one, filling them with interesting and worthwhile things.

Old Fort, NC. Nestled at the base of the Blue Ridge, Old Fort has been a working railroad town since the 1870s. Its large siding, where steam engines used to get a second "pusher" engine to help them up the mountain, has long attracted mills, and modern Old Fort has a half-dozen or so clean factories. For a visitor, Old Fort is worthwhile for its two museums: the **Mountain Gateway Museum** (on to pioneer life) and the **Old Fort Railroad Museum** (see *To See—Cultural Sites*) and its attractive little downtown. Downtown Old Fort sports a single block of 19th-century brick storefronts, a bright yellow depot containing the railroad museum, a tiny park with a gazebo, and a 25-foot-tall granite arrowhead set on a 15-foot stone plinth, erected in the 1920s as a memorial to frontier peace.

✳ Wild Places

THE GREAT FORESTS Linville Gorge Wilderness. One of the earliest wilderness areas created by Congress, this 11,000-acre tract preserves a deep, 13-mile-long gorge cut into the face of the Blue Ridge. The gorge starts with the massive hundred-foot plunge of the Linville River over **Linville Falls** (see Linville Falls Recreation Area under *To See—The Blue Ridge Parkway* in "The Blue Ridge Parkway: Blowing Rock and Grandfather Mountain"), then quickly drops away in near-vertical slopes to a river bottom that's a third of a mile below the gorge edge. The fierce river and steep slopes have prevented logging, leaving the gorge in pristine shape—a rich, riverside old-growth forest. Access to the gorge bottom is by footpaths that go straight down the gorge sides, making for an extremely difficult return. Even the riverside trail can be difficult, finding its way along the rough, rocky gorge bottom. Nevertheless, the gorge bottom is reasonably popular with day hikers, backpackers, and fishermen. Fortunately for the less athletic, the gorge rims are easier to reach (see **The Rim of Linville Gorge** under *Wandering Around—Exploring by Car*), and the finest viewpoint, **Wiseman's View,** is disabled accessible.

RECREATION AREAS ✿ ✎ ♿ **The Catawba River Greenway in Morganton** (828-437-8863), City Hall, 201 West Meeting Street, Morganton, NC. This City of Morganton park stretches along the south bank of the Catawba River for a mile, starting at **Judges Barbeque** (see *Eating Out*). It's an easy, paved walk with plenty of views over the wide Catawba as it enters the Piedmont. The upstream terminus at Judges has ample parking and picnicking facilities, as well as a canoe launch and fishing docks.

PICNIC AREAS Table Rock Picnic Area. This small primitive picnic area sits in a handsome hardwood forest on the rim of the Linville Gorge Wilderness, between the rock pinnacles of **Table Rock** and the **Chimneys.** The drive into the picnic area is worthwhile in itself (see **The Rim of Linville Gorge** under *Wandering Around—Exploring by Car*), and short hiking trails lead to stunning views (see **Table Rock Walks on the Linville Gorge Rim** under *Wandering Around—Exploring on Foot*).

Bark House Picnic Area. This small, attractive picnic area sits in a shady hardwood glade atop a small knob, an easy 6 miles south of the Blue Ridge Parkway on NC 181 in the **Linville,** NC, area. It's a lovely little place, with a low fee (free admission) that reflects its single pit toilet and water from a hand pump. Nearby,

SOUTH MOUNTAINS STATE PARK

🐾 ✂️ ♿ (828-433-4772), 3001 South Mountain Park Avenue, Connelly Springs, NC. The park is 20 miles south of I-40 off exit 104 (Enola Road). Take Enola Road south for 9 miles to its end at old NC 18, then go right 5 miles. From here, large brown state park signs will guide you in for the remaining 6 miles. Open during daylight, all year. Free admission.

This 16,000-plus-acre state park occupies the rugged central heart of the **South Mountains,** an outlier of the Blue Ridge. With about a thousand feet of valley-to-peak relief, the South Mountains are smaller than much of the Blue Ridge—but they more than make up for it with rugged scenery. Streams twist and dash through deep gorges; the sharp points of gray cliffs emerge from deep forests; truck-sized boulders litter the bottoms of steep gulches; great waterfalls plunge over cliff edges. The mixed forests are dominated by hemlocks, a conifer with pinelike bark and firlike needles that grows rapidly to great sizes. On exposed cliffs, pines and hemlocks twist into bonsai shapes.

Heavily logged in the 20th century, South Mountains State Park is laced by a network of slide roads (used to skid timber downhill), jeep trails, and even auto roads—nearly all now closed to vehicles. The best of these are marked as bicycle and/or horse trails, while other paths are strictly for foot travel only. The rugged topography makes nearly all paths difficult, but the short local relief limits the pain. The two most popular paths (see **Waterfalls and Views in the South Mountains** under *Wandering Around—Exploring on Foot)* give breathtaking (figuratively and literally) climbs to a high cliff view and an 80-foot waterfall. Many other worthwhile paths exist, some requiring backpacking. The park has an information desk (which may close when the rangers are busy elsewhere), two picnic areas (see **South Mountains Picnic Areas** under *Wild Places—Picnic Areas),* and an equestrian camping area.

two short but steep hiking trails lead down into the gorgelike Upper Creek Valley to reach the large and beautiful **Upper Creek Falls.**

🖉 ♿ **South Mountains Picnic Areas.** South Mountains State Park has two fine streamside picnic areas. **Jacob Fork Picnic Area** sits beside the main parking lot, its dozen tables spread widely underneath tall hemlocks and rhododendrons. The first-rate **Hemlocks Nature Trail,** disabled accessible, starts in the picnic area and follows the banks of Jacobs Creek for ⅜ mile. Just beyond the end of the nature trail is the primitive **Shimmy Creek Picnic Area,** with no automobile access, toilets, or water.

Old Fort Picnic Area. This lovely national forest picnic area on the back road to **Andrews Geyser** (see *To See—Historic Sites*) offers streamside picnicking in an old Civilian Conservation Corps (CCC)–style site. Tables sit under tall old trees, spaced well apart,

TABLE ROCK MOUNTAIN AS SEEN FROM THE ENTRANCE ROAD TO THE RECREATION AREA

with small stone walls and steps forming scenic accents. The entrance road furnishes a wonderful view up Mill Creek Valley, past a quiet farming community, to the forested wall of the Blue Ridge.

✴ To See

BIG DAMMED LAKES 🖉 **Lake James** (828-652-5047), Nebo, NC. Giant electric utility Duke Power created this huge reservoir at the foot of the Blue Ridge between Marion and Morganton, NC, by damming two separate watersheds—the **Catawba River** and the **Linville River**—and linking them with a canal. They actually needed three dams to do this, with the third preventing the combined impoundments from slipping into a side stream. Like all such lakes, Lake James provides lots of room for motorboat-based sports and lots of public and private boat launches. One of these is at **Lake James State Park,** along with a number of short walking trails, a sandy beach, and a very good picnic area.

Sitting at the foot of the Blue Ridge, Lake James gives exceptional mountain views—particularly toward the cliff-lined mouth of the **Linville Gorge Wilderness** (see *Wild Places—The Great Forests*). The easternmost dam, known as **Bridgewater Dam,** gives the best shore views; from the top of this tall earthen dam, traversed by a paved state road, you can see the sweep of the Blue Ridge curving in front of you, from the Linville Gorge cliffs on your right to the mile-high peaks of the Black Mountains on your left. This is a first-rate sunset spot, especially when the air is still and the water glassy. To reach the dam, take NC 126 west out of Morganton for 9 miles, then turn left at a fork onto North Powerhouse Road; Bridgewater Dam is 3 miles farther on.

HISTORIC SITES ✵ ⬆ **The Old Burke County Courthouse** (828-437-4104), Morganton, NC. Open Tuesday through Friday 10–4, all year. Free admission. This tiny old courthouse sits at the center of downtown Morganton on its nicely kept square, with its Civil War statue out front. It's a square structure whose outside stairs lead to grandly columned second-story porches, topped by an elaborate Victorian cupola. However, it's much older than its Victorian trim; it was built in 1837 as a simple, elegant Federal-style structure, and served as the summer seat of the North Carolina Supreme Court until the Civil War. Inside, the **Historic Burke Foundation** maintains a small historic museum with exhibits that change annually; the second floor is taken up by a single 150-seat auditorium, where you can view a good slide presentation on Burke County history. Also in the building are the offices of the Historic]Burke Foundation and the **Travel and Tourism Commission** (see *Guidance*), either of which will welcome your visit and your questions.

⬆ **Quaker Meadows Plantation (The McDowell House)** (828-437-4104), Morganton, NC. To reach the McDowell House, take NC 181 for 4 miles northwest from Morganton's town center to the end of the four-lane highway, then turn right on St. Mary's Church Road. Open April through November, Sunday 2–5; other times by appointment. Adults $3, students $1.

The 1812 McDowell House sits on the 6 remaining acres of the vast **Quaker Meadows Plantation.** In colonial times the McDowells were leaders of the western settlers, and their plantation hosted the gathering of the Overmountain Men as they marched to meet the British forces at Kings Mountain. The restored McDowell House shows the post-Revolution success of this early family. A high-ceilinged two-story structure made of on-site red brick, it has two front doors that show a Pennsylvania Dutch influence (even though the McDowells were Scots-Irish). Despite encroaching urbanization the house remains beautifully situated amid rolling lawns. The **Historic Burke Foundation** has carefully restored it to its 1812 appearance and rebuilt the detached kitchen, and is in the process of locating authentic period furnishings; an 1852 corncrib sits behind the house, awaiting its time.

Morganton's National Historic Districts. Morganton has nine National Historic Districts listed on the Nation-

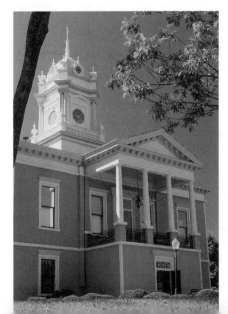

THE OLD BURKE COUNTY COURTHOUSE IS NOW A MUSEUM.

al Register of Historic Places. This adds up to a lot of old buildings. However, it means more than this; a historic district preserves the look and feel of the past, and is an experience in itself. The **Historic Burke Foundation** (828-437-4104) has an excellent color brochure listing all nine districts and giving details of the major buildings in each one. It's a good way to get a deep insight into the way an American small town used to be.

✎ **Andrews Geyser,** Ridgecrest, NC. Take US 70 west from Old Fort, NC, and follow the signs, first onto Old US 70, then up Mill Creek Road. Built as part of the **Swannanoa Grade** (see *Wandering Around—Exploring by Car or Bicycle*) railroad in the 1870s, 30-foot Andrews Geyser sits in a small park in the crook of a hairpin turn the railroad makes as it climbs the face of the Blue Ridge. Today it's kept in loving repair by locals such as innkeeper Jim Carillon of the **Inn on Mill Creek** (see *Lodging—Bed & Breakfasts*), who turns the valve on and off daily. If you are lucky, a train will pass while you visit it, looping around you with half its cars going toward you and the other half away.

⬆ **Carson House** (828-724-4948), Route 1, Box 179, Old Fort, NC. This historic home is on US 70 west of Marion, NC, near the intersection with NC 80. Open May through October, Tuesday through Saturday 10–5, Sunday 2–5; closed Monday. Open November through April by appointment. Adults $3, children $2.

Revolutionary War soldier and prominent North Carolina politician Colonel John Carson built this large family home at the center of his plantation in 1790, an elaborate two-story farmhouse built of 12-inch walnut logs. Fifty years later his son modernized this sophisticated log home by covering it in clapboard and adding the wide first- and second-story porches with their Greek Revival trim. McDowell County was organized in the Carson House; it served as the new county's first courthouse; and the Carsons donated the site of the permanent county seat, Marion, NC, 3 miles to the east (but still on the family plantation). Today, the Carson House is an independent not-for-profit museum displaying pioneer objects and furnishings.

⬆ **The Albertus Ledbetter House** (828-738-9798; 1-877-738-9798), Chimney Rock, NC. Call for directions. Open Saturday beginning at 2 PM. $5 per person. Each Saturday afternoon, innkeepers Arthur and Zee Campbell of **The Cottages at Spring House Farm** (see *Lodging—Cabin Rentals*) open their private home, the 1836 Albertus Ledbetter House, to the public. It's definitely worth the 15-mile trip south from Marion, NC, to the remote, pastoral Hickorynut Mountains.

Jonathan Ledbetter built his original log cabin in 1826, then (10 years later) used post-and-beam construction to expand it into a two-story farmhouse—the structure you see today. Ledbetter, a prosperous farmer and local postmaster, built grandly with Greek Revival detailing but still followed Southern Appalachian traditions. Two rectangular, two-story "cribs"—each an independent structure with its own stairway—were separated by an open "dogtrot," a wide hall open on both ends. Stone fireplaces were set in the gabled sides, while a wide porch ran along the long front of the house. A kitchen wing extended to the rear. Alterations in the 1940s enclosed the dogtrot to from more interior space and modernized the kitchen; otherwise, the rest of the house is unaltered. Amazingly, this includes the original 1836 paint on the planked walls and dogtrot stairs. These elaborate paintings and stencilings combine with a hand-carved vine motif—a rare survival, signed and dated by the artist "Charles Dunkin." The house also includes gun ports in the attic gables, possibly used during the Civil War.

CULTURAL SITES Senator Sam J. Ervin Jr. Library (828-438-6000), 1001 Burkemont Avenue, Morganton, NC. To reach the library, on the **Western Piedmont Community College** campus, follow the signs from exit 103 on I-40; once on campus, you'll find the library on the second floor of the Phifer Learning Resource Center. Then explore the views by strolling this compact campus. Parking is ample and no permit is needed. Open Monday through Friday 8–5. Free admission.

Those of us old enough to remember Watergate will no doubt remember the late Senator Sam Ervin, chairman of the Nixon impeachment hearings, for his fairness, shrewdness, sharp intelligence, deep knowledge of the Constitution—and frequent protestations that he was "a simple country lawyer." Senator Sam was a Morganton man, born and bred, and Western Piedmont Community College has commemorated their local hero in a most appropriate way: by preserving his large personal library. The college has gone well beyond saving the senator's personal papers and 7,500 books. It has faithfully re-created his large, wood-paneled library, every piece of furniture the way the Senator left it, every book it its original place on the shelf. Located in its own room within the college's library, the Ervin Library offers a window into a great mind.

Apart from the Ervin Library, the college is worth a visit for its wide views and handsome campus. Crowning a hillock on the southwestern edge of town, its modern buildings form a tight group surrounded by wide meadows. To the north and east are views toward the 19th-century historic districts (see **Morganton** under *Villages*) of Broughton Hospital and the North Carolina School for the Deaf, each facing the college with its own farmland and crowning its own hill with cupola-topped buildings. On the horizons are the silhouettes of the Blue Ridge and the South Mountains.

🌱 **Jailhouse Gallery (Burke Arts Council)** (828-433-7282), 115 Meeting Street, Morganton, NC. Open Monday through Friday 10–4. No Old Courthouse Square would be complete without an Old Jail. Morganton's 1950s-era Andy-of-Mayberry-style sheriff's office and jail now houses an art museum dedicated to local and regional artists. Expect more than the traditional displays of small-town art students; with national headquarters of major furniture manufacturers, Morganton is a serious venue, where artists can get their work seen and appreciated by art-buying professionals. The thoroughgoing displays, professionally presented, wander through two good-sized galleries, while a third room houses a small **gift shop.** Displays change every two months, so it's always worthwhile to stop in for another look.

✎ 🌱 **The Mountain Gateway Museum** (828-668-9259), Old Fort, NC. Located at the center of Old Fort, this small state museum features exhibits on pioneer life and folk culture in a 1936 Works Progress Administration (WPA) building made of native stone. Permanent exhibits include mountain folk arts, a log cabin reconstructed from a pioneer church, and a reconstructed still; temporary

THE OLD FORT RAILROAD DEPOT

exhibits, on a variety of topics, change every couple of months. Next door are two beautiful old log cabins, authentically furnished with period antiques.

✔ ⊤ **The Old Fort Railroad Museum.** Old Fort's canary yellow depot sits at the center of its single-block downtown, the site of the town's 25-foot-tall granite arrowhead, a monument to frontier peace. Today the depot houses a small but charming railroad museum, with rooms furnished as a late-19th-century depot, and exhibits on the dramatic **Swannanoa Grade** (see *Wandering Around— Exploring by Car or Bicycle*), 10 miles of railroad that loop up the face of the Blue Ridge just outside of town.

MYSTERIOUS PHENOMENA The Brown Mountain Lights. Since 1900 (and perhaps earlier, according to local tales), mysterious lights have danced and flickered over the 2,725-foot peak of Brown Mountain, a side ridge off the Blue Ridge 13 miles north of Morganton, NC. Attempts to explain them have all failed, including train lights (they appear when trains don't run), car headlights (no cars), and swamp gas (no swamps). Most of the remaining explanations involve ghosts in some way. So find a good viewpoint and a clear night, bring to mind your favorite campfire tale, and wait for the lights to come out. With luck, you can view the Brown Mountain Lights from **Wiseman's View** on the rim of Linville Gorge and from **overlooks along NC 181** (see The Rim of Linville Gorge under *Wandering Around—Exploring by Car*).

✳ To Do

BICYCLING Table Rock Bikes (828-437-7959; 1-800-358-2453), 133 West Union Street, Morganton, NC. Open Monday through Friday 10–5:30. This downtown bike shop offers trail bike rentals, and has loads of information and help on local trails.

GOLD MINING ✔ Thermal City Gold Mine (828-286-3016), 5240 US 221 North, Union Mills, NC. Open daylight hours, all year. The South Mountains, and the hills to their east, formed the site of America's first gold rush when a 12-year-old boy picked up a 12-pound (yup, that's pounds, not ounces) gold nugget from a Piedmont creek. Within the South Mountains, gold was quickly found along the Second Broad River, 13 miles south of modern-day Marion, NC (and 9 miles south of I-40), just off US 276. One of the first gold mines, the 1830 Thermal City Mine, is still in operation, under the ownership of the same family since 1890. Owner Lloyd Nanney offers recreational gold miners 30 acres of placer deposits along a half mile of the **Second Broad River.** (In a placer mine, gold dust and nuggets are washed from streamside sediments, not dug out of hard rock.) Panning is done with unsalted on-site deposits in an attractive riverside setting, for an authentic experience. Lloyd has an on-site **snack bar and café,** and sells a full line of gold mining equipment from a **small store** in the center of the mine. Serious gold bugs go for the three common digs held each year, where participants pay a $100 fee for 2 days of all-out collective prospecting, everyone splitting the take.

GOLF Silver Creek Plantation Golf Club (828-584-6911), 4241 Plantation Drive, Morganton, NC. Open all year. $19–31. This 18-hole, Tom Jackson–designed semiprivate course wanders along hilltops west of Morganton, with sweeping views toward the South Mountains and the Blue Ridge. **Fairway Oaks Bed & Breakfast** (see *Lodging*) is located on this beautiful course, overlooking the fifth green.

Pine Mountain Golf Course (828-433-4950), US 18, Connelley Springs, NC. This 18-hole Paul Mallard–designed course rests high in the South Mountains, adjacent to South Mountain State Park. Originally created as part of South Mountains Resort,

this golf course with its wide and lovely views continues to thrive even as the resort business is being reorganized (and largely phased out).

Old Fort Golf Course (828-668-4256), Route 2, Old Fort, NC. Take exit 73 (Old Fort) from I-40, then follow the signs south for 3 miles. $12–16. This semiprivate nine-hole par-36 course, built in 1962, sits south of Old Fort in the rolling hills of the Catawba River Valley, with views toward the Hickorynut Mountains to the south.

Marion Lake Golf Club (828-652-6232), US 126, Nebo, NC. $12 weekdays, $20 weekends. This par-70 course, first opened in 1933, wanders along hilltops on the south side of **Lake James** (see *To See—Big Dammed Lakes*), with stunning views over the water toward the cliffs of the Blue Ridge.

✳ Lodging

BED & BREAKFASTS Fairway Oaks Bed & Breakfast (828-584-7677; 1-877-584-7611), 4640 Plantation Drive, Morganton, NC 28655. It only looks like a traditional southern farmhouse, with its wide wood porches and tall windows; innkeepers Bill and Genni Poteat built Fairway Oaks as a four-room B&B in 1997. Set inside the gated golf community of Silver Creek Plantation 10 miles west of Morganton, this course-side inn has sweeping views over the links toward the majestic South Mountains. The guest lounge is warm and inviting, with hardwood accents, plush new furniture, and a gas log fireplace. Upstairs, each of the four sizable guest rooms is furnished around its own theme with antiques and reproductions and has its own phone, data port, and desk. Guests receive a discount at the semiprivate **Silver Creek Plantation Golf Club** (see *To Do—Golf*). $65, including full hot breakfast.

🐾 **College Street Inn** (828-430-8911), 204½ South College Street, Morganton, NC 28655. Located near downtown Morganton in the prestigious West Union Historic District, this four-room inn occupies a simple, well-kept cottage behind innkeepers Bill and Karen Pizzorni's bungalow. The handsomely furnished rooms are large, comfortable, and business ready, with desks, phones, and data ports. The smallest room matches that of a good hotel; the largest room has a king bed, a full-sized executive desk, and a separate sitting area with two sofas and full-sized windows. Guests with business meetings can use the cottage's conference room, with its own private entrance, fax, computer, and large-screen TV/video player. Guests receive a hot breakfast in the large and comfortable common room, or can make up their own meals in the fully furnished guests' kitchen. The inn welcomes pleasure travelers as well as business travelers and is a good choice for touring Morganton's handsome downtown and nine historic districts. $59–69, including breakfast.

The Inn at Old Fort (828-668-9384), 106 West Main Street, Old Fort, NC 28762. This large 1880 farmhouse sits on a hill in the center of Old Fort, separated from the historic depot by its own wide gardens. Simple by Victorian standards, this mountain home has a wide front porch with views over Old Fort, and high peaked gables front and side. Innkeepers Chuck and Debbie Aldridge have surrounded it with gardens. Inside, the Aldridges have decorated the three rooms and a suite with Victorian antiques and themed bric-a-brac; hardwood floors uneven from age, and 19th-century bead-board ceilings, add character, as do odd angles from the many gables. Some rooms have shared baths. $50–70, including homemade continental breakfast.

The Shamrock Inn (828-652-5773), 28 Henderson Street, Marion, NC 28752. Open all year. This downtown Marion B&B occupies a simple, red-brick boardinghouse from the turn of the 20th century, a few steps down a side street. Outside, it appears modest enough, its wide porch overlooking a well-kept front garden. Inside, it is elegantly furnished with antiques and art, with hardwood floors and trim, and hand stenciling rather than wallpaper decorating the walls. A ground-floor suite and four upstairs rooms are all individually themed and furnished with antiques. Gourmet breakfasts are served with crystal and silver. $85–150, including full breakfast.

The Inn on Mill Creek (828-668-1115; 1-877-735-2964), P.O. Box 185, Ridgecrest, NC 28770. Take I-40 to Ridgecrest (exit 66) and follow the Bed & Breakfast signs east for 3 miles. Innkeepers Jim and Aline Carillon have created this peaceful, beautiful haven deep within Pisgah National Forest, the only home on a country lane that winds up the Blue Ridge through 9 miles of forest land but still only 10 minutes from Black Mountain. Beside the inn, a 1916 dam forms a small lake stocked with rainbow and brown trout; its outfall, through a pipe regulated by Jim, feeds **Andrews Geyser** (see *To See—Historic Sites*). Uphill, carefully trimmed fruit trees march in neat rows; Aline delights in making gourmet breakfasts from the fresh fruit. Old tracks radiate through the miles of public forest that cover the Blue Ridge slope in all directions—carefully mapped by Jim and perfect for exploring on foot or mountain bike. Jim will even arrange for rental mountain bikes for guests.

Common spaces in the modern lodge are large, yet comfortable, with the homey touch of two woodstoves and a library balcony. The four en suite rooms are exquisitely furnished with reproduction antiques; three of the rooms have four-poster beds. The smallest room, Orchard View, is larger than most hotel rooms (with 350 square feet), and the largest, Lake View, is simply huge at 650 square feet, with broad windows overlooking the lake, a private screened balcony, and a bath with two showers and a whirlpool tub. Only slightly smaller is the Terrace Room, with a private terrace, fireplace, and private four-person hot tub. $90–160, including breakfast.

CABIN RENTALS ✐ **Robardajen Woods Bed & Breakfast** (828-584-3191), 5640 Robardajen Woods, Nebo, NC 28761. A 5-minute drive from I-40, halfway between Morganton and Marion, 3 minutes from Lake James, and equal distance between the Blue Ridge and the South Mountains. Owner Bill Reep moves historic log cabins onto this large forested property near Lake James, rebuilds them, and renovates them to a high degree of comfort. The result is sort of a log cabin B&B; you stay in an historic pioneer log cabin, with a porch overlooking deep woods, then join the Reeps and the other guests for a fine country breakfast. Or make breakfast in your own cabin—they all have full, well-equipped kitchens. The two-story **New Canton House,** moved from Virginia, has a wood-burning fireplace (wood provided) and a working wood-

stove (plus a working electric stove for those who must have their modcons); a wide front porch is perfect for rocking, and a roomy second story holds a large bedroom suite. The **Whisnant House,** moved from a nearby mountain, has a billiard table and a library, as well as a porch overlooking the pool. In addition, the Reeps occasionally take guests into the **Main Lodge,** their personal home—a 1790 two-story log farmhouse from South Carolina. All cabins are furnished with country antiques, as well as having access to a swimming pool and exercise room.

The Cottages at Spring House Farm (828-738-9798; 1-877-738-9798), P.O. Box 130, Chimney Rock, NC 28720. The cottages are located off Sugar Hill Road (SSR 1001), 12 miles south of exit 81 off I-40; ask for directions. These four luxury log cabins share a wooded 92-acre farm in the Hickorynut Mountains (part of the South Mountains), 15 miles south of Marion, NC. The 1836 **Albertus Ledbetter House** (see *To See—Historic Sites*), a National Register property, is on the farm, the home of owners Arthur and Zee Campbell. All cabins are privately situated deep in the woods. All have private porches or decks, full-sized outdoor hot tubs, and a wood-burning stone stove or fireplace. One boasts a view over a trout pond; another a tree growing through its deck; or a bedroom that opens onto a large, airy porch. The Craftsman-style furniture is handmade locally from lumber salvaged from the Ledbetter House restoration; the massive king-sized beds are particularly impressive. Kitchens are fully furnished and stocked with milk, sausage, Zee's fresh-made bread, real butter, local jams, and brown eggs from a neighbor's farm. $200–265.

❋ Where to Eat

EATING OUT ✐ **Yiannis Restaurant** (828-430-8700), 112 West Union, Morganton, NC. Open for lunch and dinner every day. Behind the narrow storefront is a bright, sparkling space with hand-painted murals on white walls, hardwood floors and tables, and an original high ceiling. Behind this roomy main area is an old-fashioned counter, and behind that a flight of steps leads up to a glass brick bar framed by great floor-to-ceiling windows; then up to a third level of seating, this quieter and more formal than the ground floor. The menu is large and eclectic, a mix of traditional Greek recipes and Southern and American favorites made with fresh local ingredients. Not surprisingly, this bright and airy restaurant has gained a broad audience in this sophisticated little mill town, with its appealing mix of simplicity and sophistication, quality and price. Most sandwiches are under $5; most dinners are under $10. Full bar.

✐ **Judges Barbeque** (828-433-5798), Greenlee Ford Road, Morganton, NC. Open 11–9 daily. This large new restaurant sits on a remote, shaded spot on the south bank of the Catawba River, at the end of Greenlee Ford Road, hard by the upstream terminus of the **Catawba River Greenway** (see *Wild Places—Recreation Areas*). Judges open, wood-paneled layout, floor-to-ceiling windows, and multi-level deck give wide views over the Catawba River. The menu features a variety of imaginative daily specials, but here's all you really need to know: The barbecue is great. It's fresh made, slow cooked, mild, smoky, tender, and moist, with just the right amount of crust—chopped pork, beef brisket, chicken, or ribs. The wonderfully spiced homemade hot sauce and a sweeter mild sauce are served on the side. The exceptional homemade sides include a vinegar-dressed coleslaw and thick, sweet onion rings. Sandwiches $4.75–5.95; barbecue dinners $7.25–9.95; other dinners $8.95–13.95. Wine and beer.

✐ **D&B Café** (828-668-7786), 111 Main Street, Old Fort, NC. Open Tuesday through Friday 9–4, Saturday 9–3; closed Sunday and Monday. Mom (Dee Russell) makes your food from scratch, and her daughter Brandy serves it up with a friendly smile in this delightful storefront café in Old Fort's tiny downtown (see *Selective Shopping—Old Fort*). Bright and cheerfully decorated, a table of the day's newspapers and shelves of books and magazines invite you to linger. The menu lists all the old favorites of a tradition small-town café, to which Dee adds more adventuresome specials—such as a pork tenderloin, grilled and served over noodles with a bell pepper sauce. Dee makes a wide variety of desserts, all of them wonderful. Be sure to get a few fresh cookies to take with you. Breakfast $0.75–2.25; lunch $1.95–4.25.

The Crooked Door, Marion, NC. Open Wednesday through Saturday 8 AM–10 PM. This attractive second-story coffee shop sits behind the arched windows of Marion's beautiful old Eagle Hotel, an 1895 three-story brick building on the north end of downtown. It features Italian and American coffees and homemade pastries, along lots of old Victorian wood trim, a sofa'd sitting area by a fire, and good views over downtown. It's only the first stage of the Ornburg family's plan to revive this fine old structure. If all goes well, the coffee shop will be looking out over a covered second-floor balcony by the time you read this, and an art gallery featuring regional artists will fill the large hotel area behind the shop.

Carolina Chocolatiers (828-652-4496), Marion, NC. This sandwich- and dessert-oriented restaurant in downtown Marion occupies a restored corner of an old downtown building, with wide windows, handsome interior arches, and a tin ceiling painted shocking pink. They have a large range of deli-style sandwiches and grill items, and they make their own desserts. They also make fancy gift chocolates, a real temptation as you leave.

DINING OUT King Street Café (828-437-2661), 207 South King Street, Morganton, NC. Open Wednesday through Saturday 5 PM–9 PM. This elegant little café wanders through the ground floor of a small Victorian house in the **South King Street Historic District** (see Morganton's National Historic Districts under *To See—Historic Districts*), adjacent to downtown Morganton. The menu is varied and original. Indeed, you don't expect a $15 liver entrée in most mill towns— but this café has two, one sautéed with apples and red onions, served with demiglaze; the other sautéed with mushrooms and onions in a brown sauce. Cornish game hen is served with dates, oranges, cinnamon, nutmeg, and garlic; quail is roasted with chanterelle mushrooms in a lingonberry sauce. Seafood has a special place in Malaysian chef Peter Chang's repertoire: trout, crab, salmon, shrimp, lobster, and sole blend with a variety of sauces, domestic and exotic, while pork and steak entrées receive simple, classic treatment. The café has an intelligent selection of simple and sophisticated wines, from $16–42 a bottle. Entrées typically from $15–25.

✳ Entertainment

☂ **City of Morganton Municipal Auditorium** (828-433-7469; 1-800-939-7469), 410 South College Street, P.O. Box 3448, Morganton, NC; follow the signs for "CoMMA," which stands for "City of Morganton Municipal Auditorium." This handsome auditorium, larger and nicer than you might expect for a small town, sits on a hill above downtown, surrounded by the well-kept Victorian mansions of the **South King Street Historic District** (see Morganton's National Historic Districts under *To See—Historic Sites*). Their summertime **Back Porch** series features outdoor evening concerts with a picnic dinner. Back Porch events are $7.50. Other events vary, typically from $10–45.

☂ **Old Fort Mountain Music.** Open every Friday, from 7 PM until whenever. Free admission. Old Fort Mountain Music shares space with Old Fort Emergency Medical Service (EMS) in an old brick building at the center of town. On the one hand, it doesn't provide any on-site parking, as the EMS vehicles can't be blocked. (However, there's plenty of free parking within a half-block walk.) On the other hand, the wide, empty EMS driveways provide a place for the musicians to tune up, practice, and talk. Inside, a long, narrow hall with folding chairs forms the venue for this free weekly mountain concert and jam session. Bands range from first rate to enthusiastic, playing a variety of mountain music, bluegrass, and country—but the emphasis is on mountain music.

✳ Selective Shopping

Morganton, NC

Downtown Morganton. Morganton's Old Courthouse Square, well kept and handsomely landscaped in a traditional style, sits at the center of a four-block downtown of turn-of-the-century two-story storefronts. The area still preserves the charm of a small town center, its old buildings immaculately kept and filled with clothing stores, restaurants, and boutiques. Shopping is concentrated along **Union Street** (Business US 70) on the north side of Old Courthouse Square. Traditional storefronts stretch westward from the square; to the east sits the newly restored **Morganton Trading Company** (under construction at this writing), offering more specialty shops in a restored 19th-century mill complex that includes City Hall.

♈ **Studio XI** (828-433-0056), 117 West Union Street. This unique art gallery serves as an outlet and studio for a group of artistically gifted individuals who are challenged by developmental disabilities. Walk into this gallery in the center of Morganton's small, active downtown, and you'll be greeted by sophisticated art in the primitive style, with bold colors and designs and a strong point of view, by artists who exhibit nationally and internationally. Studio XI makes a fine anchor for Morganton's lively little downtown, occupying a Union Street storefront near Old Courthouse Square and surrounded by a variety of restaurants and shops.

South Mountain Crafts Village (828-433-2836), 409 Enola Road. To reach the Crafts Village from I-40, take the Enola Road exit (exit 104), then go south 0.25 mile. Open Monday through Friday 9–4. This unique crafts shop features handmade crafts and furniture produced by the residents of **Western Carolina Center,** a large regional facility for the mentally retarded. Founded in 1980, the Crafts Village occupies seven of a mile-long line of small, square wooden houses that face Enola Road, built half a century ago as employee housing for the center. The Crafts Village exists to give training and work opportunities, and the skilled and original products found in its shop testify to its success. In it you'll find wooden craft items, pottery, woven items, candles, soaps, potpourri, quilts, early-American pine furniture, and fine finished oak tables and chairs—all handmade on the premises. In-season, you may find fruits, vegetables, and flowers grown in the village's gardens and greenhouses—although the center's kitchens get first crack at the edibles.

Apple Hill Orchard and Cider Mill (828-437-1224), Appletree Lane. Take the Enola Road exit (exit 104) from I-40 south for 4 miles, turning right onto Pleasant Hill Road at the large brick church. Open normal business hours, August through Christmas. This working apple orchard, located on the lower slopes of the South Mountains south of Morganton, has been producing apples since the 1930s. During the harvest season they open their orchard to the public and sell a variety of fresh-made apple products—including cider pressed on the site. While the well-kept buildings are modern, the site and the orchard are very scenic.

Marion, NC

Downtown Marion. Marion's downtown spreads along four blocks, centered on a 1903 bank with a fake dome and a wonderful 1922 golden brick courthouse with 12-foot art deco windows. Downtown is busy and improving steadily but is still recovering its shopping and architecture. Shops tend to be functional rather than funky, and all too many historic storefronts remain barnacled by "modernizing" facades from the 1950s and 1960s.

Old Fort, NC

Downtown Old Fort. Old Fort may well have the nicest one-block downtown in the mountains. A single row of one- and two-story turn-of-the-century stores lines one block of US 70, anchored by the old railroad depot and the giant arrowhead statue at its west end. Half of one side is taken up by a nice little park with a gazebo, while half of the other side is occupied by Old Fort Emergency Medical Service and **Old Fort Mountain Music** (mixed together in the same old brick building; see *Entertainment*). There is just enough room remaining for three nice, largish shops of antiques, collectibles, memorabilia, and stuff, as well as **D&B's Café** (see *Eating Out*). It's definitely worth poking around, particularly as it's next door to the **Old Fort Railroad Museum** and only two blocks from the **Mountain Gateway Museum** (see both museums under *To See—Cultural Sites*).

✳ Special Events

Second weekend in May: **Assault on Mount Mitchell.** Sponsored by Free-wheelers of Spartanburg, a South Carolina bicycle club, this bicycle race goes from **Spartanburg,** SC, to the top of Mount Mitchell, in **Burnsville,** NC. The thousand or so racers cover a hundred miles of road and bicycle 11,000 feet uphill; the final stretch, from Marion, NC, to Mount Mitchell, climbs 6,700 feet in 27 miles.

Fourth of July weekend: **Freedom Celebration and Rodeo,** Old Fort, NC. Old Fort Ruritans sponsor an old-fashioned cowboy rodeo as the main event in the town's celebration; there's also a parade and fireworks.

September (weekend after Labor Day): **Historic Morganton Festival,** Morganton, NC. This large downtown street fair features arts and crafts booths, food vendors, and live music.

Second Saturday in October: **Mountain Glory Festival,** Marion, NC. This two-block-long street fair in downtown Marion features a hundred booths with crafters, artists, and food vendors, plus live entertainment in front of the county courthouse. It's held in association with a month-long **Quilters' Show.**

First Saturday in December: **Appalachian Potters Market,** Marion, NC. Held annually at McDowell High School, this major regional market, open to the general public, is a serious meet between regional potters and their buyers. It draws 60 to 80 potters each year.

Asheville's Mountains

ASHEVILLE & THE BLUE RIDGE PARKWAY

WAYNESVILLE & THE BLUE RIDGE PARKWAY

ASHEVILLE'S RUGGED HINTERLANDS

THE BLUE RIDGE: CHIMNEY ROCK & SALUDA

THE BLUE RIDGE: HENDERSONVILLE
& BREVARD

ASHEVILLE'S MOUNTAINS

The highest mountains in the East mark the point where the Blue Ridge enters the Asheville, NC, region. Here the Black Mountains extend a solid wall of 6,000-foot peaks northward, including Mount Mitchell, the highest mountain in the eastern United States. The Craggy Mountains, famous for their natural rhododendron gardens, merge with the Blacks just north of Asheville. The Blue Ridge Parkway hugs these high ridgelines, furnishing easy access to spectacular tracts of Pisgah National Forest land.

Despite this rugged beginning, one of the largest and gentlest valleys in the Blue Ridge and Smoky Mountains forms behind the Blue Ridge—the valley of the French Broad River. A major tributary of the Tennessee River, the French Broad (like the geologically similar New River farther north), is one of the most ancient in North America, and perhaps the world. It twists sluggishly through a wide area, cutting through hard Blue Ridge rock like so much butter. It forms a natural path for transmountain roads and railroads, and the convergence of these roads forms the mountains' only city, Asheville.

The mountain's first stagecoach road, known as the Buncombe Turnpike, was constructed in the 1820s from Charleston, SC, to Asheville and down the French Broad into Tennessee. For decades it made much of its money from drovers, men who would drive hundreds of cattle, pigs, and even turkeys from mountain farms to markets in South Carolina. However, it quickly generated a new an unexpected industry: tourism. Rich South Carolina plantation owners would take their coaches up the turnpike to large summer estates in the cool mountains. The greatest of such early resorts settlements was at Flat Rock, well established by the 1840s, but other great summer estates of the wealthy stretched along the Blue Ridge as far as Cashiers, NC (see "The Blue Ridge: Cashiers and Highlands").

Asheville is surprisingly sophisticated for its size (fewer than 70,000 residents in 2000), with a large downtown that's both lively and historically fascinating. While its early tourism industry helped, much of its big-city air comes from its richest homeboy, George Vanderbilt, whose 1890 Biltmore Estate is now the region's premiere tourist attraction outside Great Smoky Mountains National Park. In the decades before WWI, society families flocked to Asheville to be near Vanderbilt, and society architects followed. A century later, Asheville remains

a striking early-20th-century city, resplendent in craftsman and art deco architecture.

The Blue Ridge swings due south from Asheville, once again reverting to type with
a rugged, steep eastern face and a gentle, hilly western face. In this area the gentle western slopes are heavily planted in apple orchards, the subject of apple festivals, roadside
stands, and u-pick-em's. The east face is particularly rugged, a gapless cliff that runs due
south to South Carolina, then turns westward in a line so dramatic it's known as the Blue
Wall.

Meanwhile, the mountains to the west of Asheville and the French Broad Valley rise
in a confusing mass of mile-high peaks, carrying names like the Bald Mountains, the
Newfound Mountains, the Pisgah Mountains, and the Great Balsam Mountains. The
Blue Ridge Parkway leaves the actual Blue Ridge to climb into these high peaks, reaching a mile in elevation in the Pisgahs, then climbing above 6,000 feet in the rugged
wilderness of the Great Balsam Mountains. From there, the Smokies are only a short
distance away.

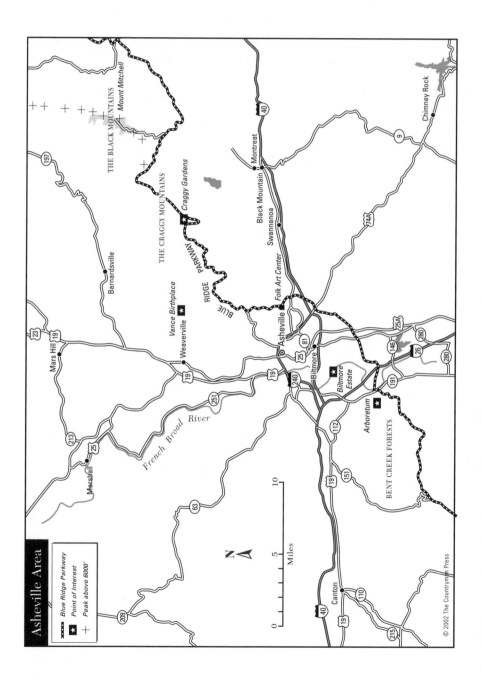

Asheville Area

- ■■■■ Blue Ridge Parkway
- ★ Point of Interest
- + Peak above 6000'

THE BLACK MOUNTAINS
Mount Mitchell

THE CRAGGY MOUNTAINS
★ Craggy Gardens

BLUE RIDGE PARKWAY

Barnardsville

197

Vance Birthplace ★
Weaverville

Mars Hill

23
19

213
25

Marshall

French Broad River

209

251

19

63

19

Canton

40
19

110

215

N

0   5   10

Miles

Folk Art Center

Montreat
Black Mountain
Swannanoa

40

744

9

Chimney Rock

Asheville

81
25

240
Biltmore

280
146
26
280

191

Biltmore
Estate ★

112

Arboretum ★

BENT CREEK FORESTS

151

25A

ASHEVILLE & THE BLUE RIDGE PARKWAY

Asheville, NC, sits behind the Blue Ridge in a huge bowl of a valley. The railroads converged here in the 19th century, followed by the interstates in the 20th. It's the major trade center for the entire mountain region.

You'll find it surprisingly sophisticated, especially for a city of not quite 70,000. It has a wonderfully retro downtown, a 60-block area with exuberant little buildings from the 1890s to the 1930s. During the day, shoppers fill a dozen or more shopping blocks lined with small, independent shops; at night, streets bustle as people explore the restaurant and music scene. Some of this sophistication is the natural result of being the only city for miles around. However, much of it springs from the influence of George Vanderbilt, who made Asheville his home in 1889 and constructed the spectacular Biltmore Estate, reputedly the largest private home in America.

Northeast of Asheville, the Great Craggy Mountains and the Black Mountains come together to form the highest mountain complex in the eastern United States. This amazing knot of mountains includes Mount Mitchell, at 6,684 feet the highest peak in the East. It also has the second-highest peak in the East (Mount Craig), as well as the 5th, 7th, 8th, 13th, 14th, 15th . . . well, honestly, it's hard to come up with an accurate count when 13 miles of near-continuous ridgeline tops 6,000 feet. Easily reached from the Blue Ridge Parkway, this high ridge provides stunning panoramas, deep forests, rough crags, and fields of wildflowers. The section of the Craggy-Black complex known as Craggy Gardens provides a large natural rhododendron garden with wide views; blooms peak in mid-June with some color lingering into mid-July.

GUIDANCE **Asheville Convention and Visitor's Bureau** (828-258-6101; 1-800-257-1300), P.O. Box 1010, Asheville 28802. This chamber covers Asheville and the surrounding area. It runs a visitors center in downtown Asheville, just off I-240's Montford Avenue exit.

Black Mountain/Swannanoa Chamber of Commerce (1-800-669-2301), 201 East State Street (US 70), Black Mountain, NC 28711. This chamber runs a visitors center out of a small storefront in the town of Black Mountain, a short distance east of downtown. It covers the four towns on the uphill side of the Blue Ridge's Swannanoa Gap—Black Mountain, Swannanoa, Ridgecrest, and Montreat, NC.

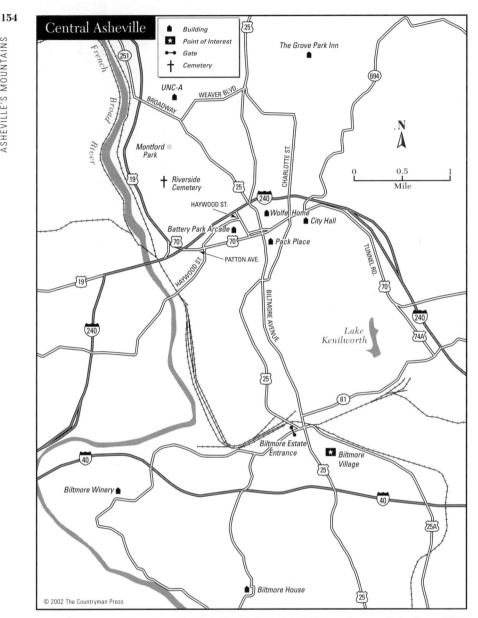

Central Asheville

	Building
★	Point of Interest
•—•	Gate
†	Cemetery

© 2002 The Countryman Press

Pisgah National Forest (828-257-4202), 160A Zillicoa Street, P.O. Box 2750, Asheville, NC 28802. The headquarters for all the national forests in North Carolina are located in Asheville, off the US 19/23 freeway (future I-26), NC 251 exit; follow the signs. They maintain an information desk and bookstore, and—like all national forest stations—are more than happy to help you. Hikers take note: This office sells U.S. Geological Survey topographic maps overprinted with current trail data.

GETTING THERE *By car:* Asheville, NC, is located at the intersection of I-26 and I-40. Downtown Asheville is several miles north of I-40 via a spur, I-240. At this writing, points north are reached via a new freeway, designated US 23 on the Asheville end and I-181 on its Tennessee end at I-81. Someday in the indefinite future this freeway is destined to become I-26; check your map.

By air: **Asheville Regional Airport** (828-684-2226), 708 Airport Road, Fletcher, NC. Asheville's small regional airport is located 15 miles south of downtown off I-26, exit 9 (NC 280). This lovely little airport is virtually unchanged since the 1950s—a low, rambling, white concrete structure with orange stripes, its boarding gates rambling outward from a central lobby. Despite its old-fashioned appearance, it has daily service from Atlanta,

CATAWBA RHODODENDRON SURROUND CRAGGY PINNACLE TUNNEL

Cincinnati, Pittsburgh, Raleigh, and Charlotte, with 20 to 25 flights daily. Several car rental agencies are located within or near the airport.

By bus: **Greyhound Bus Lines** (828-253-8451), 2 Tunnel Road (US 70), Asheville, NC. Asheville is served by Greyhound, with several arrivals each day. The terminal is located a mile east of downtown.

MEDICAL EMERGENCIES Mission St. Josephs Hospital (828-213-1111), 509 Biltmore Avenue, Asheville, NC. This major hospital complex has a large campus south of downtown Asheville, straddling Biltmore Avenue. Its Class II trauma center (the only one in western North Carolina) is a left turn as you go south on Biltmore, into the St. Josephs Hospital area of the campus. Call for directions.

✳ Wandering Around

EXPLORING BY CAR The Blue Ridge Parkway. *Leg 1:* Start at NC 80. Follow the Blue Ridge Parkway 37.8 miles to US 70.

Leg 2: From US 70 outside Asheville, follow the Blue Ridge Parkway 11.0 miles to NC 191.

Leg 3: From NC 191 follow the Blue Ridge Parkway 11.7 miles to NC 151. Easy.

The first leg follows the **Blue Ridge Crest,** climbing uphill through increasingly rugged country. The road breaks out of the forest on both sides for frequent views; **Mount Mitchell,** the highest point in the East, can be clearly seen on the right, distinguishable by its tower. In 9.25 miles the parkway leaves the Blue Ridge forever; at **Pinnacle Bald** the Blue Ridge heads south into South Carolina and Georgia, and the parkway climbs northward into the **Black Mountains** (see Mount Mitchell and the Black Mountains under *Wild Places—The Great Forests*). In 10.2 miles from NC 80, the **Mount Mitchell Spur Road** heads 4.5 miles to the right to wonderful views from the highest point anywhere east of the Rockies (see **Mount Mitchell State Park** under *To See—Along the Blue Ridge Parkway*).

The parkway continues through high spruce-fir forests and frequent views to **Craggy Gardens** (see *To See—Along the Blue Ridge Parkway*), covered in purple rhododendron blossoms in June. From here the parkway descends from its mile-high perch, passing the **Folk Art Center** (see *To See—Along the Blue Ridge Parkway*) right before the end of Leg 1.

The second leg bypasses Asheville on a series of low mountains (or high hills), a forested section with few views. You'll pass the new **Blue Ridge Parkway Headquarters Building,** opened in 2001, in 1.5 miles, with an exit onto US 74A, I-40, and I-240 just beyond. In 4 more miles (after the US 23 exit) the parkway passes through the **Biltmore Estate** (see *To See—The Biltmore Estate*), but with no special views until it reaches the **French Broad River** and **NC 191** in another 4.5 miles. The entrance to the **North Carolina State Arboretum** (see *To See—Along the Blue Ridge Parkway*) is on this exit ramp.

From here, the third leg climbs steadily away from Asheville and into the wilderness. The views start immediately, over the gorge of the French Broad River; look carefully for the **Biltmore House** (see *To See—The Biltmore Estate*). In 6.5 miles, gravel **Bent Creek Road** gives access to **Lake Powhatan Recreation Area** (see *Wild Places—Recreation Areas*). A series of tunnels brings you above 4,000 feet as you approach the **NC 151** exit. Ahead are the **Pisgah Mountains** and the **Great Balsam Mountains,** the grand finale of the parkway. NC 151 provides a beautiful drive back to Asheville.

EXPLORING ON FOOT Downtown Asheville Urban Trail (828-259-5855), Asheville, NC. This 1.6-mile loop is not your ordinary downtown historic walk. A City of Asheville public arts project, the Urban Trail marks each of its 30 interpretive stations with a unique work of art. Some are solemn historic statuary with explanatory plaques, such as the monument to Elizabeth Blackwell, MD, the Ashevillian who became the first American woman to get a medical degree. However, the most notable pieces are whimsical tributes to Asheville's past. A little girl

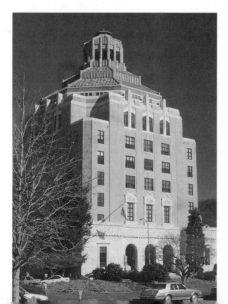

CITY HALL PLAZA IN ASHEVILLE

drinks from a fountain in City Hall Plaza; author Thomas Wolf's size-13 shoes sit outside his mother's boardinghouse; a giant flatiron, accurately reproducing one used in downtown's Asheville Laundry, stands in front of the Flat Iron Building. You might sit down on a bench to rest a spell, only to find yourself beside a bronze fiddle, a bag of apples, or a little boy; or facing dancers swirling to mountain music. Historic buildings, never completed due to timidity, rise in the glorious form imagined by their architects.

✳ Villages

Asheville, NC. Until 1889 Asheville was just another mountain town, a bit larger and more prosperous than most. By then, four rail lines had converged upon Asheville, guaranteeing its future success (at least in comparison to its neighbors). Convenient rail connections gave Asheville more than its share of the emerging mountain tourism market; from this, Asheville gained a couple of truly spectacular hotels (now, alas, gone), which in their turn attracted a more highfalutin clientele. One of these society high rollers was George Vanderbilt, grandson of the railroad magnate, who visited an Asheville hotel in 1888. A year later he returned, buying up more than 100,000 acres and creating a grand baronial estate for himself (see **The Biltmore Estate** under *To See—The Biltmore Estate*).

What followed Vanderbilt and his Biltmore Estate wasn't just more tourism. It was a cultural upheaval. Vanderbilt caused part of this directly and intentionally. Unhappy with the way American loggers destroyed their forests, Vanderbilt brought Gifford Pinchot (a German-trained forester, born in America) to his estate to develop European-style forestry practices and to teach forest conservation to the locals (see **The Cradle of Forestry in America** under *To See—Historic Sites* in "The Blue Ridge: Hendersonville and Brevard"). He founded a model village, **Biltmore Village** (see *Selective Shopping*), to provide humane and comfortable housing and stores for his workers. He started crafts schools (see **Grovewood Galleries** under *To See—Cultural Sites*), and built a cultural center for his African American workers (see **The YMI Cultural Center** under *To See— Pack Place*). All of these efforts may have fallen short of turning a raw Southern town into a sophisticated and diverse European settlement, but they certainly had their effect. Vanderbilt's indirect impact was even more important. He brought America's greatest society architect, Richard Morris Hunt, to Asheville, and America's greatest landscape planner, Frederick Law Olmsted. Hunt, in turn, hired the immensely talented Douglas D. Ellington as his chief assistant (see **Asheville City Hall Plaza** under *To See—Gardens and Parks*). Hunt, Ellington, and Olmsted all received local commissions, many from socialites attracted to Asheville by the presence of the Vanderbilts. Asheville was raw no more.

In the 1920s, Asheville's blossoming attracted investors—including land speculators looking for the next Florida. After 1925, Asheville land prices soared and building boomed, and the 1926 collapse of the Florida Land Boom only seemed to bring more land speculators to Asheville. Author Thomas Wolfe publicly ridiculed the speculators—and privately advised his mother (who ran an Asheville boardinghouse) to buy more land on credit (see **Thomas Wolfe Memorial State Historic Site** under *To See—Historic Sites*). Asheville's bubble burst in November 1930, leaving a 60-block downtown so vastly overbuilt that its gorgeous Land Boom architecture remained largely unviolated 70 years later. Careful land-use planning, instituted in the 1990s, has kept it that way, allowing the beautiful old buildings to slowly fill with wonderful small shops (see **Battery Hill Downtown Shopping District** under *Selective Shopping—Downtown Asheville*).

Black Mountain, NC. The village of Black Mountain sits in a high mountain valley 15 miles east of Asheville, NC, just off I-40. Located just below **Swannanoa Gap** on the Blue Ridge, it has historically been a major entry point to the western mountains—first by wagon road, then by the **Swannanoa Grade** railroad (see *Wandering Around—Exploring by Car or Bicycle* in "Beneath the Blue Ridge: The Catawba River Valley"). Today you'll find it a handsome small town. Its lively

THE ROADSIDE VIEW TOWARD MOUNT MITCHELL FROM LICKLOG RIDGE OVERLOOK (MP 349)

downtown fills two blocks with old brick-front stores, now filled with antiques shops, gift shops, and restaurants. Its historic train depot is now an important regional crafts gallery (see **The Old Depot Gallery and Museum** under *Selective Shopping—Black Mountain*).

Weaverville, NC. Located on the north edge of Asheville's urban area, Weaverville has managed to retain its small-town look and feel. It's one-block-long downtown lines the former US 19 with nice old brick-front stores; its handsome residential districts, with houses dating to the 1840s, host several nice B&Bs that offer a small-town ambiance within an easy drive of downtown Asheville.

Barnardsville, NC. This remote village sits along NC 197 well north of Asheville, NC, under the shadow of the **Craggy Mountains.** It has a recognizable center, but is mainly noted as a gateway to **Pisgah National Forest**'s extensive and spectacular holdings in the Craggies. You'll find the turnoff to Barnardsville (pronounced BAR-nurds-vill) well signposted on the US 19/23 freeway 14 miles north of Asheville, then 6 miles east on NC 197. To reach the Pisgah Forest lands, take Dillingham Road (SSR 2173) south from the village center—an attractive drive with some lovely surprises.

✳ Wild Places

The Great Forests Mount Mitchell and the Black Mountains. Quite simply, this is the highest mountain range in the East. In the mid–19th century New Englanders were astonished to learn that Mount Mitchell (see Mount Mitchell State Park under To See—Along the Blue Ridge Highway), the tallest of the Blacks at 6,682 feet, was taller than New Hampshire's impressive Mount Washington (6,288 feet). By the end of that century, people knew that eight Black Mountain peaks topped Mount Washington, and the entire ridgeline stayed above 6,000 feet almost continuously for 13 miles.

The Black Mountains and the **Craggy Mountains** run together at **Balsam Gap**—a beautiful 22.7-mile drive north of Asheville's US 70 on the Blue Ridge Parkway. The parkway parallels the **Black Mountain Crest** for the next 4.6 miles to the **Mount Mitchell Spur Road,** NC 128, on the left. This spur road then parallels the Black Mountain Crest for 4.8 miles, finally reaching 6,500 feet at a parking lot a quarter mile below Mount Mitchell. A short, easy path leads a quarter mile to the peak, with spectacular views. A hiking trail, made difficult by craggy, boulder-strewn terrain, continues along the crest of the Blacks to its end.

The Craggy Mountains. Rising from the northeast edge of the City of Asheville, the aptly named Great Craggy Mountains quickly reach above a mile in elevation and beyond, with the tallest peak topping 6,000 feet. The highest peaks are characterized by sharp crags and thick heath balds—a beautiful but impenetrable combination of rhododendron, mountain laurel, azalea, and blueberry. Its most beautiful peak is **Craggy Gardens** (see *To See—Along the Blue Ridge Parkway*), where the thick heath is broken by wide areas of grassy meadows and wildflowers, for wide views framed by deep purple rhododendrons. The Blue Ridge Parkway traverses the high gaps of the Craggies, passing above a mile in elevation in 17 miles from Asheville's US 70—on a hot summer day, an easy and most pleasant drive. It gives easy access to the **Mountains-to-Sea Trail** (see A Walk in the Middle Prong Wilderness under *Wandering Around—Trails of the Great Balsam Mountains* in "Waynesville and the Blue Ridge Parkway"), running along ridgetops previously too thickly grown with heath to be accessible, now giving wide views from rock ledges. The western slopes of the Craggies are mainly owned by Pisgah National Forest and have a large number of fascinating hiking trails as well as several gravel forest roads well worth exploring with a high-clearance vehicle; access is mainly from **Barnardsville,** NC (see *Villages*). The east slope, wild and stunningly beautiful, is the **Asheville Watershed,** which is closed to the public.

The Bent Creek Forests (828-667-5261), 1577 Brevard Road, Asheville, NC. This tract of Pisgah National Forest, on the southwest edge of Asheville, NC, centers on the watershed of Bent Creek, a 6,000-acre bowl surrounded by 3,500-foot ridgelines. George Vanderbilt consolidated this tract in 1909 from 70-odd small farms and homes, because it linked his estate with his huge **Pisgah Forest** (see *Wild Places—The Great Forests* in "The Blue Ridge: Hendersonville and Brevard") holdings, and because it was in the middle of the view from his terrace. Seven years later, his widow sold it to the U.S. Forest Service for $5 an acre. Since 1925, the bulk of this land, including all of the Bent Creek watershed, has been managed as the **Bent Creek Experimental Forest.** At first the forest was dedicated to experiments in regrowing healthy hardwood forests on devastated lands, but since World War II the experiments have concentrated on managing mountain hardwood forests for their logging resources. Two large tracts have been carved out of the experimental forest for recreational users: the **North Carolina State Arboretum** (see *To See—Along the Blue Ridge Parkway*) and **Lake Powhatan Recreation Area** (see *Recreation Areas*). A network of trails wanders through all parts of the forest, most of them open to mountain bikes and horses as well as walkers. Its ready accessibility (and relatively easy gradients) make this a popular area.

RECREATION AREAS Lake Powhatan Recreation Area. This Pisgah National Forest recreation area sits just outside **Asheville**, NC, off NC 191, in the **Bent Creek Experimental Forest** (see The Bent Creek Forests under *The Great Forests*). It has a large lake with a swimming beach, picnic facilities, and campgrounds. A large network of hiking trails, very popular with Ashevillians, spreads throughout the surrounding hills, and an easy gravel road leads uphill to the Blue Ridge Parkway.

PICNIC AREAS Lake Tomahawk Park, Black Mountain, NC. This town park centers on a lovely little lake surrounded by a walking path. As well as picnicking, you'll find tennis, golf (see **Black Mountain Municipal Golf Course** under *To Do—Golf*), swimming, and croquet. Lake Tomahawk is the venue for Black Mountain's **Park Rhythms** summer music series (see *Entertainment—Black Mountain*).

Montford City Park is a full-service recreational park located on Montford Avenue about a mile north of downtown **Asheville**, NC. This attractive city park has a gardenlike appearance—well kept, deeply shaded, and climbing a steep hill in stone terraces.

✷ To See

ALONG THE BLUE RIDGE PARKWAY Mount Mitchell State Park (828-675-4611), milepost 355, right on NC 128, Burnsville, NC. Open 8 AM–9 PM in summer; closes earlier at other times of the year. Free admission. This 1,700-acre state park centers on the highest peak in the East—6,684-foot Mount Mitchell, more than 1.25 miles above sea level. The park stretches along the high ridgeline of the **Black Mountains,** with three other 6,000-foot peaks in its 2.5-mile length. The remainder of the Blacks are largely owned by Pisgah National Forest (see **South Toe River Forests** under *Wild Places—The Great Forests* in "Behind the Blue Ridge: Spruce Pine and Burnsville"), with a large chunk of the western slopes in private hands. A spur road runs from the Blue Ridge Parkway to the park, a 2.5-mile drive through the Pisgah Forest lands, just below the crest of the Black Mountains (and beneath two more 6,000-foot peaks). At the park entrance the road passes above 6,000 feet, offering wide meadow views, and stays above 6,000 feet to its end on Mount Mitchell. The road continues to climb along the Black Mountain crest, through subarctic spruce-fir forests, reaching 6,200 feet at the **Mount Mitchell Restaurant** in 1.25 miles; this full-service restaurant serves up good country food and wonderful views. Beyond the restaurant, the road slabs up Mount Mitchell to gain the ridge again at 6,400 feet, with some good roadside views. From there it passes 250 feet beneath the peak of Mount Mitchell to end on the ridgeline a bit downhill from the summit. Here you'll find plenty of parking, a first-rate picnic area, a snack bar, and a small visitors center. Expect it to be cold and blowy, even in summer. The wide, easy path to the summit passes through forests and wildflower meadows to reach the peak in a quarter mile, after climbing 125 feet. A contemporary-styled concrete tower allows you to climb above the trees for a 360-degree view, with the entire eastern United States beneath your feet.

Craggy Gardens. This recreation area on the Blue Ridge Parkway takes in the three highest peaks of the Craggy Mountains: **Craggy Dome**, **Craggy Pinnacle,** and **Craggy Gardens.** The views are great—but there is more here than views from high mountains. Each June, the Craggies have one of the finest rhododendron displays in the mountains.

Driving up the parkway from Asheville, you enter the Craggies at **Potato Field Gap,** milepost 368, with views leftward over the town of Woodfin's watershed. In 0.5 mile, a paved spur road leads left 1.25 miles to **Craggy Gardens Picnic Area,** a lovely tree-shaded meadow. This is the lower end of the **Craggy Gardens Trail,** climbing 400 feet in 0.75 mile to Craggy Gardens, a stunning natural rhododendron garden. Here you'll find wide views over grassy meadows, framed in June and July by huge mounds of purple Catawba rhododendrons mixed with rosebay rhododendrons, flame azaleas, blueberries, and mountain laurels.

Back at the parkway, the road curves along a breathtaking ledge to reach **Pinnacle Gap,** with wide views in both directions. Here a tiny visitors center has several exhibits about the Craggy Mountains and a gift shop. Here too is the uphill end of the Craggy Gardens Trail. From here Catawba rhododendrons line the parkway and frame changing views over the Asheville watershed. **Craggy Pinnacle Overlook** is a half mile from the visitors center, with wide views that improve dramatically as you walk up the easy path to the rhododendron-covered summit.

 ⛰ **The Folk Art Center and Allenstand Craft Shop** (828-298-7928), milepost 382, Blue Ridge Parkway, Asheville, NC. Open daily 9–6 (9–5 January through March). Free admission. Founded in 1930 to help poor mountain folk refine their crafts skills and find markets for their crafts, the **Southern Highland Craft Guild (SHCG)** has evolved into a juried membership organization of crafts artists from a large area centered on the Southern Appalachian Mountains. In the 1970s the National Park Service collaborated with the SHCG to provide a facility to interpret Southern Appalachian mountain culture on the Blue Ridge Parkway. To achieve this, the Park Service built the present Folk Art Center, a large building on the Blue Ridge Parkway just north of US 70, and turned it over the SHCG. The guild has used this building by moving their Allenstand Craft Shop into it from downtown Asheville and by installing a medium-sized gallery in an upstairs mezzanine. Although the gallery features items from the guild's collection of 3,500 mountain-crafts pieces, for the most part it displays contemporary art by its current members, with university-trained fine artists far outnumbering native mountain folk crafters.

🐾   **The North Carolina State Arboretum** (828-665-2492), 100 Frederick Law Olmsted Way, Asheville, NC. The gardens are open daily 8 AM–9 PM. Buildings may keep shorter hours. Free admission. Founded in 1992, this 426-acre arboretum has elaborate formal and informal gardens, greenhouses, educational programs, and miles of walking paths. As part of the University of North Carolina, it is dedicated to conserving native plant resources and educating the public. Beyond that, it's darned pretty, even though (at 10 years old) few of the gardens are mature and some haven't been built yet. The entrance drive, off the Blue Ridge Parkway at the NC 191 exit, is spectacular—beautifully landscaped in an unobtrusive style that includes a viaduct over a delicate stream environment. The handsome main building of stone and gray wood combines contemporary architecture with such homey touches as a large porch with rocking chairs. Outside stretch a series of contemporary formal gardens, designed by the original architect and rather severe and intellectual. More successful is the informal garden beneath the porch and stretching down the mountainside. Known as Plants of Promise (or POP), it contains a riot of native garden plants, both showy and practical, in a setting designed by the arboretum staff and maintained with home garden equipment and methods. Behind the main building are the greenhouses, now the source of nearly all the seasonal and potted plants in the arboretum. Paths stretch downhill through forests to reach **Bent Creek** (see The Bent Creek Forests under *Wild Places—The Great Forests*), where an old road has been converted to a walking and biking path. Along the creek are more gardens, both existing and planned. The most interesting for a May visit is the **National Azalea Repository,** containing all but two of the native American azalea species. In planning is a disabled-accessible trout garden along Bent Creek, with fishing encouraged.

THE BILTMORE ESTATE The Biltmore Estate (828-255-3400; 1-800-543-2961), One North Pack Square, Asheville, NC, is located on US 25, 0.25 mile north of I 40, exit 50. The mailing address is for the administrative offices in downtown Asheville. Open January through March: all week 9–5; April through December: all week 8:30–5. Locations within the estate may have different hours. One-day admission to grounds, house, and winery: adults $29.95; youths ages 10–15, $22.50; children 9 and younger, free with paying adult; second consecutive day $7. An annual pass costs less than the price of 2 nonconsecutive days.

In 1889, 28-year-old George Vanderbilt decided to become a medieval nobleman. The grandson of railroad tycoon Cornelius Vanderbilt, George was a sensitive and intellectual young man who left the coarse work of running the family enterprises to his older brothers. Like many of the Victorian aristocracy, he looked back on medieval Europe as a happy, stable society where the laboring classes found satisfaction through fine craftsmanship while the nobility watched over all with fatherly concern. Vanderbilt wanted to create such a society with himself as the nobleman, and chose Asheville as the site.

TULIPS BLOOM OUTSIDE THE VISITORS EDUCATION CENTER AT THE NORTH CAROLINA STATE ARBORETUM

George Vanderbilt had discovered Asheville on his many travels. He loved the mild climate and the scenic beauty, and appreciated the advantages of forming a great estate from cheap Appalachian land. And Vanderbilt had a very large estate in mind. Before he was done he had purchased 125,000 acres—nearly 200 square miles stretching from the southern edge of Asheville to the Pisgah Mountains on the far horizon. He then assembled a remarkable team of experts to convert this tired-out land into a noble demesne: leading architect Richard Morris Hunt to design the house; Frederick Law Olmsted, the designer of Central Park and the U.S. Capitol grounds, to design the gardens and develop a management plan; and America's first forester, Gifford Pinchot (see **The Cradle of Forestry in America** under *To See—Historic Sites* in "The Blue Ridge: Hendersonville and Brevard"), to restore and manage 100,000 acres of logged-out forest. He had Hunt build the largest house in America, a 250-room French chateau, and emparked this house with several hundred acres of Olmsted's gardens. Beyond the gardens he laid out a thousand acres of farmland and dairy to establish the self-sufficiency of a great medieval estate. He built a medieval village at the estate gates, today's **Biltmore Village** (see *Selective Shopping*), to provide his workers with housing and shops.

After George Vanderbilt's death in 1914, his wife continued to live on the estate and manage its farms and forests, becoming the first woman president of North Carolina's agricultural society. Being more of a practical manager than a medieval baroness, she sold 87,000 acres of forest to the U.S. Department of Agriculture (run by her husband's old employee Gifford Pinchot), to form the nucleus of **Pisgah National Forest** (see Driving through Pisgah National Forest under *Wandering Around—Exploring by Car* in "The Blue Ridge: Hendersonville and Brevard"). She sold off Biltmore Village and other holdings as well, shrinking the estate to a mere 11,000 acres. When she remarried and moved north, her daughter and son-in-law, Cornelia and John Cecil, continued to live in Biltmore, opening it to the public in 1930.

The Vanderbilt heirs ceased living at Biltmore in 1958 but have continued to run it as a self-sufficient estate; it is now owned by John and Cornelia's son and grandson, who run it as a profit-making, tax-paying enterprise. Currently possessing 8,000 acres, the estate continues its extensive farming and forestry operations as well as a distinguished winery and vineyard. But the core of the estate remains the house and gardens, carefully preserved and restored to reflect the way it looked to George and Edith Vanderbilt, an Appalachian lord and lady at the height of the Gilded Age.

&. **The Biltmore House,** Asheville, NC. Open all week 9–5:30. The entrance fee is included in the price of the estate admission ticket (see The Biltmore Estate, above). "Behind the Scenes" and "Roof" tours are extra. Famed architect Richard Morris Hunt personally supervised the construction of this 250-room French chateau from 1889 to 1895, and helped its owner, George Vanderbilt, pick out the furniture in a series of European buying sprees. Today, still fully furnished as in Vanderbilt's day and immaculately preserved by his heirs, the Biltmore House is completely overwhelming.

The front entrance is a delightful surprise—a bright, open place, where white marble floors surround a glass-roofed atrium, opening into arches that lead into great spaces. This is the **Winter Garden,** with its great palms overhanging rattan and bamboo garden furniture. To one side of the entrance is the grandest room in the house, the baronial **Banquet Hall**—a huge space with a barrel-vaulted wooden ceiling 70 feet high, five gigantic 16th-century Flemish tapestries, and a leaf table that expands to hold 64 guests. Opposite the hall, the **Library** has balconied two-story-tall walls, completely covered with 10,000 books—less than half of Vanderbilts' personal collection.

Walk onto any one of a series of terraces that line the rear of the house, and one of the grandest views in the region opens up. Meadows and glades drop away from the steep stone sides of the terraces to the farmland lining the French Broad River far below. Then, after miles of steeply rolling forest lands, the grand clifflike sides of the Pisgah Range form a tall, unbroken wall along the horizon. Vanderbilt owned this view; every bit of land in this wide panorama was his.

Upstairs, on the second and third floors, are the family's private quarters and a large number of guest rooms. Vanderbilt disliked formal entertainment, but he enjoyed having house guests, informal house parties of the sort popular in the great houses of Europe. There were so many guests, and so many guest rooms, that Vanderbilt had the halls color-coded so that guests would know where they were. Downstairs, the basement housed servants' quarters, kitchen and laundry facilities, and indoor recreation rooms, including a swimming pool, bowling alley, and gymnasium.

In all, the self-guided house tour leads through 23 rooms upstairs and 11 rooms downstairs, and has disabled access. Two other tours, each requiring an additional payment and at least six flights of steps, take visitors through closed portions of the house, from the fourth-floor servants' quarters to the Victorian boilers and electric panels in the sub-basement; and up onto the roof for sweeping views.

Biltmore Gardens, Asheville, NC. Open all week 9 AM–dusk. The entrance fee is included in the price of the estate admission ticket (see the Biltmore Estate, above). Designed by Frederick Law Olmsted after he had already completed New York's Central Park, the Biltmore Gardens flow downhill from the house, covering several hundred acres. Formal gardens, patterned after Italian Renaissance styles, frame the house and offer striking views both of the house and the mountains beyond. Then, downhill from the house's Italianate gardens, an informal **Ramble** allows visitors to explore an intimate mountain draw covered with flowering shrubs. Beneath the Ramble is a large, formal **Walled Garden,** patterned after the gardens found in English country houses, and ending in a large and impressive series of glasshouses called the **Conservatory,** with displays of delicate tropical vegetation. Beneath the Walled Garden stretch a series of intriguing informal gardens spread about the mountain slopes and reaching down a long series of paths. Most notable here is the stunning **Azalea Garden,** with an extensive collection of local and exotic azaleas, and the beautiful **Bass Pond and Waterfall,** recently restored to its original appearance.

The exit road takes visitors through parts of the garden, including the Walled Garden, the Conservatory (with a parking lot), and the Bass Pond. The estate's brochure, included with the admission ticket, has an excellent and detailed map of the garden's many twisting paths.

The Biltmore Winery, Asheville, NC. Open January through March: Monday through Saturday 11–6, Sunday noon–6; April through December: Monday through Saturday 11–7, Sunday noon–7. The entrance fee is included in the price of the estate admissions ticket (see The Biltmore Estate, above). Biltmore opened its ambitious winery in 1985, in a dairy barn designed by Richard Morris Hunt and built as part of the original estate construction. The short winery tour includes a 7-minute video and a self-guided walk through the wine-making areas and the basement. The tour ends with a delightful private tasting in the old calf barn, where you can interact with wine-serving bartenders at U-shaped bars. The wines include one of Biltmore's top-end estate-grown wines,

PACK PLACE IN DOWNTOWN ASHEVILLE

plus several white and red blends of North Carolina and California grapes. Those interested in tasting more of Biltmore's estate wines and champagnes can pay $5 for an additional tasting.

Biltmore Shops and Restaurants, Asheville, NC. There is quite a variety of shops and eateries within the estate that are available only to ticket holders. The largest concentration of these is by the house, in the old stables. Here are shops that specialize in Victorian-style gifts, Biltmore wines, Christmas items, old-fashioned toys and candies, and books related to local sites, Victorian arts and crafts, and the Vanderbilts. Food service includes the **Stable Café** (open 11–5), an ice cream parlor, and a bakery. In the Winery is another gift shop with Biltmore wines and other food and gift items, as well as **The Bistro** (open 11–9), serving lunch and dinner. Finally, a **garden shop** located at the Conservatory offers plants from the Biltmore nurseries and a variety of garden items. The **Deerpark Restaurant,** also on the estate, is open to the public for buffet lunches.

The estate's eateries are not cheap. Visitors who wish to spend less on lunch can find a large variety of good local cafés in Biltmore Village (see **Trevi** under *Eating Out*) immediately outside the main gate. Your ticket allows you to leave the estate and reenter on the same day.

PACK PLACE Pack Place (828-257-4500), 2 South Pack Square, Asheville, NC. Open Tuesday through Saturday 10–5; Sunday (June through October only) 1–5; closed Monday. Pack Place will sell you combined tickets at various complex prices (every tenant sets its own price rules), or you can buy tickets separately at each venue (combined tickets are cheaper). A combined adult ticket costs $14. Located on downtown Asheville's **Pack Square,** this **arts and sciences center**'s small entrance is deceiving. Behind the entrance, a large complex of museums, public spaces, and the **Diana Wortham Theater** (see *Entertainment—Asheville*) stretches back through several buildings, including the marble-clad 1920s neoclassical **Asheville Public Library** building. The not-for-profit Pack Place Foundation runs the multilevel public area at the center of the complex, including the fascinating free exhibition on the history of the square. Off the public area are three independent museums—the art museum, the gem and mineral museum, and the hands-on health museum. Behind The Diana Wortham Theater, in its own historic building, is the YMI Cultural Center, a major part of Asheville's African American community.

&. ⊤ **The Asheville Art Museum** (828-253-3227), Pack Place, Asheville, NC. See Pack Place listing for hours. Adults $6, children and seniors $5. Additional fees may apply for selected exhibitions. Founded in 1948 by a group of Asheville-area artists, this museum has a permanent collection of over 1,500 pieces of 20th-century art. Part of the Pack Place Center, it occupies much of the Italian Renaissance public library adjacent to Pack Square. The museum wanders through three stories of display space, with two or three exhibitions going at any one time. As you might expect, the permanent exhibitions emphasize western North Carolina, with one gallery displaying art inspired by the Blue Ridge Mountains from the 19th century to the present, and another displaying pieces by the contemporary crafts masters of the western mountains. However, the displays are by no means limited to area artists, and pieces by nationally known figures are splashed throughout the museum.

✔ &. ⊤ **Colburn Gem and Mineral Museum** (828-254-7162), Pack Place, Asheville, NC. See Pack Place listing for hours. Adults $4, students $3. Founded in 1960, this first-rate museum combines an extensive collection of North Carolina gems and minerals with educational and interpretive exhibits aimed at families with children. Exhibits include locally mined precious stones, mountain building, and mountain minerals. Summer field trips lead to some of the most fascinating and little-known corners of the Asheville area.

✔ &. ⊤ **The Health Adventure** (828-254-6373), Pack Place, Asheville, NC. See Pack Place listing for hours. Adults $4, students $3. Founded in 1968, this is a hands-on health and science museum. Originally a museum for school children, the administrators have been expanding the exhibits to appeal to adults and older children, and to include biology and physics as well as health.

✔ &. ⊤ **The YMI Cultural Center** (828-252-4614), Pack Place, Asheville, NC. See Pack Place listing for hours. Adults $4, students $3. George Vanderbilt constructed this National Register Tudor-style brick building as a cultural center for his African American workmen. Originally known as the Young Men's Institute, it continues to this day as the YMI Cultural Center. Exhibitions on African American arts and history, particularly in the Asheville area, are always featured, as are plays, storytelling, and hands-on craft classes. Considered part of Pack Place, its building is across the street from Pack Place, to the south.

HISTORIC SITES &. **Vance Birthplace State Historic Site** (828-645-6706), 911 Reems Creek Road, Weaverville, NC. Only the visitors center, rest rooms, and picnic area are fully disabled accessible. Open April through October: Monday through Saturday, 9–5; Sunday 1–5. November through March: Tuesday through Saturday 10–4; Sunday 1–4. Free admission. This log farmstead east of Weaverville accurately reconstructs the early-19th-century birthplace of Zebulon B. Vance, one of North Carolina's most beloved politicians. In the mid–19th century, Vance led the movement to democratize North Carolina's patrician planter-controlled government; during the Civil War, Governor Vance (an anti-Confederate and anti-secessionist, but not a Unionist) protected North Carolina from lawlessness, preserved civil liberties, and sheltered his state from the Confederate government's worst excesses. This state historic site memorializes his life and presents an accurate picture of the frontier mountain life that shaped his boyhood.

THE KITCHEN OF A LOG FARMHOUSE IS ON VIEW AT THE ZEBULON VANCE STATE HISTORIC SITE.

167

ASHEVILLE & THE BLUE RIDGE PARKWAY

The farmstead is a well-crafted two-story log home, set on a grassy hill, shaded by large old trees, and surrounded by mountains. It has been carefully furnished to reflect the frontier period of Vance's boyhood. A vegetable garden separates the farmhouse from several log outbuildings—a weaving house with a period loom, a toolhouse, a smokehouse, a corncrib, a springhouse, and a slaves' house. Beautiful views stretch from the split-rail "worm" fence, past the log buildings, and to the mountains beyond.

Throughout the season, this is a venue for various programs interpreting early life on the mountain frontier (see **Fall Pioneer Days** under *Special Events*). There's also a visitors center with a small museum on Vance's life.

☂ **Smith-McDowell House Museum** (828-253-9231), 283 Victoria Road, Asheville, NC. Open May through December: Tuesday through Saturday 10–4; Sunday 1–4. $4.50. One of the oldest brick houses in the area, this 1840 house sits on a hilltop south of downtown Asheville, on what is now the campus of Asheville-Buncombe Technical Community College. The postfrontier farmhouse of a prominent family, this handsome, symmetric structure sports first- and second-story full front porches, and double fireplaces on each gable end. Now a historical museum, different rooms are furnished for different periods of the house's 19th-century heyday. The kitchen shows the earliest period, the 1840s; a bedroom reflects more prosperous antebellum tastes; and the parlor and dining room show the style of the succeeding generation. The garden behind the house preserves a design of Frederick Law Olmsted, executed during his days at the nearby Biltmore Estate (see **Biltmore Gardens** under *To See—The Biltmore Estate*).

Thomas Wolfe Memorial State Historic Site (828-253-8304), 52 North Market Street, Asheville, NC. Open April through October: Monday through Saturday 9–5; Sunday 1–5. November through March: Tuesday through Saturday 10–4; Sunday 1–4. Free admission. Author Thomas Wolfe, acclaimed for his autobiographical novels during the 1930s, spent his childhood in his mother's boardinghouse, **My Old Kentucky Home,** on the eastern edge of the Lexington Hill section of downtown Asheville. That boardinghouse, and the town of Asheville, became the thinly veiled subject of his most famous novel, *Look Homeward, Angel: A Story of the Buried Life,* published in 1929 to high acclaim (and great embarrassment among Asheville's worthies). Today, the boardinghouse and a modern visitors center make up the Thomas Wolfe Memorial. For many years the boardinghouse has fronted a pedestrianized street opposite a downtown hotel tower, furnished as it was when Wolfe lived there in the 1910s, and housing a considerable collection of Wolfe memorabilia and artifacts. An arsonist brought this to a halt in 1998, causing massive destruction to the house and collection. Fortunately, most of the collection has been salvaged and restored, and the house's reconstruction started in late 2001. Until the house can reopen, the visitors center houses a display of Wolfe artifacts and an audiovisual show on Wolfe's life and works. Consult the official web page for updates on the restoration.

The Grove Arcade (828-252-7799), 29½ Page Avenue, Asheville, NC. This astonishing 1920s downtown mall is expected to reopen for shopping in 2002—for the first time in 60 years. It's a five-story elaborately decorated structure covering two entire city blocks in downtown Asheville's Battery Hill shopping district (see **Battery Hill Downtown Shopping District** under *Selective Shopping—Downtown Asheville*). Outer walls are covered with terra-cotta tiles and limestone; stone-carved lions and gryphons guard the entrance. Built by the developer of the **Grove Park Inn Resort** (see *Lodging*) in 1929, it functioned successfully as an "indoor market" throughout the Depression, only to be taken over by the federal government in 1942 as part of the war effort. In 1995 the City of Asheville bought it from the Feds with the intent of restoring it to its original glory. The public market is scheduled to open in 2002, with 70 stores—all local, and many specializing in unique local products.

CULTURAL SITES Grovewood Galleries (828-253-7651), 111 Grovewood Road, Asheville, NC. Open Monday through Saturday 10–6; Sunday 1–5. This collection of two museums, a gallery, and a lovely little café occupy a group of historic buildings in their own little garden by the **Grove Park Inn Resort** (see *Lodging*). To find the Grovewood Galleries, go to the Grove Park Inn, enter its parking lot, and follow the signs. This complex was erected by the Vanderbilts (see **The Biltmore Estate** under *To See—The Biltmore Estate*) in 1901, as a training school for traditional mountain weavers and woodworkers. After George Vanderbilt's death, his widow sold the school to the adjacent Grove Park Inn Resort, which added three English cottage–style buildings to the complex in 1917. From then until the 1980s, the small complex produced fine homespun cloth for the crafts market. Independent of the Grove Park Inn since 1942, Grovewood became a crafters' center again in the 1990s. Its large fine-crafts gallery represents regional crafts artists in a wide variety of media, including a large furniture gallery. It rotates solo exhibits every two months or so, and has actively supported artists' groups in areas such as woodworking and jewelry. Adjacent are two museums, one dedicated to the Vanderbilt's school and the homespun industry of the early 20th century, and the other with a collection of 30 antique cars. All of these buildings front on a lovely tree-shaded garden, with sculptures scattered about, and a wide view over the Grove Park Inn and its golf course toward downtown Asheville.

A FOOTBRIDGE IS SURROUNDED BY SPRING BLOOM AT THE BOTANICAL GARDENS AT ASHEVILLE

Montreat (828-669-2911; 1-800-572-2257), NC 9, Montreat, NC. This retreat is located at the end of NC 9, 2 miles north of Black Mountain, NC. Of the 20 or so religious retreats and conference centers, Montreat is one of the two most worthwhile for a visit, as well as being friendly toward a casual visitor (the other being **Lake Junaluska** (see The Town of Lake Junaluska under *Villages* in "Waynesville and the Blue Ridge Parkway"). Founded in 1897 and now run by the Presbyterian Church USA, Montreat is really a town in itself, combining its major retreat center with a liberal arts college and a collection of summer homes, all grouped around a lovely recreation center on **Lake Susan.** Montreat features a major concentration of early- 20th-century resort architecture, from its impressive front gate (now permanently open) to the large and beautiful **Assembly Inn,** built of local stone. Historic stone and wood buildings face Lake Susan on one side; a gardenlike park lines the other. Uphill, winding gravel roads lead past early-20th-century cottages to reach various **hiking trails.** The best known and most popular trail follows the old Mount Mitchell Road, abandoned in 1940 in favor of the Blue Ridge Parkway.

GARDENS AND PARKS The Botanical Gardens at Asheville (828-252-5190), 151 W. T. Weaver Boulevard, Asheville, NC. Free admission. This 10-acre garden in central Asheville is dedicated to preserving and exhibiting the native plants of the western North Carolina mountains in their natural surroundings. Designed in 1960 by Doan Ogden, the gardens follow a narrow draw formed by Reed Creek. Four bridges cross the creek, each with its own view. Special environments include a Sunshine Garden, a Woods Garden, a Rock Garden, a Heath and Azalea Garden, and a Garden for the Blind, emphasizing textures and smells. Also on the property are a historic log cabin and earthworks from a Civil War skirmish. This volunteer-run garden sponsors regular walks and talks, as well as plant sales.

Asheville City Hall Plaza, Asheville, NC. This urban park covers four blocks of downtown Asheville, between Pack Square and the seats of local government—Asheville's City Hall and the **Buncombe County Courthouse.** It's a lovely place to stop and rest, with ample tree-shaded benches and well-kept flower beds. Its courthouse is an attractive 1927 neoclassical "skyscraper" of 17 stories, with an elaborately decorated interior. However, the real star of the square is City Hall, a 1927 nine-story art deco masterpiece in rich gold brick, white limestone, and rose terra-cotta trim. Its octagonal stepped roof is topped by a tall torch-shaped carillon belfry, all covered in pink terra-cotta tile with green accents. Its architect, Ashevillian Douglas D. Ellington, designed several other stunners within an easy walking distance—the adjacent **Fire Department,** the octagonal **First Baptist Church** two blocks north, and the **S&W Cafeteria Building** two blocks south.

Riverside Cemetery (828-258-8480), 53 Birch Street, Asheville, NC. Open Monday through Friday 8–4:30. Free admission. This 87-acre historic cemetery, owned by the City of Asheville and operated by the city's Parks and Recreation, features parklike grounds with winding hillside paths, large shade trees, many dogwoods and azaleas—and more than 9,000 unusual headstones, monuments, and mausoleums. In use since the Civil War, it holds the graves of such notable Ashevillians as O. Henry, Thomas Wolfe, and Governor Zeb Vance. It's a popular place to stroll on a warm spring day.

✐ ᾖ **Western North Carolina Nature Center** (828-298-5600), 75 Gashes Creek Road, Asheville, NC. Open daily 10–5. Adults $5, children $3. Run by Buncombe County Parks and Recreation, this large and sophisticated nature-study museum concentrates on the animals and plants of the western North Carolina mountains, occupying 42 acres on the east side of Asheville, off NC 81. Much of the museum is taken up with live animal and plant displays that put their subjects in their environmental context. Habitat displays include predators (red wolves, black wolves, cougars, and bobcats), river otters, turkeys, deer, and bears. A **Nocturnal Hall** displays animals found only at night—bats, owls, rabbits, flying squirrels. The **Educational Farm** has farm animals (including a petting area) and exhibits. The **Main Hall** has 75 live animal exhibits and encourages touching (except for the poisonous snakes and spiders). There are also raccoons, foxes, turtles, hawks, and eagles, as well as a log cabin, herb garden, and nature trail.

✷ To Do

BALLOONING Mount Pisgah Balloons (828-667-9943), 1410 Pisgah Highway (NC 151), Asheville, NC. Reservations are necessary. $130 per person. A hot-air balloon dealer and certified Federal Aviation Administration (FAA) repair shop with more than 20 years' experience, this company offers 1-hour flights in one of the most beautiful corners of the Asheville area. **Hominy Valley,** southwest of town, offers unspoiled pastoral beauty framed by 5,000-foot peaks, including **Mount Pisgah.**

BICYCLING Epic Cycles (828-669-5969), 108 Black Mountain Avenue, Black Mountain, NC. This full-service bike shop rents bikes and offers detailed information on area trails.

Bio-Wheels (828-232-0300), 76 Biltmore Avenue (US 25), Asheville, NC. This large bicycle shop on the south edge of downtown Asheville offers rentals and tours, with your choice of off-road mountain biking, road touring, or leisure biking.

Liberty Bicycles (828-684-1085; 1-800-962-4537), 1987 Hendersonville Road (US 25), Asheville, NC. This full-service bike shop, south of Asheville, is popular with the area's serious bicyclists and rents mountain bikes.

FISHING Lake Julian County Park, Asheville, NC, is located on Asheville's south side, off I-26, exit 6, then east 0.5 mile on NC 146. This county park centers on a large cooling pond used for a major regional power plant, "Lake Julian," covering some 300 acres. Wilderness it's not, but the fishing is excellent, with an abundance of bass, catfish, brim, crappie, and talapia. Jonboat rentals are available ($15 per day). Fishing permits $3 per day.

Hunter Banks Co. (828-252-3005; 1-800-227-6732), 29 Montford Avenue, Asheville, NC. You'll find the store located just north of downtown Asheville, off I-240's Montford Street exit. Half day $150, full day $250; includes lunch. This large fly shop, occupying a fine old brick store in Asheville's historic Montford section, offers guide services to local trout streams. Their web site is worth a peek for its detailed stream reports and fly recommendations.

Also see **Black Dome Mountain Sports** under *Rock Climbing*.

GOLF Grove Park Inn Resort (828-252-2711), 290 Macon Avenue, Asheville, NC. $80. This scenic course sits in a historic neighborhood a short distance north of downtown Asheville, overlooked by the mammoth stone-built Grove Park Inn and Beaucatcher

Mountain. Built in 1899, the course was substantially redesigned by Donald Ross in 1923; a major renovation was completed in 2001.

Great Smokies Holiday Inn Sun Spree Resort (828-253-5874), 1 Holiday Inn Drive, Asheville, NC. In the center of Asheville, the course is just off I-240. $30. This 18-hole 1976 course sits on a hilltop overlooking the French Broad River and downtown Asheville.

Buncombe County Golf Course (828-298-1867), 226 Fairway Drive, Asheville, NC. $20. Designed in 1927 by Donald Ross, this 18-hole par-72 course is located on the east side of Asheville, just off US 70. The front 9 holes parallel the Swannanoa River, while the back nine climb a fairly substantial hill with narrow, short fairways. Built as part of a 1920s subdivision, it's now surrounded by a pleasant urban neighborhood and run by Buncombe County Parks and Recreation as a fully public course.

Reems Creek Golf Course (828-645-4393), 36 Pink Fox Cove Road, Weaverville, NC. $42–49. This 1984 course, designed by English firm Hawtree and Son, sits among the Blue Ridge Mountains east of Weaverville. Rated four star by *Golf Digest*, its scenery is particularly beautiful.

Black Mountain Municipal Golf Course (828-669-2710). $20. This 1929 18-hole public course has hilly terrain, water on most holes, and spectacular mountain scenery. While most greens are short, #17 is 747 yards, par 6.

HORSEBACK RIDING Biltmore Estate Equestrian Center (828-277-4485), 1 Biltmore Estate Drive, Asheville, NC. The **Biltmore Estate**'s stables (see *To See—The Biltmore*

THE FRENCH BROAD RIVER IS THE SETTING
FOR A VARIETY OF WATERSPORTS.

Estate) offer riding on 100 miles of
estate trails constructed by George
Vanderbilt in the 1890s.

⚲ **Berry Patch Stables** (828-645-
7271), 300 Bairds Cove Road, Asheville, NC. Located just north of
Asheville off old US 19, this stable
offers trail rides, camps, lessons, and
pony rides.

ROCK CLIMBING ClimbMax (828-
252-9996), 43 Wall Street, Asheville,
NC. Located in the Wall Street shopping district, this complete climbing
shop has equipment and a large indoor
climbing wall in addition to guide services for day trips and overnighters.

⚲ **Mountain Adventure Guides,
Inc.** (828-255-7577), Asheville, NC.
This adventure guiding service offers
all levels of rock climbing that includes
equipment, with beginner instructions
for children as young as eight. They
also offer guided day hiking and backpacking.

Black Dome Mountain Sports (828-
251-2001), 140 Tunnel Road (US 70),
Asheville, NC. This large outdoor sup-
plier is located in its own building just

east of downtown Asheville and is
worth a visit. They offer guide services
for rock climbing, fly-fishing, and
backpacking.

**WHITEWATER AND STILLWATER
ADVENTURES** The **French Broad
River,** running for many miles straight
through the middle of the Asheville,
NC, area, furnishes a wide range of
recreational opportunities, from dramatic Class III and IV rapids near
Hot Springs, NC (see *Villages* in
"Asheville's Rugged Hinterlands"), to
leisurely canoeing through the heart of
the **Biltmore Estate** (see *To See—
The Biltmore Estate*). The Buncombe
County Parks and Recreation Department maintains a number of canoe and
kayak launch sites along the river. In
addition to the outfitters listed below,
check out the listings for the French
Broad River under *To Do—Whitewater Adventures* in the Hot Springs
chapter ("Asheville's Rugged Hinterlands").

Southern Waterways (828-232-1970;
1-800-849-1970), 521 Amboy Road,
Asheville, NC. Partial day $24–48.
This outfitter offers gentle, self-guided
trips on the **French Broad River** as it
cuts through the **Biltmore Estate**
(see *To See—The Biltmore Estate*)—
several miles of private wilderness, little changed since Frederick Law Olmsted designed its landscape in the
1880s. You have your choice of raft,
canoe, or kayak, or they will shuttle
your private boat for a modest fee. A
guided sunset paddle goes down the
same stretch in the twilight hours.

**Nantahala Outdoor Center in
Asheville** (828-232-0110; 1-888-622-
1662), 52 Westgate Parkway, Asheville,
NC. This large Bryson City outfitter
maintains a base and outdoor shop in

Asheville, at the Westgate Shopping Plaza off I-240, just across the river from downtown.

✴ Lodging

GUIDANCE **Blue Ridge Mountain Host of North Carolina** (1-800-807-3391), P.O. Box 1806, Asheville, NC 28802. This organization of independent hotels and B&Bs covers the area around Asheville and Boone, NC.

Asheville Bed & Breakfast Association (ABBA) (1-877-262-6867). This association is made up of 16 small B&Bs, all of them in private homes located in quiet neighborhoods in and around Asheville. You can use either their web site or their toll-free number to find and reserve the room that's right for you.

COUNTRY INNS AND HOTELS ✐ ♿
The Richmond Hill Inn (828-252-7313; 1-888-742-4550), 87 Richmond Hill Drive, Asheville, NC 28806. Open February through December. This AAA four-diamond inn, centering on an 1890s mansion built by a congressman, occupies 46 private acres on a hilltop just outside of downtown Asheville. The Richmond Hill is well known for its gracious hospitality, fine dining (see **Gabrielle's** in *Dining Out*), and luxurious comfort; the 2001 Zagat Survey has listed it as one of the top 15 small resorts and inns in America. However, it's most remarkable feature is its 6-acre Victorian garden, designed and maintained by the inn's full-time horticulturalist, Hunter Stubbs, and his staff. The inn's 36 rooms are divided between the old mansion at the top of the hill, the new **Garden Pavilion** at the base of the hill, and a row of tiny cottages around the regulation croquet court. Rooms range in size from standard size to large, and all are tastefully decorated with antiques and reproductions; some rooms have fireplaces, whirlpool baths, refrigerators, separate sitting areas, private rocking porches, and/or garden balconies. A full breakfast in the garden, and afternoon tea, are served. Rooms $155–395; suites $240–450; includes breakfast.

✐ ♿ **The Haywood Park Hotel** (828-252-2522; 1-800-228-2522), 1 Battery Park Avenue, Asheville, NC 28801. This small luxury hotel sits at the center of downtown Asheville's Battery Hill shopping district (see *Selective Shopping—Downtown Asheville*), in a recently renovated historic four-story brick building. The lobby centers on a four-story glass-roofed atrium, whose contemporary lines contrast nicely with the historic brick exterior; inside the atrium are exotic shops and restaurants. The hotel has room service, an exercise room, and a sauna, and covered valet parking. The 33 rooms are stylishly and elegantly decorated with custom-designed contemporary furniture, and all rooms have sitting areas, wet bars, and Spanish marble baths

THE GARDENS AT THE RICHMOND HILL INN

with garden tubs (with whirlpool baths in some rooms). Business travelers will appreciate the three phones and the writing desk with a computer/fax port. A continental breakfast is delivered to each room. Child-care facilities are available. $140–325; includes contintental breakfast.

🏌 ♿ **The Grove Park Inn Resort and Spa** (828-252-2711; 1-800-438-5800), 290 Macon Avenue, Asheville, NC 28804. Open all year. This impressive stone inn sits on a hillside above Asheville, just north of downtown. Built in 1913, it was a focal point for Asheville's early development; now it's at the center of an upscale historic neighborhood. The large old inn is built of huge granite stones, some as large as 10,000 pounds, and topped with a bright red roof—a grand sight viewed across its 1899 golf course (redesigned by Donald Ross in 1923; see *To Do—Golf*). The huge stones form the lobby wall, with an enormous fireplace at one end. This old inn is flanked by two modern wings, built in the 1980s; together they offer 510 rooms, all furnished in the style of the Arts and Crafts movement—reproductions in the new wings, the hotel's custom-built original furniture in the old inn. Some of the original rooms are small (labeled "value rooms" in the resort's literature), while others range from standard size to large suites. Resort activities include the 18-hole golf course with its wide mountain views; three indoor and three outdoor tennis courts; a sports complex with exercise equipment, aerobics class, and racquetball; a swimming pool; and a new 40,000-square-foot spa. The hotel also has seven restaurants, cafés, and bars, as well as a number of shops (including a golf pro shop and a tennis pro shop). This child-friendly inn offers fully supervised children's programs (ages 3–12) in a summer-camp format for half days, full days, and (some) evenings. Child-averse adults can stay in the child-free **Club Floor,** which has oversized rooms, its own private lounge, free evening cocktails, and free continental breakfast. Value rooms $135–195; standard rooms $150–299; oversized rooms and suites $235–635. Apart from the Club Floor, breakfast is not included in the tariff.

Inn on Biltmore Estate (1-800-624-1575), 1 North Pack Square (administrative offices), Asheville, NC 28801. This highly regarded inn has all of the attentions and luxuries you expect from a top-flight hotel. This 213-room hotel stands six stories tall on a hillock within the **Biltmore Estate** (see *To See—The Biltmore Estate*), about 2 miles from the house and garden. A monolithic modern structure built in 2001, it has been given exterior decorative flourishes reminiscent of the Biltmore House's French chateau architecture. The same sort of decorated modern architecture carries on in the interior, where distinctly contemporary lines and room designs serve as backdrops for English and French country-house furniture. Apart from the beautiful reproduction furniture, guest rooms are fairly standard and none too large; you'll find yourself having to pay extra for a balcony, a whirlpool bath, or a little extra room. Please note: The room rate does NOT include a ticket to the **Biltmore House and Gardens,** even though the hotel is on the estate grounds. April through December: rooms $199–359; suites: $595–2,000. January through March: rooms $139–269; suites $450–1,400. Breakfast is not included.

In Asheville

The Albemarle Inn (828-255-0027; 1-800-621-7435), 86 Edgemont Road, Asheville, NC 28801. Occupying a large Greek Revival mansion in Asheville's elegant Grove Park district, the Albemarle Inn is spacious, elegant, and quiet. Greek columns support its high front porch, an elegant place to sit and enjoy the westward view; inside, a grand oak staircase winds up past a semicircular sitting area before reaching the second story. A guest lounge has wood paneling, comfortable Victorian furniture, and a gas log fire in the old fireplace. Here guests are served wine and cheese in the early evening; the attached sunroom, roomy and bright, is the site for breakfast. The 11 guest rooms range from spacious to huge, with high ceilings, period furnishings, queen and king beds, and claw-foot tubs. Breakfasts are luxurious, ample servings of stunning gourmet treats.

Abingdon Green Bed & Breakfast Inn (828-251-2454; 1-800-251-2454), 46 and 48 Cumberland Circle, Asheville, NC 28801. This 1908 Colonial Revival mansion, listed in the National Register, sits on a large tree-shaded lot in Asheville's **Montford National Historic District,** not far from downtown. Carefully tended English gardens surround the house and fill the back of the property. Inside, antique furnishings grace the common rooms. The eight guest rooms (including three suites in the separate **Carriage House**) are theme-furnished with antiques and range in size from cozy to large. Full breakfasts are served in the elegant dining room. Rooms $125–185; suites $225–265.

Chestnut Street Inn (828-285-0705; 1-800-894-2955), 176 East Chestnut Street, Asheville, NC 28801. This large brick Victorian home is located three blocks north of downtown Asheville, in the **Chestnut Hill National Historic District.** Its wide porch looks out on a large lot landscaped as an English garden. Common areas have their original heavy woodworking and period antiques, and each of the six rooms is theme decorated in Victorian antiques. $165–235, including full breakfast and afternoon tea.

WhiteGate Inn and Cottage (828-253-2553; 1-800-485-3045), 173 East Chestnut Street, Asheville, NC 28801. Rated three diamonds by AAA and located in Asheville's **Chestnut Hill National Historic District,** just three blocks north of downtown, the hilltop WhiteGate is surrounded by gardens, with the tops of downtown Asheville's tallest buildings visible over the white picket fence. This 1889 shingle-style house, painted brick red, is elegant inside and out. Gravel paths looping through its English-style gardens, with a 1,200-square-foot greenhouse and conservatory holding a special orchid garden. Inside, the common rooms are wood paneled and decorated with Edwardian antiques. The four rooms in the main house are large, each theme decorated with period antiques; two have separate sitting rooms. A small **garden cottage,** original to the house, makes up the fifth room in the inn. $155–200.

The Wright Inn and Carriage House (828-251-0789; 1-800-552-5724), 235 Pearson Drive, Asheville, NC 28801. Rated three diamonds by AAA. and located in Asheville's **Montford National Historic District** just north of downtown, the National Register– listed Wright Inn occupies one of the largest and most elaborate Queen Anne mansions in the North Carolina mountains. The thickly gingerbreaded veranda curves around the front in a witch's-hat turret; on the side, elaborate steps lead down the rock wall foundation to the Victorian garden. The period is carefully maintained inside, with polished hardwood trim setting off the antique and heirloom furniture. The seven rooms and three suites are all elegantly decorated in-period, and range in size from cozy bedrooms to multiroom apartments. A full breakfast is served, along with afternoon tea and cookies in the gazebo. $125–235; ask about the five-room suite.

§ **The Colby House** (828-253-5644; 1-800-982-2118), 230 Pearson Drive, Asheville, NC 28801. This four-guest-room inn occupies a 1924 Colonial house in Asheville's gentrifying **Montford National Historic District,** convenient to downtown. An extrawide side porch is floored with red tile and framed by classical columns; its rockers give views over the private back garden. Common areas, furnished with a combination of Edwardian and 1920s-era furniture, include a parlor, a library, a formal dining room, and a butler's pantry where cookies, coffee, and soft drinks are always available. Rooms, ranging from cozy to large, are decorated with elegant colonial themes. A full breakfast is served on china in the dining room, and wine and hors d'oeuvres are served in the evenings. A detached garage has been converted to a two-room **cottage** with a whirlpool tub, where children are welcome; only children over 12 are allowed in the main inn. Rooms $130–150; cottage $235.

1900 Inn on Montford (828-254-9569; 1-800-254-9569), 296 Montford Avenue, Asheville, NC 28801. Tree lovers take note: The 1900 Inn on Montford has the North Carolina State Record Norway Maple in its front yard. Business travelers take note: This century-old historic house a couple of blocks north of downtown Asheville has high-speed Internet ports in every room. This fine old Victorian house in Asheville's **Montford National Historic District** is painted brick red, has flanking front gables, and a huge wrap-around porch overlooking its English-garden landscaping. Common areas as well as the five rooms are elegantly furnished in a turn-of-the-century style, allowing you to plug in your laptop with some homey comfort. Rooms $165–225; suite $295.

North Lodge Bed & Breakfast (828-252-6433; 1-800-282-3602), 84 Oakland Road, Asheville, NC 28801. This 1904 house sits on a large lot in Asheville's hospital and medical district, halfway between downtown Asheville and the Biltmore Estate. The inn is only a few blocks from both of Asheville's major hospitals. It was built in the fashionable cottage style, heavily influenced by the Arts and Crafts movement, with stone walls on the first floor and cedar shakes covering the second floor. Beautifully restored, the house is isolated from the surrounding neighborhood by its landscaped lot and long drive. Inside, it's beautifully decorated in a mixture of antiques and contemporary furnishings that go well with it's early-20th-century design features. The five en suite guest rooms are theme furnished in the same manner, and range in size from cozy to large. A sixth en suite bedroom has a single twin bed, and a greatly reduced price. Single room

$70; other rooms $105–145l; includes full breakfast.

Cedar Crest, a Victorian Inn (828-252-1389; 1-800-252-0310). This 1890s Victorian mansion graces its upscale Asheville neighborhood with a full panoply of gables, gingerbread, turrets, balconies, and verandas. The influence of the nearby **Biltmore Estate** (see *To See—The Biltmore Estate*) is clearly visible in the elaborate woodwork in the common areas and on the grand staircase. Gardens surround the property, making for a pleasant view from the rocking chairs on the porch. The nine guest rooms in this huge house are all individually decorated in period antiques. Full breakfasts are served in the formal dining room or on the veranda, and fresh cookies and lemonade are served each afternoon. Rooms $140–190; suite and cottage $205–240.

& **The Blake House** (828-681-5227; 1-888-353-5227), 150 Royal Pines Drive, Asheville, NC 28704. Built as a summer home in 1847, the Blake House sits in what is now a quiet southern suburb of Asheville, convenient to the airport. Built entirely of granite, it sports 22-inch-thick granite walls and 14-foot-high ornamental plaster ceilings, as well as a wide front porch with rocking chairs. Common rooms are beautifully decorated and quite roomy. The spacious five rooms are individually and elegantly decorated with antiques. A full breakfast is served in the dining room. Rooms $155–185; suite $225.

Engadine Inn (Owls Nest Inn at Engadine) (828-665-8325; 1-800-665-8868), 2630 Smokey Park Highway, Chandler, NC 28715. Located 0.5 mile from exit 37 on I-40, this elaborately Victorian 1885 farmhouse sits on the western edge of the Asheville area,

on 12 acres of meadowland with beautiful views. Even for a Victorian house the porches are a wonder, wrapping around both floors, with a corner turret and plenty of gingerbread and fine wood trim. The five guest rooms are decorated with Victorian antiques, and range in size from roomy to large. $120–195, including full breakfast.

In Weaverville

Dry Ridge Inn (828-658-3899; 1-800-839-3899), 26 Brown Street, Weaverville, NC 28787. This 1849 farmhouse, rebuilt into a stylish Victorian mansion in 1888, sits in a quiet residential neighborhood two blocks from Weaverville's quaint little downtown. Surrounded by a white picket fence, the house's wide front porch looks out on well-kept gardens, with a water garden in the rear. The eight rooms are individually decorated in country-themed antiques and range in size from cozy to large. A full breakfast is served, in the brightly lighted breakfast room or on the brick patio by the water garden. $95–155, including breakfast.

The Inn on Main Street (828-645-4935; 1-877-873-6074), 88 South Main Street, Weaverville, NC 28787. Built by a local doctor in 1900, this country house in Weaverville, two blocks south of downtown, represented high living in a small town. Today this late-Victorian house, with its two-story projecting bay windows and wide porches, continues to give high comfort in a small town. Its seven rooms are standard size to large, each theme-furnished in antiques and reproductions that feel comfortable in a turn-of-the-century home. $95–145, including full breakfast.

The Secret Garden (828-658-9317; 1-800-797-8211), 56 North Main Street, Weaverville, NC 28787. This elegant cottage-style 1904 home sits a few blocks north of downtown Weaverville on its busy Main Street. Its 60-foot veranda looks out over the semiformal garden, while a sunroom offers pleasant sitting in unpleasant weather. The three guest rooms are all elegantly furnished in late-Victorian antiques. $115–140, including full breakfast, and afternoon wine and snacks on the veranda.

✳ Where to Eat

Note: For more listings also see *Selective Shopping*

EATING OUT

In Asheville

✑ **Asheville Pizza and Brewing Company** (828-254-1281), 675 Merrimon Avenue, Asheville, NC. Open for lunch and dinner. Located in an old neighborhood theater on busy Merrimon Avenue north of downtown, this restaurant offers some of the best pizza in town, their own outstanding microbrewed beer, and second-run movies on a full-sized screen. Pizzas are freshly made to order, as are a good selection of hamburgers, veggie burgers, sandwiches, and other bar food— but the really outstanding menu item is their Shiva IPA, an unusually mild and rich version of this heavily hopped English-style brew. You can enjoy your food in the lobby, set up as a regular restaurant and bar with funky movie memorabilia, or in the theater, where movie-house rocking chairs face onto bench tables, and beat-up old sofas fill the empty area in front of the screen. There's a slight charge for recent movies, but various other features (including children's daytime movies) are free. $8–14; the movie is $2 extra.

The Early Girl Eatery (828-259-9292) 8 Wall Street, Asheville, NC.

Breakfast 7:30–11:30 weekdays; lunch 11:45–3 weekdays; dinner 5:30–10 Thursday–Saturdays; brunch 9–3 weekends. This small storefront in the **Battery Hill** shopping district (see Selective Shopping) specializes in original food with a Southern twang, made fresh from locally grown ingredients. The cafe is bright and airy, with windows overlooking a downtown park two floors below; service is fast and attentive. Breakfasts have traditional egg and pancake dishes, complemented with less usual courses such as shrimp in brown gravy over grits. Lunches have fresh soups and sandwiches, plus a large blackboard of specials such as shrimp and andouille sausage in a rich brown sauce full of fresh spring onions, served over stone-ground yellow grits. Dinners feature duck, chicken, salmon, and pork in a variety of blackboard specials. There are always vegetarian and vegan choices, and the extensive vegetable list will show you just what the mountain farms are harvesting right now. Beer and wine are available, with a good choice of microbrews and quality wines by the glass. Breakfast: $2–7; lunch: $3–7; dinner entrees: $11–15.

✑ **The Laughing Seed Café** (828-252-3445), 40 Wall Street, Asheville, NC. Open Monday, Wednesday, Thursday 11:30–9, Friday and Saturday 11:30–10; Sunday 10–9. This downtown Asheville vegetarian café offers awide choice of fresh, exotic produce, and imaginative preparations fusing a variety of ethnic cuisines. Reminiscent of a 1940s snack bar, it's bright and sparkling, with a big mural and lots of blond wood. The menu is huge, vegan (no dairy or egg) choices clearly labeled. All food is prepared from scratch with fresh ingredients (including the bread), and most produce comes from local organic suppliers. Organic wines, and their own brand of beer, the England-inspired Green Man (brewed downstairs). Lunch $5–9; dinner $7–14.

Trevi (828-281-1400), 2 Hendersonville Road, Asheville, NC. Open weekdays for lunch 11:30–2:30; dinner Monday–Thursday 5–9; Friday and Saturday 5–10. This Biltmore Village (see *Selective Shopping*) restaurant features Italian cuisine from the Apulia region—light sauces, fresh produce, lots of seafood, flavorful cheeses, and intense fresh herb flavors. The lunch menu includes sandwiches and salads, market-fresh fish, calzones, and a large number of pasta dishes. Sandwiches disappear from the dinner menu, replaced by a greater choice of entrées. The large and varied wine list is dominated by Italian wines, with nearly every bottle less than $25. Inside the restaurant the superb specialty grocer Baba Riche offers an amazing array of Italian and international specialty items. Lunch $5-8; dinner $9–18.

Jack of the Wood (828-252-5445), 95 Patton Avenue, Asheville, NC. Open daily 4 PM–2 AM. Free parking adjacent after 6 PM. This downtown Asheville brew pub has a distinctly Celtic slant. Located in a storefront, Jack in the Woods makes its own beer and its own food fresh daily. Simple bar meals of sandwiches, stew, curry, fish cakes, or chili complement the British-style ales brewed in the basement. An interesting and original lineup of bands entertain on Friday and Saturday nights, while jam sessions are a regular feature on Sunday (Celtic, 5 PM), Wednesday (mountain music, 9:30 PM), and Thursday (bluegrass, 9:30 PM). $6–9.

DINING OUT Gabrielle's (828-252-7313; 1-888-742-4550), 87 Richmond Hill Drive, Asheville, NC. Open 6 PM–10 PM; closed Tuesday. A coat for gentlemen is suggested. Reservations are required. The elegant paneled dining room of a 19th-century congressman serves as the venue for this classic continental restaurant, one of the few in North Carolina to receive the AAA four-diamond award. Part of the **Richmond Hill Inn** (see *Lodging—Country Inns and Hotels*), the restaurant occupies part of a hilltop 1890s mansion, whose wide front porch overlooks 6 acres of Victorian gardens. Inside are cherry paneled walls, crystal chandeliers, and live piano music; double-clothed tables are set with fine china and crystal. The single set price brings six courses: an *amusé*, a choice of four appetizers, a salad, a seasonal sorbet as a refresher, a choice of four entrées, and a choice of three desserts. You might start with wild mushroom ravioli served with Parmesan cream and squash confetti; then a simple salad of Bibb lettuce with Roquefort, pecans, and sherry vinaigrette; seared red snapper with lobster risotto, carrot and salsify ragout, and Parmesan tuile; and finish with warm molten chocolate cake with vanilla bean ice cream and coffee swirl. The more expensive Grande Menu features dishes made with caviar, truffles, foies gras, and quail eggs. The final step to this grand meal is a cup of freshly brewed coffee or tea, enjoyed from a rocking chair on the porch. $58–85 for a six-course dinner.

The Market Place Restaurant and Wine Bar (828-252-4162), 20 Wall Street, Asheville, NC. Open for dinner, Monday through Saturday. One of the attractive storefronts on Wall Street in downtown Asheville, the Market Place offers a fusion of continental and global cuisine with fresh mountain ingredients. Outside,

THE HISTORIC DOWNTOWN DISTRICT OF
BLACK MOUNTAIN

wrought-iron gates welcome strollers into a courtyard and dining patio; inside, diners are greeted by cool, contemporary lines in tall spaces, with elegant, muted colors. The dinner menu changes daily, depending on the fresh, seasonal fruits, vegetables, and seafood available. It may feature meats from local farms, perhaps smoked with apple wood, or berries from the Biltmore Estate (see *To See—The Biltmore Estate*). The wine list includes hundreds of different bottles, with many rare vintages priced over a hundred dollars, and a limited choice of wines under $30. Appetizers $7–10; entrées $13–26; desserts $4–7.

✳ Entertainment

For more suggestions also see *Selective Shopping.*

Asheville, NC

The Asheville Symphony Orchestra (828-254-7046; 1-888-860-7378). $14–38. Since 1960, this orchestra has been bringing professional symphony to the mountains. Seasons typically include six masterworks concerts, two pops concerts, and a fully staged opera in conjunction with the **Asheville Lyric Opera Company.**

Asheville Community Theater (ACT) (828-254-1320), 35 East Walnut Street. $15. Asheville's amateur theater maintains an ambitious program of eight or more sophisticated plays from their permanent downtown theater near the **Thomas Wolf Memorial** (see *To See—Historic Sites*).

The Diana Wortham Theater (828-257-4530), 2 South Pack Square. This 500-seat theater, part of the **Pack Place** complex (see *To See—Pack Place*), hosts around 150 performances a year, of every conceivable type.

Shindig on the Green (828-259-6107). Open 7 PM–10 PM, Saturday in July and August. Free admission. Asheville sponsors this weekly outdoor musical get-together on the large green in front of the downtown **City Hall** (see Asheville City Hall Plaza under *To See—Gardens and Parks*), featuring old-time mountain music, bluegrass, and dancing.

The Asheville Tourists (828-258-0428), McCormick Field, 30 Buchanan Place. Asheville's minor league baseball team has its headquarters in an handsome new redbrick stadium, **McCormick Field,** just south of downtown off US 25. Founded in 1909 as the Asheville Red Birds, the team's been known as the Tourists since 1915 and have been playing at their current site since 1924. Members of the A-rated South Atlantic League, the Tourists have been affiliated with the Colorado Rockies since 1994.

In *Eating Out* also see **Jack in the Woods** (featuring live music) and the **Asheville Brewing and Pizza Company** (movies).

BATTERY HILL DOWNTOWN
SHOPPING DISTRICT

The Battery Hill shopping district wanders through back streets lined with fine 1920s-era buildings in the western part of downtown Asheville. Start your shopping trip at the little triangular-shaped park on **Patton Avenue at Haywood Street.** Although most of the action is to your north and west, you definitely want to start by going a block east on **Patton** to the **Kress Emporium,** where the individual booths of handcrafters fill the delicious old Kress Department Store building. Back at the park, **Ten Thousand Villages** carries gifts and art objects from third world countries.

Go north, then left onto **Battery Park.** There's an amazing number of good, upscale restaurants within a block of this corner: **Uptown Café, 23 Page and The New French Bar, Laughing Seed Café** (see *Eating Out),* **The Market Place Restaurant and Wine Bar** (see Dining Out). In the lobby of the **Haywood Park Hotel** (see *Lodging: Country Inns and Hotels)* is **Himalayas Import,** with gift items from Tibet and Nepal. Straight ahead is the amazing **Grove Arcade** (see *To See—Historic Sites),* a quarter-million-square-foot 1920s-era mall, encrusted with elaborate statuary; it should be fully restored and filled with small, independent merchants by the time you visit. When you finish with the arcade, go down the alley-width **Wall Street,** pedestrianized and lined with shops. **Natural Selections,** a nature store, has regional art, books, telescopes and optics—everything that has to do with appreciating nature. Rock climbing store **ClimbMax** (see *To Do—Rock Climbing)* has gear and an indoor climbing center. At the end of Wall Street, the monolithic glass-walled **Federal Building** houses the **World Data Center for Meteorology,** our nation's major repository for global warming data.

Return along Battery Park, then go left up **Haywood Street.** There are several interesting shops and restaurants here. Be sure not to miss **Malaprop's Bookstore,** winner of the *Publishers Weekly* Bookseller of the Year 2000 Award, with a wide selection of hard-to-find titles. At the end of the long block, the **Asheville Public Library** is a friendly refuge, and library patrons who park in the garage behind it can get their parking receipts validated. Beside that is the **Asheville Civic Center** and **Thomas Wolfe Auditorium,** a popular venue for all sorts of stuff, from symphony orchestra concerts to minor league ice hockey.

Black Mountain, NC

Park Rhythms (828-669-2052). Open Thursday in July and August at 7 PM. These free concerts at Black Mountain's **Lake Tomahawk Park** (see *Wild Places—Picnic Areas*) feature a variety of bluegrass and alternative music.

Swannanoa Chamber Music Festival (828-771-3050). Open June and July. $15. This annual series consists of five weekly concerts, each one performed first at **Warren Wilson College** (between Asheville and Black Mountain, NC), then repeated at **Waynesville,** NC (see *Villages* in "Waynesville and the Blue Ridge Parkway"), and **Hendersonville,** NC (see *Villages* in "The Blue Ridge: Hendersonville and Brevard").

✳ Selective Shopping

DOWNTOWN ASHEVILLE, NC Asheville's 1920s era downtown spreads over a 60-block area, just south of I-240 at US 25 (exit 5A). Frozen in time by the Great Depression, it somehow survived the late 20th century with most of its charm intact. Nearly all of the large downtown area is dominated by two- and three-story buildings dating from the early 20th century. "Newer" buildings show art deco's industry-inspired design features, while many of the older structures sport the elaborate fillips of the 19th-century art nouveau movement. Indeed, you'll find only four modernist block buildings in the entire district, and few buildings higher than 10 stories. Without glass towers to sterilize the streets below, Asheville retains a downtown district of charm and grace. Shoppers stroll past buildings crusted with fancy brickwork, colored tile, stone trim, and sculptures small and large. Sidewalks are filled with people, and storefronts filled with shops.

Asheville's downtown is large enough to split into four districts, each with its own distinct personality. To the west, **Battery Hill** has the largest concentrations of vintage-1920s architecture and small boutiques. **Pack Square** marks the busy heart of downtown, its banking and office district, and its arts district. To the north of Pack Square, **Lexington Hill** houses businesses and people pursuing alternative or New Age lifestyles. And to the east, the **Thomas Wolfe Plaza** area (heavily urban-renewed in the 1960s) holds the institutions of urban life—the city hall, the courthouse, the glass-tower hotel, the YMCA, and lots of parking lots.

Below are descriptions of the main shopping streets of the three shopping districts. Some of the shops are mentioned by name; others are left for you to discover.

Pack Square Downtown Shopping District

Tiny Pack Square sits at Asheville's center, a classic urban square with benches, trees, sculptures, and storefronts—four-story brick buildings from the late 19th century. On its north side, two of Asheville's modernist glass towers choke off interest; paradoxically, the squat anonymous one on the right now houses the corporate offices of the **Biltmore Estate** (see *To See—The Biltmore Estate*), having been designed by I. M. Pei for a chemical company in 1979. On its south side, the city's **Pack Place museum and theater complex** sits beside the marble-clad **Asheville Public Library.** Restaurants, including **Café on the Square,** crowd around its edge.

Asheville's **arts district** extends south of the square along **Biltmore Avenue** (US 25). Its centerpiece is the large commercial gallery, **Blue Spiral I,** representing major regional artists in a 14,000-square-foot display area that wanders through a three-story brick building. Next door, the **Fine Arts Theater** plays a full schedule of independent films. Storefronts up and down the street house smaller galleries; but not all is art. A **Mast General Store** (see *To See—Historic Sites* in "Behind the Blue Ridge: Boone and Banner Elk") inhabits a 1940s-era department store building; next door, an architectural salvage firm fills a building with a range of antique items rescued from old buildings being demolished. **Barley's Taproom,** a popular regional franchise, is a good place for a pizza and a microbrew (including Asheville's own Highland Gaelic Ale, brewed in the basement). The district ends at the **French Broad Food Co-op,** with a large line of natural and organic products, and the **Asheville Wine Market,** a large wine shop with a full selection of beers and cheeses as well.

Lexington Park Downtown Shopping District

At one time, Lexington Park would be known as the Bohemian Quarter, or perhaps the hippie district. In the New Millennium, it's the place where the New Age hangs out its shingle. The smallest of the districts, it includes **Broadway** (US 25) north of the plain modernist glass towers that flank Pack Square, and **Lexington Avenue,** one block to the west. This is the least boutique-y of the three districts, and the most likely spot to find stores that decorate with spray paint. It's also the best place to find that odd-little something that would never appear inside a mall shop. The best shopping is on Lexington Avenue. A row of shops (**Native Expressions, Cosmic Vision,** and **The Natural Home**) feature gifts, clothing, jewelry, and home accessories

from third world countries. Beyond that, **Max and Rosie's** offers hearty vegetarian meals in a pleasant, deli atmosphere. **TS Morrison and Company,** a downtown department store in continuous operation since 1891, now specializes in a broad selection of nostalgia items. An equally venerable institution, **The Downtown Bookstore,** anchors the upper end of Lexington with a huge set of magazine racks.

BILTMORE VILLAGE In the 1890s, George Vanderbilt constructed Biltmore Village outside the gates of his **Biltmore Estate** (see *To See—The Biltmore Estate*) as the home for his hundreds of workers. Frederick Law Olmsted planned the village, and Richard Morris Hunt designed its buildings, giving it a unique appearance that survives to this day. Sold off after Vanderbilt's death in 1914, Hunt's handsome buildings and Olmsted's landscaping remain—now holding an upscale shopping district.

To understand the village, picture the idyllic rural world that Vanderbilt tried to create. Vanderbilt placed his village across from the main gate of his estate, separated from it by an old narrow coach road and an expanse of green lawn. On one side of the village he placed an elegant little train station to serve the needs of the estate. In the ensuing decades, a large industrial rail yard grew up beside the little depot. The narrow coach road became US 25 and slowly expanded to hold 10 lanes of traffic. The grassy lawn, sold off and divided, came to hold a motel, three gas stations, and two fast-food franchises. Fortunately, the noise and ugliness stop as if cut off by a curtain as soon as you enter the tiny back streets of the village. The center of the village remains pretty much as Vanderbilt left it.

The large selection of independently owned shops include a half-dozen antiques stores, several galleries, five clothiers, and a dozen or so gift shops. If you get a might peckish, there are nine small independent restaurants inside the village.

New Morning Gallery (828-274-2831), 7 Boston Way, Asheville. New Morning Gallery looks like a tiny storefront, sitting a half block from the center of Biltmore Village. Looks can deceive; the gallery stretches back deep into the building, then climbs up the stairs to sprawl through nearly a block of elegant second-floor space. New Morning specializes in "functional art," handcrafted stuff you can use (if only as a paperweight). It features artists from all over America, but with a special emphasis on regional artists. The gallery sponsors the annual **Village Art and Craft Fair** (see *Special Events*). An affiliated gallery in the village, **Bellagio,** offers handcrafted clothing and accessories.

BLACK MOUNTAIN, NC The Old Depot Gallery and Museum. Black Mountain's old-fashioned passenger depot anchors the southern end of this small-town downtown. Painted bright yellow, it sits hard against Sutton Avenue with a row of old brick storefronts across the street. The Old Depot Association, which took it over and renovated it in 1976, runs a good-sized crafts gallery there, dedicated to high-quality handcrafts in traditional mountain styles. The works of more than 75 local and regional mountain crafts artists can be seen at any one time, and artists frequently volunteer to run the gallery. Behind the gallery, a restored caboose houses a local history museum.

✳ Special Events

Early May: **Spring Herb Festival** (828-689-5974), **Western North Carolina (WNC) Farmer's Market,** Asheville, NC 109 at I-26. Free admission. This annual gathering brings together all of the region's many herb farmers, selling seedlings and meeting new customers.

⚘ *May and October:* **Lake Eden Arts Festival** at Camp Rockmont (828-686-8742), 377 Lake Eden Road, Black Mountain, NC. *Last weekend in May; repeated in mid-October.* Full weekend pass: adults $80 (in advance) to $90 (at gate); children $65 (in advance) to $75 (at gate). This twice-annual festival is an eclectic mix of New Age and traditional mountain elements, heavy on music and crafts, families and good times. Limited to 5,000 attendees at any one time, it's held at **Camp Rockmont,** a large and beautiful facility in the mountains west of the town of Black Mountain. People tent-camp by the lakes, go swimming and kayaking. The 3-day schedule offers music, dancing, concerts, handcrafting, healing arts, special children's programs, and workshops.

First weekend in June: **Black Mountain Arts and Crafts Show** (828-669-0433), Black Mountain, NC. This juried sidewalk art show, limited to the best 70 exhibitors, occupies downtown Black Mountain's Sutton Avenue by its historic depot. Saturday night features "A Taste of Black Mountain" ($15–18), a sampling of foods from a dozen or more Black Mountain restaurants for one ticket price. The art show is free.

Mid-June: **Asheville Gem and Mineral Show** (828-254-7162), Asheville, NC. Free admission. This weekend show at Pack Place's **Colbern Gem and Mineral Museum** (see *To See—*

Pack Place) has booths displaying crystals, gemstones, meteorites, and handcrafted jewelry from collectors and rock shops all over the East.

July Fourth: **Fourth of July Celebrations,** Asheville, NC. There is a large downtown party with live entertainment, food, children's activities, and evening fireworks. **Montreat** (see *To See—Cultural Sites*) has a street parade. **Black Mountain,** NC, has its celebration at **Lake Tomahawk Park** (see *Wild Places—Picnic Areas*).

Last weekend in July: **Belle Chere** (828-259-5800), Asheville, NC. Free admission. This annual street festival boasts of being the largest free outdoor festival in the South. Taking over most of downtown Asheville for three days, Belle Chere is best known for its multiple, ongoing music venues (featuring bluegrass, jazz, rock, pop, and whatever), its street food, its copious beer sales, and its hundreds of arts and crafts vendors.

First weekend in August: **Village Art and Craft Fair,** Biltmore Village, Asheville, NC. This large fine-crafts and arts show, held on the shaded grounds of the **Cathedral of All Souls** in **Biltmore Village** (see *Selective Shopping*), attracts 140 or more artists from all over America. Held annually since 1972, its posters are notable for their original art featuring cats. It's sponsored by the **New Morning Gallery** (see *Selective Shopping— Biltmore Village*).

First weekend in August: **The Mountain Dance and Folk Festival** (828-257-4530), Asheville, NC. Founded by Bascom Lamar Lunsford in 1927, this annual festival is dedicated to mountain folk music and dancing. It's held in the **Diana Wortham Theater** in

Pack Place (see *To See—Pack Place*).

Last Saturday in August: **Mount Mitchell State Park Heritage Day,** Burnsville, NC. Traditional mountain music and dancing on the highest peak in the East, along with a variety of traditional foods and crafts, a raptor demonstration, an annual tree-planting event, hikes, and workshops.

Last weekend in August: **Sourwood Festival** at Black Mountain, Black Mountain, NC. This annual street fair, held in downtown Black Mountain, features crafts and art exhibits and food vendors.

✍ *Third weekend in September:* **Fall Pioneer Days** (828-645-6706) at **Vance Birthplace State Historic Site** (see *To See—Historic Sites*), 911 Reems Creek Road, Weaverville, NC. This annual event has crafts and pioneer skill demonstrations with a frontier militia encampment, at this early-19th-century log farmstead.

Second Saturday in October: **Fall! By the Tracks,** Black Mountain, NC. Black Mountain's local art and history association, the Old Depot Association, sponsors this annual fall festival, featuring crafters' demonstrations, make your own mountain toys workshops, cake-walks, local honey, mountain barbeque, and made-while-you-watch apple cider.

Mid-October: **Craft Fair of the Southern Highlands** (828-298-7928), Asheville, NC, at the **Civic Center.** $5. Founded in 1930 to promote crafters of the Southern mountains, the nonprofit Southern Appalachian Craft Guild has been holding these crafts fairs since 1948. It has a large juried show of member artists, crafts demonstrations, and live music. They hold a show in mid-July as well.

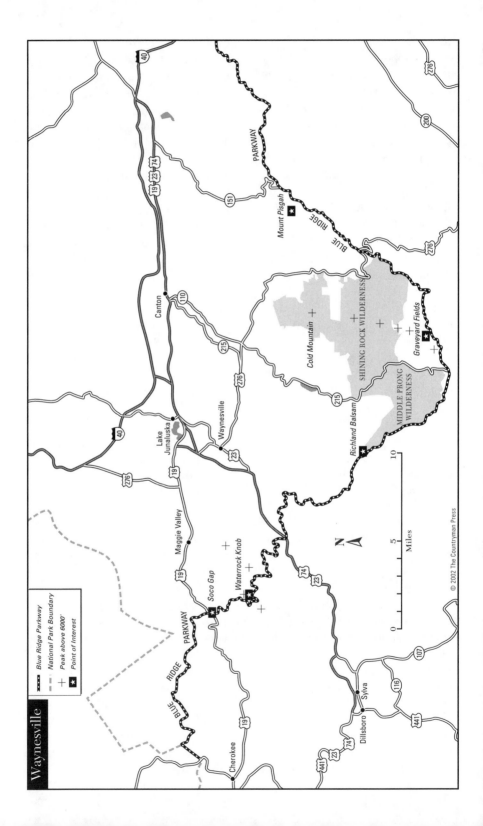

Waynesville

Blue Ridge Parkway
National Park Boundary
Peak above 6000'
Point of Interest

40

276

200

19 23 74

151

PARKWAY

Mount Pisgah

BLUE RIDGE

276

Canton

110

215

Cold Mountain

SHINING ROCK WILDERNESS

Graveyard Fields

40

276

Lake
Junaluska

Waynesville

276

215

MIDDLE PRONG
WILDERNESS

19

23

Richland Balsam

10

Maggie Valley

N

Soco Gap

Waterrock Knob

5

Miles

19

74

23

BLUE

RIDGE

PARKWAY

107

19

116

Sylva

Cherokee

441

Dillsboro

23

74

441

0

© 2002 The Countryman Press

WAYNESVILLE & THE BLUE RIDGE PARKWAY

Thе penultimate section of the Blue Ridge Parkway forms a high half circle that arcs around Waynesville, NC, for nearly 50 miles. It's the parkway's highest section, passing close to 12 peaks above 6,000 feet while peaking out at 6,158 feet (1.16 miles above sea level). Indeed, 19 miles of this drive are a mile or more above sea level, and virtually all of it is above 4,000 feet. As the parkway gets higher, its views get better—broad, panoramic views that cover ridge upon ridge, not only from overlooks but also from long roadside stretches as the roadway becomes a ledge perched high in the sky. This is the most remote section of the Blue Ridge Parkway, almost continuously bordered by giant tracts of national forest lands, including two large wilderness areas; little wonder that only three roads intersect it between its start and end points.

At the foot of these mountains, Waynesville is a classic redbrick small town with a bustling three-block Main Street filled with interesting stores; its historic neighborhoods have an astonishing selection of high-quality B&Bs. Nearby is the lovely little Methodist retreat village of Lake Junaluska, NC, with its historic center and landscaped lakeside walks.

GUIDANCE Haywood County Tourism Development Authority (828-452-0152; 1-800-334-9036), 1233 North Main Street, Suite 1-40, Waynesville, NC 28786. This quasi-governmental agency uses the room tax to promote tourism. These are the people to call to get a packet of brochures and information.

Haywood County Chamber of Commerce (828-456-3021; 1-877-456-3073), 73 Walnut Street, P.O. Drawer 600, Waynesville, NC 28786. This private not-for-profit organization promotes business members. It maintains a visitors center in a restored bungalow, on US 276 just north of downtown Waynesville.

Canton Papertown (Canton Chamber of Commerce) (828-648-7925), 36 Park Street, Canton, NC 28716. The chamber shares the town's former public library with the Canton Historic Museum, a Colonial-style brick building on the eastern edge of downtown (see *To See—Historic Sites*).

MEDICAL EMERGENCIES Haywood Regional Medical Facility (828-456-7311), 90 Hospital Drive, Clyde, NC, is 5 miles east of downtown Waynesville via US 23; take the NC 209 exit, then parallel the freeway to Jones Cove Road and follow the signs. This major regional hospital has a walk-in clinic on its campus, as well as a full-service emergency room.

✳ Wandering Around

EXPLORING BY CAR The Blue Ridge Parkway. *Leg 1:* From the parkway's intersection with NC 151, go right 17 miles to the intersection with NC 215.

Leg 2: From NC 215, continue along the parkway for 32 miles to US 19.

This starting point, already 2,200 feet above Asheville, NC, is on the crest of the Pisgah Ridge—a crest you'll be following for the next 17 miles. Your first landmark will be the short **Mount Pisgah Spur Road,** on the left. Go down it a few hundred yards for a good view over the forests of the **Mills River** (see The Pisgah Forest under *Wild Places—The Great Forests* in "The Blue Ridge: Hendersonville and Brevard"), then continue to the end if you want to pick up the popular (but steep and rocky) 2.5-mile round-trip hike to the 5,720-foot cone of **Mount Pisgah,** where an observation deck offers 360-degree views only partially spoiled by a TV tower. Back at the parkway, the **Mount Pisgah Picnic Area** (see *Wild Places—Picnic Areas*) is a short distance away, with **The Pisgah Inn** (a good place to grab a meal; see *Lodging—Resorts*) a bit farther on. From here the views open up to the south over the rhododendron covered cove known as **The Pink Beds,** with the enormous rock dome of **Looking Glass Rock** behind it; US 276 furnishes an excellent side trip to **The Cradle of Forestry in America** (see *To See—Historic Sites* in "The Blue Ridge: Hendersonville and Brevard"). Now the parkway climbs to 5,000 feet through increasingly rugged and dramatic scenery, to **Graveyard Fields** (see Graveyard Fields and **Black Balsam Knob** under *Trails of the Great Balsam Mountains*), a meadow-covered cove perched among mile-high peaks. In another mile, the **Black Balsam Spur Road** leads left to the trailhead for the **Shining Rock Wilderness** (see *Wild Places—The Great Forests*) and access to six peaks topping 6,000 feet. Back at the parkway, look for the great stone outcrop known as **The Devils Courthouse,** and don't miss the short, easy path to its top, with panoramic views.

The second leg follows the crest of the **Great Balsam Mountains,** with seven more 6,000-foot peaks along its 32 miles of ridgetop wilderness. Built in the 1960s this modern highway slashes through the wilderness landscape in huge cuts, with long sweeping views from its wide, clear shoulders. The views start suddenly as the parkway turns upward along the clifflike flanks of 6,110-foot **Mount Hardy,** with continuous and wide panoramas southward. More views open up as the parkway sweeps toward 6,000 feet in elevation, with exceptional panoramas near **Caney Fork Overlook** and at **Cowee Mountain Overlook** (see *To See—Along the Blue Ridge Parkway*). After that, the parkway reaches its highest elevation as it crests out at 6,190 feet at **Richland Balsams Overlook.** From there it follows the mile-high meadows of **The Long Swag** before it starts its long drop to Balsam Gap. On this downward leg the parkway gives impressive views of itself as it approaches the long, curving **Pinnacle Ridge Tunnel;** beyond, look for sunrise views at **Waynesville Overlook.**

The parkway dips into **Balsam Gap,** where it intersects with the four-lane **US 23/74** and the first services since Mount Pisgah (go east 1 mile). After Balsam Gap the parkway climbs steadily for the next 8 miles, then crests out as it crosses the massive side ridge known as **Plott Balsams**, at 5,710 feet. Here a spur road leads to the impressive **Waterrock Knob** overlook (see *To See—Along the Blue Ridge Parkway*), with a new visitors center, water, toilets, and picnic tables. To the left, a side trail follows a high, narrow ridgeline to form the **Plott Balsams Walk** (see **Richland Balsams Nature Trail** under *Trails of the Great Balsam Mountains*), with excellent views back toward Balsam Gap. As the parkway descends from Waterrock Knob it passes a series of good views west over the Cherokee lands, before dropping into the forests of **Soco Gap** (see *To See—Along the Blue Ridge Parkway* in "Cherokee and the Southeast Quadrant").

EXPLORING ON FOOT **A Walk around Lake Junaluska.** You'll find Lake Junaluska just off US 19, 4 miles north of Waynesville, NC; turn right on Lakeshore Drive and proceed to the large public lot by the administration center. This walk covers 2.5 miles.

After you've explored the high, windy ridges and mountaintop meadows in the rugged wilderness surrounding the Blue Ridge Parkway, you may find yourself ready for a level walk, on a paved path, through landscaped parklands along a lakeshore. If so, you're in luck. The historic Lake Junaluska retreat, run by the United Methodist Church, maintains a 3-mile parkland walk along their centerpiece lake, open to public use. Admire the stunning mountain view from the parking lot and the handsome buildings at the center of this retreat; then follow the paved path left. You'll quickly reach the monumental cross that serves as the centerpiece for the retreat, on a hill above you. Then, at a quarter mile, you'll walk across the handsome old dam that impounds the lake. For the next mile the level, paved path goes through landscaped parklands along the lakeshore, with stunning views west toward the 6,000-foot peaks of the Plott Balsams. Then the path crosses the lake on a long footbridge and reenters the main retreat area, passing historic and modern buildings still used as a center for refreshing the spirit (see **The Lambuth Inn at the Lake Junaluska Assembly** under *Lodging —Resorts*).

THE PUBLIC PARK ON THE SHORES OF LAKE JUNALUSKA IS A PLEASANT PLACE TO CATCH COOL LAKE BREEZES

✳ Villages

Waynesville, NC. In the early days of the Republic, Waynesville sat at the border of the Cherokee Nation, literally the end of the road for European settlers. As the Cherokees were pushed back into Tennessee, and then evacuated to Oklahoma, Waynesville

TRAILS OF THE GREAT BALSAM MOUNTAINS

Even compared with other parts of the Blue Ridge and Smoky Mountains, this area gives an exceptional variety of walking paths in a small area. Each of these walks gives a comparatively easy taste of a particular type of scenery found here: mountaintop meadows, backcountry waterfalls, wide views, craggy outcrops, and spruce-fir "balsam" forests.

Graveyard Fields and Black Balsam Knob. This perched valley sits nearly a mile above sea level, flanked by seven 6,000-foot peaks, just off the Blue Ridge Parkway 3 miles east of NC 215 (see The Blue Ridge Parkway under *Exploring by Car*). Once covered by huge old-growth forests—the "graveyard" refers to the gravelike mounds left by fallen giant trees as they return to the soil—it was devastated by clear-cut fires in the early 20th century and remains meadow covered to this day. A lovely system of hiking trails, most starting at the **Graveyard Fields Overlook** on the Blue Ridge Parkway, loops around the wildflower-carpeted meadows, along the clear mountain river that cuts through its center, down to the roaring waterfall that marks its foot, and up to the tall, graceful waterfall that sits at its head.

Above the fields, the 6,214-foot **Black Balsam Knob** and the adjacent 6,040-foot **Tennant Mountain** can be easily reached via the **Black Balsam Trail,** starting on the **Black Balsam Spur Road** off the parkway just west of the fields. This 1.75-mile round-trip (with 1,200 feet of climbing) follows the high ridgeline through mountaintop meadows and past large rock outcrops, with nearly continuous views over waving wildflowers. Turn around when you reach the deep gap with the old abandoned road—or continue forward into the stunning high-ridge meadows of the **Shining Rock Wilderness** (see *Wild Places—The Great Forests*) with three more 6,000-foot peaks.

A Walk in the Middle Prong Wilderness. The **Mountains-to-Sea Trail** makes for an easy 3.5-mile round-trip to the lush, spreading meadows on the 5,800-foot-tall crest of this otherwise remote wilderness area. Park your car on the

gained in importance as the gateway to the tangled valleys of the Blue Ridge and Smoky Mountains. Today it remains the main gateway and the largest of the traditional mountain towns. At first glance it's more sprawling and industrial than the other Smokies/Blue Ridge towns; however, attractive and genteel neighborhoods, rich in historic architecture, sit only a scant half block off the main drag. These his-

Blue Ridge Parkway as it traverses the **Great Balsam Mountains** (see The Blue Ridge Parkway under *Exploring by Car*), at **Rough Butt Bald Overlook** (milepost 425.3) about 2 miles from **Beech Gap** (NC 215). A path directly opposite the overlook links you to the Mountains-to-Sea Trail with its white circular blazes. Follow the blazes to your right. The trail quickly passes into the **Middle Prong Wilderness** (see *Wild Places—The Great Forests*) and follows an old logging tramway, level, wide, and easy. At 1.2 miles, the Mountain-to-Sea blazes turn uphill to the right, climbing 0.5 mile to the crest of **Fork Ridge,** remarkable for its mountaintop meadows. Formed by logging fires in the early 20th century and still occupying most of the Fork Mountain crest, the grassy meadows extend along the top of this high ridge for 2.3 miles, with a maze of paths leading through wildflowers and berries. Views are frequent and stunning, with the best views from rocky outcrops on the east side, looking over the gorge of the **West Fork Pigeon River** toward the sweeping meadows of the **Shining Rock Wilderness** (see *Wild Places—The Great Forests*).

Richland Balsams Nature Trail. This 1.2-mile nature trail climbs 350 feet to the 6,410-foot peak of Richland Balsams (10th highest in the East). A guide to this nature loop, available at its beginning, gives full information on the forest succession going on around you. Once a forest walk where giant firs and spruces shaded an open floor of needles and moss, it now crosses an ecology undergoing rapid and radical transition. Around 1980 a parasitic insect known as the wooly adelgid or aphid (an exotic introduced into Canada around 1900) reached the Balsam Mountains in its slow southward migration through the Appalachians. Within a few years all the fir trees (more than half the forest) had died, leaving the remaining spruces exposed to harsh weather and high wind, and the forest floor exposed to a whole host of sun-loving competitors. The trail now travels through wildflower meadows, thick patches of blackberry briars, stands of mountain ash (rowan) saplings, occasional groves of old spruces, and thick masses of fir seedlings and saplings competing with each other as well as the aphids. Once viewless because of the dense forest, the path now offers several views over newly formed meadows and briar patches; one such view lets you look down on the sign marking the highest point on the parkway.

toric neighborhoods have become a prime destination for knowledgeable visitors, as a dozen or more B&Bs have moved in. Waynesville has a charming downtown, three blocks of historic redbrick structure with a good choice of interesting shops. Downtown parking is free, but limited; however, there is plenty of parking on the back blocks. Every July this wonderful town center becomes the main venue for

Folkmoot USA (see *Special Events*), a large-scale gathering of 10 or more national-al dance troupes with performances throughout the Smoky Mountains region.

The Town of Lake Junaluska, NC. This small lakeside town 4 miles north of Waynesville, NC, off US 19 is dominated by its large and historic retreat, head-quarters for the **United Methodist Church** in the Southeast. The town centers on its 180-acre lake, created in the 1920s as part of a retreat for missionaries; now open to the public, the retreat remains the main focus of the village. The Methodist Church headquarters and retreat sit on the north side of the lake, an impressive grouping of buildings both historic and modern, dominated by the 1922 **Lambuth Inn** (see *Lodging—Resorts*) with its giant memorial cross. The south side, a quiet residential area, is lined by landscape parklands with by a 2-mile paved path—a wonderful lake-view walk (see **A Walk around Lake Junaluska** *under Wandering Around—Exploring on Foot*).

Canton, NC. Founded as the home of Champion Paper in 1906, Canton remains dominated by its giant mill, still one of the largest in America. Champion located here because the high-altitude forest furnished large numbers of spruce trees, val-ued for producing a high-quality pulp. Parts of these Champion forests have since become the **Shining Rock Wilderness**, the **Middle Prong Wilderness** (for both, see *Wild Places—The Great Forests*), and the **Smokemont** area of Great Smoky Mountains National Park (see *Wild Places—Recreation Areas* in "Chero-kee and the Southeast Quadrant")—all with large areas significantly altered to this day by huge clear-cut fires. Champion Paper finally left this area in the late 1990s, selling its plant to its employees and divesting itself of its last forest lands in 2001. Still a working mill town, Canton has few tourist facilities, but the small **Canton Historic Museum** (see *To See—Cultural Sites*) is worth a visit.

✳ Wild Places

THE GREAT FORESTS The Shining Rock Wilderness. The 18,400 acres of the Shining Rock Wilderness center on the high **Shining Rock Ledge,** a north-trending side ridge of the **Pisgah Range** with three 6,000-foot peaks (and four more in the protected recre-ation lands to its immediate south). Champion Paper purchased all of these lands in 1906, building the huge paper mill at Canton, NC (see *Vil-lages*), to exploit the spruces found in these high-altitude forests. This was not a success, and Champion turned to the Smokies for spruce pulp (see **Smokemont** under *Wild Places— Recreation Areas* in "Cherokee and the Southeast Quadrant"), selling Shining Rock to a succession of lum-ber companies. The loggers used tramways and locomotives to clear-cut

A BACKPACKER MAKES CAMP IN A MOUNTAIN MEADOW IN THE SHINING ROCK WILDERNESS.

the area; in 1926 sparks from a locomotive touched off a 25,000-acre wildfire that denuded the Shining Rock crest, creating the broad grassy meadows that remain the wilderness's most distinctive feature. Logging ceased after the fire, and the tract passed into the hands of Pisgah National Forest in 1935. Congress created the Shining Rock Wilderness in 1964.

Shining Rock's mile-high crest is completely covered by huge meadows, the results of that 1925 fire. The mountaintop meadows are rich in wildflowers and punctuated by unusual rock outcrops—including the large **Shining Rock,** a great mass of quartz that shines in the sun. The meadows extend southward all the way to the crest of the Pisgah Range and the Blue Ridge Parkway, and northward to **Cold Mountain** (at 6,030 feet, the 40th highest peak in the East), the same mountain used as the title for the best-selling novel. Because this 12-mile ledge is both stunningly beautiful and easily reached from the Blue Ridge Parkway, it tends to be popular. A good trail follows the crest from **Black Balsam Knob** (see Graveyard Fields and Black Balsam Knob under *Wandering Around—Trails of the Great Balsam Mountains*) all the way to Cold Mountain; it's easy going in its early sections but gets gradually more difficult as it proceeds, with the final ascent of Cold Mountain being notoriously difficult. A number of side trails, very rough and difficult, lead down the ridge to the forested valleys in the wilderness's lower slopes.

The Middle Prong Wilderness (828-877-3265), Pisgah Forest, NC. Located South of Waynesville off NC 215 and the Blue Ridge Parkway. Created by Congress in 1984, the 7,900-acre Middle Prong Wilderness occupies some of the highest, roughest, and most difficult land in the eastern wilderness system—the southern terminus of the **Great Balsam Mountains.** Within this wilderness the mountains rise from 3,200 feet to 6,400 feet—more than 3,000 feet of local relief—in only 2 linear miles. The **Middle Prong River** runs through the center of this wilderness, a mountain river in a deep, gashlike valley; **Fork Mountain** rises from it to the east, wholly within the wilderness, while the Great Balsam Mountains (with the Blue Ridge Parkway on its crest) rings the wilderness to the south and west.

Like the neighboring Shining Rock Wilderness (see above), the Middle Prong was clear-cut in the 1920s, then devastated by fire. The forests have rested since then, becoming very mature and attractive. Upper slopes are covered by balsam forests, while lower slopes are covered in maturing mixed hardwoods. The high crest of **Fork Ridge,** contained within the wilderness, is covered by a series of grassy wildflower meadows stretching for 2 miles along its ridgeline, affording spectacular views; at the south end of Fork Mountain stands 6,010-foot **Mount Hardy**. The **Mountains-to-Sea Trail** (see A Walk in the Middle Prong Wilderness under *Wandering Around—Trails of the Great Balsam Mountains*) gives safe and easy access to these mountaintop meadows; otherwise, the Middle Prong Wilderness trail system, although extensive, consists mainly of unblazed, unmaintained logging tramways, making for difficult and dangerous hiking.

PICNIC AREAS **Mount Pisgah Picnic Area,** milepost 408. This large picnic area on the Blue Ridge Parkway is part of the Mount Pisgah area, the last full-service recreation area on the parkway. It sits in a ridgeline forest just shy of 5,000 feet high—very breezy and cool on a hot summer day.

A LATE AFTERNOON VIEW WEST FROM THE RICHLAND BALSAM OVERLOOK (MP 431), NEAR CANEY FORK

✳ To See

ALONG THE BLUE RIDGE PARKWAY Caney Fork and Cowee Mountain Overlooks, mileposts 428 and 431. The mile-long stretch of parkway on either side of the Caney Fork Overlook gives dramatic roadside views (with easy verge parking) down a 3,000-foot drop into a mountain valley, and beyond to the **Tuckaseegee River, the Cowee Mountains,** and the **Nantahala Mountains.** Sunset lovers will appreciate the way the sun dips down into the lowest part of the deep valley, dropping below the horizon to throw orange sidelights on the tall ridges to its right and left, then falls behind layered mountains that recede endlessly into the background. Four miles later, Cowee Mountain Overlook gives a 270-degree view from a promontory, nearly 6,000 feet in elevation, that thrusts westward from the parkway over the deep valleys of the Balsams. A quarter mile north, **Haywood-Jackson Overlook** supplies the missing 90-degree view, eastward over the deep gorge of the **West Fork** to the mountaintop meadows of the **Middle Prong Wilderness** and the **Shining Rock Wilderness** (for both, see *Wild Places—The Great Forests*); fans of the best-selling novel *Cold Mountain* should look for this 6,030-foot peak in the far background.

Waterrock Knob. In its climb northward out of **Balsam Gap,** the parkway passes a number of good overlooks with views west and south. However, you might want to save your film for the top; as the parkway finally reaches the crest, it sends a ⅓-mile spur to a series of three overlooks with stunning 270-degree views. These overlooks (with views west, south, and north over the Balsams) occupy the high, grassy crest of a great wall-like side ridge known as **Plott Balsams,** after the local frontiersman who bred the Plott bearhound for hunting these slopes. The collection of overlooks makes up a small recreation area, with a modest visitors center, water, toilets, several tables, many wildflowers, and large grassy verges perfect for picnic blankets or tossing a Frisbee. Beyond the overlooks a wide, heavily used trail climbs very steeply to the peak of Waterrock Knob, for some good views.

CULTURAL SITES The Museum of North Carolina Handicrafts (828-452-1551), 49 Shelton Street (US 276), Waynesville, NC. Open Tuesday through Friday 10–4. $5. Located on the south edge of Waynesville, the 1875 **Shelton House**

is home to this extensive display of both home crafts and fine-art crafts from the Smokies, other parts of North Carolina, and the Navajo Nation. This beautifully restored mountain farmhouse, surrounded by meadows, has two-story verandas along its front, and walnut trim throughout its interior. Inside are traditional 19th-century farm furnishings and a wide array of mountain crafts—pottery, baskets, quilts, toys, and dulcimers. It has a large collection of Seagrove pottery, and items from fine-crafts artists throughout the state. A gift shop offers handmade crafts items for sale.

Canton Historic Museum (828-646-3412), Park Street, Canton, NC. Open Monday through Friday 10–noon and 1–4, Sunday 2–4. Free admission. This small local museum occupies the former public library in downtown Canton, next to the city hall. It has some items from the pioneer era, but most of its exhibits are about its controversial paper mill, often cited as the largest in the South, in operation next door since 1906.

✳ To Do

FISHING Lowe Fly Shop and Outfitter (828-452-0039), 977 North Main Street, Waynesville, NC. Half day: $150 for one person, $50 per additional person. Full day: $200 for one person, $75 per additional person. Fees include lunch. Roger Lowe acts as a fly-fishing guide from his fishing shop in downtown Waynesville. A specialist in hand tying flies, he offers encyclopedic information on fly patterns useful in the Smokies.

GEM MINING Old Pressley Sapphire Mine (828-648-6320), 240 Pressley Mine Road, Canton, NC. To find the mine, take exit 33 from I-40, then go north 1 mile on Newfound Road; from there, follow the signs for another 1.5 miles down back roads. Open every day 9–6. This remote mine has produced record-setting sapphires in years past. It remains one of the few recreational gem mines in these mountains to be located at an authentic mine, using unsalted ore from on-site (which you can dig yourself).

GOLF Waynesville Country Club Inn (828-452-4617; 1-800-627-6250), Business US 23, Waynesville, NC. The club is located on the edge of Waynesville, a mile west of downtown. $28. This golf resort built its first 9-hole course on a dairy farm in 1926; the barn served as the clubhouse. It now has three nine-hole courses that are played in three 18-hole combinations; views from the links extend to the surrounding mountains. The large resort has buildings from nearly every decade between the 1930s and the 1990s.

Iron Tree Golf Course (828-627-1933), Iron Tree Drive, NC 209, Waynesville, NC. Located 5 miles north of Waynesville off NC 209 (exit 24 off I-40), this 1991 course recently expanded to 18 holes. Open 7–7 every day. $22. The course is hilly, with excellent mountain scenery.

Lake Junaluska Golf Course (828-456-5777), 19 Golf Course Road (US 19), Waynesville, NC. $12. This 18-hole public course, built in 1919, is located 2 miles north of Waynesville, on the south edge of the Methodist retreat community (see The Town of Lake Junaluska under *Villages*).

Springdale Resort and Country Club (828-235-8451; 1-800-553-3027), 200 Golfwatch Road, Canton, NC. Open at 7 AM all year. $45. Despite its

Canton address, this golf resort is deep in the Pisgah Mountains, in a scenic valley 11 miles south of Waynesville, NC, on US 276. The 18-hole par-72 course offers stunning scenery, with views toward Cold Mountain and the Shining Rock Ledge, with play accentuated by hilly terrain and mountain streams.

✳ Lodging

COUNTRY HOTELS AND LODGES
The Old Stone Inn (828-456-3333; 1-800-432-8499), 109 Dolan Road, Waynesville, NC 28786. Open April through December. This highly rated lodge sits off a quiet back street in one of Waynesville's residential neighborhoods, 0.75 mile north of downtown. In operation since 1946, this rustic lodge has 23 rooms and a well-respected gourmet restaurant in its seven buildings scattered over 6 acres. The Main Lodge, with stone walls and tuliptree logs, houses the restaurant, wine bar, and two rooms; its long front porch overlooks the well-kept garden. Seventeen other rooms and four cottages (no kitchens) are found elsewhere on the property. Rooms, frequently small, are decorated in a simple, rustic manner, with wood paneling common. Breakfast, available only to guests, starts with coffee, muffin, and newspaper left outside the room, and continues with a full gourmet buffet in the lodge (table service on weekends). $89–154.

RESORTS ✍ & **The Pisgah Inn** (828-235-8228), P.O. Drawer 749, Waynesville, NC 28786. Open April through October. This modern motel-style inn fronts on the Blue Ridge Parkway in the 4,900-foot-high Mount Pisgah area—a national park concessionaire, and a good one. Two long, low buildings face over a sharp drop, giving dramatic views from every room. Standard rooms are standard hotel size, with two double beds and a private balcony with rocking chairs overlooking that fabulous view. The deluxe rooms have the same great views from the balcony but are larger and more recently renovated, and have larger windows for an unobstructed inside view. The one suite is a two-roomer with wood-burning fireplace. The attached restaurant (see *Eating Out*) is consistently good, specializing in fresh, simply prepared mountain dishes. This is the Blue Ridge Parkway's final inn, at the start of the stunning, rugged Pisgah/Balsams section—very cool, windy, remote, and quiet. Standard room $75; deluxe room $87; suite $125.

✍ & **The Lambuth Inn at the Lake Junaluska Assembly** (1-800-222-4930), Lake Junaluska, NC. Open all year. This Methodist retreat complex, owned and operated by the Southeastern Conference of the United Methodist Church (whose headquarters are on the premises), is open to individual vacationers and families, whether or not they wish to participate in any of the religious programs. The complex includes modern motels, apartments, and private cottage rentals—but the most striking property is the 1922 Lambuth Inn, with 130 en suite hotel rooms. This large hilltop hotel dominates the Lake Junaluska skyline with its bright yellow walls, white trim, and neo-Federalist classical styling. Needless to say, views from the Lambuth are first rate. The Lambuth has standard hotel rooms for one to four people, plus an on-site restaurant. The tariff includes free access to all the recreation facilities at the retreat, including golf and tennis. Alcohol is prohibited on all retreat properties. The Junaluska Assembly likes to quote prices per person, double occupancy, including meals; this listing converts this cost to the price for two people, double occupancy, without meals, at the time of writing. In-season $72; off-season $58. To include all meals, add $20 per day per person.

BED & BREAKFASTS ✿ **Windsong, A Mountain Inn** (828-627-6111), 459 Rockcliffe Lane, Clyde, NC 28721. The front of this beautifully situated modern log lodge faces uphill toward a small oriental-style garden, heated swimming pool, and tennis courts. Inside the inn, timber framing and plank log walls give a rustic counterpoint to an exotic decor that combines western furniture with folk items from around the world, while high picture windows open up the inn to the grand view outside. Four of the five theme-decorated rooms share that view with private decks or patios; the fifth has a private entrance onto the inn's flower and herb garden. All rooms have fireplaces, large whirlpool tubs (with wineglasses and opener on the side), and VCRs. Children are welcome in the adjacent **Pond Lodge,** another modern log structure, whose two suites each have two bedrooms, a full kitchen, and a private deck. Main Inn guests are served a full gourmet breakfast; Pond Lodge guests have a continental breakfast delivered to their suite. The hosts also offer guided llama treks to a mountain stream, where they serve a dinner of grilled salmon. Main Inn $120–145 off-season, $125–155 in-season; includes full gourmet breakfast. Pond Lodge suites $160–170 in-season, $170–180 off-season; includes continental breakfast. $10 weekday discount.

The Yellow House (828-452-0991; 1-800-563-1236), 89 Oakview Drive, Plott Creek Road, Waynesville, NC 28786. This outstanding luxury B&B occupies a century-old house on a pond, surrounded by beautiful gardens, in the pastoral Plott Creek Valley 3 miles from downtown Waynesville. Built by the prominent Lykes family of Tampa in the late 19th century, the Yellow House is a simple, elegant late-Victorian structure with wraparound porches and a second-story balcony. Common rooms are rich in polished hardwood and Victorian antiques; guests enjoy a wine and cheese reception in the afternoon, and a refrigerator full of beverages in the kitchen. The full gourmet breakfast is served on china and crystal in the elegant dining room. Six rooms, all en suite and more than ample in size, are in the main house, and a full cottage sits above the pond. All of the rooms are individually theme-decorated by owner Susan Smith, each reminiscent of a favorite place. There are two standard-size rooms; and two 2-room suites featuring a full sitting area with fireplace, large bed area, wet bar, and luxurious bath. Two extra-large suites have private entrances and lily pondviews: the high-ceilinged Carriage House is decorated in English Country with a peninsular fireplace and a private balcony; the low, beamed ceilings of St. Paul de Vence impart a French cottage atmosphere, with tiled floors, two-sided fireplace, and French doors leading to a private garden terrace. The recently opened Joy's Place cottage offers a French country kitchen, two bedrooms and baths, two fireplaces, and views over the pond from every room. Rooms $135–145; suites $175–250; cottage with kitchen $235;

includes full gourmet breakfast. Discounts for midweek and off-season.

Andon House Bed & Breakfast (828-452-3089; 1-800-293-6190), 92 Daisey Avenue, Waynesville, NC 28786. This large 1902 Victorian-style farmhouse sits in a quiet residential neighborhood three blocks uphill from downtown Waynesville. It features wide porches, tall ceilings, high windows, and lots of wood trim and Victorian furniture in the ample common rooms downstairs. The four rooms range from cozy to large; all are individually decorated and sound insulated, and two have private sundecks. A full breakfast, served in the dining room, runs to four courses. In-season $85–115; off-season: $95–125; includes full breakfast.

✐ **Prospect Hill Bed & Breakfast** (828-456-5980; 1-800-219-6147), 274 South Main Street (Business US 23), Waynesville, NC 28786. Built in 1902, this large late-Victorian farmhouse sits on its own hill surrounded by 1.3 acres of lawns and trees, just south of downtown Waynesville. A large, wide wraparound porch gives fine views over downtown Waynesville, and the first-floor common rooms are decorated with period antiques. The five spacious upstairs guest rooms are individually furnished with antiques and reproductions. Three more-expensive rooms have sitting areas with Victorian sofas. Morning coffee is brought to your room, and a full breakfast is served on china and crystal in the formal dining room or on the porch. Small children are welcome in the two cottage apartments on the property. $95–135 for B&B in the main house, including breakfast; cottage apartments (breakfast not included) $170 for 2 nights, $450 per week.

Haywood House Bed & Breakfast (828-456-9831), 675 South Haywood Street, Waynesville, NC 28786. This large historic house on a busy side street of Waynesville's lovely little downtown was once the home of the local historian; now it houses a five-room B&B. The cozy rooms are elaborately decorated in high Victorian style, including antiques; two share a bath. A full home-cooked breakfast is served in the dining room. $75–95, including breakfast.

& **Herrin House** (828-452-7837; 1-800-284-1932), 94 East Street, Waynesville, NC 28786. Originally built as a boardinghouse in 1897, the completely renovated Herrin House sits a short block off the center of Downtown Waynesville, on a quiet residential side street. Its large wraparound porch looks out over a garden, with a roomy gazebo. Decor, both in the ample common areas and in the six guest rooms, is elegantly Victorian, with antiques and reproductions. Rooms are individually decorated, some elaborately and others with a simpler, outdoors theme; one special room is octagonal, with an original 48 light window. Afternoon tea consists of homemade goodies, and a full breakfast is served in the dining room. $95–140, including full breakfast and afternoon tea.

Ten Oaks Bed & Breakfast (828-452-9433; 1-800-563-2925), 224 Love Lane, Waynesville, NC 28786. This large hilltop Victorian house, built for the mayor of Waynesville in 1898 and listed in the National Register of Historic Places, sits in a quiet residential neighborhood, with views over Waynesville and toward the Pisgah Mountains beyond. Common areas, with elegant Victorian decor, face a large wraparound porch and a gazebo garden.

The five large rooms all have sitting areas and individual Victorian decor, and two are two-room suites. Rooms $95–110; suites: $130–145; includes breakfast.

October Hill (828-452-7967; 1-800-628-4455), 421 Grimball Drive, Waynesville, NC 28786. This elegant 1920s mansion sits on a hill, surrounded by shaded lawns, 1 mile south of downtown Waynesville and just off Business US 23. Its four literary-themed rooms, ranging in size from standard to large, are furnished in high fashion from the 1920s, as are the comfortable common rooms. A full breakfast is served in the dining room, and afternoon refreshments are available in the Grand Room. $95–135, including breakfast.

❀ **The Grange Bed & Breakfast** (828-452-0339), 355 Grassmere Lane, Waynesville, NC 28786. This modern, purpose-built inn sits on its own 60 acres in Oxear Cove, 5 miles from downtown Waynesville. The lands include an English tea garden, meadows, forests, mountain streams, even a duck pond, all accessible to guests by a network of old farm roads. Wide covered porches offer spectacular views over Waynesville and the Pisgah Ridge, especially good at sunrise in the fall, when fog fills the valleys below. Each of the four rooms has its own balcony with a wide mountain view. $100–115, including full breakfast; discounts during the off-season.

CABIN RENTALS Rivermont Cabins (828-648-3066), 311 Rivermont Drive, Canton, NC 28716. This 70-acre wooded property has a half-mile frontage on the West Fork Pigeon River in the Sunburst area, 9 miles south of Waynesville. The nine cabins are all individual structures with their own histories, ranging from modest

cabins to full-sized houses, and from contemporary log structures to the local 1855 schoolhouse. $415–985 per week; daily rentals only during off-season.

✳ **Where to Eat**

EATING OUT ♿ **The Pisgah Inn** (828-235-8228), Blue Ridge Parkway milepost 400, Waynesville, NC. Open April through October: 7:30 AM–10:30 AM (breakfast); 11:30 AM–4 PM (lunch); 5 PM–9 PM (dinner). This national park concessionaire sits by the side of the Blue Ridge Parkway, high and remote on the flanks of Mount Pisgah. The casual, simply furnished restaurant in The Pisgah Inn (see *Lodging—Resorts*) has dramatic views from huge windows that cover its entire southern side, flanked by large timber beams. The menu emphasizes fresh ingredients and mountain recipes, although there are plenty of old favorites available too. Full breakfasts can be ordered with fresh mountain trout, and local hickory-smoked trout can be ordered from the appetizer menu. Burgers and sandwiches are available for lunch or dinner, but a more formal dinner is also available, with specials that are prepared from scratch and change daily. Wine and beer are served. Breakfast $4.75–9.95 (pastries $1–2); lunch $4.95–6.95; dinner $4.95–11.50.

Lomo Bakery and Café (828-452-1515), 44 Church Street, Waynesville, NC. Open for lunch, Monday through Saturday. This lunch spot produces fresh breads and pastries, and a fine array of first-rate sandwiches. Its big brother, the nearby **Lomo Grille** (see *Dining Out*), now opens for lunch as well to give customers better seating for the popular sandwiches and pastries, plus burgers and other hot items.

Maggies Galley (828-456-8945), 49

Howell Mill Road, Waynesville, NC. Open for lunch and dinner, Tuesday through Sunday. Despite its name, Maggie's Galley is not located in Maggie Valley; this seafood restaurant occupies a log building just off US 276 a mile north of downtown Waynesville. Built in 1975 from logs salvaged from historic log cabins, this cozy and comfortable eatery features casual dining from a menu heavy with seafood favorites. Don't expect any masterful gourmet specialties here—just good food, prepared in the traditional way.

DINING OUT The Old Stone Inn (828-456-3333; 1-800-432-8499), 109 Dolan Road, Waynesville, NC. Open April through December, 6 PM–8 PM, by reservation only. Part of a rustic lodge, this Golden Fork–winning restaurant sits in a quiet residential neighborhood 0.75 mile north of downtown Waynesville. Owner Cindy Zinser serves as the chef, designing a short but selective menu that imaginatively exploits seasonally fresh ingredients. The wine list is excellent, and the Wine Bar offers wine by the glass with hors d'oeuvres from 5 PM. The stone and log lodge, with a large porch overlooking 6 landscaped acres, has a rustic look and feel. Entrées $15–21.

The Sourwood Grille (828-235-8451; 1-800-553-3027), 200 Golfwatch Road (US 276), Canton, NC. Open for lunch and dinner, April through November. Located on the grounds of the **Springdale Resort and Country Club** (see *To Do—Golf*) 11 miles south of Waynesville, this scenic and popular spot offers fine dining. The lunch menu includes a range of interesting and unusual hot and cold sandwiches, burgers, fish cakes, salads, and pasta dishes, none of it particularly expensive. Dinners are fancier, with

fresh and highly original fare, ranging from a spinach, leek, and goat cheese phyllo pie with charred pepper and tomato coulis, to grilled spiced lamb chops with roasted sweet potato and mint cumin yogurt sauce. Lunch $6–8; dinner: $13–19.

Lomo Grille (828-452-5222), 44 Church Street, Waynesville, NC. Open for lunch 11–3 Monday through Saturday; for dinner 5:30–9:30 Thursday through Saturday and Monday. This Golden Fork winner in downtown Waynesville specializes in Italian-Argentinean cuisine—the heritage of owner Ricardo Fernadez. Its special feature is its wood-fired oven, imported from Italy. Its menu includes imported Argentine beef, as well as lamb, salmon, trout, and pasta. Chef Ricardo uses only fresh ingredients and grows many of his own vegetables and herbs. The restaurant has an extensive international wine list, as well as a wine bar where many of the offerings can be sampled by the glass.

✳ Entertainment

Haywood Arts Repertory Theater (HART) (828-456-6322), 114 Church Street, Waynesville, NC. This local theater group performs seven shows each summer season (including two musicals) in their 250-seat theater behind the **Museum of North Carolina Handicrafts** (see *To See—Cultural Sites*). $12–15.

Pickin' in the Park (828-646-3411). Canton Recreation Park. Fridays at 7 PM May through August, every Friday, 7 PM till. Free admission. The City of Canton presents local bluegrass, mountain, and country groups, free of charge, by the Pigeon River at **Canton Recreation Park.** Bring your own lawn chair.

Mountain Street Dances (828-456-3517), Waynesville, NC. Held July through August, every other Saturday, 6:30 PM–9 PM. Free admission. Clogging and square dancing to live bluegrass music on the front lawn of the county courthouse, in downtown Waynesville.

✳ Selective Shopping

Downtown Waynesville, NC, furnishes one of the more interesting and varied shopping districts in the Smokies. A classic small-town district, it stretches for three blocks along the former main highway, from the county courthouse to the city hall. Its 86 retailers and restaurants are dominated by small crafts galleries and boutiques, but you'll also find antiques stores, kitchen-supply stores, bookstores, cafés, wine sellers . . . almost anything except the franchised or the dull.

Sloan's Book Shop, 263 North Haywood Street, Waynesville, NC. This bright, pleasant bookstore one block off downtown Waynesville's Main Street goes well beyond the usual stock of best-sellers, to carry a wonderful selection of local-interest titles. Smoky Mountains history, ecology, folklore, fiction—it's all here.

Crafts Galleries and Studios in Downtown Waynesville. Twelve crafts galleries and studios group together in the three blocks of downtown Waynesville—a bonanza for the fine-crafts shopper. On the edge of downtown (Haywood and Depot Streets), sculptor Grace Cathey exhibits her nature-inspired art in a working gas station **(Walker Service Station),** with a sculpture garden in back. Then, in a two-block stretch of Main Street (US 276), are galleries displaying local professional artists' clay

sculpture, stoneware, jewelry, textiles, photographs, woodcarving, watercolors, pencil sketches, and numbered prints. Four of these shops incorporate the working studios of the artists/owners. **Twig and Leaves** (98 Main Street) features nature-inspired art and includes the studio of potter Kaaren Stoner. **Burr Gallery** (136 Main Street) features the studio and work (sculpture and stoneware) of clay artists Dane and MaryEtta Burr. **Hardwood Gallery** (102 Main Street) features crafts items and sculptures carved from local woods on the spot. And **Cross-Currents** (84 Main Street) features textiles and rugs, some handwoven on the giant loom upstairs.

✳ Special Events

Second Saturday in May: **The Garden Party** (828-642-7925), Canton, NC. This Canton street fair celebrates the coming of spring with plant sales, crafts displays, live music, and a Mad Hatter contest.

Third Saturday in June: **Art in the Mountains** (828-456-3517), Waynesville, NC. Downtown Waynesville artists open up their galleries and studios for this annual open house and walking tour.

☂ *July–October:* **Blue Ridge Reunion Arts and Crafts Show,** Balsam Gap. The wide halls of the historic **Balsam Mountain Inn** (see *Lodging—Country Inns and Hotels* under in "Near the Park: Sylva and Dillsboro") host this annual juried art show of Jackson and Haywood County artists and crafters.

Fourth of July: **Fourth of July Celebrations. Waynesville,** NC, celebrates with a downtown street fair, sidewalk sales, entertainment, and refreshments. Nearby **Lake Juna-**

luska, NC, has an 11 AM parade followed by live mountain music, clogging, and crafts displays until 3 PM. Waynesville's fortnightly evening of **Mountain Street Dances** (see *Entertainment*) starts the following Saturday.

Last two weeks in July: **Folkmoot USA** (828-452-2997; 1-877-365-5872), 282 Haywood Square, Waynesville, NC. This major folk-dance event brings 10 to 12 national dance troupes to the Smoky Mountains region, with Waynesville at the center of the action. As many as 350 dancers and musicians perform folk music and dance in native costume, at venues scattered throughout the mountains. The festivities start with a day-long street fair in downtown Waynesville, with dancers and musicians giving impromptu performances and mixing with visitors and locals. After that, the festival concentrates on indoor performances, with admissions charges partially defraying costs.

August–September: **The Canton Labor Day Celebration** (828-648-7925), Canton, NC. Canton, with its giant paper mill, makes quite a celebration out of Labor Day. Starting the Thursday before, five days of music and special events at **Canton Recreation Park** climax with a parade down Main Street on Labor Day.

Last week in September: **The Haywood County Fair** (828-456-3575), Waynesville, NC. Held at the **Hay-**

PARTICIPANTS IN TRADITIONAL COSTUME AT THE FOLKMOOT FESTIVAL IN WAYNESVILLE

wood County Fairgrounds in Waynesville, this classic county fair has carnival rides, live entertainment, and plenty of food, along with the livestock shows, home-extension exhibits, and agriculture competitions.

Second Sunday in October: **Church Street Arts and Crafts Show,** Waynesville, NC. This downtown Waynesville street fair features regional crafters along with mountain music and dance, entertainment, and food.

November–December: **Christmas Celebrations. Waynesville** has its **Christmas Parade** during the last week in November; **Canton** follows with its **Festival of Lights Night Parade** a week later. Canton continues its celebration throughout December with home tours, lighting displays, and a **"drive-through Nativity"** organized by Canton churches.

ASHEVILLE'S RUGGED HINTERLANDS

North of Asheville, NC, the mountains extend in a grand tumble for mile after mile. This is an area of tangled ridgelines where craggy tops can suddenly change to wide, broad meadows, a place where streams drop over waterfalls into sharp-sided valleys. It's also a region of broad rivers that flow through deep gorges to empty into broad, rich valleys, where isolation keeps towns tiny and unspoiled. Opportunities for outdoor enjoyment are remarkable and widespread: the French Broad River, a first-rate kayaking and rafting river with spectacular gorge scenery; The Bald Mountains, straddling the state line with 50,000 rugged acres open to the public; Max Patch, one of the most beautiful sunset peaks anywhere. Most tourism focuses on the tiny, remote town of Hot Springs, where there are a good choice of quality B&Bs and restaurants. High-quality travel services can also be found in Marshall, NC, Mars Hill, NC, and Del Rio, TN—but for the most part, this area has more outdoors opportunities than innkeepers and restaurateurs.

GUIDANCE **Madison County Tourism Development Authority** (828-680-9031; 877-262-3476), P.O. Box 1527, Mars Hill, NC 28754. This agency maintains a visitors center in a restored historic mansion near the center of Mars Hill.
Pisgah National Forest, Appalachian/French Broad Ranger District (828-622-3202), US 25, P.O. Box 128, Hot Springs, NC 28743. The French Broad Ranger District is responsible for all Pisgah National Forest lands in this region. It maintains an information desk at its office in Hot Springs.

GETTING THERE *By car:* This area is bisected by US 25/70, a two-lane U.S. highway running between Newport, TN, and Asheville, NC; all four of the region's villages are on this highway. Tennessee's Bald Mountains, in the northeast quadrant of this area, are best reached from Greeneville, via TN 107 or TN 351.

By air: **Asheville Regional Airport** (see *Getting There* in "Asheville and the Blue Ridge Parkway") is the closest to most of this area. **Tri-Cities Airport** (see *Getting There* in "The Mountains of Northern Tennessee"), near Johnson City, TN, is closer for those who are mainly interested in Tennessee's Bald Mountains.

By bus or train: This region has no scheduled passenger service by either train or bus.

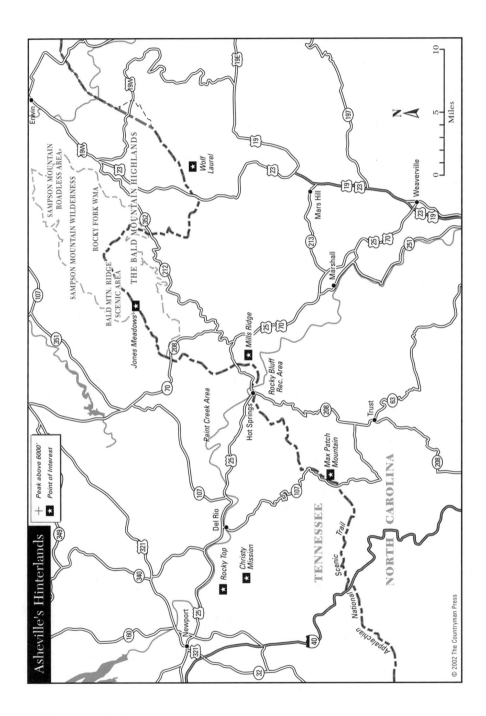

Asheville's Hinterlands

Legend:
+ Peak above 6000'
★ Point of Interest

Locations and features:
- Ervin
- SAMPSON MOUNTAIN ROADLESS AREA
- SAMPSON MOUNTAIN WILDERNESS
- ROCKY FORK WMA
- BALD MTN. RIDGE SCENIC AREA
- THE BALD MOUNTAIN HIGHLANDS
- ★ Jones Meadows
- ★ Wolf Laurel
- Mars Hill
- Weaverville
- Marshall
- ★ Mills Ridge
- Rocky Bluff Rec. Area
- Paint Creek Area
- Hot Springs
- Trust
- ★ Max Patch Mountain
- Del Rio
- ★ Rocky Top
- ★ Christy Mission
- Newport
- TENNESSEE
- NORTH CAROLINA
- Appalachian National Scenic Trail

Roads: 107, 351, 349, 340, 321, 160, 32, 40, 25, 70, 208, 112, 352, 23, 19W, 19E, 19, 197, 213, 251, 63

Scale: 0 5 10 Miles

N

© 2002 The Countryman Press

Springs Health Program is not a hospital and does not maintain an emergency room. Rather, it is a rural primary-care program with four clinics (listed below)—the only primary-care program in the area. It was founded in 1971 by two nurse practitioners who were distressed by Hot Springs's inability to obtain medical care. The rural clinic they founded—a model of its sort—now employs 11 general practitioners, an obstetrician, and a dentist, along with 130 other employees. For routine medical problems, these are good people to contact. Please note that the Mars Hill clinic (see **Mars Hill Medical Center** below) is open every day.

Mars Hill Medical Center (828-689-3507), 119 Mountain View Road, Mars Hill, NC. Open Monday through Saturday 9–9, Sunday 1–9.

Marshall-Walnut Medical Center (828-649-3500), 8625 US 25/70, Marshall, NC. Open Monday through Friday 9–5, Saturday 2–5.

Hot Springs Medical and Dental Center (828-622-3245), 66 Northwest US 25/70, Hot Springs, NC. Open Monday through Friday 9–5, Saturday 8–noon.

Laurel Medical Center (828-656-2611), 80 Guntertown Road, Laurel, NC. Open Monday through Friday 9–5.

MEDICAL EMERGENCIES: HOSPITALS **Mission St. Josephs Hospital** (828-231-1111), 509 Biltmore Avenue, Asheville, NC. With western North Carolina's only Level II trauma facility, this large hospital is located just south of downtown Asheville. This is the closest hospital for Mars Hill and Marshall, NC; for Hot Springs, NC, it's a toss-up between this hospital and the much smaller Baptist Hospital of Cocke County in Newport, TN (see below).

Baptist Hospital of Cocke County (865-625-2200), 435 Second Street, Newport, TN. Located near the center of Newport, this 74-bed hospital has the closest emergency room to the Del Rio area.

Takoma Adventist Hospital (423-639-3151), 401 Takoma Avenue, Greeneville, TN. This full-service local hospital within Greeneville is just west of the town center, off US 321. It's the closest hospital to Tennessee's Bald Mountains.

✳ Wandering Around

EXPLORING BY CAR **A Hot Springs Drive.** *Leg 1:* From Hot Springs, NC, follow US 25 north 13 miles to Del Rio, TN; then turn right on TN 107 and drive 13 miles to the state line; then continue straight ahead for 3.3 miles on gravel SSR 1182, Max Patch Road, to the Max Patch Parking Area.

Leg 2: Continue on Max Patch Road 4.5 miles to Meadow Fork Road (SSR 1175); turn left and drive 3.6 miles to Caldwell Corner Road (SSR 1165); turn right and drive 2 miles to NC 209; then turn left and drive 11.6 miles to Hot Springs.

This chapter's featured scenic drive links Hot Springs with Max Patch, visiting the western part of the district on the way there and back. Its first leg starts along the recently rebuilt US 25, switchbacking out of **Hot Springs** past a monument, then leaving town to make broad sweeps high above the **French Broad River.** As the river drops into a gorge far away on the right, the highway climbs toward the Ten-

THIS VIEW OVER THE FRENCH BROAD RIVER AND THE BALD MOUNTAINS FROM A ROADSIDE OVERLOOK ON OLD US 70 IS MAINTAINED BY A LOCAL RESIDENT

nessee border, marked by a classic state-line bar (once a common sight when much of the rural South was dry). From there the highway curves back to the French Broad River, crossing it on a long, old bridge with good views. The highway now follows the river closely, with broad views over it toward the fields and mountains beyond, reaching **Del Rio**, TN (see *Villages*), in 4.5 miles Despite its tiny size and obscurity, Del Rio featured prominently in two pop-culture icons from the late 1960s—Catherine Marshall's best-selling religious novel *Christy* (see **The "Christy" Mission** under *To See—Historic Sites*), and the ribald bluegrass standard "Rocky Top" (see **Rocky Top, Tennessee** under *To See—Historic Sites*). From there, the route runs through beautiful, hilly farming valleys, then climbs very steeply uphill to the crest of the **Bald Mountains.** Finally the road crosses the crest of the Bald Mountains into North Carolina and immediately turns into the gravel **Max Patch Road** (SSR 1182). **Max Patch** (see *Wild Places—The Forests of Hot Springs*) itself, with its wide wildflower meadows and stunning 360-degree views over the Smokies and the Balds, is just beyond.

Past Max Patch, Max Patch Road becomes a beautiful ridgetop drive that alternates between deep forests and wide views over mountaintop pastureland. From there, our route turns east off the mountaintop, dropping through lovely valleys and over a side ridge to reach NC 209. A right turn down this state highway will take you 2 miles to the tiny village of **Trust,** NC, with its beautiful roadside **Trust Chapel** (see *To See—Cultural Sites*) and, farther down NC 63, a European-style garden (see **The Herb of Grace** under *Selective Shopping—Trust, NC*). However, the scenic route goes left instead, heading back toward Hot Springs. On this stretch NC 209 passes through well-tended farm valleys with some fine old buildings, then curves steeply uphill to run along the top of the dramatic **Spring Creek Gorge.** There are three good views over the gorge, plus more views from the paths in **Rocky Bluffs Recreation Area** (see *Wild Places—Recreation Areas*). From there, Hot Springs is only 3 miles away, for a total loop of 50 miles.

Mountain Wilderness trails are known for their waterfalls, handsome forests, good views—and steep uphill pulls from the ends of valley roads. The trails that lead into the wilderness from **Horse Creek Picnic Area** (see Horse Creek Recreation Area under *Wild Places—Picnic Areas*) possess all these virtues. The easier of the two follows **Squibb Creek** uphill, climbing 600 feet in 2.2 miles, through beautiful cove forests to a small but particularly lovely waterfall. The second path, a mountain-climbing loop, leaves Squibb Creek after 0.4 mile, marked as **Turkeypen Creek Trail.** This path climbs a steady 18 percent gradient through

MAX PATCH WALKS

A 4,630-foot peak marking the western end of the Bald Mountains, Pisgah National Forest's Max Patch offers easy and dramatic walking across miles of mountaintop meadows. This walk starts at the trailhead parking lot (see A Hot Springs Drive under *Exploring by Car).* Go uphill through meadows, climbing 200 feet in a scant half mile, gaining increasingly spectacular views on the way up. You'll probably pass hay bales; the Forest Service keeps these old cattle pastures from returning to scrubby forests by regular mowing and burning. At the top you'll find a surveyor's monument marking the summit, and posts with white blazes marking the route of the **Appalachian Trail (AT)** through the grasses and flowers. Here the view is a complete circle of endlessly receding mountains. The mountains on the west are the Great Smokies; the ridges passing on to the northeast are the Bald Mountains. The **Max Patch summit** is a wonderful place for a sunset, and it's not uncommon to see people all over the ridge, picnicking and camping in an impromptu sunset party.

To extend the walk, follow the AT downhill to the left, dropping 400 feet. As the trail reaches a lower set of meadows, it briefly merges with an old farm track running along the ridge. Follow this track along the ridge for another mile of stunning meadow views. When you reach the end, don't try to explore downhill; instead, return by following the farm track all the way back to **Max Patch Road.** When you reach the road, your car is parked a thousand feet to the right.

THE APPALACHIAN TRAIL PASSES OVER THE SUMMIT OF MAX PATCH.

rich and varied forests, following a small, steep creek to finally gain a ridgeline. Then there's more steep climbing up along the ridge, whose xeric forests give way to large rock outcrops with spectacular views over the **Sampson Wilderness.** The trail reaches a ridgetop trail intersection at 2.5 miles, having gained 1,600 feet in that short distance. Turn right for a ridgeline walk back down to Squibb Creek.

✳ Villages

Mars Hill, NC. Mars Hill is a handsome hilltop college town, with a one-block downtown adjacent to the tree-shaded, redbrick campus of **Mars Hill College** (see *To See—Cultural Sites*). It's located a mile off the main freeway, US 23 (the future I-26), on NC 209. Its single traffic light marks the center of town, with the campus straight ahead, the visitors center to the left, and downtown to the right. Both the college and the village are compact, more like a New England college town than a Southern one, and people tend to get around on foot—along the downtown sidewalk with its old redbrick storefronts, through the campus on tree-shaded walks, and into the neighborhoods with their historic houses.

Marshall, NC. You'll find Marshall just off US 25, north of Asheville, NC. Madison County's seat sits deep in a gorge, stretching for six blocks along the **French Broad River.** The river here is broad enough to have an island that holds the local elementary school—a popular venue for festivals. A major railroad line stretches along the river's east bank; then the town's center stretches along the railroad; then the town's residential area terraces up the side of the gorge behind downtown. The handsome old courthouse sits in the middle of downtown, its dome set against the green forests of the gorge wall behind it—a striking sight, particularly with the unusual **Rock Café** (see *Eating Out*) adding character to the scene. A long time ago, the main road from Asheville passed through the center of town; however, Marshall was bypassed in the 1950s, then the bypass was bypassed in the 1960s. Now it looks like the bypassed bypass's bypass is going to be bypassed by the new I-26. Nowadays, Marshall is a real quiet place.

APPALACHIAN TRAIL THRU-HIKERS REST OUTSIDE THE BRIDGE STREET LAUNDRY IN HOT SPRINGS.

Hot Springs, NC. Hot Spring's old downtown tries to stretch itself to three blocks. On those blocks are a little bit of everything—restaurants, a neat hardware store, a 1950s-style motel, a Forest Service ranger station, some houses, and several shops. However, this central business district gets an unusual boost from its sidewalk; this particular stretch of concrete is known to the world as the **Appalachian Trail.** The famous Georgia to Maine path descends into town from the mountains on the west, follows the sidewalk through town and across the

French Broad River, then dives into the woods again. You'll see hikers with backpacks walking the sidewalk, sitting and resting on a bench, or inside one of the stores with their gear stored neatly in a corner.

The other notable thing about Hot Springs is its remoteness. It's 30 minutes to the nearest town in either direction, down a twisting, two-lane highway (US 25). After a 1998 ice storm it took 10 days to restore power to parts of the area. Hot Springs tends to attract people who like it quiet and isolated, making for a tightly knit community of mountain people, free spirits, and folks dedicated to serious relaxing. Most services are available at Hot Springs. US 25 runs through town from Asheville, NC, to Newport, TN; and NC 209 forks away at the center of town to wander southward toward Waynesville, NC.

Del Rio, TN, is an old depot town in the Bald Mountains of Tennessee. Sitting by a siding near the banks of the **French Broad River,** it consists of a straggle of old buildings along TN 107 just off US 25. While Del Rio itself offers little reason to slow down (aside from an occasional dog sleeping on the road), the surrounding mountains are remarkably scenic (see A Hot Springs Drive under *Wandering Around—Exploring by Car*). Del Rio was the model for "El Plano" in Catherine Marshall's 1968 novel *Christy,* and the actual mission portrayed in that novel makes for an interesting visit (see **The "Christy" Mission** under *To See—Historic Sites*).

✳ Wild Places

THE BALD MOUNTAIN HIGHLANDS For the most part, the steep-sided Bald Mountains are known for two things: dividing North Carolina from Tennessee, and carrying 20 miles of the **Appalachian Trail.** Less well known are its nearly 50,000 contiguous acres of recreational wild lands—about 75 square miles. To the hikers, fishers, hunters, and campers who use this area, it's one giant tract of remote mountain land, a land filled with craggy ridgelines, mountaintop meadows, hidden coves, waterfalls, and a single, continuous hardwood forest that has not been disturbed for more than 60 years. However, to the powers that be it's five separate tracts: one owned by Pisgah National Forest in North Carolina (Shelton Laurel Backcountry Area), three owned by the Cherokee National Forest in Tennessee (Sampson Mountain Wilderness Area, Sampson Mountain Roadless Area, and Bald Mountain Ridge Scenic Area), and one leased by the State of Tennessee from a lumber company (Rocky Fork Unit of the Cherokee Wildlife Management Area).

Shelton Laurel Backcountry Area. This remote tract of North Carolina's Pisgah National Forest was the site of one of the most notorious of the Civil War's genocides: the **Shelton Laurel Massacre,** where Confederate regulars, acting under orders, murdered 13 local Unionist farmers and hid the bodies in a mass grave. The victims were traditionalist mountain folk who believed that God had established the Union and that the flatlander Confederates were rebels against God's Will (see **Primitive Baptist Church** under *To See—Cades Cove Historic Sites* in "Townsend, Cades Cove, and the Northwest Quadrant"). In turn, the most radical Confederates considered these Unionist mountain folk to be traitors who deserved to be killed. These killings occurred throughout the mountains but were usually done by marauding gangs of irregulars. The Shelton Laurel Massacre was exceptional for its brutality—the dead included children—and for being an official act of the Confederate Army.

Today, Shelton Laurel is a backcountry forest, managed by Pisgah National Forest, for rugged outdoor recreation. Here, mixed hardwoods cover the steep southern slopes of the Bald Mountains, crossed by **hiking trails** that not uncommonly climb 2,000 feet or more. Two popular (and very difficult) loops climb from **Big Creek** to the **AT,** with stunning views back over the Laurel; to find the trailhead, take NC 212 to **Big Creek Road** (SSR 1312, opposite Carmen Church), then north to the trailhead. A second trailhead (NC 212, then north on **Hickey Fork Road,** SSR 1310) leads to an easy forest walk up and old road to remote, meadow-covered **Whiteoak Flats,** where a right turn leads half a mile to a waterfall.

The Sampson Mountain Wilderness Area and Roadless Area. Part of Tennessee's Cherokee National Forest, these two areas protect nearly 15,000 acres of the north slope of the Bald Mountains, near Erwin, TN. They cover an area of quickly maturing second-growth forest, last logged in the 1920s. These two areas are noted for their waterfalls, as well as their attractive forests and good views. They are also noted for trails with long, steep uphill pulls, starting at the ends of the valley roads and going straight up the steep flanks of the Balds. The most popular trailhead, at **Horse Creek Picnic Area** (see Horse Creek Recreation Area under *Picnic Areas*), gives a good sampling of all of these qualities (see also **Sampson Mountain Wilderness Walks** under *Wandering Around—Exploring on Foot*).

Bald Mountain Ridge Scenic Area. West of the Sampson Mountain Wilderness (see above), the Tennessee Bald Mountains are protected for recreationists as the Bald Mountain Ridge Scenic Area. Unlike a wilderness area, this scenic area allows a broad range of recreation (while prohibiting logging). Off-road vehicles are allowed on some trails, and three remote sites can be reached by passenger cars. One, **Forge Creek Campground** (a side road from Horse Creek Recreation Area; see *Picnic Areas*), is a seasonal campground and trailhead for the notably beautiful **Jennings Creek Trail.** The second, **Round Knob Picnic Area** (see *Picnic Areas*), features a hair-raising mountain drive to a lovely little Civilian Conservation Corps (CCC) picnic spot. The third leads to the remarkable **Jones Meadows** (see Jones Meadows on the Bald Mountains under *Recreation Areas*) high on the crest of the Balds.

The Rocky Fork Unit of the Cherokee Wildlife Management Area. Approach from US 23 (future I-26) south of Erwin, TN, by taking TN 352 for 4.4 miles to a right on Rocky Fork Road, then drive another 0.9 mile to the trailhead. This 10,000-acre tract of private land has been leased by the State of Tennessee as a hunting area for the past 60 years. At this writing, the state still leases it, and it remains open to hikers when hunting isn't going on. It's an important tract, separating the **Sampson Mountain Wilderness** from the **Appalachian Trail** and abutting the **Shelton Laurel Backcountry.** It shares the virtues of these publicly owned tracts—spectacular views, waterfalls, rugged and rocky scenery, and deep gorges. Trails are not developed, but hunters' trails exist, and access tracks lead deep into its center.

Just east of Hot Springs, NC, a large tract of national forest land extends upward from the **French Broad River,** with high peaks, wildflower meadows, impressive waterfalls, and a long section of the **Appalachian Trail (AT).** Historically, its most famous landmark has been **Paint Rock,** a tall red cliff that loomed above the Buncombe Turnpike, an 1820s road that opened up the mountains. Now the cliff looms above gravel **Paint Rock Road,** on the east bank of the French Broad River. The road follows the river until it passes under Paint Rock, then crosses into Tennessee and turns abruptly inland to follow Paint Creek. This is an impressive drive, hugging close to **Paint Creek** to pass a whole series of waterfalls, some quite large. There are several good picnic areas as well.

Over the river from Hot Springs and south of US 25, the AT climbs the bluffs above the French Broad River for wide, cliff-top views. From there it wanders into a series of meadows on the rolling 2,500-foot top of **Mill Ridge.** Passenger cars can make it to the near edge of the Mill Ridge meadows by taking US 25 about 4 miles west of town, then making a left onto a side road and crossing over the highway on a viaduct; from there it's only a mile up a gravel Forest Service road. There's a loop bicycle path and lots of good exploring. Nearby (at the intersection of US 25 and NC 208), another hiking/biking path leads gently downhill to the French Broad River at the remote, abandoned siding town of **Runion, NC.** The trail follows an old lumber railroad grade along the remarkably beautiful **Laurel Creek,** gently falling ever deeper into the gorge.

Max Patch. Known as the Jewel of the Appalachians, remote 4,600-foot Max Patch is crowned with wide wildflower meadows. The best-known and best-loved part of a large tract of Pisgah and Cherokee National Forest lands, Max Patch is an easy introduction to this little-visited corner of the country, with a trailhead on **Max Patch Road** (see A Hot Springs Drive under *Wandering Around—Exploring by Car*) scarcely a half mile and 200 feet from the summit. Grasslands cover its wide, rolling pinnacle, and grasslands continue to flow down to the ridgelines 400 feet below. A 360-degree panorama surrounds a mountaintop nearly always buffeted by high winds; **Great Smoky Mountains National Park** is clearly visible to the west (see **Max Patch Walks** under *Wandering Around—Exploring on Foot*). Westward from Max Patch, the **Harmon's Den Area** of Pisgah National Forest is crossed with hiking and horse trails. To the north, Tennessee's **Cherokee National Forest** conceals the lost mountain community of **Wasp, TN,** its ruins hidden deep in the forest that has taken over its high, perched cove. Farther east, the **Appalachian Trail** pokes its way through a number of interesting little corners before making its final drop into **Hot Springs**, NC.

RECREATION AREAS Jones Meadows on the Bald Mountains. Wide grassy meadows top the crest of the Balds at Jones Meadows, a remarkable site within the **Bald Mountain Ridge Scenic Area** of the Cherokee National Forest. The 8-mile gravel approach road, **Bald Mountain Road** (CR 58), can be charitably described as thrilling, with rough bumps up 4 miles of hairpin switchbacks. Nevertheless, it's worth the thrill, as wide wildflower meadows spread along the 4,500-foot crest. An attempted vacation subdivision went bankrupt here in 1989, to be snapped up by the Forest Service at auction; you'll see abandoned and decaying vacation cottages in the woods on all sides. The **Appalachian Trail** enters the meadows on your right, crosses them, and exits on your left. Park and follow it left (east). You'll quickly come to a side trail that leads 15 yards right to **Whiterock Cliffs,** with wide views south over North Carolina's **Shelton Laurel Backcountry Area** (see *The Bald Mountain Highlands*). Continue on, for another short trail left to the **Blackstack Cliffs,** with panoramic views north over the face of the Balds to Tennessee's **Great Valley.** There are no formal facilities up here, but plenty of places to spread a picnic blanket.

Rocky Bluffs Recreation Area. NC 209 twists and turns its way south of Hot Springs to hack its way along the cliffs of the **Spring Creek Gorge,** with a couple of impressive views along the way. Three miles south of town along this scenic stretch of highway, the Rocky Bluffs Recreation Area furnishes picnicking and camping on the edge of the gorge. A short loop trail goes to a viewpoint before descending into the gorge, while a longer loop trail explores the steep slopes above the road.

PICNIC AREAS Horse Creek Recreation Area. Take TN 107 to Horse Creek Road (CR 94) and follow the Forest Service signs. This Cherokee National Forest recreation area centers on a deep, clear pool in a mountain creek, a popular swimming hole. The picnic area is up the road a short distance, with several tables under tall old trees. A popular **Sampson Mountain Wilderness trailhead** is here, with some fine walking (see Sampson Mountain Wilderness Walks under *Wandering Around—Exploring on Foot*).

Round Knob Picnic Area. Find the intersection of TN 350 and TN 351 (it will be southeast of Greeneville, TN, on your map). From there, go toward the mountains (southeast) on Jones Bridge Road and stay on it 1.25 miles as it curves left and becomes McCoy Road. In another mile, go right on Greystone Road and stay on it 2.5 miles to a right on Round Knob Road. This tiny Civilian Conservation Corps (CCC)–era picnic area snuggles deep under tall trees, halfway up Bald Mountain's steep slopes. While this heavily forested site has no views, it is so high and steep that it gives the impression of an eyrie. It has a shelter built of great logs, and a hand pump, and a few tables. The 4.5-mile drive up the mountain is on **Round Knob Road** (FS 88), a one-lane gravel road, very steep and narrow, with stunning views off the side.

Morlay Branch Picnic Area. This Pisgah National Forest area has a number of tree-shaded tables beside the French Broad River, on Paint Rock Road.

✳ To See

HISTORIC SITES The "Christy" Mission (423-487-2648), 1425 Chapel Hollow Road, Del Rio, TN. To find the mission at Chapel Hollow ("Cutter Gap" in the novel), take TN 107 south from Del Rio for 1 mile, then go right on Old 15th for 4.4 miles to Chapel Hollow Road. Novelist Catherine Marshall based her bestseller *Christy*, about a young teacher in a remote Appalachian mission, on her mother's life and work in a cove above Del Rio ("El Plano" in the novel). That original Presbyterian mission site, and all that remains of its buildings, are signposted, interpreted, and preserved by local resident Larry Myers—whom fans of the novel will be delighted to learn is the grandson of the novel's "Fairlight Spencer" (Flora Corn). Such remote missions, bringing education, medicine, and religion to the inaccessible coves, were an important feature of the turn-of-the-century mountains. Times have changed, and formerly well-known missions have been lost; the Salvation Army's Max Patch Mission has long disappeared into Pisgah National Forest (see **Max Patch** under *Wild Places—The Forests of Hot Springs*), and the Methodist Church's Pittman Center Mission is now a country club and golf resort (see Bent Creek Golf Resort under *To Do—Golf* in "Gatlinburg and the Northeast Quadrant"). The "Christy" mission is now the best place to get a feel for those difficult times.

A final note for fans of the 1996 CBS TV series: The location shots were done at Townsend, TN (see *Villages* in "Townsend, Cades Cove, and the Northwest Quadrant"), 60 miles west of Chapel Hollow. The actual Chapel Hollow sites lack the breathtaking mountain backdrops of the Townsend TV sets. If you want to see the Townsend location sites, ask for directions at the visitors center (see Smoky Mountain Convention and Visitors Bureau under *Guidance* in "Townsend, Cades Cove, and the Northwest Quadrant").

Rocky Top, Tennessee. Oddly enough, Felice and Boudleaux Bryant wrote the racy bluegrass standard "Rocky Top" at about the same time Catherine Marshall was writing *Christy*. You might not recognize these two pop icons of the 1960s as being about the same place—but they are. Rocky Top is a 2,400-foot peak separating Chapel Hollow (*Christy*'s "Cutter Gap") from the town of Newport, TN. The real-life "Christy," Leonora Whitaker, ran her small mountain school and mission immediately below Rocky Top, on its eastern slope, presumably not far from where the song's good old boys were making moonshine and whooping it up with the girls. Of course, this proximity is complete coincidence; the Bryants picked "Rocky Top" merely because it sounded good in the song; they had no knowledge of the actual locale. Catherine Marshall's version is the one based in fact—not the Bryants's.

CULTURAL SITES Country Workshops (828-656-2280), 990 Black Pine Ridge Road, Marshall, NC. The school welcomes visitors, who should call ahead for directions (and to ensure that someone is there). The fees are $300–850, including dormitory-style accommodations and all meals, for 2- to 6-day courses. This crafts school for serious hand-tooled woodworking occupies a remote farmstead high in the Shelton Laurels area. Founded by Drew Langner in 1978, it offers 2- to 6-day residency seminars and workshops that cover a wide variety of woodworking with hand tools; while most courses deal with furniture making, others deal with folk vernacular styles, wood carving, green woodworking, making hand tools on a forge, and making a timber-frame building. Students stay in a dorm on the property and eat hearty homemade meals together. Anyone serious about woodworking will want to visit the school's store, with a thorough line of high-end woodworking equipment and books.

Trust Chapel, Trust, NC. Open during daylight hours, the chapel is on NC 63 just south of its intersection with NC 209. Beverly Barutio built this 12-by-14-foot log chapel, dedicated to St. Jude, in 1990 in thanks for the curing of her cancer.

It's a beautiful structure, built of logs and outfitted with a variety of handcrafted art objects. To be in it is to be moved.

&. **Mars Hill College** (1-800-543-1514), Mars Hill, NC. The town of Mars Hill remains firmly centered on its 150-year-old Baptist liberal arts school, a 4-year college with 1,100 students. Founded in 1856, it was one of a number of church-run boarding high schools, called "academies," in these mountains; such academies were the only real way that a mountain child could obtain any education beyond the local one-room schoolhouse. The college entered its modern phase in 1896, when it began the long journey to becoming a fully accredited 4-year college (in 1962). The modern campus evolved over this century. It's dominated by handsome redbrick buildings from every period of the 20th century, from elegant and beautiful late-Victorian structures to recent modernist structures, looking slightly racy on this rural Baptist campus. The grounds are shaded and parklike, beautifully landscaped with native vegetation.

AN APPLE ORCHARD OUTSIDE MARS HILL BURSTS WITH SPRING BLOSSOMS

Rural Life Museum (828-689-1424), Mars Hill, NC. **Mars Hill College**'s History Department (see above) maintains this on-campus museum dedicated to the history and culture of the Southern Appalachian Mountains. It includes a fascinating section on the hand-hooked rug industry, a Depression-era, $3 million dollar a year cottage industry in the Mars Hill area.

Weizenblatt Gallery (828-689-1396), Mars Hill, NC. Free admission. Part of the Art Department at **Mars Hill College** (see above), this on-campus gallery features the works of students, faculty, and regional artists and has regular exhibits highlighting the works of Southern artists.

✴ To Do

FISHING Metcalf Creek Outfitters (828-689-5503), 1911 Metcalf Creek Loop Road, Mars Hill, NC. Gerald Scott guides fly-fishing trips on the streams throughout this area, including equipment and hand-tied flies.

See also **Little Creek Outfitters** under *Horseback Riding and Llama Trekking*.

HORSEBACK RIDING AND LLAMA TREKKING Little Creek Outfitters (828-622-7606), 767 Little Creek Road, Hot Springs, NC. Open daily during the summer. This stable in the rural countryside west of Hot Springs offers half-day ($30–40) and full-day ($80–90) trail rides inside **Pisgah National Forest** and **Great Smoky Mountains National Park,** including trail rides over nearby Max Patch. They also offer trail riding/fly-fishing combinations.

Sandy Bottom Trail Rides (828-649-9745; 1-800-959-3513), 155 Caney Fork Road, Marshall, NC. Open April through October. This stable offers half- and full-day trail rides, as well as overnighters, from their location in a beautiful rural valley west of Marshall.

Flintlock Inn and Stables (423-257-2489). This Tennessee stable, off TN 107 east of Greeneville, offers half- and whole-day trail rides in the rolling hills near the **Nolichucky River,** and in the forests of the nearby **Sampson Mountain area** of the Cherokee National Forest. They also have a B&B, the **Flintlock Inn** (see *Lodging—Bed and Breakfasts*) in a 200-year-old log cabin on their property.

WindDancers Llama Treks (828-627-6986), 1966 Martins Creek Road, Clyde, NC. These half-day llama treks on a beautiful 270-acre private ranch include spectacular views and a gourmet meal ($40, including meal). They also offer overnight treks with four meals, coupled with a stay in their lovely B&B (see **WindDancers Lodging and Llama Treks** under *Lodging— Bed & Breakfasts*). Overnight: $150 per adult, plus the cost of one night in their B&B; includes four meals.

East Fork Llamas (828-689-5925), East Fork Road, Marshall, NC. Gourmet food is part of this llama trek (half day $50, including meal) on 60 private acres in the **Walnut Mountains** between Marshall and Mars Hill, NC. They also offer llama training and breeding, and adventure-based counseling.

Roads End Llama Treks (828-680-9429). This outfitter offers half-day llama treks with and without picnic lunch (half day $25; $31 with picnic) in the mountains between Marshall and Mars Hill, NC.

SKIING Wolf Laurel (828-689-4111; 1-800-817-4111), Route 3, Box 129, Mars Hill, NC. Day lift tickets: $24–34. This ski slope is located on the leeward side of snow-magnet **Bald Mountain,** just below its crest. Maximum vertical drop is 700 feet from a high elevation of 4,650 feet, with 14 runs and four chair lifts. All runs have artificial snow and night lights.

WHITEWATER ADVENTURES Upstream from Hot Springs, NC, the French Broad River dives into a steep and rugged gorge, surrounded on both sides by large tracts of national forest land. A number of whitewater-sports outfitters offer trips on this section, operating from a string of stations along US 25 between Marshall, NC, and Hot Springs.

WHITEWATER OUTFITTERS LINE THE BANKS OF THE FRENCH BROAD RIVER.

Huck Finn River Adventures (877-520-4658), Hot Springs, NC. Headquartered in Hot Springs, this outfitter leads whitewater rafting trips on the remote and beautiful **French Broad River** upstream from Hot Springs, and float trips on the calm waters downstream from Hot Springs. Special trips include an evening float trip with a sunset steak dinner and an overnight river-camping trip with a steak dinner and pancake breakfast. Half day $25–35; full day $35–50; overnight $125.

French Broad Rafting Company (828-649-3574; 1-800-570-7238), 376 Walnut Drive, Marshall, NC. Half day $42; full day $65. Located north of Marshall, off US 25 near the French Broad River, this outfitter offers both whitewater and calm-water trips on different sections of the French Broad.

Nantahala Outdoor Center (NOC) (1-800-232-7238), NC 25, Marshall, NC. $33–$56. This large outfitter, headquartered in Bryson City, NC, runs this outpost north of Marshall for whitewater trips on the French Broad River.

USA Raft (1-800-872-7238), US 25, Marshall, NC. $31–38. This large rafting chain headquartered in Rowlesburg, WV, maintains this outpost north of Marshall for excursions on the French Broad River.

✴ Lodging

RESORTS 🐾 𝒪 **Gannon's French Broad Outpost Ranch** (423-487-3147; 1-800-995-7678), 461 Old River Road, Del Rio, TN 37727. $250–400 per day for two adults; weekly packages at reduced rates; discounts for children; includes all meals and all activities. This dude ranch sits on the French Broad River near Del Rio, extending from the riverside meadows

to the ridges above. The central lodge and related facilities are built to look like an Old West town, which they dub "Rough Cut." Along with the four-room lodge, it contains a dining room, a dance hall, and a saloon. Accommodations consist of four good-sized lodge rooms, four ridgetop cabins, and four tiny log "pioneer cabins." Activities include 5 days of horseback trail riding, three rafting trips (including one with some Class IV rapids), a cattle drive, a fishing trip with a chuck wagon lunch, and a guided Appalachian Trail hike on **Max Patch** (see *Wild Places—The Forests of Hot Springs*). There's also nightly entertainment, which may include live bluegrass, square dancing, campfires, naturalist talks, and wagon rides. Children of all ages are welcome, and there are special activities just for kids under 12.

BED & BREAKFASTS **WindDancers Lodging and Llama Treks** (828-627-6986), 1966 Martins Creek Road, Clyde, NC 28721. Three modern log lodges group around the high meadows of a llama ranch, with wide views over the remote and little-visited Newfound Mountains, east of the Great Smokies. Each lodge has four large rooms grouped around a central common area, with decor tending toward the western or exotic. All rooms are decorated with art items and artifacts from around the world, with lounge areas, fireplaces, decks with mountain views, and two-person hot tubs. Two lodges have in-room mini-kitchens, in which a continental breakfast is left daily; the third lodge has a pool table and video room, with full breakfast served in the common area. WindDancers is a working llama ranch, offering 1- to 3-day treks with these gentle animals on their 270 acres and in surrounding Pisgah National Forest (see **WindDancers Llama Treks** under *To Do—Horseback Riding and Llama Trekking*). $130–165.

The Magnolia Mountain Inn (828-622-3543), P.O. Box 6, Hot Springs, NC 28743. This elaborate 130-year-old Victorian house has been beautifully restored to a five-room B&B. The 3 acres of gardens are beautifully landscaped, with a hundred-year-old boxwood maze, vegetable and herb gardens (used in the food prepared for guests), and rhododendrons, all framed by spectacular mountain views. The house is Victorian at its best, its elaborate exterior trim and porches in authentic multicolor paints, inside common areas furnished with period antiques. The five rooms range from cozy to large, each with its own personality, defined by the spaces of the house and the beautiful antiques within. Several of the rooms have private balconies. There's also a 20th-century **Garden Cottage,** overlooking the vegetable gardens, with a beautifully decorated open plan very suitable for retreats or family gatherings. A full breakfast is included in the price (except for the Garden Cottage). Dinner is available to guests and nonguests on Friday and Saturday, for an extra charge. Rooms $120–175; cottage $250.

The Bridge Street Inn (828-622-0002), P.O. Box 502, Hot Springs, NC 28743. Open April through October. The second story of the **Bridge Street Café's** (see *Dining Out*) old general-store home has been converted to a four-room B&B. Rooms are bright and high-ceilinged, furnished in turn-of-the-century antiques, with two shared baths. Guests are treated to a continental breakfast at the café downstairs—noted for its fresh-made breads and pastries. Early sleepers should note that the restaurant has live entertainment on Saturday (see *Entertainment*). $50–70.

✒ **Duckett House Inn and Farm** (828-622-7621), 433 Lance Avenue, Hot Springs, NC. Open all year. This 1900 Victorian-style house sits by NC 209 a half mile outside of Hot Springs. It's the sort of fancy farmhouse that a wealthy man might have built, with a nicely trimmed wraparound front porch, a full second story, and a fancy third story with a projecting gable and lots of dormers. Today it is beautifully kept, with an eye-catching red tin roof. Inside, six tastefully decorated rooms are furnished with period antiques; all share baths. Breakfasts feature homemade breads and free-range eggs. In addition, there is a two-bedroom cottage on the property. Children of all ages are welcome in the cottage, while the main house is restricted to children over 12. Rooms $85–95; cottage $125.

❀ *✒* **Marshall House Bed & Breakfast Inn** (828-649-9205), 100 Hill Street, Marshall, NC. The Marshall House rises in stone terraces above the handsome old county courthouse. Designed by the same architect who built Biltmore Village (see *Selective Shopping—Biltmore Village* in "Asheville and the Blue Ridge Parkway"), this 1903 National Register mansion is covered with pebbledash, with a 50-foot-long veranda rising from a tall stone wall and turreted on one end. The views from the veranda extend over the courthouse and town below, framed by the French Broad River and the mountains behind. Inside, the home is decorated with period antiques. One of the eight rooms has a queen bed, the remainder

having twins or doubles; some of the rooms share baths. A full breakfast is included, and pets, children, and smokers are welcome. $40–85.

Flintlock Inn (423-257-2489), 790 G'Fellers Road, Chuckey, TN 37641. Located in the broad, rolling plains of Tennessee underneath Sampson Mountain, near TN 107. Part of a stable offering trail rides (see **Flintlock Inn and Stables** under *To Do— Horseback Riding and Llama Trekking*), the Flintlock has three antiques-furnished rooms in a 200-year-old log cabin, along with a three-bedroom rental cabin on the Nolichucky River. They also offer stables for people traveling with their horses.

CABIN RENTALS ✐ **Mountain Valley View Cabins** (828-622-9587; 1-888-808-8812), 225 Mountain Valley Drive, Hot Springs, NC 28743. Open all year. Two log-clad traditional cabins sit on a grassy and shaded ridgetop 9 miles south of Hot Springs, off NC 209. These bright, one-bedroom cabins are nicely decorated in a country style, and have picnic areas with barbeque pits, full front porches with rocking chairs, living rooms with woodstoves (plus gas heat), and full kitchens, along with such amenities as phones, washer/driers, and satellite TV with HBO. $110.

✳ Where to Eat

EATING OUT **The Rock Café** (828-649-0633), 18 Main Street, Marshall, NC. Open Monday through Friday 7 AM–3 PM, Saturday 8 AM–1 PM. This downtown Marshall tradition with walls made of local rocks sits beside the handsome old county courthouse. It was prominently featured as a location (complete with name) in the movie *My Fellow Americans,* principally because it looks so much like a refuge from an earlier time, as if no one had told it that it wasn't the 1940s anymore. In real life, it lives up to all expectations. A friendly place where the locals gather, it features good, fresh cooking in a simple Southern style, with ample helpings and reasonable prices. It's a perfect distance from Asheville, NC, for a hearty breakfast before a long day's fun in the mountains.

Aunt T's Café (828-622-3663), 70 Bridge Street, Hot Springs, NC. Open for lunch. If you are ever in the Hot Springs area and stuck for a lunch place, aim for Aunt T's Café. It's a simple soup, salad, and sandwich place— or maybe not all that simple. Located in a nice old downtown building, well kept and sparkling clean, Aunt T's has a true restaurant feel, with ample inside table seating removed from the order counter. Prices are reasonable, and the generous sandwiches are made with high-quality ingredients on a choice of five types of fresh-baked breads. They have lunch specials too. Fresh-baked goods make tempting desserts. Sandwiches $3.50.

DINING OUT **The Bridge Street Café** (828-622-0002), Bridge Street, Hot Springs, NC. Open April through October, Thursday through Sunday, from 5:30 PM, plus Sunday brunch. Located in a restored general store fronting on the Appalachian Trail in the center of Hot Springs, this café offers casual fine dining with a Mediterranean flair. The inside dining area is decorated with original art, and complemented by an outside terrace overlooking a small mountain creek— a venue for live music on summer Saturdays. Its menu is noted for its fresh, organically grown produce, breads and desserts made from scratch, and Italian-style brick-oven pizzas. Pastas and entrées feature an imaginative range of fresh, seasonal vegetables and seafood along with free-range chicken. A Shrimp Trieste sautées large shrimp with fennel, sun-dried tomatoes, mushrooms, and capers in a garlic-citrus sauce; a Pizza Gorgonzola combines Gorgonzola cheese with shiitake mushrooms, caramelized onions, and rosemary. The wine list is extensive, with many offerings by the glass, and microbrews are also available. Appetizers and soups $5–7; pastas $9–14; pizzas $10–19; specialties $15–19.

✳ Entertainment

Southern Appalachian Repertory Theater (SART) (828-689-1384), Mars Hill, NC. $18–21. Located in the 175-seat **Owen Theater** on the campus of **Mars Hill College** (see *To See—Cultural Sites*), SART is a non-profit professional theater company whose performance schedule of plays and musicals always includes original plays from Appalachian authors.

The Bridge Street Café (828-622-0002), Hot Springs, NC. Open April through October, Saturday evening from 8:15 PM. The excellent Bridge Street Café (see *Dining Out*) in the center of Hot Springs offers live entertainment on its creek-side terrace every Saturday night in-season. It tends toward alternative music, with folk and blues well represented in the schedule.

⚲ Hillbilly's Music Barn (423-487-5541), Del Rio, TN. Open Saturday, 6 PM–11 PM. Free admission. To find Hillbilly's, take TN 107 for 5.4 miles south from Del Rio, make a right on Blue Mill Road, and follow the signs.

Located deep in the mountains behind Del Rio, Hillbilly's offers weekly live bluegrass music in the heart of bluegrass country—underneath the peak of Rocky Top, Tennessee (see *To See—Historic Sites*). It has a large dance floor, with country dancing a major part of the event. Family oriented, there's plenty of munchies and soft drinks, but no alcohol is permitted.

✳ Selective Shopping

Mars Hill, NC
The Gallery Main Street (828-689-5520), Located in Mars Hill's tiny brick-front downtown, adjacent to Mars Hill College, this gallery features fine arts and crafts from local and regional artists. You'll find an interesting selection of painting, sculpture, pottery, jewelry, fiber art, and photographs.

Marshall, NC
Claywaves Studio (828-649-3333), 428 North Main Street. This potter's studio on Marshall's quaint Main Street features the functional stoneware pottery of Suzanne Kraman.

Hot Springs
The White House (828-622-3456). Located in a modest turn-of-the-cen-

ALONG A COUNTRY LANE IN THE NEWFOUND MOUNTAINS

tury farmhouse at the center of Hot Springs's modest downtown, the White House presents an eclectic selection of antiques, collectibles, and local crafts.

The Yellow Teapot (828-622-9727), 152B Bridge Street. This downtown Hot Springs shop specializes in fine teas, tea accessories, and Appalachian folk arts and crafts.

Trust, NC

The Herb of Grace (828-622-7319), 1951 NC 63, Trust, NC. With acres of flower gardens and its own commercial nursery, this shop and tearoom cater to the serious gardener. Located on NC 63 two miles south of its intersection with NC 209, the shop is a replica of a 17th-century French farmhouse, its large exposed beams timbered on the property. It carries lines of garden art, botanicals and toiletries, linens, porcelains, candles, antiques, lace, and art—all from local and European artisans or small specialty companies. The tearoom serves High Teas (exquisite light luncheons with a variety of gourmet items) and Cream Teas (two English pastries with clotted cream and tea). The 5-acre garden surrounding the shop shows off the mature flowers and plants grown by, and available from, the nursery—a lush and beautiful display of specialized strains of perennials, herb, antique roses, conifers, heathers, and vines.

Trust General Store (828-622-7431), 14535 NC 209 at Trust, NC. This attractive, modern general store serves this remote community at the intersection of NC 209 and NC 63. Its wide range of items reflects this community's distance from the stores most of us now take for granted. It also has camping and outdoor supplies, and a nice lunch counter.

✳ Special Events

✍ *Fourth of July:* **Fourth of July Celebrations.** All three Madison County, NC, towns—Mars Hill, Marshall, and Hot Springs—have special Independence Day celebrations that climax with fireworks. **Mars Hill** and **Hot Springs** have live music and food (Mars Hill has a fish fry), with special attractions for the kids. **Marshall's** Volunteer Fire Department sponsors a rodeo on the island in the French Broad River opposite the courthouse.

First Saturday in October: **Madison County Heritage Festival** (828-689-9351), Mars Hill, NC. Free admission. This Mars Hill street festival, held just outside the 150-year-old Baptist **Mars Hill College,** celebrates its mountain heritage and traditions with booths and crafts demonstrations from a variety of local mountain people. You'll find rug hooking, spinning, weaving, basket making, musical-instrument making, old-time mountain music, clog dancing, shape-note singing, wreaths, quilts, dolls, and all sorts of traditional foods. In the evening, the **Bascom Lamar Lunsford Festival** honors this famous collector of Appalachian folk ballads (and Mars Hill native) with a program of mountain music and dancing at the college; admission is charged.

THE BLUE RIDGE: CHIMNEY ROCK & SALUDA

East of Asheville, NC, the Blue Ridge (the mountain, not the parkway) extends due south in a straight line, reaching South Carolina after 50 miles of rugged valleys and gray cliffs. It is quite a barrier, and towns have formed where gorges have broken through it. On its north end, the Hickory Nut Gorge carried a 19th-century coach road up the Blue Ridge, now US 64/74A; along this old road sits the village of Lake Lure, NC, and the settlements of Chimney Rock and Bat Cave, NC. On the south end of the Blue Ridge, the Pacolet River Gorge allowed the railroad to break through, bringing the handsome little depot towns of Tryon and Saluda, NC.

Between these two settled areas stretch 40 unpopulated miles of empty, rugged mountains. The southern half of this remote stretch is forest-covered wilderness, broken by the deep wilderness gorge of the Green River; much of this wild land is open to the public as part of the 18,000-acre Green River Game Lands, owned by the State of North Carolina. North of these wild lands stretches Apple Country, rolling orchard lands with wonderful views from a confusing network of back roads.

GUIDANCE **Hickory Nut Gorge Chamber of Commerce** (828-625-2725), P.O. Box 32, Chimney Rock, NC 28720. This association of merchants from Lake Lure, Chimney Rock, Bat Cave, and Gerton, NC, runs a visitors center and information desk on US 64/74A, at the center of Lake Lure on the west end of the lake.

Polk County Travel and Tourism (1-800-440-7848), 317 North Trade Street, Tryon, NC 28782. This agency, covering the Saluda, Tryon, and Columbus, NC, area, has a visitors center and information desk at the Tryon City Hall, on US 176 at the north end of downtown Tryon.

Rutherford County Tourism Development Authority (828-245-1492; 1-800-849-5998), 1990 US 221 South, Forest City, NC 28043. This agency provides tourist information for Lake Lure and Hickory Nut Gorge, NC, as well as for parts of Rutherford County east of the mountains. It's located in Forest City, a Piedmont town some distance from Lake Lure.

GETTING THERE *By car:* I-26 runs north and south up the middle of the region. The interstate-quality US 74 freeway links this region to Charlotte, NC, and points

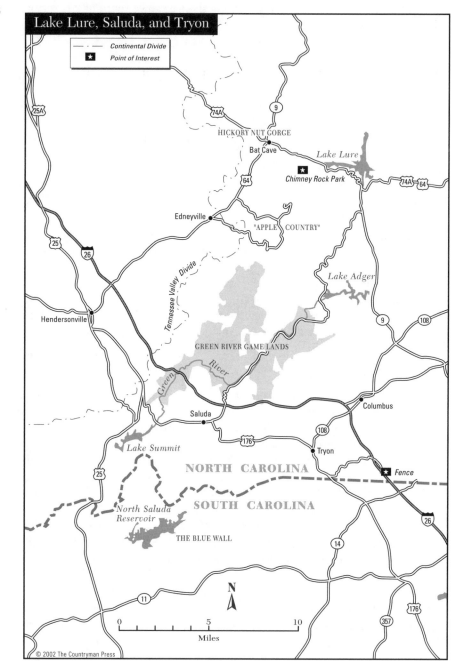

Lake Lure, Saluda, and Tryon

- - · - Continental Divide
★ Point of Interest

25A

74A

9

HICKORY NUT GORGE

Bat Cave

Lake Lure

64

★ Chimney Rock Park

74A 64

Edneyville

"APPLE COUNTRY"

25

26

Tennessee Valley Divide

Lake Adger

Hendersonville

9

108

GREEN RIVER GAME LANDS

Green River

Columbus

Saluda

108

176

Tryon

Lake Summit

NORTH CAROLINA

25

★ Fence

SOUTH CAROLINA

North Saluda
Reservoir

26

THE BLUE WALL

14

N

11

0   5   10

Miles

176

357

© 2002 The Countryman Press

east, meeting I-26 outside Tryon, NC. Everything else is a back road—including the U.S. primary highways (US 176 from South Carolina to Tryon and Saluda, NC; US 64 from Hendersonville to Lake Lure, NC; and US 74A from Asheville to Lake Lure, NC).

By air: **Greenville-Spartanburg International Airport (GSP)** is probably your best bet for an air connection, located only a short distance south of this region. **Asheville Regional Airport** (see *Getting There* in "Asheville and the Blue Ridge Parkway") is also convenient but frequently costs more.

MEDICAL EMERGENCIES **Mission St. Joseph's Hospital** (828-231-1111), 509 Biltmore Avenue, Asheville, NC. This huge regional hospital is just north of this region in the center of Asheville, via I-26 or US 74A (see also Mission St. Josephs Hospital under *Medical Emergencies* in "Asheville's Rugged Hinterlands").

Margaret R. Pardee Memorial Hospital (828-696-1000), 715 Fleming Street, Hendersonville, NC. Located in downtown Hendersonville, this hospital is closer to most parts of this region, via US 176 from Saluda, NC; I-26 from Tryon or Columbus, NC; or US 64 from Lake Lure, NC (see also Margaret R. Pardee Memorial Hospital under *Medical Emergencies* in "The Blue Ridge: Hendersonville and Brevard"). They maintain a walk-in clinic, **Pardee Urgent Care at Four Seasons** (828-697-3232), near I-26 off US 64 (see *Medical Emergencies* in "The Blue Ridge: Hendersonville and Brevard").

✳ Wandering Around

EXPLORING BY CAR **The Blue Ridge without the Parkway.** *Leg 1:* From Asheville, NC, follow US 74A to Lake Lure, NC.

Leg 2: East of the town center, turn right onto NC 9 and drive 1.25 miles; turn right onto Owl Hollow Road (SSR 1164) and drive 1.25 miles; continue straight ahead on Silver Camp Road for 6 miles; then turn right on Green River Cove Road (SSR 1151) and drive 10 miles to I-26.

Leg 3: Continue straight 1.25 miles to Saluda, NC; turn left onto US 176 and drive 8 miles to Tryon, NC; continue on US 176 for 1.4 miles to Ridge Road on the North Carolina–Tennessee state line; turn left after 0.6 mile onto Hunt Country Road (SSR 1501); then turn right and drive 3.4 miles to Foothills Equestrian Nature Center (FENCE).

This 46-mile drive follows the Blue Ridge after the Blue Ridge Parkway has deserted it, using U.S. highways and gravel back roads to stay as close to it as possible. You'll be surprised how different the Blue Ridge looks away from the care of the National Park Service. The first leg follows the **Rocky Broad River** along the base of the **Hickory Nut Gorge.** As you pass the village of **Bat Cave**, NC, you'll get good views of the rough little Rocky Broad; look to your right for views of the 400-foot **Hickory Nut Falls.** Gift shops and motels increasingly block the views as you approach the 1920 stone gates of **Chimney Rock Park** (see *To See— Gardens and Parks*), and the western edge of Lake Lure a mile later. US 74A follows the lake shore through the 1927 town center, with views backward over the lake to the cliffs of the Blue Ridge, now behind you.

As you enter the second leg you'll be on the western edge of the Piedmont, with the Blue Ridge sometimes visible as a faraway wall that rises out of rolling meadows. This route curves through lovely farmland, then quickly passes **Lake Adger,** a largish 1920s hydropower lake. A mile later the route turns to reenter the mountains, following the **Green River** upstream in a deep gorge, surrounded by the **Green River Game Lands** (see *Wild Places—The Great Forests*), with a few scatterings of vacation cottages. At the end of the gorge, the road climbs steeply up the face of the Blue Ridge, with 17 switchbacks in less than 2 miles—a startling stretch of road. By rights you should have a grand view from the top of this, but you won't. However, you'll get a chance to stop for a homemade ice cream at a good crafts shop (see **Saluda Mountain Crafts Gallery** under *Selective Shopping—Saluda, NC*)—and well earned too.

The third leg continues to lovely little **Saluda** (see *Villages*), a major crafts center despite its tiny size. From there the route once more drops down the Blue Ridge, following US 176 into the **Pacolet River Gorge.** After Green River Road this is an easy, pleasant drive; nevertheless, the railroad that wanders in and out of view on the right has the steepest grade in the East. Look for a waterfall in a rocky gorge on your left, after which the road opens up, with broad views over the gorge, right. **Tryon** sits at the bottom of the gorge; this route continues straight through downtown, past Morris the giant toy horse and the old depot (see **Tryon Depot and Polk County Historical Museum** under *To See—Historic Sites*). This route continues into "hunt country," using back roads to drive past horse farms and the trails used in the hunt. The drive ends at the **unique Foothills Equestrian Nature Center** (see *Wild Places—Recreation Areas*), with its combination of nature exploration and horse competitions.

Apple Country. Along the Blue Ridge Crest south of Hickory Nut Gorge, a maze of small, deep-sided valleys form a protected environment perfect for apples and have been covered with orchards since the late 19th century. The orchards bloom in late April, and come into full fruit between mid-August and mid-October. During the harvest, the growers put up stands along **US 64** to allow passers by to purchase bushels of fresh-picked mountain Rome apples. Behind the main highway, country lanes reach deep into the orchards and along the ridges offering beautiful scenery and stunning views.

THOMPSON'S GROCERY IN DOWNTOWN SALUDA

Here's a **back road orchards tour,** a loop just 15 miles long but with lots of scenery (and plenty of places to get lost). To start, take US 64 3.5 miles south from Bat Cave, NC, to a left on **Hog Rock Road** (SSR 1703), passing the actual **Hog Rock** on your right at 1.25 miles. From there, go left onto **Bald Rock Road** (SSR 1710), entering a valley bowl with scattered orchards. Passing through a mile of orchards, this road becomes **Sugarloaf Mountain Road** (SSR 1602), reaching a three-way fork in another mile. The left fork, still Sugarloaf Mountain Road, looks like a gravel farm lane as it climbs through orchards; then it suddenly crosses a ridge and slabs out onto the steep eastern face of the Blue Ridge, with a near-vertical 3,000-foot plummet on the right. The road tops out at the meadowed summit of **Sugarloaf Mountain,** with four or five houses and wide views.

Backtracking to the triple fork, take **Spicer Cove Road** (SSR 1708) south through orchards and along ridges with frequent views, to a right onto **Sumners Road** (SSR 1713) after 2.25 miles. Sumners Road twists through two rural valleys with many orchards, then reaches an intersection with yet another section of **Sugarloaf Mountain Road** (SSR 1602). Turn left. As this road crosses another orchard-clad valley it will also cross the **Eastern Continental Divide** twice, briefly entering, then leaving, the **Mississippi Valley.** In 2.5 miles you'll regain US 64 at the apple-packing town of **Edneyville,** NC, less than 3 miles from where you started. If you are completely turned around at this point, Bat Cave is to your right, and Hendersonville, NC, is to your left.

EXPLORING ON FOOT Walking the Green River Gorge (828-692-0385). Fifteen miles of hiking trails loop along the cliff tops over the Green River Gorge, climb down to the river's edge, and reach into the 6-foot-wide chasm known as **The Narrows.** Three paths start from **Big Hungry Road,** a country lane running from US 64 east of Hendersonville, NC, to a dead end in the **Green Mountain Game Lands** (see *Wild Places—The Great Forests*). To find the Big Hungry trailheads, leave **I-26** at exit 22, **Upward Road,** and go east approximately 1 mile to a right turn onto **Big Hungry Road** (SSR 1802). The three trailheads are on the right, the first one at 4.25 miles. The riverside trail starts at the new bridge on **Green River Cove Road,** 1.25 miles downstream from the **Fishtop Access Area** (see *Wild Places—Picnic Areas*).

The three Big Hungry trails run through rolling terrain covered in rich old forests, typically reaching the cliff edge in 2 miles for spectacular views over the gorge. Other paths run parallel to the cliffs, linking the main paths into loops, while two more paths make their way down the gorge side to the river's edge. The final trail, reached from the road that follows the gorge bottom, hugs the river's edge for approximately 3 miles to reach the Narrows.

All of these remarkable paths, constructed by a local group known as ECO, who publishes an excellent brochure on them, explore about 10 percent of the huge Green Mountain Game Lands—only about 10 percent of the total public lands. Perhaps we'll see more of this beautiful tract in years to come.

✳ Villages

⬆ **Saluda, NC.** Saluda's short downtown lines one side of US 176 with turn-of-the-century brick buildings, facing the railroad that monopolizes the opposite side of the street. The buildings are immaculately kept, and filled with fascinating places to poke into: an old-style country store with a soda fountain; a wood-floored hardware shop; a fine-crafts gallery featuring the works of the nationally known artists who live nearby (see **Heartwood Contemporary Crafts Gallery** under *Selective Shopping—Saluda, NC*); the forge of a blacksmith who incorporates his wife's hand-painted tiles in his creations; an elegant little storefront café with live music (see **The Purple Onion Café and Coffee House** under *Eating Out*). The railroad itself is well known as the steepest grade now existing in the East, the notorious **Saluda Grade,** and Saluda is the siding created to furnish the special services needed for such a steep grade. Across from the railroad, a nice little town park (see **McCreery Park** under *Wild Places—Picnic Areas*) climbs up the hillside with views of downtown, good picnicking, and lots of happy children.

⋔ **Tryon, NC.** Located at the base of the Blue Ridge, Tryon has been a summer retreat for the South Carolina aristocracy since the turn of the 20th century. The rolling hills that extend from the end of the mountains had immediate appeal to the horse-and-hounds set, and Tryon has long been a center for hunt-oriented equestrian activities (see **Foothills Equestrian Nature Center** under *Wild Places—Recreation Areas*). Its short, railroad-facing downtown has art galleries and restaurants, watched over by Morris, a giant toy horse and the town's mascot

THE SUMMIT OF CHIMNEY ROCK, WITH LAKE LURE IN THE DISTANCE

since 1928. Across the tracks, the old depot holds an excellent history museum and the hunt club (see **Tryon Depot and Polk County Historical Museum** under *To See—Historic Sites*); just uphill is the **Tryon Fine Arts Center** (see *To See— Cultural Sites*), whose galleries and gardens cover half a block.

Columbus, NC. Located at the foot of **White Oak Mountain** (see *To See—Gardens and Parks*), Columbus is an attractive, old-fashioned county seat. It has a sleepy, Piedmont flavor, a typical flatland Southern town—even though the mountains are in sight from its streets. It centers on its handsome old courthouse, sitting on a square with a Confederate soldier statue and surrounded by a downtown that's only a scattering of old brick buildings. Tourist services are limited; tourists are Tryon's job, 8 miles to the west (see above).

✳ Wild Places

THE GREAT FORESTS Hickory Nut Gorge. It's best to say it right up front: Hickory Nut Gorge doesn't look the slightest bit like a Wild Place when you drive through it on US 64/74A. This winding two-lane road, which runs down the gorge's bottom, has become lined—very close to continuously—by an assortment of businesses clamoring for tourists' attention. What many tourists never realize is that all this development is just one building lot thick. The rest of Hickory Nut Gorge is just plain beautiful.

Hickory Nut Gorge is an 8-mile slash through the heart of the Blue Ridge, a U-shaped valley 1.5 miles wide and 1,900 feet deep. Much of the gorge's upper slope is near-vertical, and its lowermost 2 miles are framed by sheer gray cliffs. Its stream, the **Rocky Broad River,** is even stranger. Above its short and narrow gorge, the Rocky Broad fans out in a series of tributaries that collect a tremendous volume of water from all over Buncombe and Henderson Counties. You can see the result clearly in the gorge—rocks the size of pickup trucks have been rolled down the streambed. As violent as this river looks on a hot summer's day, it seems unbelievable that it could roll these rocks down from Asheville. Believe it; the Rocky Broad is noted for its devastating floods. It's quite an experience to camp by the Rocky Broad, watch your kids splash around in the water, and listen to an old-timer talk about the flood of 1998.

The Hickory Nut Gorge is privately held in its entirety. The largest tract open to the public is the spectacular **Chimney Rock Park** (see *To See—Gardens and Parks*), a thousand-acre attraction and nature preserve that has stunning cliff-top views, amazing geological formations (including the **Chimney Rock,** a huge free-standing spire reachable via a long bridge over a chasm), and a 400-foot waterfall. Other areas can be reached by the guests of private resorts. **The Chalet Club** (see *Lodging—Resorts*) gives its guests access to miles of trails on the north rim opposite the Chimney Rock, while the **Hickory Nut Gap Inn's** guests (see *Lodging—Resorts*) can explore the mountains along the upper parts of the gorge. The Nature Conservancy owns a 93-acre preserve that contains a stretch of undisturbed north-facing cliff and the **Bat Cave,** believed to be the largest granite fissure cave in America; this preserve is open only to Nature Conservancy field trips. A much larger Nature Conservancy preserve—some 800-plus acres—was in the planning stage as this book went to press.

Green River Game Lands (919-733-7291). Like the Rocky Broad 13 miles to its north, the Green River drains a wide area above the Blue Ridge, then uses its heavy water flow to cut a long, deep gorge through the hard center of the mountain. However, the gorge of the Green River remains in a nearly wild state, with more than 18,000 acres protected by the State of North Carolina as the Green River Game Lands. Like other Blue Ridge gorges, the Green River Gorge is U-shaped with sheer gray cliffs common along its upper slope, its lower slopes clad in botanically rich mature cove hardwoods. The gorge starts a short distance north of Tryon, NC, at **Summit Lake Dam,** is crossed by US 176 on an impressive old bridge, then digs deeply into the mountain wilderness. The **Green River** becomes increasingly wild, with Class III and IV rapids, as it reaches its deepest and most rugged point—**The Narrows,** where the river rushes between cliffs barely 6 feet apart. After The Narrows, the gorge widens to form a flat valley floor beneath tall cliffs, the river becoming wider and much less wild. This section, called **Green River Cove,** is traversed by a back road (see The Blue Ridge without the Parkway under *Wandering Around—Exploring by Car*) and contains scattered houses between blocks of state game lands. The gorge ends suddenly as the Green River drains into the Piedmont and enters **Lake Adger.**

Kayakers enjoy both the rowdy upper section of the Green River Gorge and its less technical lower section, and the North Carolina Wildlife Resources Commission maintains a launching point just downstream from The Narrows, as well as a nice riverside picnic area (see **Fishtop Access Area, Green River Cove** under *Wild Places—Picnic Areas*). Five miles of hiking paths allow easy exploration of the deepest and most rugged section of the gorge, including The Narrows and the cliffs to its north (see Walking the Green River Gorge under *Wandering Around— Exploring on Foot*).

South Carolina's Blue Wall. South Carolina's impressive mountain escarpment, The Blue Wall (see The Mountain Bridge Wilderness of South Carolina under *Wild Places—The Great Forests* in "The Blue Ridge: Hendersonville and Bre- vard"), extends into this area as the **Saluda Mountains.** Lower and less rugged than the mountains near Brevard, they are nevertheless beautiful and full of vari- ety. Most of this section of The Blue Wall is taken up by the City of Greenville Watershed and closed to the public, and much of the remainder is in private hands. A hiking trail known as the **Blue Wall Passage** traverses Nature Conser- vancy lands and is worth the walk, passing ponds and climbing through old-growth forests to reach stunning mountain views. (Directions: Take **US 176** south of Tryon, NC, to a right at the Lake Lanier entrance just before the North Caroli- na–Tennessee state line; follow **West Lakeshore Road** around the lake for 2 miles to a right on **Dug Hill Road;** follow Dug Hill Road to the entrance of the Nature Conservancy's **Blue Wall Preserve.**)

RECREATION AREAS 🐾 ✿ ♿ **Foothills Equestrian Nature Center (FENCE)** (828-859-9021), 500 Hunting Country Road, Tryon, NC. This beauti- ful and unusual center (known as FENCE), sits in the foothills of the Blue Ridge near Tryon. It combines an educational nature center with a large, national- quality horse show and steeplechase venue. Best known as the host of Tryon's famous equestrian events, it also has 320 acres of picnic areas, walking paths, forests, and wildflower meadows. Its rolling-foothills location provides an astonish- ing variety of environments for its 5 miles of paths—hardwood forests, pine forests, hilltops, open meadows (with lovely views), marshlands, and ponds. A historic building at the center, shaped like a stable, holds the offices and a shop; next door, an herb garden surrounds a log cabin. One of the trails is disabled accessible.

On the other side of I-26 sits the equestrian center, with an eight-furlong track and stalls for 200 horses. Some sort of equestrian event is scheduled for almost every weekend and is worth looking into. Events include dressage, stadium jump- ing, cross-country, combined events, and carriage driving.

PICNIC AREAS ✿ **McCreery Park,** Saluda, NC. This small park at the center of Saluda climbs a hill opposite downtown, with good views from the picnic tables toward the Main Street shops. It's a popular playground for local kids.

Fishtop Access Area, Green River Cove. Part of the **Green River Game Lands** (see *The Great Forests*), Fishtop offers limited riverside picnicking at the deepest and most rugged part of the Green River Gorge, the mouth of **The Nar- rows** (see Green River Game Lands under *The Great Forests*).

✳ To See

BIG DAMMED LAKES Lake Lure. The village of Lake Lure, NC, includes the large hydropower lake of that name and all of the land surrounding it. The Morse family, owners (then and now), of **Chimney Rock Park** (see *To See—Gardens* *and Parks*), built the lake and founded the town in 1926. They wanted to expand Chimney Rock's appeal by adding a scenic lake, recreational opportunities, and upscale vacation development; it was the Morses who created the vintage-1928 town center and the 1926 Donald Ross golf course (see **Lake Lure Municipal Golf Course** under *To Do—Golf*). However, the Depression intervened, and Lake Lure was sold off in bankruptcy. That's too bad; the Morses have shown themselves to be masters of tasteful and environmentally friendly development at Chimney Rock Park.

Lake Lure remains an attractive little resort settlement, despite its haphazard development. The towering cliffs of the Blue Ridge form a crescent around the lake's western end, and **Hickory Nut Gorge** (see *Wild Places—The Great Forests*) cuts deeply into this gray green escarpment. This great wilderness wall frames a lakeshore largely encrusted by vacation homes of all types and sizes, extending two to five lots uphill on twisting gravel roads. Access to the town is by **US 64/74A,** a narrow prewar relic that hugs the lake's southern coastline; traveler services stretch out along this highway but become thicker toward the village center at the lake's western end. The main highway continues westward up the base of Hickory Nut Gorge, past the road-hugging tourist settlements of **Chimney Rock** and **Bat Cave,** NC.

SHUNKAWAKEN FALLS ON WHITE OAK MOUNTAIN

HISTORIC SITES ⬆ **Tryon Depot and Polk County Historical Museum** (828-859-2287), 22 Depot Street, Tryon, NC. Open Tuesday and Thursday 10–noon. Sitting across the tracks from downtown, Tryon's classic turn-of-the-century depot serves as home for a wonderful local historical museum. Exhibits include a reconstructed press for the *Tryon Daily Bulletin;* a section on William Gillette, the famous actor (and Tryon resident) who created Sherlock Holmes for the stage; a local moonshine still, complete and accurate; the depot's station master's room, furnished accurately; and a "madstone," a folk remedy for curing rabies. This delightful miscellany is pulled together into a picture of life underneath the Blue Ridge a hundred years ago—definitely worth seeing. Also in the depot are the offices of the **Tryon Riding and Hunt Club,** sponsors of several important horse events including the **Blockhouse Steeplechase** (see *Special Events*).

CHIMNEY ROCK PARK

☀ ✈ ♿ (828-625-9611; 1-800-277-9611), US 64/74A, Chimney Rock, NC. Open daily. Ticket plaza opens 8:30 AM; closes 5:30 PM, May through October; 4:30 PM, November through April. Adults $11; children 4–12, $5. Owned by the same family since 1902 (and open as a tourist attraction since 1885), Chimney Rock is a very old, traditional, and beautiful scenic attraction off US 74A in **Hickory Nut Gorge.** The park centers on a series of stunning cliffs along the south edge of the gorge, where unusual geological formations frame overwhelming panoramas over Lake Lure, Hickory Nut Gorge, and the Blue Ridge. Entering the park in the middle of **Chimney Rock Village,** you'll travel a mile through park lands before reaching the 1920 stone-built ticket booth. Two more miles bring you to the base of the cliffs, with views up to **Chimney Rock**—a 300-foot rock tower with a flat top, crowned by a giant American flag. From here you walk through a 200-foot tunnel and zoom up a 250-foot elevator to a cliff ledge large enough to hold a gift shop and snack bar. Outside are wide views from large rock-floored balconies placed in the ledge—views over to the Chimney Rock, now only a little ways up, along the cliffs, and over Lake Lure. This is the end of the disabled-accessible area. Now a cliff-side path and steps climb up to a bridge across the chasm that separates the Chimney Rock from the cliff face; the wide top of the Chimney furnishes more views. From there the trail continues, climbing the cliffs in stairs, looking down on the Chimney Rock, getting even better views from the cliff top, cutting through the cliff face on a narrow ledge, and viewing the unique cliff-side forest, stunted into bonsai shapes by harsh winds. The climax of the cliff walk: a huge, violent **waterfall** that plunges straight down for 400 feet without so much as a bounce off a ledge until it crashes to the bottom. (This is the same waterfall featured in the 1992 movie *The Last of the Mohicans.)* A separate (much easier) path leads to the bottom of the falls, with astonishing views upward. The pre-elevator steps to the Chimney, built in 1920, are still there and are a fun trip down. If you bring your dog, you are required to use the steps instead of the elevator.

Below the cliffs, an area called **The Meadows** provides a large picnic area and a museum that explains the natural history of the cliffs above. Be sure not to miss it on the way out.

CULTURAL SITES ↑ **The Upstairs Gallery** (828-859-2828), Tryon, NC. Located upstairs in the Town Hall building on the north edge of downtown. This well-respected contemporary-arts gallery displays the works of professional regional artists and fine crafters from their digs in downtown Tryon. A not-for-profit art organization, the Upstairs Gallery starting renovating a new three-story home in

an old downtown building in 2001, not yet open as of this writing. The current
gallery is the venue for the monthly **Pickin' Parlor** (see *Entertainment*).

↑ **Tryon Fine Arts Center (TFAC)** (828-859-8322), 34 Melrose Avenue, Tryon,
NC. Founded in the mid-1960s, the TFAC is an umbrella organization made up
of nine local arts groups, including the **Tryon Little Theater** (see *Entertainment*). TFAC occupies a half-block campus a block away from downtown across
the tracks, with several public gardens and art galleries. On site is **Tryon Crafts,**
a crafts school and one of the founding members. Also on site is the gallery for the
Tryon Painters and Sculptors, a coop made up of local professional artists.

GARDENS AND PARKS **Pearson's Falls.** Located off US 176 (on Pearsons Falls
Road, SSR 1102) between Tryon and Saluda, NC. Open March through October:
Tuesday through Sunday 10–6; November through February: Wednesday through
Sunday 10–5. Adults $2. Since 1931 the Tryon Garden Club has preserved this
extraordinarily beautiful and botanically rich gorge. From a small picnic area, a
quarter-mile trail climbs gently up a limestone ravine, alive with every sort of wildflower and fern imaginable, to the lovely 20-foot Pearson's Falls.

White Oak Mountain. Long a popular beauty spot outside Columbus, NC, this
tall outlier of the Blue Ridge is being loved to death, its summit taken over by con-
dominiums and vacation houses. To find it, take Houston Road (SSR 1137) north
from Columbus for 1.1 miles, to a left on White Oak Mountain Road (SSR
1136)—and a 1,500-foot climb to the summit. As you reach the top of the mountain the road will cross the beautiful and tall **Shunkawaken Falls.** Then, as you
top out on the summit, what's left of a mountaintop meadow sits in front of a
condo development, with some truly remarkable views south over the Piedmont.

✳ To Do

GOLF **Lake Lure Municipal Golf
Course** (828-625-4472), US 64/74,
Lake Lure, NC. $11–14. This nine-
hole course, designed by Donald Ross
in 1929, follows rolling terrain
between Lake Lure and US 74A.

Colony Lake Lure Golf Resort
(828-625-2626), 201 Boulevard of the
Mountains, Lake Lure, NC. $43–46.
This resort is located north of Lake
Lure at the development complex
known as **Fairfield Mountains.** It has
two 18-hole courses with notable views
of the rock cliffs of the Blue Ridge.

Orchard Trace Golf Club (828-685-
1006), 942 Sugarloaf Road, Hendersonville, NC. $10. This 1993 18-hole
course is located in **Apple Country**
(see *Wandering Around—Exploring
by Car*), just north of Hendersonville a
mile or so off US 64. It features large
greens and sloping terrain.

Pine Links Golf Club (828-693-
0907), South Orchard Road, Flat Rock,
NC. $10. This nine-hole **Apple Coun-
try** (see *Wandering Around—Exploring by Car*) course, designed in 1997 by
Sidney Blythe, features short greens
and a number of water hazards. **$12.**

Red Fox Country Club (828-894-
8251), 2 Club Road, Tryon, NC.
$30–35. This 18-hole course, designed
by Ellis Maples in 1966, sits in the
Piedmont underneath Tryon, with
views toward the Blue Ridge some distance away. Described as "scenic and

serene," it has a number of streams and a 30-acre lake in play.

HORSEBACK RIDING Cedar Creek Riding Stables (828-625-2811), 542 Cedar Creek Road, Lake Lure, NC. Located deep in the mountains north of Lake Lure, Cedar Creek offers scenic 1- and 2-hour trail rides on their own 360-acre ranch. Two-night pack trips ($400 per person) in **Pisgah National Forest** include all equipment and meals. $25–45 for half-day rides.

STILLWATER ADVENTURES Lake Lure Marina (828-625-0077; 877-386-4255), Lake Lure, NC. This marina on Lake Lure rents a variety of human- and machine-powered boats, including canoes and kayaks. Half day $40–50, whole day $65–75.

✳ Lodging

COUNTRY INNS AND HOTELS The Orchard Inn (828-749-5471; 1-800-581-3800), US 176, P.O. Box 128, Saluda, NC 28773. Sitting on its own little mountaintop, at the end of a winding private drive, and surrounded by 12 acres of gardens and woods, this 1910 National Register country hotel offers mountain views from its wide wrap-around veranda. Located near Saluda, the Orchard Inn has nine rooms furnished with antiques, along with four small kitchen-free cottages—each with fireplace, whirlpool bath, and private deck—scattered about on the property. Well known for its fine dining (see *Dining Out*), the Orchard serves a wonderful full breakfast, included in the tariff. Rooms (second floor): $119–139; first-floor room with sitting area: $169–189; cottages: $169–245.

The Pine Crest Inn (828-859-9135; 1-800-633-3001), 85 Pine Crest Lane,

Tryon, NC 28782. This highly regarded National Register 1917 hotel sits on 3 hilltop acres above downtown Tryon. Built as a meeting place for Tryon's horses-and-hounds set, today it's run as an elegant English-style country inn with a full gourmet restaurant (see *Dining Out*). The main lodge holds 4 of the 35 rooms as well as the restaurant. Long and deep, its side-on front entrance looks a bit like a farmhouse, but its long side is set upon a stone terrace and covered with a veranda overlooking gardens. Within the lodge, a parlor area is furnished in an English country-house style and is centered on a large stone fireplace, while a library is similarly furnished and stocked floor to ceiling with books. There are five multiroom cottages and five individual cottages (no kitchens) that range widely in style, from historic log cabins to contemporary buildings, with most in a 1930s style; many have separate seating areas, fireplaces, and whirlpool baths. Rooms $95–190; private cottages $170–370; includes full gourmet breakfast.

🐾 ✀ **The Melrose Inn** (828-859-7014), 55 Melrose Avenue, Tryon, NC 28782. This 1889 hotel sits on a hill above downtown Tryon, in a quiet residential neighborhood. It has wide verandas with mountain views as well as a full-service restaurant that serves lunch and dinner. Its guest rooms are individually decorated with antiques and reproductions in a late-Victorian theme. Special guest rooms are dedicated to families traveling with children or pets. The room rate includes a full breakfast. $75–115.

The Mimosa Inn (828-859-7688; 877-646-6724), Mimosa Inn Drive, Tryon, NC 28782. This 1903 mansion, built in the style of an antebellum classical plantation, sits on the north end of Tryon, in 4 acres of landscaped grounds. An impressive sight when viewed from busy NC 108, it is dominated by its 50-foot-tall veranda framed by classical columns—a popular site for breakfast on pleasant summer mornings. Extensive common rooms are furnished in elegant turn-of-the century antiques. The 10 upstairs guest rooms are also antiques furnished and individually themed. A guest house with kitchen and private entrance is also available on the property. A full breakfast is included in the room rate. $95 and up.

✔ **The Dogwood Inn** (828-625-4403; 1-800-992-5557), US 64/74A, Chimney Rock, P.O. Box 159, NC 28720. Built in 1930 to replace Hickory Nut Gorge's historic stagecoach inn (destroyed by fire), the Dogwood Inn has 11 rooms tucked away in a handsome Colonial-style white clapboard structure. Fronting right on the sidewalk in the middle of Chimney Rock Village, this B&B hotel also holds a gourmet coffee shop and a nice gift shop. The rear of the hotel has a large covered veranda overlooking the Rocky Broad River, separated from the water's edge by tree-shaded lawns. Common rooms are attractively decorated in a modest, country style well in keeping with the building's 1930s age and heritage as the heir to a coaching inn. The rooms are cozy and comfortable, with country furnishings and quilts; some have whirlpool baths. Breakfast, served in the dining room or on the porch, includes a choice of a European-style buffet or the chef's specialty of the day. $89–$145.

The Esmeralda Inn (828-625-9105), US 74A, P.O. Box 57, Chimney Rock, NC 28720. Open February through December. The modern Esmeralda Inn is a careful reconstruction of an 1890 coach-road inn that burned on this spot in 1997. It sits on a wooded site, surrounded by gardens, along side US 74 in the Chimney Rock area of **Hickory Nut Gorge.** All modern on the inside, this 2000 structure carefully re-creates the old inn as it appeared after its 1917 remodeling. The board-and-batten-clad exterior is dominated by wide porches on the first and second floors, with the eaves extending over the porches. The lobby is dominated by raw locust log columns and elaborate twig railings on the stairs and mezzanine. The 14 rooms, located on the second and third floors, are also completely modernized while looking like their historic predecessors, with simple, attractive country furnishings. A continental breakfast is included. $99–129.

RESORTS ✔ **The Chalet Club** (1-800-336-3309), P.O. Box 100, Lake Lure, NC 28746. The Washburn family has run this intimate resort above Lake Lure on the rim of **Hickory Nut Gorge** since they founded it in 1934. Even though classed as a private club, the proprietors welcome all visitors with no restrictions; the modest annual fee is used to maintain the surrounding wild lands. With five guest rooms and six cottages, it is nevertheless a traditional full-service resort, including all meals and all activities in the price; guests can also get a "bed & breakfast" limited to breakfast and only a few of the activities. The main lodge, built in 1927 as the family vacation retreat, is in a chalet style with plenty of period charm and panoramic views. It contains the five comfortable guest rooms and the large common areas with a stone fireplace, comfortable furniture, an ample library, and lots of games. The cottages were all built as private houses and range from a quaint 1927 log caretaker's cabin to a comfortable 1962 home. Meals are prepared from fresh ingredients, with breakfasts served from a menu, and a simple lunch served buffet style or taken as a picnic. Dinners are more formal, with gentlemen expected to wear a coat. Outdoor activities (no extra charge) include two tennis courts, a platform tennis court, 7 miles of hiking and biking trails, basketball, shuffleboard, and horseshoe courts, two swimming pools, lake swimming, waterskiing, canoeing, kayaking, electric boating (for lake fishing), and powerboating. Discounts or special packages are available for golf, horseback riding, rock climbing, and several nearby attractions. Rooms $156–262 per couple. Cottages $166–314 per couple. Add $30 per couple membership fee, good for 1 year. Discounts for children. Includes all meals and activities. B&B rates, which include breakfast and the use of all facilities: $40 less per couple.

Hickory Nut Gap Inn (828-625-9108), P.O. Box 246, Bat Cave, NC 28710. This mountaintop lodge with six guest rooms is notable for its remarkable building and guest facilities. It sits above **Hickory Nut Gorge** near Bat Cave, at the end of a mile-long private drive, with wide views from its 40 acres. The founder of the Trailways Bus line built the lodge in the 1940s out of wood and stone taken from his surrounding 5,000-acre estate. With a modest exterior, the lodge is sited to gain a stunning view over the cliffs of Hickory Nut Gorge. Its interior is completely paneled with fine hardwoods—including floors and ceilings. The huge living room has a cathedral ceiling and large stone fire-place, and remains furnished in the style of a 1940s vacation lodge. The game room has a full-sized bowling alley as well as pool and table tennis. All six guest rooms are furnished in simple, comfortable period furniture. The 40-acre site offers excellent walking opportunities, and horseback riding can be arranged. The tariff includes a continental breakfast on the large covered porch. Rooms $125 for a single night, $95 per night for more than one night. Two-room suite $155.

BED & BREAKFASTS **Stone Hedge Inn and Restaurant** (828-859-9114; 1-800-859-1974), 222 Stone Hedge Lane, Tryon, NC 28782. This 1934 mansion, made of stacked fieldstone taken from the property, makes a charming site for this small inn and restaurant. Located 3 miles north of Tryon in the shadow of the Blue Ridge, the original house combines its vernacular local stonework with elements of art deco and Mediterranean architecture, all framed by spectacular views over the 28-acre estate. The main house, a guest house, and a tiny poolside cottage are all made of the same stacked fieldstone; a swimming pool sits between the three buildings. All six guest rooms are large enough to have sitting areas. The two rooms in the main house are the most formal, with antique furnishings complementing their sculpted plaster ceilings. The three guest house rooms and the single-roomed poolside cottage tend to be more casual and contemporary. Its restaurateur owners run a fine small restaurant in the main house (see *Dining Out*), and the included breakfasts are predictably excellent. Rooms $100–115; suite with kitchen $130.

✍ **Tryon Old South Bed & Breakfast** (828-859-6965; 1-800-288-7966),

27 Markham Road, Tryon, NC 28782. Open all year. Located in a residential neighborhood near downtown Tryon, this 1910 restored mansion is surrounded by wide lawns, old oaks, and azaleas. Its common areas and four rooms are filled with antiques, the rooms individually themed. Also on the property is a modest 1930s house, remodeled into a handsome guest cottage with full kitchen. The rate includes a full Southern breakfast. Rooms $65–95; cottage $125.

✒ **The Foxtrot Inn** (828-859-9706; 1-888-676-8050), 800 Lynn Road, P.O. Box 1561, Tryon, NC 28782. This attractive 1915 home in a Tryon residential neighborhood has four guest rooms. It has a heated swimming pool, and mountains are visible through the old trees that frame the house. Both the common areas and the rooms are furnished in elegant antiques, with rooms attractively decorated to individual themes. Some of the rooms have separate private sitting rooms. A full breakfast is included. $75–115.

The Oaks Bed & Breakfast (828-749-9613; 1-800-893-6091), 339 Greenville Street, Saluda, NC 28773. Built in 1895 for a local banker, this fine old Victorian house in a Saluda neighborhood has a witch's-hat turret, a wraparound porch with turned woodwork, and gables in all directions. Porches have plenty of wicker furniture, and common areas (including a living room, dining room, and library) are furnished in a combination of Victorian antiques and comfortable sofas and chairs. Four rooms in the main house are elegantly furnished with antiques, and the turret room has a separate sitting room (in the turret); three of these rooms are en suite, while the turret room has a private bath down the hall. Two suites (both en suite), located in a separate guest house, have separate sitting rooms and a deck or balcony and are furnished with antiques or locally handcrafted furniture. The price includes a full breakfast. Rooms $115–125; suites $175.

✒ **Gaestehaus Salzburg** (828-625-0093; 877-694-4029), 1491 Memorial Highway, Lake Lure, NC 28746. Austrian-born innkeeper Werner Meringer and his wife, Patricia, have built their Lake Lure B&B in the folk style of the Alpine borders. Located on a woodland plot on the east side of town just off US 74A, the inn has three guest rooms, all furnished in a traditional Alpine style. There's a pool and hot tub by the gaestehaus, as well as the excellent German-Austrian restaurant **Das Kaffeehaus Austrian Pastry Shoppe** (see *Eating Out*). The included traditional German breakfast consists of fresh-baked breads and fresh fruits, the Kaffehaus's scrumptious Austrian pastries and a selection of cold cuts, cheeses, and sausages. In addition to the B&B, they have a cottage on the property and a set of eight modern condo-style efficiencies. Rooms $82–95, includes breakfast; cottage $145; efficiencies $125.

Ivivi Lake and Mountain Lodge (828-625-0601; 866-224-7740), 161 Waterside Drive, Lake Lure, NC 28746. This strikingly contemporary inn sits on a hill overlooking Lake Lure and the Blue Ridge. The imposing, modernist glass entrance is framed with undressed timbers. Inside, the house is decorated with contemporary European furniture and art objects from southern Africa. The dining room, where the full breakfast is served, is surrounded by plate glass and spills onto the adjacent flagstone patio, with wide views westward over the lake and toward Hickory Nut

THE CAFÉ AT THE WILDFLOUR BAKERY

Gorge. The seven rooms are large and luxurious, with floor-to-ceiling windows and contemporary decor with an African theme. Included in the tariff is an evening cruise on Lake Lure with wine and hors d'oeuvres. $255–350.

The Wicklow Inn (828-625-4038; 877-625-4038), P.O. Box 246, Chimney Rock, NC 28720. This attractive 1947 Colonial house sits in the middle of Chimney Rock Village on US 74A, by the Rocky Broad River. Innkeeper Jack Ryan named it after his native Wicklow Mountains in Ireland and gives the inn an Irish flavor. The six comfortable rooms are beautifully furnished in a simple, country style. The three downstairs rooms all have private entrances opening onto the garden or a deck overlooking the river. Upstairs, two charming rooms share a sitting room, while the third room has its own private sitting area and a dining alcove. Full breakfasts include seasonal fruits, muffins and scones, and specialty dishes.

CABIN RENTALS **Sandy Cut Cabins** (828-749-9555), P.O. Box 386, Saluda, NC 28773. Open all year.

These two modern cabins are located on 15 acres near Saluda, set between the North Pacolet River and the Saluda Grade, an active freight railroad. The cabins are clad in stained clapboard, one built in a simple mountain style with a full porch, the other more contemporary with a deck. Both have full kitchens with dishwashers, and either a hot tub or a whirlpool bath. First night $100–150; thereafter $75–100 per night.

✳ Where to Eat

EATING OUT **The Purple Onion Café and Coffee House** (828-749-1179), 16 Main Street, Saluda, NC. Lunch 11–3, dinner 5–8; closed Wednesday and Sunday. This small upscale eatery occupies a well-kept storefront in downtown Saluda. Its menu offers California-style cuisine, with lots of fresh and exotic ingredients. It has a good wine list and a selection of microbrews. Lunches feature salads, sandwiches, soups, and pizzas—a simple menu that conceals some exotic fare seldom spotted in Southern streetfront cafés. Dinner menus add more elegant entrées, such as London broil marinated in fresh ginger, soy, and lime; or roast pork tenderloin with fresh rosemary and portobello mushrooms.

Wildflour Bakery (828-749-9224), Main Street (US 176), Saluda, NC. Open Monday and Wednesday through Saturday 8–4, Sunday 11–3; closed Tuesday. Located at the east end of downtown Saluda on US 176, this small local bakery is well known for its scratch-made breads and pastries, fresh each morning. Breakfast pastries are featured in the morning, while lunches consist of soups, salads, and sandwiches.

Old Rock Café (828-625-2329), US 64/74A, Chimney Rock, NC. Located in Hickory Nut Gorge right outside **Chimney Rock Park** (see *To See—Gardens and Parks*), this café offers salads, burgers, trout, and seasonal specials. In addition to indoor dining, they offer tables on a large deck overlooking the Rocky Broad River.

Das Kaffeehaus Austrian Pastry Shoppe (828-625-0093), 1491 Memorial Highway, Lake Lure, NC. Open Wednesday through Saturday. Lunch 11–2:30; dinner, by reservation only, 6–8. Part of the **Gaestehaus Salzburg Bed & Breakfast** (see *Lodging —Bed and Breakfasts*) on the east end of Lake Lure, Das Kaffeehaus offers freshly made Austrian pastries and authentic German entrées. You'll find it off US 74A down its own private drive, deep in the woods, and built in the folk style found in the Alpine borders where restaurateur and innkeeper Werner Maringer was born. A selection of a dozen Austrian pastries will tickle your sweet tooth, while hot lunch entrées include sausages, goulash, potato pancakes, and crêpes. Dinners are more formal and require reservations; entrées include a variety of traditional

German pork and sausage dishes. They have a full selection of German wines and beers. Pastries $2.50–3.50; lunch $5–8; dinner $12–16.

DINING OUT The Orchard Inn (828-749-5471; 1-800-581-3800), US 176, Saluda, NC. Open 7 PM. Dinner by reservation only, Wednesday through Saturday. Well known for its fine dining, the Orchard Inn (see *Lodging—Country Inns and Hotels*) is a 1910 National Register country hotel south of Saluda off US 176 in the scenic Pacolet River Valley. Sitting on a grassy hilltop, this fine old building, with wide verandas wrapping around its front and sides, is elegantly furnished with antiques. The dining area occupies a glassed-in porch overlooking the gardens and vineyard. The elegant four-course meal includes a choice of four entrées with fresh seasonal vegetables, soup, salad, and choice of dessert, plus hors d'oeuvres. Gentlemen should wear coats and ties. The Orchard has an excellent wine list; however, the choices below $25 a bottle are extremely limited. $39 plus gratuity.

The Pine Crest Inn (828-859-9135; 1-800-633-3001), 85 Pine Crest Lane, Tryon, NC. Open for breakfast and dinner. Reservations requested. Located in the hotel's historic main lodge (see *Lodging—Country Inns and Hotels*), its two dining rooms are decorated as an English tavern. The menu, designed by Executive Chef Brian Binzer, features New American cuisine and favors original taste combinations with distinctive flavors. For an appetizer, seared scallops may be combined with celery root–sweet onion puree and an orange cream; an entrée may marry a pork tenderloin with pears, sweet onion marmalade, blue cheese, and a Marsala-scented reduction. An extensive wine list is available. Breakfast $6–8; dinner entrées $20–29.

Stone Hedge Inn and Restaurant (828-859-9114; 1-800-859-1974), 222 Stone Hedge Lane, Tryon, NC. Dinner: Wednesday through Saturday 6 PM–9 PM; reservations encouraged. Sunday brunch noon–2:30. Part of Tryon's Stone Hedge Inn (see *Lodging—Bed and Breakfasts*), this casually elegant little restaurant occupies a delightfully eccentric building, a 1934 vacation mansion built entirely of local fieldstone in a style combining art deco and Mediterranean. Views from its dining room face out over 28 rolling acres of meadows and forests toward the Blue Ridge, only a few miles away. Much of the menu is simple, elegant fare—a black Angus filet mignon, wrapped in bacon, grilled to order, and served with mushroom caps; a veal top-round cutlet, lightly breaded and sautéed in clarified butter. A unique chicken dish is prepared every evening, along with other specials. Dinner $16–25.

✳ Entertainment

The Tryon Little Theater (828-859-8322), Fine Arts Center, 34 Melrose Avenue, Tryon, NC. Plays $10, musicals $15. This local amateur theater performs four plays a year.

The Pickin' Parlor (828-894-8091). Open first Friday of each month 7 PM–9 PM. Donations at the door. This monthly jam session brings local musicians together for folk and bluegrass music. It's held in one of two Tryon art galleries, usually the **Fine Arts Center** (34 Melrose Avenue, Tryon, NC), but occasionally the **Trade Street Café and Gallery.**

The Purple Onion Café (828-749-1179), 16 Main Street, Saluda, NC. On Saturday nights, this downtown Saluda café features live acoustic performances in a coffeehouse atmosphere, tending toward folk and alternative music. Performances start at 8 dinner service ends at 9 (but you can order desserts and coffees until closing); and performances typically end at 10.

✳ Selective Shopping

Lake Lure, NC, and Hickory Nut Gorge Area

Edie's Good Things (828-625-0111; 1-888-625-8054), Chimney Rock, NC. Open daily 9–6. This Chimney Rock gallery represents the work of fine-crafts artists from the western Carolina mountains. The store features hand-woven basketry, hand-thrown pottery and clay pieces, handblown glass, hand-carved wood, handmade metal pieces, and much more.

A Touch in Time (828-625-1902), Bat Cave, NC. Open daily 10–5:30. A wide-porched 1902 Victorian farmhouse, overlooking US 74 in Bat Cave (at the high end of Hickory Nut Gorge), carries a wide variety of crafts.

Tryon, NC

Silver Fox Gallery (828-859-2259), 94 North Trade Street. This downtown Tryon gallery presents "art for living" as they put it—art for the home, practical and otherwise. Representing around 50 artists, Silver Fox has a large and varied selection of contemporary fine crafts and arts, including wall art, wearable art (including jewelry), glass art, clay, metal, papier-mâché, and wood. Their selection can have a whimsical touch, and (this being Tryon) they have a special selection of "horses and hounds."

Saluda, NC

Heartwood Contemporary Crafts

Gallery (828-749-9365), Main Street. Open Monday through Saturday 10–5, noon–5 Sunday. This downtown Saluda gallery features American fine crafts with a strong contemporary flair. Handsome, roomy, and brightly lighted, this historic storefront offers a wide range of items—handmade wearables, jewelry, paper, paintings, fine porcelain, stoneware, glass, metal, and wood.

Saluda Mountain Crafts Gallery (828-749-4341), 1487 Ozone Drive. Don't let the interstate-side location fool you; this is no chintzy gift shop. Located in a rusticized modern building by I-26's exit 28, this gallery stocks original crafts art with a traditional tone, featuring the works of local and regional artists. They carry pottery, woodworking, decoys, handmade furniture, woven art, jewelry, cornhusk dolls, children's toys, and books. They have a wide front porch with rocking chairs, and a quilter upstairs every Saturday. Best of all, the store right next door is a fine soda fountain that makes its own ice cream.

✳ Special Events

March: **St. Patrick's Day Parade and Celebration,** Tryon, NC. A parade through downtown Tryon is followed by live music, an antique car show, and plenty of food.

Late April: **The Blockhouse Steeplechase** (828-859-6109; 1-800-438-3681), P.O. Box 1095, Tryon, NC 28782. Ticket sales to the public begin on February 15. Gates open at 10 AM. Races start at 2 PM. Walk-in: $60 per person at the gate, including off-site parking. Carload: $80–125; RV: $200; must be purchased in advance. The Tryon Riding and Hunt Club has been holding this sanctioned steeplechase annually since 1947. Race-day activities include a parade of hounds, antique carriages, the Parade of the Old Tryon Foot Beagles, and awards for Best Tailgate Picnic and Most Creative Hat. The 1-mile kidney-shaped track, located at the **Foothills Equestrian Nature Center (FENCE)** (see *Wild Places—Recreation Areas*), sits in a hollow surrounded by low hills. Spectators' tickets gain them a parking space within view of the track, and they watch the races from their car (or mingle about and admire each other's tailgate picnics and hats). The cheapest seats are in the infield, while the most expensive seats are hillside and RV parking.

Mid-June: **Blue Ridge Barbeque Festival and Foothills Crafts Festival** (828-859-7427), Tryon, NC. The official barbeque competition of North Carolina combines with a high-quality juried arts fair every June in Tryon's **Harmon Fields** (on the north end of town). Eleven of the 80-plus barbeque contestants sell food to the public, and there is a large variety of other food vendors as well. The crafts fair offers a limited number of booths in each category, with booths going to the best artists; content is strictly limited to original design fine crafts and arts.

Mid-June: **Tryon Riding and Hunt Club Horse Show** (828-859-6109; 1-800-438-3681), Tryon, NC. This hunter-jumper show has been held in Tryon since 1928. It's a 4-day event held at the **Foothills Equestrian Nature Center (FENCE)** (see *Wild Places—Recreation Areas*)—one of a number of such events held throughout the spring and summer months.

Early July: **Annual Coon Dog Days** (828-749-2581), Saluda, NC. Free admission. This annual coon dog show has been held in Saluda since 1964.

Along with the coon dog judging is a coon dog race, a crafts fair, a parade, live music, and a street dance.

Early October: **Any and All Dog Show** (828-859-6109; 1-800-438-3681), Tryon, NC. A Tryon tradition since 1933, this show has categories such as Most Interesting Tail, Looks Most Like Master, Best Costume, Most Doubtful Ancestry, Best Trick, Happiest, and (of course) Best Horse-Show Dog.

First weekend in November: **Foothills Highland Games** (828-859-2050), Tryon, NC. This 2-day event, held at **Harmon Fields** on the north side of Tryon, features Scottish athletic competition, the Calling of the Clans, bagpipe bands, Scottish dance, border collie demonstrations, live (nonbagpipe) music, and Scottish food.

First weekend in December: **Tryon Christmas Stroll,** Tryon, NC. Downtown Tryon celebrates Christmas with carriage rides, refreshments, an open house, carol singing, and a crafts sale. The celebration extends to nearby towns; in the evening, **Saluda**, NC, has its **Home Town Christmas** open house and celebration, while **Columbus**, NC, has a **Christmas parade** the next day.

THE BLUE RIDGE:
HENDERSONVILLE & BREVARD

At the far northern border of South Carolina, the hot, humid southlands end abruptly at the foot of a remarkable cliff. Two thousand feet high and 35 miles long, South Carolinians call it The Blue Wall. Its western half is part of the Blue Ridge, here many miles south of the Blue Ridge Parkway; its eastern half is a side ridge called the Saluda Ridge. Its crest forms the boundary between South and North Carolina. In back of this crest, in North Carolina, sits a high perched valley, bowl-shaped, with small mountains at its center. This valley is large enough to contain two North Carolina counties, high enough to be cool and pleasant in the summer, and mountainous enough to be exceptionally beautiful. This chapter describes the Blue Wall and the valley behind it, including the small county seats of Hendersonville and Brevard, NC.

Since the construction of the Buncombe Turnpike in the 1820s, rich South Carolinians have fled here in the summer, escaping the sticky heat of Charleston and Columbia. Antebellum second homes are still scattered throughout this valley, as are vacation homes from every historic period thereafter. Today, these historic homes play host to elegant inns and sophisticated restaurants. Art galleries dot brick-front Main Streets. Two symphony orchestras and the State Theater of North Carolina headquarter in these tiny rural towns, and a major classical music festival stages full-scale operas from its own lakeside campus. Tourism here is refined, cultured, and understated.

Hendersonville and Brevard offer excellent shopping and restaurants in their revived and restored downtowns, and both have a good choice in B&Bs. Hendersonville, the larger and more industrial of the two, plays urban host to the elegant 19th-century tourist settlement of Flat Rock, NC, only a few miles south. Brevard, much deeper in the mountains, is quieter, with more of a small-town atmosphere; its summer music festival, held on its own lakeside campus, is one of the cultural highlights of the mountains. The valley itself is largely flat, so much so that the French Broad River wanders through it in a long series of tightly twisted loops. However, a series of small mountains runs up the middle of the valley; near Brevard, the westernmost of these low mountains makes up the waterfall-rich DuPont State Forest.

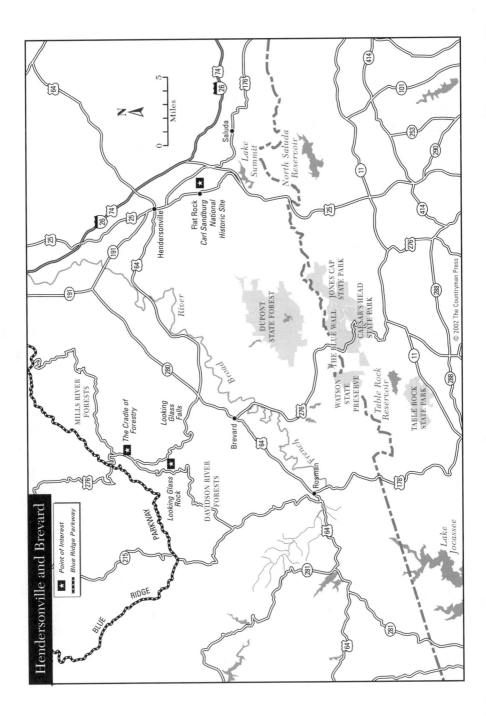

Hendersonville and Brevard

Point of Interest ★
Blue Ridge Parkway ▪▪▪▪▪

© 2002 The Countryman Press

N

0   5
Miles

GUIDANCE Henderson County Travel and Tourism (828-693-9708; 1-800-828-4244), 201 South Main Street, Hendersonville, NC 28792. Open Monday through Friday 9–5; open weekends in-season. The visitors center occupies its own building on the south edge of downtown Hendersonville, just beyond the old county courthouse.

The Greater Hendersonville Chamber of Commerce (828-692-1413), 330 North King Street, Hendersonville, NC 28792. This private organization concentrates on promoting its member businesses, leaving tourism to the county's Travel and Tourism Authority (see above).

Transylvania County Tourism Development Authority (828-883-3700; 1-800-648-4523), 35 West Main Street, Brevard, NC 28712. The visitors center for the combined Chamber of Commerce and Tourism Development Authority is in a small storefront in the center of downtown Brevard.

Pisgah National Forest, Pisgah Ranger District (828-877-3265), 1001 Pisgah Highway (US 276), Pisgah Forest, NC 28768. Located 4 miles north of Brevard, this National Forest Service visitors center has interpretive displays, a bookstore, and an information desk as well as the administrative offices of the Pisgah District.

GETTING THERE *By car:* From I-26 twenty-four miles south of Asheville, NC, take US 64 (exit 18) west. You'll hit the north edge of downtown Hendersonville, NC, in 2 miles, and the north edge of downtown Brevard, NC, in another 20 miles. Other routes, including those with U.S. highway numbers, are not recommended for any purpose other than sight-seeing down steep and winding mountain roads.

By air: **Asheville Regional Airport** (see *Getting There* in "Asheville and the Blue Ridge Parkway") is actually closer to Hendersonville than it is to downtown Asheville—9 miles compared to 13. It's 20 miles from Brevard.

By train: This is the only mountain location to have a reasonably convenient train connection. Hendersonville is 35 miles from the **Amtrak** (1-877-276-2767). depot in Greenville, SC, served twice daily by the Crescent from New York to Atlanta and New Orleans.

By bus: Hendersonville has twice daily bus service via **Greyhound Bus Lines** (1-800-229-9424); Brevard has no bus service.

MEDICAL EMERGENCIES **Margaret R. Pardee Memorial Hospital** (828-696-1000), 715 Fleming Street, Hendersonville, NC. This full-service major regional hospital offers 24/7 emergency-room services from its campus on the northwest edge of downtown Hendersonville.

Pardee Urgent Care at Four Seasons (828-697-3232), 205 Thompson Street, Hendersonville, NC. Open Monday through Saturday 9–9, Sunday noon–6. This walk-in clinic, run by the area's regional hospital, is located near the I-26 intersection with US 64, just off US 64 (behind the Taco Bell), toward Hendersonville.

Transylvania Community Hospital (828-884-9111), Hospital Drive, Brevard, NC. This small but full-service local hospital is located just east of Brevard off US 64.

EXPLORING BY CAR **Driving through Pisgah National Forest.** This 40-mile drive winds its way through the heart of the Pisgah Forest, the forests that George Vanderbilt brought into his **Biltmore Estate** (see *To See—Along the Blue Ridge Parkway* in "Asheville and the Blue Ridge Parkway") in 1889. In the early decades of the 20th century, when giant logging companies were devastating much of the Smoky Mountain forest, Vanderbilt's foresters tended these forests with thought and care. Today they are very beautiful.

Start at **Lake Powhatan Recreation Area** (see *Wild Places—Recreation Areas* in "Asheville and the Blue Ridge Parkway"), turning onto the gravel **FS 479.** Your road follows **Bent Creek** gently uphill through increasingly handsome mixed forests, then climbs steeply to the **Blue Ridge Parkway** on the crest of the Pisgah Ridge. Cross the parkway and continue downhill on the gravel Forest Service road **(FS 5000),** winding downhill for nearly 6 miles to **North Mills River Recreation Area** (see *Wild Places—Picnic Areas*). Turn right onto the gravel **Yellow Gap Road** (FS 1206). For the next 12 miles, Yellow Gap Road climbs two ridges, follows three streams, and enters four high-mountain coves. Watch how the mature forests change from the rich diversity of the coves to the dry oak and pine forests on the ridgelines. The last of the coves is known as **The Pink Beds,** named for its rhododendron displays in June, and the center of Vanderbilt's early forestry operations.

Yellow Gap Road ends at **US 276** (see above); turn left and follow the highway for 1.5 miles, passing **The Pink Beds Picnic Area** (see *Wild Places—Picnic Areas*) and the Biltmore's historic forestry school, **The Cradle of Forestry in America** (see *To See—Historic Sites*). Then turn right onto **FS 475B,** another gravel forest road. This road takes you around the west side of the gigantic schist monolith **Looking Glass Rock,** best viewed from the Blue Ridge Parkway. In 3.5 miles the road passes through **Gumdrop Gap,** the trailhead for rock climbers attacking the north face of Looking Glass Rock, and drops down into the lush valley of **Rockhouse Creek.** Look for the attractive **Slick Rock Falls** on your left about 1.5 miles into the valley. In 2.75 miles you reach the **Davidson River** at **Johns Rock** (see A Pisgah Forest Hike under *Exploring on Foot*); turn right onto **FS 475,** passing the **Pisgah Center for Wildlife Education** (see *To See—Cultural Sites*), a first-rate museum on wildlife management and conservation. This gravel road follows the Davidson River for nearly 5 miles upstream through a popular hiking area with many trailheads, topping out at **Gloucester Gap,** to descend 3 miles to **NC 215.** Turn left on NC 215 to reach **US 64** at **Rosman,** NC, in 7.6 miles; Brevard and Hendersonville, NC, are east (left) on US 64.

EXPLORING ON FOOT **A Pisgah Forest Hike.** Looming a thousand feet over the **Pisgah Center for Wildlife Education** (see *To See—Cultural Sites*), the long expanse of gray cliff known as **Johns Rock** is hard to resist. This 6-mile loop climbs from the Pisgah Center to the top of Johns Rock, with good Pisgah Forest scenery along the way and a stunning panoramic view at the top. The path, named **Cat Gap Loop Trail,** starts at the far end of the Pisgah Center's parking lot. It follows a lovely little mountain stream, then turns south and starting its steady climb up a side valley. In 1.5 miles from the parking lot (and a climb of 500 feet),

The 46-mile scenic drive down US 276 is a perfect way to get acquainted with this part of the mountains.Starting at its north end, from its intersection with the Blue Ridge Parkway, this route passes through **Pisgah National Forest** for 15 miles, descending steeply off the Pisgah Ridge. In less than 4 miles the highway passes a Forest Service picnic area at **The Pink Beds** (see *Wild Places—Picnic Areas*), named for its rhododendrons, and **The Cradle of Forestry in America** (see *To See—Historic Sites*). In the next 5 miles the highway drops into a gorgelike valley, passing **Slide Rock,** a popular swimming hole, and **Looking Glass Falls,** a classic river-over-a-cliff waterfall. A quarter mile later, a paved side road leads right to the **Pisgah Center for Wildlife Education** (see *To See—Cultural Sites*).

Leaving the national forest, US 276 immediately turns and follows four-lane US 64 to Brevard, NC, temporarily losing its charm but picking up a wide array of roadside services. After 3.4 miles of this, the highway reaches the middle of Brevard, turns, and becomes Main Street through Brevard's handsome old **downtown** (see *Selective Shopping*). It quickly leaves Brevard to follow the old, slow, meandering **French Broad River** for 2 miles, then enters a long series of straight stretches through pastoral scenery; look for crafts artists' studios and galleries scattered about. Five miles south of Brevard, the twin waterfalls of **Conestee Falls** (see *To See—Gardens and Parks*) cascade beside the highway. At 11 miles south of Brevard, a left turn onto paved **Cascade Lake Road** leads to the **DuPont State Forest** (see *A DuPont Forest Waterfall Walk under Exploring on Foot*) with its first-rate waterfall walks

Soon the highway crosses the **Blue Ridge** and suddenly tips over the edge of the world. No other road gets so up close and personal with South Carolina's **Blue Wall.** The highway follows the flat top of a side ridge for 3 miles out into the cliff lands, reaching **Caesar's Head State Park** (see *Wild Places—Recreation Areas*) with its stunning panoramic views and walks to gorges and waterfalls. Then the highway drops down off the ridgetop and switchbacks wildly down the steep slopes. In 7 miles of continuous twists the highway drops 2,200 feet to the floor of the South Carolina Piedmont. Five miles into this (it will feel longer) you'll reach a graffiti-prone roadside rocky bald called **Bald Rock,** with wide views over this sudden end of the mountains to the endless flatness of the Deep South. Four miles later, at the base of the mountain, look for **Wildcat Falls** on your left, with a nature trail following the stream. In 4 more miles the highway reaches the flatlands, with views over fields toward the Blue Wall.

a side path peels off right across the stream and up to Johns Rock, reaching the summit in another mile (and another 500 feet up). The views north take in the gorgelike valleys of the **Davidson** and **Looking Glass Rivers,** the gray cliff-sided dome of **Looking Glass Rock,** and the mile-high crest of the Pisgah Ridge. From the summit, the trail heads south along the rock's narrow ridgeline, reaching a trail intersection in 0.6 mile. While all three choices will take you back to your car, this walk follows the rightmost trail, **Cat Gap Bypass.** This path circles around the high forests above a little side valley, then merges with the Cat Gap Loop Trail. Follow the Cat Gap Loop Trail downhill along a dry ridgeline, and along **Cedar Rock Creek** to the Pisgah Center.

A DuPont Forest Waterfall Walk. Four lovely waterfalls, each with its own unique personality, group tightly together at the center of **DuPont Forest** (see *Wild Places—the Great Forests*). A single walk to all four waterfalls, following a roaring mountain river most of the way, takes a total of 5 miles with 750 feet of total climbing. To reach the trailhead parking, take **US 276** eleven miles south of Brevard, NC, to **Cascade Lake Road;** then take Cascade Lake Road north 2.4 miles to its fork with **Staton Road;** then take Staton Road 2.3 miles (passing the Agfa plant) to a parking lot on the left just after a bridge.

Your first destination is **Hooker Falls**—through the gate at the end of the parking lot, then 0.35 mile along the river on a level old road. Here the **Little River,** 130 feet wide, pours straight down over a 13-foot ledge. Retrace your steps to the parking lot, then cross the river on the paved road bridge to continue upstream on the opposite bank. As the scenery becomes more mountainous the trail ascends to a view of **Triple Falls** on the Little River—three separate cascades that together drop 120 feet. From here a path leads to the base of the fall, and a roadbed leads to a picnic shelter. Continue on the main trail, first uphill, then along the riverbank. As your trail goes uphill again, a side trail along the river leads to the base of **High Falls,** where the Little River slides straight down a 150-foot cliff. The main trail continues uphill to views from the top of High Falls, then more views from a picnic shelter.

At this point you have walked 1.75 miles and climbed 250 feet, and you are 1.4 miles from your car (downhill all the way). If you want to continue, there is one more waterfall nearby, a tall slide rock on **Grassy Creek** that will add 2 miles and 500 feet of climbing to your walk. Cross the Little River on the bridge upstream from High Falls, then continue left on **Buck Forest Road** (at one time the main road through these parts). After about a mile, you'll cross Grassy Creek on a bridge, then turn left on **Imaging Lake Trail** (another old roadbed, leading a couple of miles to a pretty little lake built by the DuPont (now Agfa) film factory in years past). The newly built path to the base of **Grassy Creek Falls** is just beyond, to your left.

Ravens Cliff Falls on The Blue Wall. South Carolina's Blue Wall is a rugged and difficult area; with few exceptions, its rewards must be earned by hard effort. This walk is comparatively easy—by Blue Wall standards. By any reasonable standard, it's a tough day hike. However, with a 400-foot waterfall at the end, it's well worth it.

The 4- to 8-mile round-trip walk to Raven Cliff Falls, one of the tallest in the East, follows a well-built footpath in **Caesar's Head State Park** (see *Wild*

Places—Recreation Areas), 13 miles south of Brevard, NC, on **US 276.** Trailhead parking is a mile north of the park's headquarters. For the first mile the path follows the gently rolling ridgeline along the top of the cliff wall, passing through handsome forests with occasional views over the Blue Ridge, with about 300 feet of climbing and dropping. At the intersection with **Gum Gap Trail,** continue left on **Raven Cliff Falls Trail,** dropping into the rugged terrain around the waterfall. The trail will drop 700 feet in the next 0.9 mile, and you'll have to reclimb every step on your way back. At the bottom of the trail is an observation deck giving a wide view across this narrow, forested gorge to the waterfall, a strong cataract that hurls down the cliff in three large jumps. When it's time to go back, you have a thousand feet of climbing to reach your car, for a round-trip of 4 miles. If you are feeling energetic, you may double this length and add 300 feet of climbing by taking the right-hand fork at Gum Gap Trail, leading around to **Naturaland Trust Trail** and a suspension bridge over the waterfall—another first-rate view from a completely different angle.

✳ Villages

Hendersonville, NC. This busy little city of 10,000 sits in a wide valley 20 miles south of Asheville, NC, via I-26. A successful small center of commerce, it's surrounded by a ring of modern, sprawling development, its highways busy and noisy.

However, its quiet little downtown is a wonderful place. Almost completely preserved from the early 20th century, it has five blocks of Italianate redbrick storefronts, with wide, landscaped sidewalks and free street parking; downtown shopping is varied and sophisticated, and the choice of restaurants is excellent (see *Selective Shopping—Downtown Hendersonville, NC*). The town's most historic (and ritzy) neighborhoods stretch westward from downtown along **Fifth Avenue,** then up a little mountain on the 1920s-era **Laurel Park Highway** —ending at **Jumpoff Rock Park,** a lovely city park with a high-view rock (*To See— Gardens and Parks*).

Flat Rock, NC. This attractive village of 2,500 residents stretches along US 25 three miles south of Hendersonville. Like many Southern settlements, it lacks a well-defined center; shops and inns are spread out along the high-

THE HENDERSON COUNTY COURTHOUSE IN HENDERSONVILLE

way, widely separated by tree-lined fields. Flat Rock has been a tourist destination since the late 1820s, when the stagecoach road known as the Buncombe Turnpike (following the route of modern US 25), made it accessible to wealthy South Carolinians. By the 1850s, Flat Rock was a fashionable summer destination for heat-struck Southerners who could afford it, and not even the Civil War could alter this. Today it remains genteel and beautiful, a village of elegant country inns and fine restaurants hidden down remote lanes. Flat Rock was the home of Carl Sandburg and his wife for 22 years (1945 to 1967); their antebellum home and modern goat farm are a National Historic Site (see **Carl Sandburg Home** under *To See—Historic Sites*), a wonderful example of an early Flat Rock plantation.

Brevard, NC. This small mountain town of 6,800 people, the seat of Transylvania County, sits on a hillside by the French Broad River, 20 miles west of Hendersonville via US 64. The main approach to town on US 64 doesn't do it justice, passing through several miles of sprawling industry and commercial development before briefly diving in and out of the town's center. However, leave the main high-

DOWNTOWN BREVARD

way to explore the traditional center of town, and you'll find a perfectly preserved redbrick downtown filled with interesting shops, galleries, and cafés (see *Selective Shopping—Downtown Brevard*) and surrounded by well-kept old neighborhoods with lovely little parks and plenty of trees. Brevard gains a surprising level of cultural sophistication from its small Methodist liberal arts college (Brevard College), and its first-rate summer program for aspiring young professional musicians, the **Brevard Music Center** (see *To See—Cultural Sites*).

✴ Wild Places

THE GREAT FORESTS The Pisgah Forest. Pisgah National Forest wanders through much of western North Carolina, with important tracts stretching from the edge of the Smokies (see **Max Patch** under *Wild Places—The Forests of Hot Springs* in "Asheville's Rugged Hinterlands") to **Roan Mountain** (see The Roan Highlands under *Wild Places—The Great Forests* in "Behind the Blue Ridge: Spruce Pine and Burnsville") and on to the slopes of **Grandfather Mountain** (see Wilson Creek National Wild and Scenic River under *Wild Places—The Great Forests* in "The Blue Ridge Parkway: Blowing Rock and Grandfather Mountain"). However, to most people in North Carolina, "The Pisgah Forest" is the great stretch of wild lands on the south slopes of the Pisgah Ridge, north of Brevard and Hendersonville, NC.

Originally part of George Vanderbilt's **Biltmore Estate** (see *To See—Along the Blue Ridge Parkway* in "Asheville and the Blue Ridge Parkway"), Vanderbilt had carefully tended and restored its forests over a 30-year period. Vanderbilt's foresters had set up America's first forestry college in log cabins on this 100,000-

LADY'S SLIPPERS DECORATE THE FOREST FLOOR.

acre tract to train the assistants they needed; its buildings, still preserved, make up the core of the forestry museum, **The Cradle of Forestry in America** (see *To See—Historic Sites*). More than a century later, Vanderbilt's Pisgah forests are remarkably diverse and beautiful, with a network of gravel roads and hiking trails leading to its scenic wonders.

The Pisgah Forest splits naturally into two halves. To the east, the **Mills River** and its tributaries drain a series of watersheds. To the west, the **Davidson River** drains southward toward the headwaters of the **French Broad River**. In the center, roughly straddling these two areas, runs **US 276** (see *Wandering Around—Exploring by Car*), a winding and scenic drive that links many of the finest sites of the forest. Gravel forest roads run cross-grain through the area, giving ready access to most corners of the forest (see Driving through Pisgah National Forest under *Wandering Around—Exploring by Car*). The **Blue Ridge Parkway,** running along the mile-high crest of the Pisgah Ridge, lets you drive up to the high points of many of these trails and enjoy their best views without raising a sweat. Trails are extensive and well developed, with the majority open to bicyclists and horseback riders as well as hikers.

DuPont State Forest (828-251-6509), 14 Gaston Mountain Road, Asheville, NC. This 10,300-acre North Carolina State Forest, purchased from the DuPont Corporation in 1997, lies in a high plateau 13 miles south of Brevard, NC, via US 276 and Cascade Road (SSR 1536). It's noted for its many waterfalls and slide rocks, and its excellent views from a number of exceptionally large rocky balds. Its forests are young and varied, and its slopes are much gentler and shorter than in other mountain tracts. It has four lakes, one of them quite large—remnants of old real estate schemes and summer camps. It has nearly a hundred named trails, most of them old roadbeds—and nearly all of these gentle, old paths are open to bicyclers and horses as well as walkers. In the middle of this large, popular recreation site sits a large film factory, formerly DuPont and now Agfa, like a hole in a doughnut. Access to the plant is strictly prohibited, and this means you. Access to everything else is free and open.

About a quarter of this forest, including nearly all of the prime recreation sites, was seized by the State of North Carolina in 2000 from a developer who had started to construct an exclusive gated community on the site; the gate is still there, now part of the state forest. At this writing, the developer is challenging the legality of the seizure in court; he currently states that he wants the land back, rather than compensation. Stay tuned. Meanwhile, you can thank him for the beautiful new picnic shelters strategically placed by streams, waterfalls, and lakes.

For the traveler, the DuPont Forest is worthwhile for its seven major waterfalls and rock slides, the views from its large rocky balds, and its refreshingly easy walking. The largest and most remarkable waterfalls are on the **Little River,** easily reached from paved roads. The **DuPont Forest Waterfall Walk** (see *Wandering Around—Exploring on Foot*) describes a stroll to three of these, from a roadside parking area at the center of the forest. A second scenic area can be reached from a trailhead parking lot on **Cascades Road,** about 2 miles north of **US 276** (10 miles south of Brevard). From here, easy trails lead to **Bridal Veil Falls,** a wide, tall waterfall with a high water volume that you can walk behind—it's featured in the movie The Last of the Mohicans; to **Cedar Rock,** claimed as the longest rocky bald in the Blue Ridge with panoramic views; and to **Corn Shoals,** a slide rock and popular swimming hole. A loop walk to all three points is 4.4 miles long with 950 feet of total climbing (hint: Do Cedar Rock first, and the Corn Shoals swimming hole last.)

The Mountain Bridge Wilderness of South Carolina. Rising 2,000 nearly straight up from the South Carolina Piedmont, this clifflike 35 miles of the Blue Ridge and Saluda Ridge is known as **The Blue Wall** (see chapter introduction). The terrain is extraordinarily beautiful, with lush forests, deep gorges, huge waterfalls, and high cliffs. It's also extremely difficult—a rough and broken land with extreme elevation changes in short distances. Much of this wild territory is protected by the government of South Carolina in a series of state parks and state heritage preserves, while other large tracts are protected by private conservation foundations and city watersheds. All together, these state, local, and private conservation tracts make up more than 40,000 acres of coterminous wild lands, termed **The Mountain Bridge Wilderness and Recreation Area** by South Carolina.

Three state parks make up the bulk of the recreational opportunities in this area. **Table Rock State Park** (see *Recreation Areas*), on the western edge of this chapters' region off **SC 11,** centers around an outlying dome of hard, gray rock that looms 2,000 feet above the park's lakeside picnic area; history buffs will want to check out its extensive Civilian Conservation Corps (CCC) architecture, listed on the National Register. **Caesar's Head State Park** (see *Recreation Areas*), bisected by **US 276** in the center of the region, protects a long series of cliffs and waterfalls (see **Ravens Cliff Falls on The Blue Wall** under *Wandering Around—Exploring on Foot*)—the only place on The Blue Wall with cliff-top views you can drive to. **Jones Gap State Park** (see *Recreation Areas*) protects the upper reaches of the **Middle Saluda River,** with some spectacular cliff scenery.

RECREATION AREAS Table Rock State Park (864-878-9813), 158 East Ellison Lane, Pickens, NC. Open every day 7 AM–9 PM. Built in 1936, this 3,000-acre park preserves a 3,100-foot mountain dome, plus enough historic Civilian Conservation Corps (CCC) architecture to place the entire park on the National Register of Historic Places. The central attraction is, of course, **Table Rock,** a cliff-sided outlier of the Blue Ridge that towers 2,000 feet above the picnic area—a horizontal distance of only 1.4 miles. Most visitors enjoy the view from the lovely little lake or the wildflower meadows at its base; but more than a few climb the very steep 3.5-mile trail to its peak, for wide views over the Blue Ridge and out over the level plains of the Deep South. The park has a CCC picnic area on a small lake, CCC-built log rental cabins, a lakeside restaurant with dining-room views toward Table Rock, and a nature center.

Caesar's Head State Park (864-836-6115), 8155 Greer Highway, Cleveland, NC. Open April through September, 9–9; October through March, 9–6. Bisected by **US 276** (see *Wandering Around—Exploring by Car*), this park occupies a 3,200-foot cliff-faced side ridge projecting out into South Carolina's **Blue Wall** (see chapter introduction) country. A roadside overlook offers stunning views over the rugged Blue Ridge, toward **Table Rock** (see above) and the plains of the Piedmont. Nearby, a visitors center has an information desk, gift shop, and exhibits on area history. **Raven Cliff Falls** (see Ravens Cliff Falls on The Blue Wall under *Wandering Around—Exploring on Foot*)**,** at over 400 feet one of the tallest in the East, is in this park.

Jones Gap State Park (864-836-3647), 303 Jones Gap Road, Marietta, NC. Open April through October, 9–9; November through March, 9–6. This 3,300-acre park protects the rare forests and unique rock formations at the foot of the **Cleveland Cliffs,** along South Carolina's **Blue Wall** (see chapter introduction). Rugged (but well-maintained) paths climb the high cliffs, follow side ridges, or explore the **Middle Saluda State Scenic River.** At the park's headquarters up a quiet rural lane off **SC 11,** the park's **Environmental Education Center** has nature exhibits, and the Civilian Conservation Corps (CCC)–era **Cleveland Fish Hatchery** has been restored and stocked as a demonstration.

PICNIC AREAS Silvermont Park, Brevard, NC. This funky Brevard city park offers good picnicking three blocks south of downtown on US 276. It takes up the house and grounds of a historic neoclassical brick mansion—but with no attempt at restoration. Quite the contrary; the house itself, used for meetings, is in bad shape, and much of its extensive formal gardens have been paved over with tennis and basketball courts. However, it has a nicely kept, shady picnic area with a good playground, as well as a lovely little herb garden and a gravel exercise path through a forest garden.

A RESTORED LOG CABIN AT THE CRADLE OF FORESTRY IN AMERICA

North Mills River Recreation Area. At the end of the paved North Mills River Road, and the start of two scenic gravel Forest Service roads, this Forest Service site offers picnicking in a great hemlock grove by a mountain river.

The Pink Beds Picnic Area. This National Forest Service picnic area sits just off the Blue Ridge Parkway on **US 276** (see *Wandering Around—Exploring by Car*). Apart from the famous rhododendrons from which it is named (and which display in June), it's notable for its attractive and level loop trail, which leads to beaver dams (and may be flooded by beaver ponds).

✳ To See

HISTORIC SITES ✧ ♿ **The Cradle of Forestry in America** (828-877-3130). Run by the National Forest Service, this historic site is on US 276, fourteen miles north of Brevard, NC, and 3.5 miles south of the Blue Ridge Parkway. Open May through October, 9–5. Adults $5, children $2.50. When George W. Vanderbilt founded Asheville's **Biltmore Estate** (see *To See—The Biltmore Estate* in "Asheville and the Blue Ridge Parkway", Introduction to the Biltmore Estate) as his private residence in the 1880s, he surrounded it with vast tracts of forest lands, including much of the Pisgah Ranger District of **Pisgah National Forest** (see The Pisgah Forest under *Wild Places—The Great Forests*). With no scientific forestry in existence in America at the time, Vanderbilt imported professional foresters from Germany to manage his forests—first the German-trained American Gifford Pinchot, then the German scientist Carl A. Schenck. With no trained assistants or staff available in the United States, these scientists were forced to start a training school on Biltmore property. This training school is now preserved as The Cradle of Forestry in America, a beautiful and fascinating collection of historic log structures. The tour starts at the large modern museum, where historic and modern forestry practices are explained. Then a loop trail leads to the historic site, with a log school room, store, and cabins (including some built in a properly German style by Dr. Schenck), where crafts demonstrations are held. A second loop trail leads through a demonstration of historic forestry practices.

✧ ♿ **Carl Sandburg Home National Historic Site** (828-693-4178), 1928 Little River Road, Flat Rock, NC. Open daily 9–5, year-round. Free admission to grounds and goat barn. House tours are $3 for adults; children under 17 free. In 1945, poet and scholar Carl Sandburg and his wife, Paula, moved from Michigan to Flat Rock, NC. Mrs. Sandburg was a dedicated goat farmer and serious goat breeder, and the mild climate of Flat Rock was a superior place to raise goats. They purchased **Connemara,** a large farm with a beautiful antebellum house and a large pond, at the center of Flat Rock. Carl Sandburg remained at Connemara until his death in 1967; a year later, Connemara became the Carl Sandburg National Historic Site, part of America's national park system.

Connemara would have been worthy of preservation under any circumstance. One of the oldest farmsteads in this region, it was built in 1838 as a vacation home for a rich South Carolinian, Christopher Memminger, later Treasury Secretary for the Confederate States of America. His heirs sold it to a Captain Smyth, and Smyth's heirs sold it to the Sandburgs with 240 acres of farmland and forest. The National Park Service has preserved the house, the grounds, and the goat farm the way Carl and Paula left them.

Connemara is an extraordinarily beautiful place, easily worth a full day's exploration. From the roadside parking lot, you walk along a lovely pond with views toward a meadow-covered hill and the house. The path crosses a wooden bridge, then climbs along wood fences and through meadows for 0.3 mile to the surprisingly modest house, with its columned porch and lush azaleas. The basement visitors center has a small bookstore and information desk. After touring the house, continue up into the farm area with 21 buildings preserved from the Sandburg era. It's still a functioning goat farm, and kids wander out from the giant red barn to greet visitors. Beyond the goat dairy, walking paths lead through woods to mountaintop viewpoints.

Historic Johnson Farm (828-891-6585), 3346 Haywood Road, Hendersonville, NC. Open May through October: 9–2:30, with guided tours at 10:30 AM and 1:30 PM; closed Sunday and Monday. November through April: closed Sunday through Tuesday. Adults $3, students $2. Run by a not-for-profit organization on behalf of the Henderson County school system, this 15-acre museum complex preserves a late-19th-century tobacco farm. It centers on a restored brick 1870s farmhouse listed on the National Register and furnished as a late-19th-century farm residence. There are nine other historic structures, all original to the farm, including a boardinghouse and a barn museum.

CONNEMARA, THE HOME OF POET CARL SANDBURG

CULTURAL SITES Brevard Music Center (828-884-2011; 1-888-384-8682), 1000 Probart Street, Brevard, NC. From its beautiful lakeside campus on the north edge of Brevard, the Brevard Music Center furnishes summer instruction in professional music practice and theory for talented, serious musicians from age 14 to post-college. Its 50 faculty members teach 400 students each summer. Brevard's unique program emphasizes performance experience with professional musicians under real-world conditions—the sorts of rehearsals and audiences that students will encounter in their first professional jobs. For this reason the center sponsors the annual **Brevard Music Festival** (see *Entertainment*)—two months of performances (50 in all) in which the center's students perform with top-ranked professionals. Founded in 1936 as a band camp, the campus consists of 145 rolling, wooded acres with around a hundred separate buildings and two lakes. Its main venue, the **Whittington-Pfohl Auditorium,** is open sided, with seating both under cover and on the open lawn by Milner Lake.

✇ ♿ **Pisgah Center for Wildlife Education** (828-877-4423), Pisgah Forest, NC. Open every day 8–5. Free admission. Located 10 miles north of Brevard, NC, this wildlife museum run by the North Carolina Game and Fish Commission is 1.5 miles off US 276, down a signposted paved forest road. Deep in Pisgah National Forest, this small museum occupies a beautiful site at a working fish hatchery, bordered by the rocky Davidson River and with views up toward the gray cliffs of Johns Rock. Inside the small museum building are a gift and bookshop; exhibits follow a stream from the mountains to the sea, including aquaria of mountain, Piedmont, and coastal species. Then the museum path leads outside for an easy streamside walk, with first-rate exhibits on Appalachian forest ecology, wildlife, and management. The museum tour ends with a walk through the working fish hatchery, its long concrete troughs filled with trout. Given the ownership of this museum, as well as its being funded by hunting and fishing licenses, expect a subtle pro-hunting (and an unsubtle pro-fishing) slant to the displays. There is a good picnic area at the far end of the parking lot, as well as trails to the top of Johns Rock, with stunning views.

A 1929 CURTISS ROBIN AT THE WESTERN NORTH CAROLINA AIR MUSEUM

Western North Carolina Air Museum (828-698-2482), Hendersonville, NC. Open afternoons on Wednesday, Saturday, and Sunday. Free admission. This museum, run by local enthusiasts, occupies a modern metal hangar on the grounds of Hendersonville's small airport, south of town, off US 25 on Brooklyn Avenue. It has beautifully restored and fully operational small historic aircraft, including WWI fighters and small private aviation craft.

The Jim Bob Tinsley Museum and Research Center (828-884-2347), 20 West Jordan Street, Brevard, NC. Open May through November: Tuesday through Saturday 10–4; December through April: Tuesday through Saturday 1–4. This not-for-profit museum in a historic downtown Brevard storefront houses the collections of cowboy singer and Brevard resident Jim Bob Tinsley. Much of it features western memorabilia and cowboy music material, while other sections contain displays of Transylvania County history. There's a special section on local waterfalls, featuring art and photos from Jim Bob and others.

255

THE BLUE RIDGE: HENDERSONVILLE & BREVARD

GARDENS AND PARKS Skytop Orchard (828-692-7930), Flat Rock, NC. Located on a side road off US 25 near the center of Flat Rock; from US 25 turn west onto Pinnacle Mountain Road and follow the signs. Open August through October, 9–6 daily. This U-pick apple orchard has stunning views from 50 acres of handsome orchards straddling the Blue Ridge. Pickers have 20 varieties of apples to choose from; there are also hayrides, farm animals to pet, picnicking, and a farm stand during the picking season.

Conestee Falls. Although signs along US 276 south of Brevard advertise a residential subdivision named Conestee Falls, there is an actual waterfall, and it is definitely worth a stop if you're in the area. You'll find it behind the development's realtor office alongside the main highway, 6 miles south of town. A well-built path leads perhaps a hundred feet to a railed overlook with an excellent view over a double waterfall.

South Brevard Park. This local park, two blocks west of downtown Brevard on US 64, offers a small but worthwhile native plant garden. Covering perhaps half a block, it has a wide range of flowers blooming from April through October, displayed from a system of wide rectangular paths with plenty of benches.

Jumpoff Rock Park. This local park outside Hendersonville offers panoramic 270-degree views over the valley of the French Broad River, toward the mile-high crest of the Pisgah Ridge, from a large projecting rock. To find it, take Fifth Avenue west from downtown Hendersonville; then continue on Laurel Park Highway, never turning off onto any of the confusing maze of side roads, until you reach its end, 4.4 miles from downtown. Actually, Laurel Park Highway is a hoot—a genuine 1920s-era main road, complete with its original concrete surface, that curves uphill through an old, wealthy mountainside subdivision with 80-year-old mansions spread through the trees. Jumpoff Rock Park, at its end, is a landscaped picnic and walking area, where the clifflike sides of this small mountain become undeniable cliffs. Apart from the views, this is a pleasant, cool, and attractive spot.

✳ To Do

BICYCLING Backcountry Outdoors (828-884-4262), 18 Pisgah Highway (US 276), Pisgah Forest, NC. $28–38 per day for trail bike rentals. This outdoor supply store, located north of Brevard, specializes in outdoor activities in Pisgah National Forest, and particularly in mountain biking. They will rent you a fine trail bike and help you find a good trail; they offer guided mountain bike tours of these forests as well.

FISHING Davidson River Out-fitters (828-877-4181; 1-888-861-0111), 4 Pisgah Highway, Pisgah Forest, NC. This full-service fly-fishing shop, located north of Brevard at the intersection of US 64 and US 276, dispenses good advice and arranges guide service ($125–200, half day; $215–325, full day) to the rich streams of **Pisgah National Forest.**

GOLF Etowah Valley Country Club and Golf Lodge (828-891-7022; 1-800-451-8174), 450 Brickyard Road,

Etowah, NC. Open all year. $31. Three nine-hole courses give a choice of play in this championship course, noted for its mountain views and beautifully landscaped floral edges.

Crooked Creek Golf Club (828-692-2011), 764 Crooked Creek Road, Hendersonville, NC. $15. Located just south of Hendersonville, this mainly rustic course follows a stream along a valley bottom, with water in play in 12 of its 18 holes. The clubhouse occupies an old Warner Brothers retreat.

Highland Lake Golf Course (828-692-0143), 111 Highland Lake Road, Flat Rock, NC. Open all year. $9 (nine holes). This nine-hole course near the center of Flat Rock (not part of the Highland Lake Inn resort) is fairly level, with four water hazards.

HORSEBACK RIDING Pisgah Forest Riding Stables (828-883-8258), Avery Creek Road, Pisgah Forest, NC. $20 per hour per person. Located north of Brevard, off scenic US 276 on a national forest road, this stable offers 1- to 3-hour trail rides inside **Pisgah National Forest,** with destinations that include views and a waterfall.

WHITEWATER ADVENTURES Headwaters Outfitters (828-877-3106), Rosman, NC. Open April through October, 9–5 every day. This is something you don't see often—a canoe outfitter in the deep mountains. Located at the start of 20 miles of serpentine stillwater, Headwaters Outfitters offers canoe and kayak sales, rentals ($30 per day), and shuttled trips ($20–37 with shuttle service) on this unique and beautiful stretch of the **French Broad River.** Other services include tubing on nearby mountain streams ($7–15 with shuttle service),

overnight canoe trips, and guided kayak tours of the gigantic wilderness reservoir, **Lake Jocassee.**

✳ Lodging

COUNTRY INNS AND HOTELS The Claddagh Inn (828-697-7778; 1-800-225-4700), 755 North Main Street, Hendersonville, NC 28792. Open all year. This large late-Victorian mansion surrounded lawn and giant oak trees is an oasis of calm, yet an easy stroll to downtown. The three-story Classical Revival house, listed on the National Register, features an extrawide wraparound front porch with interesting double columns. Inside common areas include an elegant front parlor; a cozy wood-paneled library with piano, books, and fireplace; a dining room with table seating; and a convenient second-floor parlor, all carefully furnished in the late-Victorian style. The 14 en suite guest rooms, all comfortable to large in size with telephone, television, and air-conditioning, are individually furnished in Victorian antiques and reproductions. Some have special features, such as #215's private second-story sunporch with its parquet floor and wicker furniture. The third floor is split between two suites, each with two bedrooms and a sitting room. Guests are treated to a hearty country breakfast and an evening glass of sherry. January through April: $89–125; May through December: $105–150.

The Woodfield Inn (828-693-6016; 1-800-247-2203), US 25 South, P.O. Box 98, Flat Rock, NC 28731. Open all year. In operation since its founding in 1852, this National Register antebellum stagecoach inn sits on 28 acres at the center of Flat Rock. Surrounded by landscaped parkland, the 18-room

Italianate structure has wide verandas on its first and second floor. The en suite rooms are individually themed with Victorian decor, including antiques; guests can choose rooms with private verandas, whirlpool tubs, and views. The hearty breakfast is served in the inn's restaurant, which also serves lunch and dinner to the public. April through December: rooms $119–149; suites $169–189. January through March: $79–109.

The Angelique Inn (828-883-4105; 877-698-7819), 408 South Caldwell Street, Brevard, NC 28712. Open all year. This remarkable Victorian mansion sits near the center of Brevard, a block off US 64. The house, situated on a 2-acre knoll with lawns, gardens, and shade trees, is an elaborate three-story fantasy of columns, gables, dormers, verandas, projections, bay windows, a circular whatsis at the corner of the wraparound porch, and a witches-hat turret. Inside are high-ceilinged, wood-trimmed common rooms filled with Victorian antiques. The largest (and most expensive) suite has a full kitchen, sunroom with sofa, and formal dining room; the other two suites have a large bedroom area, restricted kitchen facilities, and a small eating area. All are furnished with Victorian antiques and have private bath, TV, phone, and air conditioning. Suites $85–110. Off-season and weekly discounts apply.

RESORTS The Highland Lake Inn (828-693-6812; 1-800-762-1376), Highland Lake Road, Flat Rock, NC 28731. This 180-acre full-service resort in the center of Flat Rock has a modern inn and a historic lodge overlooking a lovely little lake. Resort amenities include fishing, lake swimming, pool swimming, canoeing, paddleboating, volley ball, horseshoes, and on-site walking trails. The site itself is beautiful, gently rolling and tree-covered, with an extensive organic-farm operation that supplies its first-rate restaurant (see *Dining Out*). The contemporary inn has 16 large and airy rooms, some with whirlpool baths, wet bars, fireplaces, or private patios, as well as several common sitting areas. The historic lodge, recently renovated, has 20 rooms, with common areas that include a recreation room and a bar. Modest cabin duplexes, simple structures with board-and-batten walls and covered porches, make up the economy end of the lodgings, while quaint cottages with full kitchens make up the high end. Inn rooms $149–215; lodge rooms $144–180; cabins $109–130; cottages $209 and up.

BED & BREAKFASTS ❧ **The Flat Rock Inn** (828-696-3273; 1-800-266-3996), 2810 Greenville Highway, P.O. Box 308, Flat Rock, NC 28731. This 1888 National Register mansion sits comfortably off US 25 on its own tree-shaded property at the center of Flat Rock village. Originally built as a summer residence for a wealthy Charlestonian, it features wraparound porches, second-story balconies, and a large, quiet lawn and garden. Homemade afternoon sweets are served from the wide porch, or in the parlor. Inside, the common rooms are beautifully decorated in Victorian antiques. Comfortable sofas and chairs face a fireplace, with plenty of interesting books to read, while a gourmet country breakfasts are served in the traditional formal dining room. A butler's pantry has tea and custom-blended coffee for guests, as well as a guest refrigerator well stocked with wine, ice cream, and the usual soft drinks. Each of the large air-conditioned guest rooms is individually furnished in Victorian antiques and has a private bath; two have private porches. $85–145.

210 Maple Bed & Breakfast (828-877-5004; 1-888-350-5004), 210 Maple Street, Brevard, NC 28712. Set on a quiet back street in a lovely residential neighborhood, 210 Maple offers the upstairs of a large and beautiful 1920s house as a single, multi-bedroom suite. It's hard to imagine a better way to enjoy life in one of the mountain's loveliest small towns. A period house in a neighborhood filled with period houses, 210 Maple sits on a tree-shaded lot, surrounded by well-kept flower gardens complete with fountain. The large rear garden, available to guests, includes an herb garden, fresh vegetables, and a table shaded by great trees. The house is furnished with antiques, including a comfortable sitting room with fireplace and TV. The three bedrooms upstairs are all ample in size, furnished with turn-of-the-century antiques. Hearty Southern-style breakfasts are made with farm eggs and fresh vegetables and herbs from the garden, and may include omelets, cheese grits, Southern-style biscuits, or French toast with huckleberry syrup. $95–210, depending on the number of bedrooms needed.

The Mary Mills Coxe Inn (828-692-5900; 1-800-230-6541), 1210 Greenville Highway (US 25), Hendersonville, NC 28792. Open all year. This seven-room inn occupies a National Register–listed mansion on the south edge of Hendersonville. Built in 1911 by a wealthy widow, the three-story pebbledash-sided Colonial Revival house is surrounded by a wraparound porch. During parts of the day and evening, the downstairs functions as

ROCKING CHAIRS BECKON ON THE FRONT PORCH OF A LOG CABIN AT THE CRADLE OF FORESTRY IN AMERICA.

the elegant **Gables Restaurant** (see *Dining Out*); in the mornings, it's the venue for elegant breakfasts served to the inn's guests. Upstairs, the seven en suite guest rooms have individual European decor; differences in the rooms give guests the choice of working fireplaces, whirlpool baths, and wet bars. $140–160.

Mélange Bed & Breakfast (1-800-303-5253), 1230 Fifth Avenue, West, Hendersonville, NC 28739. This five-room B&B occupies a 1920 Colonial Revival mansion in an upscale residential section of Hendersonville. The large house is surrounded by 3 acres of lawns and gardens in elaborate Mediterranean style, with four fountains. Surprisingly, the interior of this simple Colonial design is an elaborate French Empire concoction. Common areas—which include an foyer, parlor, living room, formal and informal dining rooms, and a book-filled study—may have 11-foot ceilings, marble floors, mahogany trim, high mirrors, and (of course) elegant furnishings. All five en suite rooms are large, with decor both luxurious and comfortable; features (varying by room) may include wood-burning fireplaces, whirlpool baths, sitting areas, wet bars, and a private deck. Full gourmet breakfasts are served on a flagstone patio in the rose garden, weather permitting. Rooms $125–155; suite $165–185.

The Apple Inn (828-693-0107; 1-800-615-6611), 1005 White Pine Drive, Hendersonville, NC 28739. Built as a vacation home by a wealthy South Carolinian, the 1930s-era Apple Inn is surrounded by 3 acres of lawns and gardens in a quiet suburb of Hendersonville. The individually decorated en suite rooms are country or Victorian in style, with antiques and reproductions. Homemade breakfasts are served on the porch or inside. Rooms $98; two-bedroom suite $250.

Rose Tree Bed & Breakfast (828-698-8912; 1-800-672-1993), One Boxwood Drive, Flat Rock, NC 28731. This B&B occupies a large 1910 home in the center of Flat Rock. The two-story house, renovated in 1998, sits on 6 acres, with a wide wraparound porch and a bright, airy interior. Common spaces include a large parlor with a fireplace, a grand piano, and plenty of books, and a traditional, formal dining room where the full breakfast is served. This classic B&B has only two rooms, both two-room suites with in-room refrigerators and flowers freshly cut from the inn's garden. $145.

The Red House (828-884-9349), 412 West Probart Street, Brevard, NC 28712. Open all year. Located four blocks from downtown Brevard and eight blocks from the **Brevard Music Center,** the Red House may be the town's most historic structure. Estab-

lished as a trading post before Brevard existed, it served as the town's first train station and as the founding location for Brevard College, a local 4-year liberal arts school. The inn sits on a hill just north of downtown, surrounded by lawns. Painted brick red, it has first- and second-story wraparound porches and third-story dormers. Inside, it's furnished with Victorian antiques in a country style, including the four guest rooms. The rate includes a full country breakfast. $65–99.

Chestnut Hill Bed & Breakfast (828-862-3540), 400 Barclay Road, Brevard, NC 28712. Open April through October. Built as a summer home in 1856, this National Register–listed antebellum mansion sits on a wooded hillock surrounded by hay meadows. Three miles south of Brevard, on a rural lane off US 276, Chestnut Hill offers lovely views over the French Broad River from its two-story gingerbread veranda, as well as gardens and woodland walks on its 80-acre tract. $125–185.

Key Falls Bed & Breakfast (828-884-7559), 151 Everett Road, Pisgah Forest, NC 28768. This large two-story farmhouse from the 1860s sits on 35 acres by the French Broad River, 3 miles east of Brevard. Its well-kept gardens and meadows give views toward the river and the mountains beyond, while the large property contains a pond, tennis courts, and hiking trails (including one to the lovely **Key Falls,** on site). Comfortable common areas and five guest rooms are furnished with Victorian decor, including antiques. The room rate includes a full breakfast. $75–95.

CABIN RENTALS Lakemont Cottages (828-693-5174; 1-800-597-

0692), 100 Lakemont Drive, Flat Rock, NC 28731. Open all year. Lakemont features 14 modestly styled modern cottages spread around a rolling, wooded tract south of Hendersonville, not far off US 176. A small lake (or large pond) makes up the centerpiece of this little village. Cottages have separate bedrooms and full kitchens, as well as enclosed porches. Credit cards are not accepted. April through October: $60–100; November through March: $60–90.

✳ Where to Eat

EATING OUT Center Stage Deli (828-694-0080), 126 Fourth Avenue East, Hendersonville, NC. Open 11–9. This storefront restaurant on a downtown side street offers authentic New York deli food. This is a sit-down restaurant with table service; it's clean and bright, with plenty of booths. The decor, in saturated primary colors, is theater themed, with an art deco–style wall mural. Many items come from the Carnegie Deli in New York—pastrami, corned beef, hard salami, knishes, and cheesecakes. Specializing in huge deli sandwiches piled thick with meat, but also offering a range of specialty sandwiches, appetizers, and salad platters. Sandwiches typically $6–8; salads $5–8.

Cypress Cellar (828-698-1005), 321-C North Main Street, Hendersonville, NC. Located in a roomy, airy space below sidewalk level in downtown Hendersonville, the Cypress Cellar features authentic dishes from southern Louisiana, for lunch and dinner. It's a bright and friendly space, with furniture made from Louisiana cypress. The lunch menu features hot Cajun dishes as well as sandwiches and burgers, including muffulettas and po-boys on bread from Gambino's of New Orleans, fried green tomatoes on jalapeño cheddar grits, gumbo, red beans and rice, jambalaya, and crawfish cakes. The dinner menu drops the sandwiches and adds a variety of steak, pasta, and seafood entrées. On weekend evenings, it's a popular venue for live music. Lunch $5–7; dinner $6–15.

Haus Hiedelberg (828-693-8227), 630 Greenville Highway, Hendersonville, NC. Open for lunch and dinner. This modest restaurant on US 25 on the southern edge of town has an impressive all-German menu prepared authentically from scratch by Chef Helge Gresser. Apart from its full selection of German entrées, this is a sausage lover's heaven, with a dozen or so sausage entrées with fresh sauerkraut and potato salad. A wine list and a selection of draft German beer are available. Sausage dinners $4–8; fancier fare $11–15.

The Wildflower Café (828-884-7311), 430 North Caldwell Street, Brevard, NC. Open Monday through Friday 11:30 AM–3:30 PM; Friday and Saturday 7 PM–10 PM. This vegetarian organic café in downtown Brevard features lunchtime sandwiches, salads, and soup on weekdays, and custom dinner specials with live music on their patios on Friday and Saturday.

Rocky's Soda Shop and Grill (828-877-5375), 38 South Broad Street, Brevard, NC. Open Monday through Saturday 11–5:30, Sunday noon–5; extended hours in summer. This nostalgic storefront in the center of downtown Brevard has burgers, hot dogs, and sandwiches, but the emphasis is on its old-fashioned soda fountain. Counter service with round stools and round tables with red-backed wire chairs, it's decor steps back in time a half century—as does its ice creams, floats, sundaes, and banana splits.

DINING OUT ⟨ **The Gables Restaurant** (828-692-5900; 1-800-230-6541), 1210 Greenville Highway (US 35), Hendersonville, NC. Open for dinner Monday through Saturday. Located in an elegant Victorian mansion (the **Mary Milles Coxe Inn;** see *Lodging—Bed and Breakfasts*) on the southern edge of town, the Gables Restaurant serves American and international dishes in a setting of European antiques. The restaurant area—downstairs of the B&B—wanders through two large parlors and fronts on the wraparound porch. Its tiny bar is paneled with bookshelves and filled with books. The menu changes daily; an appetizer of venison sausage ravioli with smoked garlic cream sauce might precede entrées of duck breast with orange zinfandel sauce or fresh Thai snapper with tomato saffron broth. $35–40 including appetizer and dessert.

The Highland Lake Inn (828-696-9094; 1-800-635-5101), Highland Lake Road, Flat Rock, NC. Closed January through April. Open for breakfast 7:30 AM–10 AM; lunch 11:30 AM–2 PM; dinner 5 PM–9 PM; closed Sunday. Many of Highland Lakes' vegetables, salads, and even their herbs and seasonings come from the inn's organic gardens. Sitting on 180 lakefront acres in Flat Rock, just off US 25, this attractive restaurant offers all three meals to nonguests. Lunches, which start at $9, offer salads and sandwich favorites with a difference—half-pound burgers topped with caramelized shallots, apple-smoked bacon, and local-farm cheese; or chicken melts with roasted breast meat, tomatoes, and chives, and topped with Muenster cheese and

oven baked on focaccia bread. The extensive dinner menu marries fish, fowl, or meat with exciting combinations of vegetables and cheeses, and includes impressive vegetarian dishes. Lunch $9 plus, dinner entrées $15–23.

✳ Entertainment

Flat Rock Playhouse (828-693-0731), US 25, Flat Rock, NC. $20–27. The **State Theater of North Carolina,** as professional Actor's Equity company, performs nine or so productions at its barnlike theater in Flat Rock.

Hendersonville Symphony Orchestra (828-697-5884), P.O. Box 1811, Hendersonville, NC 28793. $15. Hendersonville is probably the only small-town rural county seat with its own full-sized symphony orchestra. Made up of talented local musicians, it's led by Music Director and Conductor Thomas Joiner, Professor of Violin and Orchestra Activities at Furman University and Concertmaster of the **Brevard Music Festival** (see below). Performing at various local venues (including the high school auditorium), its typical concert season includes a pops concert, a Christmas concert, and a couple of traditional classical concerts with guest soloists.

✳ Selective Shopping

Downtown Hendersonville, NC

Hendersonville's five-block downtown remains utterly dominated by turn-of-the-century two- and three-story buildings, facing a landscaped Main Street. The main highway, US 25, splits down one-way streets that flank the back sides of these downtown blocks, leaving Main to shoppers and people looking for parking places. Now one of the classier shopping districts in the mountains, downtown's old storefronts are dominated by art and fine-crafts galleries, antiques shops, gift shops, specialty shops, and restaurants—90 retailers and eateries in all. The Main Street shopping district is bordered on the north by US 64, and on the south by the old and distinguished (but decrepit) Henderson County Courthouse. Parking is free along Main Street, and 25¢ for 2 hours on four metered lots along US 25.

✐ **Dad's Cats** (828-698-7525), 221 North Main Street. Dad's Cats one-ups your normal model railroad shop with a large selection of model industrial cranes and construction equipment. Owned by a retired design engineer who specialized in earthmoving equipment, they specialize in limited, serial-numbered die-cast scale models. They also have model cars, trucks, fire equipment, and—yes—train layout items, as well as educational toys and collectable model horses.

Wickwire Fine Art/Folk Art (828-692-6222), 330 North Main Street. This commercial fine arts gallery features a wide variety of arts and fine crafts from local and regional artists. Its artists include three Smithsonian artisans and two artists who have been declared North Carolina Living Treasures.

JRD's Classics and Collectibles (828-698-0075), 222 North Main Street. JRD's specializes in memorabilia and collectibles from the 1950s—particularly those from soda shops. Their ever-changing inventory of reproductions and restorations includes soda machines, jukeboxes, pinball machines, slot machines, diner decor, gas pumps, telephones, diner furniture, and neon, as well as recently issued collectibles. They perform their own restorations, including vintage slot machines.

Henderson County Farmer's Curb Market (828-692-8012), 221 North Church Street. Open May through December: Tuesday, Thursday, and Saturday 8–2; January through April: Tuesday and Saturday 9–1. Located just outside downtown behind the Old County Courthouse (facing southbound US 25), this nonprofit organization has 137 vendors, all of whom are from Henderson County and all of whom offer only locally made or grown items. In continuous operation since 1924, some of its vendors are now in their third or fourth generation.

Flat Rock, NC

Hand in Hand (828-697-7719), 2713 Greenville Highway. Open Tuesday through Saturday 10–5. This fine-crafts gallery, specializing in professional local artists, occupies an unprepossessing roadside brick building toward the center of Flat Rock. In it is a wide variety of fine crafts, both traditional and contemporary, as well as a quilting store.

Forge Mountain Foods (838-692-9470; 1-800-823-6743), 1215 Greenville Highway (US 25). This small specialty-food company maintains its outlet store in an attractive modern building along US 25. Forge Mountain makes a wide variety of traditional Southern-style gift foods—jellies, jams, fruit butters, honey, molasses, sorghum, syrups, relishes, ciders, candies, shortbreads, cakes, hams, and that sort of thing—and sells them all from this roadside company store.

Downtown Brevard, NC

This four-block classic small town Main Street centers on its beautiful and well-kept Transylvania County Courthouse. For the past decade it's been evolving from a rural downtown to an upscale shopping district; you can still get your hair cut and shoes repaired, but you can browse for art and antiques as well.

Number 7 Arts (828-883-2294), 7 East Main Street. This fine arts and crafts cooperative, sponsored by the Transylvania County Arts Council, is made up of local artists selected by an impartial jurying process. It displays a wide range of media and styles, and always has a local artist/member on hand.

Red Wolf Gallery (828-862-8620), 3 East Main Street. This fine arts gallery represents well-known professional artists, mainly from the Appalachian region, with a decidedly contemporary slant.

The Forest Place (828-884-4734), 100 South Broad Street. This ecology-oriented gift- and bookshop is owned and operated by The Cradle of Forestry Interpretive Association, a nonprofit organization that supports **The Cradle of Forestry in America** (see *To See—Historic Sites*) and other educational efforts of Pisgah National Forest. You'll find a wide range of books, gifts, art, toys, and educational material—all dealing with forest ecology in the Blue Ridge and Smoky Mountains.

Cedar Mountain Community
This rural community, stretched along US 276 ten miles south of Brevard, NC, is home to several highly respected crafts artists who maintain galleries and open studios.

Mountain Forest Studio (828-885-2149). Open 10–5, Monday through Saturday. This white stucco farmhouse on US 276 three miles south of Brevard holds the studios of potter Mary Murray. It features the work of several other local artists as well.

✳ Special Events

Last weekend in April: **Poetry Celebration at the Carl Sandburg Home** (828-693-4178), 1928 Little River Road, Flat Rock, NC. This 2-day festival, sponsored by the National Park Service on the grounds of the **Carl Sandburg Home National Historic Site** (see *To See—Historic Sites*), features poetry readings by school children, college students, and well-known guest poets, in addition to poetry workshops.

Last Saturday in April: **Johnson Farm Festival** (828-891-6585), 3346 Haywood Road, Hendersonville, NC. Adults $5, students $2. This fundraiser for the nonprofit organization that runs the **Historic Johnson Farm** (see *To See—Historic Sites*) museum fea-

BREVARD MUSIC FESTIVAL

&. (828-884-2011; 1-888-384-8682), P.O. Box 312, Brevard, NC 28712. Open June through August (box office opens in April). Events typically cost $7–25; some performances and seats may cost more. Students at the **Brevard Music Center** (see *To See—Cultural Sites*) combine with top-notch professional musicians to put on a summer-long series of performances —typically 50 or so. Events include symphony orchestras, chamber music, popular music, musicals, and fully staged operas.

tures mountain crafters and musicians (including fiddles and dulcimers), old-time mountain food, crafts exhibits, and farm demonstrations—as well as the full range of museum features.

Labor Day weekend: **The North Carolina Apple Festival** (828-697-4557), Hendersonville, NC. This 4-day festival in downtown Hendersonville celebrates the local apple industry. Six blocks of Main Street are filled with 150 vendors and two music stages, while apple-related activities and demonstrations go on throughout the county. The festival ends with a downtown **Labor Day parade.**

Great Smoky Mountains National Park

GATLINBURG & THE NORTHEAST QUADRANT

TOWNSEND, CADES COVE & THE NORTHWEST QUADRANT

BRYSON CITY & THE SOUTHWEST QUADRANT

CHEROKEE & THE SOUTHEAST QUADRANT

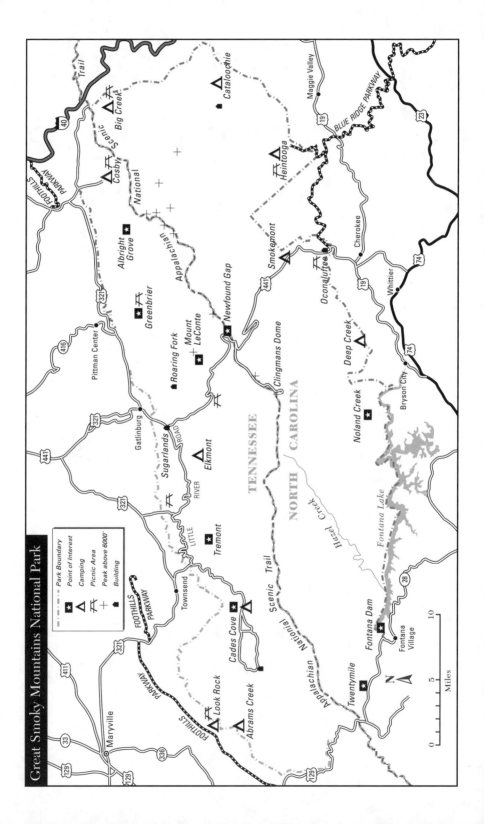

Great Smoky Mountains National Park

Legend:
- ▦ Park Boundary
- ▲ Point of Interest
- ⛺ Camping
- ⛽ Picnic Area
- + Peak above 6000'
- ■ Building

Maryville

33

411

128

129

336

321

FOOTHILLS PARKWAY

Look Rock

Abrams Creek

Townsend

Tremont

LITTLE RIVER ROAD

Sugarlands

Gatlinburg

416

Pittman Center

321

441

Cades Cove

National Scenic Trail

Appalachian

Hazel Creek

TENNESSEE

NORTH CAROLINA

Fontana Lake

Fontana Dam

28

Fontana Village

Twentymile

Noland Creek

Bryson City

74

Deep Creek

Oconaluftee

19

Whittier

Cherokee

74

Smokemont

Newfound Gap

441

Clingmans Dome

Mount LeConte

Roaring Fork

Greenbrier

Albright Grove

Appalachian

National

Scenic

Trail

40

FOOTHILLS PARKWAY

Cosby

Big Creek

Cataloochie

Heintooga

BLUE RIDGE PARKWAY

19

Maggie Valley

23

Elkmont

N

0   5   10
Miles

GREAT SMOKY MOUNTAINS NATIONAL PARK

The Great Smoky Mountains make up the craggy climax to the Southern Appalachians. While the nearby Black Mountains (see Mount Mitchell and the Black Mountains under *Wild Places—The Great Forests* in "Asheville and the Blue Ridge Highway") may be taller by a few dozens of feet, no other eastern range is steeper, more twisted and knotted, or more rugged. The Smokies run as an unbroken wall for 60 miles along the state line, blocking North Carolina from Tennessee with a cliff-walled razor's edge that has mile-high gaps and 6,000-foot peaks. Then, at Tricorner Knob, the Smokies suddenly twist south, change their name to the Balsam Mountains, and run as a mile-high wall for another 45 miles. Behind this great L-shaped range (to its south and west) lie a tangle of tall, knotted mountains with deep gaps and slashing narrow valleys.

While the Smokies may have missed the honor of having the highest peak in the East, they are without doubt the most difficult, rugged, and impenetrable range in the Southern Appalachians. Where most eastern mountains struggle to push their peaks more than half a mile above sea level, the Smokies and the Balsams quickly reach an elevation of ¾ mile above sea level—then stay there or higher for a hundred miles. Indeed, the ridge stays a mile above sea level for 50 miles (in four stretches), with 107 peaks and gaps that are a mile high. Mile-high peaks and gaps are so common in these ranges that folks haven't bothered naming 35 of them, a nonchalance unheard of in other eastern ranges. Slopes plunge 4,000 to 5,000 feet nearly straight down from these high ridges to narrow valley floors, then jump straight up to the next ridge. This tangle of valleys and ridges forms a chaotic non-pattern in which all ridge names are arbitrary.

Mountains this tall make their own climate. Valley floors as low as 800 feet above sea level have a warm Southern climate with oak and pine forests. Looming above these valleys, the mile-high ridgelines extend into a subarctic zone typical of Canada, dominated by spruces and firs (known locally as a "balsam forest"). Between these two forest types are every type of hardwood forest imaginable, changing by slope, elevation, local rainfall, exposure to the sun, history, and pure luck. The trees cover nearly every slope, no matter how steep, with the most rugged slopes covered in *laurel hells*, dense tangles of rhododendron and mountain laurel. High rainfall, on some ridges more than a hundred inches a year, can bring about a lush temperate rainforest of wondrous variety and beauty, where springs ooze out of the rocks to become raging rivers within 3 miles. With all this variety, it comes as no surprise that Great Smoky Mountains National Park is an International Biosphere Reserve, said to contain more tree species than Europe.

In these tangled ridges, stage roads and railroads followed the few river valleys with any width, while towns and farms followed the roads. Away from the railroads and turnpikes, settlements fanned out among the steep draws and coves as a thin cover of small subsistence farms. A high-mountain family would live in a one-crib log cabin and grow the food they planned to eat—mainly corn—in a small steep plot cleared by girdling trees. They would probably have a log barn with a horse or mule and a few cattle, as well as a corncrib, a chicken coop, and (perhaps) a springhouse. Uphill, where it was too steep to farm, the ancient forest spread to the ridgeline; the menfolk hunted the forest but did not log it. These small plots spread up streams wherever there was enough land to grow a little corn. Great Smoky Mountains National Park preserves quite a number of these high-mountain farmsteads, some as major open-air museums, others as cabins sitting by a path.

Great Smoky Mountains National Park combines all of these areas of interest—scenic grandeur, ecological diversity, and pioneer history. It forms a half-million-acre oval with the highest and most difficult ridges running lengthways along its center, and roads penetrating in from its periphery. Only one road, the popular

SNOW DUSTS THE HIGHEST ELEVATIONS OF MOUNT LECONTE.

Newfound Gap Road, penetrates deep into the park's interior to emerge on the other side. All other roads skitter along its edge, or run up valleys to dead-end at the mountain wall. Those roads lead to all sorts of places—wide views, deep forests, noisy rivers, beautiful waterfalls, and quaint log farmsteads. And footpaths—more than 800 miles of foot- and bridal paths penetrate the national park's backcountry. If you stay in your car, you'll miss most of the park.

Great Smoky Mountains National Park is run as a wilderness experience. Apart from campgrounds and camp stores, there are no restaurants or lodgings inside the park. The largest concentration of rooms and restaurants is at Gatlinburg, TN, a congested tourist town at the park's north entrance. To the west of Gatlinburg, the settlement of Townsend, TN, offers a quieter alternative. On the North Carolina side, much of the land bordering the park is within the Qualla Boundary, the reservation of the 10,000-member

Eastern Band of the Cherokee Nation; its tribal town of Cherokee straddles the park's main entrance in North Carolina. Not too far away are the unspoiled county seats of Bryson City and Sylva (see Sylva under *Villages* in "Near the Park: Sylva and Dillsboro"), NC, each with an excellent choice of B&Bs and restaurants.

GETTING ALONG IN THE NATIONAL PARK **Fishing.** Inside the national park, fishing for rainbow and brown trout is allowed year-round; you must have a state license, use a single hook on an artificial lure, and not take brook trout (a native specie the National Park Service is trying to restore). Despite the fact that the Park Service stopped stocking streams over 30 years ago, the fishing is excellent and most streams are at their trout population maximums. Fishing within the **Qualla Boundary** (see Fishing on the Qualla Boundary under *To Do—Fishing in* "Cherokee and the Southeast Quadrant") requires a tribal license but no state license; fishing on some streams is limited to tribal members.

Bicycling. For the most part, the National Park Service treats bicycles as vehicles on a par with cars, and requires them to follow the same rules. As a practical matter, this means that bicycling opportunities are limited, as the auto roads are narrow, shoulderless, and crowded. There are some exceptions. The scenic drive from **Cades Cove** up **Parsons Branch Road** and back on the **Foothills Parkway** (see The Foothills of Cades Cove under *Wandering Around—Exploring by Car* in "Townsend, Cades Cove, and the Northwest Quadrant") is well suited for bicycles, as is the loop around **Heintooga** (see The Blue Ridge Parkway and the Heintooga Spur Road under *Wandering Around—Exploring by Car* in "Cherokee and the Southeast Quadrant"). The Park Service allows bicycles up **Deep Creek** and **Indian Creek Trails** (see Deep Creek Trail under *Wandering Around—Exploring on Foot or Bicycle* in "Bryson City and the Southwest Quadrant") near Bryson City, even though they are closed to motorized vehicles. Last and best, the wonderful **Cades Cove Loop Road** (see *Wandering Around—Exploring by Car* in "Townsend, Cades Cove, and the Northwest Quadrant") is closed to cars Wednesday and Saturday mornings until 10, to allow bicyclists and walkers to enjoy it without noise and fumes.

Day Hiking. Day hiking is unrestricted in the national park, and this guide includes many suggested paths. Paths are normally high in quality, wide, and properly graded (although maintenance may vary in quality). Nearly all paths are forest walks, including those along ridgetops, as forests cover even the steepest slopes in the Smokies.

Two dangers confront even the casual walker. The first is bears, discussed elsewhere (see *Bears* below). The second, and by far the more deadly, is hypothermia, followed by dehydration and exhaustion. **Hypothermia**—sudden body cooling leading to disorientation—can occur in the hottest weather when altitudes exceed 5,000 feet and rainstorms blow up suddenly. **Exhaustion** and **dehydration** can occur whether or not a person is overcooled, particularly when pulling up a 25 percent gradient that stretches for miles without a break. In either case, a disoriented person can wander off the trail—a very dangerous place to be in this twisted, craggy land. The Park Service posts a daily web report on trail conditions, weather, trail closures, and bear problem locations.

Backpacking. Couch potatoes may be surprised to learn that backpacking in Great Smoky Mountains National Park is so popular that it has had to be rationed for the past 30 years. The rationing system takes the shape of backcountry camping permits, required for all overnight trail use. The most popular backcountry areas require reservations and assigned camping spots, while the less visited areas have fewer restrictions. This system has succeeded in its goal of spreading backpackers throughout the park, instead of concentrating in the hundreds along the **Appalachian Trail (AT).** You can get a permit from any of the ranger stations, or by calling in advance of your trip (423-436-4564).

Many people are interested in hiking the AT, as a special and famous place. Day hiking the trail is unrestricted, and this book includes suggestions (see **A High Ridge Walk on the Appalachian Trail** under *Wandering Around—The Heart of the Smokies* in "Cherokee and the Southeast Quadrant"). However, the AT remains badly overcrowded by backpackers at all times of the year except the dead of winter, and is strictly regulated by the permit system. Here as elsewhere, the trail has three-sided shelters with shelf bunks every 5 or so miles, but these are completely full nearly all the time. Overuse can make these camping spots unpleasant. In addition, there are bear problems, as bears have learned to raid the AT camping areas for food. It's a good idea to backpack down other park trails, or on sections of the AT outside the park. Near the park, the **Cheoah Mountains** (see *Wild Places—The Great Forests* in "The Northeast Unicois: Robbinsville and Tellico Plains") section of the AT is a good alternative, as are **Max Patch** (see *Wild Places—The Forests of Hot Springs* in "Asheville's Rugged Hinterlands") and **Standing Indian Basin** (see *Wild Places—Recreation Areas* in "Franklin and the Nantahala Mountains").

Car Camping (1-800-365-2267 for Park Service information and reservations). Most campgrounds close seasonally; ask in advance. $12–17. Car-based camping is allowed at 10 campgrounds, all of them scenic but primitive, with unheated toilet rooms, no hookups, no electricity, and no showers. Despite these conditions the national park campgrounds are extremely popular and fill up fast. You can get advanced reservations at the most popular campgrounds—**Cades Cove, Elkmont,** and **Smokemont.** Of the remaining first-come first-serve campgrounds, **Deep Creek Picnic Area** (see *Wild Places—Picnic Areas* in "Bryson City and the Southwest Quadrant") is an excellent alternative to the Big Three, with a convenient location just outside Bryson City, a fair amount of room at 92 spaces, and some neat waterfalls. But on a really hot summer's day, try to get into **Balsam Mountain Campground** on the **Heintooga Spur Road** (see The Blue Ridge Parkway and the Heintooga Spur Road under *Wandering Around—Exploring by Car* in "Cherokee and the Southeast Quadrant")—at 5,300 feet, one of the coolest places in the park. If you want remoteness 12-site **Abrams Creek** is hard to beat; you may be 2 hours from Gatlinburg, TN, or Cherokee, NC, but the campground is lovely, the footpaths are some of the park's easiest and most beautiful, and the fishing is great.

Pets. Great Smoky Mountains National Park is definitely not a pet-friendly place; the National Park Service sees them as an environmental risk, period. Pets are prohibited on all trails, to the extent that thru-hikers on the Appalachian Trail are required to kennel their dogs until they clear the park. Dogs are allowed only in the overlooks and picnic areas, and they must be on leashes at all times.

Bears. The park's first-ever black bear fatality happened in March 2000, on the Little River Trail about 4 miles from Elkmont (see Elkmont National Historic District under *To See—Other Historic Sites* in "Townsend, Cades Cove, and the Northwest Quadrant"). In this incident, two bears attacked two adult hikers without apparent provocation, killing one and guarding the body as bears do a carcass they intend to eat, until rangers could arrive and kill the bears. Bears are extremely dangerous. They should never be approached or fed.

GUIDANCE **Smoky Mountain Host of North Carolina** (1-800-432-4678), 4437 George Road (US 441), Franklin, NC 28734. This innkeepers' organization will help you find a room throughout the North Carolina side of the Smoky Mountains. They run a large, friendly visitors center south of Franklin, near the North Carolina–Georgia state line.

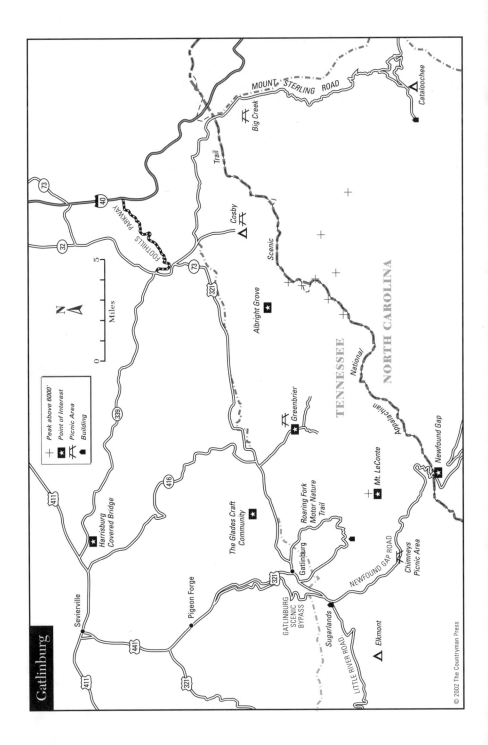

Gatlinburg

© 2002 The Countryman Press

GATLINBURG & THE NORTHEAST QUADRANT

The great majority of the 10 million people who visit the Great Smokies every year get their first sight of the national park from the tourist town of Gatlinburg, TN. With 3,800 full-time residents, this intensely busy collection of motels, restaurants, and shops straddles US 441 as it passes up a narrow valley and into the park. Brought into existence by the millions of visitors who have visited the park every year since the end of World War II, Gatlinburg tempts would-be nature lovers away from the park with a carnival-like atmosphere. It also plays host to an exceptionally large and rewarding crafts community, with 80 or more crafts artists perpetuating mountain-craft traditions.

Whatever the attractions of Gatlinburg, Great Smoky Mountains National Park is the main event, with its entrance abutting the southern edge of town. In the areas of the park nearest Gatlinburg, visitors are faced with a wide range of exceptional sites. Views encompass the great crest of the Smokies, so high that the hills around Gatlinburg appear flat next to them. Old-growth forests form groves of giants, trees that tower 150 feet in the air on trunks 15 feet across. Waterfalls range from graceful, lacy curtains to raging torrents that plunge over 90-foot cliffs. Historic log homesteads, barns, and mills remain scattered about the hills above Gatlinburg. While some of these sites can be reached by car, this is very much a walker's park, and most of the best sites are well removed from the noise and fumes of the park's busy main roads.

GUIDANCE **Gatlinburg Visitors Center (Chamber of Commerce)** (1-800-900-4148), 466 Brookside Way (US 441), Suite 8, P.O. Box 527, Gatlinburg, TN 37738. The Gatlinburg Chamber of Commerce cooperates with the National Park Service to run this large welcome center at the eastern entrance to the town. It offers help and information from both the National Park Service and the Gatlinburg Chamber, as well as a park-oriented bookstore run by the Smoky Mountains Natural History Association. It's also a major terminus (with free parking) on Gatlinburg's elaborate trolley network, making it a good place to park while visiting the rest of the town.

Gatlinburg Department of Tourism (865-436-2392; 1-800-343-1475), 234 Historic Nature Trail, Gatlinburg, TN 37738. This City of Gatlinburg agency runs the convention center, and works with the chamber (see above) to promote the area. It runs a small visitors center in the center of town, on the corner of US 441 and US 321, at traffic light 3.

Sugarlands Ranger Station (865-436-1291), 107 Park Headquarters Road, Gatlinburg, TN 37738. The administrative headquarters for the national park is located just behind the Sugarlands Visitors Center, outside Gatlinburg. If you're looking for a place for walk-in information, try either **Sugarlands Visitors Center** on the Tennessee end of the Newfound Gap Road, or **Oconaluftee Visitors Center** on the North Carolina end of the Newfound Gap Road.

Mount LeConte Geology Web Site. www./geology.er.usgs.gov/eespteam/mtleconte. This web site, sponsored by the U.S. Geological Survey (USGS) at the request of the National Park Service, gives detailed information on the geology of the Smoky Mountain Front, accompanied by a large number of color photos to aid in rock identification. Rockhounds and geology enthusiasts will want to look up the detailed descriptions (with photos) of the geology along each of the trails up Mount LeConte. The USGS team responsible for this site has compiled a similar site for Cades Cove.

GETTING THERE *By car:* To reach Gatlinburg, TN, from any direction (including south), take I-40 to TN 66 (exit 407), then go south on TN 66 to pick up US 441 in Sevierville, TN. Gatlinburg is 13 miles south of Sevierville on US 441. Don't worry about getting lost; Gatlinburg is well signposted the entire distance.

By air: If you're staying on the Gatlinburg side of the Smokies, you'll want to fly into Knoxville's **McGhee Tyson Airport** in Alcoa, TN (see *Getting There* in "Townsend, Cades Cove, and the Northwest Quadrant"), a full-service regional airport with on-site car rentals. The Knoxville airport is a 44-mile drive from Gatlinburg, TN, more than half of it down two-lane roads; expect it to take at least an hour and a quarter. If your primary destination is the Cades Cove area of the park, you should note that the Cades Cove entrance at Townsend, TN, with a full range of tourist facilities, is only a 20-mile drive from the airport via multilaned highways.

By bus: There is no regularly scheduled bus service into Gatlinburg. Many tour operators offer bus tours to Gatlinburg; check with your travel agent.

MEDICAL EMERGENCIES Fort Sanders Sevier Medical Center (865-429-6100), 709 Middle Creek Road, Sevierville, TN. Despite its Sevierville address, Sevier (pronounced severe) Medical Center is located in **Pigeon Forge,** 1.2 miles east of US 441; if you're coming from Gatlinburg, you'll find this to be a right turn, 7 miles north of downtown. A branch of Knoxville's massive regional hospital company, Covenant Health, Sevier is a small full-service local hospital with surgical facilities and a 24/7 emergency room.

Gatlinburg First Med Walk-in Clinic (865-436-7267), 1015 East Parkway (US 321), Gatlinburg, TN. Open Monday through Friday 9 AM–3 PM, Saturday 9 AM–2 PM. This walk-in clinic is located on the east end of Gatlinburg.

EXPLORING BY CAR **The Newfound Gap Road in Tennessee.** Built in 1932 as a scenic tourist highway, the Newfound Gap Road climbs up the steep Tennessee face of Great Smoky Mountains National Park to top out in the 5,048-foot-high Newfound Gap. From there the highway enters North Carolina to descend to Cherokee, a beautiful stretch with spectacular views (see The Newfound Gap Road in North Carolina under *Wandering Around—The Heart of the Smokies* in "Cherokee and the Southeast Quadrant"). This two-lane highway is a fairly easy drive as mountain roads go, but heavy traffic and inconsiderate drivers can make it slow going. You'll enjoy it more if you approach it as a recreation drive, taking plenty of time to pull over and enjoy the scenery.

Most people start this drive at the national park entrance at the south edge of Gatlinburg. A better plan is to start at the north end of Gatlinburg, entering the **Gatlinburg Bypass** from the southbound lanes of **US 441** a mile south of the **Smoky Mountains/Gatlinburg Visitors Center.** This 5-mile scenic parkway, part of Great Smoky Mountains National Park, winds along the mountain slopes

west of Gatlinburg with two stunning 180-degree views over the town and toward the high slopes of **Mount LeConte** (see The Smoky Mountains Front under *Wild Places—The Great Forests*). This little-used road will zip you around Gatlinburg and into the park just south of the **Sugarlands Visitors Center,** to join the **Newfound Gap Road** proper. For the next 2 miles the highway curves gently uphill through a young hardwood forest growing on the site of the former **Sugarlands** community. A nature trail and two "quiet walkways" give you an

MAILBOXES LINE A COUNTRY LANE OUTSIDE GATLINBURG.

opportunity to explore the forests for signs of its former inhabitants—old foundations, chimneys, tuliptrees growing in abandoned fields, even a motel and some paved roads and concrete bridges. After that the highway climbs above Sugarlands for sweeping views over the valley and toward the face of Mount LeConte. At 5 miles you'll reach the streamside **Chimneys Picnic Area** (see *Wild Places—Picnic Areas*), where a nature trail explores a virgin-cove hardwood forest. Now the highway becomes more rugged as it climbs away from the valley, with good views to **Chimney Tops,** two gigantic rock spires protruding from the ridgeline above (see Five Popular Hikes Near Gatlinburg under *Exploring on Foot*). Beyond that, the highway goes through a 360-degree pigtail curve, circling over itself to gain a high, gentle-floored stream valley. When the highway finally runs out of valley it switchbacks steeply upward to become a ledge cut into cliffs, with a low stone wall guarding its downhill edge. Finally it reaches **Morton Overlook,** with striking views into the deep valley below and receding ridges beyond. **Newfound Gap** (see *Wild Places—Recreation Areas* in "Cherokee and the Southeast Quadrant"), with its large parking lot, views, and **Appalachian Trail** access, is just beyond.

Roaring Fork Motor Nature Trail. This nature trail for the car-bound leads down old farm roads that once wandered through the settlements south of Gatlinburg, TN, passing five pioneer farmsteads along the way. This scenic drive starts in downtown **Gatlinburg,** turning onto **Historic Nature Trail** (that's the name of the street) from **US 441** at traffic light 8. Continue past the lovely little **Mynatt Park** (see *Wild Places—Picnic Areas*) to enter the national park just beyond. The road goes through gentle curves to climb through hardwood forests to the **Bud Ogle Place,** a log cabin with running water piped in using hollow logs. Just beyond, the road breaks into a mile-long one-way loop through **Cherokee Orchards,** an apple orchard and commercial nursery until 1940. As the road loops uphill and around (to return to the Bud Ogle Place), turn onto the one-lane, one-way **Roaring Fork Motor Nature Trail** to the right. Passing the **Baskins Creek Trail** (see Old Settlement Walks Near Gatlinburg under *Exploring on Foot*) in 0.25 mile, the road twists up to a set of ridgetop views, followed by the **Grotto Falls** trailhead (see Five Popular Hikes Near Gatlinburg under *Exploring on Foot*). After 0.5 mile a parking lot will mark the far end of the Baskins Creek Trail and the second historic site—a **log cabin and outbuildings** overlooking a small waterfall. Not long after, the road reaches the **Ephriam Bales Place,** a modest dogtrot log cabin and barn, with an impressive stone wall. A half mile farther, the road passes the last and most colorful of the four sites, the brightly painted **Alfred Reagan Place,** with a restored horizontal wheel "tub mill" by the stream. A double stream crossing marks a sudden drop into a small gorge, with dramatic views down the stream, and two wonderful waterfalls dripping down the rocks above the road. The road finally leaves the park to reenter Gatlinburg; return to downtown by taking the turn to the left.

EXPLORING ON FOOT Five Popular Hikes near Gatlinburg. These five hikes, all within 10 miles of Gatlinburg, TN, are overwhelmingly popular. Each is extraordinary, even by Smoky Mountain standards, with a magnificent view, remarkable feature, or beautiful waterfall. Each is well maintained (one is paved) and capable of handling its visitors, although parking can be a problem. In fact, the only thing wrong with any of these hikes is their lack of solitude. On a sunny weekend, expect them to be more like a carnival than a wilderness experience.

Laurel Falls Trail, 4 miles west of Sugarlands Visitors Center on Little River Road. This 1.3-mile paved trail, partially blasted through solid rock by the Civilian Conservation Core (CCC) in 1935, leads past a view to a strong 75-foot waterfall.

Chimneytops Trail, 6.7 miles south of Sugarlands Visitors Center on Newfound Gap Road. This 2-mile uphill slog leads through old-growth forest to a popular, but dangerous, clifftop viewpoint. This is not a place to take children.

Alum Cave Trail, 8.6 miles south of Sugarlands Visitors Center on Newfound Gap Road. The lowermost 2 miles of this **Mount LeConte** access trail feature huge boulders, an interesting geological formation known as Arch Rock, old-growth forests, and spectacular views from exposed bluffs.

Grotto Falls (on **Trillium Gap Trail**), 3.5 miles from Gatlinburg on the Roaring Fork Motor Nature Trail. This easy 1-mile walk leads through mature forests to a large waterfall.

Ramsey Cascades Trail, at the end of the left fork within the Greenbrier area (see **Greenbrier Picnic Area** under *Wild Places—Recreation Areas*). This difficult hike (8 miles round-trip with 2,000 feet of climbing) runs through old-growth forest with giant hemlocks and tuliptrees, to end at an exceptionally beautiful 90-foot waterfall.

Old Settlement Walks near Gatlinburg. One of the best ways to escape the crowds near Gatlinburg, TN, is to take a walk through the old mountain settlements of **Sugarlands** and **Baskins Creek,** abandoned in the 1930s to make way for the national park. These interconnecting paths are so close to Gatlinburg that you can start from the center of downtown, do them both in a day, and return to where you started—a total distance of 11 miles with an elevation gain of 1,600

ALBRIGHT GROVE

Named after a National Park Service administrator who did much to ensure the park's integrity from developers, Albright Grove is a remarkable stand of virgin old-growth forest. It's a moderate hike, 6.7 miles round-trip with 1,600 feet of uphill climbing, all through forests. The trailhead is hard to find. Go 15.5 miles east of downtown **Gatlinburg,** TN, on **US 321,** then turn right onto **Baxter Road,** by Smoky Mountain Creekside Rentals; from there, turn right at the T-intersection with **Laurel Springs Road,** going a short distance until you reach the Park Service sign for the **Maddron Bald Trail.** You'll hike uphill on the Maddron Bald Trail for 3 miles to reach Albright Grove, walking along an old settlement road through forests that have grown over former farms. After a 0.5 mile you'll pass one of the old farmhouses, a chestnut log cabin with a shake roof, built by Willis Baxter in 1889. The old settlement road ends after 2 miles, and the forest becomes deeper, dominated by large hemlocks; you are now entering a classic Appalachian-cove hardwood forest, with a rich variety of old, large trees. At 2.8 miles, the **Albright Grove Loop Trail** forks right to enter a segment of the forest that has never been logged. Giant tuliptrees (yellow poplars) exceed 25 feet in diameter; similar gargantuan hemlocks and beeches are scattered about, as are huge silverbells, the signature tree of the cove forest. In all, the loop trail leads through this cathedral-like forest for 0.7 mile before returning to the Maddron Bald Trail. To go straight back to your car, turn right; it's downhill all the way. Strong hikers may be interested in taking a left here, going deeper into the wilderness and higher up the mountain. This path reaches a large, wild heath bald on remote **Maddron Bald,** with 360-degree views over the **Smokies Crest** and down into Tennessee—6.5 miles and 1,800 feet of climbing added to an already long walk.

feet. If you want to try this loop hike, follow the downtown sidewalk toward the park, then continue along the pretty riverside **Gatlinburg Trail** to the national park headquarters at Sugarlands, a level 2-mile stroll past old home sites and a lovely cascade.

Old Sugarlands Trail starts near the park headquarters (where you can park)—across the **Newfound Gap Road,** over the bridge, and on your right. This little-used path follows old abandoned roads, some once paved, through the heart of the Sugarlands community. You'll walk past foundations, stone walls, stretches of abandoned macadam, old automobile bridges, and a Civilian Conservation Corps (CCC) camp beneath the trees. The walk is 4 miles to the **Cherokee Orchards Road;** the first 2 miles are particularly interesting and nearly level.

To continue the loop walk, pick up **Trillium Gap Trail** at the end of Old Sugarlands Trail. This trail goes through an old commercial apple orchard absorbed into the park in 1942; it still shows signs of its former use. This trail connects with the next walk.

Baskins Falls Walk follows a little-used path 1.75 miles through an old settlement to a lovely waterfall. Its trailhead, marked BASKINS CREEK TRAIL, is just beyond the start of the **Roaring Fork Motor Nature Trail** (see *Exploring by Car*). This trail climbs up a piney ridge, then descends into a small canyon with impressive bluffs. As the main trail turns away, a side path continues downhill along the stream to **Baskins Falls,** a 30-foot plunge that settlers used as a shower in the summer. This is the end of the official path, and most folks return to the main trail. From there you can retrace your steps to your car, or continue left along the official trail, through overgrown farms and woodlots, to an old cemetery and log cabin farther along on the **Roaring Fork Road.** If you take the latter you'll have walked 2.7 miles and will be about 2.5 miles from your car (to the left along Roaring Fork Road).

However, you may want to continue ahead, along **Baskins Creek** to **Gatlinburg,** to complete the loop. This little-used informal path (a manway in park parlance) follows the banks of the creek through the heart of another old community. This rough, overgrown walk passes many signs of the old settlement, as well as wildflowers and beautiful stream views. The path leaves the national park and enters Gatlinburg at the end of the town's **Baskins Creek Road;** follow the paved roads downhill to return to downtown.

✳ Villages

Gatlinburg, TN. In the late 1920s Gatlinburg was just another poor mountain crossroads. It was where the road up from the flatlands reached the foot of the Smokies—a fork with a general store and a gas pump. The left fork (now US 321) went to the Methodist mission at Pitman Center, which furnished limited, but lifesaving, medical services to the isolated mountain folk. The right fork (now the **Newfound Gap Road**; see The Newfound Gap Road in Tennessee under *Wandering Around—Exploring by Car*) went deep into the Smokies to dead-end at the poverty-stricken community of **Sugarlands,** also known as Blockader's Heaven, according to local moonshine expert Horace Kephart. Then came the park. Gatlinburg found itself the main entrance to a park that attracted a million automobile-driving visitors in 1941. Twenty years later, all those tourists had turned the mountain's crossroads into a small city.

Gatlinburg is a city built for tourists. It's still centered on that old fork in the road, but now the fork is a busy multilaned intersection in the middle of a crowded downtown. Here two-story buildings, jammed against the sidewalk and each other, are filled with every sort of tourist enticement imaginable—gift shops, restaurants, candy shops, old-timey photo places, side shows (labeled "museums" and "attractions"), amusement rides . . . you name it. It has more than a passing resemblance to a really large county fair, complete with bad parking, high prices, and a stiff dose of hucksterism. It's easy to complain about it, but it's a lot more fun to grab a corn dog and enjoy it.

Unlike Cherokee, NC (see *Villages* in "Cherokee and the Southwest Quadrant"), Gatlinburg is continuously tearing itself down and rebuilding itself. Its downtown is crammed into a narrow river gorge, a single block wide and a mile long, so that real estate is at a premium. The entire length is built continuously with commercial structures two to three stories high, attached to each other and the sidewalk. The latest commercial craze has been to take what had been normal-sized stores and turn them into "malls" with tiny shops opening onto a central corridor. This has allowed the number of downtown shops to multiply like rabbits, with small merchants scrambling to offer something new and different to browsing tourists. Behind this long, thin downtown strip, scores of motels with thousands of rooms climb down to the river and up the mountainsides.

Apart from this full-time street fair, Gatlinburg has a serious, mountain-oriented side. On the rural east side of town, the Glades area hosts a community of 80 crafts artists—some newcomers, others from old mountain-craft families (see **The Glades Arts and Crafts Community** under *To See—Special Places*). A series of crafter-owned shops strings out along this scenic mountain cove, with members of the community prominently displaying a logo certifying that they make what they sell. Indeed, most have their studios in their shops and will welcome you in as they work.

Gatlinburg traffic is always slow and can grind to a stop during the season. If you wish simply to get beyond Gatlinburg to the other side, take the **Gatlinburg Bypass** (see The Newfound Gap Road in Tennessee *Wandering Around—Exploring by Car*), a scenic road maintained by the National Park Service. Except in winter, there is no street parking in downtown Gatlinburg. Instead, downtown parking is in a couple of city garages at a stiffish $1.50 per hour, plus an outdoor lot near the auditorium at a somewhat lower price. As an alternative, you can park for free at the visitors center at the north end of town (see **Gatlinburg Visitors Center** under *Guidance*) or at City Hall at the east end of town on US 321, and take a trolley (cost from $0.25–$2).

Pigeon Forge, TN. This sprawling suburb of Gatlinburg, TN, 6 miles north of downtown, consists of a 2-mile string of chain restaurants and franchise motels stretching along a six-lane segment of US 441. Pigeon Forge's landscape is that of a recently built-up area on the edge of a large city, with no real mountain views or traditional mountain culture. If you long for the certainty of familiar surroundings and brand names you recognize, you'll certainly find them at Pigeon Forge. However, if you want to immerse yourself in mountain scenery and culture, you might want to look elsewhere.

Sevierville, TN. Sevierville (Se-VERE-vull) is the seat of Sevier County, TN—the county that contains Gatlinburg. Travelers along US 441 will see little of it beyond a continuous suburban-style sprawl that merges seamlessly with Pigeon Forge. However, two blocks off the highway is a quaint old downtown centering on an old brick courthouse with a statue of Dolly Parton in front. Many businesses in the foothills of the Smokies sport Sevierville addresses, even though they are not particularly near town.

A BRONZE SCUPTURE OF DOLLY PARTON BY JIM GRAY SITS OUTSIDE THE SEVIERVILLE COUNTY COURTHOUSE.

Cosby, TN. Cosby is a dispersed rural settlement with no defined village center, stretching along US 321 about 16 miles east of Gatlinburg, TN. It offers access to the little-visited northeastern fringe of Great Smoky Mountains National Park. However, services are slight and choices are limited.

✳ Wild Places

THE GREAT FORESTS The Smoky Mountains Front. A drop of rain, falling on the highest point of Mount LeConte, travels through 7 miles of wilderness before it reaches the river in downtown Gatlinburg, TN. It also drops 1 mile vertically—in all likelihood the longest slope in the eastern United States. This slope is wet as well as steep, with 7 feet of rainfall in a typical year. This combination of high rainfall and high, steep slopes does more than create big rivers and impressive waterfalls; it creates one of the richest temperate forests in the world.

Start at the top, with that drop of water on the 6,593-foot peak of **Mount LeConte.** You'll be in a boreal forest, an extension of the great subarctic forest that covers much of Canada, whose Christmas-tree species of spruce and fir form a forest canopy over thin, rocky soils. Below that will be a mosaic of forest types: New England–style hardwood forests; oak-hickory forests; beech-maple forests; pine-oak forests on warm, dry ridgelines; northern riverine forests along many stream banks. Unique to the Smokies and other nearby mountains is the **cove hardwood forest,** with the highest specie richness in temperate North America. A cove forest can mix and match as many as 25 tree species in an acre of old-growth forest, covering a thick shrubby understory that bursts into colorful blooms every spring—rhododendron, mountain laurel, flame azalea, dogwood, redbud, silverbell. These thick forests cover even the steepest slopes with trees that grow 6 to 10 stories high.

And there's a lot of slope that has to be covered. The front of the Smoky Mountains at Gatlinburg forms an unbroken wall 65 miles long. The central 56 miles of that wall, immediately behind Gatlinburg, stays continuously above 4,000 feet, with half of that length above a mile high. On the western (Tennessee) side of the crest, the Smokies drop to a valley that appears flat-bottomed from a crest-top viewpoint, and stretches off to the horizon as far as the eye can see. On the eastern (North Carolina) side, other mountains, nearly as tall, fill the view in a confused jumble.

Access to this great forest is either from the **Newfound Gap Road** (see The Newfound Gap Road in Tennessee under *Wandering Around—Exploring by Car*), or from a series of four trailheads along its perimeter: **Roaring Fork Motor Nature Trail** (see *Wandering Around—Exploring by Car*), **Greenbrier Picnic Area, Cosby Picnic Area,** and **Big Creek Picnic Area** (see all three sites under *Recreation Areas*). All five of these trailheads are gateways into rich and varied forests, with stunning wildflowers, roaring rivers, large waterfalls, and magnificent views. Almost without exception, the hiking and horse trails that lead from these trailheads are well built, well kept, and incredibly beautiful; it should go without saying that nearly all of them are very steep as well.

RECREATION AREAS Greenbrier Picnic Area. Six miles east of Gatlinburg, TN, on US 321, a right turn on a narrow paved lane leads 4 miles up a broad valley named **Greenbrier Cove.** Inhabited by scattered farms in the 1920s, Greenbrier Cove is now grown over by a young riverside forest along the noisy, boulder-strewn **Middle Prong of the Little Pigeon River.** The modest, pleasant picnic area is 2.5 miles up the lane. In another 0.5 mile, a side road crosses the Middle Prong at a particularly scenic spot, then winds through forests to the start of the **Ramsey Cascades Trail** (see Five Popular Hikes Near Gatlinburg under *Wandering Around—Exploring on Foot*). Straight ahead, the road follows **Porters Creek** to end at a gate in 1 mile. You can park here and continue up the road on foot. This was once the road to a farming community; you'll pass old stone walls, steps leading up hills, boxwoods and roses growing rank where houses once stood. At the end of the road, in a mile, a short path leads right to an old cantilevered barn in the woods, and a log cabin nearby.

COSBY CREEK

Cosby Picnic Area. Cosby Picnic Area is at the far northeast corner of the Tennessee Smokies; go 18 miles east of downtown Gatlinburg, TN, on US 321 to TN 73 at Cosby community, then right 0.4 mile to TN 32, then right 1.3 miles to a Park Service lane on the right. This lane leads 2 miles into the national park, through a rich forest growing on a fan of river deposits at the foot of the Smokies. This forest is particularly beautiful in spring, when it gets its color early, and in fall, when its color lingers a few extra days. The picnic area at the upper end of the road (there is also a campground here) is small and forest covered, along lovely Cosby Creek. Here you'll find a trailhead to the **Lower Mount Cammerer Trail**—a lengthy trail along the middle slopes of the Smokies, here lower than at Gatlinburg. The first 1.5 miles of this well-built path, climbing only 260 feet, are definitely worth your while as it rises gently to **Sutton Ridge.** Here a side trail uphill to the right leads to a wonderful view out over the **Foothills** and the **Great Valley.** Beyond, the trail descends slightly to **Riding Fork**, with a lovely little cascade upstream to your right.

Big Creek Picnic Area. This remote valley hides just over the state line in **North Carolina,** at the extreme northeast tip of the park. The drive there is part of its charm. Take US 321 east to Cosby, TN, then turn right onto TN 32. This narrow road must set a state record for twists, as it slowly feels its way through a lovely young hardwood forest on the park's northeast flank. There's a really nice view or two at first; then the forest closes in, and the road becomes a serpentine tunnel through the trees for mile after mile after mile . . . You cross the state line and the **Appalachian Trail** at the same time, then descend quickly on the now-gravel road to an intersection. The right turn takes you into the Big Creek area; straight ahead leads to **Cataloochee** (see Cataloochee Cove Drive under *Wandering Around—Exploring by Car* in "Cherokee and the Southeast Quadrant"); and the left turn takes you through the attractive settlement of **Waterville,** TN, to I-40, for a much faster return to Gatlinburg via US 321.

Once at Big Creek you'll be on a narrow gravel road that leads 1 mile into the park, to end at a creekside camping and picnic area. The picnic tables sit near the lovely Big Creek, noisy and full of rapids, and sheltered by tall, young hardwoods. Beyond the picnic area, the road continues up the stream as a foot- and horse path. At 1.4 miles up this gentle roadway is **Midnight Hole,** a 6-foot cascade between two large boulders into a deep pool. At 2.1 miles is **Mouse Falls,** where the creek pours 20 feet over gray stone.

PICNIC AREAS Chimneys Picnic Area. This large picnic area offers forest-shaded tables strung along the **Little Pigeon River,** 7 miles from Gatlinburg, TN, on the Newfound Gap Road. It's attractive, cool, and quiet, even on a busy summer day. A nature trail explores the Smokies' unique hardwood cove forest, leading 0.75 mile to a virgin old-growth stand. Picnickers should note that Chimneys is the last picnic area on the Newfound Gap Road for 22 miles—the next place to picnic is **Collins Creek Picnic Area** (see *Wild Places—Picnic Areas* in "Cherokee and the Southeast Quadrant"), on the other side of the mountain.

Mynatt Park. This attractive city park inside Gatlinburg, TN, offers a number of forested, streamside picnic tables in a quiet residential neighborhood, as well as a full range of recreational facilities (including tennis, if you remembered your racket). Parking is adequate. You'll find it a mile from downtown on **Historic Nature Trail** road.

HISTORIC SITES Harrisburg Covered Bridge. To find this bridge, go east from Sevierville on US 411 for 4 miles; then turn right onto TN 339, continuing onto TN 35, for a total of 1 mile; then turn right onto Harrisburg Road for 0.2 mile, to the bridge. Built in 1875 by a local mill owner, this simple wood-truss bridge spans a gap between two high bluffs above the **East Fork of the Little Pigeon River,** in this scenic rural location 5 miles east of Sevierville, TN. Like all true covered bridges, the cover protected the heavy wood trusses from rotting; the wood trusses, in turn, allowed the bridge to span the long distance between the bluffs. (Doubting Thomases in the Tennessee Department of Transportation have stuck a big concrete pier in the middle, just in case.) The covered truss bridge still carries local traffic on this pastoral back road, thanks to a 1972 restoration funded by the local DAR chapter.

CULTURAL SITES Sugarlands Visitors Center (865-436-1291), 107 Park Headquarters Road, Gatlinburg, TN. Located outside Gatlinburg, TN, at the start of the Newfound Gap Road, this visitors center has an information desk, gift shop, exhibits, a multimedia show, and a native plant garden. Its exhibit area, recently revamped, explores the Smoky Mountains' unique environment in detail. However, its most rewarding feature is its least visited. **Fighting Creek Nature Trail** leads you on a 1-mile ramble through forest growing on old farmland; it takes you along an old wagon track, along a stream, past stone walls and springs, to a restored log cabin deep in the woods.

Galleries and Gardens of the Arrowmont School (865-436-5860), 556 Parkway, Gatlinburg, TN. Open weekdays, normal business hours. The prestigious **Arrowmont School of Arts and Crafts** (see *To Do—Crafts and Environmental Schools*), founded by the Pi Beta Phi women's fraternity, has occupied its campus in the middle of downtown Gatlinburg since the 1920s—long before downtown Gatlinburg existed. You'll find it to be a string of handsome buildings ranging from old log cabins to contemporary structures, stretching uphill from busy downtown in beautiful parklike gardens. Five galleries in the main educational facility, a 1970 prairie-style homage that echos the mountain peaks behind it, display works of faculty and students, as does a sculpture garden farther up the site. The campus starts behind the venerable **Arrowcraft** shop (see *Selective Shopping—Downtown Gatlinburg, TN*), on US 441, in the center of downtown just south of River Road.

SPECIAL PLACES The Glades Arts and Crafts Community (865-671-3600), P.O. Box 807, Gatlinburg, TN. This scenic rural cove on the east side of Gatlinburg has been known as a center for mountain crafts for over half a century. An 8-mile loop road, well signposted off US 321 three miles east of town, runs through the center of this crafters' community, becoming increasingly beautiful as it draws away from Gatlinburg's center; along it, small crafts shops sit in meadows with views over the low mountains of the Foothills. Since 1978, the crafts artists of the Glades have formed their own association, the **Great Smoky Mountains Arts and Crafts Community** (see The Glades Arts and Crafts Community under

Selective Shopping), limited to Glades crafters who feature their own work in their own studios. There are now more than 70 such studio/galleries displaying the "Arts and Crafts Community" logo. Their president, porcelain artist Judy Baily, says, "People feel free to take their time in our shops. Many times they ask us a lot of questions about what we do, and we are glad to spend time with them." These fine crafters, rather than the downtown souvenir shops, are Gatlinburg's main attraction for serious shoppers.

Foothills Parkway East. This isolated 6-mile section of the long-delayed Foothills Parkway links I-40 with US 321—sort of a shortcut for people heading from Asheville, NC to Gatlinburg, TN. It's worth a visit, even if it's out of your way. Overlooks give panoramic views of the Great Smoky Mountains as they rise almost a mile above you; other viewpoints look westward, over the **Foothills** as they descend in waves into the **Great Valley.**

✴ To Do

FISHING Old Smoky Outfitters (865-430-1936), 511 Parkway, Gatlinburg, TN. $135 for half-day trips; $200 for full-day trips; $225 for full-day lessons. This downtown fishing shop offers guide service for both stream and lake fishing.

GOLF Bent Creek Golf Resort (865-436-2875; 1-800-251-9336), 3919 East Parkway (US 321), Gatlinburg, TN. $30–35 for nonmembers, $20 for nine holes. This par-72 golf course, designed in 1972 by Gary Players, is located at Pittman Center, TN, 10 miles east of Gatlinburg, TN. Its first nine holes play along the valley bottom, while the more challenging second nine climb up and down the mountainside. Owned by Sunterra, it has a large number of time-share condos available for rent along the course, as well as some very nice cottages.

Gatlinburg Golf Course (865-453-3912; 1-800-231-4128), 520 Dollywood Lane, Pigeon Forge, NC. Open all year. $31–55 for 18 holes. Owned by the City of Gatlinburg, TN, this 1955 Bob Cupp–designed course is noted for its dramatic 12th hole—teeing over a 200-foot drop down a near-clifflike slope to reach the green 194 feet away. This handsome 6,282-foot course offers beautiful views along its length, plus a lake on the 18th.

HIKING AND CAMPING A Walk in the Woods (865-436-8283), 4413 Scenic Drive East, Gatlinburg, TN. Half day $17–19; full day $38–50. Erik and Vesna Plakanis offer half- and whole-day guided nature walks within Great Smoky Mountains National Park, as well as custom trips and backpacking trips. All walks include a guide, car shuttles, and a picnic lunch. They also rent camping equipment. **Appalachian Trail** hikers should note that the Plakanis offer thru-hiker support.

HORSEBACK RIDING English Mountain Llama Trekking (423-623-5274), 738 English Mountain Road, Newport, TN. From a farm on English Mountain, north of Cosby, TN, Bob and Cathi MacIntyre lead llama treks in nearby **Pisgah National Forest,** as well as in the high mountains of **Nantahala National Forest** on the south side of the national park. Day treks ($60) include lunch; overnight camping treks ($225 for 1 night, $325 for 2 nights) include all gear and meals. **McCarters Riding Stables** (865-436-

5354), Smoky Mountains National Park. One of two national park concessionaires operating in the Gatlinburg, TN, area, McCarters offers trail rides in the **Sugarlands** area of the park, near the Sugarlands Visitors Center.

Smoky Mountains Stables (865-436-5634), Smoky Mountains National Park. Located on US 321, 4 miles east of downtown Gatlinburg, TN. The second of two national park concessionaires (see above) in the Gatlinburg area, this stable offers trail rides up the little-visited **Dudley Creek** area of the national park.

SKIING AND SKATING Ober Gatlinburg (865-436-5423), 1001 Parkway, Gatlinburg, TN. Open all year, except for the first 2 weeks in March (dates vary). Ski season runs December through February; summer amusement park from April through November. Cable car from downtown Gatlinburg $8 (discounted from lift ticket). Lift ticket $25–35 per day ($12 night only). Skating $7 for 3 hours. Amusement rides $2–6.

You can drive to the ski slopes of Ober Gatlinburg, but it's a lot more fun to take the Swiss-made **cable car** from downtown Gatlinburg. The enclosed cars sweep over the Gatlinburg rooftops, up a hollow, and over a ridge to a wide panorama—**Mount LeConte** towering on the right, the much lower hills of East Tennessee on the left, and Gatlinburg deep in the valley directly below. The clean and orderly ski hall, which doubles as a fun center in the summer, is a wide-panning metal building with exposed girders and a sloping floor of exposed concrete. Inside, county fair–style concessions surround a skating rink, with the floor spiraling down. The eight ski trails have a longest run of 5,000 feet

and a maximum drop of 600 feet, with a maximum elevation of 3,300 feet.

WHITEWATER ADVENTURES
✔ **Rafting in the Smokies (Pigeon River Outdoors, Inc.)** (865-436-5008; 1-800-776-7238), Gatlinburg, TN. Open March through October. From their downtown Gatlinburg location, this company runs whitewater rafting trips ($42) on the Class III to IV **Pigeon River** (shuttling a half hour to the river), and float trips ($20) on a smooth section of the same river. The intermediate-level rapids of the Pigeon—more thrilling than the better known Nantahala River (see The Nantahala Gorge under *Villages* in "Bryson City and the Southwest Quadrant")—are restricted to children over 8 who weigh more than 60 pounds, but the float trip is open to anyone over the age of 3.

✔ **Smoky Mountain Outdoors** (423-487-5290; 1-800-771-7238), 3299 Hartford Road, Newport, TN. This outfitter offers **Pigeon River** whitewater rafting adventures and leisurely floats from their headquarters deep in the country, on the banks of the Pigeon River a mile down Hartford Road from I-40's exit 447, on the Tennessee side of the state line. They maintain a location in Gatlinburg, TN, as well, on the east side of town on US 321.

✔ **USA Raft** (423-487-4303; 1-800-872-7238), 3630 Hartford Road, Newport, TN. This West Virginia rafting company maintains an outpost on the **Pigeon River** in the Hartford community, just off I-40's exit 447 and just beyond the Tennessee–North Carolina state line. They offer guided adventure rafting on the Class II to IV rapids of one section of the Pigeon, and family rafting (for children over five) on another section of the same river.

CRAFTS AND ENVIRONMENTAL SCHOOLS & **Arrowmont School of Arts and Crafts** (865-436-5860), 556 Parkway, Gatlinburg, TN. $280 per week tuition; room and board available for $205–470 per week for a single adult; other fees may apply. In the early 20th century, the Pi Beta Phi women's fraternity founded the Settlement School just south of the mountain crossroads known as Gatlinburg, a charitable effort to bring schooling into the remote coves and hollows of the Smoky Mountains. Today known as the Arrowmont School, it has evolved over the years into one of the mountain's premiere crafts schools. Still occupying its original 70-acre campus at the center of Gatlinburg (see **Galleries and Gardens of the Arrowmont School** under *To See—Cultural Sites*), it offers 1- and 2-week intensive residency courses in a wide variety of crafts arts.

The Smoky Mountains Field School (865-974-0150), 600 Henley Street, Suite 105, University of Tennessee Conference Center Building, Knoxville, TN. The Field School's headquarters is far outside the park, at the University of Tennessee's Knoxville Campus. Courses run spring through late fall. Half-day programs range from $12–18; full-day programs are typically $42; multiday programs (mostly camping) are mostly $84–148 for two or three days. This cooperative program between the National Park Service and the University of Tennessee offers outdoor walking-based courses, taught by experts. The range of courses is truly incredible, from the expected offerings on Smoky Mountain plants, animals, and history, to special programs in the arts and nature writing, to wonderfully specialized programs on such topics as land snails and slime molds. A typical course will meet in a picnic area inside the park, then travel (most likely, walk) to the course's various locations over a period of 4 to 8 hours. Many of the courses are specifically structured for parents to share with their children, with separate courses aimed at parents with teens and parents with youngsters.

✳ Lodging

BACKPACKERS' CABINS **Mount LeConte Lodge** (865-429-5704), Smoky Mountain National Park. Reservations are required and very hard to get. Try calling the first week in October for the following year. Open mid-March through mid-November. Deep within the national park's backcountry and accessible only by hikers, this lodge sits just shy of the 6,593-foot peak of Mount LeConte. Its collection of log buildings and primitive cabins is surrounded by old balsam forests, with only a short walk to wide sunset and sunrise views off clifftops. Hikers stay in bunk beds (linens and blankets supplied) in tiny board-and-batten cabins, heated by kerosene and lighted by oil lamps; there's no electricity or running water at LeConte Lodge. Meals, served in the rustic lodge and included in the price, are plain and hearty, not surprising as the food has to be packed in by llama. On any given day it's the coolest place to stay in the South—it's typically 20°F cooler than nearby Knoxville, TN. It's also one of the rainiest and foggiest (and no, they won't give you a rain check on your reservation). However, if the weather cooperates you'll experience the finest sunrises and sunsets anywhere in the South, from clifftops 1.25 miles above sea level.

COUNTRY INNS **Eight Gables Inn** (865-430-3344; 1-800-279-5716), 219 North Mountain Road, Gatlinburg,

TN 37738. This inn sits in forests on the northern edge of Gatlinburg, 2 miles from downtown and a short distance off a section of US 441 maintained as a scenic corridor. Built in the 1990s, the handsome, stylized exterior reminds one of a prosperous Victorian farmhouse, with wide porches (complete with rocking chairs, swings, and checkers), high windows, powder blue clapboarding, and two gables on each side. Inside, a large common area occupies half or more of the first floor. Comfortable sofas and easy chairs group around the large windows and the two wood-burning fireplaces. An impressive hardwood staircase splits into three spurs under an octagonal dome to reach the 8 upstairs rooms, each under its own gable. There are 16 rooms in all—8 upstairs, 4 downstairs, and 4 in an adjacent "cottage," a homelike annex that blends quietly into the woods. All rooms are comfortable and full sized, theme furnished with reproduction antiques; larger rooms are elegantly furnished, with wing-back chairs, a sofa sitting area, and a whirlpool bath. Breakfast is served promptly at nine, and consists of a main dish, sweet pastry, and fresh fruit, with orange juice. Guests typically gather before breakfast for coffee and a chat by the fire, or to read a morning paper on the wide veranda. In the evening, a homemade sweet and coffee offers another chance to socialize. At lunchtime (except Monday) the breakfast area in the common room becomes the elegant luncheon spot, **The Magnolia Tearoom** (see *Eating Out*). Low season $89–149; high season $109–189.

Hippensteal's Mountain View Inn (865-436-5761; 1-800-527-8110), P.O. Box 707, Gatlinburg, TN 37738. Open all year. Prominent Gatlinburg water-colorist Vern Hippensteal (see The Glades Arts and Crafts Community under *Selective Shopping*) and his wife, Lisa, own and operate this modern luxury inn on an hilltop deep in the countryside east of town. Set on 25 acres, the three-story inn has one of the finest views in the area, a sweeping 180-degree panorama over dense forest toward the high wall of the Great Smoky Mountains. Each of 12 rooms has a view from a wide covered porch furnished with rockers. The three-story inn and its two-story annex have an old country look about them, with covered porches on every floor, French doors, and floor-to-ceiling sash windows. The inn's ground floor is taken up by a large common area, with many sofas and easy chairs grouped around small tables and a large stone fireplace. A separate glass porch holds the elegant marble-floored dining area. Rooms are large, furnished with antique reproductions around a gas log fireplace, with two-person whirlpool baths, and separate showers. A hearty full breakfast is served from 8–10. $149 in-season and winter weekends; $95 on winter weekdays; includes breakfast.

Blue Mountain Mist Country Inn (865-428-2335; 1-800-497-2335), 1811 Pullen Road, Sevierville, TN 37862. Open all year. Built as a country inn in 1987, this AAA three-diamond B&B looks like a turreted Victorian farmhouse, powder blue and surrounded by wide porches. Located in the hills above Pigeon Forge on the innkeepers' 60-acre family farm, its hilltop vantage point offers wide views toward the Great Smoky Mountains 7 miles away. The 12 rooms are ample in size and elegantly furnished with antiques and heirloom quilts. Five simple clapboard cabins are luxuriously furnished, and include whirlpool baths and kitchenettes. All rooms and cabins include a full breakfast and evening dessert. Inn rooms $115–145; cottages $135–159.

Hilton Bluffs B&B Inn (865-428-9765; 1-800-441-4188), 2654 Valley Heights Drive, Pigeon Forge, TN 37863. Open all year. A modern cedar-sided building conveniently located just outside Pigeon Forge (on a dead-end residential road just off US 321), Hilton Bluffs has 10 nicely decorated, country-themed rooms. Each has its own door to a balcony or deck, and half have two-person whirlpool baths. Common areas, all brightly lighted and carefully decorated, include a den with a fireplace, and a recreation room with bumper pool and darts as well as table games. The cedar-clapboard building, in a plain modern style, is amply supplied with decks, porches, and balconies; it sits on a well-landscaped property surrounded by forests on all sides. $79–129, including full breakfast.

COUNTRY RESORTS The Buckhorn Inn (865-436-4668), 2140 Tudor Mountain Road, Gatlinburg, TN 37738. Open all year. Located in the beautiful, rural Glades area east of Gatlinburg, within the Arts and Crafts Community (see *Selective Shopping*), this historic inn offers an elegant and gracious experience at an old-fashioned 1930s resort. The inn is surrounded by 25 private ladnscaped acres of meadows and woodlands. From the approach road the inn appears as a simple, modest white-painted wood structure; the inn turns its more elegant side to the Smokies, with a lovely view over wildflower meadows and hemlock forests to the peak of Mount LeConte. With no TV or radio in the historic main structure, the Buckhorn Inn appeals to those who want quiet and meditation rather than bustle and noise. The grounds encourage this with profuse wildflowers, a fish pond, and a meditation labyrinth. Inside, a large common room and dining room occupies much of the ground floor, with sofas and easy chairs facing a fire. The six inn rooms are each theme decorated with English country antiques and reproductions; the least expensive room is a charming two-level retrofit on the inn's old central tower (which held a water tank during the 1930s). A new annex with has new luxury suites, each with its own sitting area, gas log fireplace, and whirlpool baths, and a large common area. Seven 1930s kitchenette cottages have porches, decks, and wide picture windows. Breakfasts are hearty and fresh; dinners are also served daily but are not included in the price (see *Dining Out*). Inn rooms $115–130; cottages $130–150; guest houses $200–250 for up to four adults.

Christopher Place, An Intimate Resort (423-623-6555; 1-800-595-9441), 1500 Pinnacles Way, Newport, TN 37821. This luxury retreat sits on a remote site, north of Cosby, TN, on English Mountain. This Colonial-style mansion perched high above the valley and surrounded by meadows with wide views has more amenities than other country inns, with a pool table, heated outdoor pool, tennis, fitness room, sauna, on-site trails, and llama trekking. Most rooms are large, and elegantly furnished, with private sitting areas. The restaurant serves a hearty breakfast, and offers an elegant table d'hôte evening meal for $25 (available to the public with a 24-hour reservation). $150–300, including breakfast.

BED & BREAKFASTS Berry Springs Lodge (865-908-7935; 1-888-760-8297), 2149 Seaton Springs Road, Sevierville, TN 37862. A farmhouse-style lodge built in 2000, this nine-room B&B is located deep in the hills above Pigeon Forge. Quiet and remote, its hilltop location offers spectacular views over the foothills toward the Great Smoky Mountains, 7 miles to the south. The rooms are handsomely theme furnished with reproduction antiques; each room has a fireplace and a private door to either a deck, porch, or balcony with a view. A large common area is comfortably furnished with plush sofas and chairs—a great place to read a book by the fire. $89–169, including full breakfast.

7th Heaven Log Inn (865-430-5000; 1-800-248-2923), 3944 Castle Road, Gatlinburg, TN 37738. This modern log home with five guest rooms faces the seventh green of the **Bent Creek Golf Resort** (see *To Do—Golf*), 10 miles east of Gatlinburg in Pittman Center, TN. Four log-walled rooms on the first floor face the green and share a common recreation room with a pool table and kitchenette. The fifth room, larger than the others, has a whirlpool bath and its own private entrance and porch, with views over the golf course to the Smokies. $87–137, including full breakfast and evening dessert.

Morley House Bed & Breakfast (865-430-3399; 1-800-299-8389), 4559 Powdermill Estates Road, Gatlinburg TN 37738. Open all year. This large private house, recently built in a traditional country style, sits on 5 wooded acres just north of the Glades Arts and Crafts Community (see *To See—Special Places*). Two guest rooms, each elegantly furnished with reproduction antiques, each have queen beds, private baths with whirlpool baths, and private entrances. $79–99, including evening dessert.

Tennessee Ridge Inn B&B (865-436-4068; 1-800-737-7369), 507 Campbell Lead, Gatlinburg, TN 37738. From its ridgetop location 1 mile west of downtown Gatlinburg, this inn offers sweeping panoramic views over Gatlinburg and toward Mount LeConte and the Smokies. This modern structure of stone and wood appears modest enough on the street side; on the outward side it drops away with three stories of glass and balconies. Rooms are beautifully decorated with king beds and range from standard sized to large; some have fireplaces and/or whirlpool baths, and five have 180-degree views. $119–159, including full breakfast.

Chilhowee Bluff Bed & Breakfast (865-908-0321; 1-888-559-0321), 1887 Bluff Mountain Road, Sevierville, TN 37876. This modern four-room B&B sits in the fascinating **Bluff Mountain** (see *To See—Special Places* in "Townsend, Cades Cove, and the Northwest Quadrant") area above Pigeon Forge, a steep, rockbound mountain on the outward edge of the Smokies, 7 miles from the national park. All four rooms are beautifully decorated with country-style antique reproductions; three have sitting areas with a fireplace and a two-person whirlpool tub. Breakfasts are large and luxurious. Standard room $85–99; suites with sitting areas and whirlpool baths, $125–159.

Gremmy's Garden (865-908-2709; 1-888-592-9518), 724 Sharp Road, Sevierville, TN 37876. This modern-built French Country-style house isn't really near much of anything, except lots of beautiful countryside; it's well out into the low mountains of Harrisburg (see **Harrisburg Covered Bridge** under *To See—Historic Sites*), east of Sevierville. What you'll find is lots of beautiful, wide views and immaculate accommodations in four rooms in the main house, plus two full "mother-in-law" apartments. Elegant country-style furnishings are found throughout the common areas and guest rooms. Amenities include walking trails, a screened gazebo, a hot tub, and a recreation room with a pool table. House rules prohibit smoking and alcohol. Standard rooms $99–129; suites with kitchens $139–149; includes breakfast and dessert.

MOTELS Gatlinburg, TN, has several thousand motel rooms, and nearby Pigeon Forge, TN, has several thousand more. Gatlinburg tends more toward independent motels, set tightly on small pieces of property, frequently with unusual architectural flourishes. Pigeon Forge units are more interstate in style—chain motels, of standard construction, surrounded by large parking lots and fronting on a six-lane highway. Some of the more interesting-looking Gatlinburg motels sit along the river, a block below downtown. Contact the Chamber of Commerce (see **Gatlinburg Visitors Center** under *Guidance*) for more information.

✳ Where to Eat

EATING OUT The **Magnolia Tearoom** (865-430-3344; 1-800-279-5716), 219 North Mountain Road, Gatlinburg, TN. The large, brightly lit dining area of the **Eight Gables Inn** (see *Lodging—Country Inns*) serves as the venue for this informal luncheon spot. Built in the style of a Victorian farmhouse, its large windows and French doors open onto a wide wrap-around porch with rockers and swings. The menu concentrates on simple, well-prepared foods—soups, salads, sandwiches, a special, and dessert—all made to order from fresh ingredients. An easy walk from the trolley terminal at the Smoky Mountains Visitors Center (see *Guidance*), the Magnolia Tearoom is a calm and quiet respite from downtown's noise and crowds.

Smoky Mountain Brewery and Restaurant (865-436-4200), 1004 Parkway, Gatlinburg, TN. Open for lunch and dinner. This two-story eatery toward the back of the Calhoun Village retail area, is decorated in rough wood and 1950s-style furniture. It's immaculately clean, the atmosphere is neat, and the food is great—but the real story is the beer. You'll want to try their fresh-brewed product, including a Czech-style pilsner, a mellow German-style black porter, an American-style light lager, an Irish-style red ale, and a mild English-style brown ale. The pizza is excellent, and the sandwiches are made with bread baked fresh on the premises. Next door, **Calhouns** is run by the same people and presumably has the same high-quality food; it is more of a sit-down restaurant with ribs and steaks dominating the menu. Sandwiches and salads $6–8; dinners $10–15.

The Fox and Parrot Tavern (865-436-0677), 1065 Glades Road, Gatlinburg, TN. Gatlinburg's best place for a friendly meal won't be found among the tourist-crowded downtown shops; instead, it sits above photographer Brian Papsworth's first-rate gallery in the **Glades Arts and Crafts Community** (see *To See—Really Neat Places*). Every item on the menu is made from scratch ingredients on the premises. A dozen items are traditional British pub fare: meat pies, bangers, ploughman's lunch, and corned beef top the list. A dozen or more American bar favorites, including a fine chili. First-rate desserts include eccles cake, a Scots pastry filled with rum-soaked raisins. Draft ales include imports and local brews from nearby towns, while the lengthy bottles list is filled with imports and microbrews; standard American beers are unavailable. Ale lovers should note that Brian tries to stock a cask-conditioned ale on a hand pump during the season. Meals $5–6.50; desserts $2.50–3; beer $3 (12-ounce bottle) to $5 (20-ounce draft).

DINING OUT **The Buckhorn Inn** (865-436-4668), 2140 Tudor Mountain Road, Gatlinburg, TN. Open all year. Gatlinburg's historic resort inn offers an elegant, yet friendly dining experience. The Buckhorn offers only one seating for the small number of tables in its 1938 main lodge, so that service is attentive and food is prepared specifically for each table. The lodge furnishes an intimate atmosphere, with sofas grouped around a large hearth, encouraging conversation. All diners are seated at one time and presented with five courses from a fixed menu; reservations are required, as preparation starts long before the seating time. The imaginative and exquisitely prepared food varies daily but tends to combine familiar favorites in new and exciting ways. Located in a dry area of the county, the Buckhorn has no wine list but welcomes you to bring your own and charges nothing for corkage. $25 per person; reservations required.

✻ Selective Shopping
Downtown Gatlinburg, TN
"We don't want to be noticed as T-shirt City, USA," the mayor of Gatlinburg once told a newspaper reporter, but "evidently it's easier to make a dollar selling T-shirts than anything else." Yes, downtown Gatlinburg has a lot of T-shirt shops. However, there are a lot of other downtown shops as well: old-timey photographs, tattoo parlors, NASCAR memorabilia, wedding chapels, souvenir stores, fudge shops, funnel cakes, gaudy jewelry, four different Thomas Kincade stores (the California-based "painter of light"), museums of the curious and weird (filling the role of side shows), amusement arcades, even carnival rides. It's easy enough to sneer at this "rundown, haphazard collection of buildings ranging from the good to the bad to the ugly," as did the Sonoran Institute in a report funded by the Gatlinburg Chamber of Commerce; "Gatlinburg is widely viewed as one of the most unattractive and inappropriate gateways to a national park in the United States," the institute sniffed. But it's also easy to relax and have fun, at Tennessee's giant unofficial permanent state fair. Message to the Sonoran Institute: Grab a funnel cake, guys, and chill.

This book finds four downtown sites particularly worth visiting. In this section you'll find Arrowcraft, a crafts shop older than the downtown that surrounds it, and Beneath the Smoke, Ken Jenkins's wonderful combination of nature shop and photographic art gallery. Elsewhere are listings for the lovely **Arrowmont School** (see Galleries and Gardens of the Arrowmont School under *To See—Cultural Sites*) and the fascinating cable lift to Ober Gatlinburg (see *To Do—Skiing*), with its sweeping panoramic views.

Arrowcraft (865-436-4604), 576 Parkway, Gatlinburg, TN. Open summer and fall: Monday through Saturday 10–8, Sunday 10–6. Off-season:

open 10–6 daily. The Arrowcraft crafters gallery predates the downtown area that crowds around it on all sides; this wandering log building has been selling fine crafts by local artists since 1926. Originally part of the adjacent **Arrowmont School of Arts and Crafts** (see Galleries and Gardens of the Arrowmont School under *To See— Cultural Sites*), it is now run by the not-for-profit Southern Highland Craft Guild and features only items hand-made by Craft Guild artists.

Beneath the Smoke (865-436-3460; 1-888-818-2262), 467 Parkway (US 441), Gatlinburg, TN. Beneath the Smoke is Gatlinburg nature photographer Ken Jenkins's homage to the Great Smoky Mountains, an 8,000-square-foot nature store, outfitter, bookshop, and gallery of Ken's stunning wildlife and scenic photography. You'll find it wandering through two stories of a storefront in the center of downtown, opposite US 321.

THE GLADES ARTS AND CRAFTS COMMUNITY Out of the 70 or more craft artists who are members of the Arts and Crafts Community in Gatlinburg's scenic, rural Glades neighborhood, it's impossible to select only three or four "best" or "most worthy." The listings that follow are more in the line of appetite whetters than anything else. Poke around and choose your own favorites.

The Historic Cliff Dwellers (865-436-6921), 668 Glades Road, Gatlinburg, TN. Constructed in 1933 as an art gallery and studio, for decades this distinctive, multigabled wood structure served as a prominent landmark in downtown Gatlinburg. When threatened with demolition in 1995, artists Chris and Jim Gray moved it to its present site at the heart of the Glades Community. Now the historic structure houses a fine-crafts cooperative, showcasing the work of its eight member artists. Owner Jim Gray has his studio and gallery next door.

Church Mouse Gallery (865-436-8988), c/o Greenbrier Incorporated, P.O. Box 735, Gatlinburg, TN 37738. Open every day 10–5. Watercolorist and sculptor Jim Gray creates a wide range of landscapes, portraits, and florals—by no means all of the Smokies, although Smoky Mountain scenes predominate. The detail and colors of his works are remarkable, as are the liveliness and sympathy of his sculpture— which includes the statue of Dolly Parton in front of the Sevier County Courthouse (see Sevierville, TN, under *Villages*).

Gatlinburg Ceramics (865-436-4315). Judy Baily has been handcrafting fine porcelains in her Glades studio/gallery for 30 years, taking each piece painstakingly from raw kaolin to finished ceramic. The bulk of her work is in a traditional, even Victorian style, but her range is wide. She is frequently in her studio, visible from the showroom, and welcomes visitors.

Ogle's Broom Shop (865-430-4402; 1-800-443-4575). One of the original crafts studio/galleries in the Glades; David Ogle is a third-generation mountain crafter, native to Gatlinburg. He produces a variety of traditional mountain brooms, walking sticks with carved handles, wooden toys, doll furniture, and carved birds.

G. Webb Gallery (865-436-3639), 2160 Tudor Mountain Road, Gatlinburg, TN. Watercolorist G. Webb specializes in highly detailed studies of local landscapes; recent works include the Temple Feed Store in Sevierville and the Emerts Cove Bridge near his home. His Glades Community gallery occupies a restored 1910 board-and-batten farmhouse surrounded by wild-flower gardens and giant hemlocks.

✳ Special Events

Last week in April: **Annual Spring Smoky Mountain Wildflower Pilgrimage** (865-436-7318), 115 Park Headquarters Road, Gatlinburg, TN. Adults $10; children under 12 free; other fees may apply. For over half a century, a group of East Tennessee organizations has sponsored this weeklong exploration of the national park's spring wildflowers. There are exhibits and vendors at the **Gatlinburg Convention Center,** but the real action takes place in a long series of field trips into the park—by foot, bicycle, and car. Wildflower walks predominate, but there are daily field trips for birders and specialized trips for geology, plant identification, medicinal plants, moss, algae, fungi, insects, spiders, salamanders, bats, bears, old-growth forests, second-growth forests, logging, history, folk art, plant sketching, photography, and environmental issues.

April: **The Cosby Ramp Festival,** Cosby, TN. Since 1954, Cosby, TN, has celebrated that pungent herald of spring, the ramp. A ramp is a type of wild onion also known as a wild leek. It has a sweet, mild taste with a hint of garlic but is notorious for the strong odor it leaves behind. One of the first plants to emerge in the spring, the ramp has traditionally been a center of community celebration in the mountains—typically a ramp supper given by the volunteer fire department. The Cosby Ramp Festival is unusual in being a big shindig thrown for tourists

as much as locals, with a full slate of mountain and bluegrass music.

Third weekend in May: **Gatlinburg Scottish Festival and Games** (1-800-568-4748), P.O. Box 1487, Gatlinburg, TN 37738. This traditional Scottish festival includes bagpipes, drums, Highlands dancers, sheep dog demonstrations, entertainment, clan tents, and Scottish food (yum!), in addition to Scottish Games. It's held in **Mills Park,** a largish city park near the Glades Arts and Crafts Community (see *Selective Shopping*).

Fourth of July: **Fourth of July Celebrations,** Gatlinburg, TN. Gatlinburg's July 4th celebrations start promptly at midnight, with a night parade through downtown that includes marching bands, lighted floats, and helium balloons. During the day there's a **River Raft Regatta** in which unmanned craft race down the river in the middle of town.

November–December: **Winterfest Kickoff,** Gatlinburg, TN. *November 14th:* Gatlinburg starts its season of winter illumination—light displays that continue through Christmas to Valentine's Day—with a festival at the new **Ripley's Aquarium**, featuring a chili cook-off, live music, clowns, and magicians, as well as trolley tours of the lights. **Christmas hayrides** start 2 weeks later and continue through most of December.

December: **New Year's Eve Space Needle Spectacular,** Gatlinburg, TN. A New Year's street party centers on downtown Gatlinburg's **Space Needle** attraction, with a ball drop and a stunning display of fireworks launched from the 340-foot observation tower.

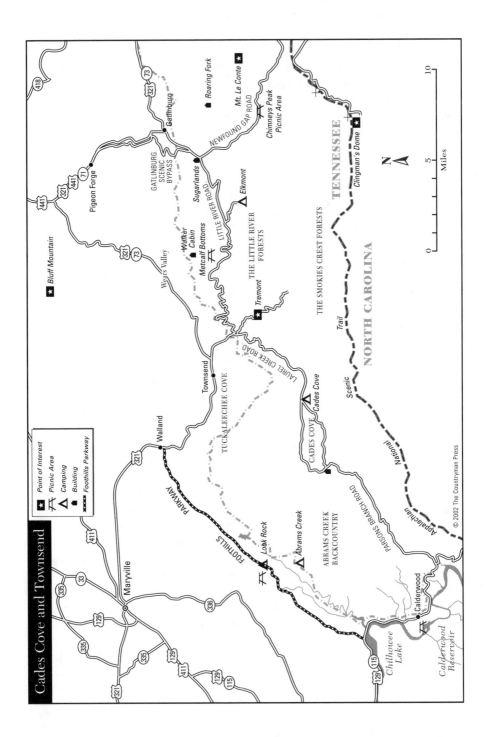

Cades Cove and Townsend

Point of Interest
Picnic Area
Camping
Building
Foothills Parkway

Maryville

Walland

Townsend

Pigeon Forge

Gatlinburg

Bluff Mountain

Wears Valley

GATLINBURG SCENIC BYPASS

Walker Cabin
Metcalf Bottoms
Sugarlands

Roaring Fork

Mt. Le Conte

Chimneys Peak Picnic Area

NEWFOUND GAP ROAD

LITTLE RIVER ROAD

Elkmont

THE LITTLE RIVER FORESTS

Tremont

THE SMOKIES CREST FORESTS

TUCKALEECHEE COVE

LAUREL CREEK ROAD

CADES COVE
Cades Cove

Clingman's Dome

TENNESSEE

NORTH CAROLINA

Scenic

Trail

PARSONS BRANCH ROAD

ABRAMS CREEK BACKCOUNTRY

Abrams Creek

Look Rock

FOOTHILLS PARKWAY

Calderwood

Chilhowee Lake

Calderwood Reservoir

Appalachian
National

N

0   5   10
Miles

© 2002 The Countryman Press

TOWNSEND, CADES COVE & THE NORTHWEST QUADRANT

T his quadrant of Great Smoky Mountains National Park contains one of the most beautiful and rewarding sites in the eastern United States—the remarkable Cades Cove, a large flat-bottomed valley covered in pastureland, dotted with log cabins, and surrounded on all sides by great mountain walls. The Park Service maintains this huge valley, 5 miles long and nearly 2 miles wide, as a 3,000-acre outdoor museum of pioneer life, with 12 major structures and many more out-buildings. An 11-mile-long, one-way loop road skirts the cove's edge, giving wide views and easy access to all of its sites.

The drive to the cove tells another story. The twisting paved road follows the bed of a historic logging tramway along a roaring mountain stream—as do most of the roads in this part of the park, the former lands of the Little River Lumber Company. The handsome young hardwood forests you see in these parts have grown since the Park Service gained control of the stripped-out land in 1940. Two old lumber camps, at Elkmont and Tremont, offer recreation opportunities, while the scattered remnants of the Little Greenbrier farming community survive in a little-visited corner of the woods.

Outside the park, another large cove straddles the main highway (US 321). Tuckaleechee Cove furnishes a scenic mountain setting for a variety of B&Bs, resorts, cabin rentals, cafés, and restaurants. It also contains the main settlement of Townsend, TN, a former logging town where restaurants, shops, and motels spread along the four-lane highway. It has a visitors center in a new log building in the center of town—a good place to get oriented. Townsend is a lot less trafficked and more mountainy than the Gatlinburg–Pigeon Forge, TN, area, for those who prefer a more personal, homelike experience and are willing to do without chain restaurants.

GUIDANCE ♿ ☂ **Smoky Mountain Convention and Visitors Bureau** (865-448-6134; 1-800-525-6834), 7906 East Lamar Alexander Parkway, Townsend, TN 37882. Open daily during business hours. This nonprofit organization, dedicated to promoting economic growth and tourism in the Blount County area of the Smokies, maintains a visitors center in a modern log building in Townsend. This visitors center has a good gift shop and displays of local artists, as well as a staffed information desk.

Great Smoky Mountains National Park—Ranger Stations. The Park Service maintains a ranger station at Cades Cove with a staffed information desk. You'll find it off to the left as you enter the cove, in the main recreation area across from the camp store. For general phone inquiries, it's best to call the **Sugarlands Visitors Center** (see Sugarlands Ranger Station under *Guidance* in "Gatlinburg and the Northeast Quadrant").

Cades Cove Web Site (www.nps.gov/grsm/cchome.htm.). Maintained by the National Park Service, this web site gives a good overview of the cove.

GETTING THERE *By car:* Townsend, TN, is on US 321 between Maryville, TN, and Gatlinburg, TN. If you're approaching *from the south or west,* take the interstate to Knoxville, TN, then take I-140 and US 129 to Maryville; Townsend is another 20 miles via US 321. *From the north or east,* follow I-40/81 to TN 66 (exit 406), northeast of Knoxville. Take TN 66 to Sevierville, TN, then follow US 441 south until US 321 branches off right at Pigeon Forge, TN; Townsend is another 15 miles farther on.

By air: **McGhee Tyson Airport** (865-970-2773), 2055 Alcoa Highway, Alcoa, TN, serves the Knoxville area and is about 20 miles from Townsend, TN. It's large enough to have all the major car rental agencies on site, which is just as well; there is no bus service into Townsend.

By bus, train, or public transportation: The Townsend area has no railroad, no bus service, and no public transportation.

MEDICAL EMERGENCIES **Blount Memorial Hospital** (865-983-7211), 907 East Lamar Alexander Parkway (US 321), Maryville, TN. Located 20 miles west of Townsend, TN, this 250-bed regional hospital serves all of Blount County from the county seat of Maryville. It has 24-hour emergency-room services.

Blount Health Clinic (865-983-0093), 1503 East Lamar Alexander Parkway (US 321), Maryville, TN. Open Monday through Friday 5 PM–10 PM; Saturday 10 AM–6 PM; Sunday noon–6. This is an after-hours walk-in clinic near Blount Memorial Hospital (see above), 20 miles west of Townsend, TN.

Park Med (865-977-1455), 117 Gill Street, Alcoa, TN. This is a walk-in clinic located just beyond downtown Maryville via TN 35, then three blocks left on Gill Street. It keeps regular business hours on weekdays and shortened hours on weekends. Open Monday through Friday 8–5; Saturday 8–1:30; Sunday 12:30–3.

✳ Wandering Around

EXPLORING BY CAR **Driving the Little River Railroad.** To the east of Cades Cove, 23 miles of park roads follow the railroad beds of the Little River Lumber Company. By the time the Little River Lumber Company finished logging in 1940 they had laid more than 400 miles of rail bed, mostly to dead ends in the valleys they were logging. These abandoned rail beds form many of the hiking trails and nearly all of the roads in this part of the park.

Starting at the **Cades Cove Picnic Area** (see Cades Cove Recreation Area under *Wild Places—Recreation Areas*), this drive follows **Laurel Creek Road** out of the Cove toward Townsend, TN. Just beyond the **Schoolhouse Gap Trailhead**

CADES COVE LOOP ROAD

The 11-mile, one-way Cades Cove Loop Road furnishes a scenic ramble through the national park's most historic and beautiful corner. Meandering through forests and fields, with sweeping views toward the Smoky Mountains, this lane passes 10 separate historic sites, each one preserving one or more pioneer-era structures from the cove's past. To reach the start of the

THE GREGG-CABLE HOUSE

Cades Cove Loop Road, enter the park at **Townsend**, TN, and follow the signs 7.3 miles to **Cades Cove.** The loop road begins with views over horse pastures to the crest of the Smokies, then wanders through forests and meadows for more than a mile to the **John Oliver Place** (see *To See—Cades Cove Historic Sites*), a handsome log cabin set back a quarter mile from the road, visible over wide meadows. Another 2 miles of winding through forests takes you to (or near) three of the cove's four 19th-century churches, including the lovely little **Methodist Church,** set splendidly in wide meadows to the right of the road. From there the loop road passes through broad hayfields for more than 2 miles, giving some of the widest views from any paved road in the national park. Two miles into the hayfields stretch, a split-rail fence on the right frames views over wildflower meadows toward a large farmstead—the **Cable Mill Area,** for many the high point of the loop with its visitors center, working water mill, restored farmhouse, cantilevered barn, collection of pioneer farm tools, and crafts demonstrations. Another good reason to stop: Cable Mill has the only toilets on the loop road.

From Cable Mill, the loop road runs through forests, passing the **Cades Cove Nature Trail** on the right, to the **Dan Lawson Place,** a log cabin behind split-rail fences. A half-mile farther on sits the elaborate **Tipton Place,** with its impressive cantilevered barn. The final cabin on the loop, the modest **Carter Shields Cabin,** is 0.85 mile beyond, in an open glade rich in spring dogwoods. The loop road reaches its end 2 miles later, after passing through young, open forests with meadow views.

A final word of warning: Loop-road traffic can be very bad. It's one lane wide with no passing, so you'll go no faster than the slowest car on the loop. On a weekend the loop road can become a parking lot, with traffic inching forward slower than a walking pace. There's a great alternative, though; on Wednesday and Saturday mornings (until 10:30 AM) the loop road is open to bicyclists and walkers only (see Bicycling in Cades Cove under *To Do—Bicycling*).

the highway takes to the old logging railbed, acquiring its even gradients and sharp curves. Frequently the road becomes a narrow shelf cut into the mountain slope, with the stream racing along on one side and a vertical rock face on the other. You'll pass a tunnel and a waterfall, then the side road to Tremont (see **Tremont Logging Camp Walk** under *Exploring on Foot*), before you reach the fork to Townsend (1 mile left) at a great swimming hole with a sandy beach. From there, the old railbed goes right, following the **Little River** upstream. Now the road-/railbed winds sharply while hugging this full-volume, cascading river. Views over the river are continuous for miles, with many opportunities to fish, wade, or admire the scenery. At **The Sinks** (parking right, over the stone bridge) there's a cliff-top view of a stone bridge framed by two large waterfalls. A few miles farther down the road you'll reach the **Metcalf Bottoms Picnic Area** (see *Wild Places—Picnic Areas*) and a side road leading to the historic **Little Greenbrier community** (see *To See—Other Historic Sites*) and **Wear Cove** (see Wear's Valley under *Villages*). When you reach the side road to **Elkmont,** take it; you'll still be following the old railbed. Abandoned buildings and a security fence mark the start of the old lumber camp, then a long straight stretch of road follows Elkmont's railroad siding. The paved road ends at the parking area for the **Little River Trail,** which continues to follow the railbed upstream. A gravel road, right, leads to the **Elkmont National Historic District** (see *To See—Other Historic Sites*), an early 20th-century vacation settlement.

The Foothills of Cades Cove. The Foothills Parkway, part of the National Park Service's scenic highway system since the 1930s, has only two short completed segments. This scenic drive follows the longer of the two segments, Chilhowee (kill-HOWee) Mountain, for 17 miles, using historic old roads to make a loop trip.

To start this scenic drive, go through **Cades Cove** to the **Cable Mill Site,** then take **Forge Creek Road** through young forests growing up on abandoned fields. In 2 miles, **Parsons Branch Road** forks right. This is one of the earlier pioneer roads out of the cove, and the only motorable road that preserves the look and feel of a 19th-century turnpike—9 miles of twisting, steep, one-lane, one-way gravel road. You'll reach the first of many fords at 2.7 miles; these fords consist of a concrete ramp into, then out of, a small stream. The road tops at **Sams Gap** (2,780 feet), then drops into a steep defile so narrow that it's forced into a dozen fords before it ends at a historic 20th-century road—**US 129.**

US 129 is a relict of the 1930s Works Projects Administration (WPA); built for a depression era when cars were few and slow, it is so curvy that motorcyclists use it for rallies. Turn right. US 129 spends the next 5 miles twisting under giant power lines that lead from ALCOA Corporation's hydropower dams upstream (see The Tapoco Lakes under *To See—Big Dammed Lakes* in "The Northern Unicois: Robbinsville and Tellico Plains"). Views climax as the highway occupies an entire ridgetop, and the **Little Tennessee River** twists through a deep canyon below. Just beyond is the turnoff to the **Calderwood Power Station Recreation Area** (see *Wild Places—Picnic Areas*). The highway finally descends to the banks of **Chilhowee Reservoir,** with 3 miles of wide and continuous views across the lakes. Turn right onto the **Foothills Parkway.**

Wide shouldered, straight, and easy, the parkway curves gently up **Chilhowee Mountain** to its dry, sandstone ridgeline. Once there, you'll get the first of many

sweeping views east toward the high crest of Great Smoky Mountains National
Park. Along this stretch, the **Look Rock Picnic Area** (see *Wild Places—Picnic Areas*) offers picnicking and 360-degree views from an observation tower. From there the Foothills Parkway goes more than 3 miles without a view, then makes up for it with a westward view over the flat **Tennessee Valley**—a great sunset location. The parkway ends a few miles later, 7 miles from Townsend on **US 321.**

EXPLORING ON FOOT ✐ **Tremont Logging Camp Walk.** The Little River Lumber Company did its best to jam a full-gauge railroad into every stream valley between Elkmont and Cades Cove, TN. Eighty years later, these old lumber railroads can make for some great walking, combining wide, even paths and easy gradients with stunning streamside views. This quiet stroll follows one such path, starting from the old logging settlement of Tremont and going up the railroad grade used to log out Lynn Camp Prong.

You'll find the trailhead, with ample parking, at the end of the **Tremont Road,** at the old town site. Constructed in 1925, **Tremont** operated for 8 years as the company stripped the upstream valleys bare of timber. Tremont had a hotel, general store, electrical generator, machine shop, doctor's office, and combination church/school/movie theater (known as the House of Salvation, Education, and Damnation)—now all gone. A brochure, available from a roadside kiosk at the end of the Tremont Road's pavement, gives details of family life in the Tremont Camp as well as a map of the town.

A footbridge perches on old railroad piers in the center of the former town; a flat place beyond marks a siding and a fork in the railroad. Take the left grade up **Lynn Camp Prong,** a strong mountain torrent full of water in the driest weather, with many cascades in its narrow, steep valley. You'll immediately notice the coolness of this valley, and the fine smell of mountain water that hangs in its moist air. In a quarter mile, the grade gives a clear view straight toward a 30-foot waterfall, where the stream slides down a great exposed dome of a rock. For the next half mile the stream continues to furnish good views of small cascades, still pools, moss-covered boulders, and trees clinging to high bluffs. Then the valley becomes more U-shaped, allowing the railroad to straighten and retreat from the more dramatic and difficult terrain to a flat valley floor. This is a good place to turn around.
Chestnut Top Trail. Cades Cove Ranger Steven McCoy calls Chestnut Top Trail "the best wildflower walk in the Smokies, both for variety and sheer numbers." Located right outside Townsend, TN, this well-maintained footpath follows the ridgeline of **Chestnut Top Lead** just inside the national park boundary. You'll find the trailhead a half mile inside the park on the Townsend entrance road, at the large riverside parking lot. The trail starts by climbing up the slope above the road, shaded by straight young hardwoods. Frequent outcrops indicate the source of the lush wildflowers—rich limestone soil, similar to that of Cades Cove, supports a diverse ecosystem here. As the path climbs away from the road, the trees become large and the forest more open. Hemlocks reach 2 feet in diameter and rhododendrons arch over the path as the trail reaches a narrow but beautiful view over Townsend and the mountains beyond the park. Then the trail gains the ridgeline and leaves the tiny limestone cove, to enter a dry pine forest with a rocky outcrop floor and a rich pine smell. As the trail continues up the ridgeline, the forest

gradually yields to a dry ridgetop pine-oak forest, very sunny and dusty with a faint smell of dry rot on a hot day. When the trail levels and enters the fourth gap, you've gone 2 miles and climbed 800 feet; it's a good place to turn back. If you continue, the path will climb another 300 feet and lose it again, before reaching the **Schoolhouse Gap Trail** in 2 more miles.

✳ Villages

Townsend, TN. Founded as a lumber-mill town in 1901, Townsend sits on the first piece of flat land outside the national park boundaries, straddling the main road into this area of the park. This makes it the closest town to Cades Cove, and the closest collection of travel facilities (including food and gasoline) for the cove's 2 million annual visitors. Nevertheless, Townsend has always been dwarfed in popularity by Gatlinburg, TN (23 miles east on US 321), and this has allowed it to retain much of the character of a quiet mountain cove. Today it consists of a scattered (but increasing) number of modest commercial buildings widely spread along a 2-mile stretch of newly four-laned US 321. It retains little of its past as a mill town apart from a worthwhile (and free) small museum at the mill site, and it lacks any real town center or historic structures. However, views are good, and the town parallels the lovely Little River as it exits the Smokies. Townsend has only a scant few franchise motels and eateries, but it does have a decent selection of crafts shops, antiques shops, souvenir shops, and independent motels and restaurants. Traffic and parking pose few problems, even at the height of the season.

VALLEY MEADOWLANDS OUTSIDE TOWNSEND LOOK TOWARD THE SMOKY MOUNTAINS

Wear's Valley (Wear Cove), TN. Wear's Valley (also known as Wear Cove) is a wide rural valley just outside the park's boundary between Townsend and Gatlinburg. Although isolated by bad roads for many years, Wear's Valley started getting tourists when US 321 entered it in 1980. Since then it has become a popular spot for second-home subdivisions; its open views over rolling meadows are increasingly apt to include a large number of modern houses. A side road, Little Greenbrier Road, leads 2 miles into the park, ending at Metcalf Bottoms (see **Metcalf Bottoms Picnic Area** under *Wild Places—Picnic Areas*).

✳ Wild Places

THE GREAT FORESTS The Forests of the Smoky Mountain Crest. The Smokies Crest forms a giant half circle around the southern edge of Cades Cove. Lower here than at Gatlinburg, TN, the crest rises abruptly from the 1,940-foot **Deals Gap** at the park's southern edge to reach 4,700 feet at **Parsons Bald**—and then sticks at that elevation for most of its 12-mile arc around the cove. Although the Smokies formed a barrier here as well as elsewhere, it was a porous barrier, broken by a network of footpaths that allowed a low but steady commerce between the cove people and North Carolina. The cove folk would use these paths to bring their cattle up to graze in the great grassy balds that straddle the ridgeline. These balds, probably formed by the Cherokees and enlarged by the cove settlers, are some of the most varied and beautiful places in the park, with stunning views over the Smokies Crest and the infinitely receding ridges of North Carolina. Today's park trails retrace the old pioneer paths, ascending steadily through handsome young forests to the great mountaintop meadows above the cove at **Gregory Bald, Russell Bald,** and **Spence Bald.** Several of these paths make a challenging but doable all day hike, with elevation gains between 2,000 and 3,000 feet and 6 to 12 miles of hiking one way.

The Forests of the Little River. When the Tennessee National Park Commission started buying land for Great Smoky Mountains National Park in 1925, the Little River Lumber Company owned the entire Little River Drainage, some 77,000 acres. The company agreed to sell the land for a national park, but only if it could retain logging rights for 15 years. The Park Commission agreed; after all, how many trees could they harvest in 15 years? The company attacked the slopes, stripping them of every tree it could sell before the deadline came and logging ended forever. They beat the deadline by a year, denuding the virgin forests of the Little River by 1939. Then they took up the last of the rails from the railbeds, disassembled the Townsend mill, and turned control of the wrecked Little River Basin over to the National Park Service. The logging company had purchased a huge tract of old-growth forest, removed every tree, left a destroyed land bereft of economic value—and sold it to the government for a 50 percent profit.

The forests you see today are a product of this clear-cut logging—a forest of young, straight hardwoods, mostly less than 70 years old. Hiking trails are more plentiful than you might expect, and many of these trails are remarkably easy and well built. Little wonder—they follow the gentle, even grades of logging rail beds, up the streams to end at the great mountainous wall of the Smokies Crest.

Lower Abrams Creek Backcountry. The national park extends westward of Cades Cove to take in 60 square miles of rugged, little-visited backcountry centered on the lower reaches of Abrams Creek. This is a jumbled region of low ridges, with elevations seldom reaching 3,000 feet—short, stubby, linear ridges, placed close together between parallel creeks. The entire backcountry is thickly forested, with dry pinelands on the ridges and rich mixed hardwoods and hemlocks along the creeks. Access is by foot and horse only, with three trails running across the lay of the land and many more occupying the linear streambeds. **Abrams Creek Trail,** the only well-used trail in the area, follows the gorge of Abrams Creek as it cuts through the middle of these ridges, while the beautiful old cove roads, **Cooper Road** and **Rabbit Creek Road,** allow easy and lonely walking through the backcountry's northern and southern marches. All three of these access trails start in Cades Cove and converge at the **Abrams Creek Ranger Station** at the western edge of the park in **Happy Valley** (best reached from **Happy Valley Road** at US 129, just east of the Foothills Parkway, then follow the signs). This ranger station has a fine little campground, a couple of picnic tables, and good fly-fishing access.

RECREATION AREAS Cades Cove Recreation Area. This large, tree-shaded recreation area sits at the beginning of the Cades Cove Loop Road, a short distance down the paved road on your left. Its lovely streamside picnic area follows **Abrams Creek** as it flows into the cove from the mountains on its east. Just beyond is the large, wooded campground, the most popular in the park. Between the two is a recreation hall and camp store in a 1950s-style building, and a ranger station with an information desk; you can rent bicycles at the camp store (see **Cades Cove Bike Shop** under *To Do—Bicycling*). Across from the ranger station, a concessionaire-run stable offers trail rides (see **Cades Cove Riding Stables** under *To Do—Horseback Riding*).

Although the official picnic area is very nice indeed, serious picnickers will want to bring a blanket and enjoy the fine meadows on the cove floor. **Hyatt Lane** is a particularly good place to look for picnic spots, as is the stretch of loop road between the **Primitive Baptist Church** and the **Elijah Oliver Place** (see *To See—Cades Cove Historic Sites*).

PICNIC AREAS Metcalf Bottoms Picnic Area. This large picnic area, 10 miles west of Townsend, TN, on the Little River Road, occupies a long, flat-bottomed wide space on the otherwise twisty and cliff-sided **Little River Gorge.** Now covered in tall forest, this used to be a small, isolated farm and a whistle-stop on the Little River Railroad. Metcalf Bottoms nearly always has a large choice of tables along its long riverfront—a particularly calm and wadable stretch of the Little River. Little Greenbrier Road sneaks out behind this picnic area to the Little Greenbrier historic area (see **Little Greenbrier Community** under *To See—Other Historic Sites*), then out of the park to **Wear's Valley** (see *Villages*).

Look Rock Picnic Area. This striking picnic area, about halfway along the **Chilhowee Mountain** section of the Foothills Parkway, features a row of picnic tables along a rock precipice, the view only partially blocked by trees stubbornly growing in the rock cracks. This is a dramatic, breezy place for a warm summer's lunch. The nearby observation tower, built in the 1960s and given to casual vandalism, offers fine views west over the flat lands of Tennessee's Great Valley.

Calderwood Power Station Recreation Area. This remote, lovely recreation area off US 129 is owned by the ALCOA corporation and is open to the public daily 8–4. The ALCOA road goes south from the highway to a lakeside fork; the right fork follows the lake through grassy meadows, then swerves left onto a short causeway pier out into **Chilhowee Reservoir.** Here you'll find a few picnic tables and a portable toilet—and views, a full circle of views over the lake to the surrounding mountains, from this quiet and serene spot well out into the lake. Returning, be sure to take the left fork 0.75 mile to admire **Calderwood Power Station,** a handsome industrial Gothic structure in red brick, built by ALCOA in 1928 and still used by them to help power their aluminum smelters in nearby Maryville, TN.

✳ To See

CADES COVE HISTORIC SITES The John Oliver Place. The first log cabin on the Cades Cove Loop Road, the John Oliver Place may well be the most visually impressive. It sits a quarter mile off the paved road, clearly visible across a meadow, framed by a split-rail "worm" fence, set against a backdrop of hardwood forest and steep slopes. Like all cove log cabins, its logs are planked, hewn with flat fronts and backs, to prevent rot from entering along the rounded undersides of the logs. It works; the John Oliver Cabin has been standing for over 180 years. It is built as a single log cube, one log in length, with logs that interlock with dovetail joints—the same type of joint still used in making good-quality cabinet drawers. The dovetail joints left large gaps between the logs, which the farmer chinked with mud mortar. Inside, the cabin has a single large room heated by a fireplace, and a second-story loft. The chimney is set outside the cabin against the gable end, and is made of local stone held with mud mortar. Southerners will see nothing unusual in this, but northerners might wonder about the heat loss from an outside chimney. The mountain people preferred it cool, particularly after a long day cooking in the middle of the summer. At night, the sparse furniture would be moved out of the way; parents and girls would sleep downstairs, while the boys would sleep in the loft. (See also **Elijah Oliver Place,** below).

Primitive Baptist Church. Cades Cove's Primitive Baptist Church was organized in 1826; the surviving church building is an 1887 white frame structure ⅓ mile down a gravel road. The **Missionary Baptist Church** (see below) is a short distance down the loop road.

Why two Baptist churches in such a small community? The Primitive Baptists were (and are) a deeply conservative and traditionalist group. They believed that every person should remain in the place given to them by God and that missionary work was interfering with God's will for the heathen and a first step toward establishing a permanent, paid priesthood. In contrast, the upwardly mobile Missionary Baptists encouraged people to improve their position through business activity, had little fear of a permanent minister class, and funded missionaries. During the Civil War the Primitive Baptists were strongly pro-Union; God had created the Union, and to rebel against it was to rebel against God's will. Although the Primitive Baptist Church stopped meeting during the Civil War, its members resisted the Confederacy and formed a

THE JOHN OLIVER PLACE

way station of the Underground Railroad that smuggled escaped Union prisoners to safety. For this they were targeted for assassination by Rebel marauders who would cross the border from North Carolina, receiving information from Rebel sympathizers in the cove. This viciously genocidal pattern repeated itself in isolated coves on both sides of the Tennessee–North Carolina border (see Shelton Laurel Backcountry Area under *Wild Places—The Bald Mountain Highlands* in "Asheville's Rugged Hinterlands").

Methodist Church. The current building is the prettiest of the cove's three churches, a beautifully proportioned 1902 white frame structure with a bell set in a small tin-roofed steeple. Built by a cove carpenter and blacksmith who later served as its minister, it replaced an old log church that the congregation had used since the 1820s. Like the other two surviving cove churches, it has a pioneer cemetery. Large meadows stretch uphill from it, a good place to ramble for views and wildflowers.

Missionary Baptist Church. The cove's Missionary Baptist Church was formed in 1839 by dissidents from the **Primitive Baptist Church** (see above). It, too, went inactive during the Civil War, its congregation split between Unionists and Rebels; it reorganized after the war without its Rebel families. The current white frame building dates from 1915 and served the congregation until it closed in 1944. Springtime visitors should look for daffodils in the back of the church, planted by the cove's Civilian Conservation Corps (CCC) troop in the 1930s to form the phrase "Co. 5427."

Elijah Oliver Place. This site is a pleasant half-mile walk from the loop road. Elijah Oliver, a son of John Oliver, built this cabin after the Civil War. It's larger and more elaborate than this father's cabin (see above), with an attached wing and a board-and-batten enclosure on the porch. It's interesting to note that Elijah used smaller logs than his paw had 40 years earlier; great trees had become harder to find in the cove.

⅖ Cable Mill Historic Area and Visitors Center. This complex of seven historic buildings occupies the site of the cove's mill, store, and most prosperous farm. When founded by John P. Cable in 1870 it had a gristmill and sawmill, both powered by a large overshot wheel that got its water down a long millrace from Mill Creek. The water mill is still in business, its overshot wheel turning its huge grist stones every weekend in-season. The short walk along the millrace to the modest milldam is interesting and peaceful. The adjacent frame house, built from lumber sawed at the Cable Mill, was a store and boardinghouse run by "Aunt Becky" Cable from 1887 until her death in 1944, 10 years after becoming part of the national park. It's now furnished like a late-19th-century cove boardinghouse. Nearby are all the outbuildings of a prosperous cove farm: a smokehouse, corncrib, barn, and sorghum mill. A large cantilevered barn houses a collection of farm wagons and implements.

When you're scheduling your cove loop tour, be sure to check for crafts demonstrations. These can include sorghum milling, blacksmithing, dying and flint knapping, as well as milling corn. Every October the hayfields beside the Cable Farm are mowed with authentic 19th-century horse-drawn equipment.

Henry Whitehead Place. In the 1880s, Matilda Gregory's husband deserted her and their son; in this emergency, her brothers quickly erected a crude log cabin for them. Then, a few years later, Matilda married Henry Whitehead, a widower with three daughters. Whitehead built them a fancy new cabin, attached to Matilda's tiny, crude one. The Whitehead Cabin is made of logs milled to 4 inches thick at the Cable sawmill (see above), fitted snugly together, and covered with milled clapboards. It's the most sophisticated log cabin in the cove, and it's attached to the crudest. You'll find it 0.7 mile down Forge Creek Road, a side road just beyond the Cable Mill entrance.

Dan Lawson Place. This well-built 1856 cabin is made of large hand-hewn logs fitted tightly together, with a frame extension added some years later. Located at the intersection with Hyatt Lane, it is the most visible log cabin from the floor of the cove. Its split-rail fences provide space for wildflowers and a favored subject for photographs.

The Tipton Place. Colonel "Hamp" Tipton, a Mexican War veteran who lived in nearby Tuckaleechee Cove, built this frame house in the early 1870s for his daughters who taught school in Cades Cove. In the 1880s, the Tiptons sold the house to a blacksmith, James McCaulley, who built a smithy that still stands behind the house. Quite a farmstead survives from McCaulley's era. In addition to the smithy, there's a smokehouse and woodshed in the front yard, and a corncrib and cantilevered barn across the road.

The Carter Shields Cabin. Little is known of the history of this modest log cabin, set in a lovely glade 2 miles from the end of the loop road. It's named after George Washington "Carter" Shields, a wounded Civil War veteran, who lived in it with his wife from 1911 to 1922.

OTHER HISTORIC SITES ℰ **Little Greenbrier Community.** Little Greenbrier Community is one of the least-known and least-visited historic sites in the national park. To find it, take Wear Gap Road from the middle of the **Metcalf Bottoms Picnic Area** (see *Wild Places—Picnic Areas*), 0.5 mile to a gravel road on the right, then another 0.5 mile up this narrow gravel road to its end. You'll be parked by a one-room log schoolhouse that started life as a church—hence the incongruous presence of a pioneer cemetery on the hill above it. The Greenbrier schoolhouse is still in use as the site of special classes for the schoolchildren of Blount and Sevier Counties. With a bit of luck you'll find it open and class in session, with a full set of turn-of-the-century texts and teaching aids. The teacher uses an old map of Greenbrier Community that shows how these woods used to be filled with a network of cabins linked by paths and tracks.

One of those cabins still survives. Across the road from the cemetery a gated jeep track dives into the forest of young, handsome hardwoods. A lovely and nearly level walk, the track follows **Little Brier Creek** upstream for a mile, then goes right at a fork to cross the stream and continue 0.2 mile to the **Walker Place.** This fine log cabin, set in a clearing with a springhouse and barn, was the home of the Walker sisters, who refused to move out of the park and continued to live in their family cabin until the 1960s. No other site in the park gives quite the feeling of remoteness, of quiet, and of simplicity as the Walker Place.

Elkmont National Historic District. In 1908, the first logging train climbed up the Little River Gorge to the new lumber camp, Elkmont—then a typical company town, temporary but with a full range of services for the lumbermen and their families. However, the 18-mile rail journey up the Little River Gorge was so scenic, and Elkmont so cool and pleasant during the summer's heat, that tourists started coming up the rail line to stay at the modest little company hotel. By 1912 there were so many tourists coming to Elkmont that the company built a luxury hotel, the Wonderland, and subdivided a lovely nearby valley for vacation homes. These early-20th-century vacation developments, popular with Knoxville's powerful elite, easily survived the lumber camp's closure in 1926. In fact, they survived until 1992, an enclave of privilege inside the national park.

Why did the National Park Service allow the vacation homes of Knoxville's socialites to survive while they systematically demolished 6,600 farms, homes, and businesses? Many have jumped to the obvious conclusion—but the Park Service maintains that no one received any special treatment. When the National Park Service condemned the privately held lands, they gave all the landowners the option of retaining a lifetime lease in exchange for giving up much of the purchase money. Mountain folk, who had to earn a living, took the money and left, while the Elkmont vacation-home owners accepted the lease option. Then, in 1972, the Elkmont elite used their clout to gain a 20-year extension from Congress. Enraged, the National Park Service formally stated their intention of tearing down every structure in Elkmont as soon as they got control. However, by then Elkmont was a National Historic District with 69 of its structures on the National Register of Historic Places. This made the park's wholesale demolition plan illegal and required independent review and approval for any substitute plan. The Park Service still insists in tearing down five dozen listed structures, and no outside agency will approve this wholesale historic destruction. The Historic District has been in this bureaucratic limbo for a decade, while the National Park Service allows its buildings to deteriorate. Meanwhile, the cottage community is unfenced and open to any who wishes to see this bit of park history. To find it, continue down the Elkmont Road past the Little River trailhead. Nearly all of the cottages have serious structural damage—so enjoy them from a safe distance, and respect the historic integrity of these listed structures.

CULTURAL SITES *&* **The Little River Railroad and Lumber Company Museum** (865-448-2211), Town Center on old US 73, Townsend, TN. Open Monday through Saturday 10–2; Sunday 2–6. Between 1902 and 1939, the Little River Lumber Company stripped more than a half billion board feet of lumber from the Great Smoky Mountains and milled it in Townsend. This small local museum seeks to preserve the memory of the days when logging, not tourism, dominated the mountains of Tennessee. Headquartered in a historic railroad depot moved in from nearby Walland, TN, this volunteer-run museum contains a first-rate collection of local logging artifacts. The artifacts are interesting in themselves, and are arranged intelligently to give a thorough and coherent picture of Smoky Mountain logging and the way of life that logging briefly created. If you're lucky, you'll be shown around by a volunteer such as Georgia Bradshaw, who can expand on the exhibits with tales from her own childhood in the lumber camps high in the mountains. Outside the museum sits one of the Little River Lumber Company's original Shay engines—an amazing site with its huge geared wheels.

Road, Townsend, TN. To find the caverns, follow the signs south from US 321, just east of Townsend. Open April through October, 9–6; late March and early November,10–5; closed mid-November through mid-March. Adults $9; children 5–11, $5; children under 5, free. The limestone-floored Dry Valley, just a mile east of Townsend, is home to one of the most dramatic show caves in the Southern Appalachians, Tuckaleechee Caverns. The 170-step descent (no disabled access) leads to a deep underground river, then follows it for a half mile. The 75-minute tour passes underground waterfalls, rapids, and sandy beaches on a gently curving stretch of stream. Long stretches of the path appear to travel through a western-style canyon, with steep rock walls rising on all sides. Stalactites, stalagmites, and flowstone of all sorts decorate the cave walls. The path ends in one of the South's largest underground rooms open to the public, big enough to hold three football fields and containing a stalactite column five stories tall. It's particularly dramatic in rainy weather, when its underground river rises and the waterfalls become lively. As the path is not a loop, the total tour requires a mile's walk and 340 steps, so be prepared.

Bluff Mountain. Any view aficionado will consider Bluff Mountain a real find. Bluff Mountain is the last real mountain in the Smokies Foothills—a steep, rocky, cliff-lined protuberance into the flatness of Tennessee's Great Valley. Bluff Mountain Road, a narrow, steep, paved lane, leads to the very top of Bluff Mountain, with wide views from (you guessed it) high rocky bluffs. Nowhere else can you see how dramatically the Appalachians rise from the flatlands below and how villages such as Pigeon Forge, TN, are jammed into deep, narrow valleys. To find Bluff Mountain Road, take US 321 three miles west of Pigeon Forge; then turn right onto Walden Creek Road for and drive 0.6 mile to Goose Gap Road; then go 0.6 mile up Goose Gap Road to turn left onto Bluff Mountain Road.

The views are at the very top of **Bluff Mountain Road** (4.3 miles from its start on **Goose Gap Road**), then left along the ridgetop on **DuPont Springs Road.** You'll find two wonderful views along the 1.2 miles of this paved dead-end lane; then a third view a short walk through the gate at the end of the road—a wide panorama over the entire flatness of the Great Valley.

✳ To Do

BICYCLING Faced with jammed auto traffic on Cades Cove Loop Road, a large number of people prefer to bicycle around the 11-mile valley-bottom loop. In order to accommodate all these cyclists, the Park Service closes the loop road to cars on Wednesday and Saturday mornings until 10 AM during the summer season. Nor is the cove the only good place to cycle; the **Smoky Mountain Convention and Visitors Bureau** in Townsend, TN, (see *Guidance*) has an excellent brochure giving detailed descriptions of eight back road jaunts throughout the area. You can rent bicycles from a concessionaire in the cove or from a shop in Townsend.

✐ **Cades Cove Bike Shop** (865-448-9034), Maryville, TN. Located at the Cades Cove Camp Store at the start of the Cades Cove Loop Road, this national park concessionaire offers reasonable day-long rentals on sturdy, well-kept machines. Open daily April through October. $3.25 per hour/ $16.25 per day.

Little River Village (865-448-2241), 8533 TN 73, Townsend, TN. This bicycle rental shop operates from a large camp store in the middle of Townsend.

ENVIRONMENTAL PROGRAMS

The Great Smoky Mountains Institute at Tremont (865-448-6709), 9275 Tremont Road, Townsend, TN. Multiday programs run all year; reservations are required. Most adult programs list 2 or 3 days, and run from $120–375; the cost includes room and board. For more than 30 years this institute at Tremont has been giving youth and adult programs in environmental topics from their headquarters in the old Youth Conservation Corps camp near Tremont. The Tremont Institute offers an immersive, intense experience with a great deal of group interaction, in the setting of a rustic camp surrounded by deep forest. While many of the activities are for school groups or professional educators, the institute also offers regular programs for the general public, typically 3- to 5-day residency programs with extensive outdoor time; meals are taken in a large mess hall. Youth and teen camps are scheduled through-out the summer, while adult multiday programs include nature observation, wildflowers, geology, fall colors, photography, backpacking, and Elderhostels.

FISHING Little River Outfitters
(865-448-9459), 7807 East Lamar Alexander Parkway, Townsend, TN. This large outdoor specialist offers fishing guides and fly-fishing school in addition to their large line of fly-fishing gear and clothing. Owner Byron Begley is a fly-fishing expert.

GOLF *Laurel Valley Country Club* (865-448-6690; 1-800-865-4770), 702 Country Club Drive, Townsend, TN. Open daily. Weekends: nonresidents $50, residents $40; weekdays: residents $40, nonresidents $30. This country club is a modest but comfortable facility at the center of a large gated community a scant 3 miles east of Townsend. Fully open to the public, its 18-hole par-70 golf course offers sweeping views toward nearby Rich Mountain (the northern border of Great Smoky Mountains National Park), only a 0.5 mile away. Despite its stunning mountain scenery, the course is not unusually hilly or dramatically sloped. Its small clubhouse has a sports bar and restaurant (both very nice), as well as a swimming pool. Guaranteed tee times are available but not required.

HORSEBACK RIDING *Davy Crockett Riding Stables* (865-448-6411), 505 Old Cades Cove Road, Townsend, TN. You can find the Crockett Stables by following the signs for Tuckaleechee Caverns, which is nearby. Located in scenic, rural Dry Valley east of Townsend, this stable specializes in groups but welcomes walk-ins for half- to 2-hour guided rides; longer rides, including overnighters, are available by appointment.

Next To Heaven Stables (865-448-9150; 1-800-407-2231), Wears Valley Road (US 321), Townsend, TN. Open Monday through Saturday 10–5:30; closed Sunday. This stable, located 3 miles east of Townsend on US 321, offers guided and unguided rides.

Cades Cove Riding Stables (865-448-6286), 4025 East Lamar Alexander Parkway, Walland, TN. Open April through October, daily 9–5; closed

November through March. This national park concessionaire operates guided trail rides within Cades Cove, from a well-kept stable across from the picnic area. If you visit the cove early in the morning, you'll see their horses grazing the wide fields at the start of the loop road. They also offer carriage rides and hay rides inside Cades Cove.

WHITEWATER ADVENTURES
River Romp Tube Rentals (865-448-9097; 1-888-862-2633), 8203 TN 73, Townsend, TN. Located at the intersection of US 321 and TN 73 at the center of town, River Romp offers tube floats (with shuttle service) on the calm in-town section of the Little River.

✳ Lodging

COUNTRY INNS **Maple Leaf Lodge and Cabins** (865-488-6000; 1-800-369-0111). This new log inn, constructed in 2000, sits on a large tract of woods and meadows adjacent to the center of Townsend. Each of its 12 rooms is individually decorated, some with elegant antique reproductions, others with handmade log furniture with lots of character. The log cabins, with either one or two bedrooms, all have whirlpool tubs inside and hot tubs on the porch outside, along with rockers and swings, woodburning fireplaces, cable TV, and private phones. The property has 3 miles of nature trails, with views over meadows toward the Smokies. January through March: rooms $110–150, cabins $90–140; April through September: rooms $120–170, cabins $100–140; October through December: rooms $130–190; cabins $110–170. Rates include a hearty country breakfast and afternoon tea.

COUNTRY RESORTS **Blackberry Farm** (865-984-8166; 1-800-862-7610), 1471 West Millers Cove Road, Walland, TN 37886. Formerly a 1920s-era summer estate on 1,100 acres adjacent to the national park, Blackberry Farm has evolved into a luxurious 44-room mountain resort. United by an architecture that combines the American Shingle Style of the original main house with motifs from England's Cotswold District, the resort's facilities spread across a hundred landscaped acres in groupings of large houses and small cottages. The landscaped grounds give the appearance of a thoroughbred horse farm through which guest can hike, bicycle, or jog on 7 miles of hiking paths and 3 miles of paved jogging trails; there are tennis, basketball, and shuffleboard courts, a swimming pool, and bicycles available to guests. All rooms are individual and unique, decorated in a simple, elegant country English style; the selection ranges from the original rooms in the historic Main House, to newer rooms in the Guest House, to suite-sized cot-

TWILIGHT SETTLES OVER THE COVE

tages, and on up to full-sized houses with all facilities. The elegant candlelight dinners are available to guests only and are fully included in the room rates (excluding wine and beer), along with breakfast, a picnic lunch, a light tea, and ample day-long snacks. Executive Chef John Fleer's Foothills Cuisine, combines East Tennessee country flavors with gourmet techniques and presentation. Standard rooms $495–695; cottage suites $845–945. A private three-bedroom house with meeting room and kitchen runs $1,895.

BED & BREAKFASTS & **The Richmont Inn** (865-448-6751), 220 Winterberry Lane, Townsend, TN 37882. Open all year. The first thing you notice about the Richmont Inn is its remarkable architecture. Inspired by the unique local cantilevered barns (see also Cable Mill Historic Area and Visitors Center under *To See—Cades Cove Historic Sites*), this small, modern hotel has a planked-log ground floor and a much larger second and third floor, cantilevered out a good 10 feet in all directions. Located on 11 wooded ridgeline acres inside the **Laurel Valley Country Club** development (golfers receive a discount on the golf course, only a short walk away; see *To Do—Golf*), the Richmont offers a quiet and intimate experience, combining spectacular views toward Rich Mountain and the national park and lovely woodland walks. But the Richmont is really distinguished by its rooms and its food. The 12 rooms, are each individually decorated around a theme from Smoky Mountain history, and each has either a fireplace, a private balcony, or both. The trio of third-floor luxury suites are beautifully decorated in Native American themes,

each with wood-burning fireplaces, private balconies, skylights over the king beds, and spa tubs for two. The very reasonable room rates include a full gourmet breakfast and a candlelight dessert worthy of the finest restaurant. Separate antique log buildings house the **Cove Café,** an intimate dinner place specializing in fondue, and a gift shop. Smaller rooms and the disabled-access Asbury $115; larger rooms $135–165. Two luxury suites (no kitchens) are available in a separate building for $220.

CABIN RENTALS Although the Townsend, TN, area has only a few B&Bs, it has an enormous number of high-quality cabin rentals at very reasonable prices. The listings below are just a sampling of the units available, chosen to give the flavor of this area. With nightly rental rates competitive with local B&Bs and Gatlinburg, TN, motels, these cabins—all with full kitchens and separate living, dining, and bedroom areas—are the bargains of the Smokies. And, while the fellowship of a B&B is nice, there is something to be said for enjoying a mountain view from your own porch.

↑ ✐ & **Mountain Mist Cabins** (865-448-6650; 1-800-686-9288), 345 Boat Gunnel Road, Townsend, TN 37882. Open all year. When Earl Lamb retired, he returned to the farm in Tuckaleechee Cove where his father had been born and raised. He found it grown up after a half century of abandonment, a pine-forested hollow along the abandoned pioneer road. On this old family farm, Earl has created a small community of country-style cabins, each set in its own woods separate from the others. Distinctive red tin roofs sit above full-sized wraparound porches; walls are sided with rough-cut

12-inch planks. Each porch has rockers and a hot tub. Inside, doors are handmade, and on-site wood is used for decorative accents with the log country furnishings. Fireplaces are finished in local stone, with gas log insets. $100–140; ask for off-season rates.

⊤ ✄ **Blue Smoke Cabins** (865-448-3068), 1233 Carrs Creek Road, Townsend, TN 37882. Open all year. Retired fireman Ron Brady and his wife, Linda, run this collection of handsome log cabins high on top of a pine ridge 3 miles north of town. These well-furnished and roomy cabins have fine views from the rocking chairs and hot tubs on their wide porches, yet each cabin is completely isolated from its neighbors. You'll find the site's gravel roads to be mountainy verging on breathtaking, but within the abilities of the family sedan. In-season $85–95; off-season $75–85.

✄ **Bradley Mountain Retreat** (865-448-6788), 339 Bradley Retreat Road, Townsend, TN 37882. Open all year. This ridgetop site southwest of Townsend offers stunning views over the town toward Rich Mountain. These roomy log cabins, set far enough apart on this wooded site to offer good privacy, are furnished comfortably and with a lot of personality; all have porches and hot tubs. Also on site is a two-story log building with three motel-style kitchenettes, at a greatly reduced price. Cabins $85–95; motel-style kitchenettes, also on site, $40.

⊤ ✄ **Carnes' Log Cabins** (865-448-1021), 214 Tom Henry Road, P.O. Box 153, Townsend, TN 37882. Open all year. Richard and Yvonne Carnes have built a lovely little community of four hand-hewn log cabins, conveniently located in a hollow above Townsend.

The cabins form a rough circle around the end of the approach drive, scattered in a wooded, grass-floored glade that gives privacy without impeding the views. The roomy cabins, which have from one to three bedrooms, feature porches with rocking chairs, fireplaces, and whirlpool baths. Small pets are allowed, with restrictions; please call ahead well in advance. Typically from $85–150 a night, with the higher rates in summer and October.

Gilbertson's Lazy Horse Retreat (865-448-6810), 938 Schoolhouse Gap Road, Townsend, TN 37882. Open all year. Melody Gilbertson boards horses and their people from her spread in scenic Dry Valley, 4 miles southwest of Townsend. Horses board in 10 indoor box stalls in a handsome and well-kept modern barn, with a half acre of paddock surrounded by wooden fences. Their guests get stabled in four cabins: two modern log cabins, a small house, and a farmhand's cabin right by the barn. This is a great location for trail riders, with 12 horse trails within 14 miles. Three large cabins $85; smaller Cowboy Cabin $65; horses $10 per night.

⊤ ✄ **Hideaway Cottages and Log Cabins** (865-984-1700), 102 Oriole Lane, Maryville, TN 37803. Open all year. These seven cottages occupy the middle portions of highly convenient Black Mash Hollow, a scenic and wooded side valley linked to central Townsend by a short one-lane mountain road. These charming cabins range from modest and homey to elaborate and luxurious. All are comfortably and handsomely furnished with a mixture of antique and modern items, with fireplaces and porches. All guests have access to a 5-acre streamside private meadow with a pavilion and picnic area. From $85–155, with price reflecting size and luxuriousness; off-season rates available.

ℐ **Old Smoky Mountain Cabins** (865-448-2388; 1-800-739-4820), 238 Webb Road, Townsend, TN 37882. Open all year. Possibly the oldest cabin rental in Townsend, Old Smoky has a wide range of properties scattered about, including a number of roomy, well-appointed log cabins. Their centerpiece property is a small modern hotel in a quiet rural location just north of town, with three suites overlooking a pool. All their cabin rentals have free access to the pool as well. $85–125; smaller, less expensive units available.

Whisperwind Cabin Rentals (865-448-1979; 1-800-993-9928), 1177 Shuler Road, Townsend, TN 37882. Open all year. Cheryl Hobbes offers seven cabins in Dry Valley, each on a separate property but none far from her house and office. These excellently kept rentals cover quite a range, from a modest little cabin to a large luxury house; all properties offer privacy, and some are very secluded. Various cabins offer log construction, mountain views, whirlpool baths, hot tubs, wide porches, and great rooms with cathedral ceilings; Cheryl's excellent brochure, with first-rate professional photography, gives a full and accurate description of each unit. $75–135.

CABIN RESERVATION SERVICES
Laurel Valley Cabin Rentals/White Oak Realty (865-448-8040; 877-448-2040), 125 Townsend Park Drive, P.O. Box 247, Townsend, TN 37882. A reservations service with many properties in the Laurel Valley development, on or near the golf course (see Laurel Valley Country Club under *To Do— Golf*). Their Sequoyah Village collection of vacation cabins, deep within a ridgetop forest in Laurel Valley, offers roomy, modern cabins, each set deep in its own woods with whirlpool bath and wood-burning stone fireplace.

"Bear"ly Rustic Cabin Rentals (865-448-6036; 1-888-448-6036), 7807 East Lamar Alexander Parkway, Townsend, TN 37882. Open all year. A reservation service for renting second homes, they offer their selection of more than two dozen homes through a color brochure and a web site.

Dogwood Cabins (1-888-448-9054), 7016 East Lamar Alexander Parkway, Townsend, TN 37886. A reservations service managing and renting second homes.

✳ Where to Eat

EATING OUT *ℐ* **Doolittles** (423-448-0199), 7837 East Lamar Alexander Parkway, Townsend, TN. This small coffee shop in the center of town offers huge deli sandwiches on Italian flat bread, a selection of fresh-ground gourmet coffees, fresh-baked cakes and cookies, and hand-scooped ice cream (a choice of locally made Mayfield or fancy import Ben and Jerry's). It's a good place to relax and cool down a bit. Sandwiches $4.95–6.95; coffee $1.50 and up.

Applejack's Restaurant (865-448-9999), 7753 East Lamar Alexander Parkway, Townsend, TN. Open all year, 7 AM–10 PM, with shortened hours off-season. East Tennessee farm cooking and plenty of it—that's the specialty of this bright, wood-toned restaurant and buffet. Everything is fresh and made to order from scratch, familiar country recipes with just enough originality to make them memorable. Breakfast is a large buffet centered around an omelet grille; the friendly grillmaster will make you fresh eggs, omelets, or pancakes as part of your buffet. Lunch is sandwiches on homemade breads, thick country soups made fresh to original recipes, and blue plate specials. The dinner menu is more ambitious, as Applejack's chef puts his own turn on country favorites—fresh, local trout dishes; chicken ranging from breast filets fried in butter to a plate of livers; pork chops, ribs, and East Tennessee country ham with redeye gravy (as well as the inevitable steaks). Breakfast buffet, served until 2 PM, $6.95; lunch sandwiches and burgers $2.75–6.95; daily specials $6.95; pinto beans and cornbread $2.95; dinner, served after 4 PM, $8.95–13.95, with steaks up to $17.95.

Trailhead Steak House (865-448-0166), 7839 East Lamar Alexander Parkway (US 321), Townsend, TN. Open for dinner all year. Grill your own steaks on the Trailhead's large, open outdoor grille! But most people prefer to let owner Tim Byrd do the work while they relax in this western-themed restaurant, enjoying the large, flavorful salad, homemade bread, and a cold beer. Apart from four types of steak, Tim will grill up Alaskan halibut or salmon, caught wild and flown in, and local trout, chicken breasts, kabobs, or shrimp; all get a treatment of his lightly seasoned olive oil. Steaks $16.95–19.95; other entrées $10.95–15.95; sandwiches $6.95–8.95.

Smokin' Joes (865-448-3212), 8215 TN 73, Townsend, TN. Open all year for lunch and dinner; hours vary with season. Smokin' Joe is producing real barbeque the old-fashioned way; as you walk up to the modest restaurant,

the aroma of oak and hickory smoke fills the air. Founder Joe Higgins is a farm-raised South Carolinian who learned the fine art of barbeque as a boy, during his family's seasonal hog-butchering. He barbeques slowly—his ribs take 8 hours—creating a meat that's moist, smoky, flavorful, and falling apart. The ribs are spectacular, with the lightest of crust on the outside. Sides are made from scratch, and include barbequed pinto beans as well as everyone's barbeque favorites. Save room for dessert, as they make their own hot cobblers. Sandwiches $2.50–4, and add $2 for two sides; dinners $6.95–10.95, including 2 sides and bread.

✳ Entertainment

The Pickin' Porch at Nawgers Nob, Townsend, TN. Twice a week, on Tuesday and Saturday, local musicians and performers show up in front of Mike Clemmerer's dulcimer shop (see **Wood-N-Strings** under *Selective Shopping*) in the Nawgers Nob Crafts Settlement. Mike will play a bit, and introduce the other acts. Dave "Buffalo Bill" Nelson is a regular with his warm cowboy whimsy, and the local Creek Mountain Band is frequently on hand for some country and bluegrass. It's free, but don't forget your lawn chairs.

🎵 **Appalachian Music at the Community Center,** Walland, TN. Free admission. Every Friday night, year-round, local musicians come to the Walland Community Center to jam. What happens next depends on who shows up; bluegrass musicians might be playing in one room, while old-time fiddlers hold court in another.

Mountain Music Program, Cades Cove, TN. This event occurs on the third Saturday of every month, from June through October; for details, call the park office (Sugarlands Ranger Station, Gatlinburg, TN; 865-436-1291). Great Smoky Mountains National Park sponsors a monthly program of authentic Appalachian mountain music at the **Cades Cove Amphitheater,** next to the camp store. In these programs, skilled musicians perform the historic music and ballads of the Smokies, and talk about this heritage music. Traditional dance may also be performed.

✳ Selective Shopping

All listings are in Townsend, TN.

🌂 **Wood-N-Strings** (865-448-6647), 7327 East Lamar Alexander Parkway. Mike Clemmer handcrafts fine Appalachian stringed instruments, from fiddles to the strange and beautiful stringed psaltery. But his favorites are dulcimers, lovingly crafted from walnut, cherry, or butternut. Wood-N-Strings is located in the Nawgers Nob Craft Settlement in the center of Townsend, a modest-looking collection of roadside shops that house several other worthwhile crafts studios. Mike's handmade dulcimers typically range from $150–500, depending on material and decoration.

✏ ♿ 🌂 **Art of the Smokies: Lee Roberson Gallery** (865-448-2365; 1-800-423-7341), 758 Wears Valley Road. You reach the well-signposted entrance 2 miles east of Townsend on US 321. Open Sunday through Friday 10–5; closed Saturday. Blount County native Lee Roberson offers collectors' prints (and an occasional original acrylic) of an idealized Smoky Mountain landscape—"the way we all wish it could be," as his literature puts it. Lee's gallery is an attraction in itself.

It's down a narrow (but paved) mile-long private road that winds through beautiful mountain farm scenery to end at a forested hollow, with walking paths along a pretty stream. The trees shelter several log buildings, modern-built from historic logs, including the spacious gallery.

♿ 🌂 **Earthtide Gallery** (865-448-1106), 7645 Lamar Alexander Parkway. Beryl Lumpkin has assembled a truly astonishing variety of fine-crafts pieces—all from local artists. Occupying a newly built log structure in the center of town, the gallery has baskets, furniture, glass, pottery, jewelry, wooden bowls, sculpture, photographs, ranging from traditional to the most vividly imaginative. One or more of their 70 represented artists is frequently on hand for crafts demonstrations.

♿ 🌂 **Larry Burton Art Gallery** (865-448-1314), 7142 East Lamar Alexander Parkway. Prominent watercolor landscape artist Larry Burton keeps his gallery of original watercolors and art prints in a modern log building next to the popular gift shop Apple Valley Farms. Larry's watercolors are highly detailed and accurate renderings of Smoky Mountain scenes using soft,

DULCIMER MAKER MIKE CLEMMER PERFORMS AT THE PICKIN' PORCH AT NAWGER NOB CRAFT SETTLEMENT

muted colors—a contrast from other artists who feature bright colors and idealized subjects.

✳ Special Events

🖉 *Last week in April:* **Townsend in the Smokies Spring Festival and Old-Timers Day** (865-448-6134; 1-800-525-6834), 7906 East Lamar Alexander Parkway, Townsend, TN. Held 9–6. Most events are free. This week-long festival, held in a large grassy field behind the **Townsend Visitors Center,** features daily live bluegrass music, crafts demonstrations, and wildflower walks, with occasional pecial features such as mountain storytelling, antique tractors, and a barbeque competition. Events include a barbeque cook-off, the **Nawgers Nob Arts and Crafts Show** at the **Nawgers Nob Craft Village** west of town, and **Old Timers Day** in **Cades Cove.**

🖉 *Last weekend in September:* **Townsend Fall Heritage Festival and Old-Timers Day,** Townsend, TN. For those who can't make it to Townsend's Spring Heritage Festival (see above), they repeat it in the fall. That's okay—it's enough fun to be worth doing twice a year. Like its spring counterpart but shorter, the fall festival fills a weekend with bluegrass music, crafts demonstrations, bake sales, and antique tractors, as well as parallel events at **Nawgers Nob** in Townsend and at **Cades Cove.**

Last week in October: **Cades Cove Fall Harvest Hayride,** Cades Cove. The National Park Service collaborates with the **Cades Cove Riding Stables** (see *To Do—Horseback Riding*) concessionaire to offer this evening hayride around the **Cades Cove Loop Road.** The cove is at its best in the evening, and never more beautiful in the fall—but this hayride has something special. As you progress around the cove you meet people from the cove's history: a cove farmer, a Cherokee, perhaps an escaping Union soldier or a Confederate raider.

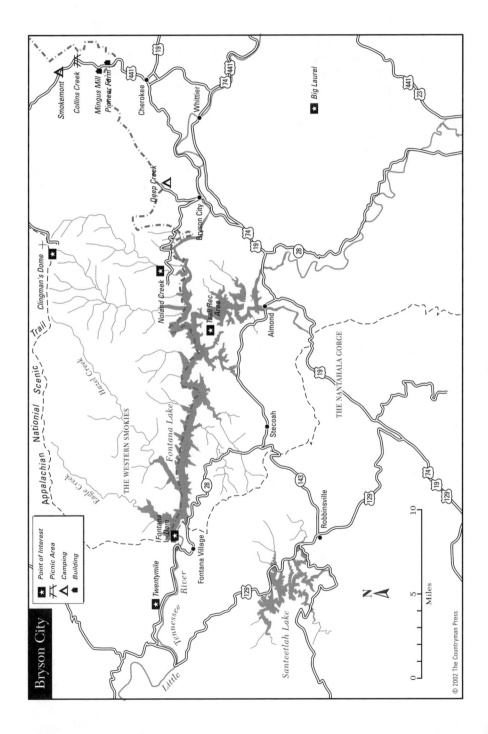

Bryson City

Point of Interest ★
Picnic Area ⛄
Camping △
Building ■

Appalachian National Scenic Trail

Clingman's Dome ★

Smokemont △
Collins Creek ⛄
Mingus Mill ■
Pioneer Farm ■
Cherokee

19
441
74
441

Whittier

Big Laurel ★

23
441

Deep Creek △

Bryson City

THE WESTERN SMOKIES

Hazel Creek

Noland Creek ★

Tsali Rec Area ★

Almond

19
28
74

Eagle Creek

Fontana Lake

Stecoah

THE NANTAHALA GORGE

Fontana Dam ★

Twentymile ★

Tennessee River

Fontana Village

Little

28

143

Robbinsville

129

129

74
19
129

Santeetlah Lake

N

0   5   10
Miles

© 2002 The Countryman Press

BRYSON CITY & THE SOUTHWEST QUADRANT

Bryson City, NC, sits at the southern edge of Great Smoky Mountains National Park, within a deep, narrow bowl surrounded by mile-high peaks. To the north looms the third-tallest peak in the eastern United States: Clingmans Dome (see *Wild Places—Recreation Areas* in "Cherokee and the Southeast Quadrant"), 6,643 feet above sea level, and 0.93 mile above Bryson City's small-town main street. To the south lie the knotted peaks of the Cowee Mountains, within Nantahala National Forest. Between these two ranges the Tuckaseegee River drains a deep, narrow valley, where fertile bottomland supplies a half-dozen produce stands. Bryson City, straddling the Tuckaseegee, is a fine old-fashioned Southern country town whose lively little downtown spreads between the former railroad depot and the old main highway.

Although (or perhaps because) the national park's tallest and steepest region abuts Bryson City, only limited areas of the park's backcountry can be reached easily by car starting from town. The Deep Creek area, down a paved local road, centers on a lovely stream noted for its waterfalls. The seldom-visited Lakeshore Drive (aka The Road To Nowhere) offers a short, scenic drive down a dead-end park road, with access to Noland Creek, a former mountain settlement cut off by the rising waters of Fontana Lake. Farther west, the waters of Fontana Lake block the park's backcountry all the way to Fontana Dam; even farther, the remote Twentymile Ranger District has worthwhile (and little visited) walks.

Thirteen miles southwest of Bryson City lies the Nantahala Gorge, a deep tree-lined canyon. US 19 runs along the floor of the gorge, allowing easy access to numerous whitewater outfitters—a popular destination on a hot summer day. There's a scenic drive for this area as well, extending well upstream from the popular areas to explore deep gorge scenery and waterfalls.

Other parts of the Bryson City area are dominated by scattered farms separated by private woodlots and the great tracts of Nantahala National Forest. Most of the national forest lands around here are used for forestry and have little recreation development. The one exception is Tsali Recreation Area on Fontana Lake, developed for off-road bicycling. In addition, a new tract of national forest land, known as Big Laurel is worth a visit, with large meadows and a stunning waterfall.

GUIDANCE **Swain County Chamber of Commerce** (828-488-3681; 1-800-867-9246), P.O. Box 509, Bryson City, NC 28713. The chamber is located at the center of downtown Bryson City, immediately adjacent to the old courthouse. You'll find it well staffed and extremely helpful. When the train is in town, they open a substation in an old red caboose within easy walking distance of the depot.

Great Smoky Mountains National Park Ranger Stations. For backcountry permits and other related questions, visit the ranger station at **Deep Creek,** in the campground (see Deep Creek Picnic Area under *Wild Places—Picnic Areas*). The nearest visitors center, with a staffed desk 7 days a week, is at **Oconaluftee,** 2 miles north of Cherokee, NC, on US 441 (see **Mountain Farm Museum** under *To See—Historic Sites* in "Cherokee and the Southeast Quadrant").

Wayah Ranger District, Nantahala National Forest (828-524-6441), 90 Sloan Road, Franklin, NC 28734. The 15,000 acres of Nantahala National Forest in the Bryson City, NC, area are run from the Wayah Ranger Station in Franklin (see **Nantahala National Forest, Wayah Ranger District,** under *Guidance* in "Franklin and the Nantahala Mountains"), 33 miles south via four-lane US 74 and US 441.

GETTING THERE *By car:* Bryson City, NC, sits at the far western end of the four-laned Smoky Mountain Expressway that links North Carolina's rugged western counties with the rest of the state. For this reason, it's almost always easiest to approach it from the east, even if it means driving out of your way. You can pick up the expressway from Asheville, NC, by following I-40 west to US 64, or from Georgia by following US 441 north into North Carolina, reaching US 74 at Dillsboro, NC.

By air: Asheville, NC, has the closest airport (see **Asheville Regional Airport** under *Getting There* in "Asheville and the Blue Ridge Parkway"). As Bryson City has no bus service from Asheville (or anywhere else), you'll have to rent a car. The 70-mile driving distance is stop-free expressway virtually the entire distance and should take about an hour and a quarter.

NINETEENTH-CENTURY BRICK BUILDINGS LINE EVERETT STREET IN DOWNTOWN BRYSON CITY.

By bus or train: Bryson City has no bus or train links to the outside world. Like most of these poor mountain counties, Swain County has no rural bus system.

MEDICAL EMERGENCIES **Swain County Hospital** (828-488-2155), 45 Plateau Street, Bryson City, NC. You'll find this hospital on an obscure residential side street, uphill from the train depot; look for the blue hospital signs on the north side of the depot. A rare survival from earlier days, this fully accredited small-town hospital has 48 beds, general surgical facilities, and a fully staffed Class II 24/7 emergency room.

✳ Wandering Around

EXPLORING BY CAR **Driving the Nantahala Gorge.** This scenic drive follows the Nantahala Gorge, a 1,600-foot-deep, heavily forested gorge carved by the **Nantahala River.** It starts 13 miles west of Bryson City, NC, on **US 19,** as that highway drops into the gorge to follow the gorge floor. The highway hugs the river closely, with many places to pull over and admire the scenery. You'll only have to wait a few minutes to see kayakers paddling furiously through the rapids, and rafters carried happily with the current. After 8 miles US 19 continues straight ahead, but the gorge swings left in an almost perfect right angle; follow the gorge left onto **Wayah Road.** Now the gorge turns rugged, its river violent and boulder-strewn beneath black rock walls—the scenery of a western gorge moved into the lush East and covered with trees. The highlight is **Camp Creek Falls,** a 200-foot jet of water pouring over the sheer rock wall of the gorge, 2.6 miles up Wayah Road. In another mile Wayah Road climbs out of the gorge without making any noticeable curve; once again, the gorge has swerved 90 degrees. Here you turn right onto **Old River Road,** a good gravel road maintained by Nantahala National Forest. You'll immediately cross **Whiteoak Creek,** with an impressive 20-foot waterfall visible on your left from the concrete bridge. Beyond, the gorge is less rugged and the river smaller. The Nantahala River passes over a beautiful small waterfall, then becomes starved for water by the Tennessee Valley Authority's **Nantahala Dam,** only a few miles upstream. In another mile the road catches up with some of that missing water—a giant penstock crosses the road, then follows it for 0.5 mile. Old River Road ends at a T-intersection with paved state secondary road **SR 1401 (Junaluska Road).** A left turn will take you 2.5 miles back to **Wayah Road;** follow it left to **US 19** in a bit less than 10 miles.

The Remote Western Smokies. The waters of giant Fontana Lake isolate much of the western Smokies from casual visitors. As a result, it has little by the way of development to intrude upon its stunning scenery. To explore this area by car, pick up **NC 28** westbound, 9 miles west of Bryson City, NC, on **US 74.** Chances are you'll find this section partly four laned and partly under construction—a regional development project surviving from Lyndon Johnson's War on Poverty in Appalachia and scheduled for completion in 2008. (If you are visiting after 2008, you may find this section named "US 74.") In 10 miles you'll pass the sleepy village of **Stecoah,** NC (see *Villages*), off on side roads to your left. Shortly beyond, NC 143 peels off to the left, a shortcut to Robbinsville, NC, and the corridor for the four-lane highway. From here, NC 28 becomes much more steep and curvy. Views will open up on your right, including a wonderful 180-degree sweep over **Fontana Lake** toward the crest of the Smokies, from a wayside picnic area.

You'll reach the turnoff to **Fontana Dam** (see *To See—Other Historic Sites*) after 22 miles. It's worth a visit for the good views and generator tours at its visitors center—but the biggest thrill is driving over the narrow dam top, high above the gorge below. Turn left at the far end (inside the national park) for a great view of the dam. Continue on NC 28 to the **Little Tennessee River;** now NC 28 hugs the river, impounded as **Cheoah Lake,** with several beautiful views. In 8 miles you'll reach the national park's remote **Twentymile** section (see A Twentymile Walk under *Wandering Around—Exploring on Foot*), then reach **US 129** in another 3 miles. Go left on US 129 for 2 miles to an old bridge over the Little Tennessee River. Here you'll get a good view of **Cheoah Dam,** a 265-foot structure built in 1919 by the ALCOA Corporation (see *To See—Big Dammed Lakes, The Tapoco Lakes* in "The Northern Unicois: Robbinsville and Tellico Plains"). This was the site of Harrison Ford's dramatic dam jump in the 1992 movie *The Fugitive.*

EXPLORING ON FOOT OR BICYCLE Deep Creek Trail. This easy path, following an old pre-park road up Deep Creek, is well known for its three beautiful waterfalls, as well as its lovely streamside scenery. The gravel-road portions are open to bicycles and make a pleasant, beautiful morning's ride; bicycles are prohibited on the footpaths. You'll find the trailhead at the end of **Deep Creek Road,** just inside the national park.

Walkers should start with the quarter-mile spur trail to **Junywhank Falls,** which leaves the northwest corner of the parking lot. Junywhank Falls is a thin trace of water that hurls itself over a 50-foot ledge, dashes under a wood log bridge, then bounces down another 30 feet of rock. Be sure to take the footpath to the log bridge for the best views, then return the way you came.

For Deep Creek Trail, walk or bike up the old roadbed 0.2 mile to view **Tom Branch Falls,** a side stream that enters Deep Creek by pouring over a 30-foot rock wall. Farther along, the track follows **Deep Creek** as it bounces over rapids and rock shelves, then climbs above it to give views up the deep V-shaped cleft. At 0.7 mile the old road forks at a bridge where **Indian Creek** pours in from the side, through a chute into a still pool that throws rippling reflections onto the overhanging rocks. Both forks are open to bicyclists. Walkers will want to take the right fork—then listen for the roar of a waterfall. A short side trail leads to the base of the third and most impressive waterfall, **Indian Creek Falls.** Here a wide wall of water pours over a 50-foot ledge into a deep, still pool with a natural pebbly beach. A short distance beyond the side trail, the main path offers a good view over the top of the falls. Return the way you came.

INDIAN CREEK FALLS IN SPRING

EXPLORING ON FOOT Noland Creek Trail. Up until 1942 Noland Creek was the site of a streamside settlement, 50 or so families in scattered farmhouses that ranged from log cabins to modern bungalows. Then the Tennessee Valley Authority (TVA) built Fontana Dam and flooded their road access. Rather than rebuild the road, the TVA condemned the Noland Creek community, evicted its residents, and donated their land to Great Smoky Mountains National Park. To visit their old community, take **Lakeshore Drive** to the trailhead at **Noland Creek Overlook.** You can go either up or down the valley—but the more interesting parts of the trail are up the valley, a 4-mile walk along an old road at a steady upward gradient of 6 percent. Although the National Park Service demolished nearly all of the structures in Noland Creek for safety reasons, signs of the settlement still remain. Boxwoods and roses grow rank around old homesites, where a set of steps or an old chimney might poke up through the trees. Because the valley was never logged, the forests are extraordinarily beautiful, a combination of old woods and young trees growing in former farmland.

At 3.7 miles, the track enters a flat-floored stretch known as **Solola Valley,** a heavily settled area named for the Cherokee word for squirrel. The remains of this settlement include the ruins of a large mill, its wheelhouse foundations emerging from the streambed. At 4 miles a side trail, the **Springhouse Branch Trail,** leads uphill to the left, passing house and field ruins to reach a large old-growth forest in 0.75 mile. At 4.2 miles an unmarked side trail leads uphill a short distance to a cemetery, still used by the families evicted from Noland Creek. Another 0.75 mile leads to a nice waterfall—a good place to turn around.

A Twentymile Walk. The western backcountry of Great Smoky Mountains National Park has numerous choices for good walks, all the more enticing for being remote and little used. Most are cut off from roads by the waters of **Fontana Dam** and require boat access. However, a collection of little-used trails radiate out from the **Twentymile Ranger Station,** on **NC 28** nine miles west of Fontana Dam (and 37 miles west of Bryson City, NC).

Like many of the trails in these parts, the **Twentymile Creek Trail** follows a pre-park road—in this case, an old narrow-gauge lumber railroad built in the 1920s and converted to a jeep track by the Civilian Conservation Corps (CCC). Closed to cars and bicycles, it makes for gentle and pleasant walking through attractive young forests, grown up since this area was logged 80 years ago. After a mile it reaches **Twentymile Cascades,** where the little **Twentymile Creek** jumps down a steep sloping rock about 40 feet high. At 3 miles the track reaches a trail intersection at **Proctor Field Gap,** where remnants of stone walls and old foundations poke up through the level forest floor.

At this point, you have climbed a thousand feet above the Twentymile Ranger Station. Should you continue on the old track (to the right), you'll gain another 1,500 feet in only 1.5 miles—a steep pull. When you finally reach the ridgeline you'll be on the **Appalachian Trail.** A third of a mile to the right (and uphill, alas) is the **Shuckstack Fire Tower,** with one of the finest panoramic views anywhere in the Smokies. To your north the entire Smoky Mountain Crest marches along the horizon, while the deep gorge of the **Little Tennessee River** cuts across the ridges that recede forever into the south.

✳ Villages

Bryson City, NC. Visitors to Bryson City will find it a handsome town of about 1,500 inhabitants, with an old-fashioned downtown stretched into a T-shape and possessing a full range of services. The **Old Swain County Courthouse** sits by the main downtown intersection and furnishes an unmissable landmark. It's guarded by a WWI doughboy instead of the traditional Confederate soldier, showing Swain County's post–Civil War origin. The town's Main Street follows US 19 east and west from the old courthouse, ending at the town's beautiful hilltop cemetery (see **Bryson City Cemetery** under *To See*).Down from the courthouse, the downtown district crosses the **Tuck-aseegee River** to reach the old railroad depot, now housing the **Great Smoky Mountain Railroad** (see *To See—Other*), with daily scenic excursions. Parking is ample and free. Apart

THE OLD SWAIN COUNTY COURTHOUSE IN BRYSON CITY

from its quaint downtown with some interesting shops, Bryson City offers some of the better lodging and dining in the mountains, with several first-rate establishments in town or nearby.

The Nantahala Gorge. Located 13 miles southwest of Bryson City, NC, along US 19, this 8-mile-long gorge has recently acquired its own community of tourist-oriented businesses, drawn by the increasing popularity of rafting and kayaking on the Nantahala River. Most of it consists of roadside businesses of recent and undistinguished architecture, separated by long stretches of beautiful national forest land. Apart from the outfitters, you'll find several places to eat and at least one good lodge (see *Lodging—Falling Waters Adventure Resorts*). Traffic can be very slow on a warm summer weekend, with lots of pedestrians, cars entering from parking lots, and old repainted busses loaded high with inflated rafts.

Almond, NC. Formerly a riverside stopping place along US 19 nine miles southwest of Bryson City, the settlement of Almond was flooded in 1942 by the rising waters of Fontana Reservoir. US 19 moved elsewhere, and the remnants of the village rose up the mountain slope until they were just above the high-water line. The NC 28 bridge over Fontana Reservoir, in the center of Almond (if Almond is big enough to have a center), gives good views over the giant Fontana Lake. Some Nantahala Gorge businesses have Almond addresses.

Stecoah, NC. This tiny village off NC 28, eighteen miles west of Bryson City, NC, is the population center of this remote corner of the Smokies. Its old stone school, now being renovated into a community center, marks the center of town. It has few services beyond gas, a café, and a couple of general stores.

Fontana, NC. Fontana Village, 31 miles west of Bryson City, NC, on NC 28, was founded in 1942 as the construction camp for **Fontana Dam** (see *To See—Other*). After the dam was completed in 1944 the construction camp became a **resort.** And so it remains—the main administrative building converted into a lodge, and the temporary workers quarters becoming a small city of modest vacation cabins. A log cabin in the center has displays on pioneer life. The surrounding countryside is very remote, with few facilities.

✳ Wild Places

THE GREAT FORESTS **The Southwest Quadrant of the Great Smoky Mountains.** The high crest of the Smokies sweeps southwest from Bryson City, NC, starting some 10 miles north of town and 4,800 feet above it. For much of this area the crest comes to a sharp, rocky point, and drops down almost clifflike—but still covered by trees more typical of New England or Canada than the South. In other places, the crest becomes wide and rolling, the scene of great open meadows. Side ridges branch off to the south, separating valleys that drop straight down to a sharp point, with scarcely enough bottomland to contain a fierce little river. Before the park was created in the 1930s, these valleys frequently contained roads that would peter out at high dead ends—some made by farmers, others by loggers. In 1944 many of these roads were cut off from the rest of the world by the waters the newly impounded Fontana Lake, running along the southern edge of the park for 24 miles. Today they are hiking trails.

Within the wild southwestern quadrant of the park, two areas are easily reached from Bryson City: **Deep Creek** (see Deep Creek Trail under *Wandering Around—Exploring on Foot or Bicycle*) and **Noland Creek** (see Noland Creek Trail under *Wandering Around—Exploring on Foot*). These valleys were once heavily settled, their upper reaches valued for hunting—effectively protecting them from the destructive large-scale logging that decimated many of the more remote valleys. Instead, these valleys had either been selectively logged, leaving a continuous cover of old hardwoods, or cleared for pasture, leaving rich, well-conserved soil that supported fast-growing, healthy forests when abandoned. Both valleys are rich in traces of their former inhabitants (although all the structures have been removed for safety reasons), and the upper slopes of Noland Creek preserve some large stands of old-growth forest.

Big Laurel. To find Big Laurel, take **US 23/74** east of Bryson City to the **Whittier** exit, then follow the signs for the **Smoky Mountain Golf Course** through Whittier and beyond; when you reach the golf course, just keep going on **Conley Creek Road,** which becomes a steep and narrow (but well-maintained) Forest Service road as it climbs up to Big Laurel. A word of caution: Visitors during the October leaf season will find the whole area taken over by bear hunters.

This newly acquired tract of national forest land centers on a high meadow-covered valley perched near the top of **Cowee Mountain,** a scenic 16-mile drive southwest of Bryson City, NC. At this time the Forest Service is protecting the meadows and keeping up the roads—and little else, leaving this little-known cove in its natural state. At the far end of the cove a jeep track heads gently downhill to your right, leading in 0.5 mile to lovely **Alarka Creek Falls,** a 30-foot set of waterfalls, framed by rhododendrons, with a Japanese garden type of beauty. (To find the waterfall, look for an unsigned side trail on your left.)

RECREATION AREAS **Tsali Recreation Area.** This large recreation area on the shores of Fontana Reservoir, devoted to off-road bicycling and horseback riding, occupies the site where the Cherokee Tsali hid with his family during the Trail of Tears—a turning point, as it happened, in the 1838 expulsion of the Cherokees from their homeland. Federal troops tracked Tsali and his people to these remote cliffs overlooking the Little Tennessee River and took them peacefully; but younger men in the group hid weapons and killed most of their captors, allowing their clan to escape. The local Qualla Cherokees—legally inhabitants of North Carolina and not part of the Cherokee Nation being expelled—saw this as simple murder and helped track down and execute the killers, taking and executing Tsali without help from federal troops. As a result of this chilling episode, the federal officer in charge of the district ruled that the Qualla could remain on their lands. Today the Qualla make up the Eastern Band of the Cherokee Nation, in Cherokee, NC (see the introduction to "Cherokee and the Southeast Quadrant").

This is the story told by the federal troop's official records. More details are available from the stories told by the Qualla and recorded by Smithsonian anthropologist James Mooney in the 1890s. Tsali's womenfolk had been attacked by federal troops, and the clan had fled to protect them. The young men were determined that no such outrage would be repeated and took murderous action to protect their family from the brutal troops. Tsali voluntarily gave himself up to his tribal leaders, knowing he would be executed, to save the remainder of the Cherokees in North Carolina.

This large recreation area features 39 miles of marked bicycle and horse paths, ranging from old roads to rough tracks. Paths lead to lake and mountain views,

BIG LAUREL FALLS ON ALARKA CREEK

wildflower meadows, and old homesites, through a predominantly pine forest. But don't expect to see the rugged gorges that sheltered Tsali's family; they are all under the waters of Fontana Reservoir. There's also a boat ramp and a small picnic area.

PICNIC AREAS **Deep Creek Picnic Area.** Small by Smoky Mountains National Park standards, this ample picnic area offers stream-cooled air under a hardwood forest. It's less than 3 miles from Bryson City, NC, by well-marked paved roads, but quiet and away from traffic. The Deep Creek walk (see **Deep Creek Trail** under *Wandering Around—Exploring on Foot or Bicycle*) starts from nearby, leading to three impressive waterfalls.

Picnicking in the Nantahala Gorge. The Nantahala Gorge's major picnic area is the **Ferebee Memorial,** 1.3 miles south of the Nantahala Outdoor Center on US 19. It centers around a memorial, carved in local marble, to Percy B. Ferebee, who donated the Nantahala Gorge to the American people. It's a very pleasant area, with a few tables scattered over a grassy, tree-shaded field; the Forest Service charges a dollar for its use, on the honor system. In addition to this major site, the North Carolina Department of Transportation operates four free roadside tables, each set a mile or so from the other, and each with a river view.

Riverfront Park in Downtown Bryson City. This fine small riverside picnic area with a pavilion is located in the center of Bryson City at the new Swain County Courthouse. The courthouse is an attractive modern structure on Mitchell Street two blocks west of downtown's Everett Street, and its picnic area is on the river. The picnic area is shaded by trees and rhododendrons and has a short, lovely riverside walk that gives you views of the backs of the downtown buildings across the river. A flock of Muscovy ducks hang along the river and will be sure to pay you a visit as soon as you start eating.

Tennessee Valley Authority (TVA) Park on Old NC 288. Old NC 288 is the gravel road along the north shore of the Little Tennessee River that was flooded by the rising waters of Fontana Reservoir in 1944. It leaves Bryson City, NC, as **Bryson Walk,** runs along the river past a large lumber drying kiln, changes its name to Old 288, then slowly drops toward the lake surface to disappear under the water. To find it, take Bryson Walk west out of town—it's the first left beyond the railroad depot, by the collection of old brick shops. The TVA has converted the last 0.5 mile of the old road into a linear picnic ground with a large boat ramp at the end. It has six tables, each set a tenth of a mile from the next. All tables are on grassy swaths with shade trees, and all have wide views over the lake toward the mountains beyond.

✳ To See

Bryson City Cemetery. Bryson City's cemetery occupies a tree-shaded hilltop at the west end of downtown. It's worth a visit for its lovely views over the town's Main Street, as well as a nice view of the Smoky Mountains. Its graves include a Thomas Wolfe angel—one of the angel statues imported from Italy by Wolfe's father and described by Wolfe in a famous passage in his novel *Look Homeward, Angel.* Another, nearly identical, angel statue sits in a cemetery in East Flat Rock, NC, but the

The Great Smoky Mountain Railroad in Bryson City

(828-586-8811; 1-800-872-4681), Dillsboro, NC. Open all year; schedule varies. $28–33 for diesel; $33–38 for steam; $5 extra for Crown Coach and $7 extra for Club Car. Rail 'n Raft excursions are $64 per adult.

As a major visitor attraction, the Great Smoky Mountain Railroad takes second place only to the national park itself. Organized to save a dead-end freight spur line from closing, its imaginative management has revamped it into a touring excursion line by day, with 53 miles of spectacular mountain sight-seeing, steam and diesel engines, and a wide variety of special events. By night, this Cinderella railroad becomes a freight line again. The railroad runs excursions from two centers, its headquarters in **Dillsboro** (see The Great Smoky Mountains Railroad under *To See—Other* in "Near the Park: Sylva & Dillsboro"), and Bryson City's historic old depot. Of the two, Bryson City has the more scenic tours, and its fine small town depot, surrounded by old brick shops (see The Depot Area under *Selective Shopping)*, is certainly charming.

The Bryson City depot hosts three basic excursions. The most common excursion crosses **Fontana Lake** on a high old iron trestle, then follows the lakeshore up into the flooded lower reaches of the **Nantahala Gorge.** It stops for lunch at **Nantahala Outdoor Center (NOC)** (see *To Do—Whitewater Adventures)*, then travels up the gorge to its end, returning the way it came. An alternative trip travels the same route but omits the lunch stop at NOC; instead, it uses the extra time to continue past the end of the gorge through spectacular mountain scenery to the small mountain town of **Andrews** (see *Villages* in "The Northern Unicois: Robbinsville and Tellico Plains"). A third variant follows the same route as the first Nantahala Gorge excursion—but its passengers disembark at the head of the gorge to raft their way back. As with the Dillsboro excursion, you'll have a choice of an open excursion car, an air-conditioned **Crown Coach**, or an adults-only **Club Car**—a beautifully restored historic lounge car; unlike the Dillsboro excursion, the Club Car has wine and beer service.

Bryson City Wolfe angel has the distinction of gazing over the Great Smoky Mountains. Nearby is the grave of writer and historian Horace Kephart, a plaque set on a large boulder.

OTHER ✄ ⟨ **Yellow Branch Cheese** (828-479-6710), Yellow Branch Farm, 136 Yellow Branch Circle, Robbinsville, NC. Open Saturday 2 PM–5 PM or by appointment; or just drop by. Free admission. This family-owned organic dairy, near

ONE OF THE MODELS FOR THOMAS WOLFE'S
NOVEL *LOOK HOMEWARD, ANGEL*

Fontana Dam off NC 28, produces farmstead cheese from their own cows. It's a pretty, little place, a ways up a valley and not far from Fontana Lake. The fat, sassy cows produce a high-quality, all-organic milk that yields a mild, buttery, full-bodied cheese. They make a jalapeño cheese from organic peppers they grow themselves. Next door is **Yellow Branch Pottery,** the studio and gallery of potter Karen Mickler, open Tuesday through Saturday 2 PM–5 PM. It's worth a visit too, and Karen sells Yellow Branch cheese. The **Mountain Hollow Bed & Breakfast** is nearby (see *Lodging— Bed and Breakfasts*).

Fontana Dam (423-988-2431), 804 US 321 North, Suite 300, Lenoir City, TN. Sitting at the base of the Smoky Mountains 22 miles west of Bryson City, NC, Fontana Dam is the tallest dam in the eastern United States, blocking the gorge of the **Little Tennessee River** with a concrete wall 480 feet high and over a half mile wide at the top. Built in a great hurry between 1942 and 1944, Fontana was an emergency wartime project, intended to insure that the Knoxville, TN, area had enough electrical power for the strategically important ALCOA aluminum plant and the top-secret **Oak Ridge Research Laboratory.** Its impoundment created the 29-mile-long **Fontana Lake,** flooding the gorge of the Little Tennessee River and forcing the abandonment of a half-dozen mountain communities.

Fontana Dam is an impressive sight, and well worth a visit. A modernist visitors center sits at its southern end, with a large observation deck giving fine views of the mammoth structure. From the center, those wanting to tour the dam take an **inclined tram** down the gorge wall to the generators at the base. A public road crosses the 2,600-foot dam top and leads to **national park trailheads** on the opposite side—a fascinating drive.

FONTANA DAM AS SEEN FROM THE FONTANA
DAM OVERLOOK

✳ To Do

BICYCLING   Euchella Mountain Bike Outfitters (828-488-8835; 1-800-446-1603), Almond, NC. $30 per day front-suspension mountain bike rental. This mountain bike outfitter offers specialized mountain bikes for riding the trails of Tsali (see **Tsali Recreation Area** under *Wild Places— Recreation Areas*), as well as guided

trips and twice-weekly (in the summer) **Youth Wilderness Sports Days** for teenagers. They headquarter from a large forested tract near the mouth of the **Nantahala Gorge,** from which they offer a variety of lodge and cabin rentals at a variety of prices.

Nantahala Outdoor Center (NOC) (828-488-2175; 1-888-662-1662), 13077 US 19 West, Bryson City, NC. $25–42 for 1-day bicycle rentals, depending on type of bike. NOC (see also *Whitewater Adventures*) offers a large range of mountain and road bicycling programs, from simple rentals to overnight trips.

FISHING Smoky Mountain Adventures (828-488-2020; 1-888-259-5106), 11460 US 19 West, Bryson City, NC. Open all year. Licensed guide Steve Claxton offers guide services for fly-fishing ($65–175), lake fishing, and backpacking, as well as fishing and backpacking equipment rentals.

GOLF Great Smoky Mountains Golf Club (1-800-474-0070), Whittier, NC. Located in Conley Creek Valley, this 18-hole par-71 course climbs up the mountainsides 500 feet above the clubhouse. Views are stunning, and the play is challenging, even though only 4 holes play uphill.

HORSEBACK RIDING Nantahala Village Riding Stables (828-488-9649), Route 1, Box 67, Bryson City, NC. Open in summer: every day 9–6:30; spring and fall: Friday through Sunday 10–5; closed in winter. $12 for 1 hour; $80 all day; $150 for a 2-day trip. This stable features guided trail rides in the **Nantahala Gorge** area, 9 miles west of Bryson City.

Appalachian Riding and Packing

(828-488-2122; 1-888-414-2122), Almond, NC. $40–50 per person for half-day guided trail rides This stable and guide service not far from **Tsali Recreation Area** (see *Wild Places— Recreation Areas*) offers a regular schedule of half-day guided trail rides on a variety of trails within **Nantahala National Forest.**

♪ **Deep Creek Stables** (828-488-8504), Great Smoky Mountains National Park. Open May through October: 9–5; June through August: every day; May and September through October: Friday through Sunday. $12 per hour. This privately run stable offers trail rides within the park, starting at the **Deep Creek Picnic Area** (see *Wild Places—Picnic Areas*).

WHITEWATER ADVENTURES Nantahala Outdoor Center (NOC) (828-488-2175; 1-888-662-1662), 13077 US 19 West, Bryson City, NC. $18–35 per person for a variety of inflatables, in both guided and unguided trips; price varies by season and day of week. This complex of a half-dozen handsome buildings straddles both the **Nantahala River** and the **Appalachian Trail** and qualifies as a tourist attraction all by itself. The employee-owned NOC offers kayaking and rafting, mountain biking, instruction at a variety of levels, three restaurants (see **Relia's Garden Restaurant** under *Dining Out*), cabin rentals, and an outdoor store.

Endless Rivers Adventures (828-488-6199; 1-800-224-7238), Bryson City, NC. $19–45 per person for a variety of inflatables, on both guided and unguided trips; price varies by season and day of week. This outfitter offers whitewater rafting on the **Nantahala** and other rivers, as well as workshops

THE NANTAHALA RIVER IS ONE OF THE MOST POPULAR VACATION DESTINATIONS IN THE REGION.

for kayaking and rock climbing, and fly-fishing guide service.

Rolling Thunder River Company (828-488-2030; 1-800-408-7238), Almond, NC. $17–32 per person, depending on type of rental, time of year, and day of the week. Rolling Thunder offers a variety of inflatable rentals as well as guided raft trips on the **Nantahala** and other rivers. They have on-site camping and a bunkhouse.

Wildwater, Ltd. Nantahala (828-488-2384; 1-800-451-9972), Almond, NC. $19–34 per person for a variety of inflatables, in both guided and unguided trips; price varies by season and day of the week. This outfitter offers a variety of guided and unguided rafting trips, as well as the popular **Raft and Rail** trip in association with the **Great Smoky Mountain Railroad** (see *To See—Other*) in Bryson City.

USA Raft (828-488-3316; 1-800-872-7238), 1104 US 19 West, Bryson City,

NC. This Rowlesburg, WV, company has a presence in the **Nantahala Gorge,** offering raft trips and inflatable rentals.

✳ Lodging

COUNTRY INNS AND HOTELS

✿ **The Fryemont Inn** (828-488-2159; 1-800-845-4879), P.O. Box 459, Bryson City, NC 28713. The main lodge and restaurant are open mid-April through Thanksgiving; suites are open all year. Built by timber baron Amos Frye in 1923, this National Register lodge sits on a hill above downtown Bryson City, with sweeping views from its wide front porch. The inn's large grounds are beautifully landscaped with native rhododendrons and hemlocks, isolated from all traffic and very quiet. The bark-clad lodge has a large, comfortable lobby filled with original craftsman-style furniture, a large wood fire on cold days and wide doors open onto the porch when it's warm. Its dining room, offering many trout specialties, is a classic early-20th-century lodge room with a fine bar (see *Dining Out*). The 37 en suite rooms in the main lodge all have wormy chestnut paneling and simple, comfortable furnishings in a country style; queen-bed rooms are small (and less expensive), while rooms with king or two double beds are quite large, with separate sitting areas. Room tariffs include a full breakfast and dinner, ordered from the menu, at the inn's dining room. A separate building, constructed in 1940 as a recreation hall, has been redone into large and comfortable "fireplace suites," each with a living room with fireplace, a separate king bedroom, and a wet bar. These suites, open all year, include breakfast and dinner during the season when the restaurant is open, with the tariff sharply discounted during the winter when the restaurant is closed and meals are not included. Children are permitted in the main lodge, but not the fireplace suites. Main lodge: $70–135, with two-bedroom units $150–186; includes breakfast and dinner. Suites $137–196, including breakfast and dinner, when the restaurant is open; otherwise, $75–150, with no meals.

Charleston Inn Bed & Breakfast (828-488-4644), 208 Arlington Avenue, Bryson City, NC 28713. Open all year. Built by a local attorney in 1927, the large and beautiful house sits on a wooded piece of property on a hillside within the town of Bryson City. Beautifully renovated in 1996, the Charleston Inn has 20 rooms—6 in the main house, and 14 in an annex built in the 1940s and converted to excellent-quality rooms. In the main house, the common rooms are elegant and comfortable; a game room opens onto a glassed porch through French doors, while a bright TV room has sofas and easy chairs. However, the main feature is the dining room where the included breakfast is served, a glassed wing with French doors on three sides, shingle walls, exposed beams, and hardwood floors. The French doors open onto an elaborate multilayer deck with mountain views over the town and a seven-person hot tub in a corner. All rooms are carefully decorated with new furniture in an elegant English country style. The main house's 6 rooms are more like bedrooms in a wealthy home, while the annex's 14 rooms are larger, with separate sitting areas and semiprivate porches. $75–165 per night.

⌖ **Historic Calhoun Country Inn** (828-488-1234), 135 Everett Street, Bryson City, NC 28713. Open all year. Innkeeper Sue Hyde was raised on her mother's stories of Bryson City's Calhoun Hotel, where she worked as a cook—the good country food and warm country welcome that the old owner, Granville Calhoun, had brought to it. Now Sue has restored this 1920s depot-area hotel to its glory days as a country hotel. Its public rooms are large, bright, and airy, with hardwood floors, oriental rugs, and comfortable plush sofas; French doors open onto an extrawide front porch, whose rockers overlook downtown Bryson City's Everett Street. The rooms are reminiscent of a fine old country hotel—small to medium in size, bright, with antiques mixed into the decor. The third-floor rooms face a large common area outfitted as a library; some have telescopes. Of the 23 rooms, 8 have shared baths; 4 on the second floor share two baths, and 4 on the third floor share one bath. A hearty country breakfast served in the sunny dining room. $65–135 per night, including breakfast.

RESORTS Hemlock Inn (828-488-2885). Galbraith Creek Road, P.O. Drawer EE, Bryson City, NC 28713. Open May through October. Built as a country inn in 1952, the Hemlock Inn sits just 3 miles from Great Smoky Mountains National Park's Deep Creek area, on its own 50 acres down a paved country lane. A low, modern structure of rustic gray wood, this AAA three-diamond rated facility has a large common area and two motel-style wings. The common area has wide views over grassy fields from its porch and deck, with comfortable country-style seating around a fireplace, and a large dining area. Breakfast and dinner are hearty country fare, authentically mountain and made fresh from scratch on the premises. Meals are served family style, with the food placed in great bowls in lazy Susans in the middle of round tables. Rooms have pine paneling and attractive country furniture but are small. $137–155, including breakfast and dinner.

BED & BREAKFASTS The Randolph House (828-488-3472), 233 Fryemont Road, P.O. Box 816, Bryson City, NC 28713. Open May through October. Amos Frye built the Randolph House in 1895 as his personal home, nearly 30 years before he built the grand **Fryemont Inn** (see *Country Inns and Hotels*) across the street. For the past quarter century it has been the seat of a fine restaurant and B&B, owned and operated by Frye's great-niece, Ruth Randolph Adams, and her husband, Bill. Downstairs is the luxurious and intimate dining area where guests take dinner as well as breakfast. Upstairs are seven cozy, romantic bedrooms, decorated with antiques—some from the original

house. $140–160 per night, including full breakfast and dinner.

Folkestone Inn Bed & Breakfast (828-488-2730; 1-888-812-3385), 101 Folkstone Road, Bryson City, NC 28713. Open all year. This beautifully restored 1920s farmhouse sits slightly off the paved Deep Creek Road, a quarter of a mile from Great Smoky Mountains National Park. It's a bit of a cross between a Victorian farmhouse and a large bungalow, set in a grove of giant spruces by a tiny stream. A wide full-front porch faces Deep Creek with comfortable chairs, with another porch on top serving the second floor. The front parlor has Victorian farm furnishings and a potbellied stove, while the rustic breakfast room is faced with tall windows on three sides. The 10 comfortable rooms feature Victorian and country reproductions, including three ground-floor rooms with stone flag floors and low tin ceilings. Summer and fall $82–108; winter and spring $75–98.

Mountain Hollow Bed & Breakfast (828-479-3608), 124 Possum Hollow Road, Robbinsville, NC 28771. This Victorian-style house, modern-built on a 35-acre tract near Fontana, NC (see *Villages*), has turrets, gables, and a wraparound rocking porch lined with gingerbread. Inside, decor is country Victorian, elegant and simple; each of the four rooms is individually theme decorated with Victorian antiques and reproductions. One room is a suite, with a separate turret sitting room and a whirlpool bath. A full breakfast is served in a turret breakfast room or on the porch. $55–125, including breakfast.

MOTEL Cold Springs Country Inn (828-488-3537; 877-500-4114), 435

Cold Springs Road, Bryson City, NC 28713. Open all year. This restored 1955 roadside motel takes you back to the early days of automobile touring. Originally known as the Sundowner Motel, this 10-room facility was built from local stone on what was then US 19, and what is now a quiet back country lane. It's a quiet, comfortable spot, with plenty of grass and shade. The comfortably sized rooms have their original paneling of locally milled tongue-in-grove wood—wormy chestnut, pine heartwood, poplar—with funky early-1950s white-tile bathrooms in fine condition. The new owners have decorated each room individually to its own theme, using all new furniture and mattresses (kings, queens, and doubles). Breakfast, included, is an ample continental buffet, served in the paneled lobby. $55–75 per night.

CABIN RENTALS Falling Waters Adventure Resort (1-800-451-9972), 10345 US 74 West, Bryson City, NC 28713. Although well known in the Pacific Northwest, luxury yurts are a new concept in the South. These are tents, round in shape, pitched on a wood platform. However, these are not ordinary tents. These tents are 16 feet in diameter, with French doors opening up onto wood decks, skylights over the queen-sized four-poster beds, and area rugs on the polished knotty pine floors. Not to mention ceiling fans, refrigerators, and coffeemakers. This is definitely the luxury end of tent camping. $72 for a luxury yurt.

Hidden Creek Cabin Rentals (1-888-333-5881), P.O. Box 973, Bryson City, NC 28713. These four cabins overlook Hidden Creek on 23 private acres just outside the Lakeshore Drive entrance to Great Smoky Mountains National Park. Two of the cabins are traditional second homes; one is a modern log cabin; and one is a 1930s farmhouse. All four are on a stocked trout stream, and each has its own seven-person hot tub on an outdoor deck. The wooded property includes an 1850 log cabin. Although the cabins have a great atmosphere of quiet and remoteness, they are actually quite convenient to Bryson City and the four-laned US 23/74, for ready access throughout the region. $100 per night; $650 per week.

CABIN RESERVATION SERVICES Yellow Rose Realty (828-488-2797), 150 Bryson Walk, P.O. Box 326, Bryson City, NC. This local realtor

FALL COLORS REFLECTED ON THE NANTAHALA RIVER AS IT PASSES THROUGH THE GORGE

manages 50 or so vacation properties throughout the Bryson City and Cherokee, NC, area.

✳ Where to Eat

EATING OUT **Everett Street Diner** (828-488-0123), 52 Everett Street, Bryson City, NC. Open Tuesday through Sunday 7 AM–3 PM. This busy café may occupy a brick storefront in downtown Bryson City, but it's no grits-and-grease small-town eatery; this diner offers an upscale menu filled with fresh foods and intelligent recipes. Inside you'll find indirect lighting, bamboo chairs, dark green carpets, and light gray walls hung with original art. A house salad is based on mixed greens (with nary a piece of iceberg lettuce in sight), its bitter peppery flavor balanced by the sweetness of the homemade raspberry vinaigrette. The chili, made fresh, is vegetarian, filled with black beans and chunks of tomatoes. Other menu items have the same twist—old favorites given a goose with fresh ingredients and imaginative combinations of flavors. Despite this decidedly big-city sophistication, you'll find the prices remain downtown Bryson City, tightly grouped between $5 and $7 dollars. Breakfast $3.65–4.95; lunch $5.25–6.95.

DINING OUT 🍷 ⚅ **The Fryemont Inn** (828-488-2159; 1-800-845-4879). Breakfast 8–10; dinner: Sunday through Thursday, 6–8; Friday and Saturday 6–9. The bar opens at 5 PM. Closed in winter. The historic Fryemont Inn (see *Lodging—Country Inns and Hotels*), on a hill overlooking Bryson City and the Great Smoky Mountains from its wide porch, opens its dining room to the public for breakfast and dinner from mid-April

through late November. This large room is well in keeping with a 1923 mountain lodge, with its wood rafters, polished hardwood floors, giant stone fireplace (with a wood fire cackling merrily away in chilly weather), and wormy chestnut paneling. Its full-service bar is comfortable and quiet, with lots of old wood and two pool tables. Chef and coowner George Brown Jr. has developed a thoughtful menu of trout (served four different ways), ham (sugar or salt cured), lamb, and beef, always cooked fresh and served with family-style side dishes. Breakfasts emphasize simple country foods, well prepared: eggs, omelets, French toast, and pancakes. Breakfast $5–6.25; dinner $12–19.

Relia's Garden Restaurant (828-488-2175), Nantahala Outdoor Center, 13077 US 19 West, Bryson City, NC. Open Sunday through Thursday noon–9; Friday and Saturday noon–10; closed in winter. Terraced herb gardens, curved and stepped like an amphitheater, flank the entrance walk to the fanciest of the **Nantahala Outdoor Center**'s (see *To Do—Whitewater Adventures and Bicycling*) three restaurants. The handsome modern building, clad in unpainted board and batten, also steps up in multiple levels, with wide porches and high pitched roofs. Entrées emphasize fresh ingredients and careful use of herbs, frequently from the garden outside. Sandwiches and salads $5.25–8.95; entrées $8.95–15.95.

Nantahala Village Mountain Resort and Meeting Center (828-488-2628; 1-800-438-1507), 9400 US 19 West, Bryson City, NC. This 200-acre resort and conference center, a local tradition since 1948, sports an excellent restaurant in its new lodge. The large dining room features a cathedral ceiling and plenty of wood trim; large windows offer a wide sunset view deep into the Nantahala Gorge, then over the mountains. Dinner entrées run from the simple (fried chicken, ribeye steak) to the imaginative (spinach mushroom strudel). Expect the simplest entrées to be fresh and well prepared; they include local trout, butterflied and sautéed in butter and herbs, and served with capered butter. Dinner entrées $8–17.

✳ Selective Shopping

Downtown Bryson City, NC. You don't really expect a small-town main street to be a center for high-fashion shopping; yet it can have its charms. Bryson City furnishes interesting storefronts in an ell-shaped district radiating from the old courthouse. Foremost among these is **Clampett's Hardware,** which maintains a separate store for farm-related products that may well have the single most compelling collection of country items in the Smokies. Next door, watercolor artist Elizabeth Ellison maintains her studio and gallery from a small storefront. A bit farther down, The **Charleston Station** offers antiques and gifts from an attractive brick bungalow. And don't forget to stop for lunch at the **Everett Street Diner** (see *Eating Out*).

The Depot Area, Bryson City, NC. Bryson City's classic small-town depot, on the north edge of downtown, is once again lively with passenger traffic—this time on the **Great Smoky Mountain Railroad** (see *To See— Other*). And just like in the old days, the depot area is coming alive with small shops. A quilt shop and discount bookshop occupy the old car dealership on one side, while the brick buildings across the street hold a variety of shops, including one specializing in mountain fiddles. Sideways across the street are more old brick storefronts with antiques and collectibles, with one shop specializing in what can only be called redneck humor (example: a skimpy bikini emblazoned with a Confederate battle flag).

✳ Special Events

Late April: **Dogwood Train Ride** (1-800-872-4681), Dillsboro, NC. Special train excursions are always extra fun (see **The Great Smoky Mountain Railroad** under *To See—Other*), and this one has the added attraction of benefiting the local Rotarians' scholarship fund. The 4-hour train ride into the **Nantahala Gorge** includes a barbeque lunch and plenty of spring color.

Memorial Day: **Heritage Day Festival** (828-488-3681; 1-800-867-9246), Bryson City, NC. This annual celebration of mountain heritage features traditional food, music, and crafts, as well as a toy duck race on the Tuckaseegee River.

First week in July: **Singing in the Smokies** (828-497-2060), P.O. Drawer JJ, Bryson City, NC. The festival is held at **Inspiration Park;** follow the signs from the Ela, NC, exit off US 23/74 east of Bryson City. Evening sings $12; all-day sings $15. This weeklong gospel music festival, sponsored by the successful Bryson City male gospel group, **The Inspirations,** features a large number of gospel groups over a week-long festival centered on the Fourth of July. Seating is on the grass, with a large covered area when it rains. You're welcome to bring a lawn chair and a picnic meal, although both are available on site from concessionaires. A shorter version of the festival is held on Labor Day weekend and in the middle of October.

Fourth of July: **Freedom Fest on the River** (828-488-3681; 1-800-867-9246), Bryson City, NC. Bryson City's town celebration takes place in its attractive Riverfront Park (see **Riverfront Park** in Downtown Bryson City under *Wild Places—Picnic Areas*), with live entertainment, food, crafts, and fireworks.

Late July: **Folkmoot USA** (828-488-3681; 1-800-867-9246), Bryson City, NC. Bryson City hosts three groups of international folk singers and dancers in their native costumes, as part of this major mountain-wide folk celebration.

Labor Day: **Fireman's Day Festival** (828-488-9410), Bryson City, NC. Apart from the music, entertainment, crafts, and barbeque dinner, this fundraiser for the local volunteer fire department features a **Parade of Fire Trucks** and a **Miss Flame** competition.

November–December: **Nantahala Village Fall Dinner Concert Series** (828-488-2826; 1-800-438-1507). $35 per person, including dinner. After the tourist season winds down and night starts falling early in the evening, the excellent restaurant at **Nantahala Village** schedules a series of dinner concerts, where musicians from the **Asheville Symphony** perform their choice of acoustic music. Typical music might include a guitar duo, a jazz trio, or a quintet playing Celtic and mountain instruments. The full dinner, included in the charge, has a choice of three entrées (one of which is a steak or prime rib, with the other two being more adventuresome chicken, fish, or vegetarian fare).

First Saturday in December: **Bryson City Merchants Christmas Parade and Festival** (828-488-3681; 1-800-867-9246), Bryson City, NC. Sponsored by the merchants of Bryson City, this Christmas celebration features a parade with floats, bands, horses, and clowns; a breakfast with Santa; an auction; special discounts for shoppers; and a local theater presentation. A week later, the Rotarians sponsor **A Visit from Inn to Inn,** visiting five historic inns decorated for Christmas, with plenty of Christmas music and hors d'oeuvre. Single ticket $15; per couple $25.

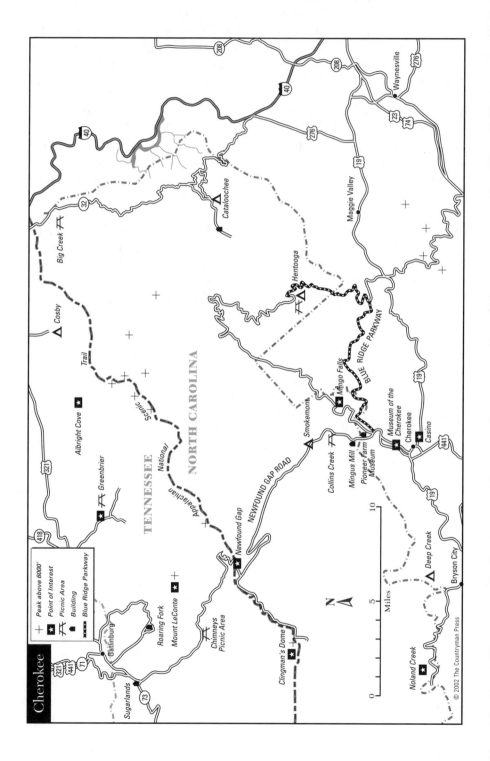

CHEROKEE & THE SOUTHEAST QUADRANT

This chapter covers the southeast quadrant of Great Smoky Mountains National Park and the adjacent lands of the Qualla Cherokees. It includes the rugged and remote ridges that run down from the Smokies Crest into the North Carolina half of the national park; the large Cherokee Reservation, properly known as the Qualla Boundary, on the park's southern edge; the populous tourist area now called Maggie Valley; and the remote mountain coves of Cataloochee and Little Cataloochee, once heavily settled and now preserving mountain heritage deep within the national park.

This corner of the Smokies was settled by traditionalist Cherokees in 1819, led by the respected Chief Yonaguska. Known as the Qualla, they wished to avoid both the white settlers and the Europeanized leaders of the Cherokee Nation; they built their riverside villages along the Oconaluftee River deep in the Smoky Mountains, on land uncoveted by whites and outside the Cherokee Nation. In 1838, President Andrew Jackson supported the State of Georgia in its efforts to expel the Cherokee Nation, seize its land for white people, and send the Cherokees west to the "Indian Territory" (now Oklahoma). The result was the genocidal Trail of Tears, where Federal soldiers forced Cherokee families from their houses at gunpoint into holding compounds, then on a long and brutal trudge in the dead of winter. However, the Qualla were not part of the Cherokee Nation, and legally not subjected to the expulsion; after much debate, federal authorities allowed the Qualla to stay (see Tsali Recreation Area under *Wild Places* in "Bryson City and the Southwest Quadrant"). Today, the Qualla are the Eastern Band of the Cherokee Nation, their tribal headquarters of Cherokee, NC, located on the border of the national park.

Great Smoky Mountains National Park wraps around the north side of the Qualla Boundary. Despite a mile-high landscape of knotted ridgelines separated by deep valleys, this quadrant offers some amazing opportunities to explore by car. The Newfound Gap Road, built in 1932 to bring tourists into the newly formed national park, runs through the center of Cherokee then up the Oconaluftee River to reach a high ridge, some of the best views in the park. From the top of the Newfound Gap Road, a side road leads along the crest of the Smokies to Clingmans Dome, the highest point in the park. From the bottom, the Blue Ridge Parkway wraps along the park's southern border, for wonderful views of the Smokies Crest and the receding ridges of the North Carolina Blue Ridge—then generates a scenic spur road that dives deep into the park's back country. East of the Qualla Boundary, the national park preserves the remote and beautiful Cataloochee Cove, with its twisting gravel roads, wide meadows, and historic farmhouses.

GUIDANCE **Cherokee Visitors Center (Cherokee Tribal Travel and Promotion)** (828-497-9195; 1-800-438-1601), P.O. Box 460, Cherokee, NC 28719. The visitors center offers information and brochures from a small stand-alone building in the center of Cherokee, by the Pizza Inn.

GETTING THERE *By car:* Cherokee, NC, is located at the main south gate of Great Smoky Mountains National Park, at the intersection of US 441 and US 19. As US 19 is a narrow, winding two-lane road between Maggie Valley, NC, and Cherokee, it's nearly always faster to use the nearby freeway, US 74 to US 441, a few miles south of town. If your destination is Maggie Valley rather than Cherokee, approach it via US 276, either from I-40 or from US 74 in Waynesville, NC.

By air: The closest airport is in Asheville, NC (see **Asheville Regional Airport** under *Getting There* in "Asheville and the Blue Ridge Parkway"). You'll need a rental car, as there is no bus service to Cherokee, NC. The 66-mile trip is on a four-lane highway all the way, and should take about an hour and a quarter. From the airport, take I-26 north to I-40; then I-40 west to US 23/74; then US 23/74 west to US 441; then US 441 north to Cherokee.

By bus or public transportation: Cherokee, NC, has no bus service, and no public transportation. **Greyhound Bus Lines** has daily bus service into Waynesville, NC, 9 miles from Maggie Valley, NC; however, no public transportation links Maggie Valley with the bus terminal.

MEDICAL EMERGENCIES **Cherokee Urgent Care Clinic and Pharmacy** (828-497-9036), El Camino Plaza, US 9 North, , Cherokee, NC. Open weekdays 9:30–4:30. This walk-in clinic welcomes travelers with non–life threatening illnesses or injuries. It's located by Harrahs Cherokee Casino and must be accessed either through the Harrahs parking lot or the parking lot of the El Camino Motel.

Serious Emergencies. From Cherokee, NC, the closest 24/7 emergency room is in the small local hospital **Swain County Hospital** (828-488-2155), at Bryson City, NC, 11 miles away (see *Medical Emergencies* in "Bryson City and the Southwest Quadrant"); the nearest full-service hospital is **Harris Regional Hospital** (828-586-7000) in Sylva, 18 miles away (see *Medical Emergencies* in "Near the Park: Sylva and Dillsboro"). Maggie Valley, NC, is about 10 miles from **Haywood Regional Medical Facility** (828-456-7311), a major regional hospital (see *Medical Emergencies* in "Waynesville and the Blue Ridge Parkway").

❋ Wandering Around

EXPLORING BY CAR **The Blue Ridge Parkway and the Heintooga Spur Road.** The Blue Ridge Parkway's final 13-mile section runs from Soco Gap on US

From **Soco Gap,** the parkway climbs uphill through forests for the next 3 miles (a particularly fine stretch for spring wildflowers), reaching the Heintooga Spur Road (described later) at **Wolf Laurel Gap.** From here the parkway picks its way down a side ridge, dropping 3,200 feet to reach the **Oconaluftee River.** Although heavily forested, the terrain is rough enough to require five tunnels, and the parkway gets its share of views. The best views are found on a 2-mile stretch between **Big Witch Gap Overlook** and **Noland Divide Overlook,** where the wall-like Great Smoky Mountains are framed in June by a stunning rhododendron display. There are more good views near the end, where the **Oconaluftee River Overlook** gives an aerial of the **Mountain Farm Museum** (see *To See—Historic Sites*). The parkway ends at an intersection with **US 441** just outside **Cherokee,** NC, and just inside Great Smoky Mountains National Park.

The parkway's Heintooga Spur Road (mentioned above) is a journey in its own right, looping 27 miles through the parks' Balsam Mountain backcountry to end deep in the Qualla Boundary. The first of the spur's three major views arrives quickly, at Mile High Overlook—as its name implies, a 5,280-foot overlook with a 180-degree view toward the Smoky Mountain Crest. At 3.6 miles the road reaches Black Camp Gap and enters the national park; the pyramidal Masonic Monument sits a short distance off the road. From here the road is a pretty forest drive that climbs gently to Balsam Mountain Picnic and Camping Area on a high ridgetop (see *Wild Places—Recreation Areas*). Shaded by a handsome old spruce forest, this high, windy spot has the second of the road's three views, known as Heintooga Overlook, at the far end of the picnic area—a fine sunset location. From the picnic area, the road becomes a one-lane, one-way gravel road, so narrow as to be a car path through the great overhanging trees. The third and last view comes 2 miles into this segment, a 90-degree view southward over deep canyonlike valleys. Six miles later the road drops away from the high ridgeline into the stream valleys below. The road bottoms out at Round Bottom Horse Camp and becomes two-way again as it follows a lovely little stream to enter the Qualla Boundary. In 3.5 more miles it reaches Big Cove Road, its first real intersection since it left the Blue Ridge Parkway. A left turn will bring you to Cherokee in 11 miles.

CYCLING ALONG CATALOOCHEE COVE ROAD

Cataloochee Cove Drive. Once the most heavily settled corner of the Smokies, Cataloochee is now the most remote part of Great Smoky National Park accessible by car. To reach it you must drive over miles of narrow, winding gravel road, through deep forest. Once there you'll find yourself in a wide valley, floored with broad meadows, dotted by historic buildings, and surrounded by mountains.

Start your drive to Cataloochee at the intersection of **US 276** and **I-40** (exit 20), 6 miles north of US 19 near Mag-

EXPLORING BY CAR: THE HEART OF THE SMOKIES

On the North Carolina side of the park, the Newfound Gap Road climbs through the heart of the Smokies to reach a mile-high gap in the center of the range. In doing so, it wanders past a pioneer log farmstead and a wooden water mill, follows a torrential mountain river, then climbs to stunning views of the endlessly receding ridges between the Blue Ridge and Smoky Mountains. Once at the top, an old spur road (unchanged in appearance from the 1930s) follows the crest of the Smokies to the park's highest peak, Clingmans Dome.

The Newfound Gap Road in North Carolina. This park road starts where US 441 ends, at the north edge of Cherokee, NC. It's good to get an early start, both to avoid the crowds and to catch a sunrise. For a sunrise go straight up to the top, then backtrack to the first overlook on the North Carolina side, where the sun rises over a deep mountain cleft. After the sun is up, you'll want to go to **Newfound Gap** (see *Wild Places—Recreation Areas*) to enjoy the way that the early-morning sun lights up the road as it dives into the deep valleys of North Carolina. From there the **Clingmans Dome Scenic Drive** (see below and *Wild Places—Recreation Areas*) has more sunrise views.

While the Newfound Gap Road continues northward to descend into Tennessee and Gatlinburg (see The Newfound Gap Road in Tennessee under *Wandering Around—Exploring by Car* in "Gatlinburg and the Northeast Quadrant"), this drive goes down the North Carolina side, south toward **Cherokee**, NC. The road drops down from Newfound Gap onto the crest of **Thomas Divide.** For the next 3 miles the road twists along the narrow ridgeline, giving panoramic views. On many mornings, the early light reflects off great sheets of fog that blanket the valleys thousands of feet below, with the ridgelines poking through like archipelagos. The road finally plunges down the side of Thomas Divide to give one final view and back up toward Newfound Gap. A quiet walkway on the left follows the original 1932 roadbed, abandoned in the 1960s; it looks like a footpath along a grassy terrace, with bits of asphalt occasionally showing through. After that, the road loops down into the valley for a long, easy streamside drive, reaching the **Oconaluftee River** at the **Kephart Prong Trail** (see *Wandering Around—Exploring on Foot*). From here the road hugs the river closely, sometimes looming over it from a high granite wall, sometimes swerving away from it through grassy meadows. Along this segment you'll pass **Collins Creek Picnic Area** (see *Wild Places—Picnic Areas*) at 10.6 miles and **Smokemont** (see *Wild Places—Recreation Areas*) at

AN AUTUMN VIEW SOUTHWEST OVER DEEP CREEK VALLEY

12.5 miles. Beyond are two first-rate historical sites: **Mingus Mill** (see *To See—Historic Sites*), a restored turbine water mill, and the Oconaluftee **Mountain Farm Museum** (see *To See—Historic Sites*), a reconstructed mountain farm complete with crops, gardens, and farm animals. At the end of this drive, the Newfound Gap Road loops around broad meadows with wide views toward the log farm museum and the mountains beyond. On the far side of the meadow, the **Blue Ridge Parkway** makes its southern terminus. Just beyond is the park boundary and the town of **Cherokee.**

Clingmans Dome Scenic Drive. This 7-mile spur road follows the crest of the Smokies westward from Newfound Gap to its dead-end at Clingmans Dome. It's the easiest way to enjoy the unusual Canadian-style spruce-fir forest found only at the highest elevations, as this high-altitude road stays inside the forest for most of its length. This forest (known locally as "balsams") is an isolated remnant of a great subarctic forest that blanketed the Southeast at the peak of the last ice age—preserved here by the cold conditions at the top of the Smokies.

More than any other park road, the **Clingmans Dome Spur Road** has the look and feel of a 1930s Works Projects Administration (WPA) scenic drive. It's narrow and twisting, shaded by the balsam forest crowding its edge, with trimmed rock walls on the downhill side. Its cuts are too modest to provide the wide views of a more modern highway, and its shoulders are frequently too narrow for pulling off to park. The first view (0.4 mile from the beginning) is one of the best, a 5,200-foot-high bird's-eye straight down **Beech Flats** gie Valley, NC. Near the intersection you'll find a side road, **Sutton Town Road (SSR 1331)** heading west. Take it; then take the right fork in 1.5 miles onto **Cove Creek Road (SR 1305).** This switchbacks steeply uphill, then over a mountain and into the national park (becoming a gravel road along the way). When you reach the bottom you'll find an intersection with a paved road, part of a long-abandoned project to turn Cataloochee into a major tourist attraction; turn left. The paved road winds through young forests, past a small campground, to an intersection with a gravel road in wide meadows. Here stands the 1905 **Will Messer Barn,** beside a small ranger station with an information desk. Continue along the

Prong to the **Oconaluftee Valley,** with the Newfound Gap Road curving away below. Your next landmarks are an **Appalachian Trail (AT)** access point (at 1.2 miles) and an **interpretive nature trail** about the spruce-fir forest (at 2.5 miles). However, you can combine both interests at the next trailhead (3.5 miles), where a short access trail leads to the AT, then 0.5 mile left and uphill through a fir forest devastated by insects (the wooly adelgid, an illegal immigrant from Europe), to views and wild berries on the peak of **Mount Collins** (6,188 feet). Then, at 5.3 miles, **Webb Overlook** gives another fine view eastward. However, save some film for the **final overlook** at the road's end, with wonderful panoramic views east, south, and west over endless mountain ranges—another good place for a sunrise. At the end of the overlook is the paved path that leads to the summit of **Clingmans Dome** (see *Wild Places— Recreation Areas)* as well as a great AT walk (see **A High Ridge Walk on the Appalachian Trail,** below). The walk to the wildflower-framed views from **Andrews Bald** starts here as well (see **Andrews Bald Walk,** below).

EXPLORING BY FOOT

A High Ridge Walk on the Appalachian Trail. This 3-mile walk follows the Smoky Mountain Crest westward from Clingmans Dome, staying above 6,000 feet with stunning views into both Tennessee and North Carolina. Starting at the **Clingmans Dome Overlook** parking lot (see *Wild Places—Recreation Areas*), go a short distance down the **Forney Ridge Trail** to the **Clingmans Dome Bypass Trail.** This little-used cutoff will save you some climbing, while leading past some good meadow views into North Carolina. After 0.3 mile you gain the **Appalachian Trail (AT)** on the high, sharp ridge of the Smokies Crest. From here are first-rate views into Tennessee, toward **Elkmont** (see Elkmont National Historic District under *To See—Historic Sites* in "Townsend, Cades Cove, and the Northwest Quadrant") and over the side ridges that fall steeply paved road to the left, passing through meadows to the lovely little 1898 **Palmer Methodist Chapel,** still occasionally used. Nearby is the 1901 **Beech Grove School,** a one-room schoolhouse authentically furnished. After that the road turns gravel, continuing through meadows with wide, pastoral views. The road passes between a large barn and a 1906 Victorian-style farmhouse, the **Caldwell House.** Beyond, the auto road ends at a gate, but the old farm road continues to the **Woody House,** an 1866 log cabin with a 1910 addition. Return to the Will Messer Barn and ranger station, then turn left onto the gravel road. In a short distance (through more meadows) you'll reach the attractive **Palmer House;** Uncle Fate

downward to the **Foothills.** Turn left onto the AT. You'll be hiking along a razorback spine of a ridge, with grass growing between exposed rocks and long views over both North Carolina and Tennessee. The trail remains more or less level to **Mount Buckley,** then starts a moderate but inexorable drop, losing a thousand feet in the next 2.5 miles. The trail remains scenic, passing through grassy areas and forests—but don't forget that going up this slope is going to be a lot more difficult than going down. When you decide to turn around, stay on the AT until it reaches the **Clingmans Dome Observation Tower,** to pick up a few good views you missed on the way out.

Andrews Bald Walk. Although Andrews Bald is a short (3 miles) hike, it's no level stroll. Starting from the high ridge at **Clingmans Dome,** it drops 600 feet in 0.9 mile, then rises 150 feet before the final 175-foot drop to the large ridgeline meadow. It offers wide views over North Carolina and **Fontana Lake,** framed by rhododendrons and azaleas in June. Not surprisingly, it's a popular walk, so expect a fair amount of company along the way.

The high grassy balds of the Smokies remain one of the most important features of the park, playing a major part in the park's environmental diversity. They are also one of the most beautiful features—wide, ridgetop meadows scattered with brushy azaleas, rhododendrons, and laurels, and a riot of wildflowers all spring and early summer. Ironically, these balds are disappearing as a result of the National Park Service's conservation efforts. It seems the balds were brought into their present form by settlers using them for summer cattle pastures—and they return to forest after grazing stops. Since the National Park Service eliminated grazing more than 70 years ago, all the balds have shrunk and some have disappeared altogether. Today the rangers maintain just two of the many balds, and those at a fraction of their former size: remote **Gregory Bald,** and Andrews Bald.

Palmer built this dogtrot log cabin in 1860, and his descendants added the hand-planed interior paneling (1905), brightly painted weatherboarding (in 1910), and kitchen wing (in 1924). Just beyond, the gravel road enters the woods, then reaches a T-intersection. The right fork goes back to Cove Creek Road and Maggie Valley. The left fork leads a few miles to an old road (now a trail) up to the **Little Cataloochee Community.** This 5-mile walk leads to three more historic sites: the 1864 log **Hannah Cabin** with its handmade brick chimney; the hilltop **Little Cataloochee Baptist Church,** topped by a handsome belfry and steeple; and the scant remains of the **Cook Place** and **Messer Farm** at the top of the road. Back at your car, continue on the gravel road, leaving the park in 3 miles to pass through 9 miles of meadows and farmlands. When you reach the road to the **Big Creek** area of the national park (see Big Creek Picnic Area under *Wild Places—Recreation Areas* in "Gatlinburg and the Northeast Quadrant") turn right into **Waterville**, NC, reaching **I-40** in 2 miles.

EXPLORING ON FOOT **Kephart Prong Trail.** Kephart Prong is a lively mountain stream named after Horace Kephart from nearby Bryson City, NC; the town's librarian, "Kep" was a prominent national park activist and an outdoor writer who authored *Our Southern Highlanders* in 1913. This easy walk on the North Carolina side of the Newfound Gap Road follows an old road for 2 miles along a lovely mountain stream to a small trail shelter. It is particularly interesting for the remains of a Civilian Conservation Corp (CCC) camp hidden in the woods along the trail. The well-signposted trailhead parking lot is 33/4 miles north of **Smokemont** (see *Wild Places—Recreation Areas*), on the right.

✳ Villages

Cherokee, NC. The main administrative center of the Qualla Boundary since the 19th century, Cherokee sits astride US 19 and US 441, hard against the southern boundary of Great Smoky Mountains National Park. It's much smaller and more modest than Gatlinburg, TN, and it's parking and traffic isn't quite so bad. Much of its modest appearance is due to rules within the Qualla Boundary that restrict land possession to tribal members; this has discouraged outside business investment and kept Cherokee in sort of a 1950s time warp.

Here's the layout. US 441 goes north and south, while US 19 goes east and west. Cherokee sits at their intersection, with modest businesses stringing outward along these highways. The most densely developed area, called Downtown Cherokee on road signs, straddles US 19 just east of US 441. Compared to Tennessee's tourist towns, Downtown Cherokee is startlingly retro, with a look and feel that's changed surprisingly little since the early days of park tourism. Old-fashioned open-front souvenir stands, bursting with an astonishing variety of trinkets, still dominate "Downtown." Shops trundle out stuffed bears on wheeled platforms. Giant sheet metal teepees sit on flat 1950s roofs, and totem poles hold up porches. "Roadside chiefs" dress up like Great Plains Indians and sit in front of fake teepees. The real center of Cherokee gathers around its government complex on US 441, about a mile north of "Downtown." The buildings here show standard government styles from the 1930s through the 1990s, with two new parks (see **Oconaluftee Islands Tribal Park and Veterans Tribal Park** under *Wild*

Indian under *To See—Cultural Sites*), and the Eastern Band's crafts cooperative (see **The Qualla Arts and Crafts Mutual** under *To See—Cultural Sites*), as well as the Cherokee Historical Association's outdoor drama (see **Oconaluftee Indian Village** under *To See—Cultural Sites*) and 18th-century Cherokee village (see **Unto These Hills** under *Entertainment*).

Big Cove, NC. One of the five original towns of the Qualla Boundary, today's Big Cove is a large, scenic mountain valley following the gorgelike Raven Fork. To a visitor, it's most significant as the site with the majority of commercial campgrounds, some good cabin rentals, and the spectacular **Mingo Falls** (see Mingo Falls Tribal Park under *To See—Gardens and Parks*).

Maggie Valley, NC. This tourist-strip town formed in the formerly beautiful Jonathan Creek Valley in the 1950s, when a new highway was built eastward from the Qualla Boundary and designated US 19. Sprawling suburban-style development slowly grew up along the new highway; now, 50 years later, the development is nearly continuous. Maggie Valley is not a convenient place to stay when visiting Great Smoky Mountains National Park, as it has no park entrance, and the Cherokee, NC, entrance is 20 miles away by a narrow, winding, steep two-lane road. However, the Blue Ridge Parkway is nearby, as is the **Heintooga Spur Road** (see The Blue Ridge Parkway and the Heintooga Spur Road under *Wandering Around—Exploring by Car*) and the **Cataloochee Cove Drive** (see *Wandering Around—Exploring by Car*).

✳ Wild Places

THE GREAT FORESTS **The Forests of the Oconaluftee Valley.** The Newfound Gap Road from Cherokee, NC, to Gatlinburg, TN, gives access to the large drainage basin of the Oconaluftee River. While this was the home of the Qualla Cherokees since 1819, the Qualla preferred the better lands toward the bottom of the drainage and left the upper slopes as hunting grounds. The tribe did not bother to purchase much of this land when they constructed the Qualla Boundary in the mid–19th century, allowing Champion Paper of Waynesville, NC, to acquire it in the 1890s.

As with their Waynesville tracts (see **The Middle Prong Wilderness** under *Wild Places—The Great Forests* in "Waynesville and the Blue Ridge Parkway"), Champion's doubtful stewardship led to large-scale ecological catastrophe. Fires and floods swept over their badly managed clear-cuts so viciously as to destroy large forests, creating meadows and even rocky cliffs that exist today. Paradoxically, the largest of these sites is now a renowned beauty spot, **Charlie's Bunion,** 4.5 miles west of Newfound Gap on the **Appalachian Trail**—an excellent, if long and tiring, day hike. Champion prized these high upper slopes for their giant spruce and fir trees, which yielded superior paper pulp. However, they logged the lower slopes with similarly enthusiastic abandon, removing every tree they could sell. They stopped logging the Oconaluftee Drainage in 1929 as a result of the Great Depression. The forests you see have been recovering since that date.

At the northeast edge of this forest, Great Balsam Mountains split off from the Great Smoky Mountains to run south for another 45 miles. Nearly all of this length is above 4,000 feet (there is one deep gap, **Balsam Gap** (see The Blue Ridge Parkway under *Wandering Around—Exploring by Car*—in "Waynesville and the Blue Ridge Parkway"), and a majority of it tops a mile in elevation. The Balsams have 14 peaks over 6,000 feet, while the Smokies get the credit for another five 6-ers at the Smokies-Balsams intersection. This remote and beautiful area is best reached from **Pin Oak Gap** (see The Blue Ridge Parkway and the Heintooga Spur Road under *Wandering Around—Exploring by Car*).

RECREATION AREAS   Balsam Mountain Picnic and Camping Area. To reach Balsam Mountain from Cherokee, NC, go 12 miles up the Blue Ridge Parkway, then 7 miles up the Heintooga Spur Road. Part of Great Smoky Mountains National Park, Balsam Mountain (also known as Heintooga) is certainly the place to be on a hot summer day. At 5,300 feet above sea level, it's the highest, coolest, and windiest picnic area and campground in the park. A very short walk takes you to **Heintooga Overlook,** with a sweeping 180-degree view over the entire Smoky Mountain Crest—probably the best place in the park to enjoy a sunset.

Smokemont. Smokemont was originally constructed as a timber camp, the general headquarters of Champion Paper's logging operations in the Oconaluftee drainage during the first three decades of the 20th century. Champion valued the high ridges above the Oconaluftee River for their spruce trees, which produced high-quality pulp for paper; Champion's aggressive logging practices led to the disastrous fires that created the meadows and cliffs around **Charlie's Bunion** (see Newfound Gap, below). Today Smokemount holds a large campground, a livery concessionaire (see **Smokemont Riding Stables** under *To Do—Horseback Riding*), and a variety of trailheads.

Newfound Gap. This high gap marks the point where the Newfound Gap Road crosses the crest of the Smokies. Not surprisingly, it's heavily visited, with a huge parking lot. A monumental stone platform at its eastern edge served as the site of the 1940 dedication ceremony, personally attended by President Franklin Roosevelt. The **Appalachian Trail** runs by the dedication platform and furnishes a steep but beautiful day hike (9 miles round-trip) to **Charlie's Bunion,** a massive cliff with sweeping panoramic views. An overlook south of the platform has interpretive plaques and a handsome 180-degree sweep over the upper Oconaluftee drainage basin on the North Carolina side.

Clingmans Dome. At 6,643 feet, Clingmans Dome is the highest point in the national park and the third-highest peak in the eastern United States. Access is by the **Clingmans Dome Spur Road** (see Clingmans Dome Scenic Drive under *Wandering Around—The Heart of the Smokies*), which is closed in winter. The dome offers some of the best views in the Smokies. Many of these views can be found at its large crescent-shaped parking lot, almost 0.2 mile long, with a continuous south-facing panorama so broad that you have to walk its entire length to take it all in. The rest of the views are from the dome's large, modern observation deck, a concrete pillar surrounded by a huge spiral ramp, a steep quarter mile up a paved trail from the parking lot. Clingmans Dome is a major trailhead, where the **Appalachian Trail** reaches its highest point (see A High Ridge Walk on the Appalachian Trail under *Wandering Around—The Heart of the Smokies*) and the

Forney Ridge Trail descends to beautiful **Andrews Bald** (see Andrews Bald Walk under *Wandering Around—The Heart of the Smokies*) before it plunges deep into the North Carolina backcountry. It has flush toilets and drinking water in-season but no picnic tables.

PICNIC AREAS **Collins Creek Picnic Area.** This large, lovely picnic area is scattered through a cool, streamside forest, 6.65 miles up Newfound Gap Road from the park's boundary in Cherokee, NC. Although it is the only picnic area on the North Carolina Newfound Gap Road, it is little used, possibly because it has no recreation opportunities besides eating outdoors. Even its one Civilian Conservation Corps (CCC) hiking trail has been closed for 30 years—a pity, as it climbed through a virgin forest to a good view.

Oconaluftee Islands Tribal Park and Veterans Tribal Park. Isolated from the center of Cherokee, NC, by the waters of the Oconaluftee River, Islands Tribal Park is an oasis of cool, quiet loveliness. Its picnic tables are widely scattered through a forested glade and linked by an interpretive nature-history trail. Unfortunately, there is only limited parking on the gravel-road shoulder by the bridge. Nearby Veterans Tribal Park, in the center of the town's government district, has picnic facilities as well as ample parking. Both parks have full facilities.

✳ To See

THE BLUE RIDGE PARKWAY **Soco Gap.** The parkway intersects with US 19 in this high (4,345-foot) gap. Soco Gap has had some sort of trail in it since the early 19th century, but its great elevation and clifflike sides have always prevented it from being a major entry point to the Smokies; it received its current highway, US 19, only in the 1950s. Apart from its height and steepness it's had another barrier to travel: It may well be the snowiest U.S. highway in these mountains, frequently having deep snow when most other areas have had only a cold drizzle. This is not always a bad thing. Although this section of the Blue Ridge Parkway is invariably closed in winter, you can drive up to Soco Gap on the plowed and salted **US 19,** park on the intersection verge, and join in the other families sledding, cross-country skiing, throwing snowballs, and building snowmen along the closed parkway. For other times of the year, if you need facilities at the US 19 exit of the parkway, drive 4 miles east on US 19 to Maggie Valley, NC (see *Villages*).

HISTORIC SITES **Mountain Farm Museum.** Located in Great Smoky Mountains National Park on the Newfound Gap Road, 1.35 miles outside Cherokee, NC, this museum is one of the most complete, and one of the most handsome, exhibits on mountain farm life anywhere in the Southern Appalachians. Unlike sites in the more famous Cades Cove, the Mountain Farm Museum portrays a full-sized operating farm—flowers along the porch, furniture in the house, corn in the field, chickens in the coop, and a horse in the barn.

The farmstead consists of log structures, all built around 1900, moved in from remote areas of the park (where other such buildings were being destroyed as safety hazards). The log farmhouse is a solid two-story built in 1902 by local farmer

John Davis; you'll find it furnished in late-19th-century style, surrounded by hand-split pickets and planted with beds of native flowers. The barn anchors the other end of the site. Original to this location, it's a large cantilevered log barn holding late-19th-century farm equipment, a horse, several stray chickens from the nearby coop, and a cat. The horse is a friendly old creature who loves to meet gentle and well-behaved children.

Between the two main structures lies a working late-19th-century farmstead. Corn grows behind high, strong split-rail fences; beans and squash grow among the corn, a standard mountain practice. A vegetable garden, protected by pickets, grows a riot of tomatoes, squash, beans, and peas, as well as flowers for the kitchen table. Gourd birdhouses provide natural insect control. Log outbuildings include a corncrib, a chicken house, a springhouse, a smokehouse, an apple house with a stone foundation, a gear shed, a blacksmith shop, a pigpen, hollow log beehives, and a sorghum press.

Adjacent to the Farm Museum is the modest **Oconaluftee Visitors Center,** with an information desk, bookshop, and interpretive exhibits housed in a classic Depression-era stone building.

Mingus Mill. Mingus Mill, located on the Newfound Gap Road a short distance beyond the Mountain Farm Museum (see above), is a late-19th-century gristmill restored to operation. In its time it was a modern facility, with two grist stones powered by an efficient store-bought turbine instead of the old-fashioned hand-carpentered overshot wheel. You can scramble under this large clapboarded building to see the turbine in operation, then go inside to watch the miller operate the great grist stones and buy a pound of stone-ground cornmeal. However, its most impressive part is its elevated millrace, standing 20 feet off the ground as it passes into the building to fall into the turbine. There's a short, pleasant walk that follows the millrace to the mill's small log dam on Mingus Creek.

WATER SPILLS OVER THE MILLRACE AT MINGUS MILL.

CULTURAL SITES **The Museum of the Cherokee Indian** (828-497-3481), Drama Road (US 441), Cherokee, NC. You'll find the museum in a handsome 1970s wood building in town at the intersection of Drama Road and US 441, 1.25 miles north of US 19. Adults $6, children $4. This is one of the most intriguing, involving, and moving museum experiences in the western mountains. The museum's displays mix carefully chosen artifacts with artworks and state-of-the-art museum technology to tell the story of the Cherokees clearly, simply, and beautifully. And storytelling is just what it does. Starting with the Cherokees' creation myth, the museum leads visitors gently through the ages, from

THE FARMYARD AND BARN AT OCONALUFTEE
RANGER STATION

Archaic times to the pre-Columbian Cherokees' culture and way of life, through their contact with Europeans and the chaotic dislocations that ensued, and ending with an emotional account of the Trail of Tears, the violent relocation of most of the Cherokees to Oklahoma. The museum, which is a wholly independent not-for-profit, has a first-rate gift shop (see **The Drama Road Gift Shops** under *Selective Shopping*).

Oconaluftee Indian Village (828-497-2315), , Cherokee, NC. Open May 15 through October 25, daily 9–5:30. Adults $12, children $5. Built in 1952 by the Cherokee Historical Association, the Oconaluftee Indian Village authentically re-creates an 18th-century Cherokee settlement. Thatched log cabins group around a seven-sided council house, where Cherokee crafters in period costume demonstrate traditional tribal arts.

The Qualla Arts and Crafts Mutual (828-497-3103), Cherokee, NC. The Qualla Mutual is in a low-slung 1960s-era building across the street from the Museum of the Cherokee Indian (see above). This is a crafts cooperative and gallery for several hundred crafters who are enrolled members of the Eastern Band. A museum area has a series of glass-case wall displays that explain the varieties of contemporary Cherokee crafts, including their history, style, materials, and methods: stone carving, basket weaving (several kinds), pottery, mask making, doll making, wood carving, jewelry making. The main area of the building contains a large shop that wanders through several rooms, offering every kind of Cherokee crafts at a wide range of prices. All crafts for sale are handmade by members and carry an authentication mark.

GARDENS AND PARKS Mingo Falls Tribal Park. You'll find these falls 6 miles north of Cherokee, NC, on Big Cove Road; turn left at Scenic Village, then just keep going. One of the most beautiful waterfalls of the Smokies, Mingo Falls is the highlight of a modest tribally run park and campground in Big Cove. A short, steep track leads a quarter mile uphill to the base of the falls—a lacy curtain of water hung over a hundred-foot cliff.

✳ To Do

FISHING Fishing on the Qualla Boundary (828-497-5201). North Carolina's record brown trout (at 15 pounds, 2 ounces) was caught on the Qualla Boundary in 1990. The boundary has 30 miles of trout streams open to visitors, plus several trout ponds.

The tribe stocks these streams twice a week in-season, and has a creel limit of 10 fish per day. Unlike the national park, you need no state fishing license; however, you must have a Tribal Fishing Permit, which costs $7 per day (children under 11 free with permitted adult). Permits are sold in most campground stores, outfitters, tackle stores, and general stores in the boundary.

GOLF Maggie Valley Resort (828-926-6013; 1-800-438-3861), 1819 Country Club Road, Maggie Valley, NC. $51 for 18 holes. This 18-hole par-72 course, constructed in 1961, winds uphill from the center of Maggie Valley, with excellent views of the surrounding peaks.

HORSEBACK RIDING Smokemont Riding Stables (828-497-2373), Smoky Mountains National Park. Open May through October. This national park concessionaire offers guided horseback rides in the **Smokemont** area (see *Wild Places—Recreation Areas*).

Cataloochee Ranch Stables (828-926-1401; 1-800-868-1401), 119 Ranch Drive, Maggie Valley, NC. Open April through November. Half day (2-3 hours): $45, with $5 discount to ranch guests. Full day (7 hours), including lunch: $100, with $10 discount to ranch guests. Part of Cataloochee Ranch (see *Lodging—Resorts*), this stable offers trail rides on the ranch's spectacular thousand acres of mile-high ridgetop meadows and forests and into the adjacent Great Smoky Mountains National Park.

✳ Lodging

If you're looking for a B&B in Maggie Valley, NC, you'll find quite a choice. However, at this writing Cherokee, NC, has only motel rooms (2,500 of them) and cabins—no B&Bs, country lodges, or resorts. A sampling of good Cherokee cabin rentals is given below. You can also rent a private vacation home in the Cherokee area from either **Apple Realty** in Dillsboro, NC

(see *Lodging—Cabin Reservation Services* in "Near the Park: Sylva and Dillsboro"), or **Yellow Rose Realty** in Bryson City, NC (see *Lodging—Cabin Reservation Services* in "Bryson City and the Southwest Quadrant"). There are a number of first-rate B&Bs and small country hotels a short drive from Cherokee, listed in the Sylva, NC, and Bryson City chapters.

COUNTRY RESORTS The Swag (828-926-0430), 2300 Swag Road, Maggie Valley, NC 28751. This large log inn sits in a grassy swale 5,000 feet high, at the end of a 2.5-mile driveway that climbs over a thousand feet in elevation. Remote and quiet, the views from its wide porches and balconies are spectacular. Rooms range in size from cozy to huge, each distinctively decorated with antiques and heritage quilts. Each room has its own special features—log walls, stone accents, fireplace, balcony, view, hot tub, steam shower, or loft. Three log cabins (one with its own billiard room) give additional choices. The tariff includes three gourmet meals each day: a full breakfast, a picnic lunch, and an elegant, relaxed dinner. The 250-acre site includes a pond, a waterfall, a 3-mile nature trail with fine views, and four sheltered hideaways for a little private relaxing in the woods. Rooms $265–515; cabins $395–580.

Cataloochee Ranch (828-926-1401; 1-800-868-1401), 119 Ranch Drive, Maggie Valley, NC 28751. The Cataloochee Ranch has been operating from its current thousand-acre ridgetop spread since 1938, under the ownership of the same family. It sits in sweeping mountaintop meadows above 5,000 feet elevation, directly above central Maggie Valley at the end of Fie Top Road. Its main compound has a log lodge with six rooms, a modern conference building with four rooms and two suites, and nine log cabins. The tariff includes a buffet breakfast and a family-style dinner with traditional Southern cooking; there are frequent barbeques as well. The ranch offers horseback rides at an extra fee, as well as hiking trips (both on its beautiful site and into the adjacent Great Smoky Mountains National Park), pond fishing, an outdoor swimming pool, and such activities as storytelling, clogging, square dancing, wagon rides, bonfires, and marshmallow roasts. Rooms $145–200; suites $210; cabins $195–275.

BED & BREAKFASTS Brookside Bed & Breakfast (828-926-0708; 1-800-754-1288), 213 Walnut Drive, Maggie Valley, NC 28751. This modern A-frame sits in a large wooded lot in a quiet residential area high above Maggie Valley. Common areas include a screened porch, a wood-paneled den with plush sofas and chairs around a fieldstone fireplace, and a large gazebo, which shelters a hot tub. Its four rooms, spread across three levels, are all roomy and comfortably furnished. Prices include a full breakfast, fresh-made afternoon sweets, and complimentary beverages. $75–155 per night.

Timberwolf Creek Bed & Breakfast (828-926-2608), 391 Johnson Branch Road, Maggie Valley, NC 28751. This classic luxury three-room B&B is in a modern ranch-style house by a mountain stream, on a side road convenient to central Maggie Valley. The rooms are beautifully furnished with antiques, and have views (either mountain or stream) and two-person hot tubs. The common area has plush country furniture around a stone fireplace, with beverages and fresh-baked goods on the counter. $195–245.

CABIN RENTALS Grandview Cabins (828-497-5849), P.O. Box 1503, Cherokee, NC 28719. Located a few hundred yards uphill from the intersection of US 19 and US 441 in the center of town, with a wide and unobstructed view toward the western mountains. The four log cabins are roomy and well appointed, with covered porches that face the sunrise, rockers, fireplaces, and good kitchens. The two-bedroom units are small houses with roomy living rooms and separate bedrooms, perfect for a family or two couples. The one-bedroom units are studios, each with an ample great room/kitchen and large offset baths, and each beautifully decorated. $100.

Sycamore Log Cabins (828-497-9068). Joyce Welch's three log cabins form a quiet little group alongside Big Cove Road adjacent to the boundary of Great Smoky Mountains National Park. These well-kept, recently built log homes have a great room with kitchen, plus two bedrooms. Each has a porch with rocking chairs and is furnished in a rustic style. $65–95, depending on season.

Great Smoky Mountain Log Cabins (828-497-6182), 1056 Adams Creek Road, Cherokee, NC 28719. Bud and Sheila Lambert keep two sets of cozy log cabins, one in the pastoral Olivet Church area south of Cherokee, and another up Owl Branch, a more heavily settled section of the Qualla Boundary. All but two of the cabins are modern log structures with a combined living area and kitchen, plus two bedrooms and either a hot tub or a whirlpool bath. All of the cabins have wide covered porches with rocking chairs, and gas fireplaces in the living areas, and all are furnished with comfortable new furniture in a country style that fits the spaces well. Most beds are doubles, with a few queens. $85–95.

Boyd Mountain Log Cabins (828-926-1575), 445 Boyd Farm Road, Waynesville, NC 28786. Set on a 150-acre private farm in Maggie Valley's scenic Hemphill Creek area, these six log cabins are all authentic, restored pioneer structures ranging from 150 to 200 years old. Cozy and comfortable historic cabins, they're set in beautiful meadows, by or near a fishing pond; all have full porches and fireplaces, with upstairs bedroom(s). $130.

✳ Where To Eat

EATING OUT Frankly, this is not a good area to search for a memorable meal. The three restaurants inside **Harrahs Cherokee Casino** (see *Entertainment*) all serve reliably good food, and there are several decent buffets for the all-you-can-eat crowd. Motel restaurants at Cherokee's **Holiday Inn** and **Best Western** are also reliable. For a number of recommended eateries and restaurants nearby, see the chapters on Sylva and Bryson City, NC (both near Cherokee, NC), as well as Waynesville, NC (near Maggie Valley, NC).

✳ Entertainment

OUTDOOR DRAMA **Unto These Hills** (828-497-2111), Cherokee, NC. Open June 14 through August 26, except Sunday; pre-show entertainment starts around 7:45 PM. Adults $14–16, children $6–16. Founded in 1950 by the nonprofit Cherokee Historical Association, this large-scale outdoor pageant, performed by a hundred actors and dancers over three stages, presents the history of the Cherokee people, from their contact with Hernando de Soto to the Trail of Tears.

CASINO **Harrahs Cherokee Casino** (828-497-7777; 1-800-427-7247), 777 Casino Drive, Cherokee, NC. Open 24 hours a day, 7 days a week. The Eastern Band owns, and Harrahs operates, this large, luxurious video gaming emporium, a short distance east of Cherokee on US 19. This new facility includes three restaurants and a 1,500-seat theater. At this writing the tribe and Harrahs are collaborating on an adjacent high-rise luxury hotel, so that the serious gamer need never walk outside into the mountain air.

✳ Selective Shopping

The Drama Road Gift Shops, Drama Road (US 441), Cherokee, NC. Not surprisingly, the first-rate Museum of the Cherokee Indian (see *To See —Cultural Sites*) has a first-rate gift shop. Spacious, handsome, and full of stuff, it has Cherokee art and crafts, books, children's toys and books related to the museum, as well as a fascinating selection of tasteful and relevant gewgaws and knickknacks. **The Qualla Arts and Crafts Mutual** (see *To See—Cultural Sites*), a Cherokee crafters' cooperative, is just across the street and simply bursting with even more good stuff—all of it handmade on the Qualla Boundary and carrying a certificate of authenticity from the U.S. Bureau of Indian Affairs. You'll find these two locations on US 441 and Drama Road, 1.25 miles north of US 19.

Great Smokies Fine Art Gallery (828-497-5444), Cherokee, NC. This storefront in the Scenic Village area of

Cherokee combines limited-edition prints by Native American artists with Native American crafts and North Carolina handcrafted furniture. With this mix, the shop has the comfortable feel of a luxuriously furnished home. Western Native American artists as well as Eastern Band artists are among those represented.

Bigmeat House of Pottery (828-497-9544), US 19, Cherokee, NC. The Bigmeat family has been noted for their fine pottery for generations. Today, Louise Bigmeat Maney carries on her family's tradition from this gallery on US 19 on the east side of town. A North Carolina Folk Heritage Award recipient, Mrs. Maney's work emphasizes preservation of Cherokee culture and the use of traditional motifs.

The Old Mill (282-497-6536), 3082 US 441 North, Whittier, NC. Located south of Cherokee, NC, outside the Qualla Boundary, this large old clapboard mill, painted white and with a huge steel overshot wheel, ground corn through most of the 20th century. Nowadays it sells a wide variety of items, including locally made jams and honeys, stone-ground cornmeal (ground at a nearby mill—the Old Mill's workings were destroyed in a 1980s burglary), salt-cured country hams, Coca-Cola memorabilia, rocks, local and Cherokee crafts, and rural antiques and collectibles. It's a fun place to browse, with all sorts of neat stuff jammed into odd corners.

✳ Special Events

Mid-March: **Honor the Elders Day,** Cherokee Ceremonial Grounds, Cherokee, NC. Cherokee stickball, a ceremonial (and very exciting) sport, combines with traditional dances and food.

First weekend in April: **Ramp and Rainbow Festival,** Cherokee Ceremonial Grounds, Cherokee, NC. Ramps—the wild mountain leek, redolent of both onion and garlic—traditionally herald the coming of spring throughout the Blue Ridge and Smoky Mountains. This festival celebrates spring with ramp and rainbow trout dinners, along with crafts and fishing vendors.

Fourth of July weekend: **Fourth of July Powwow,** Cherokee Ceremonial Grounds, Cherokee, NC. The tribe celebrates Independence Day with a powwow dance competition, arts and crafts displays, Native American foods, and a fireworks display.

Second weekend in July: **Maggie Valley Arts and Crafts Festival,** Maggie Valley, NC. Sponsored by the Maggie Valley Civic association, this festival at the **Maggie Valley Civic Center** features over a hundred crafts vendors, plus food and entertainment.

Third weekend in October: **Maggie Valley Arts and Crafts Festival** (see above).

South of the Smokies

NEAR THE PARK: SYLVA & DILLSBORO

THE BLUE RIDGE: CASHIERS & HIGHLANDS

FRANKLIN & THE NANTAHALA MOUNTAINS

THE NORTHERN UNICOIS: ROBBINSVILLE & TELLICO PLAINS

THE SOUTHERN UNICOIS: MURPHY & THE COPPER BASIN

SOUTH OF THE SMOKIES

Mountains extend southward from the Great Smokies through North Carolina, to meet the Blue Ridge near the North Carolina–Georgia state line. These ridges are high and steep sided, with most peaks above 4,000 feet and many topping a mile high. They zig and zag around with no obvious reason, hemming in narrow-bottomed little valleys. The major rivers—the Tuckaseegee, the Nantahala, the Little Tennessee, the Valley River, the Hiwassee, the Tellico—can run obediently between two low ridges, then turn suddenly to cut a deep gorge straight through a high barrier.

Early roads and railroads tried to pick their ways through the least-difficult gaps and gorges, with settlements following. The state legislatures broke the mountains into increasingly small counties in a vain attempt to create courthouses within horseback distance of most of the settlers. Today, these courthouses sit at the center of compact, old downtowns in small county seats—Sylva, Franklin, Robbinsville, Hayesville, Murphy (all in North Carolina).

These are the lands in which the Cherokees made their last stand in the East. The Cherokee Nation gave up their most rugged areas to the European invaders, hoping to satisfy the land hunger and live unmolested in the lower mountains of north Georgia and southeastern Tennessee. When the invasion failed to abate, the tribe fought its battles in the American courts—only to discover that the whites simply ignored their own courts when they did not like the results. In 1838 the Jackson administration, disobeying a U.S. Supreme Court order, forcibly removed the Cherokees from their lands, marching them to Oklahoma on the bitter Trail of Tears on which many hundreds died. The modern town of Murphy, seat of Cherokee County, occupies the site of one of the concentration camps used to gather the Cherokees for the forced march. Today, the Robbinsville grave of Chief Junaluska, who had saved Jackson's life during the battle of Horseshoe Bend, is the sole monument to the Cherokee Nation in these lands. (The Qualla Boundary—modern home of the Eastern Cherokees, is outside the final boundaries of the old Cherokee Nation.) Some 600 descendants of Cherokees who escaped the expulsion form a community at Snowbird, also near Robbinsville.

More than most other eastern mountains, these southern ridges are dominated by public ownership, with settled areas sometimes little more than islands in a sea of forest. In North Carolina, Nantahala National Forest owns the majority of the mountain slopes; in Tennessee, it's the Cherokee National Forest. Where the Blue Ridge overlaps into South Carolina, the Sumter National Forest takes over, and in Georgia the Chattahoochee National Forest rules the roost. All four of these national forests maintain ranger stations in the major towns throughout this area, and these stations always have staffed information desks, books, and maps. As with all national forests, public recreation (including hunting) is permitted nearly everywhere; however, these are not national parks or conservation areas, and active logging continues on many government-owned tracts.

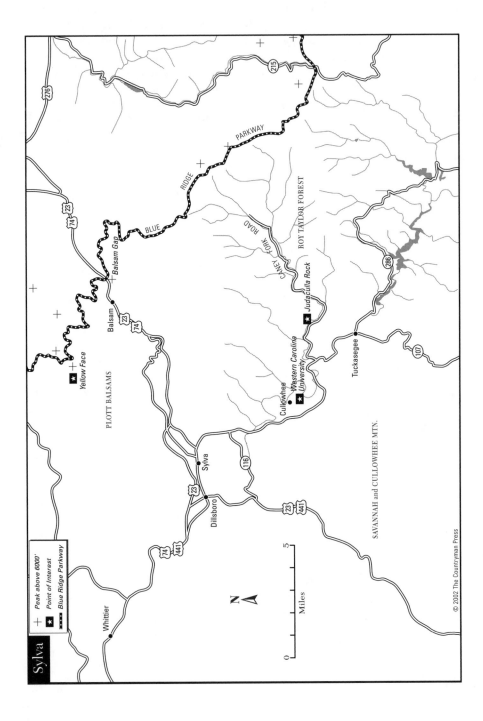

NEAR THE PARK: SYLVA & DILLSBORO

The tall, jumbled ridges of the Smokies don't end at the national park boundaries. The high peaks and deep valleys continue south of Great Smoky Mountains National Park to encircle the beautiful little county town of Sylva, NC, and its sister burg, Dillsboro, NC. Nestled deep in a valley formed by the Tuckaseegee River, Sylva and Dillsboro remain redbrick and white-clapboard villages, surrounded by deep forests and mile-high summits. Other places have more chain restaurants and franchised motels; Sylva and Dillsboro are rich in authentic, old-fashioned comfort.

Sylva and Dillsboro command a deep mountain valley that has long served as the gateway to North Carolina's western mountains, including the Smokies. Ten miles to the east, the unusually deep and gentle Balsam Gap furnishes the only real break in the solid wall of the Great Balsam Mountains. In pioneer days the Rutherford Trace, a glorified footpath through Balsam Gap, served as the main route westward as late as the 1850s. In 1855 the Smoky's first wagon road, the Nantahala Turnpike (see *Wandering Around—Exploring by Car*), opened through Balsam Gap to Dillsboro and Bryson City, NC, then on through the Nantahala Gorge to Tennessee. It took the railroad almost 30 more years to reach this isolated backwater, paralleling the Nantahala Turnpike the entire way. US 74 roughly follows the turnpike, while the Great Smoky Mountains Railroad (see The Forests of the Little River under *Wild Places—The Great Forests* in "Townsend, Cades Cove, and the Northeast Quadrant") carries passengers on the old railroad. Dillsboro was the original pioneer settlement; nearby Sylva, founded as a railroad siding, slowly acquired most of the businesses and jobs. Today, Sylva is the main town, a sleepy county seat little changed from the 1940s, with brick storefronts marching up to a grand old county courthouse crowning a green hill. Adjacent Dillsboro is a village of nicely kept white clapboard Victorian buildings, with one of the Smoky Mountain's finest concentration of crafts and gift shops. Throughout this area, the choice of restaurants and B&Bs is unusually good, the towns are small and unspoiled, and the scenery is spectacular. Access is good, with expressways leading to the Great Smoky Mountains in 15 miles and the Blue Ridge Parkway in 10 miles.

GUIDANCE Jackson County Chamber of Commerce (828-586-2155; 1-800-962-1911), 773 West Main Street, Sylva, NC 28779. This county-wide chamber handles both Sylva and Dillsboro, NC, tourist information. Its new walk-in visitors center occupies part of the beautifully renovated **Hooper House,** right by the old courthouse on Main Street.

The Jackson County Home Page (http://main.nc.us/jackson/). Sponsored by the mountains' not-for-profit Internet cooperative, MAIN (Mountain Area Information Network), this home page is a thorough and well-designed repository of community information and links about the western slopes and valleys of the Great Balsam Mountains.

MAIN STREET IN DOWNTOWN SYLVA

GETTING THERE *By car:* Sylva and Dillsboro, NC, sit near the intersection of US 441 and US 23/74, both excellent four-lane highways. Visitors from points north will find Great Smoky Mountains National Park firmly in the way; while sightseers will enjoy crossing the park on the scenic Newfound Gap Road (formerly US 441) from Gatlinburg, TN, anyone wishing to make time should take I-40 around the east side of the Smokies, picking up US 23/74 at Canton, NC, about 30 miles east of Sylva.

By air: The nearest airport is **Asheville Regional Airport** (see *Getting There* in "Asheville and the Blue Ridge Parkway"), 45 miles east of Balsam Gap. You'll need to rent a car, as the Sylva area has no bus service. It's a 45-minute drive, four-lane all the way, via I-26, I-40, and US 74.

By bus, train, or public transportation: There is no bus or rail service to this area, and there is no local bus service.

MEDICAL EMERGENCIES Harris Regional Hospital (828-586-7000), 68 Hospital Road (Business US 74), Sylva, NC. Sylva's regional hospital is small but full service. It's a mile east of town on Business US 74, just off the easternmost of the three Sylva exits on US 23/74.

✳ Wandering Around

EXPLORING BY CAR The Nantahala Turnpike. In 1855, when most of America was being linked together by iron rails, the Smokies finally got their first wagon road, the Nantahala Turnpike. This 14-mile scenic drive gives the look and feel of traveling down the old turnpike. On the way it gives good views of the 1882 railroad, including two fine old trestles and the second-steepest railroad grade in the East.

Start 10 miles east of **Sylva** on the four-laned **US 23/74** in **Balsam Gap** near the Blue Ridge Parkway; follow the signs to the old resort settlement of **Balsam.**

This road (**SSR 1701**) quickly reaches the railroad and runs parallel to it, past the abandoned Knights General Store, then crosses the railroad to pass the grand old **Balsam Mountain Inn** (see *Lodging—Country Inns and Hotels*), a 1905 railroad hotel still in operation and restored to elegance. Continue past the inn (**on SSR 1700**), then make a right on **Dark Ridge Road (SSR 1705).** Here you'll follow an isolated mountain valley downhill through lovely remote scenery. Soon both the road and the stream cross under a fine old steel-truss railroad bridge, a working piece of history from the late 19th century. After another mile of this remote mountain valley, this route turns left onto the former Works Progress Administration (WPA)–era main highway, **Old US 19/23,** at a T-intersection. This particularly scenic section snakes through the gorge carved by **Scott Creek,** zigging and zagging past the railroad. At one point the road passes over the railroad just as the railroad passes over the creek—a double bridge. A half mile later, the railroad flies over both the road and the creek. From here, the road (and the railroad) passes into wide valleys.

As you enter the town of Sylva some miles later, **Old 19/23** bends left to return to the main highway. You can stay on the turnpike by taking a right on **Chipper Curve Road,** then another right uphill onto the alleylike **Allen Street.** At first it seems odd that the turnpike avoids entering Sylva—but, of course, Sylva didn't exist when the turnpike was built. The turnpike was actually trying to miss valley mud and floods, pretty typical behavior for an early-19th-century coach road. As Allen Street enters Sylva, follow residential streets down and left to **City Hall,** then right on **Municipal Street** to **Grindstaff Cove Road** and a quick right zag onto **Old Dillsboro Road.** You have now recovered the turnpike route as it climbs and twists along hillsides to a panoramic view of the town of Sylva, which fills the valley bottom the turnpike was so careful to avoid. At the bottom of the hill, the Old Dillsboro Road returns you to **Business US 23,** the early 20th-century auto road that replaced the turnpike.

EXPLORING ON FOOT **Plott Balsams Walk.** Close to the popular **Waterrock Knob** (see *To See—The Blue Ridge Parkway* in "Waynesville and the Blue Ridge Parkway"), this little-used 2.6-mile round-trip walk follows the spectacular 5,800-foot ridgeline of Plott Balsams (see also *Wild Places—The Great Forests*) to the 6,032-foot peak of Yellow Face. Recently blazed, it's part of the Town of Sylva's effort to open up Plott Balsams for outdoor recreation. You'll find the trail along the side of the parkway opposite the intersection with the **Waterrock Knob Spur;** the closest parking is an eighth of a mile up the spur road at the **Cut-off Ridge Overlook.**

The trail immediately dives into a high-altitude "balsam" forest. Like all such forests in the Balsam Mountains, it's undergoing a drastic ecological transition, as the deaths of most of the firs (due to wooly adelgid infections) clears out the forest canopy and allows a host of other species to gain a foothold. Look for berries and wildflowers where forest giants once shaded a floor of needles, moss, and rocks. In a quarter mile the path reaches an open meadow with sweeping views east and south along the plunging slopes of the Balsams. Beyond, the trail climbs up a narrow, rocky ridgeline, occasionally clambering up a rocky outcrop where mosses and dwarf trees give the look of a Japanese garden. Near the top of the peak, the trail scrambles left around a large outcrop to another stunning view. From here you can see the little settlement of **Balsam** hugging the slopes of the mountain, with **Balsam Gap** slashing through the mountain; on a roiling summer day, rain clouds will sail through the gap a half mile below you. The viewless 6,032-foot peak of **Yellow Face,** covered in blueberry and blackberry meadows, is a short distance beyond. This is a good place to turn back. If you decide to go on, the trail continues through high mountain meadows, knife-edged outcrops, and balsam forests to reach **The Pinnacle,** with panoramic views, adding 6 miles and 2,100 feet of rugged climbing to your journey.

✳ Villages

Whittier, NC. At the turn of the century Whittier was the roughest town in the district, well known for its brawls along its saloon-lined main street. A hundred

SYLVA

The county seat of Sylva snuggles in a narrow side valley of the Tuckaseegee River, under the mile-high peaks of Plott Balsams (see *Wild Places—The Great Forests*). Its four-block downtown hugs the hillside above Scotts Creek, so that each old brick storefront has a basement on Main Street that comes out at street level on Mill Street. Its **Main Street** is not so much restored as unchanged, frozen in a time where people went downtown to shop in tiny old brick buildings. With stores such as **Jackson's General Store, Schulman's Department Store** (still run by Sol Schulman after more than 50 years), and **Hooper's Lunch Counter,** it's like stepping back into the 1940s. Main Street ends at a flight of steps climbing a tall green hill—past a fountain, then past a Confederate-soldier statue, and on up to the column-and-dome **Old Courthouse.** With its exterior recently restored, the Old Courthouse makes a stunning landmark visible as far away as the Blue Ridge Parkway (from Grassy Mine Ridge Overlook, milepost 437). The Old Courthouse is especially beautiful in the spring when framed by dogwoods but is worth a visit at anytime for its views over Main Street toward the Blue Ridge Parkway and the 6,000-foot peaks of the Great Balsam Mountains. Downtown street parking is free and plentiful.

Dillsboro. During the 19th century Dillsboro was the main town of the Tuckaseegee Valley, thriving decades before a nearby railroad siding was named "Sylva." However, a series of floods inundated Dillsboro's low-lying downtown, driving its businesses uphill to the Sylva siding. By 1970, upstream dams had solved the flood problem, but it seemed too late—Dillsboro was little more than a ghost town, with most of its old buildings abandoned. Then things started to years of time and a modern freeway have both taken their toll, and Whittier is now a sleepy collection of a few scattered buildings 7 miles south of Cherokee, NC. Two of the oldest surviving structures now house **Whittier, a Dream Remembered** (see *To See—Cultural Sites*), a delightful museum run as a labor of love by a townswoman. Three miles east of town on US 74 you'll find the Smoky Mountains' largest collection of **flea markets,** open weekends from May through October. Whittier is off US 74 at a marked exit, 12 miles west of Sylva; you'll pass the flea markets on the way there, about 9 miles west of Sylva.

Balsam, NC. The village is a quarter mile south of the four-lane US 23/74, signposted down local roads. When the railroad finally crossed the 3,550-foot Balsam Gap in the 1880s, it became the highest point in the East to receive regular passenger service, and a resort village grew up around its small depot. By 1908 it had acquired a large wooden hotel, the **Balsam Mountain Inn** (see *Lodging—Coun-*

change. Crafts artists discovered that its roomy old buildings could be rented cheaply and started moving in. The Hartbarger family acquired the town's railroad hotel, the **Jarrett House,** and returned it to its former glory as a fine old B&B and country-style restaurant (see *Lodging—Country Inns and Hotels*). Then a set of investors bought out the recently abandoned freight railroad and turned it into a successful excursion line, the **Great Smoky Mountains Railroad** (see The Great Smoky Mountains Railroad under *To See—Other*). Now Dillsboro is a beautiful old-fashioned village, reminiscent more of Old New England than the New South. Its two-block historic district, made up largely of original buildings tastefully restored, is crammed with more than 40 shops and crafts studios. Opposite the historic district The Great Smoky Mountains Railroad hauls freight at night and tourist excursions during the day, with scenic journeys departing from the nearby towns of Andrews and Murphy, NC, as well as Dillsboro.

THE OLD JACKSON COUNTY COURTHOUSE IN SYLVA

try Inns and Hotels)—now beautifully restored to a luxury full-service country inn, with gourmet food. It remains the highest and coolest place to stay in this area, as well as the closest to this section of the Blue Ridge Parkway.

Cullowhee, NC. Settled in the 1850s, this rural community in the Upper Tuckaseegee Valley has been home to **Western Carolina University** since 1889 (see *To See—Cultural Sites*). Cullowhee remains unincorporated and has only a scattering of businesses on the northern edge of the university.

✳ Wild Places

THE GREAT FORESTS **Plott Balsams.** Plott Balsams is a high side ridge running at right angles to the main crest of the Great Balsam Mountains from Sylva to Waynesville, NC. Stretching for 23 miles, it has four peaks over 6,000 feet in a central section that maintains continuous mile-high elevations for 7.5 miles. The eastern two peaks, **Plott Balsam** (6,088 feet) and **Mount Lyn Lowry** (6,240 feet), are on private lands; Mount Lyn Lowry is topped by a giant electrified cross, the site of an annual Easter-morning prayer service. The western half of the range, with 6-footers **Waterrock Knob** (6,292 feet) and **Yellow Face** (6,032 feet), is largely public, split between the Blue Ridge Parkway, Nantahala National Forest, and the Town of Sylva Watershed—now being developed by the Town of Sylva into **Pinnacle Park.** Much logged in the early 20th century to support a Sylva paper mill, Plott Balsams is covered in a variety of mature second-growth hardwood. The high crest is mainly covered in the subarctic spruce-fir "balsam" forest, with isolated meadows and rocky outcrops offering impressive views. Waterrock Knob (see *To See—The Blue Ridge Parkway* in "Waynesville and the Blue Ridge Parkway") has a popular (and very steep) 1-mile trail to its summit, while Yellow Face can be easily reached in a pleasant 2.6-mile forest walk (see Plott Balsams Walk under *Wandering Around—Exploring on Foot*).

National Forest Lands near Sylva. In addition to Plott Balsams (see above), this area has two substantial national forest tracts, both beautiful and worthwhile, and neither with any meaningful recreation development. To the south of Sylva the large **Roy Taylor Forest,** named after a former congressman, lies on the west slope of the Balsam Mountains below the Blue Ridge Parkway; it's mainly a logging area for Nantahala National Forest. Across the Tuckaseegee River, the **Savannah Mountain/**Cullowhee Mountain tracts occupy the broken peaks to the south and west of Cullowhee—a large and beautiful tract of mature second-growth hardwood forest that the National Forest Service has not developed for public use in any way. In both cases, recreational use is possible (including camping, fishing, hiking, and hunting) but is limited by a lack of trails, out-of-date maps, and possible logging operations.

PICNIC AREAS **East Laporte River Access Area.** Open every day 8 AM–dusk, this shady riverside picnic area, run by Jackson County Parks and Recreation, sits on the **Tuckaseegee River** 4 miles south of Cullowhee, NC, on NC 107. It offers several simple recreational facilities, the best of which is a little pebble beach where kids can splash in this calm mountain river.

Mark Watson Park. Open daylight and early evening hours, this Jackson County park sits on the west side of town, on Business US 23, just behind the old courthouse. Although mainly a neighborhood recreation park, it has a number of tables under a pavilion, well away from highway noise, has a number of Works Progress Administration (WPA)–style stone structures, including a long set of steps going up to Sylva's beautiful Old Courthouse with its sweeping views.

Dillsboro River Access Area. Open daylight hours, this pretty little City of Dillsboro, NC, park sits on the **Tuckaseegee River** across the street from the Riverwood Crafters (see *Selective Shopping—Dillsboro, NC*) on River Road, a short distance east of US 441; its entrance might be hard to spot. It has a handful of tables and barbeque pits on a scenic riverside location.

✳ To See

HISTORIC SITES   Judaculla Rock. A state historic site in scenic Caney Fork Valley south of Cullowhee, NC, Judaculla Rock is a large boulder completely covered by pictograms, sitting in on the edge of a lovely mountain meadow. It's signposted off NC 107 three miles south of Cullowhee. The Cherokees credited the rock to their god of the hunt, Judaculla, a terrifying giant who lived in Judaculla Old Fields on the high Balsams crest. Examine the rock closely, and you can see the imprint of Judaculla's seven-fingered hand. Scholars cannot agree on the age or meaning of these carvings, or even if they were carved by the Cherokees. This mysterious site is located in a beautiful mountain valley with lovely views over its meadow. There is no office, visitors center, or even toilets on site—just a few parking spaces in a field, and the strange stone.

CULTURAL SITES ⬆ Mountain Heritage Center (828-227-7129), Western Carolina University, Cullowhee, NC. Open all year, weekdays 8–5; April through October, Sunday 2–5. Closed on university holidays. Free admission. Run by Western Carolina University and located in its administrative building, this small museum tells the story of the pioneers who settled the deep coves and high hollows of the Smokies and their descendants who followed the pioneer way of life. In addition to this permanent display it has changing displays on such diverse topics as blacksmithing, mountain trout, and handcrafting. In addition to running the small museum and maintaining its 10,000-item collection of mountain artifacts, the center publishes scholarly and educational material, puts on educational programs, and cosponsors the highly popular **Mountain Heritage Day** (see *Special Events*) in Cullowhee on the last Saturday in September.

MADISON HALL AT WESTERN CAROLINA UNIVERSITY

Western Carolina University (828-227-7122), Cullowhee, NC. The campus, Hunter Library, and A. K. Hinds University Center are open at all reasonable hours. The Belk Building Art Gallery is open weekdays 8–noon and 1–5. Free admission. The most beautiful of the mountain colleges and universities, "Western" (as it is known) is a collection of redbrick buildings crowded into the narrow head of the Tuckaseegee Valley. Founded as a high school for teachers in 1889, materials for its earliest buildings had to be carried in by pack mules. One of the 16 campuses of the University of North Carolina, this 6,500-student university offers bachelor and graduate degrees in the liberal arts, sciences, business, and education.

Visitors can enjoy Western's superb native mountain landscaping, particularly lovely in the late spring when the rhododendrons and flame azaleas bloom. Western also sponsors the **Highlands Botanical Garden** (see *To See—Gardens and Parks* in "The Blue Ridge: Cashiers and Highlands"), the premiere botanical collection in the Smoky Mountains. Western's large **Hunter Library** houses a first-rate collection of mountain historic material, including the **Kephart diaries.** Casual visitors should enjoy the scenery and the views, visit the on-campus museum at **Mountain Heritage Center** (see above), then check out the two permanent **art galleries,** one in the Belk Building and the other in the A. K. Hinds University Center.

♪ ⊤ **Whittier, a Dream Remembered** (828-497-7589), 29 Main Street, Whittier, NC. Take US 74 twelve miles west of Sylva to exit 72, then take the first left onto Main Street. Open Friday and Saturday 10 AM–5 PM and 7 PM–8:30 PM; Sunday noon–3 PM. Free admission. Whittier resident Gloria Nolan runs a home repair service during the week and opens her wonderful small museum in an old wooden storefront on the weekends. Centered on the history of Whittier, it features a 150-square-foot scale model of Whittier at the turn of the century, as well as a collection of artifacts, family names, old photos and newspaper articles. The front of her museum contains her delightful display of Christmas miniatures and toy trolley engines, "A Little Bit of Christmas." A first-rate gift shop (see **Stuff and Such** under *Selective Shopping—Whittier, NC*) adjoins the museum.

✳ Special Places

♪ ⊤ **The Great Smoky Mountains Railroad in Dillsboro** (828-586-8811; 1-800-872-4681), Dillsboro, NC. When the Norfolk and Southern Railroad announced that they would close the dead-end spur that passed through Dillsboro to Murphy, NC, the western mountain counties faced the loss of their only railroad. To prevent this, private investors bought the hundred-year-old freight line and formed it into the Great Smoky Mountains Railroad. As a small spur line, this dead-end run to the back of beyond would make money where the giants failed by using a simple formula: carry freight at night, but tourists during the day. It's been wildly successful. The railroad runs year-round excursions on both steam and diesel engines (diesel tickets are cheaper) from Dillsboro and Bryson City, NC, on its 53 miles of track—and you'd better get a reservation if you want to make sure you have a seat. Regular excursions from Dillsboro follow the **Tuckaseegee River** downstream, passing mountain settlements and forest-covered slopes. Highlights include a long tunnel dug by convicts, and the site of the train wreck staged for the movie *The Fugitive* (including the wrecked engine, still lying on its side by the tracks). The Dillsboro excursion ends at a historic depot in the center of the pretty little county seat of **Bryson City** (see *Villages* in "Bryson City and the Southeast Quadrant"), where passengers have time to try the local shops and restaurants before the return trip. Prices depend on the comfort level of the passenger car, with the cheapest being open cars and the most expensive being reconditioned club cars. The open cars give the best views and are great fun in good weather; but on a hot or rainy day most grown-ups will prefer the air-conditioned **Crown Coach** cars with their extralarge windows. In addition to these regular excursions the railroad runs many special trains: twilight dinner trains, murder-mystery trains, trains that take in the entire 53 miles in one go, special **Tommy the Tank Engine** trains (with a real steam engine), a local microbrew train, an annual **Santa Train,** and a **New Year's Gala Train.** Open all year; schedule varies. Diesel engine: adults $26, children $13, for open or standard cars. Steam engine: adults $31, children $15, for open or standard cars. More luxurious cars cost extra. Special trains cost extra.

✳ To Do

FISHING Smoky Mountain on the Fly (828-586-4787), 100 Round Top Trail, Sylva, NC. Open all year. William R. Cope specializes in fly-fishing for trout in mountain streams. A local resident from an old pioneer family (try counting all the local places with "Cope" in their names), Willie will not only take you to the good places but will also teach you what you need to know to catch the big one. A full-time guide, Willie is licensed by the State of North Carolina and permitted for guide service within **Great Smoky Mountains National Park** and **Nantahala National Forest.** He offers half-day, full-day or backcountry trips, and will provide equipment if needed.

Appalachian Fly Shop and Guide Service (828-631-9648; 877-433-0332), 180 River Road, Dillsboro, NC. Open 7 days a week 8–6. $150 for a full day; inquire for other rates. Alan Belcher runs this fly-fishing shop and guide service out of a cute old house across the Tuckaseegee River from Dillsboro. Not surprisingly, his guide service specializes in fly-fishing for trout.

Great Smokies Guide Service (828-631-0221), 168 Happy Hollow Road, Sylva, NC. Danny Brower is a lake fishing guide. He offers year-round guiding service, for a wide variety of fish, on the multitude of **Tennessee Valley Authority (TVA) lakes** that dot the western North Carolina mountains. He uses a 17-foot-deep vee boat with three fighting chairs, fish finders, and all Coast Guard equipment.

WHITEWATER ADVENTURES ✐ **Tuckaseegee Outfitters** (828-586-5050; 1-800-539-5683), US 74/441, Dillsboro, NC. You'll find this outfitter on the river, 5 miles west of Sylva, NC. Open May through October daylight hours,. $15–28 per person, depending on the type of inflatable. Dillsboro's Tuckaseegee River is much gentler than the raging Nantahala at nearby Bryson City, NC; you might not want to train for the Olympics on the Tuckaseegee, but (unlike the Nantahala) you can take small children on it. Tuckaseegee Outfitters offers nonguided rentals of inflatables for downstream floats and paddles. They drop you off at Dillsboro and give you a map; you make your own way downstream for a very pretty, and mildly exciting, 4.5 miles.

🛶 **Blue Ridge Outing Company** (828-586-3510; 1-800-572-3510), P.O. Box 86, Whittier, NC. Open May through October daylight hours. Adults $32–42; teenagers $27–37; children $22–32. Located in the flea market complex 8 miles west of Sylva, NC, this outfitter offers guide-assisted (a guide with every group) float trips on the **Tuckaseegee River,** open to families with children as young as 4. Trips are 3½ hours, of which 2¼ hours are spent on the river.

🛶 **Carolina Mountains Outdoor Center** (828-586-5285; 1-888-785-2662), P.O. Box 592, Dillsboro, NC. Open May through October daylight hours. $10–15 per person. Located on the **Tuckaseegee River** in Dillsboro, this outdoor center offers immediate starts with a shuttle at the end of the 4.5-mile downstream float. All trips are unguided on inflatables. Their handsome modern facility has changing rooms.

WILDERNESS EXCURSIONS Slickrock Expeditions (828-293-3999), Cullowhee, NC. Burt Kornegay has been a professional guide since 1971, as well as being a freelance writer and past president of the North Carolina Bartram Trail Society. His Slickrock Expeditions offers several unusual and interesting wilderness excursions in the western mountains of North Carolina.

✳ Lodging

COUNTRY INNS AND HOTELS ♿ **The Balsam Mountain Inn** (828-456-9498; 1-800-224-9498), P.O. Box 40, Balsam, NC 28707. This beautiful-

ly restored Victorian railroad hotel is located well off the main road in Balsam Gap, 0.7 mile from the Blue Ridge Parkway's intersection with US 23/74. Current owner Merrily Teasley has restored the 1908 inn to a high degree of comfort. The inn's hundred-foot-long front is completely lined with first- and second-story columned porches filled with rocking chairs. The large, comfortable lobby has polished hardwood floors, country antique furniture, a games area, and a 2,000-volume library. The 50 rooms all have pastel bead-board walls and ceilings. The comfortable furniture is rustic in style, covered in bright fabrics. Original prints decorate the guest room walls, and each has either two double beds or a king bed; 16 of the rooms are expanded to include a large sitting area, and 8 rooms are 2-room suites. The en suite bathrooms are generally small but well appointed, with either a modern shower or a claw-foot tub. Breakfast is cooked to order and extremely good, while dinners (extra, by reservation) are of truly exceptional quality (see *Dining Out*). The inn has wine and beer service in the restaurant but no bar or hard liquor. There are no televisions, radios, or in-room phones, and the inn enforces a quiet time after 10:30 PM. Standard room: $100–110; larger room $110–130; 2-room suite (no kitchen) $135–160.

The Jarrett House (828-586-0265; 1-800-972-5623), P.O. Box 219, Dillsboro, NC 28725. Open May through December. This three-story wood hotel in central Dillsboro has been in continuous operation since 1884, when it was built to serve the railroad depot. Like everything else in Dillsboro it had fallen on hard times when Jim and Jean Hartbarger bought it in 1975 and converted it to a modern high-quality inn. The hotel's most dramatic feature is its triple level porches, allowing plenty of cool rocking on every floor. Most of the first floor is taken up by its well-known and popular restaurant (see *Dining Out*), with seating for more than 200. Its rooms have been restored to the look and feel of an old country hotel, furnished in antiques, including many 19th-century pieces from the original hotel. All rooms are en suite, and nearly all rooms have from one to three double beds. A full country breakfast is served in the restaurant. $70–95.

BED & BREAKFASTS The Chalet Inn (828-586-0251; 1-800-789-8024), 285 Lone Oak Drive, Whittier, NC 28789. Located in the Barkers Creek section of Jackson County down a tangle of paved country lanes, the Chalet Inn is only 2.4 miles from the four-laned US 23/74/441. George and Hanneke Ware have created this Alpine-style gasthaus on 22 wooded acres. The large, luxurious chalet boasts an ample great room, seven guest rooms ranging in size from comfortable to huge, and an array of private balconies and porches. The inn's grounds are beautifully landscaped around a spring-fed mountain stream, and the surrounding acres are woven with graded footpaths; a grassy lawn is the setting for picnics, barbeques, and lawn games. Rooms are simply but beautifully decorated; all are are en suite and air-conditioned. The traditional German breakfast buffet includes authentic breads, Swiss muesli, German cold cuts, fresh-baked pastries, fresh fruit, and egg casserole—all served up by George and Hanneke in Alpine dress. Rooms $80–102; suites $130–180; includes full breakfast. Cabin rentals $450 per week.

The Freeze House (828-586-8161), 71 Sylvan Heights, Sylva, NC 28779. This large, hilltop redbrick bungalow sits in a quiet Sylva neighborhood, on a shaded property large enough to be registered as a Backyard Nature Preserve by the National Wildlife Federation. Its L-shaped porch, is the setting for full-sized country breakfasts as well as a view over the old Nantahala Turnpike to Sylva's **Mark Watson Park** (see *Wild Places—Picnic Areas*). The Freeze House has been in the same family since it was built, and has been open to visitors just as long. Restored and modernized in 1995, the it offers three large and comfortable upstairs rooms, flooded with light from banks of gable-end windows, and comfortable, homey furnishings. Each room is en suite and air-conditioned, and has one double bed. Two guest houses adjacent to the property are available for weekly and monthly rental. B&B rooms, including full breakfast $75; cottages $400–600 per week.

♥ ✿ The Dillsboro Inn (828-586-3898), 146 North River Road, P.O. Box 270, Dillsboro, NC 28725. Open all year. This small B&B lodge overlooks a dam waterfall on the Tuckaseegee River, a short distance outside Dillsboro. It has 300 feet of landscaped riverfront, including a small fishing pier and a sitting area. Guests can enjoy wide views over the river and the falls from a large deck, or from a wood-fired hot tub. The inn has two rooms and three suites (without kitchen facilities). All of the rooms are large and comfortable, with contemporary decor that contrasts pleasantly with the rustic exterior, exposed beams, and board-and-batten walls. $80–140 for the rooms; $140–180 for the suites.

The Olde Towne Inn (828-586-3461; 1-888-528-8840), 300 Haywood Road, P.O. Box 485, Dillsboro, NC 28725. Open February through December. This large 1878 wood farmhouse in the center of Dillsboro has a wide, full-length front porch where you can sit in a rocking chair and watch the town's historic center immediately below. The old farm parlor now furnishes a homelike lounge, while halls remain lined with original bead board. Its four rooms and a suite are spacious and comfortable, with country-style furnishing and quilts. (A fifth room, less expensive than the others, is much smaller and shares a bath with the owner.) While this inn has many steps, both down from the covered parking and up from the street, it gives ready access to the heart of Dillsboro. Rooms $75–90; suite $105–135; all tariffs include full breakfast.

&. **The Applegate Inn** (828-586-2397), 163 Hemlock Street, P.O. Box 1051, Dillsboro, NC 28725. Located on Scotts Creek in the center of Dillsboro, the Applegate Inn sits secluded by trees and its roomy garden, yet separated from the Great Smoky Mountain Railroad and the Front Street shops by only a footbridge. A large, screened gazebo is cantilevered over Scotts Creek, directly opposite the track where the steam engine is prepared for its tasks. With only a single level and no steps, the Applegate looks like a modern ranch house. However, its five rooms and three mini-suites (two with kitchens) are first rate and recently redecorated. Breakfast is served on the covered porch overlooking the garden and the creek. Ask innkeeper John Faulk about a hayride pulled by his restored John Deere tractor. $70–100, including full breakfast.

The Squire Watkins Inn (828-586-5244; 1-800-586-2429), P.O. Box 430, 657 Haywood Road, Dillsboro, NC 28725. Open all year. This large 1880 Queen Anne mansion is decorated with Victorian antiques and bric-a-brac. When it was built, the Squire Watkins had a sweeping view over the Nantahala Turnpike and the brand-new railroad depot. Now trees screen the turnpike's successor, US 441—but the railroad's steam engine still passes by the inn's gardens. And those gardens are spectacular. Designed by the prominent mountain landscape architect Doan Ogden in the early 1950s, they step down the slope in a series of rock wall terraces. The four upstairs rooms are spacious and comfortable, and furnished in Victorian antiques; all rooms are en suite and air-conditioned. Three housekeeping units are behind the main house, 1930s style board-and-batten kitchenettes, very well kept and charmingly furnished in a country style. Rooms $75–85, including full breakfast. Housekeeping units $68–95 per night; $375–400 per week.

The River Lodge (828-293-5431; 877-384-4400), 619 Roy Tritt Road, Cullowhee, NC 28723. River Lodge would be notable for its friendly hosts, Cathy and Anthony Sgambato, for its 6 carefully landscaped acres with sweeping views, for its peaceful 600-foot waterfront on the trophy fish–producing Tuckaseegee River, for its comfortable and well-decorated rooms, or for its gourmet breakfasts. But what you really notice is the great room, a gigantic space serving as the guest lounge. Its walls are of century-old hand-hewn logs, each a foot in diameter, salvaged from derelict local cabins and barns by the building's architects in 1970. Inside, a huge stone hearth dominates one wall, old barn timbers support the massive roof span, while stairs made of

THE SQUIRE WATKINS INN, A FORMER 19TH-CENTURY MANOR HOME

half-logs flow up to the second story. Individually furnished guest rooms mingle Victorian oak, country vernacular, mission-style designs, and Native American motifs. Guest beds, either queen or two twins, are handmade in the Smokies of whole logs. All rooms are en suite; most have either a claw-foot tub with a separate shower, or a double-sized shower. A suite has a sitting area with its own stone fireplace and whirlpool bath, with a wood spiral staircase to the loft sleeping area. Rooms $109–139 peak season, $99–129 off-peak; suite $200 peak, $190 off-peak.

CABIN RENTALS 🐾 𝒮 ♿ **Mountain Creek Cottages** (828-586-6042), P.O. Box 178, Dillsboro, NC 28725. Open all year. Located 2.5 miles up a paved mountain road from the four-lane US 23/74/441, these four cabins share a beautiful streamside grove of giant hemlocks, laced with paths and centered on a log gazebo. These older cabins have been recently renovated by new owners Marybeth Druzbick and Patrick Hinkle; all are bright, clean, roomy, and comfortably fur-

nished with full kitchens and queen or king beds. They also own the three small houses that make up the **Eagle's Nest Cottages,** and manage four private homes for weekly rentals. Cabins and cottages: $70–90 per day, $420–540 per week; houses: $105–150 per night, $630–900 per week.

🐾 𝒮 **Fox Den Cottages** (828-293-9847; 1-800-721-9847), P.O. Box 129, Cullowhee, NC 28723. It's 30 miles from Great Smoky Mountains National Park, but less than 4 miles from Western Carolina University. Open all year. These remote, rural cabins cabins are completely modern, roomy, well furnished, and immaculately kept. They are set together on their own high-slope tract, with enough land to give privacy and a feeling of remoteness. Some cabins have mountain views, and all have large porches and rockers, wood-burning fireplaces, and oak floors. $375–600 per week; daily rates available during the off-season.

CABIN RESERVATION SERVICES
𝒮 **Apple Realty** (828-586-3450; 1-800-766-2775), US 441, P.O. Box 396, Dillsboro, NC 28725. Located on US 441 immediately south of town, this Dillsboro realty company leases and maintains over 50 private units. Extra 3 percent fee for credit card payments. Rates are typically $512–877 per week.

✳ Where to Eat

EATING OUT Hooper's Snack Bar (828-586-9877), 606 Main Street, Sylva, NC. Open Monday through Saturday 8–4. This classic 1940s-era snack bar, with a long lunch counter and a few tables, seems right at home on Sylva's Main Street, snuggled in among the redbrick storefronts. It features plain, freshly prepared breakfasts, sandwiches, and burgers, as well as old-fashioned ice cream dishes and shakes. Breakfast $1.50–2.29; lunch $1.89–3.29.

Meriweather's (828-586-4409), 617 Main Street, Sylva, NC. Open Monday through Saturday 11:30 AM–3 PM and 5 PM–9 PM. A comfortable lunch and dinner restaurant in a downtown brick building, Meriweather's features a menu of American favorites, all made to order from fresh ingredients. They maintain a varied menu, with a variety of salads and sandwiches for lunch with a number of dinner entrées and specials added after 5 PM. The cooking is straightforward, without exotic ingredients or unfamiliar courses, but always ample and well prepared. Their burgers and chili are among the best in the mountains. They have beer and wine service, with a limited selection. Salads, burgers, and sandwiches $4.95–5.95; dinner entrées $8.45–10.45.

Golden China Restaurant (828-586-9079), 744F East Main Street, Sylva, NC. Open Sunday through Thursday 11 AM–9:30 PM; Friday 11 AM–11 PM; Saturday 5 PM–10 PM. This modest restaurant in an old motel is a pleasant surprise—friendly, sparkling clean, with food that's fresh, imaginative, and authentic. De Tong Chen and his family offer wonderful specialties, perfectly spiced and beautifully presented, along with a long list of traditional favorites prepared with equal care. The Golden China has wine and beer service, so you can enjoy an ice cold Tsing Tao with your meal. Specialties, $8.95–15.95; Dinner $5.95–8.95; seafood $8.95–12.95.

Dillsboro Smokehouse (828-586-9556), 267 Haywood Street, Dillsboro, NC. Open Monday through Saturday 11 AM–8 PM; Sunday 11 AM–3 PM. This friendly spot in central Dillsboro is where the locals go. It features hearty, fresh food, including old-fashioned mountain barbeque. Typically $5–11 per person.

The Well House (828-586-8588), US 441, Dillsboro, NC. Open Saturday through Wednesday 11–5; Thursday and Friday 11–8. This Dillsboro café, in the basement of the **Riverwood Crafters** (see *Selective Shopping—Dillsboro, NC*) across the river from the main town, specializes in deli sandwiches, fresh salads, homemade soups, and made-from-scratch desserts. Owner and manager Mike Dillard has been in charge for 16 years and continues to pursue quality over convenience. Inside it's roomy, if a bit dark, with many booths and an actual 19th-century well in one corner (still used for irrigation water). Long a popular lunch stop, they've recently added dinner entrées on Thursday and Friday evenings, including prime rib, Cuban pork chops, and chicken with saffron rice. They'll pack you a picnic box if you ask them. Salads and sandwiches $2.95–4.95.

DINING OUT The Balsam Mountain Inn (828-456-9498; 1-800-224-9498), Balsam, NC. Open 6 PM–10 PM, by reservation. This 1908 railroad hotel (see *Lodging—Country Inns and Hotels*), 0.7 mile off US 74/23 and the Blue Ridge Parkway, offers fine dining in a remote, rural setting. The hotel's old dining hall has now become an exquisite restaurant without losing any of its authenticity. A small side room displays early tourist maps of the Smokies, and an enclosed porch offers more seating with large, bright windows. The menu typically combines several traditional items, such as fresh-baked mountain trout or filet mignon, with two or three surprises, such as shrimp and crabmeat au gratin in a sherry cream sauce, or apple-smoked pork with caramelized leek sauce. A sophisticated wine list completes the experience. Typically $15–25 per person, excluding alcohol.

🍴 **The Jarrett House** (828-586-0265; 1-800-972-5623), P.O. Boc 219, Dillsboro, NC. Open May through December. Lunch daily 11–2; dinner Friday and Saturday 4–8. This historic inn in central Dillsboro, in continuous use for 120 years, continues its history hotel tradition of good, plain food and plenty of it. Choices never vary; it's salt-cured ham (fried or baked), fried chicken, or deep fried fish—catfish for lunch, local trout for dinner. Meals are served with sides of coleslaw, candied apples, buttered potatoes, green beans, pickled beets, and hot biscuits. Lunch is served as a plate, while dinner is served family-style, out of big bowls. Desserts consist of vinegar pie, cobblers, and French silk pie. No beer or wine service. Lunch $9; dinner $11–12.50; dessert $1.25–2.25.

Lulu's Café (828-586-8989), 612 Main Street, Sylva, NC. Open Monday through Saturday 11:30–9. This handsome restaurant, occupying three redbrick storefronts in downtown Sylva, has gained a wide reputation for its sophistication and intelligence. Dishes might include a pecan-crusted catfish sandwich, or portobello mushrooms grilled in a basil-orange glaze. The lunch menu offers original salads and sandwiches, with specials such as black bean and sweet-potato enchiladas and seafood gumbo. At dinner the sandwiches disappear, replaced by a selection of entrées and specials, typically nontraditional and frequently adventurous. Lulu's wine list is sophisticated; beers include several microbrews and imported ales. $7–12.

Spring Street Café (828-586-1800), Spring Street, Sylva, NC. Lunch and dinner, Tuesday through Saturday; brunch Sunday; closed Monday. This café has acquired quite a reputation in the very short time it has been open. Located in a bookstore basement down a side street from Sylva's downtown, it's a full-service lunch and dinner restaurant. Its menu is adventuresome, with exotically spiced free-range chicken, trout, shrimp, and vegetarian dishes. Despite this distinctly un-mountain cuisine, it has become instantly popular with the locals, and comes highly recommended. Lunch salads and sandwiches $3–7.95; lunch entrées $5.25–7.85; dinner $5.95–13.95; Sunday brunch $3.75–7.95.

✳ Selective Shopping
Sylva, NC
Jackson's General Store (828-586-9600), 582 West Main Street. Open Monday through Thursday 9–7; Friday and Saturday 9–9; closed Sunday. For many years occupied by Sylva Dry Goods, this two-sided downtown store has old wood fixtures, a mezzanine balcony, and a worn hardwood floor that date straight back to the Depression. One side has casual clothes with an outdoors bent, while the other side is filled with country-style crafts, cards, and doodads.

Livingston's Photo (828-586-2814), 526 West Main Street. It's always good to know where you can find a good camera shop when you're on the road. This full-service shop in downtown Sylva, with a wide selection of equipment and supplies spread over two storefronts, is as good as anyplace in the mountains.

SOUTH OF THE SMOKIES

Dillsboro, NC

Nearly all of Dillsboro's 40-odd stores are interesting. This sampling is slanted toward those shops that feature local artists and crafters—truly unique offerings.

L. Kotila Art Gallery (828-631-1996), 72 Front Street. Open Monday through Saturday 10–5. Linda's subtle and highly detailed watercolors treat contemporary rural life with affection and respect. One series portrays Dillsboro's unique village atmosphere through winter festivities and merry-making.

Dogwood Crafters (828-586-2248), 90 Webster Street. Open all week 9:30–5:30. This modest log building at the western edge of Front Street hides a half-dozen rooms jammed floor to ceiling with every kind of country crafts and fine art imaginable. As the outlet store for Jackson County's **Dogwood Crafters Cooperative,** this volunteer-staffed shop offers the work—handmade and deeply original—of the cooperative's hundred local members. You'll find quilts, wall hangings, stained glass, watercolors, fancy birdfeeders, Christmas decorations, pottery, baskets, calligraphy, lace, knickknacks, bric-a-brac, and souvenirs of all sorts.

Mountain Pottery (828-586-9182), 152 Front Street. Open normal retail hours in-season, restricted hours off-season; may close for lunch. This brightly lit shop, with full windows running down to its wood floors, offers a large and varied selection of fine-arts pottery by owner Rick Urban and other mountain potters. You'll find pottery that's bright, earthy, traditional, sexy, humorous—anything but ordinary. More often than not, Rick will be working on new pieces in a large open studio area on one side of the gallery.

☂ **The Riverwood Crafters** (828-

BRANT BARNES OF RIVERWOOD CRAFTERS THROWING A POT

586-2547), US 441 South. Open normal retail hours all year, Monday through Sunday; individual shops' hours may vary. Located across the Tuckaseegee River from the main part of town, this fine old Victorian structure now houses a fine-crafts gallery, a pewter maker, a potter, a stained-glass maker, a café, a used bookstore, and a couple of first-rate gift shops. All three of the crafters welcome visitors into their studios, adjacent of each of their shops. Potter Brandt Barnes combines a sense of the traditional with a vivid and subtle color sense—and perhaps a touch of whimsy as well. Stained-glass artist Ivor Pace operates in a more romantic style, reminiscent of Tiffany, lush with nature motifs; a partially enclosed porch has been converted into a perfect display area. The Riverwood Pewterers are the oldest crafters in the area, authentic mountain crafters with a continuous history in Dillsboro, dating back to the Depression; their simple, elegant hand-hammered ware speaks to an earlier time.

The Dillsboro Chocolate Factory (828-631-0156; 877-687-9731), 27

Church Street. Open Monday through Saturday 10–5. The aroma of melting chocolate mixes heavily with that of hot espresso as you walk in the door of this tiny candy and coffee factory. Owners Randy and Susan Lyons make their own fine chocolate candies and scratch fudges, while stocking several varieties of gourmet chocolates. There's only one table inside, but outside are café tables under some fine old birches.

Whittier, NC

𝕋 **Stuff and Such** (828-497-7589), 29 Main Street. Open Friday and Saturday, 10 AM–5 PM and 7 PM–8:30 PM; Sunday noon–3 PM; closed Monday through Thursday (but check, as Gloria opens when she is working in her museum). This gift shop features a large selection of homey, locally made crafts in one of the few old wooden storefronts surviving in Whittier. It's run by Gloria Nolan as part of her local museum, which is attached to this gift shop (see Whittier, a Dream Remembered under *To See—Cultural Sites*).

Cherokee Daylily Garden (828-497-7722), 380 Union Hill Road, Cherokee. Open May through September, every day 9–6. Cherokee tribal member Norma Moss and her husband, Ted, run a professional daylily nursery, which they keep open to the public as a working garden. It's a beautiful place in the summer, with a fine view over the thriving daylilies. Their selection is astonishing, with scores of different varieties available. If you like something, they'll gladly dig you a healthy clump.

✳ Special Events

Late April: **Greening Up the Mountains Festival,** Sylva, NC. This downtown street party combines Appalachian heritage with environmental themes.

Mid-June: **Dillsboro Heritage Festival,** Dillsboro, NC. This large and popular street fair features local craftspeople and musicians.

Fourth of July: **Sylva Independence Day Celebration,** Sylva, NC. Bluegrass street dances, and fireworks over the beautiful hilltop courthouse.

Last Saturday in September: **Mountain Heritage Day,** Cullowhee, NC. The largest and most distinguished heritage festival in the North Carolina Smokies, **Western Carolina University**'s (see *To See—Cultural Sites*) Mountain Heritage Day features live performances, crafts demonstrations, and a midway with over 200 mountain crafters and artists. This annual event draws tens of thousands of people to Western's beautiful rural campus.

First two weekends in December: **Dillsboro Lights and Luminaire,** Dillsboro, NC. Dillsboro merchants close out the season with a nighttime program of Christmas lights, candle-lined streets, regional music, and homemade treats and hot beverages served in the shops. A special train, sponsored by the **Great Smoky Mountains Railroad** (see *To See—Other*), brings families in from Sylva, NC.

EASTER SUNDAY

Dillsboro Easter Hat Parade, Dillsboro, NC. Months before tourist season begins, Dillsboro residents celebrate the coming of the first flowers of spring by dressing up in creative hats and parading through the center of town, escorted by antique cars. Totally uncommercialized and completely local, this is great fun.

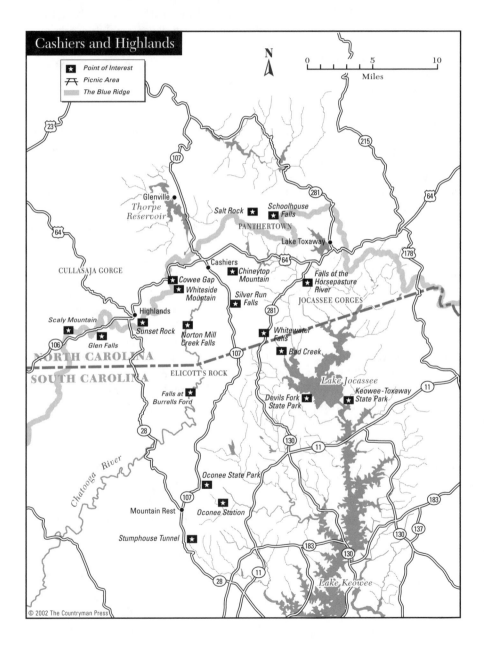

Cashiers and Highlands

Point of Interest
Picnic Area
The Blue Ridge

N

0   5   10
Miles

Glenville ●
Thorpe Reservoir
Salt Rock ★
Schoolhouse Falls ★
PANTHERTOWN
Lake Toxaway ●

CULLASAJA GORGE

Cashiers ●
Chineytop Mountain ★
★ Cowee Gap
★ Whiteside Mountain
Silver Run Falls ★
Falls of the Horsepasture River ★
JOCASSEE GORGES

Scaly Mountain ★
● Highlands
★ Sunset Rock
★ Norton Mill Creek Falls
Whitewater Falls ★
★ Glen Falls
★ Bad Creek

NORTH CAROLINA
SOUTH CAROLINA
ELICOTT'S ROCK

Falls at ★ Burrells Ford

Lake Jocassee
Keowee-Toxaway State Park ★
Devils Fork ★ State Park

Chatooga River

Oconee State Park ★

Mountain Rest ●
★ Oconee Station

Stumphouse Tunnel ★

Lake Keowee

23
107
215
281
64
64
178
106
107
28
130
11
11
183
137
130
130
183
28
11

© 2002 The Countryman Press

THE BLUE RIDGE: CASHIERS & HIGHLANDS

In this area the Blue Ridge has one of its more creative moments. Just to the east, it has just come off its long run as The Blue Wall (see The Mountain Bridge Wilderness of South Carolina under *Wild Places—The Great Forests* in "The Blue Ridge: Hendersonville and Brevard"), a solid granitic mass rising straight up from the plains of South Carolina. Now it retreats suddenly to the north, its crest lined up with the North Carolina towns of Lake Toxaway, Cashiers, and Highlands. Extending south of this crestline, well into South Carolina, it twists into a mass of hard rock ridges, many separated by deep gorges in which rivers rage over high waterfalls. Here the scenery mixes charming valleys with great gray cliffs; lovely little streams drain these valleys, only to fall off their edges in a fierce plunge over a waterfall. Much of this scenery is highly accessible from US 64, which runs east–west near the crest of the Blue Ridge, or from NC/SC 107, which runs north–south.

GUIDANCE **Cashiers Travel and Tourism Authority** (828-743-5192), P.O. Box 238, Cashiers, NC 28717.

Highlands Area Chamber of Commerce (282-526-2112), US 64, P.O. Box 404, Highlands, NC 28741. This chamber maintains a visitors center in the middle of downtown, just off Main Street.

Nantahala National Forest, Highlands Ranger District (828-526-3765), 2010 Flat Mountain Road, Highlands, NC 28741. The ranger station for this part of Nantahala National Forest is located down rural Flat Mountain Road east of Highlands; follow the signs from US 64. They have an information desk and a small bookshop.

Sumter National Forest, Andrew Pickens Ranger District (864-638-9568), 112 Andrew Pickens Circle (SC 28), Mountain Rest, SC 29664. In South Carolina, most of the public forests are within Sumter National Forest. The ranger station is located at the southern end of this chapter's area, on SC 28 just north of its intersection with SC 107.

GETTING THERE *By car:* This isolated area straddles the Blue Ridge Crest between the towns of Franklin and Brevard, NC. No modern, high-quality road enters this area. Even its one U.S. highway, US 64, was engineered in 1923 and never upgraded (see The Cullasaja Gorge under *Wandering Around—Exploring by Car*). The best of the bunch is SC/NC 107, heading north from Walhalla, SC, to Cashiers, NC; it's two lanes are full sized, and it has a real shoulder most of the way. All the other roads are substandard.

By air: The closest and most convenient airport is **Greenville-Spartanburg International Airport** (see *Getting There* in "The Blue Ridge: Chimney Rock and Saluda"), although **Asheville Regional Airport** (see *Getting There* in "Asheville and the Blue Ridge Parkway") isn't much farther. In both cases you'll have to drive a rental car some distance on mountain roads. Atlanta's airport is about 3½ hours away.

By bus or train: Highlands and Cashiers, NC, like the rest of the western mountains, have no bus or train service. However, Highlands does have a shuttle service, the **Highlands Transportation Company** (828-526-4113), that will pick you up from any of the regional airports (Asheville, Atlanta, Greenville-Spartanburg), as well as take you to a restaurant once you're in Highlands.

✳ Wandering Around

EXPLORING ON FOOT **Walking the Blue Ridge.** The Blue Ridge in this area is best explored on foot. Here is a list of the best places, each described more fully in its own listing. **Panthertown Valley** (see *Wild Places—The Great Forests*) is certainly one of the best walking and biking areas, although you'll need to buy a map from the forest service (see Nantahala National Forest, Highlands Ranger District, under *Guidance*) if you intend to stray off its gravel roads. The **Chimneytop and Rocky Mountains** (see *To See—Along the Blue Ridge*) are probably the most exciting hikes in the area. Of course, the view off the highest cliff in the East, at **Whiteside Mountain** (see *To See—Along the Blue Ridge*), is pretty hard to beat. The rivers that drain the Blue Ridge are impressive, too. The **Horsepasture River** (see Falls of the Horsepasture Wild and Scenic River under *To See—Waterfall Country*) has a whole series of waterfalls in a deep gorge—remarkable, but just a taste of 60,000-acre **Jocassee Gorges** (see *Wild Places—The Great Forests* and **Falls of the Jocassee Gorges** under *To See—Waterfall Country*) now under development. And for a quiet riverside walk, the upper **Chattooga River** from **Bull Pen Bridge** is exceptional (see **Norton Mill Creek Falls** under *To See—Waterfall Country*).

✳ Villages

Highlands, NC. The town of Highlands sits in a large bowl at the crest of the Blue Ridge, at an elevation above 4,000 feet. It was founded as a resort town in the 1870s, and numerous buildings date from the 19th century. It remains a high-end resort town, with a large summer population of Atlanta and Florida socialites. Strict zoning have left it looking more like a New England village than a Southern town, nearly devoid of sprawl and chain stores. It is a desert for those reliant on McDonald's and their ilk, and heaven for travelers who appreciate local, inde-

West of Highlands, NC. **US 64** follows the bottom of the 8-mile-long Cullasaja (Cul-la-SAY-jah) Gorge. The current roadway isnearly unchanged since the 1920s—when it was designed for farm wagons and Model Ts—and is lined with national forest sites with lovely CCC architecture. Leaving **Highlands,** it passes by **Lake Sequoyah,** one of several lakes that meander through the town's neighborhoods; look for the dam on your left. A half mile farther, lacy **Bridal Veil Falls** drops 30 feet from an overhanging cliff. Modern US 64 passes in front of the falls (a concession to safety made in 1954), while the **original highway's roadbed still goes underneath the falls,** maintained and drivable—very possibly the only such highway in existence. In 0.75 mile on the left, the Cullasaja River plunges 50 feet over a large overhang to form **Dry Falls,** so named because the footpath passes underneath the overhang, allowing walkers to pass dry (mostly) behind it. A mile farther, **Cliffside Lake Recreation Area** (see *Wild Places—Recreation Areas*), with lakeside and clifftop walks, and a CCC picnic area, turns off to the right. Shortly after that the gorge road becomes rough and wooly, with plenty of twists and turns. Four miles from Cliffside the road becomes a narrow ledge carved into a perpendicular granite cliff, with barely enough room for two cars to pass each other. Views over the gorge are spectacular. However, there is only one place to park, on the left, with room for only about four cars. Don't miss it—it's your only chance to view 200-foot Cullasaja Falls, a stunning double cataract. The gorge drive ends suddenly, dropping out onto flat farmlands in a suddenly widened valley.

DRY FALLS IN CULLASAJA GORGE

pendent shops and cafés. It has a four-block downtown lining its Main Street, with a wide variety of shops in an eclectic mix of buildings from every era. Parking is free and plentiful. Still true to its 19th-century origins, Highlands has quite a choice among small independent hotels, and almost no motels.

Cashiers, NC. Pronounced "CASH-ers," this town was until recently little more than a crossroads post office and general store at the intersection of US 64 and NC 107. Since 1845, when South Carolina's Hampton family established their **High Hampton** hunting lodge there (see High Hampton Inn and Country Club under *Lodging—Resorts*), Cashiers has drawn wealthy South Carolina socialites. In recent decades its popularity with the wealthy has increased. The low hills around High Hampton have become crossed with narrow roads and crusted with hidden mansions, and a downtown area has slowly grown up around the old crossroads. You'll now find Cashiers a full-service town, although you might have to ask where to find something.

Lake Toxaway, NC. This town was founded in 1903 as a resort for the ultra-wealthy, but its fortunes collapsed when its dam broke in 1916. With the dam rebuilt in 1961 the settlement has come back to life, but remains mostly a crossroads community at the intersection of US 64 and NC 281, east of Cashiers, NC.

✳ Wild Places

THE GREAT FORESTS Panthertown Valley. Panthertown Valley (locals say "Painter-town") is a wide, flat-bottomed bowl perched high up on the crest of the Blue Ridge, between Cashiers and Lake Toxaway, NC. The valley has two access points, one on each side. The western gate is reached from **Cashiers,** an interesting and beautiful drive that crosses the Blue Ridge Crest twice: Take **US 64** west 1.8 miles to a left on **Cedar Creek Road (SSR 1120),** then climb 2.1 miles to a right on **Breedlove Road (SSR 1121),** which you follow to its end in 3.5 miles. The eastern gate is reached from **Lake Toxaway:** Take **NC 281** north from US 64 for 0.8 mile to **Cold Mountain Road (SSR 1301),** which you follow to its end in 5.5 miles.

Part of Nantahala National Forest since 1989, the valley is noted for its high cliffs, waterfalls, sandy-beached swimming holes, and incredible biological diversity. Previous private owners installed a network of gravel roads and rough tracks, making the valley easy to get around by foot or mountain bike—motor vehicles are strictly prohibited.

The Jocassee Gorges. In this area the Blue Ridge shifts north, leaving a maze of hard rock side ridges and outliers extending into South Carolina. While this terrain stretches between Lake Toxaway and Highlands, NC, the eastern half (between Lake Toxaway and Cashiers, NC) is the rougher—a land of narrow, cliff-sided gorges and tall waterfalls. Duke Power acquired most of this area for its hydroelectric potential during the 1960s, building **Lake Jocassee** (see *To See—Big Dammed Lakes*) in the 1970s and the **Bad Creek Project** (see Bad Creek Power Station under *Recreation Areas*) in the 1980s. In the 1990s Duke negotiated with a group of governments and conservation organizations to convert most of the remaining land into public conservation lands, with the remaining Duke properties having conservation easements and public access via wildlife management

Gorges Tract had been created.

The tract possesses immense value for its biological diversity, rugged scenery, and many waterfalls. However, it's now split between six different entities (North Carolina State Parks, South Carolina State Parks, North Carolina Wildlife Resources, Nantahala National Forest, Sumter National Forest, and Duke Power), and recreational plans are not yet complete. Meanwhile, existing recreational facilities at **Horsepasture River** (see Falls of the Horsepasture Wild and Scenic River under *To See—Waterfall Country*) and **Whitewater Falls** (see *To See—Waterfall Country*) give some taste of the wonders to come. By the time you read this, more facilities will almost certainly be available.

Chattooga Wild and Scenic River and Ellicott Rock Wilderness. The Chattooga River rises at the base of **Whiteside Mountain** (see *To See—Along the Blue Ridge*), then flows southward through deep, boulder-strewn gorges. Lower sections may be known for their kayaking, but this area is much too rough and dangerous. Instead, it's the haunt of hikers and bank fishers, with most of its length within national forests and followed by footpaths. Public access starts at **Whiteside Cove Road (SSR1107**, off **NC 107** 1.7 miles south of Cashiers, NC), where this country lane crosses a clear mountain stream—the **Chattooga** near its headwaters. A short walk upstream on a fisherman's trail leads to a pretty little waterfall and a sand beach. Downstream are more waterfalls and a rough gorge, reached by walking trails from **Bull Pen Bridge** (see **Norton Mill Creek Falls** under *To See—Waterfall Country*). From here the river runs through **Ellicott Rock Wilderness,** declared by Congress in 1975. Easiest foot access to the wilderness is from **Burrells Ford** in South Carolina (see Falls of the Chattooga at Burrells Ford under *To See—Waterfall Country*), where the **Chattooga River Trail** follows the left bank both up and downstream.

RECREATION AREAS **Cliffside Lake Recreation Area.** This Nantahala National Forest recreation area, inside the **Cullasaja Gorge** (see *Wandering Around—Exploring by Car*), has a lovely little lake underneath cliffs. Paths lead around the lake shore and up the cliffs for really excellent views. The park features classic Civilian Conservation Corps (CCC) architecture from the 1930s, including a gazebo at the top of the cliff and a number of picnic shelters. The picnic area sits by the lake, under a canopy of tall old trees.

Bad Creek Power Station. You'll find this power station just inside South Carolina on NC 281/SC 130; you'll need to sign in at the visitors' gate. This Duke Power–pumped storage facility floods a bowl-shaped valley perched high in the mountains near the South Carolina–North Carolina border, just south of **Whitewater Falls** (see *To See—Waterfall Country*). Its purpose is to create extra hydropower during peak demand periods; Duke pumps water up to this reservoir during slack times, then runs it through the **Lake Jocassee** (see *To See—Big Dammed Lakes*) turbines when its needed. Duke occasionally opens the station for tours. More to the point, they always allow recreationists to enter the site during daylight hours (you can leave, but not enter, after dusk), to use the network of hiking trails. The most prominent feature is **Lower Whitewater Falls,** over 300 feet high and every bit as beautiful as the more famous waterfall upstream. As the lands are closed to hunting, this is a good place for October backcountry walking.

PICNIC AREAS Ravenel Park, Highlands, NC. Adjacent to the **Highlands Botanical Garden** (see *To See—Gardens and Parks*), this town park follows a narrow, winding lakeshore through a residential area. Such lakes are a typical and charming feature of Highlands neighborhoods, and Ravenel makes for a good picnic spot.

Oconee State Park (864-638-5353), 624 State Park Road, Mountain Rest, NC. Located at the far southern end of the Blue Ridge's craggy outliers, just off SC 107, this South Carolina state park offers lakeside recreation as well as picnicking. The Civilian Conservation Corps (CCC) built most of this lovely little park's buildings in the 1930s.

In addition to Oconee State Park, there are several **Sumter National Forest picnic areas** along SC 107, starting just below the state line.

✳ To See

ALONG THE BLUE RIDGE The Blue Wall (see South Carolina's Blue Wall under *Wild Places—The Great Forests* in "The Blue Ridge: Chimney Rock and Saluda") section of the Blue Ridge ends suddenly. The crestline of the Blue Ridge sweeps backward, well into North Carolina, and the space between the retreating crest and the line of The Blue Wall is filled with a jumble of hard rock ridges. Those jumbled ridges are separated by spectacular gorges, with an incredible concentration of waterfalls (see *Waterfall Country*). Back at the crest—now running from Lake Toxaway through Cashiers and into Highlands, NC—the Blue Ridge is up to its old tricks, with great gray cliffs plunging down its south face, and gentle slopes leading to high valley bowls on its north face. This makes for a unique treat: wide views from the highest cliffs in the East, over a massive jumble of deep gorges and craggy mountains—and all of it easy to reach from those gentle north slopes. Here are a few of the best spots, from east to west.

Schoolhouse Falls. Here the headwaters of the **Tuckaseegee River** plunge over an overhanging 20-foot ledge into a large pool, not 0.5 mile from the crest of the Blue Ridge. Schoolhouse Falls are located on the western edge of **Panthertown Valley** (see *Wild Places—The Great Forests*) in Nantahala National Forest, only 0.7 mile from the gate at the end of **Cold Mountain Road (SSR 1301).** Schoolhouse Falls is the most accessible of Panthertown Valley's waterfalls; like many such falls, it has formed a grotto that protects a variety of rare ferns and other plants. The large pool is a popular swimming hole.

Salt Rock. Salt Rock sits above the western end of Panthertown Valley (see *Wild Places—The Great Forests*) in Nantahala National Forest. You'll find this bald after a very easy 0.2-mile walk down the gravel road from the gated end of **Breedlove Road (SSR 1121),** with the bald on the left through a tree belt. Naturalist and biographer George Ellison has called this "one of the most delightful views in the southern highlands." It's a large rocky bald, decorated with moss and wind-dwarfed trees, that gives a wide panorama of the cliff face of the Blue Ridge rising straight up from Panthertown Valley.

Chimneytop Mountain and Rocky Mountain (828-743-2411). Cashiers, NC, sits at the feet of these two craggy outliers of the Blue Ridge. Rocky Mountain, on the north, provides a long, smooth, gray cliff that serves as backdrop to Cashiers and the **High Hampton** golf course (see *To Do—Golf*). To its immediate south, Chimneytop pokes a tall, narrow black crag up through the trees. The **High Hampton Inn and Country Club** (see *Lodging—Resorts*) includes both peaks in their 1,400-acre resort, and maintains exciting (and none too easy) hiking trails to the tops of both. These trails lead to breathtaking views over Cashiers, along the cliff-sided Blue Ridge and toward **Whiteside Mountain** (see below).

Cowee Gap. Here's one you can drive to. When US 64 crosses the Blue Ridge Crest between Cashiers and Highlands, NC, it opens up a broad panorama over the headwaters of the **Chattooga River. Rocky** and **Chimneytop Mountains** (see above) are ahead of you; the part of **Whiteside Mountain** known as the **Devils Courthouse** is to your right. This overlook comes up quickly on a very sharp bend, so be alert.

Whiteside Mountain. Reputed to be the highest continuous cliff in the East, Whiteside projects a mile out into the valley of the **Chattooga River** from the Blue Ridge Crest. Its gentle north slope, typical of the Blue Ridge, makes for a moderate walk to the cliff top. The view must be seen to be believed—and the loop path follows this cliff top for a mile, opening up new vistas at every turn. Like most Blue Ridge cliffs, these start off as a gentle rock slope that gets gradually steeper; a foolhardy hiker can get quite a ways down before noticing the extraordinary danger. A failed tourist attraction in the 1950s, the attraction's old tram bed makes for an easy but viewless walk to the top, where a loop trail follows the cliff line back to the parking lot. Whiteside is part of Nantahala National Forest, which may charge a parking fee.

Sunset Rock. Part of the Town of Highland's **Ravenel Park** (see *Wild Places—Picnic Areas*), Sunset Rock is a large bald overlooking Highlands, NC. It sits on one side of the Blue Ridge Crest, here an unimpressive little ridgeline, with Sunrise Rock on the other side. From Sunset Rock this little mountaintop town looks particularly quaint and attractive, its downtown surrounded by forests and framed by mountain ridges. On the other side of the ridge, **Sunrise Rock** gives more limited views over the face of the Blue Ridge. You can walk up to Sunrise Rock from the **Highland's Nature Center** (see **Glen Falls,** below), or drive up a rough gravel road that goes right from **Horse Cove Road (SSR 1603)** to follow the Blue Ridge.

WHITESIDE MOUNTAIN, VIEWED FROM WHITESIDE COVE

Glen Falls. Just west of Highlands, a violent little stream called the East Fork throws itself straight down the Blue Ridge escarpment, dropping 800 feet in a half mile. On the way down it forms three impressive waterfalls, each one bigger than the last. The Nantahala National Forest path goes straight down as well, using interminable steps to drop through old growth forest to views of the waterfalls.

Scaly Mountain. From NC 106 south of Highlands, NC, turn right on **Turtle Pond Road (SSR 1620),** then left onto gravel **Lickskillit Road (SSR 1621);** as you top a gap, look for a place to park. Access is by the **Bartram Trail,** a long-distance path that retraces the steps of 18th-century naturalist William Bartram. The trail goes left 1 mile to Scaly Mountain, a 500-foot climb. Scaly anchors the western end of this segment of the Blue Ridge. It has a large, south-facing rocky bald that gives broad views over the low ridges that drop into Georgia.

WATERFALL COUNTRY Between Highlands and Lake Toxaway, NC, great jumbled knots of ridges extend into South Carolina, separated by deep valleys cut through the hard rock. Underneath one of these narrow gorges, a particularly hard and stubborn layer of rock will suddenly give way, letting flood waters crash down into softer stone, breaking it, carrying it downhill into the flatlands. This is waterfall country.

Falls of the Horsepasture Wild and Scenic River. In 1986 the U.S. Congress acted to stop a California carpetbagger from destroying the little Horsepasture River in a hydroelectric scheme, by declaring it a Wild and Scenic River—the result of an extraordinary campaign by local residents. Waterfalls—five of them—were the reason for this unusual Congressional action. Three are easily accessible from **NC 281** south of **Sapphire,** NC, via a Nantahala National Forest path. Nearest the highway is **Drift Falls,** a 30-foot slide rock with a large swimming hole at the bottom. Ten minutes farther down the excellent path is **Turtle Back Falls,** which looks like water rolling over a turtle's back, with a 15-foot drop into the pool beneath. Some of the foolhardy (and one may doubt the "hardy" part) use this as a slide rock as well. Nobody uses the next waterfall as a slide rock. **Rainbow Falls** drops 150 feet straight down in a roar of water that puts up a perpetual mist in which rainbows form. Farther downstream the path becomes much steeper and quite difficult, leading to **Stairstep Falls** and **Windy Falls.**

Whitewater Falls. One of several waterfalls claimed as the "tallest in the East," Whitewater Falls is an impressive sight. Located in Nantahala National Forest, off **NC 281** near the North Carolina–South Carolina state line, it carries a huge flow of water 450 feet straight down in three great jumps. A short, flat walk from the parking lot leads to an unobstructed view of its entire length. The old pioneer-era road ran right by this waterfall, and its roadbed can be walked to its top. Downstream, **Lower Whitewater Falls** can be reached from Duke Power's **Bad Creek Power Station** (see *Wild Places—Recreation Areas*), just south of the state line; just drive right up and ask the guard at the gate.

Falls of the Jocassee Gorges (828-966-9099 for North Carolina's Gorges State Park), Sapphire, NC. In a very real sense, the above entries are classic Jocassee Gorges waterfalls, fortunate enough to have public protection for many years. As this book went to press, North and South Carolina were still making plans on how they intend to develop the remaining 53,000 acres of the Jocassee Gorges, purchased in 1999 from Duke Power. Neither state has designed a trail network, much less started construction. A pity—the 7,500-acre Gorges State Park in North Carolina has inventoried 13 major waterfalls on only 14 percent of their land, and this may be an undercount. Stay tuned.

Silver Run Falls. The only difficulty in exploring this isolated piece of Nantahala National Forest is finding the parking area. It's on **NC 107,** 3.92 miles south of US 64, near **Cashiers,** NC. It's a wide gravel area on the left; and, if it's summer, there are cars parked there. This is a justifiably popular swimming hole. The falls are lovely, one of those active little rivers that throws itself over a 15-foot ledge.

Norton Mill Creek Falls. One of the finest swimming holes in the mountains, this gem is little known and little visited—possibly because it's a bit of a walk. From **US 64** in **Cashiers,** NC, go south on **NC 107** for 6.9 miles to **Bull Pen Road, SSR 1603,** then west 5.1 miles to the spectacular steel-truss bridge with wonderful views of the **Chattooga River** far below; park where you can. From the steel bridge, the Chattooga River trail leads upstream 3 miles through a lovely riverine forest in a deep gorge, to this small, beautifully formed waterfall with a large, deep pool and sand beach. There's a steel footbridge over it, which the Forest Service helicoptered in.

WHITEWATER FALLS

Falls of the Chattooga at Burrells Ford. The rough side mountains of the Blue Ridge extend deep into South Carolina. Three attractive waterfalls can be found grouped around the **Burrells Ford Bridge** over the Chattooga River. (You'll find Burrells Ford Road 13 miles south of **Cashiers,** NC, on **NC/SC 107,** on the right.) Burrells Ford forms a sort of mini-recreation area along a smooth stretch of the Chattooga River, in South Carolina's **Sumter National Forest;** it has many good places to fish, a primitive camping area that can double as a picnic area, and a network of trails that leads to (among other things) three waterfalls. You'll find trailhead parking a bit uphill from the bridge. For **Spoonauger Falls,** go to your right up the **Chattooga River Trail** for a short half mile; this small stream stairsteps 40 feet down a cliff on your left. Straight ahead, the path continues to the **Ellicott Rock Wilderness,** following the Chattooga. However, for more waterfalls, return to Burrells Ford and continue across the road on the Chattooga River Trail. Very shortly (inside the camping area) a side trail will lead 0.3 mile uphill to **Kings Creek Falls,** another 40-foot drop but much more violent than Spoonauger. Return to the Chattooga River Trail and continue downstream for another 3 miles to reach **Big Bend Falls,** down a fisherman's path on your right (listen for the noise of the waterfall). This is a 25-foot waterfall stretching the width of the Chattooga, with a 12-foot plummet over an overhang onto an equally large cascade. The trail doesn't end here—it continues another 4 miles, following the Chattooga through a deep gorge, reaching **SC 28** in 10.5 miles from Burrells Ford.

BIG DAMMED LAKES Lake Glenville, Glenville, NC. This large lake, 3,500 feet in elevation, sends out long, thin arms into many former valleys in the Glenville area, north of Cashiers, NC, on **NC 107.** The highway skirts the lake for some distance before swerving away as it reaches the dispersed community of Glenville. Lakeside scenery is very mixed, with much forest, a number of farms and meadows, and a slowly but steadily increasing number of subdivisions. A winding narrow lane (**SSR 1157**) turns left off NC 107 on the north end of Glenville, first reaching a nice county park with picnicking and a boat ramp, then crossing the impressive World War II–era dam (with a free boat launch on the other side). The lake is owned by Duke Power; water from the lake flows through a giant pipeline to a hydropower station at Tuckaseegee. By the way, it's officially known as "Thorpe Reservoir," but if you call it that no one will know what you are talking about.

Lake Toxaway (1-800-443-0694), Lake Toxaway, NC. This is the lake that would not die. The Toxaway Company, established in 1896, aggressively developed Sapphire and Toxaway as resorts for the rich. In 1903 they built Lake Toxaway and place a giant luxury hotel on its shore. It seemed to be a roaring success, filling with millionaires who would park their private railroad cars on a special siding built for that purpose. However, the Toxaway Company flared out in 1911, going into bankruptcy. In 1916 the Lake Toxaway Dam failed, sending a wall of 5.4 billion gallons of water straight down the mountainside; you can still see the scoured-out trail it left just below the US 64 bridge. The grand inn was abandoned, then dismantled for scrap in 1947. In 1961 a group of investors purchased the dried-up lake bed and rebuilt the dam, selling lots once again around the lakeside. Only a few of the original mansions remain along the rebuilt Lake Toxaway, the most remarkable being the **Moltz Mansion,** now the **Greystone Inn** (see *Lodging—Resorts*). The lake itself is private, closed to the public.

Lake Jocassee. Lake Jocassee floods 7,600 acres of Blue Ridge valleys in South Carolina, just below the state line. It's part of a massive hydropower operation by Duke Power, in combination with Lake Keowee to the south and **Bad Creek Power Station** (see *Wild Places—Recreation Areas*) to its north. Most of the lands to the north of Jocassee have been owned by Duke Power since the 1960s, protecting them from development; now they are in public ownership as the 60,000-acre **Jocassee Gorges** area (see The Jocassee Gorges under *Wild Places— The Great Forests*). Lake Jocassee sends long, thin arms deep into this wilderness, allowing easy access to some remarkably remote areas. There are boat ramps at **Devils Fork State Park,** on SC 11 east of SC 107.

HISTORICAL SITES Stumphouse Tunnel, Mountain Rest, SC. This local park, on SC 28 at the far southern edge of the Blue Ridge's outliers, preserves the mortal remains of an extraordinarily overambitious antebellum railroad project. In 1850—a time when no accurate maps existed of the Blue Ridge and Smoky Mountains—the **Blue Ridge Railway** made a serious attempt to run a road straight across the Southern Appalachians. At Stumphouse Tunnel, the railroad tried to breach the first rock face of the Blue Ridge and failed. The tunnel was to be well over a mile long and was mainly completed when the venture collapsed in 1859. Today, this local park keeps the south end of the tunnel open for 500 feet, with a nice picnic area nearby. (Up to 1994 you could go 1,600 feet into the tunnel, viewing a giant air shaft at midway, but a roof collapse has closed that part of the tunnel.)

Oconee Station State Historic Site (864-638-0079), 500 Oconee Station Road, Walhalla, SC. Open for tours on weekends. This stone-built colonial Cherokee trading post sits in grassy fields at the bottom of the Blue Ridge's last outlier. The adjacent **Richard's House** dates from the same era. Now a South Carolina state park, you'll find it 2 miles off SC 11 north of Walhalla—by coincidence, just downhill from **Oconee State Park** (see *Wild Places—Picnic Areas*).

GARDENS AND PARKS

HIGHLANDS BOTANICAL GARDEN

(828-526-2602), Western Carolina University, Highlands, NC. At the center of Highlands sits a very special botanical garden. Run by Western Carolina University (see *To See—Cultural Sites* in "Near the Park: Sylva and Dillsboro"), this 30-acre site is a biological reservoir of native species and a serious research station for mountain botany, ecology, and biology. The garden is highly informal in its design and layout, a skillful modification of the found environment. Paths loop around a lakeshore thick with lily pads, climb along sheltered stream banks, and break into old cove forests. The gardens were established in 1962, but the research station has been there since the 1930s, and has the look and feel of an old-time ranger station. On site, facing Horse Cove Road, is the **Highland Nature Center,** a nature museum open seasonally. **Ravenel Park** is adjacent (see *Wild Places—Picnic Areas*), and **Sunset Rock** is an easy walk up a footpath (see *To See—Along the Blue Ridge*).

The Church of the Good Shepherd, Cashiers, NC. This lovely little Episcopalian church, located off NC 107, was built in 1896 to serve Cashier's summer colony. Listed in the National Register, it's a particularly handsome example of the rustic Gothic style then favored by the Episcopal and Catholic churches. It's still in use, the center of a year-round parish since 1982.

✳ To Do

GOLF High Hampton (828-743-2450), US 107 South, Cashiers, NC. $35. Designed by George Cobb in 1956, this 18-hole course is noted for its outstanding beauty, including wide views of the cliffs of the Blue Ridge reflecting in the glassy surface of Hampton Lake.

Trillium Links (828-464-3800), 48 Links Drive, Cashiers, NC. $95–125. Designed by Morris Hatalsky in 1998, this 4,000-foot-high course is part of a land development project in the Glenville Lake area north of Cashiers.

Sapphire Mountain Golf Club (828-743-1174), 50 Slicers Avenue, Sapphire, NC. $65. This 1982 Ron Garl course, part of a large modern resort and subdivision development east of Cashiers, NC, on US 64, features mountain scenery from its narrow and undulating fairways (including a hole that plays over a waterfall).

HORSEBACK RIDING Arrowmont Stables and Cabins (828-743-2762; 1-800-682-1092), 276 Arrowmont Trail, Cullowhee, NC. Open all year, Monday through Saturday 8–5. $25–50. Arrowmont provides horses for guided trail rides on 6 miles of trail on their remote 200-acre property in the high mountains north of Cashiers, NC, near Glenville, NC. They also have two cabins, older but clean and well kept, as well as group camping in bunk cabins left over from when the property was a boys' camp.

Sapphire Valley Stables (828-743-9574), US 64 West, Cashiers, NC. Part of a large resort development at Sapphire, NC, east of Cashiers on US 64, this stable offers 1-hour trail rides ($25).

Giddy Up N Go Riding Stables (828-526-4531), Buck Knob Road, Highlands, NC. Located in the Highlands area, this stable offers half- to 2-hour trail rides.

JUST FOR KIDS ❧ Highlands Youth Adventures (828-526-2174), Highlands, NC. Open in summer. $59–89. This organization sponsors summer weekday trips for kids ages 9 to 15, with a different program each day. They furnish lunch and snacks, equipment, and transportation, for daily programs of horseback riding, mountain biking, whitewater rafting, tubing, rock climbing and rappelling, and high ropes and zip lines.

WHITEWATER ADVENTURES Rafting the Chattooga River. The Chattooga River does not become floatable until it has put the high cliffs of the Blue Ridge well behind. The National Forest Service, which owns nearly all of the river, sets the upper limit of the floatable river at the SC 28 highway bridge—the southern end of this chapter. Two large regional float companies are licensed by the Forest Service to run trips on the Chattooga below SC 28: the **Nantahala Outdoor Center** and **Wildwater, Ltd. Nantahala** (for both, see *To Do—*

Whitewater Adventures in "Bryson City and the Southwest Quadrant").

✳ Lodging

COUNTRY INNS AND HOTELS

The Old Edwards Inn (828-526-9319; 1-888-526-9319), Fourth and Main, P.O. Box 1778, Highlands, NC 28741. Open all year. The oldest building in downtown Highlands, this 1878 inn is a country hotel in the grand old manner. It's a distinctive three-story brick building with a beautiful stone entrance (an early owner ran a rock quarry); a long wooden annex with a second-story veranda, almost as old as the main building, houses the excellent **Central House Restaurant** (see *Dining Out*) and additional rooms. A lovely little garden sits in the space between the two buildings, separated from the Main Street sidewalk by a hedge. Furnishings are elegant late-19th-century country in style, with beautiful wall stenciling a major feature found in all 20 rooms; most rooms have balconies, and some have sitting areas. A full breakfast (included) is ordered off the menu in the Central House Restaurant. April through December $115–150; January through March $85–105.

The Highlands Inn (828-526-9380), Corner of Fourth and Main, P.O. Box 1030, Highlands, NC 28741. This classic wood coaching inn, listed on the National Register, has dominated downtown Highlands since 1880. A long, low three-story building, its second-story veranda covers the sidewalk for most of a block. Completely renovated in 1989, it has been carefully decorated with authentic antiques and reproductions typical of a late-19th-century inn. The 31 rooms range from cozy to large, and some have separate sitting areas. $94–174; includes extended continental breakfast.

The Main Street Inn (828-526-2590; 1-800-213-9142), 270 Main Street, Highlands, NC 28741. Built in 1885 and restored in 1998, this farmhouse sits in the middle of the Main Street shopping district, surrounded by its own oak-shaded lawns. The 20 guest rooms are individually theme furnished in antiques and reproductions; some have individual sitting areas or balconies. In some rooms, cathedral ceilings reveal the original hardwood beams from 1885. A large country breakfast is served, and afternoon tea greats guests as they come in from shopping or touring. $95–185.

🐾 🦴 Kelsey and Hutchinson Lodge (828-526-4746; 1-888-245-9058), 450 Spring Street, Highlands, NC 28741. Located on a side lane two blocks from downtown Highlands, the Kelsey and Hutchinson (named after Highlands' founders) is a 1997 reconstruction of the 1883 Lee's Inn, a favorite Highlands' destination for many decades until it burned in the 1980s. The 3.5 acres of land includes several surviving outbuildings of the Lee's Inn, two of which have been beautifully restored for additional rooms. More business-friendly than many historic inns, the K&H has meeting rooms, concierge services, a gift shop, data ports in every room, and 24-hour voice mail service. Rooms are beautifully decorated with knotty-pine paneling and gas fireplaces; most have whirlpool baths, and some are available with balconies or porches, and sitting areas. The **Chestnut House,** also on the property, has two bedrooms, a living room, a dining room, and a full kitchen. The K&H is pet friendly, with a special VIP program for pets. Rooms $82–222; Chestnut House $162–262; $15 pet fee; includes a continental breakfast.

The Chandler Inn (828-526-5992; 1-888-378-6300), US 64 and Martha's Lane, P.O. Box 2156, Highlands, NC 28741. Open all year. This three-diamond AAA inn is one of the more unusual facilities in Highlands. Located on the east side of town, it consists of several wooden buildings grouped tightly around a central garden area, linked by decks and walkways. A modern complex, it has a rustic look and feel, with well-tended gardens; although convenient to the main highway, it's very quiet. All 15 oversized rooms have private entrances onto the interconnecting decks. A hospitality room hosts morning coffee and home-baked goods; guests eat their breakfast by the fireplace, or take it out onto the decks or back into their rooms. $65–160, including continental breakfast.

RESORTS High Hampton Inn and Country Club (828-743-2411; 1-800-334-2551), P.O. Box 338, Cashiers, NC 28717. This 1,400-acre resort, originally built by Confederate General Wade Hampton as a summer home in 1845, has been run by the McKee family in Cashiers since 1922. The entire resort is a National Historic District, with 17 of its buildings listed on the National Register. The main inn is a classic rustic lodge built in 1933, noted for its walls clad in chestnut bark and for the wide views from its wraparound veranda. Hampton Lake opens up vistas to the wide front of the Blue Ridge, which flanks the lake with great gray escarpments and granite crags. Two wonderful hiking trails lead to the tops of these crags—all on High Hampton property. The 117 rooms are rustic,

with board-and-batten paneling from wood logged on the estate, and simple country furniture. The inn serves three meals a day, plus afternoon tea on the veranda; meals are hearty country fare, prepared fresh from scratch and served buffet style. Jackets are required for gentlemen at dinner. Wine and beer are available, and an adjacent bar has mixed drinks. The resort has an impossibly scenic golf course (see *To Do—Golf*), tennis, and boat rentals, all at a reduced tariff for guests. $178–228 for two people in one room; includes all meals.

The Greystone Inn (828-966-4700; 1-800-824-5766), Greystone Lane, Lake Toxaway, NC 28747. This resort complex centers on a six-level 1915 Alpine-style mansion; it occupies a grassy hilltop peninsula in Lake Toxaway, and stairsteps down the slope in stone terraces to the waterside. The 13 guest rooms and suites in the Moltz Mansion are supplemented by 14 suites in two new buildings; all rooms are individually decorated with antiques and reproductions. Gourmet meals include a full breakfast, afternoon tea on the sunporch, evening wine and hors d'oeuvres, and a formal dinner. An evening champagne cruise is offered free to guests, as is canoeing, kayaking, powerboating, waterskiing, tennis, and lawn games. Golf privileges are available at nearby Lake Toxaway Country Club. Rooms: $315–415; suites: $415–595; includes all meals and activities.

BED & BREAKFASTS 4th Street Inn (828-526-4464; 1-888-799-4464), 55 4th Street, Highlands, NC 28741. Located in a residential neighborhood a few blocks from downtown Highlands, this inn occupies a sprawling old farmhouse with a wraparound porch

A MISTY MORNING ON LAKE SEQUOYAH

and a large back deck. Comfortable and homey, its 10 rooms have handmade quilts on the beds and terry cloth bathrobes in the closets. They serve a full gourmet breakfast (including homemade granola and cheese grits), fresh homemade cookies, and an afternoon wine hour with hors d'oeuvres.

Colonial Pines Inn (828-526-2060), 541 Hickory Street, Highlands, NC 28741. Located in a residential neighborhood not far from downtown Highlands, the Colonial Pines occupies a large mid–20th century plantation-style house on 2 acres. It's surrounded by landscaped, shaded lawns, with gardens that supply the breakfast table with fresh produce and herbs. Common rooms have a cozy 1940s look with country furniture, a redbrick fireplace, and knotty-pine paneling. The knotty pine carries throughout the six rooms and one kitchenette apartment, which range from cozy to large. $85–150; includes a full breakfast.

Toad Hall Bed & Breakfast (828-526-3889), 61 Sequoyah Point Way, Highlands, NC 28741. Open all year. This five-room B&B occupies a former family complex, built in the 1950s on a peninsula in **Lake Sequoyah,** an easy mile's drive from downtown Highlands. This small man-made lake, wandering through the hills on the west side of town, offers lovely views, the inn has a nice dock and canoes for guests. Toad Hall the main building of the complex, is principally the owners' residence and the elegant, log-sided dining room, with a large picture window overlooking the lake. Four of the rooms are in the next building, Badger Hall; all are large, individually decorated, with whirlpool tubs and either a balcony or terrace. The fifth room is a cottage with a separate living room, a stone wood-burning fireplace, and a kitchenette. All five rooms enjoy the full breakfast in the main hall. Rooms $120–200; cottage $130–225.

Innisfree Victorian Inn (828-743-2946), US 107 North, P.O. Box 469, Glenville, NC 28736. This small country hotel is an elaborate Victorian fantasy on the shore of **Glenville Lake,** 6 miles north of Cashiers, NC, off NC 107. The three-story modern structure, built in a Victorian style, has full wraparound verandas and decks on the first two floors, with wide views over the lake. Victorian antiques fill the bright common rooms, and an octagonal table in a turret room serves as the formal dining area for breakfast. The 10 rooms, ranging from standard size to very large, are individually decorated, each with its own Victorian theme. Whirlpool baths, private verandas, and fireplaces are available. $119–300.

Millstone Inn (828-743-2737; 1-888-645-5786), P.O. Box 949, Cashiers, NC 28717. Open March through December. This 1933 vacation lodge, a mile west of Cashiers and well off US 64, faces its two bark-shingled bay wings over the headwaters of the **Chattooga River** toward a tree-framed view of crag-topped **Whiteside Mountain** (see *To See—Along the Blue Ridge*). It features wide lawns with spectacular views, a large sitting room with a millstone embedded in the fireplace, and 11 comfortable rooms. The rooms are decorated in a country rustic style, with local hardwood paneling. The main lodge has 7 of the rooms, with 4 more in an annex built in 1952; some have balconies, while others have separate sitting rooms. $131–198.

CABINS The Cabins at Seven Foxes (828-877-6333), P.O. Box 123; on Slick Fisher Road, Lake Toxaway, NC 28747. Located 4 miles north of Lake Toxaway on the Blue Ridge, this group of five new cabins sits on 6 wooded acres. These one- and two-bedroom cabins, modestly styled on the outside, are comfortably furnished with antiques and reproductions, each with its own theme. All cabins have porches, gas fireplaces, fully equipped kitchens, and quilts. $100–255 per day; $630–1,395 per week.

The Cottage Inn (828-743-3033; 877-595-3600), 71 Brocade Drive (US 64 East), Cashiers, NC 28717. This collection of 14 cottages sits on 10 acres just east of Cashiers, off US 64. The cottages range widely in size and style but tend to be modest and simple, yet handsome and well kept. All have efficiency kitchens (some lack ovens), a living area, and a porch or deck, and all but one have fireplaces. On the property, and open to all cottage renters, are an indoor swimming pool and a hard-surface tennis court, as well as hammocks and a picnic area. A lodge, with four en suite rooms and a conference room, provides a venue for business meetings or family reunions. $90–155 per night.

✿ ♿ **Devil's Fork State Park** (864-944-2639), 161 Holcombe Circle, Salem, SC 29676. This South Carolina state park, located on the western shore of **Lake Jocassee** (see *To See—Big Dammed* Lakes), has 20 large modern cabins in a contemporary-rustic style, with a large screened porch. Each has a living room with a fireplace, a kitchen, and either two or three bedrooms, and 11 have lake views. $99–132.

✳ Where to Eat

EATING OUT Pescado's Highland Burrito (828-526-9313), North Fourth Street, Highlands, NC. Open for lunch and dinner. This downtown Mexican eatery prepares its food from scratch using fresh ingredients. Their specialty is large California-style burritos, tacos, quesadillas, and salads, with plenty of fresh-made salsa.

Carolina Smokehouse (828-743-3200), US 64 West, Cashiers, NC. If you find yourself at a loss for a good, simple roadside eatery, this is your place. It occupies a plain little building with a covered deck, west of Cashiers. Inside it's just as plain, but clean and with a decor centering on old automobile tags. The barbeque is fresh and tasty, with a sweet tomato-based sauce and served up with the classic sides, and reasonably priced.

DINING OUT On the Verandah (828-526-2338), 1536 Franklin Road (US 64), Highlands, NC. Open for dinner daily; Sunday brunch. Located west of Highlands, this family-owned restaurant occupies an old 1920s speakeasy overlooking **Lake Sequoyah,** with lovely views over the lake from its deck or enclosed-veranda dining areas. Inside, the bright and attractive dining room is dominated by founding owner Alan Figel's collection of more than 1,300 bottles of chili sauce (any one of which diners are welcome to try). The menu features a fusion of Caribbean, South American, and Asian approaches, always emphasizing fresh, local ingredients. As you might expect from someone with 1,300 bottles of hot sauce, at least a couple of items will feature fresh, unusual chile peppers, and the mild dishes tend to be richly flavored. This restaurant has a 200-bottle wine list, and a wine bar with an extensive choice of wines by the glass.

Ristorante Paoletti (828-526-4906), 440 Main Street, Highlands, NC. Open for dinner June through October, Monday through Saturday. This downtown storefront restaurant offers fine Italian dining with a rich choice of foods that go well beyond red sauce on pasta. The Paoletti has a long menu of gourmet pastas with a wide variety of treatments, any of which may be ordered as a main dish or as a side to one of their entrées—veal, lamb, fish, chicken, and filet mignon. Their wine list includes over 800 bottles. Appetizers: $6–9; pastas: $14–19 à la carte, $9–14 as an accompaniment; entrées: $19–33.

The Central House Restaurant (828-526-9319; 1-888-526-9319), Fourth and Main, Highlands. Located in the center of downtown Highlands, in the **Old Edwards Inn** (see *Lodging—Country Inns and Hotels*), the Central House offers a casual lunch for shoppers and a gourmet dinner after the day is done. Crab soup, onion soup, an array of fresh green and fruit salads, imaginative sandwiches, and fresh fish entrées highlight lunch, which may be served inside or in the inn's lovely garden. Dinner menus have a large selection of fresh seafood, cooked to your order the way you prefer, with steak, chicken, pork, and lamb entrées also available. Recipes are simple, merging fresh flavors in straightforward ways.

✳ Entertainment

Highlands Playhouse (828-526-2695), Oak Street, Highlands, NC. This respected summer theater performs plays and musicals in its shingle-clad playhouse behind downtown Highlands.

Highlands Chamber Music Festival (828-526-9060), Highlands, NC. This summer series of chamber music performances is held at the **Episcopal Church of the Incarnation,** in July and August.

✳ Selective Shopping

Highlands, NC

Highlands' large concentration of million-dollar vacation cottages ensures that it has an equally large concentration of antiques shops and art galleries. In fact, Highlands has had a first-class collection of antiques shops for a number of decades, about half in its quaint downtown and the other half scattered about town. The chamber of commerce lists 16 antiques shops and art galleries, with 5 more crafts galleries and shops, 14 gift shops, and 2 bookstores.

Scudders Gallery (828-526-4111), 352 Main Street. Open all year. Established in 1925 (in Silver Springs, FL), Scudders has antiques auctions every night at 7:30 PM. During the off-season, it can be the town's primary form of evening entertainment. Catalog sales are held the second and fourth Saturday, June through November, at 11 AM. Definitely a high-end antiques dealer, its stocks include oriental carpets, estate jewelry, furniture, silver, paintings, and other art.

Country Inn Antiques (828-526-5036), Fourth and Main. Specializing in antiques from the American South, this downtown shop is filled with furniture and knickknacks. The shop features American country furniture and accessories, vintage glass, and decorative smalls, as well as early textiles and architectural adornments.

The Old Red House (828-526-9201), Fifth and Main. This shop has two locations; the original Old Red House is south of downtown Highlands on NC 106, while the new shop is downtown. It specializes in fine handmade quilts, with a choice of around 250 antique quilts and 75 modern quilts handmade by six local quilters; the provenance of each quilt is known in detail. The shop also offers vintage linens, antique fishing equipment, and local crafts.

The Christmas Tree (828-526-3687). In downtown Highlands for over a quarter of a century, the Christmas Tree offers just about everything you could put on, under, or near a tree. It has a particularly large selection of miniatures, and is a Department 56 Gold Key Dealer.

Cashiers, NC

Lyn K. Holloway Antiques (828-743-2524), US 64 and NC 107. Located behind the bank at the center of town, this cottage-based shop is set off by its attractive gardens. It features French, English, and American antiques, and specializes in American lazy Susan tables.

Basketworks (828-743-5052), NC 107 South. Located south of Cashiers' center, this shop features locally made smoke vine baskets, as well as Shenandoah Valley antiques, 18th-century antique botanicals, dried and handmade silk flowers, and a range of gift items.

✳ Special Events

Fourth of July: **Symphony Under the Stars** (828-743-9941), Cashiers, NC. The **Charleston Symphony Orchestra** performs on the banks of Lake Sapphire, east of Cashiers, NC.

Mid-September: **Cashiers Annual Chili Cook-Off,** Cashiers, NC. This annual chili cook-off, sponsored by the Cashiers Chamber of Commerce, has live music.

FRANKLIN & THE NANTAHALA MOUNTAINS

The headwaters of the Little Tennessee River carve out two of the Southern Appalachian's most impressive ridgelines: The Cowee Mountains and the Nantahala Mountains. Between the two lies the deep, flat valley of the Little Tennessee, and the little gem-mining town of Franklin, NC.

The Nantahala Mountains (pronounced Nanna-HAY-luh) dominate this area, with their stunning waterfalls, spectacular cliff views, wilderness rivers, and quaint Civilian Conservation Corps (CCC) picnic areas. The Nantahala ridgeline forms a straight, steep edge running north between the Little Tennessee River and its western tributary, the Nantahala River. From its southern end, where it intersects with the Blue Ridge at Big Butt (near Pickens Nose), to its northern terminus at Wesser, the Nantahala ridgeline carries the Appalachian Trail through 30 miles of thick, deep forest little disturbed since logging stopped.

East of this mountain system lies the Little Tennessee Valley and the bustling county seat of Franklin. For centuries before the coming of the Europeans, this valley was the center of Cherokee civilization. It supported a chain of settlements known as the Middle Villages, each village ranging from a half-dozen homesteads to groups of 30 or more dwellings. In 1817, the Cherokee Nation ceded the upper Little Tennessee Valley to the government of North Carolina and retreated to the lands west and south of the Nantahalas. Settlers trickled in; after 10 years the valley had enough population to warrant its own county government, with its seat at the Cherokee village of Nikwasi, now named Franklin after a former governor. Another 30 years after that the valley received its first decent road, a turnpike that linked Franklin with Asheville and Murphy, NC, crossing the Nantahalas at Wayah Gap.

Gem mining started in the upper Little Tennessee Valley in the 1870s. To be more accurate, corundum mining started in the 1870s, and the corundum mines kept kicking up gem-quality rocks. Corundum was (and is) a valuable industrial abrasive, being the second-hardest substance found in nature and considerably more plentiful than the first-hardest, diamonds. Usually corundum is found as an opaque, milky-white rock, but when crystallized in an exceptionally pure form it becomes either rubies or sapphires (depending on the trace elements that add color). While the quality of the occasional gemstone impressed Tiffany's and attracted investors in the 1890s, a reliable source for the gemstones was never found. Commercial corundum mining ended with WWII, and today gemstone mining is a popular recreational pursuit.

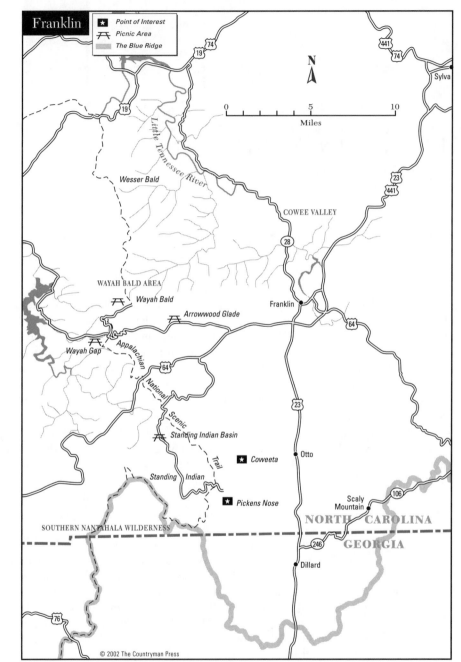

Franklin

★	Point of Interest
⛱	Picnic Area
	The Blue Ridge

© 2002 The Countryman Press

GUIDANCE Franklin Area Chamber of Commerce (828-524-3161; 866-372-5546), 425 Porter Street (Business US 441), Franklin, NC 28734. The Franklin Chamber handles tourism promotion and visitor relations for all of Macon County. Their visitors center is located south of downtown Franklin.

THE CIRCA-1911 WILSON LICK RANGER STATION

Nantahala National Forest, Wayah Ranger District (828-524-6441), 90 Sloan Road, Franklin, NC 28734. The ranger station for the Nantahala Mountains is located 1.6 miles west of downtown Franklin, just off old US 64 (now known as Old Murphy Road, SSR 1442). They have a staffed information desk during business hours, and can help with maps of the Nantahala backcountry.

GETTING THERE *By car:* Franklin has excellent highway connections with the outside world. Its main north–south highway, US 441, is a modern four-lane road. From the west, US 64 is a well-engineered highway with gentle curves and wide shoulders. However, US 64 from the east is a mess, unmodernized since it was built in 1923 (see The Cullasaja Gorge under *Wandering Around—Exploring by Car* in "The Blue Ridge: Cashiers and Highlands"); take US 74 to US 441 at Dillsboro, NC, instead.

By air: Franklin is more than an hour from Asheville, NC (see **Asheville Regional Airport** under *Getting There* in "Asheville and the Blue Ridge Parkway"), and about 3 hours from Atlanta, GA, on good roads. Atlanta is usually cheaper.

By bus or train: Franklin has no bus or passenger train service. **Road Runner Driving Services** (828-524-3265) in Franklin offers shuttle services from all regional airports, as well as driving services within the area.

MEDICAL EMERGENCIES
Angel Medical Center (828-524-8411), 120 Riverview Street, Franklin, NC. This local hospital is located a few blocks north of downtown Franklin.

✳ Wandering Around

EXPLORING BY CAR The Nantahala Mountains. *Leg 1:* Take US 64 west from Franklin 3.8 miles; turn right onto Old Murphy Road (SSR 1442), then drive 0.2 mile; turn left onto Wayah Road (SSR 1310) and drive 8.7 miles; turn right onto Wayah Bald Road (forest service road) and drive 4.2 miles. Return to US 64. Many curves; steep gravel forest road.

Leg 2: Continue on US 64 westbound for 2.2 miles; turn left onto Old US 64

(SSR 1448), then drive 6.4 miles to Wallace Gap; turn left onto paved FS 71, then drive 1.7 miles to end of the pavement at a national forest campground; continue left uphill on gravel FS 71 to Pickens Nose.

These two legs use the predecessors to modern US 64 to explore the Nantahala Mountains, topping the crest both times. The first leg follows the 19th-century coach road, while the second follows the early-20th century's first attempt at a paved auto road.

The first leg follows a handsome creek valley up past a Civilian Conservation Corps (CCC) picnic area (see **Arrowwood Glade Picnic Area** under *Wild Places—Picnic Areas*), then leads into deep woods. It switchbacks steeply up to **Wayah Gap;** only ignorance of the mountain's true layout could be responsible for putting the 1850 coach road through this high, cold pass. Look for **Bertie's Falls** on the left as you switch upward. Once in **Wayah Gap,** this leg turns up a very steep gravel side road that leads 4 miles to the peak of Wayah Bald. Be sure to stop for the **Wilson Lick Ranger Station** on your left, an attractive historic site preserving one of the earliest national forest stations in the east. Once at the top, you'll get good views from the picnic-area parking lot, but be sure to walk up the quarter mile to the stone **Wayah Bald Tower** for some remarkable panoramas. Go back the way you came.

The second leg leaves modern US 64 to the left, to follow the original US 64 auto road designed and constructed in the 1920s, replaced only in the late 1970s. It's a dramatic climb; try to picture a fully loaded semi, circa 1975, coming downhill toward you with smoking brakes. When you top out, leave the old highway to take the paved Forest Service road into the **Standing Indian Basin.** This is a beautiful forest drive along a lovely wild river, then uphill on a good gravel road to waterfalls (see **Waterfalls of Standing Indian** under *To See—In the Mountains*) and a stunning clifftop view (see **Pickens Nose** under *To See—In the Mountains*).

EXPLORING ON FOOT Standing Indian. The **Standing Indian Basin** (see *Wild Places—Recreation Areas*) is an outstanding hiking area, with varied and interesting scenery easily reached by a variety of loop trails. For an easy leg stretcher that samples the best of Standing Indian, take in the two waterfalls (see **Waterfalls of Standing Indian** under *To See—In the Mountains*), then follow up with a walk out to **Pickens Nose** (see *To See—In the Mountains*).

✳ Villages

Franklin, NC. An early pioneer town, Franklin has been a major market center for the surrounding mountains since stagecoach roads converged here in the 1850s. Today it has a handsome and shoppable downtown of three square blocks, with lots of businesses sprawling outward along its U.S. highways, US 441 Bypass, Business US 441, and US 64. It sits in the middle of a broad flat valley, straddling the Little Tennessee River with low hills that wouldn't look out of place in the Piedmont. However, when the mountains get started they kick in with a vengeance, with all local ridgelines surpassing 4,000 feet and the Nantahalas reaching well above 5,000 feet.

Cowee Valley. This remote and pastoral valley is dotted with so many old farm-

STANDING INDIAN BASIN

From Old US 64 **(see** *Wandering Around—Exploring by Car)* a gravel road, **FS 71,** cuts southward to the heart of this district. It is a worthy drive, passable by all but the wimpiest cars all the way to Pickens Nose; SUVs can continue down it into **Coweeta Hydrologic Laboratory** (see *To See—In the Mountains)* without difficulty.

Established as a Nantahala National Forest campground in the 1950s, on the site of a logging camp from the 1940s, Standing Indian Basin has evolved into a major outdoor destination. It encompasses the headwaters of the **Nantahala River,** surrounded by the 5,000-foot peaks of the Blue Ridge and the Nantahala Mountains. The highest peaks on its south are protected in the **Southern Nantahala Wilderness** (see *The Great Forests).* Lower down, the lands are open to logging and other such operations.

No doubt much of the interest in this area comes from the fact that the **Appalachian Trail (AT)** makes a three-quarter circle around the **Standing Indian Campground,** allowing weekenders to do a two night backpack on the AT and return to their car. There are now a large number of trails that loop down and up, allowing any number of different routes from a single camping space at the center. For the car-bound hiker, this is a unique place.

The scenery is worth the attention it gets. The Nantahala River runs merrily through a narrow flat-bottomed valley lined with meadows. The trout fishing is excellent, and there are lots of places to pitch a tent. While all of the upstream slopes were logged in the early 20th century, they were selectively cut and recovered quickly to form impressive forests. The side streams are violent and lovely, and higher streams have mighty waterfalls (see **Waterfalls of Standing Indian** under *To See—In the Mountains).* The high ridgeline of the Blue Ridge and the Nantahalas has wide views from grassy balds at Standing Indian, and from sheer crags at **Pickens Nose** (see *To See—In the Mountains).*

houses and barns that it has been declared a National Historic District. Its rolling farmlands are framed by the tall forested peaks of the Cowee Mountains, and easily visited from a network of country lanes. But that's not why it's famous: it's the rubies. Not crummy, cloudy little industrial corundum specks either, but big star rubies and sapphires, gem quality and weighing hundreds of carats. Cowee Valley has produced gem-quality rubies since the 1870s and has a number of recreational mines. Here we list only those mines that provide unsalted pay dirt from their own property (see *To Do—Gem Mining*).

✳ Wild Places

THE GREAT FORESTS The Southern Nantahala Wilderness. Congress created this 24,500-acre wilderness to protect the great knot of mountains at the juncture of the Blue Ridge and the Nantahalas, including large tracts in Georgia's Chattahoochee National Forest. The **Appalachian Trail (AT)** follows the crest of the Blue Ridge from Georgia to the Nantahala Mountains, then follows the Nantahalas north.

These lands are extremely rugged, with knotted ridgelines and steep slopes. Nearly all of the forests are second-growth hardwoods, as the entire area was logged between 1910 and 1940. The logging camp was located at the modern Standing Indian Campground, and logging railroads were built up the stream valleys. Some of these old railroad grades now make for attractive walking through nicely recovered riverine and cove hardwood forests.

The National Forest Service owns perhaps twice again as much land in the immediate area that is not included in the wilderness but remains open to public recreation. This includes the entire **Standing Indian Basin** (see *Recreation Areas*), adjacent to the wilderness on its north. Many good-quality trails start in the Standing Indian area, with good trailheads on its gravel access road, and extend into the wilderness; by connecting these trails, hikers and backpackers can make a wide variety of loops. One ambitious loop day hike (or good overnighter) starts at the **Standing Indian Campground** (see Standing Indian Basin under *Recreation Areas*) trailhead, hikes up the railroad grade along **Kimsey Creek** to the **AT,** then climbs **Standing Indian** (see Standing Indian—The Mountain under *To See—In the Mountains*) on the AT for wonderful views; hikers can return to their cars by a half-dozen alternative paths.

LAUREL FALLS IN THE SOUTHERN
NANTAHALA WILDERNESS

The Wayah Bald Area. The highest peak in the northern Nantahalas is not Wayah Bald; it's Wine Springs Bald, a mile to the south and a good hundred feet higher. No one cares. Everything in this area is named after Wayah Bald, including Nantahala National Forest's ranger district. It has its own gravel road, 4.5 miles long, climbing 1,100 feet just to reach it. It has one of the oldest ranger stations in the East on its slopes, preserved as a historic site. It has a **stone lookout tower** (see Wayah Bald under *To See—In the Mountains*) that's been there since 1912 and is simply beautiful. And it has views that just won't quit.

Wayah Bald marks a rough halfway point in the northward march of the Nantahala Mountains. It's surrounded by huge expanses of Nantahala National Forest, a lot of it purchased as soon as the Weeks Act established the national forest system in 1911. Nearly all of the recreational development has centered on the **Nantahala Crest,** traversed by the **Appalachian Trail** from one end to the other. Downslope, the public lands roll on and on, cut by logging roads and open to those who don't mind entering trailless areas armed only with 50-year-old United States Geological Survey (USGS) maps.

PICNIC AREAS Arrowwood Glade Picnic Area. Located on the road to **Wayah Gap (Wayah Road, SSR 1310),** this is a classic Civilian Conservation Corps (CCC) picnic area, little changed since the 1930s. If you miss it, there is another nice national forest picnic area in Wayah Gap (on the left as you crest out), named **Wayah Crest.**

Standing Indian Picnic Area. The picnic area, by the **Nantahala River,** is very beautiful and makes a great starting (or ending) place for further exploration.

✳ To See

IN THE MOUNTAINS The Nantahala Mountains dominate the Franklin area. Running almost due north from the Blue Ridge, the Nantahalas have always been a great green barrier, with more than a dozen peaks over 5,000 feet and only three gaps that barely dip below 4,000 feet. The Blue Ridge, running east and west, merges with the southern end of the Nantahalas to form the backbone of the **Southern Nantahala Wilderness** (see *Wild Places—The Great Forests*), and to wall off the **Standing Indian Recreation Area** (see Standing Indian Basin under *Wild Places—Recreation Areas*). There are many things worth exploring in these mountains, all of them in **Nantahala National Forest** (see Nantahala National Forest, Wayah Ranger District, under *Guidance*); a few of them are listed below, from south to north.

Standing Indian—The Mountain. Well over a mile high, Standing Indian dominates the Southern Nantahala Wilderness. It's also one of the tallest peaks on the Blue Ridge, just a foot shy of 5,500 feet. Known as "the grandstand of the Southern Appalachians," it has wide rocky balds with 180-degree views over the headwaters of the **Nantahala River,** framed by the 5,000-foot wall of the Nantahala Mountains. Paths up from Standing Indian Recreation Area are good, but climb a whopping 2,100 feet before reaching the top.

Waterfalls of Standing Indian. Two worthwhile waterfalls can be easily reached from the gravel road through the Standing Indian area (see Standing Indian Basin under *Wild Places—Recreation Areas*). At Big Laurel Falls, 4.9 miles up from the campground, a large stream makes a 20-foot plunge over a ledge; the trail to it is 0.5 mile long. At 5.6 miles past the campground, Moony Falls is just off the road to the right.

Pickens Nose. This easily reached high bald has wide and wonderful views over the much lower Georgia mountains to the south, and over the rich valley of the **Little Tennessee River.** A side ridge of the Nantahalas, it forms the eastern edge of the **Southern Nantahala Wilderness** (see *Wild Places—The Great Forests*). The path to it leaves the Standing Indian gravel road on the right, 8.7 miles from the campground (see **Standing Indian Basin** under *Wild Places—Recreation Areas*), then follows a ridgeline for 0.75 mile, climbing 200 feet.

Coweeta Hydrologic Laboratory. Located on the eastern slopes of the Nantahala Mountains, off US 441 south of Franklin. The National Forest Service established this forest in 1933 to perform a series of in-depth, long-term experiments that would map out the precise relationship between forest cover and stream flow—at the time a hotly controversial subject on which there was almost no data. These experiments have been crucial in improving land conservation practices on public and private lands throughout the South. Today's Coweeta continues these long-term experiments, using a multidisciplinary approach that includes detailed ecological studies, yielding data capable of addressing such questions as the effects of controlled burning or climate change. While there are no developed recreational opportunities, Coweeta is happy to answer questions and give tours. The main Forest Service road through the center of Coweeta, FS 83, is usually passable by passenger car (though steep, rough, twisty, and ill-marked); it connects with the road through Standing Indian (see Standing Indian Basin under *Wild Places—Recreation Areas*), FS 71, at Pickens Nose.

KILTS ON EXHIBIT AT THE SCOTTISH TARTANS MUSEUM

Wayah Bald. The 5,350-foot peak of Wayah Bald is crowned by a two-story stone tower that gives a full-circle panorama in all directions, as well as a nice picnic area. The gravel Forest Service road to Wayah Bald climbs 1,100 feet in 4.5 miles (see *Wandering Around—Exploring by Car*).

Wesser Bald. The last and the lowest of the Nantahala's major peaks, Wesser Bald (4,630 feet) may well have the best views. A viewing platform built on top of its old fire tower gives a complete circular panorama whose views down into the valleys below are unobstructed. It requires a 2-mile round-trip hike on the **Appalachian Trail** with an 800-foot climb; the trailhead, at **Tellico Gap,** is a 30-mile drive from Franklin, NC. (Directions: Go as to Wayah Gap [see The Nantahala Mountains under *Wandering Around—Exploring by Car*], then continue straight ahead on paved **SSR 1310** for 13.4 miles; then turn right onto gravel **Otter Creek Road [SSR 1365]** and drive 3.9 miles to the Forest Service parking lot in Tellico Gap.)

CULTURAL SITES Macon County Historical Museum (828-524-9758), 36 West Main Street, Franklin, NC. Open Monday through Friday 10–4. Free admission. Downtown Franklin's 1904 **Pendergrass Store** still has the appearance of a turn-of-the-century small rural department store, with its wood paneling and central stairs to a mezzanine balcony. Today it's filled with historical artifacts and displays about the Franklin area, as part of a local history museum and research center run by the Macon County Historical Society.

The Franklin Gem and Mineral Museum (828-369-7831), 25 Phillips Street, Franklin, NC. Open May through October, Monday through Friday 10–4. Free admission. The old **Macon County Jail** in downtown Franklin housed prisoners from 1850 until 1970. In 1976 it became the site of the Franklin Gem and Mineral Museum, run by the local rockhound club, the Franklin Gem and Mineral Society. The building remains very much an old jail, with gem and mineral exhibits in the cells. One such exhibit contains gems and minerals from North Carolina, including a most rare and valuable piece—an 18th-century Wedgewood porcelain made from clay taken from Franklin (then a Cherokee village). Another exhibit has minerals from every state in the union. There are displays of wire-wrapped jewelry, fluorescent minerals, native American artifacts, and fossils.

Scottish Tartans Museum (828-524-7472), 86 East Main Street, Franklin, NC. Open Monday through Saturday 10–5, Sunday 1–5. $1 donation per adult requested. The official North American museum of the Scottish Tartan Society—the governing society for all tartans worldwide, located in Pitlochry, Scotland—occupies a storefront in downtown Franklin. Its museum displays Scottish tartans, and relates the tartans to Scottish history and culture. It has facilities for looking up family tartans, and a really great gift shop. The museum sponsors the annual **Taste of Scotland Festival** (see *Special Events*).

PARKS AND GARDENS **Perry's Water Gardens** (828-524-3264), 136 Gibson Aquatic Farm Road, Franklin, NC. Open Monday through Saturday 9–5, Sunday 1–5. Free admission. Located in Cowee Valley (see *Villages*), these extensive water gardens are on the site of one of America's largest commercial aquatic nurseries. Here you'll see every conceivable type of water plant, but most especially water lilies, lotuses, and irises. Every pond has its own population of giant goldfish, who keep the area mosquito free.

✳ To Do

FISHING **Great Smoky Mountain Fish Camp and Safaris** (828-369-5295), 81 Bennett Road (NC 28), Franklin, NC. This **Little Tennessee River** outfitter, just north of Franklin (near Cowee Valley; see *Villages*), offers guided fishing trips, canoeing and kayaking, biking (including rentals), and a gourmet food store, in addition to its campground.

GEM MINING **Mason's Ruby and Sapphire Mine** (828-369-9742), 6961 Upper Burningtown Road, Franklin, NC. Open April through October, daily 8–5. This ruby mine in the Nantahala Mountains west of Franklin allows miners to dig their own dirt and does not practice salting. This mine is different from, and unconnected with, Mason Mountain Mine (which is near Cowee Valley and salts its dirt with foreign stones).

Sheffield Mine (828-369-8383), 385 Sheffield Farms Road, Franklin, NC. Open April through October, daily 9–5 (admissions close earlier). This long-

YOU'LL FIND DOZENS OF MINES ALONG RUBY MINE ROAD

established **Cowee Valley** (see *Villages*) mine—open to the public since the 1940s but in existence before then—features unsalted dirt from its own property. They are one of the few places in the world where star rubies (purple red rubies that form a star when cabachoned) can be mined. They also sell salted dirt, clearly labeled as such; they do not salt rubies or sapphires.

GOLF Mill Creek Country Club (828-524-6458; 1-800-533-3916), Mill Creek Road, Franklin, NC. $40. This 18-hole course, located on the west side of Franklin adjacent to Nantahala National Forest lands, offers very scenic play with wide mountain views.

Franklin Golf Course (828-524-2288), 255 First Fairway Drive, Franklin, NC. $10. This nine-hole course was built in 1929 as part of a subdivision just south of downtown Franklin. It offers convenient in-town play.

Holly Springs Golf Course (828-369-8711), 115 Holly Springs Golf Village, Franklin, NC. $20. This nine-hole golf course near Franklin was built in 1976 as part of a housing subdivision.

WHITEWATER ADVENTURES The Little Tennessee River. The Little Tennessee is wide, smooth, and beautiful, passing through handsome farmland with broad views toward the Nantahala and Cowee Mountains. Popular with local canoeists and kayakers, it is undiscovered by the raft-trip operators. However, the **Smoky Mountain Fish Camp and Safaris** (see above), on its banks near Cowee Valley (see *Villages*), offers canoeing, kayaking, and tubing.

✳ Lodging

COUNTRY INNS AND HOTELS The Summit Inn (828-524-2006), 210 East Rogers Street, Franklin, NC 28734. This 1898 mansion, built as a private house, sits on a hilltop overlooking downtown Franklin, one block to its south. A white clapboard structure, its large veranda extends outward to flank the front entrance with two room-sized extensions—one of which has been converted into a sunroom, the site of the **Summit Inn Restaurant** (see *Dining Out*). Downstairs, the **Down Under Bar** fills the cellar's river-stone walls with nightly music and dancing; its stone fireplace, pool table, and large screen TV are always open to guests. The hotel has 14 rooms, individually decorated; only 6 have private baths. $59–99.

The Franklin Terrace Hotel (828-524-7907; 1-800-633-2431), 159 Harrison Avenue, Franklin, NC 28734. This distinguished white wooden building, listed on the National Register, originally housed a school when it was constructed in 1887; it's been the Franklin Terrace Hotel since 1915. Extrawide verandas cover both stories of the building's long front, and columned porticos shelter the side entrances. Nowadays the B&B shares this building with an **antiques shop**— the shop taking up the downstairs and the B&B upstairs. The B&B has been returned to its 1915 original style, with period antiques in its nine carefully decorated rooms. $52–69, including full breakfast.

BED & BREAKFASTS The Snow Hill Inn (828-369-2100), 531 Snow Hill Road, Franklin, NC 28734. This large 1914 house, once used as a schoolhouse, occupies 14 acres with views over the Little Tennessee Valley. A classic white clapboard farmhouse, its wide front porch looks out over gardens with a gazebo and benches, framing a view that takes in six mountain peaks. The eight rooms, all with private baths, are decorated with antiques and reproductions in a simple country style. A full breakfast is served in the bright and airy sunroom. $67–97, including full breakfast.

Mulberry Mountain Country Retreat (828-524-8519), 444 Mulberry Gap Road, Otto, NC 28763. Twelve miles south of Franklin, NC, this Colonial-style brick house sits in the woods on the lower slopes of the Nantahala Mountains, adjacent to Nantahala National Forest. Rocking chairs on the front porch look into the woods; inside, the roomy common areas are comfortably and attractively furnished. This B&B has three guest rooms with private baths, and the option of a suite where two bedrooms share a bath. Rooms $85–95; suite $145; includes full breakfast and evening refreshments.

Hummingbird Lodge (828-369-0430), 1101 Hickory Knoll Ridge Road, Franklin, NC 28734. This all-log home sits on a mountainside, 8 miles south of town and more than 2 miles from US 441. A long, low lodge-style structure, it has a view porch runs full length along the home, facing over the well-tended garden. The entire main floor is given over to the B&B's guests, with a stone fireplace in the great room and three en suite guest rooms. The rooms are theme decorated with items from local crafters and artisans, including a room with handcrafted Cherokee items from the nearby Qualla Boundary. The premium room is quite large, with a whirlpool bath and a bay window. $85–95, including full breakfast and an evening sweet or wine with hors d'oeuvres.

Heritage Inn (828-524-4150; 1-888-524-4150), 43 Heritage Hollow Drive, Franklin, NC 28734. This attractive, old-fashioned house sits a short block away from downtown Franklin in a quiet residential neighborhood. Its wide wraparound veranda overhangs an old stone terrace, right above the side street. It has five en suite rooms, one with a kitchenette $75–95, including breakfast and evening wine and hors d'oeuvres; discounts available for longer stays.

Blaine House Bed & Breakfast (1-888-349-4230), 661 Harrison Avenue (NC 28), Franklin, NC 28734. This 1910 cottage sits on lightly traveled NC 28 on the north end of Franklin. With elaborate gables and dormers, its entrances framed with neoclassical columns and pediments, it has a lot of personality. Inside, it's carefully decorated with family antiques and heirlooms. Two cozy rooms are decorated in a simple, country style with quilts on the beds; the two large suites, with separate sitting areas, are more formally decorated. Gourmet breakfasts are served in a bright and airy sunroom. Rooms $79; suites $99–109; discounts for longer stays.

✳ Where to Eat

EATING OUT Mama's (828-369-8185), 21 Heritage Hollow Drive, Franklin, NC. Open Tuesday through Saturday 6:30 AM to 9 PM. Located in a wandering gray-sided building set among trees a scant block south of downtown Franklin, Mama's features standard American fare at reasonable prices, three meals a day. They make their own yeast rolls, vegetable soup, and pies fresh from scratch, and have a full line of sandwiches as well as hot entrées. Breakfast $2–4; lunch $4–6; dinner $6–11.

The Frog and Owl Kitchen (828-349-4112), 46 East Main Street, Franklin, NC. Open Monday through Saturday 11–3. This downtown Franklin storefront café serves American fusion cuisine for the casual lunch crowd. It's a rare small-town treat,

when you're looking for a lunch that's light and sophisticated. Wine is available. $6–12.

The Chef and His Wife (828-369-0575). This popular eatery sits on Courthouse Square in the center of downtown Franklin. Lunch features hot dogs (good ones), fresh half-pound burgers, and a variety of sandwiches (from roast beef on a kaiser roll to goat cheese and roasted red pepper on French bread). Dinners range from meat loaf and ribs, through a variety of steaks, to a good selection of fresh seafood. Lunch $4–6; dinner $9–15.

Fat Buddies Ribs and Barbeque (828-349-4743), 311 Westgate Plaza (US 64 West), Franklin, NC. Open Monday through Saturday 11–2:30 and 5–9. You'll find this authentic pit barbeque in a suburban shopping plaza off the freeway portion of US 64 west. Meats are slow cooked over a blend of hardwoods and basted with the house sauce. They smoke pork, beef, chicken, and baby back ribs, and serve it as a sandwich with fries, or as a platter with two sides. They also have a good choice of well-thought-out salads for the barbeque impaired, as well as Brunswick stew and black-eyed pea stew. They make four different barbeque sauces and five salad dressings, all from their own recipes. Most meals are in the $5–9 range; ribs cost more.

DINING OUT The Summit Inn Restaurant (828-524-2006), 210 East Rogers Street, Franklin. NC. Franklin's Summit Inn (see *Lodging—Country Inns and Hotels*) serves lunch and dinner in its sunroom, with views over downtown Franklin to the Nantahala Mountains. Weather permitting, there is additional dining on an outside patio. Its straightforward menu fea-

RICKMAN'S GENERAL STORE IN COWEE VALLEY

tures hand-cut steaks, seafood, and vegetarian entrées. A wine list is available. In the inn's cellar, a large bar has walls of native rock from the Little Tennessee River, a stone fireplace, pool, and live music and dancing nightly.

✴ Entertainment

Pickin' on the Square (828-349-1212), Franklin, NC. There's free music and dancing every Saturday night at the gazebo on the square in downtown Franklin, in front of the county courthouse. It starts with an open mike at 7 PM, with the main band—either bluegrass or gospel—coming on at 8.

✴ Selective Shopping

Franklin, NC

Franklin is an important market center for its surrounding region, and so takes on more of the look of a contemporary Southern town than many of its peers in the mountains. Its three-block downtown is definitely worth a stroll, with gift, antiques, and gem shops as well as two museums and a nice town square. Beyond that, a large number of shops string out for 2 or 3 miles

along all of the main highway: at the exits along US 441 Bypass, US 441 south of town (the biggest concentration), US Business 441 north and south of downtown, and US 64 east and west of downtown.

Michael M. Rogers Gallery (828-524-6709; 877-918-5888), 18 West Palmer Street, Franklin. This well-known water color artist lives in Franklin and maintains a gallery downtown. He paints highly detailed and accurate scenes of nature in the Blue Ridge, the Nantahalas, and the Smokies, showing how weather highlights seasonal changes.

MACO Crafts, Inc. (828-524-7878), 2846 Georgia Road (US 441 South). Located 2.5 miles south of town, this crafters' cooperative maintains an inventory of 10,000 items—all handmade by local crafters. The selection is juried for quality but not for style; every possible kind of craft is here, from simple grandma-style crafts to sophisticated contemporary art. MACO is noted for its handmade quilts and carries a good selection of quilting supplies and fabrics.

Otto, NC

Spring Ridge Creamery (828-369-2958), 11856 Georgia Highway (US 441 South). This small dairy sells its fresh products by US 441 north of the North Carolina–Georgia state line (about 10 miles south of Franklin, NC). The Spring Ridge Creamery's Jersey cows graze in the meadows beside their shop. The shop carries only the products of their own dairy: milk, butter, and ice cream. Stop by Spring Ridge and get the real stuff.

Cowee Valley

Rickman's General Store (828-524-2223), 259 Cowee Creek Road, Franklin, NC. This traditional general store has stood at the entrance to Cowee Valley (see *Villages*), north of Franklin off NC 28, since time out of mind. It beckons to visitors with its door-side collection of flags, stuffed bears, and whatnot; inside you'll find gift items as well as the stock of a functioning general store.

Cowee Creek Pottery (828-524-3324), 20 West Mills Road, Franklin, NC. Located a few blocks from Rickman's General Store, the former West Mills General Store is now a gallery of handmade pottery, made in a studio in the back of the old store.

✴ Special Events

Mid-June: **Taste of Scotland Festival** (828-524-7472), Franklin, NC. This annual downtown Franklin festival, sponsored by the Scottish Tartans Museum (see *To See—Cultural Sites*), features haggis, bagpipes, dancing, sheepdog demonstrations, and lots of Scottish stuff for sale.

✐ Fourth of July: **Fourth of July Celebration,** Franklin, NC. The chamber of commerce sponsors Franklin's annual Independence Day parade at the **Macon County Recreation Park**. Athletic competitions include a rubber-ducky derby, a horseshoe tourney, a watermelon roll, a plunger toss, cow-patty bingo, and—for the under-5 set—a tricycle race. There's plenty of food, and fireworks begin at dark.

Last week in July: **Macon County Gemboree,** Franklin, NC. Adults $2, children free. This annual rock show brings in gem and mineral dealers from all over, as well as custom jewelers. Sponsored by the Gem and Mineral Society of Franklin, it has been running every year since 1965.

Last week in July: **Folkmoot** (828-452-2997). This major gathering of national folk-dancing troupes, headquartered out of Waynesville, NC (see Folkmoot USA under *Special Events* in "Waynesville and the Blue Ridge Parkway"), uses Franklin as one of its venues.

Labor Day Weekend: **Gem Capital Auto Club Antique Auto Show** (828-369-0557), Franklin, NC. This annual auto show, held at the **Macon County fairgrounds,** features a wide assortment of antique automobiles and trucks.

Mid-September: **Macon County Fair,** Franklin, NC. Free admission. This classic county fair, held at the **Macon County fairgrounds,** features livestock shows and sales, agriculture displays, food, crafts, and entertainment.

✐ Last Saturday in October: **Pumpkin Fest,** Franklin, NC. This downtown Franklin street fair has food, entertainment, crafts, games, a costume parade and contest, a pumpkin cook-off, a pumpkin rolling contest, and trick or treating for kids.

THE NORTHERN UNICOIS:
ROBBINSVILLE & TELLICO PLAINS

South of Great Smoky Mountains National Park, the Little Tennessee River cuts a deep gorge through the mountains, marking the end of the Smokies. However, the mountain range picks up again on the other side of the gorge, under a new name—the Unicoi Mountains. As with the Smokies to the north, the Unicois mark the line between North Carolina and Tennessee, and between the Nantahala and the Cherokee National Forests. The eastern side of the mountains, in North Carolina, looks to the tiny county seat of Robbinsville, NC, for shopping and services. The western side, in Tennessee, looks to the remote village of Tellico Plains, TN.

Between these two small towns lies 40 miles of nearly unpopulated forest land. These huge, empty stretches of public land include 35,000 acres of congressionally declared wilderness and another 20,000 acres of roadless and primitive areas—a wonderful, and little-visited, recreational opportunity. Here you'll find huge waterfalls, wide mountaintop meadows, thousands of acres of virgin and old-growth forest, and incredible views from high crags. You'll also find long lakes that probe thin arms of stillwater deep into this wilderness, impounded behind four hydropower dams.

Until recently these two sides of the mountain could have been on different continents for all the interaction between them. There wasn't even a road between them until 1931—and that highway, US 129, has never been modernized. However, in 1997 the stunning recreational parkway known as the Cherohala Skyway finally opened after 20 years of construction. The Cherohala flies high above the valleys in broad sweeps along the crest of the Unicois, with constantly changing panoramas along its 25-mile length. It now links Robbinsville directly with Tellico Plains, bringing these two areas very close together and opening their huge wilderness to the outside.

GUIDANCE **Graham County Chamber of Commerce** (828-479-3790; 1-800-470-3790), P.O. Box 1206, Robbinsville, NC 28771.

Monroe County Tourism Council (423-442-9147; 1-800-245-5428), 4765 US 68, Madisonville, TN 37354. These are the people to contact for help in visiting Tellico Plains, TN, and the northern Unicoi Mountains of Tennessee. They have a visitors center at the county seat of Madisonville, TN, about 10 miles north of Tellico Plains on TN 68.

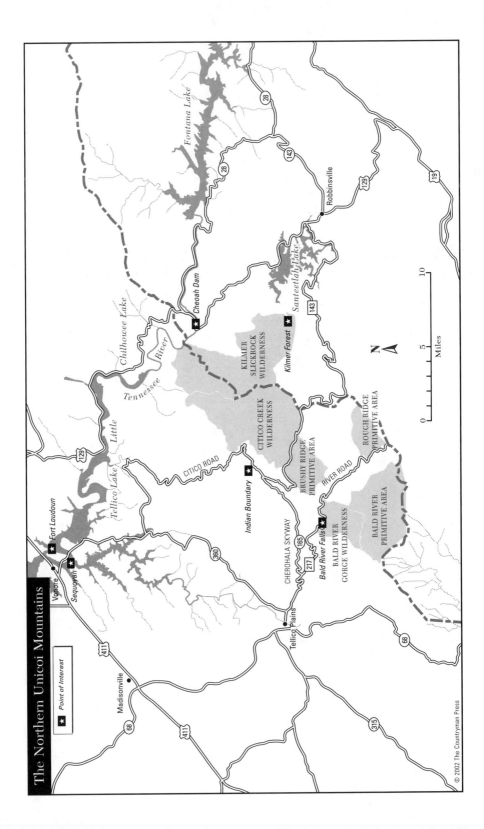

The Northern Unicoi Mountains

Point of Interest

© 2002 The Countryman Press

Nantahala National Forest, Cheoah Ranger District (828-479-6431), Robbinsville, NC 28771. The ranger station for the eastern side of the Unicoi Mountains, including all national forest land around Robbinsville, is located on NC 143 northwest of Robbinsville, near Santeetlah Lake. This station is on the site of a historic Civilian Conservation Corps (CCC) camp, and has some interesting exhibits and a nature trail on the subject.

Cherokee National Forest, Tellico Plains Ranger Station (423-253-2520), 250 Ranger Station Road, Tellico Plains, TN. This ranger station, set in a lovely little cove off the Tellico River (see The Tellico River and the Bald River Gorge Wilderness under *Wild Places—The Great Forests*), has an information desk and a bookstore, with a staff that is eager to answer your questions. It's also a fascinating and beautiful historic site in its own right, and has its own listing (see *To See— Historic Sites*).

Tennessee Overhill Heritage Association (423-263-7232), P.O. Box 143, L&N Depot, Etowah, TN 37331. This private not-for-profit association promotes tourism development in the southern Tennessee Mountains.

GETTING THERE *By car:* The Tennessee area around Tellico Plains is easily reached from I-75; take the TN 68 exit and follow TN 68 east to Tellico Plains. At anytime other than winter, this is the best approach to Robbinsville, NC, from the west as well, following the Cherohala Skyway eastward from Tellico Plains. From any other direction (and from the west in winter), approach Robbinsville by following US 19 to US 129.

By air: Knoxville's **McGhee Tyson Airport** in Alcoa, TN (see *Getting There* in "Townsend, Cades Cove, and the Northwest Quadrant"), and **Chattanooga Metropolitan Airport in** Chattanooga, TN (see *Getting There* in "The Southern Unicois: Murphy and the Copper Basin"), are the two closest airports.

By bus or train: There is no bus or train service to this area.

MEDICAL EMERGENCIES **Medical Emergencies in Tennessee: Sweetwater Hospital** (865-213-8200), 304 Wright Street, Sweetwater, TN. The nearest hospital to Tellico Plains, TN, is this hospital in Sweetwater, 23 miles north on TN 68.

Medical Emergencies in North Carolina: Murphy Medical Center (828-837-8161; see *Medical Emergencies* in "The Southern Unicois: Murphy and the Copper Basin"). There is no hospital in Robbinsville or Graham County, NC. The nearest hospital is in Murphy, NC, 36 miles away via US 129 and US 19 South. Murphy also has an urgent-care clinic, open every day. A call to **911** will bring the **Robbinsville Rescue Squad** and you'll be glad you supported them with a ramp dinner (see Graham County Ramp Festival under *Special Events*).

✴ Wandering Around

EXPLORING ON FOOT **A Slickrock Wilderness Walk.** Cut off from the rest of the world when Calderwood Lake flooded its entrance in 1928, Slickrock Creek has always been a difficult area to penetrate. Part of a national wilderness area (see **Kilmer-Slickrock Wilderness** under *Wild Places—The Great Forests*) since

EXPLORING BY CAR: THE CHEROHALA SKYWAY

Leg 1: Start on NC 143 at Stecoah Gap (off NC 28 between Fontana and Bryson City, NC). Take NC 143 west to the start of the Cherohala Parkway. 17.9 miles.

A TRAIL AND FOOTBRIDGE LEAD TO AN OVER-LOOK ON THE CHEROHALA SCENIC PARKWAY

Leg 2: Continue on NC 143 uphill, now known as the **Cherohala Parkway.** As the highway crosses into Tennessee its designation changes to TN 165. End at the village of Tellico Plains, TN. 39.7 miles. No services available before Tellico Plains.

This drive enters the area as would a traveler from the Great Smoky Mountains, crossing the Cheoah Mountains at **Stecoah Gap.** Here the **Appalachian Trail** crosses the highway as it follows the crest of the **Cheoah Mountains** (see *Wild Places— The Great Forests*). The parking lot gives views back toward the Smokies, while the road ahead gives a broad view over Robbinsville, NC, toward the **Unicoi Mountains**—our destination, 35 miles away. The highway drops into **Robbinsville** (see *Villages*), using a nondescript bypass to go around it; the three-block drive downtown is worthwhile. At **Santeetlah Lake, NC 143** turns off the main highway to follow the south side of the lake, passing the Forest Service headquarters (see Nantahala National Forest, **Cheoah Ranger District,** under *Guidance)* and attractive views over pastoral scenery. On this stretch the state highway is a twisting, intimate lane through remote countryside.

The start of the Skyway is obvious, not only because of its sign, but also because of NC 143's sudden return to full modern width and shoulders. With a design patterned after the Blue Ridge Parkway, the next 26 miles feature sweeping and ever-changing views. The Cherohala slabs and switches up a major side ridge of the Unicois, reaches the top, then slabs from gap to gap along the crest of the Unicois. Along the way it will reach elevations well over a mile high, and pass near wide mountaintop meadows. For the first 15 miles the views are all eastward over the endlessly receding ridges of North Carolina. Then, as the Skyway crosses the state line at **Beech Gap** the scenery changes, to the abrupt and rugged drop of the Unicois into the **Great Valley.** At the bottom of the mountain the road turns left for a long, easy 12-mile ramble into the attractive village of **Tellico Plains** (see *Villages).*

1975, its network of hunters' paths have had little improvement beyond getting signs. Even a level hike is tiring and difficult, because of the rough trail.

This walk takes the only reasonably level path into Slickrock, starting at **US 129** at the **Cheoah Dam** (see *To See—Historic Sites*). From the south side of the highway bridge, a Forest Service trail heads west along the steep slopes above **Calderwood Lake** (see *To See—Big Dammed Lakes*), following the top of the **Little Tennessee River**'s drowned gorge. After 0.5 mile the trail climbs to an intersection; continue straight. When the trail starts to fall, it is turning the bend to enter the **Slickrock Creek** basin; a sign marks the wilderness boundary. From here the trail follows the old lumber railroad along the creek, very rough from long abandonment, and a mere ledge in some places. Nevertheless, the forests are handsome and the stream is beautiful. At 2.6 miles from the trailhead the path reaches **Lower Falls,** an attractive 20-foot waterfall with a high volume. This is a good destination for a 5-mile return trip. However, the creekside trail continues another 6 miles past a gorge and two more waterfalls. The many side trails lead high into the Unicoi Mountains, over into **Joyce Kilmer Memorial Forest** or the **Citico Creek Wilderness** (see both under *Wild Places—The Great Forests*).

✳ Villages

Robbinsville, NC. The county seat of Graham County, NC, Robbinsville is a tiny (2000 population: 747), down-at-the-heels town where life centers on the hardwood lumber mill and the small string of new franchise restaurants along the US 129 Bypass. It's Main Street, one block off US 129, has a one-block downtown next to the handsome **1942 Courthouse,** clad in local stone. Downtown Robbinsville was the location for the small-town shots for the 1994 movie *Nell* (starring Jodie Foster and Liam Neeson), playing itself; interiors depicting local stores (including 80-year-old **Sniders Department Store,** the local pool hall, and the local café), were shot in the actual businesses, sometimes with the employees as extras.

Tellico Plains, TN. This small town sits at the feet of the **Unicoi Mountains** in Tennessee, tucked among low ridges and drained by the **Tellico River.** For many

THE GRAHAM COUNTY COURTHOUSE IN ROBBINSVILLE

years Tellico Plains was a small industrial town, appealing to businesses that needed to reach mountain resources with a railroad. In the last few decades, tourism has grown as industry retreated, as visitors learn about the immense amount of **Cherokee National Forest** wilderness and recreation lands that extend for dozens of miles from the town center. Today's Tellico Plains has a small, handsome downtown with antiques shops and art galleries, as well as good places to eat and stay. The beautiful **Cherohala Parkway** (see The Cherohala Skyway under *Wandering Around—Exploring by Car*) starts (or ends) here on its long run along the **Unicoi Crest,** and the county is anchoring this scenic highway with a visitors center and museum on the town square. A colony of fine artists and crafters has been growing in the surrounding valleys, with the downtown **Tellico Arts Center** (see *Selective Shopping—Tellico Plains, TN*) putting the spotlight on their work.

✳ Wild Places

THE GREAT FORESTS Joyce Kilmer Memorial Forest. In the 1930s the National Forest Service decided to dedicate a large, virgin forest to the poet Joyce Kilmer, author of "Trees," killed in WWI. They chose the forests of **Little Santeetlah Creek,** northwest of Robbinsville, NC, calling them "some of the finest original growth in the Appalachians." Today this watershed contains thousands of acres of never-cut old-growth forest, with trees reaching 20 feet in diameter. A 2-mile loop trail leads through some of the most dramatic forest, climaxing in a grove of huge yellow poplars. A separate trail, **Naked Ground Trail** (Trail 55), follows the valley uphill to its end, reaching the Unicoi ridgeline in 5 miles after a 2,700-foot climb; at the crest, the path to the right leads another 2 miles to stunning views from **Hangover Lead.** The original "Memorial Forest" has now become part of the much larger **Kilmer-Slickrock Wilderness** (see below), which extends into Tennessee and combines with the **Citico Creek Wilderness** (see below) to protect 33,000 acres. With all this wilderness surrounding it, the original Joyce Kilmer Memorial Forest remains one of the best places to see the forests of the Appalachians as they appeared to Cherokee hunters and European settlers.

FERNS FLOURISH IN THE RICH SHADE OF JOYCE KILMER MEMORIAL FOREST.

Kilmer-Slickrock Wilderness. This 17,400-acre wilderness, created in 1975, combined the **Joyce Kilmer Memorial Forest** (see above) with the adjacent stream basin drained by **Slickrock Creek.** The Slickrock Creek basin was partially logged in the mid-1920s, but the 1928 impoundment of **Calderwood Lake** (see *To See—Big Dammed Lakes*) drowned the loggers' railroad; after that, logging was abandoned, the land visited only by hunters and fishers. Today the Slickrock trails remain

SASSAFRAS FALLS

largely unimproved except for signage, and the Slickrock experience remains one of deep and difficult backcountry (see **A Slickrock Wilderness Walk** under *Wandering Around—Exploring on Foot*). Trails interconnect between Slickrock, Kilmer, and the adjacent **Citico Creek Wilderness** (see below), creating a large number of possible ridge and valley trips that combine old-growth forests with waterfalls and mountaintop meadows.

The Snowbird Creek Forests. Snowbird Creek drains the uppermost heights of the **Cherohala Skyway** (see *Wandering Around—Exploring by Car*), west of Robbinsville, NC, in the Unicoi Mountains. Nantahala National Forest owns all of the Snowbird drainage and protects it as a backcountry primitive area. A network of good-quality Forest Service trails follow the main creek (actually a tumultuous little river), its major side creek, and several nearby ridgelines. A 3-mile walk into the area brings you to a whole series of lovely waterfalls, including the beautiful **Sassafras Falls** on Trail 65 along **Sassafras Creek.** (Directions: Follow **NC 143** west of Robbinsville toward the **Cherohala Skyway** for 5.4 miles; turn left **onto Snowbird River Road, SSR 1115,** and drive 3.1 miles; turn left onto **SSR 1120** to its end at a Forest Service parking lot.)

The Cheoah Mountains. The Cheoah Mountains form an east–west barrier between Robbinsville, NC, and the Great Smoky Mountains, with peaks as high as 5,000 feet and gaps above 3,000 feet. The **Appalachian Trail (AT)** runs along its crest, after first climbing 3,300 feet from the bottom of the **Nantahala Gorge** (see *Villages* in "Bryson City and the Southwest Quadrant"). The slopes of the Cheoahs have been subjected to logging by Nantahala National Forest over the years, so that the AT remains the main recreation resource of these mountains. The AT is most easily reached from **NC 143** as it crosses the Cheoahs at **Stecoah Gap,** between Robbinsville and Fontana, NC. A 5.5-mile hike eastward (with 1,800 feet of climbing) leads to **Cheoah Bald** with a famous panoramic view.

Citico Creek Wilderness. Created in 1984, this 16,300-acre wilderness protects the western slopes of the Unicoi Mountains as they extend into Tennessee. The eastern slopes had already been protected by the 1936 **Joyce Kilmer Memorial Forest** and the 1975 **Kilmer-Slickrock Wilderness** (see both above); together, these areas protect 33,200 contiguous acres of mountain wilderness. Citico is noted for its deep stream valleys and violent little rivers, most with extraordinarily clean water. Its lower slopes were extensively and destructively logged in the 1920s, but a huge forest fire in 1926 destroyed the logging operation so thoroughly that it was abandoned, leaving the upper slopes untouched. Today's hiking trails follow the old lumber trams up the streams, past rapids and waterfalls, to enter the old-growth forest, and eventually reach the crest of the Unicois. The **Cherohala Skyway** (see *Wandering Around—Exploring by Car*) follows a side ridge along the southern edge of the wilderness, creating additional trailheads into the Citico's 57-mile trail system. If you have time for only a brief taste of this large area, take the short **Fall Creek Falls Trail** from the Skyway's **Rattlesnake Rock Parking Lot;** it leads 1.3 miles (with a 400-foot climb on the return) to a lacy waterfall on an 80-foot cliff.

The Tellico River and the Bald River Gorge Wilderness. The upper reaches of the Tellico River are almost entirely owned and controlled by the National Forest Service, mostly within Tennessee's Cherokee National Forest and easily reached from **Tellico Springs,** TN. A paved scenic road, **FS 217,** runs along the river's bank, frequently flanked by gray cliffs as the Tellico digs its way deep into a gorge. At one point, FS 217 passes immediately by a huge waterfall, a hundred feet tall and carrying a huge volume of water. This is **Bald Creek Falls,** and behind it is the 3,700-acre **Bald Creek Gorge Wilderness**, with a fine hiking path following the gorge bottom. Another 10,000 acres upstream from the Bald Creek Gorge Wilderness have received administrative protection as a series of Primitive Areas and provide some more remote opportunities for hiking, camping, and fishing. Not all of the stunningly beautiful wild lands of the Tellico River have received such careful handling by the National Forest Service. At the end of FS 217 at the North Carolina–Tennessee state line, North Carolina's Nantahala National Forest sponsors the heavily used 8,000-acre Upper Tellico Off Road Vehicle Area in the high-mountain basin that gives rise to the Tellico River.

RECREATION AREAS Indian Boundary Recreation Area. This small man-made lake nestles at the base of the Unicoi Mountains in Tennessee, 2 miles from the place where the **Cherohala Skyway** (see *Wandering Around—Exploring by Car*) finishes its descent. A recreation area of the Cherokee National Forest, it has a picnic area by a sandy swimming beach, with impressive views over the lake toward the Unicoi Mountains. Take the easy loop path around this lake for more views and pleasant woods walking. There's also a fairly large campground in this area.

PICNIC AREAS Joyce Kilmer and Vicinity. Joyce Kilmer Memorial Forest (see *The Great Forests*) has a nice picnic area at its trailhead parking lot; however, it does tend to fill up during the busy season. Heading back toward the **Cherohala Skyway** (see *Wandering Around—Exploring by Car*) and Robbinsville, NC, you'll find a table with a fabulous view toward the Unicois 2 miles from the Kilmer entrance road. Another 5.3 miles down NC 143 toward Robbinsville, a small national forest picnic area with a nature trail sits beside **Lake Santeetlah.**

Cheoah Point. This Nantahala National Forest recreation area sits on the shore of **Santeetlah Lake,** 7 miles north of Robbinsville, NC, off US 129. It has a nice picnic area and a sandy swimming beach on the lake, with views over the lake to the mountains beyond.

Along the Tellico River. Northeast of Tellico Plains, TN, the Tellico River forms a recreation corridor within the Cherokee National Forest. Because of steady tourist use along its scenic road, FS 217, the Forest Service has developed several picnic areas along it, as well as creating parking for fishers and trail users, and designating several small primitive camping areas.

✷ To See

BIG DAMMED LAKES The Tapoco Lakes. People frequently assume that the lakes that stretch through this area are part of the Tennessee Valley Authority (TVA), a Great Depression hydropower project (still going strong). Not so. Only the huge Tellico Lake, completed in 1979, was a TVA project (along with Fontana Lake, upstream, completed in 1943; see **Fontana Dam** under *To See—Special Places* in "Bryson City and the Southwest Quadrant"). The four other lakes in this area are part of Tapoco, a completely private initiative of the ALCOA Corporation, still known as Tapoco. Tapoco (which stands for "Tallassee Power Company") is a wholly owned subsidiary of ALCOA that owns and runs four major dams and the lakes behind them: Chilhowee, Calderwood, Cheoah, and Santeetlah. Built between 1917 and 1957, these four dams supply about half the power sucked down by ALCOA's giant aluminum smelter at nearby Maryville, TN, outside Knoxville. Although privately owned, all four lakes are open to recreational boating.

Chilhowee Lake. The newest of the four Tapoco projects, the 1957 Chilhowee Dam is just up the Little Tennessee River from the TVA's new Tellico Lake (see below). It floods a deep gorge, providing a long, serpentine lake that extends 8.5 miles upstream but covers less than 3 square miles. The lower parts of the lake are hugged by US 129, with picnic tables and a boat launch. The upper half of the lake is remote from roads, accessible only from ALCOA's shoreline recreation site, open to the public (see **Calderwood Power Station Recreation Area** under *Wild Places—Picnic Areas* in "Townsend, Cades Cove, and the Northwest Quadrant").

Calderwood Lake. ALCOA built Calderwood Dam in 1928, the third of its four Tapoco dams. It's located a mile upstream from the end of their Chilhowee Lake (see above)—a mile that's typically dry, as ALCOA reroutes the river water through a large pipe to the downstream power plant. The narrow lake backs up into a deep gorge for 7 miles, lined by wilderness its entire length. No roads follow it, but US 129, meandering along a ridgeline high above it, gives a spectacular bird's-eye view (see **The Foothills of Cades Cove** under *Wandering Around—Exploring by Car* in "Townsend, Cades Cove, and the Northwest Quadrant"). The long lake finally ends at the base of the next dam, **Cheoah Dam** (see *To See—Historic* Sites), where US 129 gives access to it.

Santeetlah Lake. ALCOA added Santeetlah to its Tapoco project in 1926. Its big dam blocks the Cheoah River, turning it dry for 9 miles as it sends its waters through a pipeline to a power station on Cheoah Lake, far below and far away. Santeetlah Lake has the best-developed recreational opportunities of all the lakes in this area, with two private marinas and a Nantahala National Forest boat ramp at **Cheoah Point** (see *Wild Places—Picnic Areas*). Santeetlah has a long and highly convoluted shoreline, most of it owned by Nantahala National Forest; there are many shoreline camping spots within the national forest, and views are spectacular.

Tellico Lake. With nearly 25 square miles of surface area, this huge TVA lake backs up from the foothills of Tennessee to the feet of the Unicoi Mountains. In the late 1970s it became a symbol to environmentalists of development out of control, and a symbol to developers of environmentalism out of control, as the U.S. Supreme Court stopped the entire dam project to save an endangered species known as the snail darter. Congress sided with developers and emended the law to allow the dam to be completed, snail darters or not, and the giant Tellico Lake started backing up in 1979. The entire lake is public land, as is much of its shore.

HISTORIC SITES **Fort Loudoun State Historic Area** (423-884-6217), 338 Fort Loudoun Road, Vonore, TN. This scenic state park occupies part of a forested island within large **Tellico Lake** (see *To See—Big Dammed Lakes, The Tapoco Lakes*). Its centerpiece is a careful reconstruction of Fort Loudoun, a large British fortification that figured prominently in the conflicts between the Cherokees, the British, and the colonials. This palisaded fort, with formidable walls overhanging

THE RECONSTRUCTED COLONIAL ERA FORT ON THE SHORES OF TELLICO LAKE AT FORT LOUDOUN STATE HISTORIC AREA

any attacking force, encloses a variety of military log structures furnished according to their original uses. Views from the fort are impressive, sweeping over the length of the large Tellico impoundment to the great wall of the Smokies and the Unicois. This is a favorite place for reenactment encampments, and the white tents and colorful uniforms add great charm to the scenery. A small museum sits near the fort; elsewhere on the grounds are walking paths and a very nice picnic area. (To find **Fort Loudoun** follow the brown signs south off US 411 at Vonore, just south of the bridge over Tellico Lake. Don't be confused by signs north of the bridge pointing to Fort Loudoun Reservoir; that's a different place altogether, and in the wrong direction.)

The Stewart Cabin. This minor site is a fun side trip from the **Joyce Kilmer Memorial Forest** (see *Wild Places—The Great Forests*) or the **Cherohala Skyway** (see *Wandering Around—Exploring by Car*). From the start of the Skyway, 2 miles south of Kilmer, **FS 81** drops down to the right to cross **Santeetlah Creek** in a mile, with good views over this handsome creek (and good access for fishers) from the bridge. Another 2 miles farther, the Stewart Cabin sits in riverside meadows by the gravel road. It's a modest, handsome log cabin, framed by wildflowers and a split-rail fence. Nantahala National Forest restored it and preserves it as a historic site. Return the way you came.

Junaluska's Grave. Chief Junaluska was a respected Cherokee warrior who fought with General Andrew Jackson against the Creeks at the Battle of Horseshoe Bend in Alabama. Junaluska and his warriors saved Jackson's European troops from near-certain defeat, and turned the battle. The victory opened Alabama to European settlement. Years later, President Andrew Jackson signed the order that expelled Junaluska from his home near Robbinsville, NC, sending him with his tribesmen on the Trail of Tears to Oklahoma. In old age, Junaluska was given permission to return to Robbinsville; his grave, immediately outside town, is a sacred site of the Cherokee Nation.

THE STEWART CABIN

Cheoah Dam. This is the most easily viewed of the Tapoco dams (see *To See—Big Dammed Lakes*), built by ALCOA to supply electricity to their aluminum smelter in Maryville, TN. Built in 1919, Cheoah was the tallest dam in the world at the time (at 225 feet) and had the largest turbines. It is now best known as the site of Harrison Ford's famous dam jump in the movie *The Fugitive*—accomplished by tossing a dummy off the dam. US 129 crosses the river just in front of the dam, with wonderful views of it, and more views from the side of the road. Take a gander at the industrial Gothic turbine station in the gorge under the dam, a beautiful piece of architecture instantly recognizable in the movie. The dam remains impressive nearly a century later and gives you a good idea of the scale of ALCOA's early electrical project, very successful and still going full tilt. Incidentally, this section of highway is historic in itself—essentially unchanged since it was built in 1931, the first paved road into this remote corner of the mountains. The trailhead for the **Slickrock Wilderness Walk** (see *Wandering Around—Exploring on Foot*) is downstream on the left.

Tellico Plains Ranger Station (423-253-2520), 250 Ranger Station Road, Tellico Plains, TN. Open Monday through Saturday 7–5. Free admission. The earliest Civilian Conservation Corps (CCC) camp in Tennessee, still in pristine condition, houses the offices of the Tellico Ranger District of the **Cherokee National Forest**. It's a nice place to drop by—scenic, historic, and friendly. You'll find it off the Tellico River Road—or FS 217—about 5 miles north of Tellico Plains via the Cherohala Skyway (see *Wandering Around—Exploring by Car*)—down a scenic little drive that winds along a mountain stream through a lovely old forest. The station is a collection of white clapboard buildings, built in 1937, centered on a small white-columned headquarters building. It's the administrative headquarters for about a sixth of the 633,000-acre Cherokee National Forest, and forest crews frequently come and go from its large, neat maintenance yard. The pine-paneled headquarters building welcomes visitors with an information desk and bookshop, as well as exhibits on the Civilian Conservation Corps (CCC) at Tellico, including a 1931 map of the Cherokee National Forest and 19th-century geological maps of the area.

CULTURAL SITES **Sequoyah Birthplace Museum** (423-884-6246), Citico Road, Vonore, TN. To find the Sequoyah museum, follow the brown signs south off US 411 at Vonore, just south of the bridge over Tellico Lake. It's only a short distance beyond Fort Loudoun State Park, on the right.) Open Monday through Saturday 9–5, Sunday noon–5. Adults $3, seniors $2, children $1. In 1821 Sequoyah, a nonliterate Cherokee silversmith living in northern Alabama, introduced a Cherokee *syllabary*—an alphabet in which each symbol represents a syllable rather than a sound. This astonishing feat made him the first, last, and only historic figure to invent an alphabet from scratch, having no previous knowledge of the concept of reading or writing. This museum, operated by the Eastern Band of the Cherokee Nation, presents exhibits on Sequoyah's life and accomplishments, as well as a full presentation of the succession of native peoples in the Tennessee Valley along with the archeological artifacts through which we know them. It also features a small exhibit area of Native American art, and a very nice gift shop with a good selection of Cherokee and other Native American arts and crafts (see **Sequoyah Birthplace Museum Gift Shop** under *Selective Shopping—Vonore, TN*).

Cherohala Visitors Center at Tellico Plains. A joint project of Monroe County, TN, and the Monroe Chamber of Commerce, this new visitors center on Tellico Plains's town square combines an information desk and exhibits on the new Cherohala Parkway (see *Wandering Around—Exploring by Car*) with a historical museum about the Tellico Plains area. Unfinished at press time, it should be open by late 2002.

✳ To Do

FISHING **Cherohala Outfitters** (828-479-4464), 260 Snowbird Road, Robbinsville, NC. Open all year. This guide and outfitting service, headquartered north of Robbinsville near **Lake Santeetlah, the Snowbird Area, and the Kilmer-Slickrock Wilderness,** offers guided trips for both fly-fishing and lake fishing, as well as hunting trips for the Russian blue boar found in this area. They will guide for backpacking trips as well and will arrange for prepared camping; they furnish all equipment, except a sleeping bag, and set up the site in advance for you.

Cherokee Guide Service (423-261-2747), 130 Payne Mountain Road, Tellico Plains, TN. This guide service offers fishing and hunting services throughout the Tellico River area, on lands of the **Cherokee National Forest.**

STILLWATER ADVENTURES San-teetlah Marina (828-479-8180), 1

Marina Drive, Robbinsville, NC. This full-service marina is located on **Lake Santeetlah,** 5.2 miles north of Robbinsville just off US 129. Open daily April through October. They rent canoes, ski boats, and pontoon boats, as well as slips by the night, and provide overnight vehicle and RV storage. If you are interested in boat camping, they have information on more than 50 informal camping spots on the long lakeshore within the national forest.

Dayton Camp Boat Rentals (828-479-7422). Located on the south shore of **Lake Santeetlah,** on NC 143 near Robbinsville, NC, Dayton Camp rents canoes, jonboats, ski boats, and pontoon boats. Open daily, spring through fall.

✳ Lodging

COUNTRY INNS AND HOTELS
Snowbird Mountain Lodge (828-479-3433; 1-800-941-9290), 4633 Santeetlah Road, Robbinsville, NC 28771. Open April through November. This 1941 rustic-style lodge sits high in the mountains above Lake Santeetlah, very near the Cherohala Parkway and Joyce Kilmer Forest and features wide, spectacular views from its native stone terrace. The library and lobby are paneled in wormy chestnut taken from the site, and feature a stone fireplace and picture window facing the view; the furniture includes pieces made by local craftsmen for the original inn's opening. The lodge's rooms all have en suite private baths and are paneled in a variety of local hardwoods. An adjacent cabin has been recently renovated to hold two more rooms; a new building holds the six largest and most luxurious rooms. The room tariff includes a full breakfast buffet, a picnic lunch, and a gourmet dinner; the dinner varies daily, featur-

ing fresh local ingredients in imaginative, international recipes. $175–320.

⚓ **The Blue Boar Inn** (828-479-8126), 1283 Blue Boar Road, Robbinsville, NC 28771. Located on Lake Santeetlah, just off NC 143 near the Cherohala Skyway and Joyce Kilmer Forest. Built in 1950 as a hunting lodge by Cincinnati's Bruckmann Brewery, the Blue Boar combines features of both lodge- and cottage-style architecture with some inspiration from early tourist camps. The eight guest rooms all have outside private entrances with private porches. Inside, a sitting area is separated from the roomy sleeping area by an open-arched wall. The decor is simple and elegant throughout. A full breakfast is served in dining room, as is lunch (open to the public), and dinner by reservation (see *Dining Out*). $95–135, including breakfast; plus 15 percent service fee.

RESORTS Tapoco Lodge Resort (828-498-2435; 1-800-822-5083), 14981 Tapoco Road, Robbinsville, NC. ALCOA constructed Tapoco Lodge in 1930, using it as a corporate retreat center until 1997. The well-preserved main lodge is an ivy-covered Georgian structure, simple and elegant in red brick, and a series of classic 1930s white clapboard cottages wander up the hill. Amenities include a swimming pool, tennis courts, and a large game room with pool tables and table tennis. Furnishings are simple, 1930s style, with many original pieces. The resort has 150 acres of property and adjoins Nantahala National Forest; hiking trails extend from the lodge deep into the **Kilmer-Slickrock Wilderness** (see *Wild Places—The Great Forests*), including full breakfast, light lunch, and hearty Southern-style dinner.

BED & BREAKFASTS The Magnolia House (423-253-2022; 1-800-323-4750), 305 US 165, P.O. Box 269, Tellico Plains, TN 37385. Located conveniently near the town square on a large and grassy tract of land, this roomy and historic old farmhouse, with its friendly large porches, was built in several phases in the 19th century. Each of its three guest rooms has a king bed (one of which can be converted to two twins) and a comfortable sitting area with a sofa or futon, a small refrigerator, and a coffeemaker. The rooms are English style, with a wash basin and water closet in each room,

WILD GERANIUM IN BLOOM AT THE EDGE OF A HARDWOOD FOREST IN STANDING INDIAN RECREATION AREA

and a common shower for all three rooms. Downstairs, a roomy and comfortable sitting area has coffee, a microwave, and a refrigerator stocked with juice and plenty of ice. Continental breakfasts include fresh muffins and other breads, cereal, milk, and juice. Rates start at $49.95 single, $54.95 double.

Riverview Bed & Breakfast (828-479-2765), 32 Summit Drive, Robbinsville, NC 28771. This classic two-room B&B is part of a private home halfway between Robbinsville and the Cherohala Parkway. Located

in a bend of the Snowbird River, the house is contemporary on the outside; on the inside it's beautifully furnished in a late-19th-century style. Both rooms have private baths; one has a king bed, while the other has two twins. $65, including full breakfast.

CABIN RENTALS Tellico Vacation Rentals (423-253-2253), 113 Scott Street, P.O. Box 906, Tellico Plains, TN 37385. These seven private cabins, scattered around the Tellico Plains countryside, offer the comfort of an immaculately kept and handsomely furnished private house. Owned by Sandra and Weldon Pyron of the **Tellico Arts Center** (see *Selective Shopping—Tellico Plains, TN*), this rental service offers a careful selection of fine private homes, ranging from small and simple rustic structures to luxurious chalets. All are beautifully set in the East Tennessee countryside; some have mountain views, others views over fields, rivers, or woods. $70–150.

The Historic Donley Cabin (423-253-2520), Tellico Ranger Station, Tellico Plains, TN 37385. Of all the lodgings listed in this guide, the Donley Cabin comes closest to an authentic pioneer experience. Owned and operated by the Cherokee National Forest, the cabin is located in the Tellico River area (see **The Tellico River and the Bald River Gorge Wilderness** under *Wild Places—The Great Forests*), 20 miles from Tellico Plains by gravel road—and a quarter mile walk into the forest. The two-crib cabin dates from the 1860s and 1870s; the earlier and cruder crib is said to have been built by a Civil War draft dodger who was hiding out, while the later, much more sophisticated crib was added by Jack Donley, a prominent local settler. The Forest Service has since restored the cabin to its 1880 condition, as a typical example of a log farmstead that has grown organically through multiple ownerships and generations. It's a beautiful little cabin, sitting in a little wildflower meadow with a nice front porch. Guest accommodations are in period as well: two slab beds without mattresses, a table with chairs, and a fireplace. That's it. No bedding; no shower; no water; no toilet. There's a stream and an outhouse nearby. Despite the less than luxurious conditions it stays booked up, and reservations are required. $35.

✳ Where to Eat

EATING OUT Cardin's Landing (423-253-7800), 222 Rafter Road, P.O. Box 759, Tellico Plains, TN. Dwight Cardin cooks his Boston butt pork and beef barbeque slowly over a hickory or apple wood fire outside his handsome log restaurant by the Tellico River. The results are incredibly tender and moist, served plain with house-made tomato-based sauce on the side. The barbeque menu includes ribs, pork, chicken, and steaks; sandwiches, salads, burgers and fresh seafood are also available. Sides include fried okra, french-fried sweet potatoes, corn on the cob, and Dwight's own scratch-made barbeque beans. Homemade desserts include cream pies and cobblers. Budweiser beer is available. Sandwiches and salads: $4–7. dinners: $7–13.

Tellahala Café (423-253-2880), 228 Bank Street, Tellico Plains, TN. Open Sunday through Thursday 11–8:30, Friday and Saturday 11–9:30. Don't be deceived by this café's modest appearance and strip-mall location; the ambitious and imaginative menu features fresh seafood, chicken, steak, and pasta, imaginatively seasoned and presented. Our meals included fillet of chicken breast grilled with fresh rosemary, and a large salmon fillet crusted with pecans and broiled to bring out the natural sweetness of the nuts. All food is made from scratch on the premises by a staff of experienced, trained chefs. Owners Rich and Donna Leudemann are always on hand in the kitchen or in the dining room. BYOB. Sandwiches, burgers, and salads $4–6; entrées $8–14, with steaks higher.

Town Square Café and Bakery (423-253-2200), 704 US 165, Tellico Plains, TN. Open Monday through Thursday 6 AM–8 PM; Friday and Saturday 6 AM–9 AM; Sunday 7 AM–7 PM. This spotlessly clean eatery is paneled with warm pine planks and matching pine tables. The menu focuses traditional Southern favorites. Breakfast (served anytime) features biscuits (with sausage gravy or spread), pancakes, and eggs, bacon, and sausage. Dinners feature country favorites such as fried chicken, country fried steak, pork chops, country ham, and catfish; all dinners come with two sides, soup, and cornbread. They also serve a full range of salads, sandwiches, and burgers. Breakfast $2–7; sandwiches and burgers $2.50–5; dinner $6–9.

DINING OUT The Blue Boar Inn at Lake Santeetlah (828-479-8126), 1283 Blue Boar Road, Robbinsville, NC. The Blue Boar is located near Joyce Kilmer Memorial Forest and the Cherohala Parkway, off NC 143. The first-rate restaurant of this elegant little B&B (see *Lodging—Country Inns and Hotels*) opens to the public for lunch, and for dinner by reservation only. The lunch menu focuses on sandwiches and salads, made with flair. A steak or chicken sandwich has thinly sliced meat grilled, then served on a fresh-baked baguette with provolone cheese, sautéed onions, and green peppers. Or try a sausage on a bun—in this case a 1/3 pound of wild boar or venison sausage on a fresh-baked French roll with sautéed onions, green peppers, mustard, and mayo.

✳ Entertainment

The Tellico Arts Center (423-253-2253), 113 Scott Street, Tellico Plains, TN. The center (see *Selective Shopping*) sponsors eight or so events a year, centering on mountain music and storytelling.

✳ Selective Shopping

Robbinsville, NC

Snowbird Indian Trading Post and Gallery (828-479-8653), Cornsilk Branch Road. (Directions: Follow NC 143 west of Robbinsville toward the Cherohala Skyway for 5.4 miles; turn left onto Snowbird River Road, SSR 1115, and drive 1.8 miles; then turn left onto Cornsilk Branch Road, SSR 1119, and drive 0.7 mile.) Open normal business hours in-season; call for appointment in winter. This modest building at the heart of the Snowbird Cherokee community has been a trading post since the early 20th century. Now it houses a crafts cooperative for the Snowbird community, featuring the work of local native American artisans.

Tellico Plains, TN

Tellico Arts Center (423-253-2253), 113 Scott Street. Located a block off the village's Town Square, this excellent not-for-profit gallery hosts the work of 74 local artists. A wide variety of fine art and crafts fill the handsome old redbrick building. You'll find fabric and fiber arts; metal artists; and pottery, beading, weaving, leather work,

stained glass, photography, soaps, candles, paintings and mixed media. Founders Sandra and Weldon Pyron are often on hand to talk about East Tennessee art and artists, and to direct people toward other area galleries and open studios.

Coker Creek, TN

Coker Creek Gallery (423-261-2157), 206 Hot Water Road. The gallery is 9 miles south of Tellico Plains via TN 68, to Hot Water Road, then a short distance west; the turn-off is well signposted. Open April 1 through December 21, Tuesday through Saturday 10–5. All other times and dates by appointment. Owners Kathleen and Ken Dalton, crafts artists well known for their white-oak basket weaving, have assembled a fine collection from 50 local and regional artists. You'll find baskets, pottery, fine hand textiles, toys, metal sculpture, dolls, wood carvings, paintings, and more, all marked by a high degree of technical competence and originality. Unlike most galleries, the Daltons buy their pieces outright from their artists—so they feature nothing that they wouldn't buy themselves. Prices are nearly always under a thousand dollars, with a wide selection of pieces under $60.

Coker Creek Village (423-261-2310). Coker Creek Village is 11 miles south of Tellico Plains on TN 68. For many years Sanford Gray ran one of the more eccentric and entertaining sites of the Southern mountains—a large "general store," where some items were for sale but most were his huge collection of antiques, memorabilia, and bygones. Unfortunately, the entire facility and its contents burned to the ground in the fall of 1999. Now Sanford has designed and built this new structure, combining planked log walls with a post-and-beam central area. Although much of the new Coker Creek Village caters to groups and retreats, Sanford has recreated his general store in one part of his building, and given another corner to the Cherokee National Forest as a staffed information center. It's definitely worth a stop.

Vonore, TN

Sequoyah Birthplace Museum Gift Shop (423-884-6246), Citico Road, Vonore, TN. Open Monday through Saturday 9–5, Sunday noon–5. Concentrating on Native American art, with a special emphasis on Eastern Cherokee artists, this museum gift shop offers a wide variety of jewelry, pottery, sculpture, and other items. The gourd pots are particularly remarkable and attractive. Book lovers will enjoy browsing the small but extremely well selected collection of Cherokee titles.

✳ Special Events

Last Sunday in April: **Graham County Ramp Festival,** Robbinsville, NC. This festival is held at the Rescue Squad building on Moose Branch Road in Robbinsville. Small communities throughout the North Carolina mountains traditionally support their volunteer fire departments and rescue squads with a dinner featuring this broad-leafed wild leek with a strong onion-garlic flavor. Here ramps are served cooked with mountain trout, chicken, baked beans, hushpuppies, cornbread, potato salad, and dessert.

April: **Fort Loudoun Bagpipes and Revelries** (423-884-6217), 338 Fort Loudoun Road, Vonore, TN. The Fort Loudoun Association sponsors this annual musical event in the center of the reconstructed fort. It features bag-piping, Highland dancing, Celtic music, and living history reenactments.

Mid-April: **The Telliquah Native American Gathering,** Tellico Plains, TN. This annual gathering of tribes features native American ceremonies and crafts. Contact the Tellico Plains Chamber of Commerce, who sponsors the event.

Fourth of July: **Graham County Heritage Festival,** Robbinsville, NC. This day-long Independence Day festival has events throughout the county but centers on Robbinsville. There's a parade, a duck race, tributes to war veterans, a town-wide crafts fair, and (of course) fireworks.

Second weekend in September: **Cherokee Arts and Crafts Festival** and the **18th-Century Trade Faire.** The **Sequoyah Birthplace Museum** (see *To See—Cultural Sites*), in Vonore, TN, sponsors an annual celebration, the Cherokee Arts and Crafts Festival, that mixes native American handmade crafts with Cherokee dancing, stick-ball, games, art, reenactments, and storytelling. Meanwhile, the European settlers are whooping it up at the 18th-Century Trade Faire, a few blocks down the road at **Fort Loudoun State Historic Area** (see *To See— Historic Sites*), also in Vonore. Hundreds of reenactors attract thousands of visitors to an authentic 18th-century trade fair at the gates of the fort, with period wares, food, and entertainment from music to fire-eaters.

THE SOUTHERN UNICOIS:
MURPHY & THE COPPER BASIN

T he great massed knot of mile-high mountains that characterizes the Blue Ridge and Smoky Mountains starts to slowly drop away as their ridgelines head south to the Georgia border. The area remains ruggedly mountainous; however, 4,000 feet becomes a high peak instead of a low one, and valley widths start being measured in miles instead of feet.

In this area, Murphy, NC, serves as the main town for a broad valley that stretches for 60 miles east and west, and can reach 10 miles wide in spots. Drained by the Hiwassee and Ocoee Rivers, this valley can be softly pastoral in some places, ruggedly handsome in others. Apart from Murphy, the Hiwassee Valley contains the towns of Andrews and Hayesville in North Carolina, and Ducktown, Copperhill, and Reliance in Tennessee.

Here tourism turns from the mountain summits to the rivers beneath them. The Ocoee River, site of the 1996 Olympic whitewater competitions, furnishes nearly continuous Class III to V rapids. The Hiwassee River in Tennessee, noted for its exceptional beauty, is popular with fishers, canoeists (rapids are Class I to II), and hikers. A series of five large Tennessee Valley Authority (TVA) lakes gives a wide choice of stillwater boating; this definitely includes wilderness exploration, as several of these lakes extend long, narrow arms for dozens of miles into remote national forest lands.

GUIDANCE **Cherokee County Chamber of Commerce** (828-837-2242), 805 West US 64, Murphy, NC 28906. The Cherokee County, NC, Chamber covers Robbinsville, NC, and the surrounding countryside.

Andrews Chamber of Commerce (828-321-3584; 877-558-0005), 345 Locust Street, Andrews, NC 28901. The small town of Andrews, 16 miles north of Murphy, NC, on US 19, has its own chamber, with a visitors center in the center of town.

Clay County Chamber of Commerce (828-389-3704), P.O. Box 88, Hayesville, NC 28904. The Clay County, NC, Chamber covers the mountainous area east of Murphy, NC, including the county seat of Hayesville.

Polk County–Copper Basin Chamber of Commerce (423-496-9000; 877-790-2157). The Polk County, TN, Chamber covers all of the Tennessee mountains

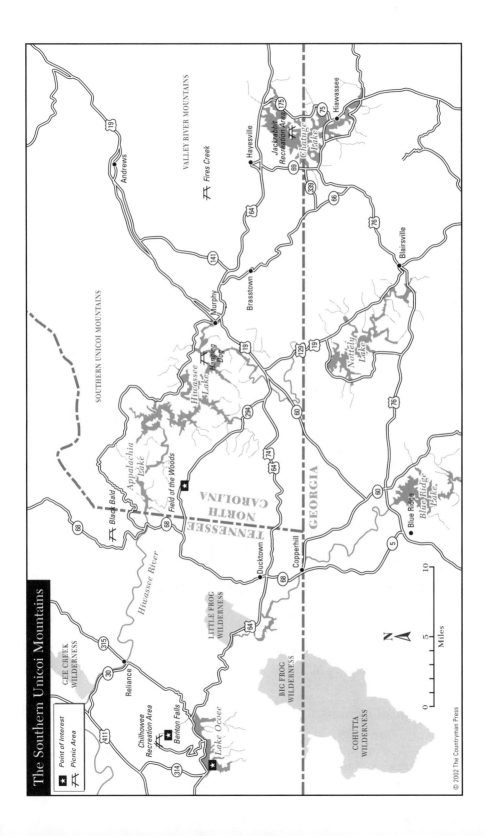

The Southern Unicoi Mountains

Point of Interest
Picnic Area

VALLEY RIVER MOUNTAINS

SOUTHERN UNICOI MOUNTAINS

Fires Creek

Hiawassee

Hayesville

Jackrabbit
Recreation Area

Chatuge
Lake

Andrews

Blairsville

Brasstown

Murphy

Nottely
Lake

Hiwassee
Lake

Hanging
Dog

Black Bald

Appalachia
Lake

Field of the Woods

Blue Ridge

Blue Ridge
Lake.

TENNESSEE
NORTH CAROLINA

GEORGIA

Ducktown

Copperhill

Hiwassee River

GEE CREEK
WILDERNESS

LITTLE FROG
WILDERNESS

Reliance

Chilhowee
Recreation Area

Benton Falls

Lake Ocoee

BIG FROG
WILDERNESS

COHUTTA
WILDERNESS

N

0   5   10
Miles

© 2002 The Countryman Press

in this chapter, including Ducktown, TN, and the Copper Basin. They maintain a visitors center in Ducktown.

Cherokee National Forest, Ocoee Ranger District (423-338-5201), Route 1, Box 348D, Benton, TN 37307. The national forest ranger station for this part of the Tennessee Mountains is located on US 64 by Lake Ocoee. They have an information desk and a bookstore.

Nantahala National Forest, Tusquitee Ranger District (828-837-5152), 201 Woodland Drive, Murphy, NC 28906. This ranger station covers all of Nantahala National Forest around Murphy and Hayesville, NC. Located off US 64 east of Murphy, it has a staffed information desk and sells maps of the forest.

OcoeeWhitewater.com (423-496-2275). This Copperhill, TN, organization acts as a central information point for whitewater sports events on the Ocoee River.

GETTING THERE *By car:* This region's modern four-lane highway still follows (at least roughly) the tracks of the 1850s wagon road that crossed through this area from Asheville, NC, to the rich farmlands of Tennessee. Whether you approach from Asheville and I-40, or from Chattanooga, TN, and I-75, you need to take US 74.

By air: **Chattanooga Metropolitan Airport** (423-855-2200), 1001 Airport Road, Suite 14, Chattanooga, TN. Chattanooga's airport is the closest, being only 80 miles from Murphy, NC, via US 74. Knoxville's airport (see **McGhee Tyson Airport** under *Getting There* in "Townsend, Cades Cove, and the Northwest Quadrant"), is an extra 20 mile's journey, at 100 miles away via I-75 and US 74. **Asheville's airport** (see **Asheville Regional Airport** under *Getting There* in Asheville and the Blue Ridge Parkway") is 35 miles farther, and Atlanta's airport (which may be cheapest) is 50 miles farther than Chattanooga. You'll have to rent a car in any case; none of the towns in this chapter have bus or train service.

By bus or train: This region has no scheduled bus or train service.

MEDICAL EMERGENCIES **Murphy Medical Center** (828-837-8161), 2002 US 64 East, Murphy, NC. This 50-bed local hospital is the closest 24/7 emergency facility for the Murphy area. It's a short distance east of town.

District Memorial Hospital (828-321-1200), 415 Whitaker Lane, Andrews, NC. This 40-bed hospital in Andrews has a 24/7 emergency room and an evac helicopter. It may be closer than Murphy Medical Center (see above) for many locations in the Hayesville, NC, area.

Copper Basin Medical Center (423-496-5511), TN 68, Copperhill, TN. This 44-bed local hospital has 24/7 emergency-room services from its facility on TN 68 near Copperhill, TN.

✴ Wandering Around

EXPLORING BY CAR **Driving the Southern Unicois.** *Leg 1:* From Andrews, NC, follow Old US 19 (Main Street in town, Andrews Highway/SSR 1428 out of town) and US 19 south to Murphy, NC.

Leg 2: At Murphy, turn right (into town) at the traffic light where US 64 is

FARMLAND IN THE UNICOI FOOTHILLS NEAR MURPHY

entering from the left. Go downhill through downtown to Lake Hiwassee; turn left onto Joe Brown Highway (SSR 1326). Follow Joe Brown Highway westward through many intersections for 19.9 miles; turn right onto SSR 1322 and drive 4.7 miles to a T-intersection; then turn right onto River Road and drive 2.1 miles to TN 68.

Leg 3: Take TN 68 south to Ducktown, TN; then take US 64/74 west to Lake Ocoee.

The first leg starts in downtown **Andrews,** an area of brick storefronts with a pretty, old depot. From downtown, stay on the old highway (crossing four-lane US 19) for the next 7 miles for a taste of old-style country driving with wide mountain views. This passes through the former town of Marble, once a major marble quarry but now mainly abandoned; the courthouse in Murphy is clad in stone from this mine. The scenery continues to be pleasant as you regain the four-lane highway and enter Murphy.

Entering **Murphy,** you'll see a pretty wood church on the left, a good example of rural Gothic design favored by 19th-century Episcopalians. The **courthouse** is the main feature, looming over the entire downtown, and worth stopping to admire. Downtown continues to the bottom of the hill, lined continuously with shops worth exploring. Past town, the road sweeps by **Hiwassee Lake** (see *To See—Big Dammed Lakes*), then winds into farming valleys, over low ridges, and back to the lake several times. As this slow and pretty drive continues, the scenery becomes wilder, more wooded, with fewer homes. At the end of the drive the road follows a tumultuous creek down to the **Hiwassee River,** then follows the riverbank over the North Carolina–Tennessee state line to a paved Tennessee highway.

The third leg follows **TN 68** south through the wide valley that sweeps through the center of this region, then into the **Copper Basin** and **Ducktown** for a view of the old copper mines and the devastation they caused. (This view is being preserved as both a historic site and a reminder—the rest of the devastation is being cleaned up.) Heading west on **US 64/74,** the route follows the **Ocoee River Gorge,** with frequent view of this violent river and the three lakes that tame it.

Near its end the road follows **Ocoee Lake** for 7 miles, with many views; **Chilhowee Mountain,** a fine recreation spot, is on the right up **FS 77.**

EXPLORING ON FOOT **Hiking the Hiwassee River.** The two great rivers of Tennessee's Unicoi Foothills, the Hiwassee and the Ocoee, are both completely controlled by upstream dams. Despite that, the two are a study in contrasts; the Hiwassee River is as mild and beautiful as the Ocoee River is rugged and violent. The Ocoee is best explored by raft or kayak; but the Hiwassee can be fully enjoyed on foot. The 19-mile **John Muir National Recreation Trail** follows the north bank of the river.

The most popular section of the John Muir trail is its western end, reached from **FS 108,** off **TN 315** just north of **Reliance, TN.** This level section follows the river, with wide views of its rapids and rock formations; tall gray river bluffs tower on the left.

At the trail's halfway point, a remote and difficult trailhead gives access to its more remote and difficult areas. To reach the trailhead: From Coker Creek (see **Coker Creek Village** under *Selective Shopping—Coker Creek*, in "The Northern Unicois: Robbinsville and Tellico Plains"), go south on **TN 68,** then follow the signs for Coker Creek Falls onto **Duckett Ridge Road (FS 22)** and south onto **FS 228** to its end. The Coker Creek Falls access road is impassible by passenger cars at this writing; FS 228 may be in very bad shape as well.

From this trailhead, follow the **John Muir Trail** right (west) to switchback up to the top of one of those river bluffs, with broad views over the river south. At the base of this climb, a short, hard side trail goes to the right, leading to the bluff's foot for an intimate view of a riverine cliffside. Also from this remote trailhead, **Coker Creek Trail** goes uphill through a deep defile along a raucous stream to reach **Coker Creek Falls;** this entire walk has been declared a National Scenic Area.

Exploring the Unicoi Foothills Wilderness. Despite their low size, the Unicoi Foothills are true mountains with rugged terrain, clifflike slopes, turbulent streams, and rich environments. Within these foothills, two small tracts of Tennessee's Cherokee National Forest have been declared wildernesses by the U.S. Congress (see *Wild Places—The Great Forests*). The Gee Creek Wilderness, with only 2,500 acres, occupies a small but rugged gorge on what is geologically the same mountain as the **Chilhowee Mountain Recreation Area** (see *Wild Places—Recreation Areas*), just north of the Hiwassee River off US 411. The **Little Frog Wilderness** contains 4,600 acres of twisted mountain wilderness just west of Ducktown, TN.

The **Gee Creek Wilderness** centers on a small but extremely broken and rugged gorge carved into the hard rock side of the mountain. The trailhead is reached from a paved road off **US 411,** 1.8 miles north of the **Hiwassee Bridge;** there should be signs. Two worthwhile trails extend from the trailhead. The first is a rough fisherman's path that follows the creek upstream, splashing through the creek and climbing over boulders. It leads through deep hemlock forests to three lovely waterfalls and a beautiful glade underneath a 150-foot cliff. The second trail climbs the ridgeline left to reach the mountain crest in 3 miles and a 1,400-foot climb—a difficult day trip rewarded by wide views from the cross path that follows the level ridgeline.

The **Little Frog Wilderness** protects a range of 2,000- and 3,000-foot peaks just east of Ducktown, TN. Despite being adjacent to the Copper Basin areas devastated by acid rains in the 1860s and 1870s, the Little Frog's young hardwood and pine forests are lush and beautiful, with a large number of wildflowers. Two trails penetrate the wilderness from **US 64/74** west of **Ducktown.** The first climbs a mountain ridge uphill from the **#3 Powerhouse on US 64,** for varied ridgeline forests and occasional views; if you stay on it to its end, you'll travel 11 miles round-trip and climb 900 feet. A few miles closer to Ducktown, a second trail starts on **US 64/74** to climb through the center of the wilderness. This is a more difficult hike, crossing several creek valleys as it climbs into a gap, then descends to lovely little **Pressley Cove.**

✳ Villages

Murphy, NC. The largest town of this area, Murphy is a good-size place at the center of a very large valley. It has a lovely, well-developed old downtown that climbs a hill, making for interesting strolling. Within North Carolina it is famous for its early-20th-century **courthouse,** reputed to be the most beautiful in the state—a large and stately neoclassical structure completely clad in locally quarried marble. **Hiwassee Lake** (see *To See—Big Dammed Lakes*), which starts 10 miles east of town, backs up into the village's residential areas.

Hayesville, NC. The tiny seat of Clay County (population just 350), Hayesville sits 2 miles off the main highway, US 64, east of Murphy, NC. Isolated by the rugged **Valley River Mountains,** Hayesville remains nearly unchanged, a 50-year step back in time. It has a wonderfully beautiful **Town Square**—a 19th-century redbrick courthouse, framed by azaleas and rhododendrons, shaded by oaks, and with a little gazebo in front. The square is surrounded by tiny shops, forming Hayesville's downtown. East of town, US 64 gives wonderful views as it climbs out of Clay County.

THE COUNTY COURTHOUSE AND POLICE DEPARTMENT MUSEUM IN MURPHY

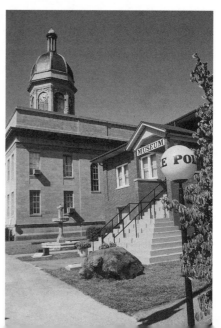

Andrews, NC. The small town of Andrews sits at the dead end of a wide, flat-bottomed river valley stretching northeast from Murphy, NC, to the **Nantahala Gorge** (see *Villages* in "Bryson City and the Southwest Quadrant"). The first large piece of flatland on the far side of the Nantahala Gorge, it was a natural location for a major siding on the railroad passing through the gorge. Like many railroad towns, Andrews declined for decades along with its line—now the **Great Smoky Mountains Railroad** in Bryson City (see *To See—Other* in "Bryson City and the Southeast Quadrant"). In the past few years its fortunes have been reviving, and its small but well-formed downtown of old brick storefronts is begin-ning to attract new businesses. Andrews is the closest town to isolated and beauti-ful **Nantahala Lake** (see *To See—Big Dammed Lakes*); the road from Andrews to the lake, Junaluska Road, follows the 1855 stagecoach turnpike.

Ducktown and Copperhill, TN. Ducktown is a small, compact hilltop village just off US 64/74. Reliant on copper mining from 1850 to 1987, it's a neat, white-washed town dominated by modest workers' housing and a few small stores. Five miles south, Copperhill is considerably larger, with a well-formed downtown of brick storefronts facing the **Ocoee River.** The area between Ducktown and Cop-perhill, known as the **Copper Basin,** was utterly stripped of vegetation by acid rain during the 1860s and 1870s, a by-product of the crude copper-smelting meth-ods then in use. The worst of the pollution ended in the 1880s, when local mines started recovering and selling the acidifying sulfur instead of spewing it into the air. However, the vegetation did not start to grow back until a revegetation effort in the late 20th century, and rural landscapes remain immature. Ironically, the sul-fur extraction outlasted the copper mining by almost two decades, the last sulfur plant closing in 2001.

Reliance, TN. This small town sits in the gorge of the **Hiwassee River,** tightly hugging TN 30. Noted for its concentration of old-fashioned small town buildings, it's now a National Historic District. Look for the **L&N Watchman's House,** the **Vaughn-Webb Homeplace,** the **Hiwassee Union Church/Masonic Lodge, Higdon Hotel,** and **Webb Brothers' General Store** (see Webb Brothers' Gen-eral Store under *Selective Shopping*)—all listed on the National Register. Just over the river north of the village, the **John Muir National Recreation Trail** gives an easy walk along the beautiful Hiwassee River (see **Hiking the Hiwassee River** under *Wandering Around—Exploring on Foot*).

✳ Wild Places

THE GREAT FORESTS The Southern Unicoi Mountains. The Unicoi Moun-tains end north of Murphy, NC, and Ducktown, TN, in a series of 4,000-foot ridge-lines. Heavily logged in past years, it's covered in second-growth hardwoods. Most of these mountains are in public ownership within Nantahala and Cherokee National Forests. Nevertheless, recreational opportunities are few, and these peaks remain remote and little visited. Lacking formal trails, hunters and hikers use Forest Service logging roads and other old tracks, poorly documented on topo-graphic maps.

The Unicoi Foothills. The Unicois do not end suddenly and dramatically. Instead, they decline into smaller ridges and wider valleys. These foothills remain mountainous in character, but with only a thousand feet or less local relief they lack the drama found only a few miles farther north. This is a land of wide valleys filled with attractive farms, with meadow views toward low mountains. It has a sur-prising amount of Cherokee and Nantahala National Forest land, including two Cherokee National Forest wildernesses, **Little Frog Wilderness** and **Gee Creek Wilderness** (see Exploring the Unicois Foothills Wilderness under *Wan-dering Around—Exploring on Foot*). Particularly on the Tennessee side, creeks tend to be full of water, dashing over cascades into lush, steep-sided gorges.

The Valley River Mountains. This 4,000-foot ridgeline isolates Hayesville, NC, from nearby Murphy and Andrews. Here two gapless ridges run southwest, surrounding **Fires Creek**. The entire mountain complex is owned by the Nantahala National Forest and made open to public recreation by a series of hiking paths, reached from the road to and past the **Fires Creek Picnic Area** (see *Picnic Areas*). The terrain is quite rugged and covered with second-growth hardwoods, with few if any views; all the best scenery is along the creek. The area is very popular with local fishers and hunters.

The Cohutta and Big Frog Wilderness. Located at the southwest corner of this area, straddling the Tennessee-Georgia state line, this is one of the East's largest congressionally declared wildernesses, at 45,000 combined acres. It encompasses a wild and rugged zone of 4,000-foot ridges, separated by violent rivers in steep defiles. It can be a real surprise; the approaches to it are through the much lower relief of the **Unicoi Foothills** (see above), or the nearly level Great Valley. Although heavily logged in the early 20th century, this area has rested for decades and now is covered by lush and attractive forests. The extensive trail network leads through every sort of mountain scenery imaginable, and the large size allows multiday backpacking loops. Like all national forest wilderness areas, it's open to hunters who wish to confront the wilds without their pickup trucks and off-road vehicles; game is plentiful and wildlife observation is excellent.

RECREATION AREAS **Ocoee Whitewater Center** (423-496-5197). Built by the Cherokee National Forest for the 1996 Olympic Whitewater Slalom Races, this whitewater racing channel looks like an accidental product of nature. Not true—this course is completely man-made, carefully designed to test the skills of the world's top athletes. This stretch of the **Ocoee River** appealed to Olympic officials precisely because it was (and is) dewatered by its upstream dam, which pipes its water to a downstream power station. This allows large-scale manipulation of the Ocoee's dry riverbed with planned water releases flooding the course. The center also includes a native plant garden, paved walkways, a hiking and biking trail on the **Historic Old Copper Road,** pools of water for wading or feeding fish, and a regional visitors center.

Jackrabbit Recreation Area. Jackrabbit is a large and handsome Nantahala National Forest site on the shores of **Chatuge Lake** (see *To See—Big Dammed Lakes*), south of Hayesville, NC. It occupies a pine-covered peninsula extending far out into the lake. Its pine-shaded picnic area has excellent views over the lake toward the Valley River Mountains.

Hanging Dog Recreation Area. Three miles east of Murphy, NC, this attractive Nantahala National Forest recreation site gives access to **Hiwassee Lake** (see *To See—Big Dammed Lakes*). It has a lovely picnic area, nice walking paths, a little pioneer cemetery, and lake views. You'll find it off the **Joe Brown Highway,** heading west from Murphy's town center (see Driving the Southern Unicois under *Wandering Around—Exploring by Car*).

Chilhowee Mountain Recreation Area. To reach this recreation area, take US 64/74 west from Ducktown, TN, to Lake Ocoee, where FS 77 is on your right. Chilhowee Mountain forms a thousand-foot-high barrier on the far western edge of this district. Oval-shaped, its sides are even and clifflike, but its top is a broad, gently sloping basin. The Cherokee National Forest's Chilhowee Mountain Recreation Area occupies that mountaintop basin. Its access road, FS 77, makes a dramatic climb straight up from **Lake Ocoee** (see *To See—Big Dammed Lakes*). At the top are wide panoramas toward the Unicoi Mountains, over the **Ocoee Gorge,** and over the Great Valley of Tennessee. Recreation facilities center on a lovely little lake and include a fine picnic area. Walking paths lace through the mountaintop basin, including one to a 65-foot waterfall.

PICNIC AREAS **Fires Creek Picnic Area.** To reach the picnic area from the Hayesville Town Square, go north on Anderson Street (SSR 1307) 0.4 mile; then turn left onto Mission Dam Road (SSR 1300) and drive 4.5 miles; then turn right onto Fres Creek Road and drive about 2 miles. Located in the **Valley River Mountains** (see *The Great Forests*) north of Hayesville, NC, this small national forest picnic area has streamside tables shaded by a deep forest. The base of **Leatherwood Falls** is visible from the picnic area, and a short path leads to the top. The good forest road that leads to the picnic area, Fires Creek Road, continues on to explore Forest Service lands in the Valley River Mountains, with many trailheads.

Buck Bald. This bald is located in Cherokee National Forest north of Ducktown, TN; drive north on TN 68 for 18.2 miles; then turn right onto gravel FS 311, following the signs on this rough but passable road for about 2 miles. The site of an old fire tower, this conical 2,350-foot mountain is crowned with open grassy lawns and a handful of picnic tables. Remarkable views in all directions make this a popular spot, despite its remoteness.

Hiwassee Dam. From Murphy, take US 64/74 west 7.6 miles to a right on NC 294; then head north for 8.6 miles to a right turn onto SSR 1314; then head north for 5.2 miles to the dam. This Tennessee Valley Authority (TVA) picnic area sits on a grassy hill, shaded by large old trees, with sweeping views over **Hiwassee Lake** (see *To See—Big Dammed Lakes*) and Dam. The paved back road to it goes right over the top of the dam.

Sugarloaf Mountain State Park (423-338-4133). This Tennessee state park sits at the base of **Ocoee Dam #1,** giving access to the calm Lower Section of the **Ocoee River** as it flows out of the mountains and into the Great Valley. The park includes a scale model of the 1996 Olympic Whitewater Slalom Race Channel that is located upstream at the **Ocoee Whitewater Center** (see *Recreation Areas*).

✳ To See

BIG DAMMED LAKES The Tennessee Valley Authority—universally known as TVA—owns and operates six hydropower dams in this area. Chatuge Dam near Hayesville, NC, controls the Hiwassee River's upstream flow, Hiwassee Dam backs up the Hiwassee River below Murphy, NC, and Appalachia Dam, blocks the Hiwassee near the North Carolina–Tennessee state line. On the Ocoee River in Tennessee, the unimaginatively named Ocoee #1, #2, and #3 break this fierce river to harness its power. The TVA, "a corporation clothed with the power of government," as Franklin Roosevelt described it, uses these and 43 other hydropower dams to produce much of Tennessee's electrical power. (The rest is produced by coal and nuclear plants, also owned by the TVA.)

Lake Ocoee. Sometimes known as "Ocoee #1 Lake," this large lake was built in 1910 by a local power company and purchased by the TVA, who now runs it. It's a long, thin lake that floods the Ocoee Gorge, with a main pool over 7 miles long but with only 3 square miles of water surface. US 64/74 follows Ocoee Lake for its entire 7-mile length, giving continuous views and many recreational opportunities, and ending with a good view of the old dam. Needless to say, this lake is a popular spot.

Upstream is **Ocoee #2 Dam,** built in 1913 and later purchased by the TVA. It serves merely to divert the river into a wooden flume that carries it to a downstream power plant, so that its impoundment is really very tiny. If you're interested in this old complex, you can see it from US 64/74. As you drive west from the **Ocoee Whitewater Center** (see *Wild Places—Recreation Areas*), look for the #2 Dam on your left at 2.3 miles; watch for its flume on the other side of the Ocoee River for the next 4 miles; then look for the #2 Powerhouse.

Ocoee #3 Lake. Built by the TVA during World War II, this small, narrow lake covers a bit more than 4 miles of the Ocoee River downstream from Copperhill, TN. Recreational access is from US 64/74, 3.1 miles west of the TN 68 intersection. The **#3 Dam** controls the flow of the Ocoee River's Upper Section, the site of the 1996 Olympics (see **Ocoee Whitewater Center** under *Wild Places—Recreation Areas*).

Apalachia Lake. TVA's Apalachia Lake (yes, it's spelled with only one *p*) covers 9 miles of narrow Hiwassee River gorge between the North Carolina–Tennessee state line and Hiwassee Dam. It's little used by fishers and other boaters, probably because it has no marinas, and its only boat ramp is in an isolated location. You'll find the single boat ramp a short distance from the **Hiwassee Dam** (see *Wild Places—Picnic Areas*).

Hiwassee Lake. Water from the TVA's Hiwassee Dam backs up into the town of Murphy, NC, 10 miles away. This long, skinny lake with many arms floods a long gorge of the Hiwassee River, with steep-sided hills rising out of the water, and the tall Unicoi Mountains visible to the north. Its main channel takes 20 miles to travel the 10 miles from the dam to Murphy, and its largest side channels extend another 10 miles—and nearly all of this 163 miles of shoreline is national forest lands. Recreational access is provided by the national forest at **Hanging Dog Recreation Area** (see *Wild Places—Recreation Areas*) and by TVA at the dam (see **Hiwassee Dam** under *Wild Places—Picnic Areas*).

Chatuge Lake. This large lake, built by the TVA in 1942 for wartime power production, sprawls over 11 square miles of surface, extending from Hayesville, NC, south to the town of Hiwassee, GA. It has a broad open central area from which many arms extend deep into mountain valleys. This is a prime recreation lake, with private marinas and a nice national forest recreation area (see **Jackrabbit Recreation Area** under *Wild Places—Recreation Areas*). It is particularly noted for its beautiful views toward the Valley River Mountains to its north. There is a large amount of privately owned land along its 128 miles of shoreline, and many second homes.

Nantahala Lake. One of the most remote and beautiful hydropower lakes in the region, Nantahala was built in the 1940s by this region's local power company, Nantahala Power and Light (now Duke Power). It floods a rugged mountain valley 14 miles east of Andrews, NC; to reach it, take Junaluska Road 13 miles to a right on Aquone Road (SSR 1310). Nantahala Lake has a T-shape, with each of its arms 2 or 3 miles long and a quarter to a half mile wide. It's surrounded by 4,000- and 5,000-foot peaks on all sides, which rise straight up out of the water; the west side, and nearly all of the surrounding mountains, are primitive national forest

Field of the Woods

(828-494-7855), NC 294, Murphy, NC. Field of the Woods is 18 miles west of Murphy; take US 64/74 west for 10 miles, then turn right onto NC 294 and drive 8 miles to the park. Free admission. This "biblical theme" park, run by the Church of God of Prophe-

THE RECONSTRUCTION OF GOLGOTHA AT FIELD OF THE WOODS BIBLE PARK

cy, commemorates its founding with monumental art deco sculptures in poured concrete, including the world's largest Ten Commandments. It occupies the spot where A. J. Tomlinson professed to have received the revelation (in 1903) that led to the founding of the Church of God. (Tomlinson led a split from the Church of God in 1923, his group becoming the Church of God of Prophecy. Both groups are now major Pentecostal denominations.) It's a remarkable place, with a white arched entrance leading into a landscaped valley filled with Christian monuments. The most striking monuments date from the park's founding in the 1940s and show a brilliant vernacular use of art deco elements in their curved, whitewashed concrete. The enormous **Ten Commandments** are the most famous, covering a grassy hillside with 7-foot-tall concrete letters. However, the most impressive monument is the **Place of Prayer,** a 320-step landscaped path lined with gigantic concrete tablets engraved with biblical verses, leading to a prayer garden with wide views. Other monuments include a reconstruction of **Golgotha** and the tomb in which Jesus was buried and a hilltop garden displaying the flags of all nations where the Church of God has congregations. There is also a large gift shop.

lands. This makes the lakeside scenery wild and remote, particularly when viewed from Aquone Road, which follows it for some length. There's a public boat ramp on Aquone Road.

Release water from Nantahala Lake provides the dependable, high-quality whitewater sports in the downstream **Nantahala Gorge** (see *Villages* in "Bryson City and the Southwest Quadrant"). Like several other hydropower sites in these mountains, Nantahala's power station is located some miles from the dam; the river water is carried to it through pipes, leaving the channel "dewatered" (see **Driving the Nantahala Gorge** under *Wandering Around—Exploring by Car* in "Bryson City and the Southwest Quadrant").

HISTORIC SITES **Ducktown Basin Museum and Burra Burra Mine Site** (423-496-5778), 701 Burra Burra Street, Ducktown, TN. Open Monday through Saturday 10–4. When copper mining came to Ducktown in the 1850s, it was a remote and inaccessible mountain community. The ore was mined in the crudest way possible, using techniques already long abandoned in most of the industrialized world. These mining methods, practiced by dozens of independent miners scattered throughout the valley, pumped so much sulfur into the air that the mountain rains turned into a sulfuric-acid bath, killing all the vegetation for miles around. This high a degree of acid rain ended in the 1880s when more modern facilities recovered and sold the sulfur, but by then it was too late. A hundred years later the Copper Basin was still stripped bare of vegetation, restored only in the late 20th century at great effort and expense.

The Ducktown Basin Museum tells the story of the copper mines from the site of the 1899 Burra Burra Mine. Here the desolate ochre landscape survives, preserved as a National Historic District. Owned and operated by the Tennessee State Parks system, the museum sits above the mine, with exhibits (redesigned in 1996) that tell the story of the Cherokees' expulsion from this valley, the subsequent European settlement, and the devastating copper mining. An overlook gives impressive views over the mine's flooded pit, and guided tours visit the mine's buildings.

CULTURAL SITES ♿ **John C. Campbell Folk School** (828-837-2775; 1-800-365-5724), One Folk School Road, Brasstown, NC. From Murphy, NC, go east on US 64 for 4.6 miles, to a right turn onto Settawig Road, and look for the signs. Founded in 1925 by New England social worker Olive Campbell and named for her late husband, the Campbell School occupies 380 acres in the rural community of Brasstown, 7 miles east of Murphy. The beautiful and well-kept campus looks like a large and prosperous farmstead, complete with barn and farm-

THE CANTRELL BLACKSMITH SHOP AT THE JOHN C. CAMPBELL FOLK SCHOOL IN BRASSTOWN

house; but these buildings hold studios and classrooms. The school sponsors an incredible list of 6-day courses, with a large number going on at once and the courses changing every week. While every aspect of folk and fine-art crafts are covered, the school is particularly strong in wood, textiles, and baskets. They run a first-rate crafts store (see **John C. Campbell Folk School Craft Store** under *Selective Shopping*) and sponsor weekly concerts and bimonthly dances (see **Friday Night Concerts at the John C. Campbell Folk School** and **Saturday Night Dances at the John C. Campbell Folk School,** both under *Entertainment*).

✳ To Do

BICYCLING **Ocoee Adventure Center** (423-496-4430; 1-888-723-8622). Rentals $30 per day; guided rides $39–75. This rafting company on the **Ocoee River** (see also *Whitewater Adventures*) offers mountain bike tours and rentals.

FISHING **Dry Flyer Outfitters** (423-338-6263), This fly-fishing guide service specializes in the gentle and beautiful **Hiwassee River,** draining the Unicoi Mountains north of the Ocoee.

GLIDING **Chilhowee Gliderport** (423-338-2000), US 411, Reliance, TN. Open weekends; weekdays by appointment. Rides $69–99. This full-service glider aircraft operation is located at the foot of Chilhowee Mountain, just outside Benton, TN. They offer 20- and 30-minute rides, for a high, quiet perspective on the mountains.

GOLF **Mountain Harbour Golf and Yacht Club** (828-389-4111), 100 Mountain Harbour Drive, Hayesville, NC. $32–38. This 18-hole Hayesville course was built on rolling terrain in the early 1990s as part of a housing subdivision.

Chatuge Shores Golf Course (828-389-8940), 260 Golf Course Road, Hayesville, NC. $18. This 18-hole course was built in 1972 as part of a lakeside subdivision on **Chatuge Lake** (see *To See—Big Dammed Lakes*) near Hayesville. It features scenic views over the lake toward the mountains.

Cherokee Hills Golf and Country Club (828-837-5853), Harshaw Road, Murphy, NC. $25. Located east of Murphy, this 18-hole 1969 course has a reputation for difficulty, with hilly terrain and water hazards.

ROCK CLIMBING **Outdoor Adventure Rafting** (1-800-627-7636). $11–29. This local rafting company (see also *Whitewater Adventures*) sponsors rock climbing and rappelling instructions on a 75-foot limestone bluff on their own 20-acre compound, with all equipment provided.

High Country Outfitters (1-800-233-8594). $125–245. This **Ocoee River** whitewater outfitter runs rock climbing and rappelling instructions, and offers a guide/instructional service on the slope of your choosing.

STILLWATER ADVENTURES **Lake Ocoee Inn Marina** (423-338-5591), Benton, TN. This marina on **Lake Ocoee** (see *To See—Big Dammed Lakes*) rents pontoon boats, fishing boats, and canoes.

WHITEWATER ADVENTURES The Ocoee River gained fame with whitewater enthusiasts as the site of the 1996 Olympic Games's whitewater competition (see **Ocoee Whitewater Center** under *Wild Places—Recreation Areas*). The river drains northward out of Georgia (where it is named the Taccoa River), through the center of downtown Copperhill, and then down through the mountains into Tennessee's Great Valley. In that final downhill stretch the Ocoee is controlled by three dams: Ocoee #3 dam on the uphill end (see **Ocoee #3 Lake** under *To See—Big Dammed Lakes*), then the much smaller Ocoee #2 Dam in the middle, and finally the large Ocoee #1 Dam at the downstream end (see **Lake Ocoee** under *To See—Big Dammed Lakes*). Below the Ocoee #3 Dam is a long dewatered stretch of river, as the river is piped from the dam to a downstream power station. This forms the "Upper River Section," the site of the Olympics, bone dry unless Ocoee #3 releases water. Downstream, between Ocoee #2 Dam and Lake Ocoee, is the "Middle River Section," which receives regular water releases from Ocoee #2, specifically for whitewater sports—a practice that started in 1976. Both of these sections offer nearly continuous Class III and IV rapids, with predictably optimal water flows because of the dam controls. Trips that combine the two sections run the Upper Section, paddle into #2 Lake, have lunch on the lakeshore, and then portage around #2 Dam to start the Middle Section. Downstream from Ocoee #1 the river enters the Great Valley, becoming much calmer; this is where tubing trips are held.

Ocoee Outdoors (1-800-533-7767), Ocoee, TN. This local company was one of the earliest to lead rafting trips on the Ocoee and has been operating here since 1977. They offer trips on the beautiful and mild-mannered

Hiwassee River (see Hiking the Hiwassee River under *Wandering Around—Exploring on Foot*), also in this area, as well as the exciting **Ocoee River.**

Outdoor Adventure Rafting (1-800-627-7636), Ocoee, TN. This company has a 20-acre site on the **Ocoee River,** from which they run rafting and tubing trips, and hold rock climbing instruction.

Ocoee Adventure Center (423-496-4430; 1-888-723-8622), Copperhill, TN. This outfitter runs both the upper and the middle **Ocoee River** by raft and by kayak, has kayak instructions, and does mountain bike tours and rentals.

High Country Outfitters (1-800-233-8594). This company maintains a 30-acre compound on the **Ocoee River,** with rental cabins and a campground. They run the **Hiwassee River** as well as the Ocoee. They also do rock climbing instruction, lead backpacking trips (and do backpacking instruction), and run retail stores in Atlanta and Birmingham, Alabama.

Nantahala Outdoor Center (423-338-5901; 1-800-232-7238), Ocoee, TN. This large outfitter in nearby Bryson City (see *To Do—Whitewater Adventures* in "Bryson City and the Southwest Quadrant") maintains this location for its **Ocoee River** runs.

Wildwater, Ltd. (423-496-4904; 1-800-451-9972). This South Carolina company maintains an outpost for **Ocoee River** rafting.

✳ Lodging

BED & BREAKFASTS The White House (423-496-4166; 1-800-775-4166), 104 Main Street, Ducktown, TN 37326. This National Register–listed B&B sits within the Ducktown Historic District, in a residential area a block from the town center. It's a large white clapboard house with a wide wraparound porch, shaded by large trees. A classic B&B, it has three guest rooms, all with private baths and furnished with antiques. $75–79, including full breakfast.

The Company House B&B (423-496-5634; 1-800-343-2909), 125 Main Street, Ducktown, TN 37326. This 1850 white clapboard house has wraparound porches that overlook the center of Ducktown's Historic District. Listed in the National Register, it was built by the local doctor, remembered for his service to the copper miners in those rough early years. The six guest rooms, furnished in antiques, are named after local mines. $69–79, including full breakfast.

Maloof Bed & Breakfast (423-496-7442), P.O. Box 1166, Copperhill, TN 37317. These four suites occupy the second story of a series of downtown Copperhill brick-front stores. However, this is no old-time hotel—these suites are tastefully furnished, with full-sized, separate sitting areas; most have wet bars with refrigerators. $80, including a voucher for breakfast at one of four local restaurants.

The Lodge at Copperhill (423-496-9020), 12 Grande Avenue, P.O. Box 247, Copperhill, TN 37317. This European-style B&B is owned by gold-medal Olympic canoeist Joe Jacobi and his wife, Lisa. A large bungalow-style house built by the town doctor just off downtown Copperhill, this B&B has a large, attractively furnished common area. Like a French pension, the six guest rooms share four baths. The full breakfast may include fresh eggs, local cheeses, or mountain trout. $50 for two; set price of $25 per person, regardless of occupancy; includes breakfast.

Bradley Inn Bed & Breakfast (828-321-2391; 1-800-581-2360), 983 Main Street, Andrews, NC 28901. The Bradley Inn renovates an upstairs hotel in downtown Andrews. Located over owners Greg and Carol Long's charming coffee shop, the Bradley Inn has a roomy and comfortable common area furnished in antiques. The four oversized rooms are each theme furnished with late-Victorian antiques, and all are big enough to have sitting areas with sofas. $85, including full breakfast.

✒ **The Hawkesdene House** (828-321-6027; 1-800-447-9549), Phillips Creek Road, Andrews, NC 28901. Located in a mountain cove above Andrews, Hawkesdene House is nestled in the arms of the 4,000-foot Valley River Mountains. It's a modern-built house, looking like a large old farmhouse with dormers, sitting in broad meadows with the mountains towering above. Llamas graze the meadows, ready to participate in treks to uphill waterfalls. The interior is elegantly furnished in antiques, with a great room dominated by a large stone fireplace. The five private-bath guest rooms continue the elegant country theme; all have sitting areas and one has its own kitchen. A set of 1940s-era two-bedroom cabins are elegant and fully furnished; a very roomy three-bedroom cabin is off-site. Young children are welcome in the cabins only. $85–110, including breakfast.

Huntingdon Hall Bed & Breakfast (828-837-9567; 1-800-824-6189), 272 Valley River Avenue, Murphy, NC 28906. This first-rate B&B is located in a homey 19th-century lawyer's house, not two blocks from downtown Murphy, its five guest rooms furnished in comfortable antiques. Common rooms have the same Victorian feel, and the sense of comfort continues with a bed turn-down and a locally made chocolate in the evening. Business travelers appreciate the fax machines, phones, and data ports (though not in the rooms). The excellent full breakfast is available on weekdays as early as 6 AM and as late as 9 AM. $75–98.

Park Place Bed & Breakfast (828-837-8842), 54 Hill Street, Murphy, NC 28906. This circa 1900 farmhouse-style B&B is located in a quiet residential section of Murphy, across from a city park. This comfortable private house is furnished with antiques and hand-knotted oriental rugs; the two guest rooms are furnished in Victorian decor. $80, including full gourmet breakfast.

CABIN RENTALS Stone Creek Cabins (423-338-2674; 1-800-780-3459), 662 Mountain View Road, Benton, TN 37307. Open all year. These five rustic cabins sit at the base of Chilhowee Mountain, on 20 acres adjacent to Cherokee National Forest lands. These recently built cabins are sided with stained logs or clapboards; furnishings are country style, simple and comfortable, with wood paneling and floors. There's a volleyball court and fishing pond (catch and release) on site. $76–105; discounts for longer stays.

Mountain Shadow Cabins (423-338-0652; 877-338-0652), 185 Locke Lane, Benton, TN 37307. These two modern log cabins sit in broad meadows by the **Hiwassee River,** north of Benton off scenic TN 30 (see Driving the Southern Unicois under *Wander-*

ing Around—Exploring by Car). Cabins have wide front porches, exposed log walls, fireplaces, and wood floors; furnishings are new and comfortable. Both cabins have full kitchens. Porches face the river, while the rear of the cabins have a view toward nearby Chilhowee Mountain over wide meadows. $100–110.

Welcome Valley Village (423-338-9499; 1-800-542-8567), P.O. Box 577, Benton, TN 37307. This 17-acre property fronts the **Ocoee River,** just under Chilhowee Mountain and a short distance from US 64. Four modern individually decorated log cabins are spaced apart for privacy. All have full kitchens and porches, wood floors, and exposed log walls. Guests have a choice of cabins with river views, whirlpool tubs, and/or wood-burning fireplaces. The property is nicely landscaped, with a riverside dock and a meadow for outdoor activities. $60–155.

☻ ᶑ **Cobb Creek Cabins** (828-837-0270), 106 Cobb Circle, Murphy, NC 28906. The collection of seven cabins occupies a quiet, rural site just off US 19, southwest of Murphy. Each cabin is unique (one is an apartment in the owner's 140-year-old farmhouse), but all share a high level of comfort. The site has a fishing pond, volleyball, and a horseshoe pitch. $65–88; discounts for longer stays; surcharge for hot tub use.

✳ Where to Eat

EATING OUT El Rio Authentic Mexican Restaurant and Cantina (423-496-1826), 23 Ocoee Street, Copperhill, TN. This downtown Mexican restaurant occupies a large, attractive two-story storefront, nicely decorated, with mezzanine seating and a tin ceiling. The menu includes the old favorites, then adds old family recipes, topping them off with vegetarian specialties. All food is made fresh from fresh ingredients.

Iron Horse Grill (423-496-9991), 50 Ocoee Street, Second Floor, Copperhill, TN. Open Tuesday through Sunday 11–9. Located in downtown Copperhill, this walk-up pub has a railroad theme, British beer, and some interesting and ambitious entrées among the sandwiches and burgers. Friday and Saturday nights feature live acoustic guitar and fiddle playing.

ShoeBooties Café (828-837-4589), 25 Peachtree Street, Murphy, NC. This downtown storefront eatery has deli sandwiches and salads for lunch, and steak, seafood, chicken, pasta, and chef specialties for dinner. Wine is available.

✷ Entertainment

The Licklog Players (828-389-8632; 877-691-9906), 131 Herbert Hills Drive, Hayesville, NC. Organized in 1977, the Licklog Players are named for the notched log used to hold salt for grazing livestock (and a common place-name in the mountains). This community theater presents amateur productions from Hayesville's **Peacock Playhouse.**

Friday Night Concerts at the John C. Campbell Folk School (828-837-2775), One Folk School Road, Brasstown, NC. Free admission. Most Friday nights the John C. Campbell Folk School (see *To See—Cultural Sites; and Selective Shopping*, below) sponsors a showing of student work at 6:40 PM, followed by a music concert at 7:30, featuring old-time mountain instruments and music. When weather permits, concerts are held in the **Fes-**tival Barn,** so bring a lawn chair or be prepared to sit on a hay bale.

Saturday Night Dances at the John C. Campbell Folk School (828-837-2775), One Folk School Road, Brasstown, NC. Held twice a month, Saturday 8 PM–11 PM. Adults $5, children $2. These community square and contra dances, with live music, welcome couples, singles, and beginners. See also John C. Campbell Folk School under *To See—Cultural Sites.*

✷ Selective Shopping

John C. Campbell Folk School Craft Store, One Folk School Road, Brasstown, NC. Located on the beautiful campus of this school (see *To See—Cultural Sites* and *Entertainment*) east of Murphy, this crafts shop has a juried selection of folk and fine arts by students, faculty, and alumni.

Webb Brothers' General Store, TN 30, Reliance, TN. This general store has been serving Reliance since 1936, from its store on the banks of the **Hiwassee River** on TN 30.

✷ Special Events

First weekend in May: **Murphy Spring Festal** (828-837-6821), Murphy, NC. This downtown Murphy street festival features crafts, fun, food, and music.

Fourth week in April: **Polk County Ramp Tramp Festival** (423-338-4053), **McCroy 4-H Camp,** near Copperhill, TN. This annual event, held since 1958, begins with a trip to **Big Frog Mountain** to gather ramps, the pungent and delicious wild leek that heralds the coming of spring, followed by bluegrass music and dinner.

🐾 ✂ *Last week in May:* **Ocoee White-**

water Games (423-496-2275; Ocoee-Whitewater.com), Copperhill, TN. Adults $6; students $4; children under 10 free; $5 pets on a leash. This multiday series of professional whitewater competitions, held at the 1996 Olympics venue (see **Ocoee Whitewater Center** under *Wild Places—Recreation Areas*), is always lively. In a typical year there are multiple whitewater sports competitions here; check with OcoeeWhitewater.com to find out what's happening during your visit (see also **Lake Ocoee Inn Marina** under *To Do—Stillwater Adventures*).

✍ *First weekend in October:* **Fall Festival at the John C. Campbell Folk School** (828-837-2775; 1-800-365-5724), One Folk School Road, Brasstown, NC. Held annually since 1973, this festival at the famous folk school (see *To See—Cultural Sites*) features crafts, food, live music, dance, children's activities, and live demonstrations.

December: **Christmas Celebrations,** Murphy and Andrews, NC. **Murphy** has a downtown **Christmas street festival** on the first weekend in December, with a Christmas parade, arts, crafts, food, and entertainment. A week later, nearby **Andrews** has its **nighttime Christmas Parade.**

December: **Annual Possum Drop at Clay's Corner,** Brasstown, NC. Every *New Year's Eve* the good people of Brasstown, 7 miles east of Murphy, NC, down a back road, gather at Clay's Corner (that's the general store) and bring in the new year with a ceremonial **Lowering of the Possum.** There's a Miss Possum contest, a possum song contest, bluegrass music, and the Little Brasstown Church Choir. You can even buy a can of USDA-approved possum from Clay's Corner.

INDEX

A

Abingdon Green Bed & Breakfast Inn, 175

Ablemarle Inn, 175

Abrams Creek campground, 270, 302

Adele's Cabins at Turkey Hill, 48

Adger, Lake, 223, 227

Afternoon Delight, 109

Airports, 15

Alarka Creek Falls, 323

Albertus Ledbetter House, 139–140, 144

Albright Grove, 277

Allegheny Mountains, 12–13

Almond, North Carolina, 322, 327, 329

Alpine Inn, 68

Altapass, North Carolina, 17, 64

Altapass, Orchard at, 54, 62, 63, 111

Alta Vista B&B, 88

Amtrak, 15

Amusement parks, 15–16

Andon House Bed & Breakfast, 198

Andrews, North Carolina, 326, 426, 428, 429, 431–432, 436, 440, 443

Andrews Bald, 342, 343, 347

Andrews Geyser, 131, 137, 139, 143

Angelique Inn, 257

Antique shops and shows, 16, 49, 126, 148, 201, 220, 262, 394, 405, 407–408

Apalachia Lake, 435

Appalachian Cultural Museum, 82

Appalachian Mountains, 12–13

Appalachian State University, 77, 82, 83, 92

Appalachian Trail (AT), 16.
Franklin & Nantahala Mountains area, 399–402

Great Smoky Mountains National Park, 270, 275, 282, 321, 342–343, 345, 346

Hot Springs area, 207–212, 216

northern Tennessee, mountains of, 114–117, 119–120

Pisgah National Forest, 98

Roan High Knob/Grassy Ridge Bald, 105

Robbinsville & Tellico Plains area, 412, 415

Appalachian Trail Conference, 16

Applegate Inn, 370

Apple Hill Orchard and Cider Mill, 147

Apple Inn, 259

Applejack's Restaurant, 312–313

Apple Realty, 350, 371

Apples, 16–17, 221, 224–225, 255, 264. See also Orchards

Archers Mountain Inn, 87, 91

Area codes, 15

Arrowmont School of Arts and Crafts, 283, 286, 292

Arrowwood Glade Picnic Area, 398, 401

Art galleries, studios, and shows, 17. See also Crafts galleries, studios, shows, and schools

Asheville, NC, hinterlands of, 214, 219–220

Asheville & the Blue Ridge Parkway, 168, 182–185

Blue Ridge Parkway: Blowing Rock & Grandfather Mountain, 70–72

Boone, NC, area, 92

Cashiers & Highlands, NC, 394

Catawba River Valley, 140, 147, 148

Cherokee, NC, area, 352–353

Chimney Rock & Saluda, NC, area, 226, 230–231, 238

Franklin, NC & Nantahala Mountains, 407

Gatlinburg, TN, area, 279, 291–293

Hendersonville & Brevard, NC, area, 263

northern Tennessee, mountains of, 126

northern Unicois: Robbinsville, NC & Tellico Plains, TN, 414, 424–425

Spruce Pine & Burnsville, NC, area, 103, 110

Sylva & Dillsboro, NC, area, 366, 374–375

Townsend & Cades Cove, TN, area, 314–315

Asheville, North Carolina &

the Blue Ridge Parkway, 19, 20, 36, 129, 152–185.
City Hall Plaza, 170
information, 15, 32, 152–155, 173, 205, 223, 338
lodging, 173–178
reservoir, 181
restaurants, 160, 178–180, 183
sights/activities, 17, 33, 155–173, 180–185
Asheville, North Carolina, hinterlands of, 203–220
information, 203–205
lodging, 216–218
restaurants, 218–219
sights/activities, 205–216, 219–220
Asheville, North Carolina, mountains in area of, 151–271.
Asheville Art Museum, 166
Asheville Bed & Breakfast Association (ABBA), 173
Asheville Community Theater, 180
Asheville Pizza and Brewing Company, 178
Asheville Regional Airport, 15
Asheville Symphony Orchestra, 180
Asheville Tourists baseball team, 180
Assembly Inn, 169
Atlanta, Georgia, 15
Aunt T's Café, 218
Azalea Inn, 88

B

Backpacking, 270, 286
Bad Creek Power Station, 380, 381–382, 386
Baird House, 87–88
Bakersville, North Carolina, 96, 99, 104, 108, 110, 111, 127
Bald Creek Gorge Wilderness, 416
Bald Mountain Ridge Scenic Area, 210, 211
Bald Mountains, 203, 206, 209–212, 215
Bald Rock, 245
Balds, grassy and rocky, 17–18
Ballooning, 170

Balsam, North Carolina, 360–364, 368, 372
Balsam Gap, 159, 188, 194, 201, 346, 359, 360, 362
Balsam Mountain, 339
Balsam Mountain Inn, 201, 361, 363–364, 368, 372–373
Balsam Mountain Picnic and Camping Area, 270, 346
Banner Elk, North Carolina lodging, 87–89
sights/activities, 75–77, 80, 84–86, 92–93
Banner Elk Inn Bed & Breakfast, 88–89
Barbeque, 18
Bark House Picnic Area, 133, 136
Barley's Taproom, 183
Barnardsville, North Carolina, 97, 158, 159
Baseball teams, 126, 180
Baskins Creek and Falls, 277, 278
Bass Lake, 57, 58
Bat Cave, North Carolina, 221, 223, 227, 229, 238
Bear Den Creekside Cabins, 68
"Bear"ly Rustic Cabin Rentals, 312
Bed & breakfasts, 19
Asheville, NC, hinterlands of, 216–218
Asheville & the Blue Ridge Parkway, 175–178
Blue Ridge Parkway: Blowing Rock & Grandfather Mountain, 66–68
Blue Ridge Parkway enters North Carolina, 47–48
Boone, NC, area, 87–89
Bryson City, NC, area, 331
Cashiers & Highlands, NC, 390–392
Catawba River Valley, 142–143
Cherokee, NC, area, 351
children at, 22
Chimney Rock & Saluda, NC, area, 234–236
Franklin, NC & Nantahala Mountains, 405–406
Gatlinburg, TN, area, 288–290

Hendersonville & Brevard, NC, area, 257–259
northern Tennessee, mountains of, 124–125
northern Unicois: Robbinsville, NC & Tellico Plains, TN, 422
pets at, 28
southern Unicois: Murphy, NC & Copper Basin, 439–441
Spruce Pine & Burnsville, NC, area, 107–108
Sylva & Dillsboro, NC, area, 369–371
Townsend & Cades Cove, TN, area, 310
Waynesville, NC, area, 197
Beech Grove School, 343
Beech Mountain, North Carolina, 31, 75–78, 84, 85, 90, 91
Bee Cliff Cabins, 125
Bent Creek, 244
Bent Creek Forests, 159–160, 162
Bent Creek Golf Resort, 213, 289
Benton, Tennessee, 428, 438, 441
Berry picking, 19
Berry Springs Lodge, 289
Bertie's Falls, 398
Bicycling, 19
Asheville & the Blue Ridge Parkway, 159, 170–171
Blue Ridge Parkway enters North Carolina, 47
Boone, NC, area, 83–84
Bryson City, NC, area, 320, 323–325, 327–328
Cashiers & Highlands, NC, 388–389
Catawba River Valley, 130–131, 141
Great Smoky Mountains National Park, 269, 302
Hendersonville & Brevard, NC, area, 255
southern Unicois: Murphy, NC & Copper Basin, 438
Townsend & Cades Cove, TN, area, 307–308
Big Butt, North Carolina, 395
Big Cove, North Carolina, 345
Big Creek, 210, 344

Big Creek Picnic Area, 281, 282

Big Laurel Branch Wilderness, 113, 116–118, 317, 323

Biltmore Estate, 150, 156, 157, 162–165, 171–172, 182
Inn on, 174

Biltmore Village, 157, 163, 183–184

Bilton, Kathy, Appalachian Trail (AT) Web site, 32

Black Balsam Knob, 188, 190, 193

Black Camp Gap, 339

Black Mountain, North Carolina, 129, 131, 153, 157–158, 160, 169, 182, 184–185

Black Mountains, 95, 97, 100, 150, 153, 155, 158–160

Blaine House Bed & Breakfast, 406

Blake House, 177

Blevins Store, North Carolina, 45, 50

Blowing Rock, North Carolina, 36, 37, 51, 73, 123
lodging, 65–68
restaurants, 68–70
sights/activities, 54, 55, 57, 64, 70–72

Blowing Rock, The, 64

Blowing Rock Stage Company, 70

Blue Boar Inn at Lake Santeetlah, 421, 423

Blue Mountain Mist Country Inn, 287–288

Blue Ridge Café, 49–48

Blue Ridge Crest, 155, 338, 378, 382

Blue Ridge Mountain Host of North Carolina, 173

Blue Ridge Mountains, 10–13, 15, 18, 378. *See also* Blue Wall; Cashiers & Highlands, North Carolina; Chimney Rock & Saluda, North Carolina, area; Hendersonville & Brevard, North Carolina, area; Northern mountains

Blue Ridge Parkway, 10, 17–20, 28, 36, 96, 150, 244, 249, 345. *See also* Asheville, North Carolina & the Blue

Ridge Parkway; Boone, North Carolina, area; Catawba River Valley; Chimney Rock & Saluda, North Carolina, area; Hendersonville & Brevard, North Carolina, area; Spruce Pine & Burnsville, North Carolina, area; Waynesville, North Carolina, area
bicycling, 19
crest of, 42, 54–56, 64
at Great Smoky Mountains National Park, 337–339, 341, 346, 347
Headquarters Building, 156
liquor laws, 23
mountaintops, 27

Blue Ridge Parkway: Blowing Rock & Grandfather Mountain, 51–72. *See also* Blowing Rock, North Carolina; Grandfather Mountain
information, 51–53
lodging, 65–68
restaurants, 60, 68–70
sights/activities, 53–65, 70–72

Blue Ridge Parkway enters North Carolina, 38–50
information, 39–40
lodging, 47–48
restaurants, 48–49
sights/activities, 40–47, 49–50

Blue Ridge Railway, 387

Blue Smoke Cabins, 311

Bluestone Lodge, 88

Blue Wall, 228, 241, 245, 250, 251, 377, 382

Bluff City, Tennessee, 125

Bluff Mountain, 289, 307

Bluff Mountain Preserve (The Nature Conservancy), 79

Bookstores, 71, 92, 110, 183, 201, 263, 273, 334

Boone, Daniel, 37, 46, 73, 82

Boone, Daniel, Gardens, 82

Boone, Daniel, Scout Trail, 54, 56

Boone, North Carolina, area, 15, 16, 22, 37, 73–93
information, 40, 53, 73–75
lodging, 82, 86–89

restaurants, 87, 89–91
sights/activities, 75–86, 91–93

Boone Greenway, 76–77

Boone's Fork National Forest, 58

Botanical Gardens at Asheville, 169

Boyd Mountain Log Cabins, 352

Bradley Inn Bed & Breakfast, 440

Bradley Mountain Retreat, 311

Brasstown, North Carolina, 17, 442, 443

Brevard, North Carolina. *See* Hendersonville & Brevard, North Carolina, area

Brevard College, 248

Brevard Music Center and Festival, 27, 248, 253–254, 259, 261, 263

Briar Patch B&B, 48

Bridal Veil Falls, 379

Bridge Street Café, 218–219

Bridge Street Inn, 217

Bridgewater Dam, 137

Brights Trace, 98

Brinegar Cabin, 40, 44

Bristol, Tennessee, 15

Brookside Bed & Breakfast, 351

Brown Mountain Lights, 141

Broyhill Inn and Conference Center, 82, 86, 90–91

Broyhill Park and Annie Cannon Gardens, 58, 64

Bryson City, North Carolina, area, 29–30, 33, 269, 316–335, 367
information, 318–319
lodging, 329–333
restaurants, 333–334
sights/activities, 319–329, 334–335

Bryson City cemetery, 322, 325–326

Buck Bald, 434

Buckhorn Inn, 288, 291

Buckley, Mount, 343

Buffalo Tavern Bed & Breakfast, 89

Buncombe Turnpike, 150, 241, 248

Burgiss Barn Mountain Music Jamboree, 48, 49

Burgiss Farm Bed & Breakfast, 47–48
Burnsville, North Carolina. See Spruce Pine & Burnsville, North Carolina, area
Bus service, 20. See also Greyhound Bus Lines
Butler, Tennessee, 123–125

C
Cabin rentals, 20, 236
Asheville, NC, hinterlands of, 218
backpackers' cabins, 286
Blue Ridge Parkway: Blowing Rock & Grandfather Mountain, 68
Blue Ridge Parkway enters North Carolina, 48
Boone, NC, area, 89
Bryson City, NC, area, 332–333
Cashiers & Highlands, NC, 392
Catawba River Valley, 144
Cherokee, NC, area, 351
Gatlinburg, TN, area, 286
Hendersonville & Brevard, NC, area, 259–260
northern Tennessee, mountains of, 119, 125
northern Unicois: Robbinsville, NC & Tellico Plains, TN, 422–423
southern Unicois: Murphy, NC & Copper Basin, 441
Spruce Pine & Burnsville, NC, area, 108
Sylva & Dillsboro, NC, area, 371
Townsend & Cades Cove, TN, area, 310–312
Waynesville, NC, area, 199
Cabins at Seven Foxes, 392
Cable Mill Historic Area and Visitors Center, 304
Cades Cove. See Townsend & Cades Cove, Tennessee, area
Cades Cove Loop Road, 269, 297, 307
Cades Cove Picnic Area, 296
Cades Cove Recreation Area, 302
Caesar's Head State Park, 245–247, 250, 251

Calderwood Lake, 411, 413, 414, 417
Calderwood Power Station Recreation Area, 298, 302
Caldwell House, 343
Calhouns, 290
Campbell, John C., Folk School, 437–438, 442, 443
Camp Creek Falls, 319
Camping, 20–21
Asheville, NC, hinterlands of, 210
Franklin, NC & Nantahala Mountains, 399–400
Gatlinburg, TN, area, 284
Great Smoky Mountains National Park, 268, 270, 302, 346
Cane River/Cane River Gap, 95, 97, 101
Canoeing, kayaking, and whitewater rafting, 21, 33
Asheville, NC, hinterlands of, 215–216
Asheville & the Blue Ridge Parkway, 172–173
Blue Ridge Parkway: Blowing Rock & Grandfather Mountain, 65
Boone, NC, area, 85–86
Bryson City, NC, area, 328–329
Cashiers & Highlands, NC, 388–389
Chimney Rock & Saluda, NC, area, 232
Franklin, NC & Nantahala Mountains, 404
Gatlinburg, TN, area, 285
Hendersonville & Brevard, NC, area, 256
northern Tennessee, mountains of, 123–124
northern Unicois: Robbinsville, NC & Tellico Plains, TN, 420–421
southern Unicois: Murphy, NC & Copper Basin, 428, 433, 438–439
Spruce Pine & Burnsville, NC, area, 106
Sylva & Dillsboro, NC, area, 367–368
Townsend & Cades Cove, TN, area, 309
Web site, 428

Canton, North Carolina, 187, 192, 195, 199–202
Canton Historic Museum, 192, 195
Cardin's Landing, 423
Caribbean Café, 90
Carl Sandburg Home National Historic Site, 28, 248, 252–253, 263
Carnes' Log Cabins, 311
Carolina Chocolatiers, 146
Carolina Hemlocks Recreation Area, 101, 102
Carolina Smokehouse, 392–393
Carson House, 139
Carter Mansion, 121
Carter Shields Cabin, 305
Carvers Gap, 96–98, 101, 118
Cascade Falls and Picnic Area, 43, 45
Cashiers & Highlands, North Carolina, 15, 32, 376–394
information, 377–378
lodging, 380, 383, 386, 389–392
restaurants, 389
sights/activities, 378–389, 393–394
Casino, Harrahs Cherokee, 352
Cataloochee Cove, 282, 337–345
Cataloochee Ranch, 350–351
Catawba River, 137
Catawba River Greenway, 135, 145
Catawba River Valley, 128–148
information, 129–130
lodging, 131, 135, 139
restaurants, 145–146
sights/activities, 130–142, 146–148
Caves and caverns, 64, 307
Cedar Crest, a Victorian Inn, 177
Cedar Mountain, 263
Cedar Rock Creek, 246
Celo, North Carolina, 96
Celo Inn, 107–108
Center Stage Deli, 260
Central House Restaurant, 389, 393
Chalet Club, 227, 233–234
Chalet Inn, 369
Chalet Restaurant at Switzerland Inn, 70
Chandler Inn, 390

Chapel Hollow, 212–213
Charleston Inn Bed & Breakfast, 330
Charlie's Bunion, 345, 346
Charlotte/Douglas International Airport, 15
Chattahoochee National Forest, 29, 357
Chattanooga Metropolitan Airport, 15
Chattooga Wild and Scenic River, 21, 378, 381, 383, 385–386, 392
Chatuge Lake, 433, 435, 438
Chef and His Wife, The, 406
Cheoah Dam, 320, 417, 419
Cheoah Mountains, 270, 415
Cheoah Point, 417, 418
Cherohala Skyway, 409, 412, 413–414, 416, 419, 423. *See also* Northern Unicois: Robbinsville, NC & Tellico Plains, TN
Cherokee, North Carolina, area, 16, 337–353
    information, 338
    lodging, 350–352
    restaurants, 350
    sights/activities, 338–350, 352–353
Cherokee Daylily Garden, 375
Cherokee Forest Mountain Cabins, 125
Cherokee Indian, Museum of the, 345, 348–349
Cherokee Nation, 21, 37, 73, 117, 121, 324, 356, 395, 419, 424–425. *See also* Qualla Boundary
Judaculla Rock, 365
Waynesville, NC, area, 189–190
Cherokee National Forest, 29, 113, 211, 357, 411, 413, 416, 417, 419–420, 422, 425, 428, 432, 441. *See also* Sampson Mountain Wilderness
    Bald Mountain Ridge Scenic Area, 210, 211
    Chilhowee Mountain Recreation Area, 433–434
    Horse Creek Recreation Area, 207, 210, 212
    Ocoee Ranger District, 428

Ocoee Whitewater Center, 428, 433
    Watauga Ranger District, 113
Cherokee Orchards, 276, 278
Cherokee Reservation. *See* Qualla Boundary
Cherokee Wildlife Management Area, Rocky Fork Unit, 210
Chestnut Hill Bed & Breakfast, 259
Chestnut Street Inn, 175
Chestnut Top Trail, 299–300
Children, attractions for, 21–22
Chilhowee Bluff Bed & Breakfast, 289
Chilhowee Lake, 417
Chilhowee Mountain, 298–299, 302, 430, 441
Chilhowee Mountain Recreation Area, 430, 433–434
Chilhowee Reservoir, 298, 302
Chimney Rock Park, 223, 227–230
Chimney Rock & Saluda, North Carolina, area, 139, 144
    information, 221–223
    lodging, 227
    restaurants, 225, 236–238
    sights/activities, 223–232, 238–240
Chimneys, the, 133–135
Chimneys Picnic Area, 275, 282
Chimneytop Mountain, 378, 382–383
Chimney Tops, 275
Christopher Place, An Intimate Resort, 288
"Christy" Mission, The, 206, 209, 212–213
Chuckey, Tennessee, 218
Churches. *See* Historic sites; *specific churches*
Citico Creek Wilderness, 413, 414–416
Claddagh Inn, 256
Clear Creek Guest Ranch, 66
Cleveland Fish Hatchery, 251
Cliffside Lake Recreation Area, 379, 381
Clinchfield Railroad Loops, 29, 54, 63, 96, 102, 103, 113, 115, 116, 122

Clingmans Dome, 317, 337, 340–342, 346–347
Clyde, North Carolina, 187, 197, 215
Cob Creek Cabins, 441
Coffee Company, The, 125–126
Cohutta and Big Frog Wilderness, 433
Coker Creek, Tennessee, 424–425, 430
Colburn Gem and Mineral Museum, 166, 184–185
Colby House, 176
Cold Mountain, 193
Cold Springs Country Inn, 331–332
College Street Inn, 143
Collins, Mount, 342
Collins Creek Picnic Area, 282, 340, 347
Colonial Pines Inn, 391
Columbus, North Carolina, 226, 231
Company House B&B, 440
Conestee Falls, 245, 255
Connelley Springs, North Carolina, 142
Connemara, 252–253
Continental Divide, Eastern, 225
Cook Place, 344
Copper Basin, 432. *See also* Southern Unicois: Murphy, NC & Copper Basin
Copperhill, Lodge at, 440
Copperhill, Tennessee, 15, 426, 428, 432, 439, 440, 442, 443
Corner Palate, The, 90
Cosby, Tennessee, 280, 288, 293
Cosby Picnic Area, 281–282
Cottage Inn, 392
Cottages at Spring House Farm, 139, 144
Cottages of Glowing Hearth, The, 89
Country inns and hotels
    Asheville & the Blue Ridge Parkway, 173–174
    Blue Ridge Parkway enters North Carolina, 47
    Bryson City, NC, area, 329–330
    Cashiers & Highlands, NC, 389–390

Chimney Rock & Saluda, NC, area, 232–233

Gatlinburg, TN, area, 286–288

Hendersonville & Brevard, NC, area, 256–257

northern Unicois: Robbinsville, NC & Tellico Plains, TN, 421–423

Sylva & Dillsboro, NC, area, 368–369

Townsend & Cades Cove, TN, area, 309–312

Waynesville, NC, area, 196–197

Country stores, 22. See also Shopping

Country Workshops, 213

Cove Café, 310

Cove hardwood forest, 280

Covered bridges, 120, 283

Cowee Gap, 383

Cowee Mountains, 194, 317, 323, 395

Coweeta Hydrologic Laboratory, 399, 402

Cowee Valley, 398–400, 404, 407–408

Crabtree Falls Recreation Area, 54, 63

Cradle of Forestry in America, The, 157, 163, 188, 244, 245, 249, 252, 263

Crafts galleries, studios, shows, and schools. See also Art galleries, studios, and shows; Penland School of Crafts

Asheville, NC, hinterlands of, 213, 219–220

Asheville & the Blue Ridge Parkway, 157, 185

Blue Ridge Parkway: Blowing Rock & Grandfather Mountain, 58–59, 70–71

Blue Ridge Parkway enters North Carolina, 49–50

Bryson City, NC, area, 334

Cashiers & Highlands, NC, 394

Catawba River Valley, 147, 148

Cherokee, NC, area, 352–353

Chimney Rock & Saluda, NC, area, 224, 225,
230–231, 238–239

Franklin, NC & Nantahala Mountains, 407–408

Gatlinburg, TN, area, 286, 291–292

Hendersonville & Brevard, NC, area, 262–263

northern Unicois: Robbinsville, NC & Tellico Plains, TN, 424–425

southern Unicois: Murphy, NC & Copper Basin, 438, 442, 443

Spruce Pine & Burnsville, NC, area, 109–110

Sylva & Dillsboro, NC, area, 363, 374–375

Townsend & Cades Cove, TN, area, 314

Waynesville, NC, area, 194–195, 201–202

Craggy Gardens, 153, 156, 159, 161

Craggy Mountains, 150, 158–159, 161

Craig, Mount, 153

Crest, Blue Ridge Parkway. See Blue Ridge Parkway

Cribs, 26

Crippen's Country Inn and Restaurant, 66, 69

Crooked Door, The, 145–146

Cullasaja River and Gorge, 379, 381

Cullowhee, North Carolina, 364, 365–366, 370–371, 375, 388

Cullowhee National Forest, 364

Cultural sites. See also Historic sites; Museums

Asheville, NC, hinterlands of, 213–214

Asheville & the Blue Ridge Parkway, 168–169

Blue Ridge Parkway enters North Carolina, 46

Boone, NC, area, 82–83

Catawba River Valley, 140–141

Cherokee, NC, area, 348–349

Chimney Rock & Saluda, NC, area, 230–231

Franklin, NC & Nantahala Mountains, 402–403

Gatlinburg, TN, area, 283

Hendersonville & Brevard, NC, area, 253–255

northern Tennessee, mountains of, 122

northern Unicois: Robbinsville, NC & Tellico Plains, TN, 420

southern Unicois: Murphy, NC & Copper Basin, 437–438

Spruce Pine & Burnsville, NC, area, 104–105

Sylva & Dillsboro, NC, area, 365–367

Townsend & Cades Cove, TN, area, 306–307

Waynesville, NC, area, 194–195

Cumberland Knob Recreation Area, 40, 43, 44

Cypress Cellar, 260

D

Dan'l Boone Inn, 90

Darby, North Carolina, 47

Das Kaffeehaus Pastry Shoppe, 235, 237

Davidson River, 244, 246, 249

D&B Café, 145

Deals Gap, 300

Deep Creek, 317, 320, 323

Deep Creek Picnic Area, 325, 328

Defiance, Fort, 46

Dellinger's Mill, North Carolina, 96, 104

DeLorme's maps, 26

Del Rio, Tennessee, 203, 205, 206, 209, 212, 219

Dennis Cove, Tennessee, 115

Devils Courthouse, The, 188

Devil's Fork State Park, 387, 392

Dillsboro, North Carolina. See Sylva & Dillsboro, North Carolina, area

Dillsboro Inn, 369

Dillsboro River Access Area, 365

Dillsboro Smokehouse, 372

Dobson, North Carolina, 48

Doe River and Gorge, 117, 122

Doe River Covered Bridge, 120

Doe River Inn, 124

Dogtrot, 26
Dogwood Cabins, 312
Dogwood Inn, 233
Dollywood, 16
Donley Cabin, Historic, 422–423
Dooley, Tom, Museum, 45–46
Doolittles, 312
Doughton-Hall Bed & Breakfast, 48
Doughton Park, North Carolina, 36, 40, 41, 43, 44
Dry counties, 22–23
Dry Falls, 379
Dry Ridge Inn, 177
Duckett House Inn and Farm, 217
Ducktown, Tennessee, 426, 428, 429, 431–433, 437, 439–440
Ducktown Basin Museum and Burra Burra Mine Site, 437
DuPont State Forest, 241, 245, 246, 249–250

E

E. B. Jeffress Park, 41, 44–45
Eagle Hotel, 135
Eagle's Nest Cottages, 371
Early Girl Eatery, 178
Eastern Band, Cherokee Nation, 21
Eastern Continental Divide, 225
East Laporte River Access Area, 364
Edgemont, North Carolina, 57
Edneyville, North Carolina, 225
Edwards-Franklin House, 45
Eight Gables Inn, 286–287, 290
Elijah Oliver Place, 302
Elizabethton, Tennessee, 37, 113, 116, 120–121, 123–127
Elizabethton Twins, 126
Elkmont campground, 270
Elkmont National Historic District, 298, 305–306, 342
Elk Mountain, 32
Elk River Falls Recreation Area, 102
Ellicott Rock Wilderness, 381
El Rio Authentic Mexican

Restaurant and Cantina, 441–442
Emergencies, medical, 23, 360
   Asheville, NC, area, 155, 205
   Blue Ridge Parkway, 39–40, 53
   Boone, NC, area, 75
   Bryson City, NC, area, 318–320
   Catawba River Valley, 130
   Cherokee, NC, area, 338
   Chimney Rock & Saluda, NC, area, 223
   Franklin, NC & Nantahala Mountains, 397
   Gatlinburg, TN, area, 274
   Hendersonville & Brevard, NC, area, 243
   northern Tennessee, mountains of, 114
   northern Unicois: Robbinsville, NC & Tellico Plains, TN, 411
   southern Unicois: Murphy, NC & Copper Basin, 428
   Spruce Pine & Burnsville, NC, area, 96
   Sylva & Dillsboro, NC, area, 360
   Townsend & Cades Cove, TN, area, 296
   Waynesville, NC, area, 187–188
Engadine Inn (Owls Nest Inn at Engadine), 177
Entertainment, 14, 27–28. *See also* Special events
   Asheville, NC, hinterlands of, 219
   Asheville & the Blue Ridge Parkway, 180–182
   Blue Ridge Parkway: Blowing Rock & Grandfather Mountain, 62, 70
   Blue Ridge Parkway enters North Carolina, 49
   Cashiers & Highlands, NC, 393
   Catawba River Valley, 146
   Cherokee, NC, area, 350
   Chimney Rock & Saluda, NC, area, 238
   Franklin, NC & Nantahala Mountains, 407
   Hendersonville & Brevard,

   NC, area, 261
   northern Tennessee, mountains of, 126
   northern Unicois: Robbinsville, NC & Tellico Plains, TN, 424
   southern Unicois: Murphy, NC & Copper Basin, 442
   Spruce Pine & Burnsville, NC, area, 109
   Townsend & Cades Cove, TN, area, 313–314
   Waynesville, NC, area, 200–201
Environmental programs. *See* Nature centers
Ervin, Senator Sam J., Jr., Library, 140
Erwin, Tennessee, 98, 113, 115, 116, 122–124, 127
Eseeola Lodge, 55, 56, 66
Esmeralda Inn, 233
Estes Mountain Retreat, 108
Etowah, Tennessee, 411
ET & WNC (Tweetsie) Railroad, 16, 29, 117, 121–123
Everett Street Diner, 333

F

Fairway Oaks Bed & Breakfast, 142–143
Fall Creek Cabins, 48
Fall foliage, 23
Falling Waters Adventure Resort, 332
Famous Louise's Rockhouse Restaurant, 69–70
Farm implements, old, 16
Fat Buddies Ribs and Barbeque, 406
Ferguson, North Carolina, 45–46
Field of the Woods, 436
Fifty Hikes in Tennessee, 31
Fifty Hikes in the Mountains of North Carolina, 31
Fires Creek Picnic Area, 433, 434
Fisher River Valley, 45
Fishing, 23
   Asheville, NC, hinterlands of, 214
   Asheville & the Blue Ridge Parkway, 171
   Boone, NC, area, 84
   Bryson City, NC, area, 328

Cashiers & Highlands, NC, 381

Catawba River Valley, 143

Cherokee, NC, area, 349–350

Franklin, NC & Nantahala Mountains, 403

Gatlinburg, TN, area, 284

Great Smoky Mountains National Park, 269

Hendersonville & Brevard, NC, area, 255

northern Tennessee, mountains of, 123

northern Unicois: Robbinsville, NC & Tellico Plains, TN, 419, 420

southern Unicois: Murphy, NC & Copper Basin, 438

Spruce Pine & Burnsville, NC, area, 105, 106

Sylva & Dillsboro, NC, area, 367

Townsend & Cades Cove, TN, area, 308

Waynesville, NC, area, 195

Web site, 32

Fishtop Access Area, Green River Cove, 225, 227, 228

Flat Rock, North Carolina, 150, 231, 241, 247–248, 255–257, 259–262

Flat Rock Inn, 257–258

Flat Rock Playhouse, 261

Flat Top, 58

Flattop Mountain, 102

Flea markets, 363

Fleetwood, North Carolina, 48, 89

Flintlock Inn, 215, 218

Fodderstack Knob, 41, 44

Folk Art Center and Allenstand Craft Shop, 17, 156, 161

Folkestone Inn Bed & Breakfast, 331

Fontana, North Carolina, 322–323

Fontana Lake and Dam, 317, 319–323, 325–327, 343, 417. See also Tsali Recreation Area

Foothills Equestrian Nature Center (FENCE), 224, 226, 228, 239

Foothills Parkway, 269, 284, 298–299

Forest City, North Carolina, 221

Forests. See also Great Smoky Mountains National Park; National forests; State parks, forests, and natural areas; Wild places/wilderness preserves

Little River, 301

Oconaluftee Valley, 345

Smoky Mountain Crest, 300–301

Smoky Mountains Front, 280–281

Fork Mountain, 193

Fork Ridge, 191, 193

Fort Defiance, 46

Fort Loudoun State Historic Area, 418

Fort Watauga, 117, 120–121

4th Street Inn, 390–391

Fox and Parrot Tavern, 290–291

Fox Den Cottages, 371

Foxtrot Inn, 235

Franklin, NC & Nantahala Mountains, 16, 194, 356, 395–408

information, 396–397

lodging, 404–406

restaurants, 406–407

sights/activities, 397–404, 407–408

Franklin Gem and Mineral Museum, 403

Franklin Terrace Hotel, 405

Freeze House, 369

French Broad River, 21, 33, 150, 156, 203, 205–206, 208, 209, 211, 215–216, 241, 245, 249, 255, 256

French Knob Inn, 89

Frescoes, The Churches of the, 46

Frog and Owl Kitchen, 406

Fryemont Inn, 329–330, 333

G

Gables Restaurant, 261

Gabrielle's, 179

Gaestehaus Salzburg, 235

Gamekeepers Restaurant, 68–69

Gannon's French Broad Outpost Ranch, 216

Garden Creek Church. See

Hutchinson Homestead and Garden Creek Church

Garden Deli, 108–109

Gardens and parks. See also specific gardens and parks

Asheville, NC, hinterlands of, 206, 220

Asheville & the Blue Ridge Parkway, 169–170

Blue Ridge Parkway: Blowing Rock & Grandfather Mountain, 64

Blue Ridge Parkway enters North Carolina, 46–47

Boone, NC, area, 83

Cashiers & Highlands, NC, 387

Cherokee, NC, area, 349

Chimney Rock & Saluda, NC, area, 231

Franklin, NC & Nantahala Mountains, 403

Hendersonville & Brevard, NC, area, 255

northern Tennessee, mountains of, 122–123

Spruce Pine & Burnsville, NC, area, 105

Sylva & Dillsboro, NC, area, 375

Gatlinburg, Tennessee, area, 16, 268, 272–293

information, 272–274

lodging, 286–290

restaurants, 290–291

sights/activities, 275–286, 291–293

Gatlinburg Bypass, 275, 279

Gee Creek Wilderness, 430, 432

Gem mining, 30, 195, 395, 403–404

General Wilder's Bed & Breakfast, 124–125

Gideon Ridge Inn, 67

Gilbertson's Lazy Horse Retreat, 311

Glades Arts and Crafts Community, 279, 283–284, 290, 292–293

Glendale Springs, North Carolina, 42, 46, 47, 49

Glendale Springs Inn and Restaurant, 47, 49

Glen Falls, 384

Glenville, Lake, 386, 391

Glenville, North Carolina, 386
Glowing Hearth, The Cottages
    of, 89
Golden China Restaurant, 372
Gold mine, 30, 141–142
Golf
    Asheville & the Blue Ridge
        Parkway, 171
    Blue Ridge Parkway: Blow-
        ing Rock & Grandfather
        Mountain, 65
    Blue Ridge Parkway enters
        North Carolina, 47
    Boone, NC, area, 84
    Bryson City, NC, area, 328
    Cashiers & Highlands, NC,
        388
    Catawba River Valley, 142
    Cherokee, NC, area, 350
    Chimney Rock & Saluda,
        NC, area, 229, 231–232
    Franklin, NC & Nantahala
        Mountains, 404
    Gatlinburg, TN, area, 284
    Hendersonville & Brevard,
        NC, area, 255–256
    northern Tennessee, moun-
        tains of, 123
    southern Unicois: Murphy,
        NC & Copper Basin, 438
    Spruce Pine & Burnsville,
        NC, area, 105
    Townsend & Cades Cove,
        TN, area, 308
    Waynesville, NC, area, 195
Good Shepherd, Church of
    the, 388
Gorges State Park. See Jocassee
    Gorges
Grandfather Mountain, 36, 40,
    53, 54, 72, 248
Grandfather Mountain Park,
    53, 55, 60
    backcountry, 54, 56
    entertainment at, 72
Grandview Cabins, 351
Grange Bed & Breakfast, 199
Grassy Ridge Bald, 98, 105
Gravel-surfaced roads, 24
Graveyard Fields, 188, 190
Great Balsam Mountains, 151,
    156, 188, 190–191, 193,
    345–346, 359, 364
Great Craggy Mountains, 153
Great Smoky Log Cabins,
    351–352

Great Smoky Mountain Rail-
    road, 326, 334
Great Smoky Mountains Insti-
    tute at Tremont, 308
Great Smoky Mountains
    National Park, 10, 28, 211,
    265–353, 367. See also
    Bryson City, North Caroli-
    na, area; Cherokee, North
    Carolina, area; Gatlinburg,
    Tennessee, area; Qualla
    Boundary; Smokies/
    Unakas; Sylva & Dillsboro,
    North Carolina, area;
    Townsend & Cades Cove,
    Tennessee, area
    amusement parks near, 16
    Appalachian Trail (AT) in, 16
    bears in, 34, 271
    cabins, backpackers', 286
    camping in, 268, 270, 302,
        346
    information, 271, 273–274,
        295–296, 318, 338
    Masonic Monument, 339
    mountaintops, 27
    Northeast Quadrant,
        272–293
    Northwest Quadrant,
        294–315
    overview, 267–269
    pets in, 28, 270–271
    ranger stations, 274, 296,
        301, 317, 321, 342
    Southeast Quadrant,
        336–353
    Southwest Quadrant,
        316–335
    trail rides, 285, 328, 350
    Web sites, 32, 274, 296
Great Smoky Mountains Rail-
    road, 29–30, 359, 363,
    366–367
Greenbrier Cove, 281
Greenbrier Picnic Area, 277,
    281
Greeneville, Tennessee, 205,
    212, 215
Green Mountain, 97
Green Mountain, North Caroli-
    na, 106
Green River and Gorge, 221,
    223, 225, 227–228
Green River Game Lands, 221,
    223, 225, 227–228
Greenville-Spartanburg Inter-

national Airport, 15
Gregory Bald, 301, 343
Gremmy's Garden (B&B),
    289–290
Greyhound Bus Lines, 20, 114,
    130, 155, 338
Greystone Inn, 386, 390
Grotto Falls, 276
Grove Park Inn Resort and
    Spa, 168, 174
Grovewood Galleries, 168
Gully Creek, 44

H
Hampton, Tennessee, 115
Hampton Creek Cove State
    Natural Area, 118,
    122–123
Hanging Dog Recreation Area,
    433, 435
Hannah Cabin, 344
Hardy, Mount, 188, 193
Harmon's Den Area, 211
Harrahs Cherokee Casino, 352
Harrisburg, 290
Harrisburg Covered Bridge,
    283
Haus Hiedelberg, 260
Hawkesdene House, 440
Hayesville, North Carolina,
    356, 426, 431, 433, 438,
    442
Haywood Arts Repertory The-
    ater, 200
Haywood House Bed & Break-
    fast, 198
Haywood Park Hotel, 173–174
Health Adventure, 166
Heintooga Overlook, 346
Heintooga Spur Road, 269,
    270, 338–339, 345
Hemlock Inn, 331
Hendersonville & Brevard,
    North Carolina, area, 15,
    17, 20, 182, 223, 231,
    241–271, 378
    information, 242
    lodging, 256–260
    restaurants, 260–261
    sights/activities, 243–256,
        261–264
Hendersonville Symphony
    Orchestra, 261
Herb of Grace, The (garden),
    206, 220
Heritage Inn, 405–406

Heritage Museum, 115, 122
Herrin House, 198
Hickory Nut Gap Inn, 227, 234
Hickory Nut Gorge and Falls, 221, 223, 224, 226–227, 229, 230, 233, 235–236, 238
Hickory Regional Airport, 15
Hickory Ridge Homestead, 82, 83
Hidden Creek Cabin Rentals, 332
Hideaway Cottages and Log Cabins, 311–312
High Hampton Inn and Country Club, 380, 383, 390
Highland Lake Inn, 257, 261
Highlands, North Carolina. See Cashiers & Highlands, North Carolina
Highlands Botanical Garden, 366, 382, 387
Highland's Crafts Guild, 17
Highlands Inn, 389
Highlands Nature Center, 383, 387
Highlands of Roan. See Roan Highlands
Highlands Playhouse, 393
High Shoals Creek and Falls, 132–133
Highways. See Roads and highways
Hiking/walking, 23, 31
  Asheville, NC, hinterlands of, 207–212
  Asheville & the Blue Ridge Parkway, 155–160, 169
  Blue Ridge Parkway: Blowing Rocks & Grandfather Mountain, 54–57, 59–61
  Blue Ridge Parkway enters North Carolina, 41–42, 44, 45, 47
  Boone, NC, area, 76–77, 79
  Bryson City, NC, area, 320–321
  Cashiers & Highlands, NC, 378, 381, 383–384
  Catawba River Valley, 131–134
  Cherokee, NC, area, 344–347
  Chimney Rock & Saluda, NC, area, 225, 227–228
  Franklin, NC & Nantahala

  Mountains, 398–402
  Gatlinburg, TN, area, 276–278, 284
  Great Smoky Mountains National Park, 268, 269–270
  Hendersonville & Brevard, NC, area, 244–247
  northern Tennessee, mountains of, 115–119, 122
  northern Unicois: Robbinsville, NC & Tellico Plains, TN, 411–416
  southern Unicois: Murphy, NC & Copper Basin, 430
  Spruce Pine & Burnsville, NC, area, 98, 100–102, 105
  Sylva & Dillsboro, NC, area, 361–362
  Townsend & Cades Cove, TN, area, 299–301
  Waynesville, NC, area, 189–191
Hilton Bluffs B&B Inn, 288
Hippensteal's Mountain View Inn, 287
Historic Burke Foundation, 138–139
Historic Calhoun Country Inn, 330
Historic Johnson Farm, 253, 263–264
Historic Nature Trail, 276, 282
Historic sites. See also Carl Sandburg Home National Historic Site; Cultural sites; Log cabins; Museums
  Asheville, NC, hinterlands of, 212–213
  Asheville & the Blue Ridge Parkway, 162, 166–168
  Blue Ridge Parkway: Blowing Rock & Grandfather Mountain, 63–64
  Blue Ridge Parkway enters North Carolina, 41–43, 45–46
  Boone, NC, area, 80–82
  Cashiers & Highlands, NC, 387–388
  Catawba River Valley, 138
  Cherokee, NC, area, 342–344, 347–348
  Chimney Rock & Saluda, NC, area, 229

  Gatlinburg, TN, area, 283
  Hendersonville & Brevard, NC, area, 252–253
  northern Tennessee, mountains of, 120–122
  northern Unicois: Robbinsville, NC & Tellico Plains, TN, 418–420
  southern Unicois: Murphy, NC & Copper Basin, 437
  Spruce Pine & Burnsville, NC, area, 103–104
  Sylva & Dillsboro, NC, area, 365
  Townsend & Cades Cove, TN, area, 297, 302–306
Hiwassee Dam, 434, 435
Hiwassee Lake, 429, 431, 433, 434
Hiwassee River, 356, 426, 429, 430, 432, 434, 435, 438, 439, 441, 442
Hiwassee Valley, 426
Holiday Inn, 352
Holy Communion, Parish of the, 42, 46
Holy Trinity Church, 46
Hooper's Snack Bar, 371–372
Horn in the West, 83
Horseback riding, 24. See also Foothills Equestrian Nature Center
  Asheville, NC, hinterlands of, 214–216
  Asheville & the Blue Ridge Parkway, 159, 171–172
  Blue Ridge Parkway: Blowing Rock & Grandfather Mountain, 59, 65
  Blue Ridge Parkway enters North Carolina, 47
  Boone, NC, area, 84
  Bryson City, NC, area, 323–325, 328
  Cashiers & Highlands, NC, 388
  Cherokee, NC, area, 350
  Chimney Rock & Saluda, NC, area, 232
  Gatlinburg, TN, area, 284–285
  Hendersonville & Brevard, NC, area, 256
  northern Tennessee, mountains of, 123
  Spruce Pine & Burnsville,

454

INDEX

NC, area, 105–106
Townsend & Cades Cove, TN, area, 302, 308–309
Horse Creek Picnic Area, 207, 210, 212
Horsepass River, 378
Horsepasture Wild and Scenic River, 381, 384
Hotels. *See* Country inns and hotels; Lodging
Hot Springs, North Carolina, 203, 205, 208–209, 211, 214–220
Houses, historic. *See* Historic sites
Howard Knob Park, 80
Hughes Gap, 100–101
Hummingbird Lodge, 405
Hunting, 24–25, 106
Huntingdon Hall Bed & Breakfast, 440–441
Hutchinson Homestead and Garden Creek Church, 41–43, 45

I

Indian Boundary Recreation Area, 416
Indian Creek and Falls, 320
Indian Grave Gap, 98
Inn at Old Fort, 143
Inn at Ragged Gardens, 67
Innisfree Victorian Inn, 391–392
Inn of the Red Thread, 48
Inn on Main Street, 177
Inn on Mill Creek, 131, 139, 143–144
Inns. *See* Country inns
Insects, 20
Iron Horse Grill, 442
Iron Mountain, 116–117
Iron Mountain Inn, 124
Ivivi Lake and Mountain Lodge, 235–236

J

Jackalope View, The, 87, 91
Jack of the Wood, 179
Jackrabbit Recreation Area, 433, 435
Jacob Fork Picnic Area, 131, 137
Jailhouse Gallery (Burke Arts Gallery), 140
James, Lake, 137–138, 142

Jane Bald, 98
Jarrett House, 364, 368–369, 373
Jefferson, Mount, Summit, State Park, and Natural Area, 41, 76, 78, 80
Jefferson, North Carolina, 37, 40, 75–76, 78, 84, 86
Jeffress, E. B., Park, 41, 44–45
Jim Bob Tinsley Museum and Research Center, 254–255
Jocassee, Lake, 256, 380, 381, 386–387, 392
Jocassee Gorges, 378, 380–381, 384–386
John C. Campbell Folk School, 17
John Muir National Recreation Trail, 430, 432
John Oliver Place, 302–303
Johnson City, Tennessee, 15. *See also* Tri-Cities Airport
Johnson Farm, Historic, 253, 263–264
Johns River, 56
Johns Rock, 244
Jones Gap State Park, 250, 251
Jones House Community and Cultural Center, 83
Jones Meadow, 210, 211–212
Joyce Kilmer Memorial Forest, 29, 413, 414, 416–417, 419, 423
Judaculla Rock State Historic Site, 365
Judges Barbeque, 145
Julian Price Park, 53, 55, 59
Jumpinoff Rocks, 41, 44
Jumpoff Rock Park, 247, 255
Junaluska, Lake, 189
Junaluska's Grave, 419
Junywhank Falls, 320

K

Kaolin, 30
Kayaking. *See* Canoeing, kayaking, and whitewater rafting
Kelsey and Hutchinson Lodge, 389–390
Kephart Prong, 344
Key Falls Bed & Breakfast, 259
Kilmer, Joyce, Memorial Forest. *See* Joyce Kilmer Memorial Forest
Kilmer-Slickrock Wilderness, 411–416, 419, 421

Kingsport, Tennessee, 15
King Street Café, 146
Kistler Memorial Highway, 133
Knoxville, Tennessee, 15, 286
Kona, North Carolina, 96, 103

L

Lake James State Park, 137
Lake Junaluska, North Carolina, 169, 187, 192, 195, 196–197, 201–202
Lake Lure, North Carolina, 221, 223, 228–229, 231, 232, 235, 237, 238
Lakemont Cottages, 259–260
Lake Powhatan Recreation Area, 156, 159, 160, 244
Lakes, 25. *See also specific lakes*
Lake Tomahawk Park, 160, 182
Lake Toxaway, North Carolina, 377, 380, 382, 386, 390, 392
Lambuth Inn at the Lake Junaluska Assembly, 189, 192, 196–197
Lansing, North Carolina, 49
Laughing Seed Café, 178–180
Laurel, North Carolina, 205
Laurel Creek and Gorge, 118, 211
Laurel Falls, 115–116
Laurel Fork and Laurel Fork Gorge, 115–116
Laurel hells, 267
Laurel Oaks Farm, 108
Laurel Springs, North Carolina, 47–48
Laurel Valley Cabin Rentals/ White Oak Realty, 312
Lawson, Don, Place, 305
Leatherwood Falls, 434
LeConte, Mount, 274–276, 280, 285
Ledbetter, Albertus, House, 139–140, 144
Lees-McRae College, 77, 92
Lenoir, North Carolina, 46, 71
Lenoir, William, house, 46
Linn Cove Viaduct, 53–55, 59–61
Linville, North Carolina, 36, 51, 55, 57, 66, 71, 72, 132, 136. *See also* Grandfather Mountain Park
Linville Caverns, 64

Linville Falls, 51, 53–55, 61,
133, 135
Linville Falls, North Carolina,
55, 64, 69–70
Linville Falls Recreation Area,
54, 57, 61
Linville Gorge Wilderness, 54,
55, 63, 65, 132–135, 137,
141
Linville River, 61, 137
Little Brier Creek, 305
Little Cataloochee Baptist
Church, 344
Little Cataloochee Cove, 337,
344
Little Frog Wilderness,
430–432
Little Glade Mill Pond, 43
Little Greenbrier Community,
298, 302, 305
Little Hump Mountain, 98
Little Laurel Branch Waterfall,
119
Little Pigeon River, 281–283
Little River, 298
forests of, 301
Little River Gorge, 302
Little River Railroad, driving,
29, 296–298
Little River Railroad and Lum-
ber Company Museum,
306–307
Little Switzerland, North Car-
olina, 51, 54–56, 62–64,
68, 70, 71, 111
Little Tennessee River, 21, 32,
298, 320, 321, 327, 356,
402, 404, 413
Little Tennessee Valley, 395
Llama trekking, 215, 284
Loafers Glory, North Carolina,
96
Lodge at Copperhill, 440
Lodging, 14. See also Camping
Asheville, NC, hinterlands
of, 216–218
Asheville & the Blue Ridge
Parkway, 173–178
Blue Ridge Parkway: Blow-
ing Rock & Grandfather
Mountain, 65–68
Blue Ridge Parkway enters
North Carolina, 47–48
Boone, NC, area, 82
Bryson City, NC, area,
329–333

Cashiers & Highlands, NC,
380, 383, 386, 389–392
Catawba River Valley, 131,
135, 139, 142–144
Cherokee, North Carolina,
area, 350–352
Chimney Rock & Saluda,
NC, area, 227, 232–236
Franklin, NC & Nantahala
Mountains, 404–406
Gatlinburg, TN, area,
286–290
Hendersonville & Brevard,
NC, area, 256–260
northern Tennessee, moun-
tains of, 119, 124–125
northern Unicois: Rob-
binsville, NC & Tellico
Plains, TN, 421–423
southern Unicois: Murphy,
NC & Copper Basin,
439–441
Spruce Pine & Burnsville,
NC, area, 106–108
Sylva & Dillsboro, NC, area,
361, 363–364, 368–371
Townsend & Cades Cove,
TN, area, 309–312
Waynesville, NC, area, 189,
192, 196–199
Log cabins, 25–26, 44, 252, 323
Brinegar Cabin, 40, 44
Cascades Overlook, 41
E. B. Jeffress Park, 45
Great Smoky Mountains
National Park, 276, 297,
302–305, 343–344
lodging, 48, 68, 108, 125,
144, 197, 215, 218, 309,
311–312, 351–352,
422–423, 441
Sheets Cabin, 40–41
Lomo Bakery and Café, 199
Lomo Grille, 200
Looking Glass Falls, 245
Looking Glass River, 246
Looking Glass Rock, 18, 188,
244
Look Rock Picnic Area, 299,
302
Lost, getting, 26
Lost Cove, 102
Lovill House Inn, 87
Lower Abrams Creek Back-
country, 301
Lower Falls, 413

Lulu's Café, 373
Lump, The, 41, 44
Lure, Lake, 228–229, 236
Lyn Lowry, Mount, 364

M
Macon County Historical
Museum, 402
Madisonville, Tennessee, 409
Maggies Galley, 199–200
Maggie Valley, North Carolina,
16, 337, 344, 345, 350–351
Magnolia House, 422
Magnolia Mountain Inn, 217
Magnolia Tearoom, 287, 290
Main Street, Inn on, 177
Main Street Inn, 389
Maloof Bed & Breakfast, 440
Mama's, 406
Maple Leaf Lodge and Cabins,
309
Maple Lodge Bed & Breakfast,
67–68
Maps, 26–27
Marion, North Carolina, 64,
129, 130, 134–135, 137,
143, 145–148
Market Place Restaurant and
Wine Bar, 179–180
Mark Watson Park, 364–365,
369
Marshall, Catherine. See
"Christy" Mission, The
Marshall, North Carolina, 203,
205, 208, 213–20
Marshall House Bed & Break-
fast Inn, 217–218
Mars Hill, North Carolina, 203,
205, 208, 214, 215, 219,
220
Mars Hill College, 208, 214,
219, 220
Mary Mills Coxe Inn, 258, 261
Maryville, Tennessee, 296, 307,
311, 419
Mason's Ruby and Sapphire
Mine, 30, 403
Mast Farm Inn, 86–87
Mast Gap Inn, 88
Mast General Store, 22, 76, 77,
81, 183
Max and Rosie's, 183
Max Patch, 203, 205–207, 211,
213, 216, 248, 270
McCreery Park, 226, 228
McDowell House, 138

McElroy House, 103–104
McGhee Tyson Airport, 15
McKinney Gap, North Carolina, 64
Medical emergencies. *See* Emergencies, medical
Mélange Bed & Breakfast, 258–259
Melrose Inn, 232
Meriweather's, 372
Messer, Will, Barn, 342
Messer Farm, 344
Metcalf Bottoms Picnic Area, 298, 302, 305
Micaville, North Carolina, 96, 99, 109
Micaville Grille, 99
Middle Prong Wilderness, 190–194, 345
Middle Saluda State Scenic River, 250, 251
Mile High Swinging Bridge, 56, 60
Mill Creek, Inn on, 131, 139, 143–144
Miller, Dave, Homestead, 118, 121
Mill Pond, 77, 80
Mill Ridge, 211
Mills River, 188, 249
Millstone Inn, 392
Mimosa Inn, 232–233
Mines, 30, 99, 141–142, 437. *See also* Gem mining
Mingo Falls, 345
Mingo Falls Tribal Park, 349
Mingus Mill, 341, 348
Missionary Baptist Church, 303–304
Mississippi Valley, 225
Mitchell, Jordan, mountain biking Web site, 32
Mitchell, Mount, 32, 54, 95, 96, 100, 148, 150, 153, 155, 158
Montford City Park, 160
Montreat, North Carolina, 153, 169
Morganton, North Carolina, 15, 129, 130
  lodging, 142–143
  restaurants, 145–146
  sights/activities, 133–135, 137–142, 146–148
Morlay Branch Picnic Area, 212

Morley House Bed & Breakfast, 289
Mortimer Recreation Area (Wilson Creek Area), 57–58
Moses Cone Park, 53, 57, 58–59
Motels, 290, 331–332, 350, 352
Mountain biking Web site, 32
Mountain Bridge Wilderness, 250
Mountain Creek Cottages, 371
Mountain Farm Museum, 25, 339, 341, 347–348
Mountain Gateway Museum, 131, 135, 140–141
Mountain Harbor B&B, 125
Mountain Heritage Center, 365–366
Mountain Hollow Bed & Breakfast, 327, 331
Mountain Lake Wilderness Resort, 123, 125
Mountain Mist Cabins, 310–311
Mountain music. *See* Music
Mountain Rest, South Carolina, 377, 382, 387
Mountain Shadow Cabins, 441
Mountains-to-Sea Trail, 159
Mountaintops, 27
Mountain Valley View Cabins, 218
Mount Burnsville, North Carolina, 111
Mount Jefferson State Park. *See* Jefferson, Mount, Summit, State Park, and Natural Area
Mount LeConte Lodge, 286
Mount Mitchell Restaurant, 160
Mount Mitchell Spur road, 155, 159
Mount Mitchell State Park, 155, 160
Mount Pisgah Picnic Area, 193
Mulberry Mountain Country Retreat, 405
Mulberry National Forest, 58
Murphy, North Carolina. *See* Southern Unicois: Murphy, NC & Copper Basin
Museums. *See also* Cultural sites; Historic sites; Nature centers

Asheville, NC, hinterlands of, 214
Asheville area, 166–168, 184–185
Blowing Rock & Grandfather Mountain area, 54, 63, 111
Blue Ridge Parkway enters North Carolina, 45–47
Boone, NC, area, 82
Catawba River Valley, 130, 131, 134, 135, 140–141
Cherokee, NC, area, 341, 345, 347–349
Chimney Rock & Saluda, NC, area, 224, 226, 229
Franklin & Nantahala Mountains, 402–403
Hendersonville & Brevard, NC, area, 252–255
Murphy & Copper Basin area, 437
northern Tennessee mountains, 115, 122
Robbinsville, NC & Tellico Plains, TN area, 420
Spruce Pine & Burnsville area, 96, 103–104
Sylva & Dillsboro area, 363, 365–366
Waynesville, NC, area, 192, 194–195
Music, 27–28. *See also* Entertainment; Special events
Mynatt Park, 276, 282
My Old Kentucky Home, 167–168

N

Nantahala Dam, 319
Nantahala Gorge, 317, 319, 322, 325, 326, 328, 329, 334, 415, 431, 437
Nantahala Lake, 432, 436–437
Nantahala Mountains. *See* Franklin, NC & Nantahala Mountains
Nantahala National Forest, 29, 317, 328, 356–357, 397–402, 411, 412, 415, 417, 418, 428, 432, 433. *See also* Tsali Recreation Area; Whitewater Falls
Cheoah Ranger District, 411, 412
fishing, 367

Highlands Ranger District, 377
llama trekking in, 284
Panthertown Valley, 378, 380, 382
Salt Rock, 382
Tusquitee Ranger District, 428
Wayah Ranger District, 317, 397
Nantahala Outdoor Center, 33, 326, 328, 333
Nantahala River, 21, 319, 328–329, 356, 399, 401
Nantahala Turnpike, 359, 360
Nantahala Village Mountain Resort and Meeting Center, 333–334
National Azalea Repository, 162
National forests, 26, 28–29, 105, 411, 412. *See also* Cherokee National Forest; Joyce Kilmer Memorial Forest; Nantahala National Forest; Pisgah National Forest; Wild places/wilderness preserves
bicycling, 19
Boone's Fork, 58
Chattahoochee National Forest, 357
Citico Creek Wilderness, 414–416
Kilmer-Slickrock Wilderness, 411–415
Mulberry, 58
rockhounding, 30
Roy Taylor, 364
Savannah Mountain/Cullowhee Mountain, 364
South Toe River, 100, 102, 160
Sumter National Forest, 357
Wilson Creek National Wild and Scenic River, 56–58
National Historic Districts
Asheville, NC, 175–176
Elkmont, 298, 305–306
Mast Farm Inn, 86–87
Morganton, NC, 134, 138–139, 146
Reliance, TN, 432
National Park Service, 28. *See also* Blue Ridge Parkway;

Carl Sandburg Home National Historic Site; Great Smoky Mountains National Park
Nature centers. *See also* Foothills Equestrian Nature Center
Grandfather Mountain Park, 60
Great Smoky Mountains Institute at Tremont, 308
Highlands, 383
Highlands Nature Center, 387
Jones Gap State Park Environmental Education Center, 251
Pisgah Center for Wildlife Education, 244, 245, 254
Smoky Mountains Field School, 286
Western North Carolina Nature Center, 170
Nature Conservancy, 79, 227, 228
Nebo, North Carolina, 137, 142, 144
Newfound Gap, 275, 340, 346
Newfound Gap Road, 268, 275, 278, 281, 337, 340–341, 345, 347–348
Newland, North Carolina, 105, 110
Newport, Tennessee, 205, 213, 284, 285, 288
New River, 21, 33, 36, 73, 76–77, 84–86
South Fork, 76, 79–80, 85–86
1900 Inn on Montford, 176
Noland Creek, 317, 320–321, 323
Nolichucky River and Gorge, 65, 97, 101, 106, 113, 123–124, 215
North Carolina Forest Service, 46–47
North Carolina Handicrafts, Museum of, 194
North Carolina Minerals, Museum of, 54, 63, 111
North Carolina State Arboretum, 156, 159, 161–162
Northern mountains, 36–148. *See also* Blue Ridge Parkway: Blowing Rock &

Grandfather Mountain; Blue Ridge Parkway enters North Carolina; Boone, North Carolina, area; Catawba River Valley; Northern Tennessee, mountains of; Spruce Pine & Burnsville, North Carolina, area
Northern Tennessee, mountains of, 112–127
information, 113–114
lodging, 119, 124–125
restaurants, 125–126
sights/activities, 114–124, 126–127
Northern Unicois: Robbinsville, NC & Tellico Plains, TN, 331, 356, 409–425
information, 409–411
lodging, 421–423
restaurants, 423–424
sights/activities, 411–421, 424–425
North Lodge Bed & Breakfast, 176–177
North Mills River Recreation Area, 244, 252
North Toe River, 103
Norton Mill Creek Falls, 385
Nu Wray Inn, 99, 106, 108

O

Oak Ridge Research Laboratory, 327
Oaks Bed & Breakfast, 235
Ober Gatlinburg, 31, 285
Ocoee, Tennessee, 439
Ocoee Dams, 434–435
Ocoee Lake, 430, 434, 435, 438–439
Ocoee River and Gorge, 21, 33, 426, 429, 433–434, 438, 439, 441
Ocoee Whitewater Center, 428, 433–435, 439, 442–443
Oconaluftee Indian Villages, 345, 349
Oconaluftee Islands Tribal Park, 344, 347
Oconaluftee River, 339, 340
Oconaluftee Valley, 342
forests of, 345
Oconaluftee Visitors Center, 348

Oconee State Park, 382, 387
Oconee Station State Historic
    Site, 387
October Hill, 199
Old Burke County Courthouse,
    134, 138
Old Edwards Inn, 389, 393
Olde Towne Inn, 370
Old Fort, Inn At, 143
Old Fort, North Carolina, 129,
    130–131, 135, 139,
    140–143, 145, 148
Old Fort Picnic Area, 131, 137
Old Fort Railroad Museum,
    130, 131, 135, 141
Old Pressley Sapphire Mine,
    30, 195
Old Rock Café, 237
Old Smoky Mountain Cabins,
    312
Old Stone Inn, 196, 200
On the Verandah, 393
Orchard Inn, 232, 237
Orchards, 221, 224–225, 255
    Altapass, Orchard at, 54, 62,
        63, 111
    Apple Hill Orchard and
        Cider Mill, 147
    Cherokee Orchards, 276, 278
Original Emporium Restau-
    rant, 68
Otto, North Carolina, 405, 407
Our Daily Bread, 90
Overlooks, Blue Ridge Park-
    way, 40–41, 44, 45
    Blowing Rocks & Grandfa-
        ther Mountain area,
        53–55, 59, 61, 63–64
    Cherokee, NC, area, 339
    Waynesville, NC, area, 188,
        190, 191, 194
Overmountain March, 126
Overmountain Victory National
    Historic Trail, 98, 118, 123

P

Pack Place, 165–166
Pacolet River Gorge, 221, 224
Paint Creek, 211
Paint Rock, 211
Palmer House, 343–344
Palmer Methodist Chapel, 343
Panes, The: A Residential Spa
    Retreat, 106–107
Panthertown Valley, 378, 380,
    382

Parish of the Holy Commu-
    nion, 42, 46
Park Place Bed & Breakfast,
    441
Parks. *See* Gardens and parks;
    State parks, forests, and
    natural areas; *specific
    parks*
Parkway Playhouse, 109
Parsons Bald, 300
Pearson's Falls, 231
Pendergrass Store museum,
    402–403
Penland, North Carolina, 17,
    96, 104–105
Penland School of Crafts, 17,
    71, 96, 104–105, 110
Perry's Water Garden, 403
Pescado's Highland Burrito,
    392
Pets, 28, 270–271
Pickens Nose, 398, 399,
    401–402
Picnic areas
    Asheville, NC, hinterlands
        of, 212
    Asheville & the Blue Ridge
        Parkway, 160
    Blue Ridge Parkway: Blow-
        ing Rock & Grandfather
        Mountain, 57–60
    Blue Ridge Parkway enters
        North Carolina, 43, 45, 57
    Boone, NC, area, 80
    Bryson City, NC, area, 325
    Cashiers & Highlands, NC,
        382
    Catawba River Valley,
        135–137
    Cherokee, NC, area, 347
    Chimney Rock & Saluda,
        NC, area, 228
    Franklin, NC & Nantahala
        Mountains, 401
    Gatlinburg, TN, area, 282
    Hendersonville & Brevard,
        NC, area, 251–252
    northern Tennessee, moun-
        tains of, 119–120
    northern Unicois: Rob-
        binsville, NC & Tellico
        Plains, TN, 416–417
    southern Unicois: Murphy,
        NC & Copper Basin, 434
    Spruce Pine & Burnsville,
        NC, area, 102–103

Sylva & Dillsboro, NC, area,
    364–365
Townsend & Cades Cove,
    TN, area, 302
Waynesville, NC, area, 193
Piedmont, 55, 57, 129, 250
Pigeon Forge, Tennessee, 16,
    279–280, 284, 288, 290
Pigeon River, 285
Pinebridge Inn, 106
Pine Crest Inn, 232, 237–238
Pines Restaurant, 49
Pink Beds, The, 188, 244, 245,
    252
Pinnacle Bald, 155
Pinnacle Park, 364
Pin Oak Gap, 346
Pisgah, Mount, 188
Pisgah, North Carolina, 256
Pisgah Center for Wildlife
    Education, 244, 245, 254
Pisgah Forest, North Carolina,
    255, 259
Pisgah Inn, 188, 196, 199
Pisgah Mountains, 156, 158,
    192, 196
Pisgah National Forest, 29, 56,
    95, 98, 101–102, 118, 130,
    131, 143, 150, 154, 160,
    163, 188, 232, 244–246,
    248–249. *See also* Cradle
    of Forestry in America,
    The; Max Patch; Middle
    Prong Wilderness; Roan
    Highlands
    Bent Creek Forests,
        159–160, 162
    Grandfather Ranger Dis-
        trict, 130
    Harmon's Den Area, 211
    llama trekking in, 284
    Morlay Branch Picnic Area,
        212
    Pisgah Ranger District, 243
    Toecane Ranger District, 95
Placer gold mine, 30
Plott Balsams, 189, 194, 361,
    364
Pond Mountain Wilderness,
    113, 118, 120
Poplar, North Carolina, 97
Porters Creek, 281
Primitive Baptist Church, 209,
    302, 303–304
Prospect Hill Bed & Breakfast,
    198

Public lands, 28–30. *See also*
National forests; National
Park Service; State parks,
forests, and natural areas;
Wild places/wilderness
preserves
Purple Onion Café and Coffee
House, 225, 236–238

Q

Quaker Meadows Plantation,
138
Qualla Arts and Crafts Mutual,
345, 349
Qualla Boundary, 21, 268–269,
324, 337–339, 345. *See
also* Cherokee, North Carolina, area
fishing licenses, 23, 269,
349–350

R

Rafting. *See* Canoeing, kayak-
ing, and whitewater rafting
Ragged Gardens, Inn at, 67
Railroads, 29. *See also* Clinch-
field Railroad Loops; ET
& WNC (Tweetsie) Rail-
road; Great Smoky Moun-
tains Railroad; Swannanoa
Grade
Amtrak, 15
Blue Ridge Railway, Stump-
house Tunnel, 387
Great Smoky Mountain
Railroad, 326, 334
Little River Railroad, driv-
ing, 29, 296–298
Little River Railroad and
Lumber Company Muse-
um, 306–307
museum, Old Fort, 130
Saluda Grade, 225–226
tunnels, Old US 70 area, 131
Yancey, 99
Randolph House, 331
Ranger district stations, 30
Ranger-led talks, 19
Rattlesnake Ridge, 119
Raven Cliff Falls, 246–247, 251
Ravenel Park, 382, 383, 387
Ray-Cort Recreation Park,
102–103
Recreation areas
Asheville, NC, hinterlands
of, 211–212

Asheville & the Blue Ridge
Parkway, 160
Blue Ridge Parkway: Blow-
ing Rocks & Grandfather
Mountain, 57
Boone, NC, area, 80
Bryson City, NC, area,
323–325
Cashiers & Highlands, NC,
381–382
Catawba River Valley, 135
Cherokee, NC, area,
346–347
Chimney Rock & Saluda,
NC, area, 228
Franklin, NC & Nantahala
Mountains, 399
Gatlinburg, TN, area,
280–282
Hendersonville & Brevard,
NC, area, 250–251
northern Tennessee, moun-
tains of, 119
northern Unicois: Rob-
binsville, NC & Tellico
Plains, TN, 416
southern Unicois: Murphy,
NC & Copper Basin,
433–434
Spruce Pine & Burnsville,
NC, area, 102
Townsend & Cades Cove,
TN, area, 302
Red Fork Falls, 115
Red Hill, North Carolina, 97
Red House (B&B), 259
Red Onion Café, 89–90
Red Thread, Inn of the, 48
Reliance, Tennessee, 426, 430,
432, 438, 442
Relia's Garden Restaurant, 333
Relief, North Carolina, 97
Rendezvous Mountain Educa-
tional State Forest, 46–47
Resorts
Asheville, NC, hinterlands
of, 216
Bryson City, NC, area, 331,
333–334
Cashiers & Highlands, NC,
390
Cherokee, NC, area,
350–351
Chimney Rock & Saluda,
NC, area, 233–234
Gatlinburg, TN, area, 288

Gatlinburg & the Northeast
Quadrant, 213
Grove Park Inn Resort and
Spa, 174
Hendersonville & Brevard,
NC, area, 257
northern Unicois: Rob-
binsville, NC & Tellico
Plains, TN, 421
Spruce Pine & Burnsville,
NC, area, 106–107
Townsend & Cades Cove,
TN, area, 309–310
Waynesville, NC, area,
195–196, 200
Restaurants, 14
Asheville, NC, hinterlands
of, 218–219
Asheville & the Blue Ridge
Parkway, 160, 178–180,
183
Blue Ridge Parkway: Blow-
ing Rock & Grandfather
Mountain, 60, 68–70
Blue Ridge Parkway enters
North Carolina, 48–49
Boone, NC, area, 87
Bryson City, NC, area,
333–334
Cashiers & Highlands, NC,
389, 392–393
Catawba River Valley,
145–146
Cherokee, North Carolina,
area, 350
Chimney Rock & Saluda,
NC, area, 225, 236–238
Franklin, NC & Nantahala
Mountains, 406–407
Gatlinburg, TN, area,
290–291
Hendersonville & Brevard,
NC, area, 260–261
northern Tennessee, moun-
tains of, 125–126
northern Unicois: Rob-
binsville, NC & Tellico
Plains, TN, 423–424
southern Unicois: Murphy,
NC & Copper Basin,
441–442
Spruce Pine & Burnsville,
NC, area, 99, 108–109
Sylva & Dillsboro, NC, area,
361, 371–373
Townsend & Cades Cove,

TN, area, 310, 312–313
Waynesville, NC, area,
  199–200
Reynolds, Lee and Vivian,
  Greenway Trail, 76–77
Richland Balsams Nature Trail,
  189, 191
Richmond Hill Inn, 173, 179
Richmond Inn Bed & Break-
  fast, 108
Richmont Inn, 310
Rich Mountain, 58
Ridgecrest, North Carolina,
  139, 143, 153
Ridgewood Barbeque, 125
Ripshin Ridge, 133
Ristorante Paoletti, 393
River Farm Inn, 89
Riverfront Park, 325
River Lodge, 370–371
Rivermont Cabins, 199
Rivers. *See specific rivers*
Riverside Park, 103
Riverview Bed & Breakfast,
  422
Riverwood, The, 70
Road maps, 26
Roads and highways, 13, 23–24
  Asheville, NC, hinterlands
    of, 203–206
  Asheville & the Blue Ridge
    Parkway, 154–156
  Blue Ridge Parkway: Blow-
    ing Rock & Grandfather
    Mountain, 53–54
  Blue Ridge Parkway enters
    North Carolina, 39–42
  Boone, NC, area, 75–76
  Bryson City, NC, area,
    318–320
  Cashiers & Highlands, NC,
    378
  Catawba River Valley,
    130–131
  Cherokee, NC, area,
    338–344
  Chimney Rock & Saluda,
    NC, area, 221–225
  Franklin, NC & Nantahala
    Mountains, 397–398
  Gatlinburg, TN, area,
    274–275
  Hendersonville & Brevard,
    NC, area, 243–245
  northern Tennessee, moun-
    tains of, 113–115

northern Unicois: Rob-
    binsville, NC & Tellico
    Plains, TN, 411–412
  southern Unicois: Murphy,
    NC & Copper Basin,
    428–430
  Spruce Pine & Burnsville,
    NC, area, 96–98
  Sylva & Dillsboro, NC, area,
    360–361
  Townsend & Cades Cove,
    TN, area, 296–299
  Waynesville, NC, area,
    188–189
  Web site, 33
Roan High Knob, 105
Roan Highlands, 18, 95, 97, 98,
  100–101, 113, 118–119.
  See also Hampton Creek
  Cove State Natural Area
Roan Mountain, 32, 96, 97, 248
Roan Mountain, Tennessee,
  122–125, 127
Roan Mountain Gardens, 97,
  101, 105
Roan Mountain State Park,
  118, 119, 121, 125, 127
Roaring Creek Valley, 101
Roaring Fork Motor Nature
  Trail, 276, 281
Roaring Gap, North Carolina,
  42, 47
Robardajen Woods Bed &
  Breakfast, 144
Robbinsville, North Carolina.
  See Northern Unicois:
  Robbinsville, NC & Tellico
  Plains, TN
Rock Café, 208, 218
Rock climbing
  Asheville & the Blue Ridge
    Parkway, 172
  Blue Ridge Parkway: Blow-
    ing Rock & Grandfather
    Mountain, 65
  Boone, NC, area, 84–85
  Cashiers & Highlands, NC,
    388–389
  southern Unicois: Murphy,
    NC & Copper Basin, 438
Rock Creek Falls, 119
Rock Creek Recreation Area,
  119
Rockhounding, 30, 274. *See
  also* Mines
Rockhouse Creek, 244

Rocksberry Bed & Breakfast, 68
Rocky balds. *See* Balds
Rocky Bluffs Recreation Area,
  206, 212
Rocky Broad River, 223, 227
Rocky Fork, Cherokee Wildlife
  Management Area, 210
Rocky Mountain, 378, 382–383
Rocky's Soda Shop and Grill,
  260–261
Rocky Top, Tennessee, 206,
  213
Rose Tree Bed & Breakfast,
  259
Rosman, North Carolina, 256
Round Bald, 98
Round Knob Picnic Area, 210,
  212
Roy Taylor National Forest,
  364
Runion, North Carolina, 211
Rural Life Museum, 214
Rush Wray Museum of Yancey
  County History, 103–104
Russell Bald, 301
Russell Creek, 86

S

St. Mary's Church, 46
Salem, South Carolina, 392
Salt Rock, 382
Saluda, North Carolina. *See*
  Chimney Rock & Saluda,
  North Carolina, area
Saluda Grade, 225–226
Sampson Mountain Wilder-
  ness, 207–208, 210, 212,
  215
Sams Gap, 115, 298
Sandburg Home. *See* Carl
  Sandburg Home National
  Historic Site
Sandy Cut Cabins, 236
Santeetlah Creek, 419
Santeetlah Lake, 417, 418, 421
Sapphire, North Carolina, 388
Sassafras Creek and Falls, 415
Savannah Mountain National
  Forest, 364
Scaly Mountain, 384
Schoolhouse Falls, 382
Scott Creek, 361
Scottish Tartans Museum, 403
Second Broad River, 142
Secret Garden (B&B), 177–178
Sequoyah, Lake, 379, 391, 393

Sequoyah Birthplace Museum, 420
Seven Devils, North Carolina, 84
Seven Foxes, Cabins at, 392
7th Heaven Log Inn, 289
Sevierville, Tennessee, 274, 280, 287, 289
Shamrock Inn, 135, 143
Sheets Cabin, 40
Sheffield Mine, 30, 403–404
Shelton House, 194–195
Shelton Laurel Backcountry Area, 103–104, 209–210, 212
Shenandoah National Park, 19
Shining Rock Wilderness, 188, 192–194
ShoeBooties Café, 442
Shook Branch Recreation Area, 120
Shopping, 14
  Asheville, NC, hinterlands of, 219–220
  Asheville & the Blue Ridge Parkway, 165, 182–184
  Blue Ridge Parkway: Blowing Rock & Grandfather Mountain, 70–71
  Blue Ridge Parkway enters North Carolina, 41, 49
  Boone, NC, area, 91–92
  Bryson City, NC, area, 334
  Cashiers & Highlands, NC, 393–394
  Catawba River Valley, 147–148
  Cherokee, NC, area, 350–351
  Chimney Rock & Saluda, NC, area, 238–239
  Franklin, NC & Nantahala Mountains, 407–408
  Gatlinburg, TN, area, 291–293
  Hendersonville & Brevard, NC, area, 261–263
  northern Tennessee, mountains of, 126
  northern Unicois: Robbinsville, NC & Tellico Plains, TN, 424–425
  southern Unicois: Murphy, NC & Copper Basin, 442
  Spruce Pine & Burnsville, NC, area, 109–110

Sylva & Dillsboro, NC, area, 363, 373–375
Townsend & Cades Cove, TN, area, 314–315
Waynesville, NC, area, 201
Shuckstack Fire Tower, 321
Shunkawaken Falls, 231
Silver, Frankie and Charlie, 95, 96, 103
Silver Cemetery, 103
Silvermont Park, 251
Silver Run Falls, 385
Six-thousand-foot peaks, 30
Skating, 285
Ski Beech. See Beech Mountain, North Carolina
Skiing, downhill, 31, 77, 85, 215, 285
Skytop Orchard, 255
Slickrock. See Kilmer-Slickrock Wilderness
Smith-McDowell House Museum, 167
Smokemont, 192, 340–341, 344, 346, 350
Smokemont campground, 270
Smokies/Unakas, 10, 12–13, 98, 114. See also Great Smoky Mountains National Park; Northern mountains; South of the Smokies; Unaka Mountain Wilderness
  area codes, 15
  Cherokees, home of, 21
  Chimney Rock & Saluda, NC, area, 346
  crest of Smokies, 338
  grassy balds, 18
  remote western Smokies, 319–320
Smoky Mountains Front, 280–281
Smokin' Joes, 313
Smoky Mountains Brewery and Restaurant, 290
Smoky Mountains Field School, 286
Smoky Mountains Natural History Association, 273
Snowbird Creek Forests, 415
Snowbird Indian Trading Post and Gallery, 424
Snowbird Mountain Lodge, 421
Snow Hill Inn, 405
Soco Gap, 339, 347

Sourwood Grille, 200
South Brevard Park, 255
Southern Appalachian Repertory Theater (SART), 219
Southern Highlands Craft Guild, 58–59, 161
Southern Nantahala Wilderness, 400–402
Southern Unicois: Murphy, NC & Copper Basin, 15, 356, 411, 426–443
  information, 426–428
  lodging, 439–441
  restaurants, 441–442
  sights/activities, 428–439, 442–443
South Mountains, 129, 142
South Mountains State Park, 131–134, 136–137
South of the Smokies, 356–443. See also Cashiers & Highlands, North Carolina; Franklin, NC & Nantahala Mountains; Northern Unicois: Robbinsville, NC & Tellico Plains, TN; Southern Unicois: Murphy, NC & Copper Basin; Sylva & Dillsboro, North Carolina, area
South Toe River, 96, 102, 108
South Toe River Forests, 100, 101, 160
South Toe River Valley, 96
Sparta, North Carolina, 36, 42
  lodging, 48
  restaurants, 48–49
  shopping, 49
  special events, 49–50
Spartanburg, South Carolina, 15, 148
Spas, 65–66, 106–107
  Grove Park Inn Resort and Spa, 174
Special events, 14. See also Entertainment
  Asheville, NC, hinterlands of, 220
  Asheville & the Blue Ridge Parkway, 184–185
  Blue Ridge Parkway: Blowing Rock & Grandfather Mountain, 71–72
  Blue Ridge Parkway enters North Carolina, 49–50
  Boone, NC, area, 92–93

Bryson City, NC, area, 334–335

Cashiers & Highlands, NC, 394

Catawba River Valley, 148

Cherokee, NC, area, 351

Chimney Rock & Saluda, NC, area, 239–240

Franklin, NC & Nantahala Mountains, 408

Gatlinburg, TN, area, 293

Hendersonville & Brevard, NC, area, 263–264

northern Tennessee, mountains of, 126–127

northern Unicois: Robbinsville, NC & Tellico Plains, TN, 425

southern Unicois: Murphy, NC & Copper Basin, 442–443

Spruce Pine & Burnsville, NC, area, 110–111

Sylva & Dillsboro, NC, area, 375

Townsend & Cades Cove, TN, area, 315

Waynesville, NC, area, 201–202

Spence Bald, 301

Spring Creek Gorge, 206

Springdale Resort and Country Club, 195–196, 200

Springhaven Inn, 67

Spring House Farm, Cottages at, 139, 144

Spring Street Café, 373

Spruce Pine & Burnsville, North Carolina, area, 37, 66, 68, 89, 94–111

information, 40, 95–96

lodging, 106–108

restaurants, 99, 108–109

sights/activities, 96–106, 109–111, 148

Squibb Creek, 207

Squire Watkins Inn, 370

Stamping Ground, 115

Standing Indian Basin and Mountain, 270, 398–402

State historic sites

Fort Loudoun, 418

Judaculla Rock, 365

Oconee Station, 387

Sycamore Shoals, 117, 120–121, 126

Vance Birthplace, 166–167, 184–185

Wolfe, Thomas, Memorial, 157, 167–168

State parks, forests, and natural areas. *See also* State historic sites

Caesar's Head State Park, 245–247, 250, 251

Devils Fork State Park, 387

Devil's Fork State Park, 392

DuPont (*See* DuPont State Forest)

Gorges State Park (*See* Jocassee Gorges)

Hampton Creek Cove, 118, 122–123

Jones Gap State Park, 250, 251

Lake James, 137

Mount Jefferson, 76, 78, 80

Mount Mitchell, 155, 160

Oconee, 382, 387

Rendezvous Mountain, 46–47

Roan Mountain, 118, 119, 121, 125, 127

South Mountains, 131–134, 136–137

Stone Mountain, 40–43, 45

Sugarloaf Mountain, 434

Table Rock State Park, 250–251

State Theater of North Carolina, 261

Stecoah, North Carolina, 319, 322

Stewart Cabin, 419

Stillwater activities. *See* Canoeing, kayaking, and whitewater rafting

Stone Creek Cabins, 441

Stone Hedge Inn and Restaurant, 234, 238

Stone Mountain State Park, 40–43, 45

Stone Pillar Bed & Breakfast, 68

Storie Street Grille, 68

Stumphouse tunnel, 387

Sugar Grove, North Carolina, 88, 93

Sugarlands, 275, 277, 278

Sugarlands Ranger Station, 274

Sugarlands Visitors Center, 274, 275, 283, 285, 296

Sugarloaf Mountain, 225

Sugarloaf Mountain State Park, 434

Sugar Mountain, 31, 77, 85, 90

Summit Inn and Restaurant, 404–407

Summit Lake Dam, 227–228

Sumter National Forest, 29, 357, 377, 382

Sunset Rock/Sunrise Rock, 383, 387

Surry County Historical Society, 45

Susan, Lake, 169

Swag, The (resort), 350

Swannanoa, North Carolina, 153

Swannanoa Gap, 157

Swannanoa Grade, 130–131, 139, 141, 157

Sweetwater, Tennessee, 411

Swimming, wilderness, Web site for, 32–33

Switzerland Inn, Chalet Restaurant at, 70

Sycamore Log Cabins, 351

Sycamore Shoals State Historic Site, 117, 120–121, 126

Sylva & Dillsboro, North Carolina, area, 269, 356, 359–375

information, 360

lodging, 361, 363–364

restaurants, 361, 371–373

sights/activities, 360–368, 373–375

T

Table Rock State Park, 250–251

Table Rock/Table Rock Picnic Area, 65, 133–136, 250–251

Tapoco Lakes, 417

Tapoco Lodge Resort, 421

Telephones, 15

Tellahala Café, 423

Tellico Lake, 418

Tellico Plains, Tennessee. *See* Northern Unicois: Robbinsville, NC & Tellico Plains, TN

Tellico Plains Ranger Station, 411, 419–420, 422

Tellico River, 356, 416, 417, 422

Tellico Springs, Tennessee, 416
Tellico Vacation Rentals, 422
Tennessee Eastman Hiking and
    Canoeing Club, 30
Tennessee Ridge Inn Bed &
    Breakfast, 289
Tennessee Valley, 299
Tennessee Valley Authority
    (TVA), 119, 120, 320–321,
    367, 418, 426, 434–435
Tennessee Valley Authority
    (TVA) Park, 325
Ten Oaks Bed & Breakfast,
    198–199
Terrell House, 107
Thermal City Gold Mine, 30,
    141–142
Thomas Divide, 340
Three Top Mountains Game
    Lands, 79
Ticks, 20
Timberwolf Creek Bed &
    Breakfast, 351
Tinsley, Jim Bob, Museum and
    Research Center, 254–255
Tipton Place, 305
Toad Hall Bed & Breakfast,
    391
Todd, North Carolina, 76,
    79–82, 85
Todd National Historic Dis-
    trict, 80–82
Toe River, 95, 97, 100, 101,
    103, 108. See also North
    Toe River; South Toe
    River
Tom Branch Falls, 320
Townsend & Cades Cove, Ten-
    nessee, area, 213, 268,
    269, 294–315
    Cades Cove Foothills,
        298–299
    campground, 270
    information, 295–296
    lodging, 309–312
    restaurants, 310, 312–313
    sights/activities, 296–309
Town Square Café and Bakery,
    423
Toxaway, Lake, 386
Trailhead Steak House, 313
Trails. See Hiking/walking
Transportation, 15, 20. See also
    Railroads
Tremont Logging Camp, 298,
    299

Trevi, 179
Tri-Cities Airport, 15
Trust, North Carolina, 206,
    213, 220
Trust Chapel, 206, 213–214
Tryon, North Carolina, 221,
    223, 224, 226, 228, 231,
    232, 234–235, 237–240
Tryon Depot and Polk County
    Historical Museum, 224,
    226, 229
Tryon Fine Arts Center, 226,
    231
Tryon Old South Bed & Break-
    fast, 234–235
Tsali Recreation Area, 19, 317,
    323–325, 328
Tuckaleechee Caverns, 307
Tuckaleechee Cove, 295
Tuckaseegee River, 194, 317,
    356, 364–368, 370, 382
Tuckaseegee Valley, 32
Turchin Center for the Visual
    Arts, 83
Tweetsie Railroad. See ET &
    WNC (Tweetsie) Railroad
Twentymile section, Great
    Smoky Mountains Nation-
    al Park, 320, 321
210 Maple Bed & Breakfast,
    258

U
Uhler, John William, Great
    Smoky Mountains Nation-
    al Park Web site, 32
Unaka Mountain Scenic Road,
    115
Unaka Mountain Wilderness,
    113, 115, 118–119
Unakas. See Smokies/Unakas
Unicoi, Tennessee, 113, 122,
    123, 127
Unicoi Foothills Wilderness,
    430, 432, 433
Unicoi Mountains. See North-
    ern Unicois: Robbinsville,
    NC & Tellico Plains, TN;
    Southern Unicois: Mur-
    phy, NC & Copper Basin
Union Mills, North Carolina,
    141–142
United Methodist Church
    headquarters, 192
Unto These Hills, 345, 352
Upper Creek Falls, 137

Upstairs Gallery, 230–231
U.S. Forest Service. See
    National forests
USGS topographic maps,
    26–27

V
Valle Crucis, North Carolina,
    73, 76, 77, 81, 86–89, 92
Valley River, 356
Valley River Mountains, 431,
    433, 434
Vance, Zeb, 45–46
Vance Birthplace State Historic
    Site, 166–167, 184–185
Vanderbilt, George, 150, 153,
    157, 159, 162–164, 168,
    244, 248–249, 252
Veterans Tribal Park, 344, 347
Vilas, North Carolina, 89
Villages, 13
    Asheville, NC, hinterlands
        of, 208–209
    Blue Ridge Parkway: Blow-
        ing Rocks & Grandfather
        Mountain, 55–56
    Blue Ridge Parkway enters
        North Carolina, 42
    Boone, NC, area, 77–78
    Bryson City, NC, area,
        321–323
    Cashiers & Highlands, NC,
        378–380
    Catawba River Valley,
        134–135
    Cherokee, NC, area,
        344–345
    Chimney Rock & Saluda,
        NC, area, 225–226
    Franklin, NC & Nantahala
        Mountains, 398–400
    Gatlinburg, TN, area,
        278–280
    Hendersonville & Brevard,
        NC, area, 247–248
    northern Tennessee, moun-
        tains of, 116–117
    northern Unicois: Rob-
        binsville, NC & Tellico
        Plains, TN, 413–414
    southern Unicois: Murphy,
        NC & Copper Basin,
        431–432
    Spruce Pine & Burnsville,
        NC, area, 99
    Sylva & Dillsboro, NC, area,

INDEX

362–364
Townsend & Cades Cove,
TN, area, 300
Waynesville, NC, area,
189–192
Vonore, Tennessee, 418, 420,
425

W

Walhalla, South Carolina, 378
Walker Place, 305
Walking. See Hiking/walking
Walland, Tennessee, 306, 308,
309, 313
Walnut Mountains, 215
Warren Wilson College, 182
Wasp, Tennessee, 211
Watauga, Fort, 117, 120–121
Watauga Colony, 37
Watauga Lake and Dam,
116–117, 119, 120, 125
Watauga River and Gorge, 65,
73, 76, 85–87
Waterfalls, 31, 384–386
    Blue Ridge Parkway: Blow-
        ing Rock & Grandfather
        Mountain, 63
    Blue Ridge Parkway enters
        North Carolina, 42, 44, 45
    Bryson City, NC, area, 317,
        319, 323
    Cashiers & Highlands, NC,
        379–382, 384–386
    Catawba River Valley,
        131–133, 136, 137
    Chimney Rock & Saluda,
        NC, area, 223, 230, 231
    Franklin, NC & Nantahala
        Mountains, 398, 401
    Gatlinburg, TN, area, 276,
        278
    Hendersonville & Brevard,
        NC, area, 245–247, 250,
        251, 255, 259
    Linville Falls, 51, 53–55, 61,
        133, 135
    northern Tennessee, moun-
        tains of, 115–116, 119
    northern Unicois: Rob-
        binsville, NC & Tellico
        Plains, TN, 413, 415, 416
    southern Unicois: Murphy,
        NC & Copper Basin, 430,
        434
    Spruce Pine & Burnsville,
        NC, area, 102

Townsend & Cades Cove,
    TN, area, 320
Waterrock Knob, 189, 194,
    361, 364
Waterville, North Carolina, 344
Waterville, Tennessee, 282
Watauga River, 117
Wayah Gap and Bald Area,
    398, 400–402
Waynesville, North Carolina,
    area, 187–202, 338
    information, 20
    lodging, 189, 192, 196–199
    restaurants, 199–200
    sights/activities, 182,
        188–196, 200–202
Wear's Valley (Wear Cove),
    Tennessee, 300, 302
Weather, 31–32, 269
Weaverville, North Carolina,
    158, 166, 171, 177–178
Web sites, use of, 19, 32–33,
    274, 296, 360, 428
Weizenblatt Gallery, 214
Welcome Valley Village, 441
Well House, 372
Wesser, North Carolina, 395
Wesser Bald, 402
Western Carolina University,
    364, 365–366, 375, 387
Western North Carolina Air
    Museum, 254
Western North Carolina
    Nature Center, 170
Western Piedmont Community
    College, 140
West Fork Pigeon River, 191
Westglow Spa, 65–66
West Jefferson, North Carolina,
    46, 75, 76, 78, 84, 89, 92
Whippoorwill Academy and
    Village, 45–46
Whisperwind Cabin Rentals,
    312
WhiteGate Inn and Cottage,
    175
Whitehead, Don, Place,
    304–305
White House, The, 439–440
White Oak Mountain, 226, 231
Whiteside Mountain, 378, 381,
    383, 392
Whitewater Falls, 381–382, 384
Whitewater sports. See Canoe-
    ing, kayaking, and white-
    water rafting

Whittier, A Dream Remem-
    bered, 363, 366
Whittier, North Carolina, 328,
    362–363, 366, 368, 369,
    375
Wicklow Inn, 236
Wilbur Lake, 116, 119, 120,
    125
Wildcat Falls, 245
Wildflour Bakery, 237
Wildflower Café, 260
Wildlife, 34, 271. See also Pis-
    gah Center for Wildlife
    Education
Wild West attractions, 16
Wilkesboro, North Carolina, 45
Wilson Creek National Wild
    and Scenic River, 53,
    55–58, 85–86
Wilson Creek Wilderness
    Study Area, 57
Wilson Lick Ranger Station,
    398
WindDancers Lodging and
    Llama Treks, 215–217
Window Views B&B, 87
Windsong, A Mountain Inn,
    197
Wiseman's View, 133, 135, 141
Wolfe, Thomas, Memorial
    State Historic Site, 157,
    167–168
Wolf Laurel, 31, 215
Wolf Laurel Gap, 339
Woodfield Inn, 256–257
Woody House, 343
Wray House, 107
Wright Inn and Carriage
    House, 175–176

Y

Yancey Railroad, 99
Yellow Branch Farm/Pottery,
    326–327
Yellow Face, 362, 364
Yellow House (B&B), 197–198
Yellow Rose Realty, 332–333,
    350
Yiannis Restaurant, 145
YMI Cultural Center, 157, 166
Young's Mountain Music, 109

Z

Zoo, Grandfather Mountain
    Park, 60